# Research Anthology on Securing Medical Systems and Records

Information Resources Management Association
*USA*

## Volume I

Published in the United States of America by
IGI Global
Information Science Reference (an imprint of IGI Global)
701 E. Chocolate Avenue
Hershey PA, USA 17033
Tel: 717-533-8845
Fax: 717-533-8661
E-mail: cust@igi-global.com
Web site: http://www.igi-global.com

Library of Congress Cataloging-in-Publication Data

Names: Information Resources Management Association, editor.
Title: Research anthology on securing medical systems and records /
  Information Resources Management Association, editor.
Description: Hershey, PA : Information Science Reference, [2022] | Includes
  bibliographical references and index.
Identifiers: LCCN 2022016825 (print) | LCCN 2022016826 (ebook) | ISBN
  9781668463116 (hardcover) | ISBN 9781668463123 (ebook)
Subjects: MESH: Medical Records Systems, Computerized | Confidentiality |
  Security Measures | Internet of Things | Big Data
Classification: LCC R864 (print) | LCC R864 (ebook) | NLM WX 175 | DDC
  610.285--dc23/eng/20220527
LC record available at https://lccn.loc.gov/2022016825
LC ebook record available at https://lccn.loc.gov/2022016826

British Cataloguing in Publication Data
A Cataloguing in Publication record for this book is available from the British Library.

The views expressed in this book are those of the authors, but not necessarily of the publisher.

For electronic access to this publication, please contact: eresources@igi-global.com.

# List of Contributors

# Table of Contents

**Section 2**
**Securing Medical Devices**

**Section 3**
**Securing Medical Images**

## Section 4
## Securing Patient Data and Medical Records

# Preface

With the influx of internet and mobile technology usage, many medical institutions—from doctor's offices to hospitals—have implemented new online technologies for the storage and access of health data as well as the monitoring of patient health. Telehealth was particularly useful during the COVID-19 pandemic, which monumentally increased its everyday usage. However, this transition of health data has increased privacy risks, and cyber criminals and hackers may have increased access to patients' personal data. Medical staff and administrations must remain up to date on the new technologies and methods in securing these medical systems and records.

Thus, the *Research Anthology on Securing Medical Systems and Records* seeks to fill the void for an all-encompassing and comprehensive reference book covering the latest and most emerging research, concepts, and theories for those working in healthcare. This two-volume reference collection of reprinted IGI Global book chapters and journal articles that have been handpicked by the editor and editorial team of this research anthology on this topic will empower security analysts, data scientists, hospital administrators, leaders in healthcare, medical professionals, health information managers, medical professionals, mobile application developers, security professionals, technicians, students, libraries, researchers, and academicians.

The *Research Anthology on Securing Medical Systems and Records* is organized into four sections that provide comprehensive coverage of important topics. The sections are:

1. Securing Healthcare Systems;
2. Securing Medical Devices;
3. Securing Medical Images; and
4. Securing Patient Data and Medical Records.

The following paragraphs provide a summary of what to expect from this invaluable reference tool.

Section 1, "Securing Healthcare Systems," explains the threats, challenges, and strategies in healthcare system security. The first chapter, "Cyber Threats in the Healthcare Sector and Countermeasures," by Prof. Mohamed Amine Ferrag of Guelma University, Algeria and Profs. Leandros Maglaras and Muhammad Mashhood Ahmed of De Montfort University, UK, presents all cyber threat actors that exist in the healthcare sector, common cyber-attacks that can be launched against all actors, and real incidents that took place during the past years. Based on these, the authors propose in a tabular form a set of recommendations that can be used as countermeasures against any type of attack. The next chapter, "Digital Healthcare Security Issues: Is There a Solution in Biometrics?" by Profs. Punithavathi P. and Geetha Subbiah of VIT Chennai, India, examines how biometric technology can be applied to the digital healthcare services. The following chapter, "Biometric Technologies in Healthcare Biometrics," by Prof. Dakshina Ranjan Kisku of National Institute of Technology Durgapur, India and Prof. Rinku Datta Rakshit of Asansol Engineering College, India, introduces biometrics systems and discusses the essential components of biometrics technologies in the healthcare system. The discussion also includes the state-of-the-art biometrics technologies, selection criteria of a suitable biometrics system, biometrics identity management, and multi-biometrics fusion for healthcare biometrics system. The next chapter, "Cyber-Physical Security in Healthcare," by Profs. Vasiliki Mantzana, Eleni Darra, and Ilias Gkotsis of Center for Security Studies (KEMEA), Greece, presents healthcare critical asset vulnerabilities, cyber-physical threats that can affect them, architecture solutions, as well as some indicative scenarios that are validated during the project. The following chapter, "Applying Blockchain Technologies in Healthcare: A Scientometric Analysis," by Profs. Serhat Burmaoglu, Zehra Ozge Candereli, Levent B. Kidak, and Dilek Ozdemir Gungor of Izmir Katip Celebi University, Turkey, explores blockchain applications in healthcare with an explorative perspective with a scientometrics analysis. With this analysis, the trends and evolutionary relations between health and blockchain technology are examined via the queries in the Web of Science database. The next chapter, "Multi-Keyword Searchable Encryption for E-Health System With Multiple Data Writers and Readers," by Prof. Devesh C. Jinwala of S. V. National Institute of Technology, India and Prof. Dhruti P. Sharma of Sarvajanik College of Engineering and Technology, India, proposes a multi-keyword SE for an e-health system in multi-writer multi-reader setting. With this scheme, any registered writer could share data with any registered reader with optimal storage-computational overhead on writer. The proposed scheme offers conjunctive search with optimal search complexity at server. It also ensures security to medical records and privacy of keywords. The theoretical and empirical analysis demonstrates the effectiveness of the proposed work. The following chapter, "Internet of Things (IOT) in Healthcare – Smart Health and Surveillance, Architectures, Security Analysis, and Data Transfer: A Review," by Profs. Parthasarathy Panchatcharam and Vivekanandan S. of VIT University, Vellore, India, displays the idea of solving health issues by utilizing a recent innovation, the internet of things (IoT). The next chapter, "Healthcare IoT Architectures, Technologies, Applications, and Issues: A Deep Insight," by Profs. Karthick G. S. and Pankajavalli P. B. of Bharathiar University, India, analyzes the applications of IoT in healthcare systems with diversified aspects such as topological arrangement of medical devices, layered architecture, and platform services. This chapter focuses on advancements in IoT-based healthcare in order to identify the communication and sensing technologies enabling the smart healthcare systems. The following chapter, "IoT-Based Smart and Secure Health Monitoring System," by Prof. Parul Verma of Amity University, Lucknow, India and Prof. Brijesh Khandelwal of Amity University, Raipur, India, focuses on how IoT can be integrated with healthcare systems and draw maximum benefits from its ubiquitous presence. The chapter also covers various security concerns of an IoT-based healthcare system and their suggested solutions to overcome those concerns. The next chapter, "Advanced Cyber Security and Internet of Things for Digital Transformations of the Indian Healthcare Sector," by Profs. Esha Jain and Jonika Lamba of The NorthCap University, Gurugram, India, methodically reviews the need for cybersecurity amid digital transformation with the help of emerging technologies and focuses on the application and incorporation of blockchain and the internet of things (IoT) to ensure cybersecurity in the well-being of the business. The final chapter, "Healthcare Security Assessment in the Big Data Era: Lessons From Turkey," by Profs. Ionica Oncioiu and Oana Claudia Ionescu of Titu Maiorescu University, Romania, contributes to the decrease of the shortcomings that exist in the healthcare security assessment by focusing on data mining for public institutions and organizations in Turkey.

Section 2, "Securing Medical Devices," reviews the protocols, challenges, and strategies in medical device security including wearable technologies and apps. The first chapter, "Cyber Security in Health: Standard Protocols for IoT and Supervisory Control Systems," by Profs. Bruno J. Santos and Rachel P. Tabacow of Instituto Federal de São Paulo, Brazil; Prof. Marcelo Barboza of Instituto Federal de São Paulo, Brazil & Escola Politécnica da Universidade de São Paulo, Brazil; and Profs. Tarcisio F. Leão and Eduardo G. P. Bock of Instituto Federal de São Paulo, Brazil, explains that increasing collaboration in terms of medical equipment, artificial organs, and biosensors is a way to facilitate H4.0. As a result, cyber security budgets have increased, new technology has been purchased, and healthcare organizations are improving at blocking attacks and keeping their networks secure. The next chapter, "Medical Device Security," by Prof. Md Abdullah Al Momin of University of Louisiana at Lafayette, USA, provides an overview of these security risks, their proposed solutions, and the limitations on IMD systems which make solving these issues nontrivial. The chapter further analyzes the security issues and the history of vulnerabilities in pacemakers to illustrate the theoretical topics by considering a specific device. The next chapter, "Quantum Cryptography for Securing IoT-Based Healthcare Systems," by Prof. Anand Sharma of Mody University of Science and Technology, Lakshmangarh, India and Prof. Alekha Parimal Bhatt of Capgemini IT India Pvt. Ltd., India, describes that it is necessary to use quantum cryptography system to make sure the security, privacy, and integrity of the patient's data received and transmitted from IoT-based healthcare systems. Quantum cryptography is a very fascinating domain in cyber security that utilizes quantum mechanics to extend a cryptosystem that is supposed to be the unbreakable secure system. The following chapter, "Constructive Solutions for Security and Privacy Issues at the Edge: Securing Edge Framework – A Healthcare Application Use Case," by Profs. Indra Priyadharshini S. and Pradheeba Ulaganathan of R. M. K. College of Engineering and Technology, India; Prof. Vigilson Prem M. of R. M. D. Engineering College, India; and Prof. Yuvaraj B. R. of Anna University, India, explains some of the serious and non-discussed security issues and privacy issues available on edge. The next chapter, "Personalized Mobile eHealth Services for Secure User Access Through a Multi Feature Biometric Framework," by Profs. Emmanouil G. Spanakis, Marios Spanakis, and Georgios C. Manikis of Institute of Computer Science, Foundation for Research and Technology Hellas, Heraklion, Greece, argues how a biometric identification system can greatly benefit healthcare, due to the increased accuracy of identification procedures. The following chapter, "'Sensitive but Essential Information': Policy Debates on Fitness Application Privacy and Data Security," by Prof. Alison Nicole Novak of Rowan University, USA, explores how government representatives, industry leaders, regulators, and politicians discursively constructed and critiqued data privacy in fitness applications in congressional contexts. The next chapter, "Role of Wearable Technology and Fitness Apps in Obesity and Diabetes: Privacy, Ownership, and Portability of Data," by Profs. Shariq I. Sherwani and Benjamin R. Bates of Ohio University, USA, addresses the concerns about health data privacy, personal ownership, and portability. The following chapter, "DeTER Framework: A Novel Paradigm for Addressing Cybersecurity Concerns in Mobile Healthcare," by Prof. Rangarajan (Ray) Parthasarathy of University of Illinois at Urbana-Champaign, USA; Prof. David K. Wyant of Belmont University, USA; Prof. Prasad Bingi of Purdue University, Fort Wayne, USA; Prof. James R. Knight of The Ohio State University, USA; and Prof. Anuradha Rangarajan of Indiana State University, USA, presents a comprehensive framework (DeTER) that integrates all three perspectives through which cybersecurity concerns in mobile healthcare could be viewed, understood, and acted upon. The next chapter, "A Lightweight Three-Factor Anonymous Authentication Scheme With Privacy Protection for Personalized Healthcare Applications," by Profs. Mengxia Shuai and Nenghai Yu of University of Science and Technology of China, Anhui, China; Prof. Hongxia Wang of

Southwest Jiaotong University, Chengdu, China; Prof. Ling Xiong of Xihua University, Chengdu, China; and Prof. Yue Li of Southwest Jiaotong University, Chengdu, China, proposes a lightweight three-factor anonymous authentication scheme with forward secrecy for personalized healthcare applications using only the lightweight cryptographic primitives. The final chapter, "My Health Record and Emerging Cybersecurity Challenges in the Australian Digital Environment," by Prof. Anita Medhekar of Central Queensland University, Australia, discusses the challenges of embracing e-health digital technologies and assurance of advancing cybersecurity of online My Health Record, which will transform e-health provision and empower patients and healthcare providers.

Section 3, "Securing Medical Images," reviews the technologies and techniques involved in ensuring that medical images are protected. The first chapter, "Secure Access to Biomedical Images," by Prof. Tariq Javid of Hamdard University, Pakistan, introduces a framework for secure access to biomedical images. In this chapter, a cryptocompression system is also proposed which integrates both encryption and compression to fulfill the requirements of electronic protected health information records. The next chapter, "Medical Signal Security Enhancement Using Chaotic Map and Watermarking Technique," by Profs. Chittaranjan Pradhan and Ajita Sahay of KIIT University, India and Prof. Amandip Sinha of West Bengal University of Technology, India, explores medical signal security enhancement using chaotic map and watermarking techniques. This new approach provides security to both the medical image and also maintains the confidentially of both the patient and doctor. The following chapter, "Integer Transform-Based Watermarking Scheme for Authentication of Digital Fundus Images in Medical Science: An Application to Medical Image Authentication," by Prof. Poonkuntran Shanmugam of Velammal College of Engineering and Technology, Madurai, India and Prof. Manessa Jayaprakasam, Independent Researcher, India, presents an integer transform-based watermarking scheme for digital fundus image authentication. It is presented under multimedia applications in medicine. The chapter introduces image authentication by watermarking and digital fundus image. The key requirements in developing watermarking scheme for fundus images and its challenges are identified and highlighted. The next chapter, "Multiple Blind Watermarking Framework for Security and Integrity of Medical Images in E-Health Applications," by Profs. Abdallah Soualmi and Adel Alti of LRSD Lab, Computer Science Department, Faculty of Sciences, University of SETIF-1, Algeria and Prof. Lamri Laouamer of Department of Management Information Systems, College of Business and Economics, Qassim University, Saudi Arabia, gives a new secure framework to protect medical data based on blind multiple watermarking schemes. The proposed approach consists of combining LWT (lifting wavelet transform), QR decomposition, and Arnold chaotic map in transform domain for the first watermark, while for the second watermark is encrusted in the spatial domain. The final chapter, "Implementation of a Reversible Watermarking Technique for Medical Images," by Prof. Abhishek Basu of RCC Institute of Information Technology, India and Prof. Ranit Karmakar of Tata Consultancy Services, India, proposes a reversible data hiding algorithm which also is capable of holding a large chunk of data without affecting the cover media.

Section 4, "Securing Patient Data and Medical Records," examines threats to patient's data and strategies for protecting their privacy. The first chapter, "Healthcare Information Security in the Cyber World," by Prof. Subrata Acharya of Towson University, USA and Prof. Brian S. Coats of University of Maryland – Baltimore, USA, presents a cognitive science-based solution by addressing comprehensive compliance implementation as mandated by the Health Insurance Portability and Accountability Act, the certified Electronic Health Record standard, and the federal Meaningful Use program. The next chapter, "Applicability of WSN and Biometric Models in the Field of Healthcare," by Prof. Aditya Khamparia of Lovely Professional University, India; Prof. Bharat Bhushan of HMR Institute of Technology and Management, Delhi, India; Prof. Ila Kaushik of Krishna Institute of Engineering and Technology, India; and Profs. Nikhil Sharma and Siddharth Gautam of HMR Institute of Technology and Management, Delhi, India, presents the role of WSN and biometric models such as two factor remote authentication, verifying fingerprint operations for enhancing security, privacy preserving in healthcare, healthcare data by cloud technology with biometric application, and validation built hybrid trust computing perspective for confirmation of contributor profiles in online healthcare data. The following chapter, "Implementation of Encryption and Data Hiding in E-Health Application," by Prof. Muzafer H. Saracevic of University of Novi Pazar, Serbia; Prof. Aybeyan Selimi of International Vision University, North Macedonia; and Prof. Selver Pepić of Higher Technical Machine School of Professional Studies in Trstenik, Serbia, presents the possibilities of applying cryptography and steganography in design advanced methods of medical software. The next chapter, "Advancements in Data Security and Privacy Techniques Used in IoT-Based Hospital Applications," by Prof. Dinesh Bhatia of North Eastern Hill University, India and Profs. Ankita Tiwari and Raghuvendra Pratap Tripathi of Amity University, India, delves upon understanding the working of a secure monitoring system wherein the data could be continuously observed with the support of MSNs. The following chapter, "Quantum Security for IoT to Secure Healthcare Applications and Their Data," by Prof. Binod Kumar of JSPM's Rajarshi Shahu College of Engineering, India; Prof. Sheetal B. Prasad of SRM Institute of Science and Technology, India; Prof. Parashu Ram Pal of ABES Engineering College, India; and Prof. Pankaj Pathak of Symbiosis Institute of Digital and Telecom Management, Symbiosis International University, India, proposes that there should be a strong mechanism to combat the security gaps in existing healthcare industry. If the healthcare data are available on the network, an attacker may try to modify, intercept, or even view this data stream. With the use of quantum security, the quantum state of these photons changes alert the security pros that someone is trying to breach the link. The next chapter, "A HIPAA Security and Privacy Compliance Audit and Risk Assessment Mitigation Approach," by Prof. Young B. Choi of Regent University, USA and Prof. Christopher E. Williams of Regent University, USA, explores network design in order to meet the complexity standards and unpredictable measures posed by attackers. Additionally, the network must adhere to HIPAA security and privacy requirements required by law. Successful implantation of network design will articulate comprehension requirements of information assurance security and control. The following chapter, "A New Perspective on the Swiss Cheese Model Applied to Understanding the Anatomy of Healthcare Data Breaches," by Prof. Faouzi Kamoun of ESPRIT School of Engineering, Tunisia and Prof. Mathew Nicho of Zayed University, UAE, reveals how Reason's swiss cheese model (SCM) provides a powerful analytic model to explain the human, technical, and organizational factors of healthcare data breaches. The next chapter, "Exploring System Thinking Leadership Approaches to the Healthcare Cybersecurity Environment," by Prof. Maurice Dawson of Illinois Institute of Technology, USA; Prof. Amalisha Sabie Aridi of Capitol Technology University, USA; Prof. Calvin Nobles of University of Maryland Global Campus, USA; Prof. Anton Shufutinsky of Cabrini University, USA; Prof. Quatavia McLester of The Chicago School of Professional Psychology, USA; Prof. Darrell Norman Burrell of The Florida Institute of Technology, USA & Capitol Technology University, USA; and Prof. S. Raschid Muller of Capitol Technology University, USA, explores the nuances and complexities around systems thinking in the healthcare cybersecurity environment. The following chapter, "Adopting Organizational Cultural Changes Concerning Whistle-Blowing in Healthcare Around Information Security in the 'Internet of Things' World," by Prof. Maurice Dawson of Illinois Institute of Technology, USA; Prof. Sharon L. Burton of Grand Canyon University, USA; Prof. Darrell Norman Burrell of The Florida Institute of Technology, USA; Prof. Nimisha Bhargava of AUL Corporation,

Napa, USA; Prof. Delores Springs of Regent University, USA; Prof. Damon P. Anderson of Capitol Technology University, USA; and Prof. Jorja B. Wright of The University of Charleston, USA, presents a foundation to establish techniques and practices for open door policies. The next chapter, "Opinions on Cyber Security, Electronic Health Records, and Medical Confidentiality: Emerging Issues on Internet of Medical Things From Nigeria," by Prof. Ibrahim Taiwo Adeleke of Federal Medical Centre, Bida, Nigeria and Prof. Qudrotullaah Bolanle Suleiman Abdul of University of Ilorin Teaching Hospital, Nigeria, deploys a cross-sectional design to determine perceptions of Nigerian healthcare providers toward medical confidentiality and cyber security in the wake of electronic health records and IoMT. The following chapter, "Impact of Information Technology on Patient Confidentiality Rights: A Perspective," by Prof. Abba Amsami Elgujja of University of Salford, UK, undertakes a general review of the benefits and dangers of embracing these new information technologies and their impact on the confidentiality of sensitive health data. The next chapter, "Blockchain for Healthcare and Medical Systems," by Profs. Sanaa Kaddoura and Rima Grati of Zayed University, UAE, studies the opportunity of blockchain to leverage biomedical and healthcare applications and research. Blockchain also contributes to the medication manufacturing area. The following chapter, "Security and Privacy for Electronic Healthcare Records Using AI in Blockchain," by Profs. Ramani Selvanambi, Samarth Bhutani, and Komal Veauli of Vellore Institute of Technology, Vellore, India, proposes the use of blockchains to store and secure data will not only ensure data privacy but will also provide a common method of data regulation. The next chapter, "Geo-Location-Based File Security System for Healthcare Data," by Prof. Govinda K. of VIT University, India, provides a mechanism to create a secure file storage system that provides two-layer security. The first layer is in the form of a password, through which the file is encrypted at the time of storage, and second is the locations at which the user wants the files to be accessed. The following chapter, "Electronic Health Record Security in Cloud: Medical Data Protection Using Homomorphic Encryption Schemes," by Profs. Desam Vamsi and Pradeep Reddy of VIT-AP, India, explains the homomorphism encryption (HE) method is very suitable for the electronic health record (EHR), which requires data privacy and security. The next chapter, "Provably Secure Data Sharing Approach for Personal Health Records in Cloud Storage Using Session Password, Data Access Key, and Circular Interpolation," by Prof. Naveen John of Nesamony Memorial Christian College, Marthandam, India and Prof. Shatheesh Sam of Manonmaniam Sundaranar University, India, develops a secure data sharing mechanism using the proposed session password, data access key, and circular interpolation (SKC)-based data-sharing approach for the secure sharing of PHR in the cloud. The following chapter, "TBHM: A Secure Threshold-Based Encryption Combined With Homomorphic Properties for Communicating Health Records," by Prof. Abdus Samad of University Women's Polytechnic, Aligarh Muslim University, Aligarh, India; Prof. Hitendra Garg of GLA University, Mathura, India; and Prof. Lalit Mohan Gupta of APJ Abdul Kalam Technical University, Lucknow, India, proposes a novel and secure threshold based encryption scheme combined with homomorphic properties (TBHM) for accessing cloud based health information. The next chapter, "Secure Healthcare Monitoring Sensor Cloud With Attribute-Based Elliptical Curve Cryptography," by Profs. Rakesh Kumar and Rajendra Kumar Dwivedi of Madan Mohan Malaviya University of Technology, Gorakhpur, India and Prof. Rajkumar Buyya of The University of Melbourne, Melbourne, Australia, proposes a security mechanism called attribute-based elliptical curve cryptography (ABECC) that guarantees data integrity, data confidentiality, and fine-grained access control. The following chapter, "Risk Reduction Privacy Preserving Approach for Accessing Electronic Health Records," by Prof. V. K. Saxena of Vikram University, Ujjain, India and Prof. Shashank Pushkar of Birla Institute of Technology, Mesra, India, introduces a novel risk reduction strategy for the healthcare domain so that the risk related with an access request is evaluated against the privacy prefer-ences of the patient who is undergoing for the medical procedure. The following chapter, "An Extended Attribute-Based Access Control (ABAC) Model for Distributed Collaborative Healthcare System," by Profs. Rabie Barhoun, Maryam Ed-daibouni, and Abdelwahed Namir of Hassan II University, Faculty of Science Ben M'sik, Casablanca, Morocco, proposes a new access control model, called Medical-Activity-Attribute-Based Access Control (MA-ABAC), which can effectively enhance the security for healthcare system and produce more perfect and flexible mechanism of access control; order to strong-ly respond to the requirements of the distributed healthcare environment. The next chapter, "Cybercrime and Private Health Data: Review, Current Developments, and Future Trends," by Prof. Athanasios An-astasiou of AiM Research Team, Biomedical Engineering Laboratory, National Technical University of Athens, Greece; Prof. Stavros Pitoglou of National Technical University of Athens, Greece & Com-puter Solutions SA, Greece; Prof. Dimitra Giannouli of Computer Solutions SA, Greece & University of Leeds, UK; Prof. Vassilia Costarides of Institute of Communication and Computer Systems (ICCS), Greece; and Prof. Thelma Androutsou of National Technical University of Athens, Greece, provides a historical review of recorded data breaches that resulted in extensive patient data leaks as well as sub-sequent efforts of monetization via black market structures that utilize the anonymity and counter-tracking environment that the dark/deep web and cryptocurrency provide. It also focuses on the methods and tools used by the villains, the types of vulnerabilities that can result in a successful attack, as well as latest developments and future trends in the field of scientific, technical, and legal/regulatory coun-termeasures that can be employed in order to prevent sensitive health data from falling into the wrong hands. The following chapter, "Assessing HIPAA Compliance of Open Source Electronic Health Record Applications," by Profs. Hossain Shahriar, Hisham M. Haddad, Maryam Farhadi of Kennesaw State University, USA, identifies HIPAA technical requirements, evaluate two open source EHR applications (OpenEMR and OpenClinic) for security vulnerabilities using two open-source scanner tools (RIPS and PHP VulnHunter) and maps the identified vulnerabilities to HIPAA technical requirements. The final chapter, "Electronic Healthcare Records: Indian vs. International Perspective on Standards and Privacy," by Prof. Aashish Bhardwaj of Guru Tegh Bahadur Institute of Technology, India and Prof. Vikas Kumar of Chaudhary Bansi Lal University, Haryana, India, explores the different aspects of health privacy and health records.

Although the primary organization of the contents in this work is based on its four sections offering a progression of coverage of the important concepts, methodologies, technologies, applications, social issues, and emerging trends, the reader can also identify specific contents by utilizing the extensive index-ing system listed at the end. As a comprehensive collection of research on the latest findings related to medical system and record security, the *Research Anthology on Securing Medical Systems and Records* provides security analysts, data scientists, hospital administrators, leaders in healthcare, medical pro-fessionals, health information managers, medical professionals, mobile application developers, security professionals, technicians, students, libraries, researchers, and academicians, and all audiences with a complete understanding of the challenges that face healthcare administrators and their patients. Given the need for medical system and record security, this extensive book presents the latest research and best practices to address these challenges and provide further opportunities for improvement.

# Section 1
# Securing Healthcare Systems

# Chapter 1
# Cyber Threats in the Healthcare Sector and Countermeasures

**Muhammad Mashhood Ahmed**
https://orcid.org/0000-0001-9825-3476
*De Montfort University, UK*

**Leandros Maglaras**
https://orcid.org/0000-0001-5360-9782
*De Montfort University, UK*

**Mohamed Amine Ferrag**
https://orcid.org/0000-0002-0632-3172
*Guelma University, Algeria*

## ABSTRACT

*Healthcare is one of the most targeted industries by cybercriminals. The healthcare sector is far behind in cybersecurity as compared to other organizations. The vulnerabilities in the system open the door for cybercriminals to exploit it and get unauthorized access into the system or network to do a malicious activity. Healthcare should have to take cyber threats seriously and follow a security framework that detects and mitigates cyber threats. This chapter presents all cyber threat actors that exist in the healthcare sector, common cyber-attacks that can be launched against all actors, and real incidents that took place during the past years. Based on these, the authors propose in a tabular form a set of recommendations that can be used as countermeasures against any type of attack.*

## INTRODUCTION

A Cyber threat is a malicious act by an individual or organisation to steal the data and damage the computer, systems and networks. The threats include in cyber-attacks are malware, phishing, denial of services and data breaches. In 1971, Bob Thomas was the first person who created the first virus and named Creeper. He just wanted to create a self-duplicating program. Creeper is a worm which replicates

DOI: 10.4018/978-1-6684-6311-6.ch001

itself and spreads from one computer to another computer. It displayed the phrase "I am a creeper, catch me if you can" on the computer screen. It was not like a today modern era virus who cause damage, steal information, encrypt the files or demand for a ransom (Parikka, 2007). In 1986, Clifford Stoll who was the system administration at the Lawrence Berkeley National Laboratory, notice a suspicious activity in accounting data. He Found out that unauthorised person was hacking in to his system. Robert Tappan Morris is the son of cryptographer Robert Morris. He graduated from Cornell University. In 1988, he did the first cyber-attack with good attention but ended with horrible consequences. He wanted to know how big the internet is so he developed the Morris worm virus which travels the web, installs itself automatically on other systems and then counts how many duplicate copies it created (Orman, 2003). The consequences caused by this worm was a horrible nightmare and it damaged approximately 6000 computers and total estimated damage of $98 million. His program was the first type of cyber-attack called "distributed denial of services". Morris was charged fines and three years of trial to violate the Computer Fraud and Abuse Act.

There are different types of cyber threat actors who do cyber-attacks for their own benefits or as a revenge from the company. These actors cause damage to the organisations, steal the data or demand a ransom. Cyber criminals are also targeting the healthcare sector because it is an easier task to do. Healthcare sector is spending very limited budget in IT department to secure their systems or networks so there are few back doors for the hackers to get unauthorized access in to the system and cause damage. The systems are not secure because they are using almost out-dated software and old version of operating systems.

The main reason for targeting the healthcare sector is that the patient sensitive information is valuable and worth a lot of money. It is more valuable than the credit card and provides a decent amount of money to hackers if they sell the information. Cyber criminals also use the information to make fake ID to take full advantage of the healthcare facilities and claim the insurance as well.

There are many cyber-attacks are happening in the healthcare sector which are causing a lot of damages economically and reputation. For example, in UK, USA and many other countries healthcare sector was hacked and the damage it causes was too much. In most cases data breaches and ransomware attacks took place. Common impacts on the healthcare sector when an incident happened were loss of reputation and patient's trust, compromised medical data and risk of patient safety. Newly trends of cyber-attacks are hackers that sell out the medical information on the black market. Ransomware and phishing emails both are the most attack happen in the healthcare sector cause data breach and loss of billions of dollars.

The UK has identified sixteen critical infrastructure sectors including the healthcare and protection of these infrastructures is very important. The UK and every other country must use a security framework in order to detect and mitigate the cyber incidents. NIS directive is the cyber security law implemented across the EU countries. The objective of the directive is to create a common framework that EU countries can use in order to detect and protect the systems and networks from cyber-attacks (Maglaras, 2018).

When people are aware about the cyber threats and know how much damage they cause then they are ready to take action that could mitigate these attacks. There are many different ways to mitigate cyber-attacks which are really helpful in order to secure the systems or networks. In this chapter, different types of countermeasures are discussed and also their advantages and disadvantages as well. Once a healthcare provider is secure the can be more competitive against their competitors (Makarona E, 2019), (Kavoura A. a., 2017) and should incorporated in the strategic design of new co mpanies in the field (Kavoura A. a., 2016).

As stated in the latest report from ENISA (ENISA, 2020) cybersecurity becomes more of a priority for hospitals and it is essential to be integrated holistically inside all processes, components and stages that may influence the healthcare ICT ecosystem. During the coronavirus pandemic a lot of cyber incidents using or targeting the Health sector globally since January 2020 were reported. The Coronavirus (COVID-19) pandemic is used as the vehicle to attack and the vast majority of the incidents are related to cybercrime, using Spearphishing, Malware, Ransomware, DDoS, Misinformation campaign, and even mobile telephony attacks (SMShing). Moreover, in order to showcase the importance of cybersecurity on healthcare the European cyber exercise that ENISA organizes every two years (Cyber Europe 2020) is focused on healthcare and involves national/governmental CSIRTs, Cybersecurity Authorities, Ministries of Health, healthcare organisations (e.g. hospitals/clinics), eHealth service providers, and health insurance providers.

Based on these findings this book chapter presents all cyber threat actors that exist in the healthcare sector, common cyber-attacks that can be launched against all actors and real incidents that took place during the past years. Based on these, the current chapter, proposes in a tabular form a set of recommendations that can be used as countermeasures against any type of attack. These recommendations can be incorporated into a cybersecurity framework or cyber security assessment model that healthcare providers could use in order to perform a gap analysis, assess their security level and take appropriate mitigation actions.

## Cyber Threat Actors

Cyber threat Actor can be anyone individual person or group of people from any organisation who just do malicious things for their own benefits and revenges (Ayres, 2016). Some of the cyber threat actors are as follows which include:

- Individual users who are alone and using their own software tools to create an attack.
- Organisations that are running criminal stuff like developing and executing attacks.
- Insider who is unhappy from their bosses.
- Terrorists
- Hackers
- Business competitors (who wants to know new ideas or plans from their competitor)
- Nation State (Countries who want to know other's country secrets)
- Spy

Cybercriminals are targeting the healthcare industry for many years. The main reason behind it is that healthcare data is more valuable than many traditional resources. On dark web, cyber criminals buy and sell patients records for various purposes, like identity theft. Healthcare sector has a vast amount of data such as bank account details, personal information, transaction records, and diagnosis, and these types of data is the main target for the cyber criminals.

From the past few decades until now, healthcare sector remains on a low priority in order to spend the money in IT security as compared to other big organisations. Previously hospitals used to record their health data on paper-based system such as registers and after that when they change their system to electronic system they created more entry points for cyber criminals (Evans, 2019).

The IoT medical devices like the ones used for monitoring heart rate or insulin levels were initially designed without the security aspect in mind. These devices can be used from cyber criminals in order to launch an attack on a hospital server that contains critical and valuable information. Cyber criminals see the medical devices as an easy target as well as other devices like mobile phones and laptops which are not really secure (Ferrag, 2018). These devices are the biggest issue for healthcare sector since they open back doors for attackers to get access into the network and cause damage.

Hospitals store a large amount of patient's data on their server that worth more money than the actual financial data such as credit cards, debit cards. Cyber criminals use the patient information to create the fake ID and buy the medical equipment's or medicines and can claim insurance by using the false patient ID number along with the provider number.

In most of the cases people discover after a long-time when cyber criminals already take benefits of health services from their personal medical ID. If patient data contain sensitive protected health information (PHI) such as sexually transmitted diseases or psychological problems cyber criminals can use this information to blackmail the patients. This is actually a hospital responsibility to secure their patients data (Zhang, 2018). When cyber criminals exploit the vulnerability and get inside the targeted system then they can install a ransomware and block out the user access to the systems and ask for ransom payment in order to unblock the sensitive data.

The healthcare industry is using out dated operating systems such as window XP or window 7 due to their limited budget. The second issue is that staff hesitate to learn new systems. An expert report found out that about "76% of healthcare sectors are using window 7 on their systems and 22% of healthcare customers browse on unsupported versions of internet explorer". The outdated software contains bugs and that is the biggest problem for the healthcare sector while updated versions contain bug fixes in order to secure the systems. Healthcare sector has responsibility to quickly act on any latest threat in order to protect the patient data.

## Common Cyber Threats

Cyber-attacks are growing now a days and every organisation in every country including healthcare system are also being targeted by cyber criminals. The worst thing is the impact and damage the cyber-attack caused. The problem is in the systems and networks, which are vulnerable and opens the back door for the attacker to get inside and stole the confidential data.

According to the researcher's report there are common cyber threats that are causing serious damages to the healthcare industry as well. The most common types of cyber threats are as follows:

## Malware

Malware is a piece of software which is developed by cyber criminals to gain unauthorized access into the computers or networks to cause damage and steal sensitive data. It consists of executable code, malicious content and scripts. It is sent in the form of file or a link via email. In order to execute the malware, the user has to click on it. There are different types of malware, like viruses, Trojans and worms.

A Virus is the most common type of malware. A Virus is a malicious piece of software that when executed, creates copies of itself by modifying other computer files and programs. Virus can spread too quickly from one computer to another computer and damage core functionality, corrupting software operation and locking users out of the systems. Cyber criminals before writing a virus make use of social engineering techniques and exploit the knowledge they obtain about security vulnerabilities that exist into the networks. Usually viruses mostly target system that are using Microsoft windows and by using a complex anti-detection technique manage to avoid being captured by anti-virus software.

There are different types of viruses which are affecting the systems on daily basis. For example; Resident Virus, Multiple Virus, Direct Action Virus, Overwrite Virus, Browse Hijacker, Web Scripting Virus, Boot Sector Virus, Directory Virus, Macro Virus, Polymorphic Virus, Encrypted Virus, File Infector Virus, Companion Virus, Non resident Virus, Network Virus, Stealth Virus, Space filler Virus, Sparse Infector and FAT Virus. (Subramanya, 2001).

A worm is a common type of malware which has the ability to replicate itself and spread from computer to computer without any human interaction. It does not need to attach itself to any software to cause damage to the systems. A Worm can get into the systems as an attachment file via spamming email or messages. When the user opens the attachment file, he automatically downloads the worm into the system. When it is installed, it goes in the system and infect it without the knowledge of the user. A worm can add other malicious software as well in the computer. Worms have the ability to modify and delete files and give access to the cyber criminals so they can control the system and its settings. There are different types of worms such as email worms, Instant message worms, Internet worms, file-sharing network worms and IRC worms (Weaver 2003).

A Logic bomb is another type of malware that is activated when specific conditions are met such as when the pre-defined date or time is reached. Cyber criminals can add a malicious code of logic bomb in a fake application or with another malware such as spyware so they can steal users' credentials and cause more damage. It is not like virus or worms that spread from one computer to another.

Ransomware is a malicious malware that takes over your system, prevents the users from accessing their data and ask for ransom payment in order to provide access to the data. First ever ransom was developed in 1980's and payment were sent via snail mail but today cyber criminals demand for ransom payment to be sent via cryptocurrency because it is safe and do not leak the information who is the sender and receiver of the payment. Most common way to send ransom is malspam. Cyber criminals deliver ransom via emails by attaching a PDF or Word files. Attackers use social engineering techniques to trick people to open attached files or click specific links by faking friend or trusted institution name. Another way to send ransom is malvertising in which they advertise an attractive ad on an internet. While browsing, user see an ad which seems interesting and clicks on it (Sood, 2011). There are different types of ransomware such as scareware, screen lockers and Encrypting ransomware.

Spyware is a software that can hijack your system. It is installed in the system to track and monitor the user activity on the web. It is not a virus to replicate itself and damage the systems but it is a software which gives access to your computer without your permission. Some organisations intentionally install this software in the systems in order to monitor user activity. There are four types of spyware: adware, system monitors, trojans and tracking cookies.

Adware is a software that pops-up advertisements or banners on your screen within a web browser on a computer screen. Developers add an adware software in their websites or software so it can automatically generate revenue for them. It is also used as a malicious adware software like virus or trojan to steal credentials of the users. For example: adware enter in to your system when user download a peer-to-peer file in which the adware is hidden then the pop-up ads begins to show after the program files are loaded on your system and add tracking cookies, key loggers or hard drive scans so it may transfer passwords, documents, credit card numbers and pictures to the cyber criminals.

## MAN IN THE MIDDLE ATTACK

During a Man-in-the-middle attack an attacker secretly intercepts the communication between two parties in order to steal sensitive credentials, corrupt the data or spy on the victims. This attack always has three players: Victim, Man in the middle (who is intercepting the communication) and Third party (to whom victim is communicating).

For example: user gets an email from the bank asking him to log in to the account and confirm the information. The user does not know about the middle of the man in this scenario. The attacker has actually created a fake website and send the email to the user which looks like one that originated from the bank so the user clicks on it and logs in without hesitation. This means that the user itself handed over the credentials to the cybercriminal.

Session Hijacking is a malicious activity also known as a TCP session hijacking. It is a technique in which the attacker hijacks the trusted web user session by secretly getting the session ID. After accessing the User's session ID then attacker can do anything on the network that the legitimate user is authorized to do. To do a session hijacking, hackers use a sniffer application such as wireshark or OWASP Zed to capture the network traffic which has the session ID between website and client. When capturing the string which is known as token the attacker can use the valid token to get the unauthorised access in to the web server.

IP spoofing is a hacking technique in which the attacker creates an internet protocol (IP) with the fake IP address in its header. The purpose of creating the fake IP address is to hide the attacker own identity when attacking a server or any other device. Ip spoofing is not illegal because since users can fake their IP address to hide their internet activities and enjoy online privacy. It is illegal if someone uses the spoofing in order to pretend being someone else and do criminal acts such as identity theft.

A reply attack is a malicious attack in which the attacker secretly intercepts on a secure network communication and fraudulently delays or repeats the valid data transmission. This attack helps the attacker to get the authorised access in a network to steal the information or complete a duplicate transaction.

It is important to note here that humans need to cooperate with start-ups, university hubs and or governments in order to find ways to deal with attacks that may also contribute in other sectors apart from health (Filkins, 2004)

## PHISHING ATTACK AND SPEAR PHISHING ATTACK

Phishing attack is a hacking technique in which attacker sends a fake call, email or message in the form of a link or attachment file through any bank or organisation in order to acquire details of a targeted person such as account number, credit or debit card or password for a malicious purpose. The cyber criminals send a fake email or message so the target user click on it, which is similar to any organisation or bank webpage. Phishing emails or messages are send to a very large number of people with the expectation that few will respond to it. Phishing attacks typically rely on a social engineering technique which is applied to emails or other electronic communication such as direct messaging sent over social networks, SMS text messages and other instant messages. Phishers may also use other social engineering and other information gathering techniques in order to get the information from LinkedIn, Twitter or Facebook to gather background information about the targeted personal and work history, interests and activities.

Spear phishing attack works like a phishing attack but the difference is that the attacker carefully design the emails to target to a single user in order to make him replay back. Cyber criminals select individual persons to target in an organisation using social media or other information gathering techniques to get some confidential information and then use them in order to create a fake email or message for the targeted individual.

## PASSWORD ATTACK

Password attack or cracking is a technique to recover the passwords which has been forgotten or to gain an unauthorised access to the targeted system. Organisations system administrators usually use this technique to check easily crackable passwords in order to suggest the staff to use a strong password to protect their system from any cyber activity. Cracking a password is not an easy task because most of the services lock down the accounts on repeated login attempts. Once an attacker gets a complete list of cracked passwords then he will try his best to break it. The goal of the attacker is to look for large number of targets so they crack down their target's password one by one rather than just to crack the password of an individual person.

Brute-force attack is a technique to get the information such as username, passwords and PIN. Brute-force can be done by using an automated software which is used to try to guess the combinations of passwords such as administrator password, encryption key or a hash key of the password. This technique is used by cyber criminals to decrypt the encrypted data. Organisations security analyst also used the brute-force to test the network security in order to make it more secure. Brute-force techniques happen in the early stages of attack when attackers are trying to get authorised access in to their targeted systems. Attackers use the brute-force in order to check hidden web pages which are not linked to other web pages and which can be exploited easily. Computers are incredibly fast so cyber criminals can do a brute-force in order to crack the password 8 character long in just 2 hours and decrypt the weak encryption hash in just a month. If the password is longer 8 characters, with a combination of Capital or small alphabets and special characters then it makes brute-force more difficult and takes years to guess it.

Dictionary attack is a technique which is used to crack or recover the password by using an actual dictionary list. The type of passwords includes in dictionary list are common password list such as pet names, famous names of television character and other words. Dictionary attack can be used where password is weak and easy to guess such as words, numbers or just phrases. It does not mean if the password is weak then attacker can easily crack the password, it takes a long time and a many attempt.

## SQL INJECTION ATTACK

SQL Injection attack is a technique which is used to hack a website by inserting malicious SQL statements which make some condition give as outcome always true. A website has two important components, one is the html code and the second is database server. The SQL statements control the database server. These database servers contain username and passwords which are the main target for cyber criminals. Cyber criminals use SQL statement in order to add, delete and modify the data or queries from the database to gain the full control of the database server. To do a SQL injection attack, the attacker has to find the vulnerabilities in the web application and then put the malicious SQL code on a user login form in order to get the unauthorised access in to the database.

For example; In the user login page, write the SQL condition in the password field e.g. 1' or '1'='1 then it will show the list of usernames and their passwords if there is a vulnerability in the web application code. This condition 1' or '1'='1 always makes the query 'TRUE' in the database. After getting the username and passwords, hackers easily get access in to the system.

## CROSS-SITE SCRIPTING ATTACK

A Cross-site scripting attack is an activity in which the malicious code is injected into trusted websites. Cross-site scripting is known as XSS. XSS attack happen when the cybercriminal uses the website as a vehicle to transport the malicious code to the targeted user in the form of a HTML script. When the user visits the web application then the code executes. Vulnerabilities in the websites allows the attacks to be successfully occur. The most commonly vulnerable vehicle used for the XSS attack are web pages comment section and forums. XSS attack mostly happen in JavaScript. XSS vulnerabilities are less dangerous as compared to the SQL injection vulnerabilities. There are three types of Cross-site scripting attacks: DOM-based XSS, Reflected XSS and Stored XSS.

## EAVESDROPPING ATTACK

Eavesdropping attack in which attacker intercepts the communication between the sender and the receiver. In this attack, cybercriminal steals the information that smartphones, computers and other electronic devices send over a network. Eavesdropping attacks are not easy to be detected because they do not cause any abnormal activity in a network transmission.

Cybercriminals can intercept the data which is transmitting between sender and receiver over a network by installing a network monitoring software on their computer or server. Attacker can insert or install a software in the targeted system directly or by malware then come back later in order to check the retrieved data. Data sniffing can be done easily on the local network as well as on the wireless networking. In local networks, data is sent to all ports and sniffer can easily accept all incoming data. In wireless networks, the data is broadcast so if the sniffer is using a proper tool then he can receive the data.

## DENIAL OF SERVICES ATTACK AND DISTRIBUTED DENIAL OF SERVICE ATTACK

Denial of service is a cyber-attack in which cybercriminals aims to interrupt the devices normal functioning so that devices are unavailable for the users. Dos Attack is done by flooding the network or servers with requests so it is difficult for the authorised victim to access it. It is difficult to recover from a denial of service attack. When attack crashes the server, sometimes it can be handled by just rebooting the system. A Dos attack can be launch by using a single computer. The US-CERT team provide some guidelines and indications that can be used in order to discover a Dos attack such as difficulties to access the website, higher number of spamming emails than usual and bad network performance. The motive behind this attack is to harm the organisation or the individual target but sometimes cyber criminal demand for the payment from the victim to end the DOS attack.

A Distributed denial of service attack is the most powerful cyber-attack on the internet. Cyber criminals aim is to send too much traffic to make a server or network unavailable for the user by flooding a website. The traffic used to make server unavailable contains fake packets or requests for connections. Botnets plays an important role to launch the DDos attack.

Buffer overflow is a type of Denial of service attack when more data insert in to the limited length of buffer and the extra data start to corrupting or overwriting the data in that limited space which causes the overflow and results in system crash. The malicious overflow data also creates the opportunity for the cyber criminals to run the script in order to do a malicious activity.

Flood attack is a kind of distributed denial of service attack in which it consumes all the available server resources in order to make a server unavailable for the target. Three-way handshake of TCP connection could be exploited by a flood attack. The attacker floods the victim device with the connection requests and when the victim device replies back the attacker the attacker system does not respond back due to which the victim system causes to time out and force the system to crash.

A Smurf Attack is a type of distributed denial of services attack. It uses ICMP request packets and IP spoofing to the targeted system. Smurf attack has a potential to exploit the broadcast networks IP addresses. The ICMP echo requests start from the fake targeted address.

Ping Death is a malicious type of denial of service attack. The attacker aim is to crash or freeze the victim computer or network by sending a large number of packets by using a ping command. POD attack can exploit the vulnerability which is already patched in the targeted system and for the unpatched systems, this attack is very dangerous.

Botnets are systems controlled by the cybercriminal which were infected in a previous stage with a specific malware. These botnets are very difficult to locate because bots are located in different locations in the world. These bots are used to launch an attack on the target system in order to consume the bandwidth and increase the processing tie of the victim's system.

## LOT ATTACKS

Internet of things are those advance tech devices which are smart enough to do their tasks and can work wirelessly and do not need to connect to other devices to communicate by wire such as mobile phones, tablets, pagers, wearable tech which measure heart rate and insulin level, cameras, headphones, cars, etc. In modern era, broadband service is growing, gadgets with Wi-Fi capabilities are introudced day by day and processors are more efficient and affordable. The devices makers are creating the devices that can collect, send and shares the data. These gadgets make the life of users a lot easier. In hospitals, modern tech devices are able to monitor the patients more efficiently and make the communication easy between the staff and doctor. Cyber criminals are targeting these devices because these devices are not very secure.

### Insider threats

Insiders are those one who know everything about the organisation, such as employees, former employees or business associates. Insider threat may occur by the three different kinds of people:

- **Malicious Insiders:** employees of an organization who take advantage of their rights for harming an organisation for their personal benefits.
- **Negligent Insiders:** employees of an organisation who are not following the policies and take the organisation at risk.
- **Infiltrators:** not part of the organisation but secretly gather information.

## CYBER ATTACK INCIDENTS

### Singapore

In 2018, a report published stated that Singapore was hit by a major cyber-attack. SingHealth is the largest Singapore healthcare group that was targeted by state-sponsored hackers. They stole the healthcare data of 1.5 million people and approximately 160,000 medical reports including the prime minister Lee Hsien Loong by exploiting an unpatched version of Microsoft outlook. They used a hacking tool which is available publicly and allowed them to install the malware on their vulnerable systems. In the published report, it was explained that the attack campaign lasted more than 10 months and stole the medical data as well as confidential data such as names, address, numbers and National identity card IDs. The main purpose was to target the higher-level individuals from politicians to industrial mangers (Quah, 2014). SingHealth has been fined $250,000 and the IT agency (IHiS) who is responsible for Singapore health sector get financial penalty of $750,000 for failing not to take the security measures to protect the information so the total sum is $1 million fine. Based on the success of the attack we can conclude that the staff of IHiS did not have the proper cyber security awareness and training which was the reason staff did not respond quickly and effectively to the attack. Moreover, there were mis-configurations and vulnerabilities in the SingHealth Network and SCM system that should have been resolved before the attack. Finally, the IT security incident response team of an IHiS failed to take an appropriate or timely action to prevent data stealing.

Based on the findings of the analysis of this incident the recommendations that could be given to the organizations would include the improvement of cyber security policies, the redesign of their incident response plans, the scheduling of appropriate training of key staff of the organization, the installation of IPS and IDS systems and the overall change of the governance model in terms of cyber security.

### United Kingdom

The year 2017 was a nightmare in the history of cyber World because of a global cyber-attack known as WannaCry ransomware. A report from the department of health and social care found that NHS is attacked by the cyber criminals which costs NHS a total estimated amount of £92m. The WannaCry attack caused a serious damage to more than 80 trusted hospitals and 8% of GP practices. The total of 200,000 computers were shut down and lock out the users with the error messages demanding the ransom payment through Bitcoins. According to the report, WannaCry attack cancelled a number of total 19,000 appointments which costed the NHS £20 million and £72 million in order to clean up the mess and upgrades the IT systems. After the Investigation the attack is blamed on the North Korea Hackers. When the attack happened, NHS was using outdated operating system and software such as Windows XP which is vulnerable and allowed attackers get unauthorised access in to their systems. NHS had increased the infrastructure investment of £60 millionin 2018 and Government said that they will spend the total of £150 million to upgrade their IT technology over the next three years. The results have shown that organisations have made good progress in implementing data security standards related to people and process, but that those relating to technology continue to be challenging.

One year before the incident, NHS was warned about the cyber-attack because their two local healthcare branches were infected previously by a ransomware attack. One major reason that attack was successful was that NHS was running old operating system (Window XP) in their systems. Based on the findings of the analysis of this incident the recommendations that could be given to the organizations would include the update of the operating systems, the development of appropriate incident response plans, the scheduling of appropriate training of key staff of the organization, the installation of antivirus, antimalware, IPS and IDS systems and the overall change of the governance model in terms of cyber security.

## Data Breach:

After the devastating WannaCry attack, NHS was affected by a data breach in 2018. NHS accidentally shared the sensitive data of 150,000 patients. The reason behind is a coding error in the IT system known asSystmOne used by GPs and developed by the TPP. Confidential data were given to the healthcare on the basis that it was used to provide the medical care to the people but it was exploited for research purposes and clinical audit by the NHS without the knowledge of patients. All the GPs and the patients have been informed about this issue. The Software Developer TPP apologised for the fault in the system and working with the NHS digital to resolve the issue. TPP clinical director John Parry said the privacy of patient data "is a key priority for TPP, and we continually make improvements to our system to ensure that patients have optimum control over information". This attack was due to a coding error in the SystmOne software. A correct countermeasure for this attack is the testing of any new software before deployment by the software assurance team.

## United States of America

UnityPoint Health data breach was the biggest breach in the history of the US. A total of 1.4 million patient records has been breached. A Phishing attack was used in order to compromise their business system. In 2018, there are two data breaches in UnityPoint health. First breach happened in its Madison campus by a phishing attack on a staff member email account and breached the total of 16,000 patient's confidential data. According to the report, the staff of the UnityPoint health received the attachment file in the email, used to trick them to give the login information which led the hacker get access into their internal email system. According to the forensics investigators and law enforcement research, the purpose of the attack was financially based because the hackers were trying to use the email system of the staff to make changes in the payroll payments.

The unauthorised access to their patient confidential data have happened but there is no misuse of the patient data is still reported. The main focus of the hackers was to divert the business funds of an organisation. This attack exploited the human factor that is responsible for the majority of the cyber attacks. In this instance proper training along with specific technologies that can secure email applications (mail filters, IDS and IPS) along with proper incident response plans are the first recommendations to give to this organization.

On the 18th of March of 2018, another cyber-attack which compromised the confidential data of 500,000 patients of LifeBridge took place. The EMR server of the LifeBridge Health that shared the registration and billing system for the other LifeBridge providers was infected with a malware that compromised the confidential information of patients. According to the investigation report, the hackers first got the access in to the servers on 2016 and compromised the data such as patient name, dates of birth, medical history, treatment information and insurance data of patients. Hackers also compromised the social security number of some patients. This attack exploited a vulnerability in the EMR server of the LifeBridge Health which allowed hackers to install malware in the system. Key recommendations for this incident would be the use of a secure SSL/HTTPS encryption protocol, installation of antivirus, patching and update of software and routers proper configuration.

## RECOMMENDATIONS

The table that follows states all recommendations that need to be taken in order to secure a hospital from cyber attacks., based also on the findings from the real incidents that happened during the past years. Other security measures can also be applied (Cook, 2017). Education of employees is an important aspect of cyber security and dedicated cyber ranges can be used (Hallaq, 2018). These recommendations can be used as a basis for building a cyber security framework that can be used from healthcare providers in order to perform a gap analysis and conduct cyber security assessments. These assessments can reveal the security gaps in the organization, help organize the mitigation plans and their immediate actions. A standardized maturity assessment model could be used a trademark for organizations to showcase their increased cyber security level and thus improve their entrepreneurial position.

The proposed countermeasures can be grouped in several categories. Technical measures consider the technological tools (software and hardware) to prevent, detect, mitigate, and respond to cyber-attacks. Organizational measures are important for the proper implementation of any type of national initiative or policy. Capacity building measures aim to enhance knowledge and know-how in order to promote cyber security. Finally, legal measures aim to provide legislations and an implementable regulatory framework to protect the cyber space.

## CONCLUSION

In Conclusion, Healthcare is the biggest industry in the world. Every country has its own healthcare system such as hospitals, care centres but they are not secure. The systems in the healthcare sector are vulnerable and software is most of the times outdated. Cyber criminals are targeting the healthcare sector because it is easy to exploit the vulnerabilities and steal the medical data which is valuable and worth a lot of money. Medical Information is a sensitive data of patient such as names, address, medical ID number and diagnosis.

There are many cyber threats which can affect the healthcare system in a second and cause a lot of damage which we cannot imagine. The impact of cyber-attacks is devastating. Millions of patient records were compromised during several attacks that took place in recent years which cost the loss of billions of dollars.

*Table 1.*

| No | Cyber Threats | | Recommendations |
|---|---|---|---|
| 1 | Malware | Virus | • Always keep your software updated and apply patches when released<br>• Do not click on links or download files if any untrusted email you get<br>• Always install an antivirus in your systems<br>• Always backup your data if you do not want to lose it. For backup use external hard drives or private cloud storage<br>• Use a strong password which includes Capital and small alphabets, numbers and special characters<br>• Turn on and configure properly firewalls which are built-in in your system<br>• On your browser always use an ad pop-up blocker<br>• Do not download files from untrusted websites. |
| | | Trojans | |
| | | Worms | |
| | | Logic bombs | |
| | | Ransomware | |
| | | Adware | |
| | | Spyware | |
| 2 | Ma-in-the-Middle Attack | Session Hijacking | • Use the secure SSL/HTTPS encryption protocol in order to secure your communication<br>• Always install antivirus software in your systems<br>• Always keep your software updated and patch which has a bug fix when release |
| | | IP spoofing | • Use secure encryption protocols like HTTPS<br>• Use a software like network blocker<br>• Configure your routers and switches in a way that they block the packets that are coming from other networks, not from your local network if supported |
| | | Replay | • Encryption: encrypt your messages |
| 3 | Phishing and Spear Phishing attack | | • Use ad pop-up blocker<br>• Install anti-virus software<br>• Always update software<br>• Always turn on firewalls |
| 4 | Password Attack | Brute-Force | • Use a two-factor authentication method<br>• Use a Multi-factor Authentication which is more secure |
| | | Dictionary Attack | |
| 5 | SQL Injection | | • Always update and apply patches<br>• Always turn on the web application firewalls<br>• Avoid using dynamic SQL queries<br>• Use encryption and password hashing to secure your data<br>• Install monitoring tools |
| 6 | XSS attack | | • Use SDL standard when you are developing the website<br>• On each page Use the right Meta tag to declare characters in your website<br>• Sanitize the data<br>• Add functions which validate the data |
| 7 | Eavesdropping | | • Encrypt your emails<br>• Use the secure SSL/HTTPS encryption protocol in order to secure your communication<br>• Use VPN's<br>• Use the secure SSL/HTTPS encryption protocol in order to secure your communication |
| 8 | Dos and DDos | Buffer overflow | • Disable the services which are unneeded<br>• Use a firewall<br>• Use an Intrusion prevention system |
| | | Flood overflow | • Use a firewall before servers<br>• increase the connection queue size and decrease the open connection timeout. |
| | | Smurf | • disable the router IP-directed broadcast |
| | | Ping Death | • use a firewall to block the ping death attack |
| | | Botnets | • Use the RFC3704 filtering which blocks the traffic from spoofed addresses<br>• Black-hole filtering which stops the undesirable traffic to enter in the network |
| 9 | IoT Attack | | • Use strong encryption<br>• Strong and unique passwords for the Wi-Fi network<br>• Keep your software updated<br>• Use a two-factor authentication method<br>• Try to avoid public free wi-fi<br>• Update your network devices like routers and switches which are offering strong security |
| 10 | Insider Threat | | • Monitor the activity<br>• Organisation must provide cyber security training to their employees to notice the suspicious activity and benefit of cyber security<br>• Publish a security policy<br>• Apply Physical security<br>• Secure the systems and use a secure authentication finger print scanner in the building |

It is always the organisation staff and higher rank officers' fault that they do not take the cyber-attack seriously and do not take the action immediately in order to secure their systems or networks. There are few security solutions that could be applied but healthcare sector should have to follow a proper security framework. There must be set of rules and regulations and policies. There must be an incident response team ready and well trained which immediately can act and try to mitigate an attack once happened. There are security mechanisms like an Intrusion detection system and an intrusion prevention system, that are really helpful in order to detect and block attacks that can be used in order to increase the security level of the healthcare sector.

This book chapter presents major cyber threat actors that exist in the healthcare sector, common cyber-attacks that can be launched against all actors and real incidents that took place during the past years. Based on these, the current chapter, proposes in a tabular form a set of recommendations that can be used as countermeasures against any type of attack. These recommendations can be incorporated into a cybersecurity framework or cyber security assessment model that healthcare providers could use in order to perform a gap analysis, assess their security level and take appropriate mitigation actions. A proper assessment can reveal any security gaps in the organization, help organize the mitigation plans and their immediate actions. A standardized maturity assessment model could be used a trademark for organizations to showcase their increased cyber security level and thus improve their entrepreneurial position.

## REFERENCES

Ayres, N., & Maglaras, L. A. (2016). Cyberterrorism targeting the general public through social media. *Security and Communication Networks*, *9*(15), 2864–2875. doi:10.1002ec.1568

Cook, A. J., Janicke, H., Maglaras, L., & Smith, R. (2017). An assessment of the application of IT security mechanisms to industrial control systems. *International Journal of Internet Technology and Secured Transactions*, *7*(2), 144–174. doi:10.1504/IJITST.2017.087163

Evans, M. H., He, Y., Maglaras, L., & Janicke, H. (2019). Heart-is: A novel technique for evaluating human error-related information security incidents. *Computers & Security*, *80*, 74–89. doi:10.1016/j.cose.2018.09.002

Ferrag, M. A. (2018). *Authentication schemes for Smart Mobile Devices: Threat Models, Countermeasures, and Open Research Issues.* arXiv preprint, arXiv:1803.10281

Gozzi, R. (2000). The Trojan horse metaphor. *ETC: A Review of General Semantics, 57*(1), 80-84.

Hallaq, B. N. (2018). CYRAN: a hybrid cyber range for testing security on ICS/SCADA systems. In Cyber Security and Threats: Concepts, Methodologies, Tools, and Applications (pp. 622-637). IGI.

Kavoura, A. a. (2017). Polish Firms' Innovation Capability for Competitiveness via Information Technologies and Social Media Implementation. Factors Affecting Firm Competitiveness and Performance in the Modern Business World. In A. N. Vlachvei (Ed.), Factors Affecting Firm Competitiveness and Performance in the Modern Business World. Academic Press.

Kavoura, A., & Andersson, T. (2016). Applying Delphi method for strategic design of social entrepreneurship. *Library Review*, *65*(3), 185–205. doi:10.1108/LR-06-2015-0062

Kenkre, P. S. (2014). Real time intrusion detection and prevention system. In *3rd International Conference on Frontiers of Intelligent Computing: Theory and Applications (FICTA)* (pp. 405-411). Springer International Publishing.

Kenkre, P. S. (2014). Taxonomy and survey of collaborative intrusion detection. *ACM Computing Surveys, 47*(4), 55.

Maglaras, L. A., Kim, K.-H., Janicke, H., Ferrag, M. A., Rallis, S., Fragkou, P., Maglaras, A., & Cruz, T. J. (2018). Cyber security of critical infrastructures. *ICT Express, 4*(1), 42–45. doi:10.1016/j.icte.2018.02.001

Makarona, E. K. A. (2019). Redesigning the Ivory Tower: Academic entrepreneurship as a new calling supporting economic growth, The Malopolska School of Economics. *Tarnow Research Papers Collection, 42*, 15–26.

Orman, H. (2003). The Morris worm: A fifteen-year perspective. *IEEE Security and Privacy, 1*(5), 35–43. doi:10.1109/MSECP.2003.1236233

Parikka, J. (2007). *Digital contagions: A media archaeology of computer viruses.* Peter Lang.

Quah, J. L., Yap, S., Cheah, S. O., Ng, Y. Y., Goh, E. S., Doctor, N., Leong, B. S.-H., Tiah, L., Chia, M. Y. C., & Ong, M. E. H. (2014). Knowledge of signs and symptoms of heart attack and stroke among Singapore residents. *BioMed Research International, 2014*, 1–8. doi:10.1155/2014/572425 PMID:24812623

Sadeghi, A. R. (2015). Security and privacy challenges in industrial internet of things. In *52nd Annual Design Automation Conference* (p. 52). ACM. 10.1145/2744769.2747942

Sood, A. K., & Enbody, R. J. (2011). Malvertising–exploiting web advertising. *Computer Fraud & Security, 2011*(4), 11–16. doi:10.1016/S1361-3723(11)70041-0

Subramanya, S. R., & Lakshminarasimhan, N. (2001). Computer viruses. *IEEE Potentials, 20*(4), 16–19. doi:10.1109/45.969588

Woo, P. S. (2015). *Towards Cyber Security Risks Assessment in Electric Utility SCADA Systems. Electrical Engineering and Technology, 10*(3), 888–894.

Zhang, X. L., Liu, S., Chen, X., Wang, L., Gao, B., & Zhu, Q. (2018). Health information privacy concerns, antecedents, and information disclosure intention in online health communities. *Information & Management, 55*(4), 482–493. doi:10.1016/j.im.2017.11.003

## ADDITIONAL READING

Andreasson, K. J. (Ed.). (2011). *Cybersecurity: public sector threats and responses.* CRC Press. doi:10.1201/b11363

Coventry, L., & Branley, D. (2018). Cybersecurity in healthcare: A narrative review of trends, threats and ways forward. *Maturitas, 113*, 48–52. doi:10.1016/j.maturitas.2018.04.008 PMID:29903648

Maglaras, L., Ferrag, M. A., Derhab, A., Mukherjee, M., Janicke, H., & Rallis, S. (2019). Threats, Protection and Attribution of Cyber Attacks on Critical Infrastructures. *arXiv preprint arXiv:1901.03899*.

Mariani, D. M. R., & Mohammed, S. (2015). Cybersecurity challenges and compliance issues within the US healthcare sector. *International Journal of Business and Social Research*, 5(02).

Rowe, B. R., & Gallaher, M. P. (2006, March). Private sector cyber security investment strategies: An empirical analysis. In *The fifth workshop on the economics of information security (WEIS06)*.

Shackelford, S. J., Proia, A. A., Martell, B., & Craig, A. N. (2015). Toward a global cybersecurity standard of care: Exploring the implications of the 2014 NIST cybersecurity framework on shaping reasonable national and international cybersecurity practices. *Tex. Int'l LJ*, *50*, 305.

## KEY TERMS AND DEFINITIONS

**CSIRT:** Computer security incident response team.
**ENISA:** European Union Agency for Cyber Security.
**ICT:** Information and communication technology.
**IDS:** Intrusion detection system.
**IPS:** Intrusion prevention system.

*This research was previously published in Entrepreneurial Development and Innovation in Family Businesses and SMEs; pages 109-124, copyright year 2020 by Business Science Reference (an imprint of IGI Global).*

# Chapter 2
# Digital Healthcare Security Issues:
## Is There a Solution in Biometrics?

**Punithavathi P.**
*VIT Chennai, India*

**Geetha Subbiah**
*VIT Chennai, India*

## ABSTRACT

*Digital healthcare system, which is undergoing transformation phase to provide safe, swift, and improved quality care, is experiencing diverse problems. The serious threats to the digital healthcare system include misidentification of patients and healthcare-related frauds. Biometrics is a cutting-edge scientific field which overcomes the weaknesses of password-based authentication methods while ensuring a friction-free user experience. It enables unprecedented authentication capabilities based on human characteristics that cannot be replicated by fraudsters. The growing demand for biometrics solutions in digital healthcare system is mainly driven by the need to combat fraud, along with an initiative to preserve privacy of the patient besides with healthcare safety. This chapter examines how biometric technology can be applied to the digital healthcare services.*

## EVOLUTION OF DIGITAL HEALTHCARE

Digital healthcare is the combination of both digital and genomic technologies with healthcare and society such that the efficiency of healthcare delivery is enhanced, and medicines are made more personalized and precise. The health problems and challenges faced by patients have been addressed simultaneously by both information and communication technologies. Digital healthcare involves both hardware and software solutions and services, including web-based analysis, email, telemedicine, text messages, mobile phones and applications, and clinic or remote monitoring sensors. Commonly, digital healthcare involves development of interconnected health systems to improve the use of computational technolo-

DOI: 10.4018/978-1-6684-6311-6.ch002

gies, computational analysis techniques, smart devices, and communication media to aid patients and healthcare professionals manage health risks and illnesses, as well as promote health and well-being.

In simple words, the growth of Internet of Things (IoT) (Gubbi, Buyya, Marusic, & Palaniswami, 2013) has revolutionized healthcare domain too. The multi-disciplinary digital healthcare involves many stakeholders, including researchers, clinicians, and scientists with a wide range of expertise in engineering, healthcare, public health, social sciences, health economics and management. Several personal healthcare tools like wearable sensors are the most popular elements of the healthcare domain. These wearables can be a device to measure physical parameters such as pulse, blood pressure, muscle exertion, blood oxygen, etc., or a sweat biosensor embedded on smartwatch to measure biochemical parameters such as hydration levels, body electrolytes, etc.

India Brand Equity Foundation has estimated that there are currently 930 million mobile users, 360 million internet users, and half a billion new smartphone users projected in the next five years. With these developments, it has been assessed that India will be a money-spinning market for sensors and mobile-based apps, especially in healthcare. Soon the doctor may be just a click away.

The digital healthcare is the confluence of healthcare and technology which are pivot elements in improving the efficiency of the healthcare management. The digital healthcare applications are still in budding stage in India while significant inroads have been made in the use of digital health and healthcare IT initiatives globally. The "E-health" (National Health Portal of India, n.d.) initiatives under the Government of India's "Digital Healthcare Program" aimed at addressing the healthcare gap in the country are slowly but surely revolutionizing the public health scenario in the country. Coupled with the large number of start-ups that are driving the penetration of technology in the healthcare sector, this joint public private focus on digital is paving the way to the future.

Cloud based services are gaining traction in the digital healthcare community. The combination of reliability, cost effectiveness and security has prompted many healthcare organizations to move data to the cloud for storage and analysis. New cloud opportunities are arising in promoting collaboration among care givers and in analysing large data sets (e.g. genomics). A GI cloud initiative under "MeghRaj" Policy (National Cloud of India, n.d.), Ministry of Electronics and Information Technology, Government of India, proves to be a cutting edge in providing seamless digital health services to rural people of India.

## THREATS TO DIGITAL HEALTHCARE

In the United States (US), healthcare is one of the biggest industries in trillion dollar club. The US has spent more on healthcare per person than any other nation in 2011 (Biometric Identification in Healthcare, n.d.), as per the World Health Organization (WHO). This trillion-dollar industry has always been under threat from malicious intruders as shown in Figure 1, compared to other sectors with huge economy.

The healthcare fraud consumes $80 billion a year in the US, as shown in Figure 2, according to an estimate by Federal Bureau of Investigation (FBI). Currently threats are even coming from the internet other than usual healthcare fraud like duplicate claims, fake billing, etc.

A study conducted by NTA in 2002 on 500 participants with approximately 21 passwords each, has revealed that about 81% of the participants use same password and about 30% of the participants write their passwords in a file. In 2017, "WannaCry" malware (What is Wannacry Ransomware, n.d.) attack badly affected the hospitals of several nations. Due to this attack, several computers and devices were left encrypted. It has become evident that the higher the dependency on information technology, the higher is the cyber-attack on healthcare facility mainly the patient records. The healthcare facilities have several operational challenges like patient identification and patient record maintenance.

*Figure 1. Data Breaches in Various Industries*

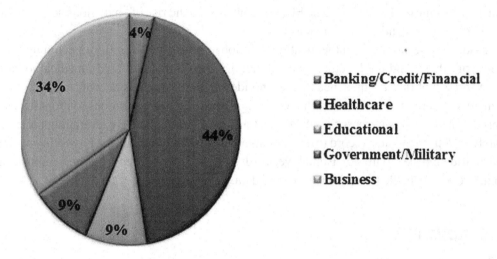

*Figure 2. Impacts of healthcare data breaches during the period of 2015-2019*

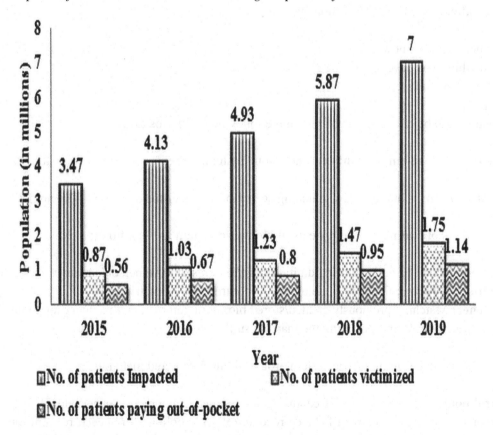

The hazards of stolen health care data to name a few are financial loss, inaccurate medical records and, thus, misdiagnosis. In last four years, there has been a steep increase of criminal intrusions into health care systems have risen 100% in the past four years, according to a recent Ponemon report (https://www.ponemon.org/library). In several incidents improper identification of patients has led to death of patients. A severe warning has been given by FBI to ward of serious cyber threats during mandatory migration to electronic health records. The FBI has emphasized the rise of "malicious actors" who target on medical device fields and health care data.

At a broader level, biometric authentication solutions prevent patients from becoming victims of medical identity theft. And unlike other types of identity theft (i.e. credit card), medical identity theft victims are rarely notified by their healthcare provider about suspicious account activity. Given the highly-sensitive nature of electronic health records, it is critical for organizations to properly secure patient information and restrict access to only a select group of individuals. By leveraging biometric data to accurately match the medical record to the patient, organizations eliminate the possibility of fraudsters accessing confidential data with stolen employee cards or passwords. Moreover, cybercriminals entering a system network are unable to steal the protected data.

## WHAT IS BIOMETRICS?

The term "Biometrics" is a means to verify or identify living subjects. The biometrics is physical or behavioural characteristic which is unique, permanent and quantitatively measurable identity of each and every individual. In a nut shell biometrics is:

1. "Something you know"
2. "Something you have"
3. "Something you are"

Biometrics can be effectively deployed in the following scenarios as follows:

1. **Verification/Authentication:** Is a one-to-one matching scenario to verify the claim "I am Mr. / Mrs. ...."
2. **Identification:** Is one-to-many matching scenario to answer the question "Who am I?"

The functions of four major components of biometric system are as follows:

1. **Scanner:** Scanning and capturing digital image/features of alive person's biometric characteristic
2. **Feature Extractor:** Creating template from captured raw biometric data
3. **Matcher:** Matching previously created/stored biometric template with a query template
4. **User Interface:** Communicating the match result

There are two stages in biometric system process – enrolment and matching.

- **Enrolment:** It is the process of capturing the biometric sample of an individual (e.g., using a sensor for fingerprint, camera for face recognition, microphone for speech recognition, camera for iris recognition). The unique features are then extracted from the biometric sample to create a template and store it in database.

- **Matching:** It is the process of matching a query template acquired from user during authorization grant with the template stored in database. A matching score is generated based on a determination of the common elements between the two templates. The threshold value for generating matching score is determined by the system designers based upon the convenience requirements of the system and security level.

## BIOMETRIC MODALITIES

Biometrics enables automated identification or verification of individuals based on their unique traits. Biometric modalities can be classified as follows:

### Physiological/Static Biometrics

Static biometrics refers to inherent physiological traits of an individual such as fingerprint, iris, hand-geometry, Deoxy-ribo Nucleic Acid (DNA), ears and other traits as shown in Figure 3. These attributes are acquired by each and every human during birth. In practice it is very hard to replicate them. Hence these attributes are highly reliable when used for identification.

### Behavioural/Dynamic Biometrics

Dynamic behavioural characteristics can be related to the behavioural characteristics of an individual. The examples include walking gait, voice, keystroke dynamics, mouse dynamics, etc. as shown in Figure 4. Brainwave signals are one among the latest dynamic behavioural area currently being explored. It is used to determine a person's mental state. These biometric traits ensure a high level of accuracy when tested in real time. Dynamic biometrics proves to be an active trait among the behavioural biometrics and they can be easily tracked in real time using emerging technologies. Several security experts prefer applied dynamic biometrics for verification purposes because of the fact that the process of acquiring static biometrics is a time-consuming process. The static biometrics is susceptible to several threats too.

### Selection of Biometric Modality

The process of selecting an appropriate biometric modality depends on the following factors:

1. Based on the nature of environment in which verification or identification process is performed
2. Based on the user profile, requirements for matching accuracy and throughput
3. Based on the cost and capabilities of the system
4. Based on the cultural issues which affects user acceptance

The comparison of between different biometric technologies is shown in Table 1. It also rates the performance of the metrics.

*Figure 3. Physiological biometrics*

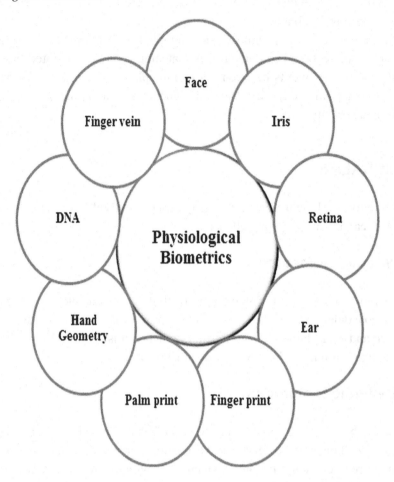

## WHY BIOMETRICS?

The healthcare identification is secured and enhanced by biometric technology. It is evident from the following claims:

1. Authenticating the patient in the provider's location will prevent card sharing and patient identity theft
2. Provider is prevented from billing for "phantom claims" or services when a patient is not at the provider location on the service date
3. Managing and verifying "encounter data" or services from providers so that data for setting of managed care rates
4. Checking the level of potential fraud called "upcoding" by creating an "audit trail" comprising check in and check out times for comparison against type of service provided

The additional benefits will be the following:

*Figure 4. Behavioural biometrics*

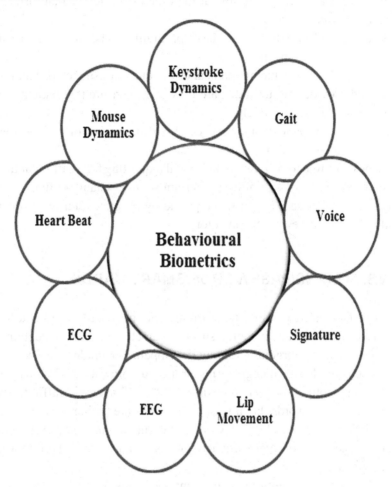

*Table 1. Comparison of popular biometric modalities*

| Biometric Modality | Accuracy | Uniqueness | Failure-to-Enrol Rate | Record Size | Universality | Durability |
|---|---|---|---|---|---|---|
| Face | M | M | L | H | H | M |
| Fingerprint | H | M | M | M | H | H |
| Hand Geometry | L | L | L | L | M | M |
| Iris | M | H | L | M | M | H |
| Signature | L | M | L | M | M | M |
| Vein | M | H | L | M | H | H |
| Voice | L | M | M | H | H | L |

(https://fas.org/irp/agency/dod/dsb/biometrics.pdf)
*H- High, M- Medium, L- Low

1.  Providers can verify if a patient is eligible at the time of service so that faster payments can be collected for services rendered
2.  Costs and risks associated with the 'pay & chase' programs can be reduced hence attempt to recoup inaccurate and fraudulent payments
3.  Patient safety is increased by reducing medical errors due to mismatch or incomplete records
4.  Unique patient and provider master index are provided to ensure that patient records in multiple provider locations are linked accurately
5.  Secured authentication of patients and providers; and protection of patient identity and patient health care information go hand-in-hand
6.  Biometrics can be employed to verify if an individual requesting for a particular treatment is eligible in cases where the individuals' eligibility for certain services changes often
7.  Inventory theft can be reduced. For instance providing accurate audit trails detailing the way in which the individual has accessed the inventory

## BIOMETRICS VS. TOKENS/PASSWORDS/SMART CARDS

With their increasingly frustrating parameters (warnings like password must be at least 12 characters long, should contain a capital letter, a number, a special character, and cannot contain a word, name, or a place), passwords can easily be forgotten, forcing developers to include a password reset feature that can be bypassed through simple social engineering or a brute force attack. The hackers can easily tap into a user terminal's Bluetooth or Wi-Fi connection and "sniff" network traffic to swipe both locally stored passwords as well as passwords that unsuspecting users are typing in when checking their bank account balance, for instance. Concisely, passwords represent an antiquated system of authentication, one that has no place in the world of internet, where the stakes and risks of both monetary and identity theft are among the greatest.

The front lines of security are identity management and access control. The insiders are separated from outsiders accurately by identifying the users and controlling what they do within your systems. The traditional tool for this task – the password – is apparently inadequate for the job. The emerging alternative solution is biometrics.

Passwords are the most common user authentication methods. It is comprised of a sequence of alphanumeric characters typed through a keypad or keyboard. For instance we largely use the Personal Identification Number (PINs) in bank applications. The followings claims prove that the password and PIN have not been an effective method:

1.  Mostly the users choose date of birth of them or their partner, telephone number, names, children/ pets, and other obvious choices. This has prone to be susceptible to guessing attacks. A test has shown that there is 90% chance of guessing the password correctly and gaining access to a system
2.  The users tend to write the passwords on a sheet of paper for future use. In such case the password is revealed to the external world easily. A poll conducted in United Kingdom has revealed that nearly one out of three people write down the PIN for their bank card. It has also been estimated that about one out of five people have been unable to withdraw money from an automatic teller machine due to the reason that they have been unable to remember their PIN
3.  An imposter may steal the password just by observing the owner entering it into a system

4.    In case if an owner wants to grant certain privilege to a colleague or a friend, the password is deliberately lent thus causing password breach

The user is not required to remember the password or PIN just by putting it into a Smart Card or Magnetic Strip Card. On the other hand the system can track the log details of the person at certain point of time. It becomes impossible to determine if the card has been used by an authorized user or an imposter. It becomes evident that the smart cards or other tokens are robust against the problems arisen by claims 1 and 2 but are susceptible to the claims 3 and 4.

The only way to solve all the above problems is to use biometrics. This is an efficient way to guarantee the presence of the owner at the place where a transaction is made. It is very difficult to counterfeit the biometric characteristics. The biometrics cannot be forgotten or lent like smart cards.

## BIOMETRICS IN DIGITAL HEALTHCARE

The term "healthcare biometrics" refers to biometric applications in doctors' offices, hospitals, or for use in monitoring patients. This can include access control, identification, workforce management or patient record storage. Biometrics in healthcare often takes two forms: providing access control to resources and patient identification solutions. Many hospitals and healthcare organizations are currently deploying biometric security architecture. Secure identification is critical in the healthcare system, both to control logical access to centralized archives of digitized patients' data, and to limit physical access to buildings and hospital wards, and to authenticate medical and social support personnel.

There is also an increasing need to identify patients with a high degree of certainty. Identity verification solutions based on biometric technology can provide identity assurance and authentication, thereby lowering healthcare fraud instances, while increasing privacy and security. Biometric technology can add operational efficiencies to the healthcare system that reduce costs, reduce fraud, and increase patient satisfaction by reducing medical errors. As electronic health records and personal health records become more commonly used, biometrics are being utilized as an authentication mechanism by medical facilities, patients and insurers.

The primary focus of using biometrics in healthcare sector is for providing solutions to staff authentication and patient identification. The biometrics can also be combined with smart cards or passwords to secure access to sensitive patient records and to assist with patient registration requirements. A research study performed by Biometrics Research Group, Inc. (n.d.) has revealed that by 2020, the phase value of biometric solutions in the healthcare market will reach up to a value of US$5 billion. Biometric use will reflect the growing demand for healthcare fraud prevention, along with the need to improve patient privacy and healthcare safety.

The Government of India has planned to make the healthcare plan accessible through Aadhaar which is the world's largest biometric database, governed by the Unique Identification Authority of India (UIDAI, n.d.) and is currently used to authenticate delivery of social services including school attendance, natural gas subsidies to India's rural poor, and direct wage payments to bank accounts. In its first budget, the government has allocated $340 million to speed up the Aadhaar registration process. The government's objective is now to enrol the citizens with Aadhaar. UIDAI has already enrolled about 700 million people and issued unique identification numbers to 650 million. The introduction of universal healthcare to India's citizens will arguably be the most ambitious use of the biometric database. The process of linking healthcare services in India would help in keeping a check on any fraudulent insurance claims or ghost beneficiaries.

## Biometrics for Authenticating Healthcare Practitioner/Patient

To prevent any errors which could mean the difference between life and death, there is a pressing need to find a highly accurate method to secure critical healthcare information and prevent any errors. Biometric modalities like fingerprints, face, iris, voice, etc., can be used to uniquely identify individuals from an entire population even in case of twins. The usage of biometric identification systems in hospitals will increase security and privacy as well as accuracy of patient identification. The patient safety is thus ensured.

Government regulations mandate the tracking of electronic records each time a physician or healthcare professional accesses a patient's record. Such tracking is extremely important to maintain confidentiality of patient data and avoid any cases of medical fraud. Implementing fingerprint authentication makes it extremely convenient for medical personnel to access patient data with a simple fingerprint swipe. It ensures that the person accessing the record is definitely who they claim to be and also have the right to see the patient's record. Any mismatch can be flagged instantly and notified to the appropriate authorities that some intruder is trying to access the secure medical records.

## Biometrics for Patient Identification

When patients are not identified correctly, bad things happen. Critical health information can be linked to a duplicate medical record or the wrong record. This affects patient safety, data integrity, and healthcare costs. Inaccurate patient identification costs the average hospital several million per year from denied claims and that's just the tip of the iceberg. Patient safety and lives are also at risk when data is matched to the wrong patient or missing from the patient record. Biometric patient identification offers numerous advantages over manual identification of patient record in Master Patient Index (MPI). These are:

1. **Accuracy:** Biometrics offers unmatched accuracy. The whole process from capture to authentication is digitized. There is no human element of error involved in matching the scanned biometric of a new patient against the stored records and is fully automated. This results in high accuracy. Overlays and duplicate medical records cannot happen with biometric patient identification.
2. **Reliability:** Biometrics technologies such iris recognition, fingerprint matching etc., have evolved to very high standards. The False Acceptance Ratio (FAR) and False Rejection Ratio (FRR) occur at very low and insignificant levels. The results of matching against the database are consistent and reliable.
3. **Speed:** Automatic scans and high-speed matching lead to quick authentication in a few seconds. This is a major improvement over manually going through all the MPI records with similar data and trying to identify the correct one.
4. **Patient Enrolment and Admission Process is Streamlined:** The process of patient enrolment and admission becomes fast and hassle free as a simple biometric scan is all it takes to identify and admit a patient.
5. **Security:** Biometric patient identification eliminates medical identity thefts. Instances of medical identity thefts have caused huge financial losses to patients and healthcare providers alike. There are

certain stringent Health Insurance Portability and Accountability Act (HIPAA) standards (https://www.hhs.gov/hipaa/for-professionals/security/laws-regulations/index.html) around the same.

## Biometrics for Workforce Management in Hospital

Authentication implies identification and access control for premises and system networks while monitoring includes surveillance, time, and attendance. The market is mainly driven by the need for organizations to adopt biometric workforce management to replace traditional security systems. These include identity cards, passwords and keys that are traditionally used to record clock in and clock out.

Market segmentation of biometrics in workforce management by application

1. Identification
2. Access control
3. Monitoring

Biometric access control systems restrict unauthorized access, thus ensuring safety of employees and mitigating the risk of tampering important data. People are granted access only when their identity is confirmed by the information stored in the database of the enterprise.

## Biometrics for Financial Sector in Digital Healthcare

One area where biometrics has begun to take hold is healthcare insurance. A study by the Ponemon Institute (https://www.ponemon.org/library) found nearly 1.5 million Americans to be victims of medical identity theft. Healthcare fraud is estimated to cost between $70 billion and $255 billion a year, accounting for as much as 10% of total US healthcare costs. Many insurers are using biometrics to help reduce billing fraud by eliminating the sharing of medical insurance cards between patients, or by making it more difficult for a person to assume another's identity. For example, as an alternative to paper insurance cards, a biometric iris scan can immediately transport proof of a patient's physical presence at a healthcare facility.

Biometric technology is also assisting healthcare insurers with compliance and data integrity standards — in particular with those set by the HIPAA. For example, in addition to adhering to requirements for automatic logoff and user identification, insurers must implement additional safeguards that include PINs, passwords and some method of biometrics. Fingerprint biometrics helps hospitals to ensure compliance to government regulations such as the HIPAA and other such laws worldwide that mandate protection of patient privacy. With fingerprint authentication, only those who are authorised can access patient data. Every time a patient record is accessed, a concrete audit trail is created that helps to ensure compliance and ensures true accountability. Thus patients and healthcare professionals can feel very secure and confident about the privacy of their healthcare data with fingerprint technology.

## Biometrics in Public Health Surveillance

The new trend is driven by the need for early detection of surreptitious biological attacks. The trend is likely to accelerate because evidence is accumulating and these new approaches are successful. They can detect outbreaks earlier than existing methods and even identify outbreaks that have previously gone unnoticed. This trend has important implications for researchers and developers in clinical informatics because it is creating new design requirements for clinical information system.

## Biometrics in Remote Patient Monitoring

Bioelectrical signals especially, the Electro Cardio Gram (ECG) and the Electro Encephalo Gram (EEG) are emerging biometric identities. Unlike anatomical biometric identities that have two-dimensional data representation, the ECG or EEG is physiologically low-frequency signals that have one-dimensional data representation. Using the ECG or EEG signals as biometric may offer the following characteristics: universality, measurability, uniqueness, and robustness. Universality refers that each (live) individual must possess the ECG or EEG signals. Measurability refers that the ECG or EEG signals can be recorded using electrodes placed on the body surface near to the particular organ (e.g., chest, hands, and legs for the ECG and along the scalp for the EEG) as shown in Figure 5.

The biological information of a person genetically governed from deoxyribonucleic acid or ribonucleic acid proteins. Eventually, the proteins are responsible for the existence of uniqueness in the certain body parts. Similarly, the organs like heart and brain are composed of protein tissues called myocardium and glial cells, respectively. Therefore, the electrical signals evoked from these organs show uniqueness among individuals. Last but not the least, the replay or reproduction of the ECG or EEG signals is very difficult until the same individual is not called for the re-enrolment. Therefore, the proposed methods using the ECG or EEG as biometric are sufficiently non-vulnerable to spoof attacks. Consequently, the fact of using the ECG or EEG signals as biometric modalities yields an assurance that the biometric data is coming from the legitimate individual who is indeed present during the enrolment. It is an essential condition for the perfect working of a practical biometric system.

## CONCLUSION

A blooming digital health care sector should be able to provide world class service to all people. The vision of the digital healthcare should be imparting secure and reliable health care service. The health-care data should be accessible whenever required by authorized personnel alone. Biometrics plays a vital role in authenticating the medical personnel and controlling/managing the workforce. The most pressing challenge of healthcare industry in today's society is patient safety. The elimination of medical identity theft and prevention of duplicate medical records stand out as two of the main culprits which jeopardize the integrity of the healthcare industry. Biometrics plays a key role in combating the health-care data breaches. The root cause of several problems in healthcare industry is generally inaccurate patient identification. This costs millions of dollars per year including legal and administrative expenses and liabilities. This problem can be rectified only through the adoption of biometric technology. The biometric template can be directly linked to an electronic medical record for accurate credentialing on subsequent visits. This ensures that no duplicate medical records can be created, and the right care is delivered to the right patient.

*Figure 5. Architecture of remote patient monitoring system*
*(http://iot4health.utu.fi/?p=53)*

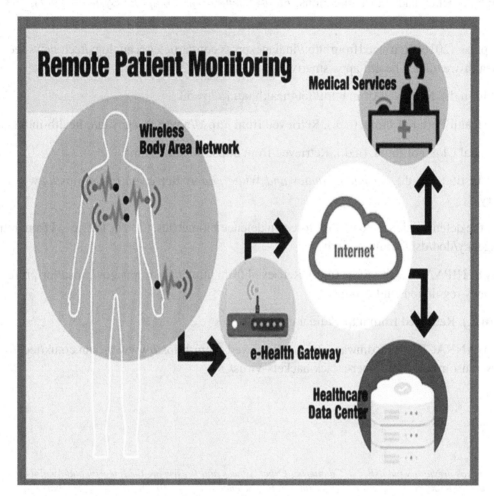

## REFERENCES

Biometric Identification in Healthcare. (n.d.). Retrieved from https://www.bayometric.com/biometric-identification-in-the-healthcare-sector/

Biometrics Research Group Inc. (n.d.). Retrieved from https://in.linkedin.com/company/biometrics-research-group-inc-

Data Breaches. (2013). Retrieved from http://www.idtheftcenter.org/ITRC-Surveys-Studies/2013-data-breaches.html

Digital Health: A Review. (n.d.). Retrieved from https://www.accenture.com/us-en/insight-revenue-risk-healthcare-provider-cyber-security-inaction

Gubbi, J., Buyya, R., Marusic, S., & Palaniswami, M. (2013). Internet of Things (IoT): A vision, architectural elements, and future directions. *Future Generation Computer Systems*, 29(7), 1645–1660. doi:10.1016/j.future.2013.01.010

Indian Express. (2016). Retrieved from http://indianexpress.com/article/technology/tech-news-technology/digital-health-wearables-health-apps-smartwatch-health-apps-2797787/

Iot4Health. (n.d.). Retrieved from http://iot4health.utu.fi/?p=53

National Health Portal of India. (n.d.). Retrieved from https://www.nhp.gov.in/e-health-india_mty

NIC, National Cloud of India. (n.d.). Retrieved from https://cloud.gov.in/

Ponemon Institute. (n.d.). *Research studies and White paper*. Retrieved from https://www.ponemon.org/library

Report of the defense science board task force on defence biometrics. (2007). Retrieved from https://fas.org/irp/agency/dod/dsb/biometrics.pdf

Summary of HIPAA Security Rule. (n.d.). Retrieved from https://www.hhs.gov/hipaa/for-professionals/security/laws-regulations/index.html

UIDAI. (n.d.). Retrieved from https://uidai.gov.in/

What Is WANNACRY Ransomware. (n.d.). Retrieved from https://www.thesun.co.uk/tech/3562470/wannacry-ransomware-nhs-cyber-attack-hackers-virus/

*This research was previously published in Countering Cyber Attacks and Preserving the Integrity and Availability of Critical Systems; pages 290-306, copyright year 2019 by Information Science Reference (an imprint of IGI Global).*

# Chapter 3
# Biometric Technologies in Healthcare Biometrics

**Rinku Datta Rakshit**
*Asansol Engineering College, India*

**Dakshina Ranjan Kisku**
*National Institute of Technology Durgapur, India*

## ABSTRACT

*The aim of this chapter is to introduce biometrics systems and discuss the essential components of biometrics technologies in the healthcare system. The discussion also includes the state-of-the-art biometrics technologies, selection criteria of a suitable biometrics system, biometrics identity management, and multi-biometrics fusion for healthcare biometrics system.*

## INTRODUCTION

Recently the concernment for biometrics is increasing swiftly to safeguard a patient's secrecy and the confidentialness of patient's actuality in the healthcare system. Identifying a patient and protecting a patient file is a ticklish task in any healthcare system. Due to improper identification, patients may lose their life in some cases. An unconscious patient cannot present an ID. The traditional patient tagging or mismatch between patient tag and hospital records are not free from flaws due to clerical mistakes or errors. This type of error can raise the inaccurate identification, wrong blood transfusion, or deceitful medicine infliction, which may be very dangerous for a patient's life. Therefore, there is a need for robust identification using biometrics in the healthcare system.

The term biometrics is a combination of two terms – 'bios' means life and 'metrics' means assessment. It refers to the metrics related to the physical and behavioral traits of human beings. The biometrics technology is implemented to analyze people for their identification, access control or surveillance by means of their biological information. Every person is unique and comprises a separate identity in the form of physical traits like fingerprint, face, iris, hand geometry and behavioral traits like voice, typing rhythm, and gait. Biometrics technologies are defined as automated way of recognizing or ascertaining

DOI: 10.4018/978-1-6684-6311-6.ch003

the identity of an individual arisen on an idiosyncratic biological (anatomical or physiological) or behavioral characteristics. It is very ticklish to feign a biometrics authentication system as biometrics can give invulnerable and competent recognition of a person and they cannot be plundered or unremembered. A biometrics system comprises four major modules –

- A device is used to take sample of a particular biometrics trait of an individual. These devices capture biometrics sample in some digital form.
- A feature extraction software module is used to transform the input biometrics sample into a template that is the fundamental component of the matching phase.
- A matching software module perpetrates comparison of an input biometrics sample with previously stored biometrics templates.
- An interface facilitates the communication of a person with the application system.

The choice of the applicable biometrics technology is a crucial task. It depends on the circumstance where the identification or verification system is enacted, the user scheme, needs for matching precision, and the implementation cost of the system and strengths, and cultural convention that could influence user adoption. To choose the proper biometrics technology, the prime factor which is used is its accuracy.

Biometrics identity is the physical or behavioral traits of a human being. Using biometrics identity of a patient, a healthcare system can simplify patient admission and immediately get entree to previous medical files. Biometrics identity also facilitates to recognize senseless or wretched patients easily, find out abuse of medical services, and establish an unprecedented way of identification across all medical services.

Biometrics identity management in healthcare is a combination of computer security and business management to ascertain that resources are to be accessed by patients, physicians, and the right healthcare personnel must be available for the right reasons. As the healthcare systems are growing exponentially and related records are accessed by several healthcare personnel concurrently, therefore the records must be protected securely. Resources in a healthcare system are very important artifacts for patients, doctors, and other healthcare personnel, so assuring that resources are protected against unauthorized access become crucial. Biometrically authenticated identity ensures that only authorized user is accessing the resources, not by imposters using fabricated identity token. Biometrics identity management eliminates the likelihood of spoofing.

Sometimes unimodal biometrics identification systems fail to produce the expected level of accuracy due to image quality, intra class variability, sensitivity to noise, non-universality, and various factors. To enhance the perfection of the biometrics system, multibiometrics system is required, which required many biometrics samples as a proof of the same individual. The fusion in biometrics system refers to the process of combining two or more biometrics modalities together. Multimodal biometrics fusion is possible using different fusion strategies and various levels of fusions. The fusion of separate modalities can ameliorate the overall perfection of the biometrics system in the different challenging environments. This provides additional tools to healthcare to accurately identify patients, physicians, and other healthcare related personnel.

Correct identification of physicians, supporting staffs and patients along with patient record maintenance, assignment of access permission for healthcare providers are major challenges in any healthcare system. These challenges can be overcome by integration of biometrics technology with healthcare system, due to its ability to provide a mechanism for verification or identification of individuals. However, biometrics technologies are vulnerable to spoofing from the faked copies of different biometrics samples. The development of biometrics authentication systems will recline on its efficiency to refuse fraud biometrics samples. Therefore liveness detection could be an important addition to biometrics technologies.

Integration of biometrics technology in healthcare system has closed doors for offenders to thieve the most worthy health information and stopped unauthorized access to laboratory apparatus in healthcare. Biometrics is the application of automated ways to identify an individual by using physiological or behavioral characteristic of that person. Biometrics systems are fitting the ground of an expansive array of extremely invulnerable identification and verification resolutions. Different instances of biometrics systems include fingerprint, face, retinal, palm print, foot print, iris recognition and hand geometry. As the security requirements are very high in healthcare sectors, therefore biometrics are to be used to control physical as well as logical access to restricted area and resources. There is no other worthy option than biometrics for person authentication in healthcare which is more safe, secure, affordable and efficient.

The aim of this chapter is to introduce biometrics and its propriety in healthcare system. This chapter comprehends the need of biometrics technologies in healthcare, state-of-the-art biometrics technologies, selection criteria of a biometrics technology, biometrics identity, and biometrics identity management in healthcare system, and multi-biometrics fusion for healthcare biometrics. Finally, this chapter discusses the various challenges of biometrics technology.

## BACKGROUND

Biometrics recognition (Jain, Ross, & Prabhakar, 2004) is the way of identifying a person by his/her biometrics traits. Necessity of improving performance of person authentication by biometrics is increases day by day. A lot of exploration has been done on the improvement and deployment of biometrics authentication systems based on fingerprint, face, iris, retina, voice, palm print, hand geometry, voice, signature, ear etc. These biometrics technologies are already used for border control, passport verification, and attendance system and in some other sensitive places. However, recently it felt that biometrics could be a value added service to the healthcare system as it needs protection of patient identity, patient record, patient insurance documents and other valuable belongingness along with personal identification and access control.

In these days, society needs a faultless security measurement that will be very natural, serviceable and favorable at any costs. Biometrics based authentication systems make this requirement possible. Biometrics is a good means of automatic recognition of an individual based on their physiological and behavioral traits. These systems give safety founded on "what you are" rather than "what you possess" and "what you remember". Therefore, such systems are very useful in healthcare system where patients need not to get anything like passwords and is permanently with a person unlike smart-card etc. This type of security measure cannot be shared or used by any other person. Different systems based on various physiological and behavioral traits have been raised which cover fingerprint (Maltoni, Maio, Jain, & Prabhakar, 2009), face (Chellappa, Wilson, & Sirohey, 1995), iris (Bowyer, Hollingsworth, & Flynn, 2008; Ng, Tay, & Mok, 2008), retina (Tabatabaee, Milani-Fard, & Jafariani, 2006), voice (Kinnunen, & Li, 2010; Campbell, 1997), hand geometry (Sanchez-Reillo, Sanchez-Avila, & Gonzalez-Marcos, 2000) (Sidlauskas & Tamer, 2008), ear (Choras, 2007), Palm print (Harb, Abbas, Cherry, Jaber, & Ayache, 2015), palm vein (Han & Lee, 2012) (Mirmohamadsadeghi & Drygajlo, 2011), and signature (Faundez-Zanuy, 2005). To exceed the difficulty of traditional biometrics measures some new biometrics measures have been introduced like ECG (Shen, 2005; Riera, Soria-Frisch, Caparrini, Grau, & Ruffini, 2008), foot-print (Jia et al., 2012; Kumar & Ramakrishnan, 2010), and tongue print (Zhang, Liu, & Yan, 2010; Zhang, Liu, Yan, & Shi, 2007; Diwakar & Maharshi, 2013)etc. Some of these have been already used in forensic applications. Deployment of biometrics solution in healthcare is the best alternative for security measure.

Safety and privacy are the utmost stringent issues for data transmission in healthcare system. A biometrics based security resolution for encryption and authentication is proposed by (Zhang, Poon, & Zhang, 2009) for Tele-Healthcare systems. Without an authentication mechanism, the distant physicians will not know who sends the physiological signals. An invader can pose to be a genuine user and send false data which leads to a wrong diagnosis. A survey (Chandra, Durand, & Weaver, 2008) is carried out on healthcare consumers and providers. According to this paper, biometrics attained excellent adoption from providers than consumers. A web-based, biometrics-enabled, patients and Electronic Medical Record (EMR) management system BEPOC is presented in (Nwosu & Igbonagwam, 2014), which practically and efficiently addresses the issue of patient identification during medical mission. (Leonard, Pons, & Asfour, 2009) proposed the fingerprint, iris, retina scan and DNA (FIRD) framework that take advantage of a patient's biometrics prominences to uniquely connect them to their medical data. The framework makes an infrastructure that will distinctively recognize a patient by his or her complete Electronic Health Record (EHR) with accurate precision. A face recognition system is discussed by (Sumathi & Malini, 2010) to enhance E-health. (Kumar et al., 2017) proposed an anonymous and biometrics based authentication scheme for the Naked hospital environment. This paper considers a hospital scenario and show how patients can get authenticated without using gadgets to entree services from their circumstance. Medical sensors embedded in the environment will deliver them the requisite digital services after invulnerable authentication. Also, this work can resists various well known attacks such as insider attack, replay attack and identity privacy attack. (Jahan, Chowdhury, & Islam, 2017) presents extensive overview of biometrics technology in addressing E-Health security challenges. This paper proposed a robust and efficient biometrics scheme for user verification and authentication using fingerprint biometrics to enhance privacy and security in E-Health system. (Mohammedi et al., 2018) proposed a new biometrics-based authentication scheme for mobile healthcare system using mobile devices, biometrics inputs and Elliptic Curve Cryptography (ECC). The security solution and simulation outcomes exhibit that the proposed approach is applicable for use in practical healthcare applications.

## NEED OF BIOMETRICS IN HEALTHCARE

Most of healthcare systems are maintaining Electronic Health Records (EHR) of their patients to provide fast, secure, and cost-effective care. Mainly passwords are used to safeguard computer systems in healthcare from unauthorized users. A patient health records may be mixed up or misplaced which might aftereffect in wrong medication. Moreover, medical information of one patient could be shifted to another person's record or to a deceitful person which causes medical identity theft. To keeping EHRs data integrity is a stringent feature. To secure critical health records of patients, passwords are not the best solution because often people forget or share their passwords. Password needs memorization. Biometrics offers a powerful solution for replacing password based authentication. Biometrics based authentication approach help healthcare workers to provide timely and quality care to their patients.

Also in healthcare sector healthcare professional have to give a lot of time on patient identification. But this worthy time could be spent on attention and treatment of other patients, if conventional patient identification system can be replaced by biometrics based patient identification. Identifying a patient correctly at healthcare facility is a crucial job. Producing an ID for patient identification is very difficult for senseless patients. Conventional patient tagging is not free from deficiency. Other important needs of biometrics in healthcare sector are to maintain security and access control because healthcare frauds like duplicate claims, fake billing and medical identity theft or theft of patient records are increasing day by day.

The acceptance of a particular biometrics depends on the adroitness of that biometrics technology to evolve the challenges of healthcare personnel identification as well as patient identification effectively with the help of their unique biometrics trait. The real-time patient identification as well as healthcare personnel identification decreases amount of stored data those are used for patient identification and healthcare personnel identification and related cost of data storing. Healthcare biometrics enables only authorized healthcare personnel to access patient's health record which eliminates the chances of medical identity theft and other healthcare insurance related thefts.

Integration of a biometrics trait with healthcare system boosts in different ways –

- Biometrics solution helps a healthcare system to verify a patient on each visit reliably.
- It dispels duplicate medical record keeping.
- It facilitates instant and secured access of patient records.
- It grants permission to only authorized healthcare personnel to access secure health records of patients.
- Accurately connect patients with their medical records.
- Maintain data integrity of patient record.
- It grants permission to only authorized persons to access a room or building physically.

## BIOMETRICS TECHNOLOGIES

Biometrics technologies are widely used in different fields, mainly for secure access control and true person identification. Already biometrics technologies are used in a number of airports, for well protected building access, in cars (for unlocking the vehicle), in schools, at border crossing. Biometrics based systems use biometrics traits as powerful authentication tool. Biometrics traits are metrics related to human prominences. Biometrics systems are mainly based on two types of human characteristics – physiological and behavioral. Physiological characteristics comprise fingerprint, face, palm print, hand geometry, iris, retina etc. Whereas behavioral characteristics use pattern of human behavior like typing rhythm, gait, voice and signature. Biometrics identifiers of every person are unique. These are more feasible in identity verification than knowledge-based and token-based systems because biometrics traits are unique for a person. To ensure high security, biometrics based authentication systems are acceptable technology because every human being possesses the biometrics traits. The block diagram of a biometrics authentication system is shown in Figure 1.

Every biometrics system contains four main modules – sensor module, preprocessing module, feature extraction module, and matching module.

*Figure 1. The block diagram of a biometrics authentication system*

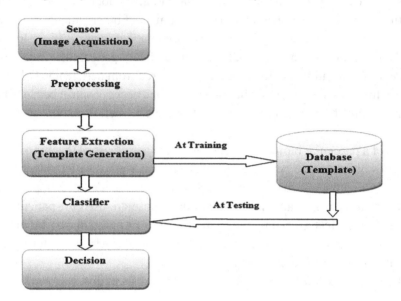

1. **Sensor Module**: This module provides an interface through which an individual interact with the system. This module captures all necessary data for identification or verification purpose. In most biometrics systems, this module is also known as image acquisition system.
2. **Preprocessing Module**: This module dispels artifacts from the data captured by a sensor to enhance the quality of the input biometrics sample, e.g. removing background noise or adding up missing information to the biometrics template. Image normalization, de-noising, filtering, histogram equalization are some of preprocessing techniques.
3. **Feature Extraction Module**: This module is very significant module of a biometrics system. Any extracted characteristic from the image is referred to a feature. Invariant features from biometrics samples are extracted using some algorithms and then templates are generated from these extracted features in this module.
4. **Matching Module**: In this module, probe sample is send to the classifier that compares it with stored templates and produces the decision.

There are two phases of every biometrics system – enrollment and testing. When an individual uses a biometrics system for first time, he/she enrolled himself/herself by his/her biometrics traits. In posterior uses, biometrics sample is captured from an individual and compared with the template stored at the time of enrollment.

Every biometrics based authentication system works either in identification mode or in verification mode. In identification mode the biometrics system compares a probe sample with all templates (one-to-many) present in the biometrics database. In verification mode the biometrics system compares a probe sample with a particular template (one-to-one) stored in the database in order to ascertain the identity.

## Finger Print Recognition

Fingerprint recognition (Maltoni, Maio, Jain, & Prabhakar, 2009) is the automated process of assimilating the pattern of furrows, ridges and minutiae points of the fingers to identify a person based on the comparison of two fingerprints. Fingerprint is very effective biometrics to restrain unauthorized personnel from accessing patient's records and used for true healthcare personnel as well as true patient identification. A fingerprint pattern of any human consists of dark lines of ridges along with white lines or valleys between them on the skin surface of a finger. The flow of ridges and their features are used for fingerprint recognition. Research reveals that fingerprints of two persons were not found to be the same, not even for the identical twins and fingerprint patterns remains same for a person throughout his/her life. The fingerprint images those are used for automatic identification can be acquired using different sensors. Actually digital imaging technology is used in capturing, storing and analyzing the fingerprint data.

There is a concern to search an extremely accurate and feasible way to secure critical healthcare records and restrain any faults which could lead the dangerous problem for life. Fingerprints which are accurate form of identification can be used to identify a person uniquely. The fingerprint biometrics mainly needed in healthcare systems to prevent unauthorized access of patient record, true patient identification as well as healthcare personnel identification. The use of fingerprint biometrics in healthcare system will raise secrecy and indemnity of patients by assuring unerring identification.

Fingerprint biometrics facilitate hospitals to ascertain consent to government rules such as the Health Insurance Portability and Accountability Act (HIPAA) and other such laws worldwide that decree safeguard of patient's privacy. Fingerprint authentication allows only authorized persons to access patient's data. Therefore, with fingerprint authentication patients and healthcare professionals can grope very sure and certain regarding the privacy of their healthcare data.

Hospitals and healthcare organizations can implement fingerprint technology effectively for registration of new patients, controlling visitors, proper distribution of medicines, executing payments for medical claims, maintaining the privacy of patient's information and impenetrable entree to the premises. Also fingerprint readers can be used in hospitals to access medical cabinets for maintaining patient's security. This facility will help to manage both medical supplies and medications efficiently. This process has been implemented in a number of major US hospitals and used by millions of healthcare related personnel.

Fingerprint systems have several advantages. Fingerprints are always undeniably tied to the actual user and always on them. A fingerprint system relieves the user from the liability of recalling to bearing their smart cards or tokens or to remember passwords. Fingerprint system gives very high accuracy and it is very cheap in terms of cost. This system is very simple to use. Fingerprint system requires small storage space to store biometrics templates. However, this system is not also free from flaws and safe to use. Temporary or permanent injury on finger, dryness or dirty of the finger's skin can cause some serious problem for fingerprint system. In addition, fingerprint spoofing is also considered as a major concern for successful identity verification.

Already the fingerprint identification system has been effectively implemented in different departments such as law enforcement and government agencies. It is an existing system which shows a high level of validity that can be used for strengthening physical as well as logical entree within a healthcare facility. Fingerprint systems are accepted extensively by hospitals because of its credibility, favor and the efficiency to be spread out in a wide range of circumstances.

## Advantages

- Accuracy is very high.
- It is most economical biometrics authentication technique.
- It is a developed biometrics technology
- Easy to use.
- The memory required to store template in database is less.

## Disadvantages

- Most devices are incapable to enroll a little percentage of users.
- Perfection of the system can come off over time
- It can make mistakes with the dryness or dirty of the finger's skin.

## Face Recognition

Face is another physiological modality which can be used to identify and authenticate a person in healthcare. Face is an individual characteristic of a person. In our daily life, a person is identified by his/her face. Remembering and distinguishing different faces is possible because human brains have natural ability to do this. It is important application to have a human visual system in machines where machines can behave like a human brain and have the capability to recognize different faces with different identity.

Face recognition (Chellappa, Wilson, & Sirohey, 1995) system is an automated technology which is able to identify or verify a person by processing their digital image or a video frame from a video source if their face recognition individuality has been pre-introduced. The face recognition algorithm extracts discriminating facial features like shape and position of nose, eyes, jaw and cheekbones stored these extracted features in the form of templates in a database. This type of system can be feasible to identify a patient at the time of registration, at the time of admission and at the time of medication. Face recognition systems are also very useful to identify healthcare personnel and restrict the access of patient's health record as well as cabinet of the patient.

The social acceptability of face recognition technology is very high and implementation cost of this system is low. Automated face recognition technology can identify a person in the crowd without letting him know, if it installed properly in airports, multiplexes and other public places. The system does not crave the assistance of the probe subject to work which makes it most suitable for healthcare system because in healthcare system, in some critical cases, patient can not cooperate with the system. Face recognition is a clean process because the patient never needs to touch it or have direct contact with anything, which could create a major problem in healthcare due to deadly infection.

Further, face recognition is considered a complicated problem in computer vision due to changes in pose, illumination, occlusion, facial expression, head rotation, and scale. Face image quality is very significant in face recognition systems as great degrees of changes are feasible in face images. Among all biometrics systems, facial recognition has the highest false acceptance and rejection rates, which raise questions on the usefulness of face recognition software in cases of high security application area. Face recognition system performs well in case of full frontal faces along with neutral facial expression and capturing of full frontal faces with neutral facial expression of patients and healthcare personnel are possible because overt (user aware) application of face recognition system might be useful in healthcare.

Health record privacy is the main disquiet when it is secured by storing biometrics data tag with health records. Data stored by face biometrics can be attained by third party if not stored properly. Face recognition technology can be spoofed by intruders by using facial mask, digital images or printed images of a person.

## Advantages

- No direct contact is required.
- Implementation cost is less.
- Easy for people to verify.

Disadvantages

- Perfection of the system is deteriorated by changing the image acquirement environment.
- Recognition rate is also decreased by changing in physiological characteristics.
- Propensity of privacy misuse is high due to non-cooperative enrollment and identification ability.

## Retinal Scan

A retinal scan (Tabatabaee, Milani-Fard, & Jafariani, 2006) is a biometrics authentication technique that uses the unique patterns of retina blood vessels to identify or verify a person. The human retina is located in the rear portion of the eye. This is thin tissue made of neural cells. Each person's retina is unique due to the depth form of the capillaries that supply the blood to retina. Even identical twins do not have an identical pattern. The retinal pattern typically remains unaltered from birth until death. Due to the permanence of unaltered pattern of retina, it is the most accurate and feasible biometrics, that can be used for authentication. Retinal scan can be used in healthcare system for true patient identification, healthcare personnel identification and physical as well as logical access control.

A retinal scan is made possible by using an unperceived beam of infrared ray having low energy into an individual's eye when they look via the scanner's eyepiece. This ray of low energy infrared light quests a standardized path on the retina as retinal blood vessels imbibe light more spontaneously than the neighboring tissue and the extent of reflection varies at the time of scan. These variations of pattern is digitized and stored as templates in database.

Retinal scanners are mainly used for authentication and identification purposes. Retinal scanning has been exploited by different government agencies including the FBI, CIA, and NASA. Recently, retinal scanning gains major popularity in commercial fields.

Retinal scanning has several advantages. Biometrics authentication using retinal scanning has low occurrence of false positives. False negative rate is extremely low (almost 0%). Retinal scanning is a speedy approach which identifies a person very quickly and it is highly feasible because no two people have the identical retinal pattern even also in identical twins. This is very hard to replicate a retina. The eye from a dead person would collapse very fast, therefore in retinal scanning liveness detection is not required. Retinal scanning also has some medical application. Retina scan based biometrics is more hygienic because the patient never has to touch anything. Though retinal scanning gives very high accuracy, it can be affected by several factors.

## Advantages

- False positive rate is very low.
- False negative rate is extremely low (almost 0%).
- It is highly reliable.
- Result produced very fast by this technology.
- Highly accurate.
- Replicate a retina is impossible.

## Disadvantages

- Measurement accuracy can be affected by several diseases like cataracts and severe astigmatism.
- Retinal scanning is not very user friendly because it requires very close contact of the person with the camera while scanning is done.
- Equipment cost of retinal scanning is very high.
- Regular uses of this technology leads to serious eye problems.

## Iris Recognition

Iris recognition (Bowyer, Hollingsworth, & Flynn, 2008; Ng, Tay, & Mok, 2008) is an automated method to identify an individual based on one or both of the irises of a person's eyes by using mathematical pattern-recognition techniques. The complex patterns of irises are permanent, unique, and can be observed from some distance.

Iris recognition uses fine near infrared illumination to capture complex patterns of iris images by video camera technology. Digital templates are generated from iris images by computational techniques and stored in database. These stored templates are further used for identification of an individual. The speed of iris recognition is very high with low false match rates.

Iris recognition technology is already implemented in several countries around the world for the use of some national ID programs and passport-free automated border-crossings. Besides the speed of matching and utmost counteraction to false matches of iris recognition technology, another advantage of it is the permanence of the iris as a protected, internal and externally visible part of the eye.

As people's eyes are unique, iris scanners are more suitable in high-security applications. The uniqueness and permanence nature of iris and the technology's contactless and non-intrusive nature make it more suitable for healthcare system to safely recognize a patient at the reception desk, blood drawing room or doctor's room, or to identify a doctor and other healthcare personnel. Also iris recognition technology can be used by people after eye surgery because eyes also are same after surgery, and iris scanners can be used by blind people as long as their eyes have irises. Generally, eyeglasses and contact lenses do not cause improper readings.

## Advantages

- **Accuracy:** Iris recognition is the ideal biometrics recognition technology with respect to accuracy while compared to other biometrics. The false acceptance rate as well as false rejection rate is extremely less in this modality which ascertains high recognition accuracy in its results.

- **Scalability:** This technology can be used for both large and small scale applications because it is highly scalable.
- **Distance:** Iris scanning can be possible from a usual distance.
- **Stable:** Iris patterns are permanent in a person's whole life.
- **Easy to Use:** Iris recognition system is very easy to use. A person only need to stand still in front of the camera and the task of capturing image is done immediately. It is a comfortable process for everyone.

## Disadvantages

- **Expensive:** Iris scanners are very expensive in terms of cost.
- **Distance:** Iris is very tiny in size and can't be captured from a several meters space.
- **Movement:** A person has to be standing steady in front of the scanning instrument to be enrolled by iris scanners and movement cause serious problem.
- **Reflection:** The presence of reflections sometimes causes a problem for iris scanning. Mainly it could occur due to lenses, eyelashes that would cause a reflection.
- **Infrared Light:** The constant use of this system may damage the iris due to the scanning with infrared light.
- **Storage Requirement:** A large memory space is required for storing the data.
- **Eyelids:** It is very difficult to control frequent blinking of eyelids.
- **Transformation:** Iris may disfigure non-elastically as its size may be changed due to some medical conditions or other conditions.

## Hand Geometry Recognition

Hand geometry (Sanchez-Reillo, Sanchez-Avila, & Gonzalez-Marcos, 2000; Sidlauskas & Tamer, 2008) is a biometrics cue that might be used to recognize users by the appearance of their hands. Hand geometry scanner measure different dimensions of a hand and compare those measurements to the stored templates in database.

Hand geometry devices have been made since the early 1980s, making hand geometry the first biometrics to trace extensive computerized use. It mainly includes applications like time-and-attendance management and access control.

Hand geometry is not thought to be as unique as other biometrics technology for high-security applications. Hand geometry can give increased accuracy when combined with other forms of biometrics traits or other forms of identification, such as identification cards or PIN. In large demography, hand geometry is not a good choice for one-to-many applications, where a user is recognized from his biometrics except any other identification.

Hand geometry is mainly feasible for practical usage in real-world applications where security in an important concern. A hand geometry recognition process mainly captures geometry of the hand like length, width and other qualities of the finger. In any hand geometry based recognition system, hand image segmentation is an important step. The accuracy of hand geometry based system is mainly depends on the quality and exactness of the segmented hand image.

## Advantages

- Its cost is medium as it only requires a medium resolution CCD camera and a platform.
- Mainly algorithms having low computational cost are used for this system which increases the speed.
- The template size is very small (9-25 bytes) which reduces storage requirement.
- It is very simple and striking to users which leads to a null user rejection
- It can be easily combined into other systems.

## Disadvantages

- It has limited accuracy.
- It is not competent for arthritic person, as placing the hand on the scanner is very difficult.

## Palm Print Recognition

Palm print (Harb, Abbas, Cherry, Jaber, & Ayache, 2015) recognition is an authentication process founded on the distinctive patterns of palm prints of a person's hands. Palm print recognition systems usage a scanner or a camera to capture the palm print images, and software that processes image of biometrics sample of a person's palm and assimilates it to a template of that person stored in database. Palm print scanners use thermal, optical or tactile processes to express the details in the pattern of ridges and bifurcations in an image of a human palm, also details like, scars, creases and texture are also considered. These three systems lean on heat-emission analysis, visible light analysis and pressure analysis, respectively. To capture images of palm print persons must touch their hands to a screen of palm print scanner or may be contactless.

Fingerprints and Palm prints are often used simultaneously to improve the exactness of identification. A handprint covers more skin area which includes more details, since making false positives is improbable and simultaneously generating intended falsification is very difficult. In other circumstances, such as criminal inquisition, a partial or full palm print may be acquired when fingerprints are not present. For example, a criminal might endue gloves to avoid giving up fingerprints but unknowingly leave a partial palm print when a glove slips at the time of a crime.

The handprint recognition was first used in 1858, when Sir William Herschel records the prints of Indian civil service employees working under him and assimilated them to new handprint samples taken on paydays to ascertain identification.

Friction ridge impression is used in both palm and finger print biometrics to represent the useful information. This information assembles ridge structure, ridge flow, and ridge characteristics of the raised part of the epidermis. The data illustrated by these friction ridge impressions authorizes a decision that similar areas of friction ridge impressions either risen from the same person or could not have been made by the same person.

## Advantages

- The palm area is much larger than fingerprint, hence it generate more distinguishable features which makes it more worthy in identification process.

- Palm prints are easily taken by low resolution devices

## Disadvantages

- Generally the palm print scanners are heavy and costly as they required to take a larger area of the hand.
- It requires more processing time.

## Footprint Recognition

Footprint recognition (Jia et al., 2012; Kumar & Ramakrishnan, 2010) is an automated system which measures the features of footprint for knowing the identity of an individual. A footprint is a natural measure for taking a particular identifier which does not vary much over time. Footprint identification is relatively a new technology which is a substitute to access control in health domains such as thermal baths and spas. This technology can be facilitating healthcare personnel to identify new born babies at hospitals. Different research groups from all over world proposed different novel approaches for foot-print identification. Footprint technology utilizes texture, foot shape, foot silhouette and friction ridge to identify a person.

Infant fingerprints are not suitable for identifying a baby, but infant footprints are more suitable for scanning and captured footprints are further processed by algorithms to extract invariant features from the footprint which are used for identification.

In many countries recording footprint of infant are mandatory. Currently maximum hospitals use ink for the foot to capture footprint on a paper. This method has various restrictions and well trained healthcare personnel are required for this.

Though several biometrics applications are available in the market, there is a concernment of low cost authentication technology that can authenticate a low quality test image which is captured in low resolution. Still footprint is a forlorn field of research. But footprint biometrics has both the behavioral and physiological characteristics to identify a person. The footprint recognition needs removal of shoes and socks to capture the image of bare foot which increases the extra concern of the user. Also dirty feet or cracked heels make the image noisy which reduces the accuracy of this technology. Physiological and behavioral biometrics characteristics makes footprint more suitable for authentication. Foot print has geometric features which helps the system at the time of recognition. Minutia features of foot biometrics are considered completely unique to an individual. The minutiae characteristic is already experimented in fingerprint analysis for its uniqueness. A healthcare system can use footprint system for authentication in those places where people strictly enter in bare foot to maintain cleanliness.

## Advantages

- Footprint recognition is very attractive for newborn babies due to its easy applicability.
- Implementation cost is low.
- This technology is widely accepted.
- Image acquisition is very fast.
- Very fast and accurate identification.
- Using high resolution scanner better accuracy can be obtained.

- It is a non-invasive method.

## Disadvantages

- Performance of footprint system is affected due to dirty feet and cracked heels that make the image noisy which reduces the accuracy of this technology

## Palm Vein Recognition

Palm vein (Han & Lee, 2012; Mirmohamadsadeghi & Drygajlo, 2011) recognition is a biometrics authentication tool which is used to recognize a person uniquely based on vascular patterns of his/her palm. A palm has an extensive and more intricate vascular pattern which comprises enormous discriminating features for personal identification. An infrared ray is used to capture the palm vein image of the user's. The lighting of the infrared ray is limited by the illumination on all direction of the sensor, and the sensor is capable to take the palm image irrespective of the location and stroll of the palm. The palm vein recognition system matches the transformed vein pattern with the enrolled vein pattern, while measuring the location and orientation of the palm by a pattern matching algorithm. The palm is an ideal portion of the body for this system; it usually does not have any obstruction (like hair) for taking the image of blood vessel pattern. Also the palm vein pattern does not affected by the skin color. In vein vessels the deoxidized hemoglobin takes up light having a wavelength of about $7.6 \times 10^{-4}$ mm within the near-infrared area.

Palm vein biometrics-based authentication is much more advantageous because it can identify a patient accurately as well as increase patient safety in healthcare. Palm vein biometrics for patient identification eliminates false medical records and protects medical identity theft and cheat at the point of health service by attaching a patient's biometrics profile to true Electronic Health Record (EHR) to ascertain accurate and safe treatment at healthcare organization. At first palm vein based biometrics authentication generates a palm vein map from the image of a patient's palm which is captured by using near-infrared light. Then using this palm vein pattern unique electronic medical record of a patient is extracted. Actually, a palm vein recognition reader is an automated system which scans palm of a patient and automatically fetch their electronic medical record. This technology is 100% safe. The palm vein recognition is safe for a user as near-infrared light used in the scanner is not so harmful. Already palm vein biometrics has been experimented and certified to be out of danger for use in healthcare as an access control and identification tool.

## Advantages

- **Security:** Palm vein patterns are very secure and tenacious to imitate as palm vein patterns subsist inside the body.
- **Usability:** The palm vein biometrics reader is very simple to use for patients. People needs to only place a flattened hand on the palm vein hand guide and deploy their fingers. The palm vein sensor then takes the image of the biometrics sample.
- **User Acceptance:** User acceptance of palm vein biometrics is very high.
- **Increasing Data Integrity:** At appropriate patient care touch points palm vein biometrics accurately links a patient with his/her electronic health records and maintains patient data integrity.

- **Accuracy:** The FAR and FRR are generated by this system is very low, hence it is deliberated as a more accurate biometrics modality.
- **Long Term Stability:** Palm vein biometrics is not changed over a long period of time.

## Disadvantages

- **Cost:** Implementation cost of palm vein technology is very high.
- Palm vein print can be affected by the humidity, body temperature, heat radiation, nearness of vein to surface, focus and camera calibration.

## DNA Recognition

DNA profiling (Gehring et al., 1995) is also known as DNA testing, DNA fingerprinting or DNA typing is the method of deciding an individual's DNA features, which are unique to a person. DNA testing desired to identify a species, more than an individual, is known as DNA bar coding.

DNA recognition is generally used as a forensic tool in criminal inquisitions, for example assimilating one or more individuals' profiles to DNA found at a crime scene so as to measure the possibility of their presence in the crime. Also, it is used in medical research and parentage testing.

DNA profiling can also be used to prevent medical identity theft and patient identification. DNA profiling is highly accurate. Recently, DNA records are maintaining in file by most countries. DNA profiling has various practical uses. It can used to match tissues of organ donors with those of people, who need transplants. It helps to identify diseases that are passed down through a family, and helps to find medication for some hereditary diseases.

## Advantages

- It is an easy and painless method for the person being tested.
- It is an affordable and unfailing technique.
- It is less time consuming.
- Anyone at any age can be tested with this method without any major concerns.
- This can be used for several cases like legal claims, missing person's cases, identification for the military, and paternity and prenatal testing.
- The technique is highly developed and improved.
- Its accuracy is very high.
- Error in this system is impossible.
- It is a standardized method.

## Disadvantages

- The sample of DNA can easily be ruined before testing.
- This process is very complex and tiring, and results produced by it may be hard to interpret.
- Multiple samples are required to test. Therefore much more time is required for ideal accuracy.
- This approach is very expensive.

## ECG Recognition

The electrocardiogram (ECG) is a pathology tool that is regularly used to measure the muscular and electrical operations of the heart. The heart is an electrical pump and the heart's electrical alacrity can be assessed by electrodes given on the skin. The electrocardiogram can assessed the rhythm and rate of the heartbeat, and also give imperceptible proof of blood flow to the heart muscle.

In healthcare system the electrocardiogram (ECG) biometrics process can authenticate the patient's identity as well as protect the privacy of their sent electrocardiogram signal. In ECG recognition discriminating features are extracted from heartbeat waveforms.

The ECG can be used as a biometrics tool (Shen, 2005; Riera, Soria-Frisch, Caparrini, Grau, & Ruffini, 2008) because it satisfies the requirements of biometrics characteristics. The ECG pattern of each individual is unique, it can easily measure, and this characteristic of a person does not change over time. The use of a biometrics reclines on the purpose and application of the system.

### Advantages

- ECG recognition is a non-expensive approach.
- It is safe, and easy to perform.
- The necessary equipments of this technology are easily available.

### Disadvantages

- It doesn't constantly give the proper diagnosis.
- ECG signals are influenced by different noise sources such as power line or electromyographic noise and motion artifacts.

## Tongue Print Recognition

Tongue print (Zhang, Liu, & Yan, 2010; Zhang, Liu, Yan, & Shi, 2007; Diwakar & Maharshi, 2013) is a new biometrics tool that can be used for user authentication. Tongue print is unique to a person and cannot be easily counterfeit because no two tongue prints are same. Tongue contains several identifiers such as ridges, wrinkles, seams, and marks. Tongue print recognition captured digital image of the tongue and matched with a database for verification. Research on tongue prints is at an initiatory stage.

The presence of fissures was the most common morphological characteristic noticed in the surface of the tongue. The fissures were mainly located in the central region of the tongue. The predominant shape of the tongue in both males and females was "U shape." V-shaped tongue with a sharp tip was also observed in a substantial sample of females. Due to uniqueness of tongue prints, it can be used as a powerful biometrics tool in healthcare organization for person identification and access control.

### Advantages

- The shape and surface textures of tongue is unique to each person.
- This organ that can be freely and completely exposed for test.

- **Inner part:** Tongue is a vital internal organ that is well protected from environment and enclosed in mouth.
- **Liveness:** Tongue is an important biometrics by which liveness of a person is detected easily. Sticking out one's tongue is an undeniable proof of life.

## Disadvantages

- Tongue is affected by diseases, which reduce the accuracy of person identification.

## Ear Recognition

Automatic identity recognition by ear biometrics (Choras, 2007) is a new biometrics research field, but has attained a rising amount of effort over the past few years. The ear images can be easily captured from a distance without the knowing of a person. This advantage makes ear recognition competent for security and surveillance applications. The ear biometrics can be implemented via ear photographs for automated identification applications. The use of 2D or 3D ear images for human recognition varies from the use of ear prints. Many countries have commenced ear prints as physical proof in different criminal happenings. Ear prints are not widely adopted in court due to the absence of scientific consonance as to their identity. The usage of ear thermo grams helps to alleviate the matter of occlusion due to accessories and hair. In addition, the adjacent background of the ear is very predictable, as it is permanently present on the side of the head. The ear biometrics does not crave closeness to capture images. Ears have performed an important preface in forensic science.

Like all other biometrics ear recognition consists of four stages. The first step is ear detection which localizes the ear's position in an image. The ear recognition system generally uses a rectangular border to imply the ear's spatial border from the side profile of an image of face. Ear detection is a complex task and errors at this step can affect the perfection of the system. Second step is feature extraction which extracts the discriminating feature from ear. Third step is matching which assimilates the extracted features of the test ear image to the templates stored in the database to make the ear's identity. The matching stage yields scores introducing the matching proximity to other ear images. Last stage is matching which uses the match scores to generate a final decision.

## Advantages

- Ear does not change over time during a human life.
- Colour distribution is more uniform in ear.
- Ear is not sensitive to expression or colour changes.
- Images of ear can be taken from a distance without knowing of a person.
- Ear is also works in low resolution.

## Disadvantages

- Sometimes ear is partially covered by hair; in those cases capturing image of ear is very difficult.
- The uniqueness of ear is moderate.

## Voice Recognition

Voice recognition or speech recognition (Kinnunen & Li, 2010; Campbell, 1997) is an automated system which used computer software program or hardware device having ability to decode the human voice. To handle a device or enact commands without using a mouse, keyboard, or any buttons, voice recognition is mainly used. Recently Automatic speech recognition (ASR) software requires the user to train the ASR software to identify the voice of a person.

A single digit spoken by a user is first recognized ASR device in 1952 and it was not computer driven. Nowadays, ASR programs are used in many fields like Healthcare, Military, Telecommunications and personal computing.

The main use of voice recognition system in healthcare organization is the generation of customized patient's room that will deliver unique services and technology. For example, researchers rely on the future hospitals that will launch using touch screen monitors having voice recognition software in every patient's room. These will support the health care personnel to access patient health records very quickly with simple voice commands. According to the National institute of Health (NIH), speech-recognition technology should be accepted by every health care organization due to its excellent benefits. The success of voice recognition technology in healthcare organization is depends on proper employee training and implementation.

## Advantages

- Voice recognition increases productivity.
- It helps with menial computer tasks, such as scrolling and browsing.
- It can support people who have trouble using their hands or trouble in movements.
- It can help people who have cognitive disabilities.

## Disadvantages

- Voice recognition can be hacked easily with prerecorded vocal messages.
- It needs some time to adjust to each user's voice.
- Its accuracy affected due to background noise.
- It can be problematic in a dense circumstance.
- Sometimes the monopoly of software companies causes a problem.

## Signature Recognition

Writing is human's behavioral characteristics as well as an acquired skill. Signature recognition (Faundez-Zanuy, 2005) is a simple means of person identification which is used in banks, offices, and different sectors. Signature recognition demands a person to show a specimen of text which induced as a basis of measure of their writing. The aim of the signature recognition system is to recognize the writer of a given signature. There are two different ways to recognize a signature.

The first technique is static which demands the individual to write their signature on paper. Then this signature will be digitized by a camera or an optical scanner. The digitized data then recognized by some software algorithm that checks text of the signature by testing its shape. This approach is known as an "off-line" mode or static mode of recognition.

The off-line mode of handwriting recognitions are a socially adopted identification process which are formerly used for bank, offices, credit card and different business transactions. Off-line signature processing can be used for healthcare organizations to identify patients, healthcare personnel, validate the contracts and past health record's documents.

Another approach for signature recognition is dynamic which used dynamic characteristics of the signature, like, acceleration, velocity, pressure, timing, and direction of the signature strokes which are very difficult to replicate. Static signature can be replicated by a trained human counterfeiter or manipulation by a computer, but dynamic characteristics are unique and very complicated in nature to the handwriting style of a person. These strengths of dynamic signature recognition make it suitable for true person authentication in healthcare.

An electronic signature system enables a healthcare organization to speed up admission, registration, and documentation processes and reduce errors while saving on printing and filing costs. Signature pads are the ideal choice for capturing electronic handwritten signatures at the admission desk or at the point of medical care. It seems like a conventional ink pen. Patients can read information regarding their healthcare services on the screen and see their signature in real-time when signing.

These reliable devices guarantee a low total cost of ownership (TCO) and ensure a Return on Investment in less than 1 year.

## Advantages

- **Speed:** This reduces paper documents maintained by healthcare organizations. Within very short amount of time patients can get registered, healthcare personnel as well as patients can be identified.
- **Costs:** The digital signatures on electronic documents are cheap compared to paper documents
- **Security:** The risks of healthcare documents being intercepted, read, dilapidated, or deflect are reduced by digital signature.
- **Authenticity:** Like signed paper document, a digital signature which is present in a digital document can stand up in court.

## Disadvantages

- **Expiry:** Technological products which use digital signatures are highly dependent on the technology used by it and technological productions have a low life span.
- **Certificates:** Digital certificates are required from trusted certification authorities to use digital signatures.
- **Software:** Some verification software at any cost is required to work with digital signature.
- **Law:** In some states and countries, laws regarding cyber and technology-based issues are powerless or even non-existent. In these cases digital signature is very risky.

*Table 1. Comparative study of some biometrics traits*

| Biometrics Technology | Accuracy | Cost | Equipment used | Social acceptance | Use | Interference |
|---|---|---|---|---|---|---|
| Fingerprint | High | Medium | Scanner | Medium | Patient, healthcare personnel identification and access control | Cut or wound on finger, dirtiness and roughness of finger. |
| Face Recognition | Medium | Medium | Camera | High | | Illumination, facial expression, pose, occlusion |
| Retinal Scan | High | High | Camera | Low | | Irritation |
| Iris Recognition | High | High | Camera | Medium | | Glasses |
| Hand Geometry Recognition | Medium | Low | Scanner | High | | Rheumatism, arthritis |
| DNA | High | High | Test equipment | Low | | Multiple samples are required, complex |
| Signature Recognition | Low | Medium | Touch panel, optic pen | High | | Changeable |
| Voice Recognition | Medium | Medium | Microphone | High | | Cold, noise |

## Selection Criteria of Biometrics Technology

The selection criteria of biometrics for healthcare system will rely on several application-specific factors and the circumstances in which the recognition process is completed. The factors those are very important while selecting a biometrics technology are throughput, the user profile, the overall system cost, requirements for matching perfection, complexity, long term maintenance cost, abilities, and cultural and social issues that could affect the adoption of user.

The main criterion in the election of appropriate biometrics technology is its perfection. When the probe biometrics sample is assimilated to the templates stored in the database for verification process, a matching score is used to assure or refuse the identity of a person. A threshold for this matching score is decided by the system designers to provide the intended level of matching perfection for the system. The perfection of a biometrics based authentication system is generally standardized by the false acceptance rate (FAR) and false rejection rate (FRR). The system administrators can adjust sensitivity to FAR and FRR to get to the intended level of matching accuracy protecting the security need of system. The false acceptance rate means the possibility that an individual is verified incorrectly by a biometrics system or accept an imposter. The false rejection rate means the possibility that a correct person is rejected by a biometrics system.

A comparative study of some biometrics traits is given in Table 1.

## Biometrics Identity and Identity Management

Biometrics identity refers to the biological characteristics of a person which help to identify a person successfully. Identity Management or Identity and Access Management (IAM) is mainly used to ensure that resources are accessed only by the right people, at the correct time and for the true causes in the field of computer security and business discipline. Biometrics authentication is used in computer science as a tool for access control and identification. Also, it is used to recognize individuals in crowd that are under surveillance.

Also, it comprises the management of explicative information of the user and how and by whom that information can be attained and changed. Identity management manages entities like users, hardware, network resources and software applications. Biometrics identity management gives the authority to set biometrics to that system as a substitute for users' credentials.

Today keeping the security of patient's data is a high priority for healthcare systems. As more organizations replace data by electronic medical records, healthcare identity management resolutions can aid to restrain unauthorized access. Biometrics identity management provides faster access to patient's data as well as securing patient's information. Users can simply interact with biometrics sensor and immediately access their remote session.

Biometrics identity management can be deployed in various environments like self-service kiosks to the emergency room, patient's identification for different healthcare services and access to their Electronic Health Records accurately. Biometrics identity management provides several facilities to healthcare users -

1.  **Token Replacement:** Biometrics identity management eliminates token based identity management (token can be lost or stolen) and improves security using biometrics. It eliminates the task of using and managing tokens in healthcare facilities.
2.  **Insurance Fraud Prevention:** To acquire valuable private data hackers is targeting healthcare databases. Mainly health records are stolen from doctor's offices or major health insurer. Biometrics identity management through biometrics authentication adds an extra layer of security that can significantly reduce insurance frauds by ensuring that every patient is exactly who he or she claims to be. Biometrics identity management reduces fraudulent services. It replaces insurance cards totally by biometrics or adds biometrics as a second factor. For this, patients can easily sign in at the doctor's office, hospital or pharmacy.
3.  **Electronic Health Records (EHRs) Maintenance:** To protect the Electronic Health Records (EHRs) from unauthorized access is the biggest challenge in medical industry. Biometrics identity management enables very fast and secure access to the patient's records. It also controls who can access patient's medical records. It generates reports on any type of access request.
4.  **Physical Access Control:** Medical facilities require high security to protect patients or their private data. Replacing token with a biometrics identity access management solution will provide a better security in accessing any building or a room in healthcare system. Biometrics identity access management keeps records of people entering any facilities (building or room). It secures any facility in healthcare system with biometrics authentication. It reduces the cost associated with the loss of tokens.

## Multi-Biometrics Fusion for Healthcare Organization

Most of existing biometrics systems use a single biometrics trait for verification or identification. However, monomodal biometrics systems are unable to fulfill the needs of large-scale biometrics systems such as larger population coverage, varied deployment circumstance, and more demanding perfection requirements. To fulfill the demands of large-scale biometrics systems, integration of extra sources of information is required to tighten the decision process. A multi-biometrics system integrates useful data from multiple biometrics traits or from algorithms or from sensors, and other elements to create a recognition procedure more harden. The fusion of biometrics has various benefits such as growing population coverage, impeding spoofing activities and decreasing enrolment failure.

Although it is evident that the biometrics technology based applications are already received a considerable amount of attention and they also reached a particular level of maturity, however, any biometrics system is not free from challenges which are to be addressed to minimize their risks. Multi-biometrics system (Jain & Ross, 2004) is a way that takes advantage of uniqueness of various physiological and behavioral characteristics of a person and combines data at different fusion levels. This gives additional tools to healthcare for identifying patients in the cases of injury or trauma correctly.

To solve problems faced by the conventional uni-modal biometrics systems, multi-biometrics fusion provides more discriminating information by combining multiple biometrics evidences at different implementation levels to generate a more accurate result or description. Multi-biometrics systems are proposed with a motive to raise the perfection and robustness to intra-person changes and to noisy data. Fusion in multi-biometrics is mainly introduced to make an identification or verification decision based on the information combined from various biometrics traits.

## Uni-Biometrics vs. Multi-Biometrics Systems

Uni-biometrics systems use a single biometrics trait while multi-biometrics systems use multiple biometrics traits of a person. Multi-biometrics system can enhance matching perfection, security and reliability of user authentication method. Multi-biometrics systems have efficiency to address inabilities of unibiometrics systems like, noise in data that is captured by a sensor, non-universality, impressibility to spoof attacks, and large intra-class changes.

## Types of Multi-Biometrics Systems

Multi-biometrics systems use multiple samples captured from more than one biometrics trait or a single biometrics trait. This type of system uses one of the following integration cases to test biometrics features:

## Multi-Sensor Systems

Multi-sensor systems utilize various sensors to generate more robust feature using a fusion methodology. For example, an optical and a capacitive sensor can be used to capture fingerprint samples of biometrics data, and then integrate it using sensor level fusion process.

## Multi-Modal Systems

Multi-modal systems exploit multiple biometrics traits to recognize an individual. For example, a person provides his/ her fingerprint and iris scan for authentication on a multi-biometrics system.

## Multi-Instance Systems

Multi-instance biometrics system integrates multiple instances of a single biometrics trait to recognize a person. For example: A multi-instance system may give fingerprints of more than one finger to identify a person. If this system uses single sensor to capture multiple instances, then cost of these systems will reduce.

## Multi-Sample Systems

Multi-sample systems capture multiple samples of a same biometrics trait. For example, a multi-sample face recognition system may want left and right (both) profiles of the face along with frontal profile. Taking different samples of a biometrics trait is very useful to capture changes that can occur in a biometrics trait and at the same time get a more complete representation of a given trait.

## Multi-Algorithm Systems

Multi-algorithm systems use multiple algorithms for feature extraction as well as matching on a single biometrics trait. These systems are very cheap and simple as they use single sensor to take biometrics samples.

## Multi-Biometrics Fusion Techniques

In a multi-biometrics system, fusion (Ross &Jain, 2003) can be done on different levels to consolidate sampled data collected from different biometrics traits.

Multi-biometrics fusion techniques are categorized into two ways –

1.  Fusion Prior to Matching
    a.  **Sensor Level Fusion:** In this fusion, data collected at sensor level from multiple biometrics traits are combined.
    b.  **Feature Level Fusion:** In this fusion, feature sets generated from multiple biometrics traits are combined to form a new feature set.
2.  Fusion After Matching
    a.  **Decision Level Fusion:** Decision level fusion works by taking the decisions generated by different biometrics matching modules. An ultimate decision is taken by getting individual decision of various biometrics traits.
    b.  **Score Level Fusion:** The score level fusion technique fused match scores (similarity or difference between the probe sample and enrolled templates) to get the final decision.
    c.  **Rank Level Fusion:** Rank level fusion integrates ranks assigned to each enrolled user by different sub modules to get a new rank for each user.

## Challenges of Biometrics Technologies

Designing a robust biometrics authentication system is a challenging task. Two biometrics samples of same biometrics trait of a person may not be the same due to several factors. Sometimes two biometrics samples of same biometrics trait of two different persons may appear to be the same like face images of twins or look-alikes. There are several challenges of a biometrics authentication systems and they are summarized as follows:

- **Variation Within Persons:** Biometrics samples taken by biometrics authentication systems may be influenced by several factors like, changes in environment, age, stress, disease, occupational factors, socio-cultural aspects of the circumstance, changes in human interface with the system, and so on. Therefore, every time when a person interacts with the biometrics system he/she may provide different biometrics information. This type of situations leads uncertainty in biometrics authentication systems.
- **Sensors:** Performance of sensor plays a significant role in biometrics authentication system. Sensor age, the sensitivity of sensor performance, and interface of a sensor affect the perfection of a biometrics authentication system.
- **Feature Extraction and Matching Algorithms:** Biometrics traits cannot be directly associated for authentication. Therefore robust feature extraction algorithms are required to extract durable and distinguishable features. Designing robust feature extraction and matching algorithms are challenging tasks.
- **Data Integrity:** Information may be changed through transformation, manipulation or mismanagement, inappropriate compression, or some other means.

No any single biometrics trait is known to be fully durable and distinguishable across all groups. Biometrics traits have primary distinguishable statistical features and varied degrees of durability under ordinary physiological situations as well as challenging circumstances. The several aspects of biometrics traits are not well convinced, specifically at large scales. Complicating phenomenon, the fundamental biological features and distribution of biometrics traits in demography are usually seen only through filters arbitrate by assessment procedures, devices and subsequent biometrics feature extraction. Better understanding of biometrics traits in human beings can be possible by sufficient data collection and analysis. It is very important to understand fundamental discriminating features of a biometrics trait and also the durability, exactness, and implicit variableness of a given measure.

Another main feature of biometrics based authentication system is to make decision under ambiguous situations. A biometrics match yields not definite recognition but a probability of true recognition and a non-match yields a probability that an individual is unknown to the system.

## Future Trends

It is very important to identify the tools and technologies which facilitate true user identification. Currently the papers which are available and information about biometrics disclose that the main contention for applying biometrics solutions is high security. This aspect is permitted by policy makers, governments for fighting against terrorism, help to identify criminals, or immigrants at border crossing etc. Therefore, the best solution for person identification is biometrics (using biometrics cues) through some automatic devices. Biometrics readers are now used in homes, offices, computers, machines, devices, etc to get security. In near future biometrics technology will be the largest technology in market which will be used in everywhere. However, for the most part, the use of these technologies will only replace existing user authentication and access control methods, giving increased security and amenities. There will be no need to take keys, identity cards, personal documents and don't even remember passwords, etc. This implementation of biometrics will assemble to the overall security solution: counteracting the possibility of theft or illegal use of equipments/technologies. Biometrics devices will grant new attributes and approaches towards security solutions.

## CONCLUSION

Identity verification of human beings plays a significant role in today's linked and fast going world that can give entree to very secure facilities, perform transactions and also used for the tasks like border crossing, passport verification, banking transactions, etc. User authentication is very important for security measures. As biometrics is being used for physical as well as digital identity recognition, therefore it is essential to enhance the performance as well as use in new domain like healthcare of current biometrics technologies. Biometrics systems could be found useful in healthcare domain due to its irreplaceable properties towards successful person identification. As biometrics are used for personal identification for accessing high security facilities where security is susceptible to attack, it becomes necessary to increase performance and reliability of these systems more and more. To increase the accuracy and develop robust biometrics systems, multi-biometrics systems can be found competitive over monomodal biometrics. This chapter presents a comprehensive study on different biometrics systems including physiological and behavioral biometrics traits and their suitableness for healthcare domain where every live entity is important to be authenticated successfully. Besides, challenges and future scopes of biometrics systems are also discussed in this chapter. As healthcare organizations play a serious role in our daily life as well as the security is an important concern in healthcare system, therefore choosing appropriate unibiometrics or multi-biometrics systems and then integrate with healthcare systems would be an imperative aspect for keeping things secure.

## REFERENCES

Bowyer, K. W., Hollingsworth, K., & Flynn, P. J. (2008). Image understanding for iris biometrics: A survey. *Computer Vision and Image Understanding*, *110*(2), 281–307. doi:10.1016/j.cviu.2007.08.005

Campbell, J. P. (1997). Speaker recognition: A tutorial. *Proceedings of the IEEE*, *85*(9), 1437–1462. doi:10.1109/5.628714

Chandra, A., Durand, R., & Weaver, S. (2008). The uses and potential of biometrics in health care: Are consumers and providers ready for it? *International Journal of Pharmaceutical and Healthcare Marketing*, *2*(1), 22–34. doi:10.1108/17506120810865406

Chellappa, R., Wilson, C. L., & Sirohey, S. (1995). Human and machine recognition of faces: A survey. *Proceedings of the IEEE*, *83*(5), 705–741. doi:10.1109/5.381842

Choras, M. (2007, June). Image feature extraction methods for ear biometrics--a survey. In Null (pp. 261-265). IEEE.

Diwakar, M., & Maharshi, M. (2013). An extraction and recognition of tongue-print images for biometrics authentication system. *International Journal of Computers and Applications*, *61*(3).

Faundez-Zanuy, M. (2005). Signature recognition state-of-the-art. *IEEE Aerospace and Electronic Systems Magazine*, *20*(7), 28–32. doi:10.1109/MAES.2005.1499249

Gehring, W. J., Yan, Q. Q., Billeter, M., Furukubo-Tokunaga, K., Schier, A. F., Resendez-Perez, D., . . . Wüthrich, K. (1995). Homeodomain-DNA recognition. In Nmr In Structural Biology: A Collection of Papers by Kurt Wüthrich (pp. 493-505). Academic Press. doi:10.1142/9789812795830_0042

Han, W. Y., & Lee, J. C. (2012). Palm vein recognition using adaptive Gabor filter. *Expert Systems with Applications*, *39*(18), 13225–13234. doi:10.1016/j.eswa.2012.05.079

Harb, A., Abbas, M., Cherry, A., Jaber, H., & Ayache, M. (2015, September). Palm print recognition. In *Advances in Biomedical Engineering (ICABME), 2015 International Conference on* (pp. 13-16). IEEE. 10.1109/ICABME.2015.7323239

Jahan, S., Chowdhury, M., & Islam, R. (2017, December). Robust fingerprint verification for enhancing security in healthcare system. In *2017 International Conference on Image and Vision Computing New Zealand (IVCNZ)* (pp. 1-5). IEEE.

Jain, A. K., & Ross, A. (2004). Multibiometrics systems. *Communications of the ACM*, *47*(1), 34–40. doi:10.1145/962081.962102

Jain, A. K., Ross, A., & Prabhakar, S. (2004). An introduction to biometrics recognition. *IEEE Transactions on Circuits and Systems for Video Technology*, *14*(1), 4–20. doi:10.1109/TCSVT.2003.818349

Jia, W., Cai, H. Y., Gui, J., Hu, R. X., Lei, Y. K., & Wang, X. F. (2012). Newborn footprint recognition using orientation feature. *Neural Computing & Applications*, *21*(8), 1855–1863. doi:10.100700521-011-0530-9

Kinnunen, T., & Li, H. (2010). An overview of text-independent speaker recognition: From features to supervectors. *Speech Communication*, *52*(1), 12–40. doi:10.1016/j.specom.2009.08.009

Kumar, T., Braeken, A., Liyanage, M., & Ylianttila, M. (2017, May). Identity privacy preserving biometrics based authentication scheme for Naked healthcare environment. In *Communications (ICC), 2017 IEEE International Conference on* (pp. 1-7). IEEE.

Kumar, V. A., & Ramakrishnan, M. (2010). Footprint recognition using modified sequential haar energy transform (MSHET). *International Journal of Computer Science Issues, 7*(3).

Leonard, D. C., Pons, A. P., & Asfour, S. S. (2009). Realization of a universal patient identifier for electronic medical records through biometrics technology. *IEEE Transactions on Information Technology in Biomedicine*, *13*(4), 494–500. doi:10.1109/TITB.2008.926438 PMID:19273015

Maltoni, D., Maio, D., Jain, A. K., & Prabhakar, S. (2009). *Handbook of fingerprint recognition*. Springer Science & Business Media. doi:10.1007/978-1-84882-254-2

Mirmohamadsadeghi, L., & Drygajlo, A. (2011, October). Palm vein recognition with local binary patterns and local derivative patterns. In *Biometrics (IJCB), 2011 International Joint Conference on* (pp. 1-6). IEEE.

Mohammedi, M., Omar, M., Aitabdelmalek, W., Mansouri, A., & Bouabdallah, A. (2018, April). Secure and lightweight biometrics-based remote patient authentication scheme for home healthcare systems. *In Programming and Systems (ISPS), 2018 International Symposium on* (pp. 1-6). IEEE.

Ng, R. Y. F., Tay, Y. H., & Mok, K. M. (2008, August). A review of iris recognition algorithms. In *Information Technology, 2008. ITSim 2008. International Symposium on* (Vol. 2, pp. 1-7). IEEE. 10.1109/ITSIM.2008.4631656

Nwosu, K. C., & Igbonagwam, O. (2014, October). BEPOC: A biometrics-enabled point-of-care patients and electronic medical records management system for medical missions. In *Healthcare Innovation Conference (HIC), 2014 IEEE* (pp. 223-226). IEEE.

Riera, A., Soria-Frisch, A., Caparrini, M., Grau, C., & Ruffini, G. (2008). Unobtrusive biometrics system based on electroencephalogram analysis. *EURASIP Journal on Advances in Signal Processing, 2008*, 18.

Ross, A., & Jain, A. (2003). Information fusion in biometrics. *Pattern Recognition Letters, 24*(13), 2115–2125. doi:10.1016/S0167-8655(03)00079-5

Sanchez-Reillo, R., Sanchez-Avila, C., & Gonzalez-Marcos, A. (2000). Biometrics identification through hand geometry measurements. *IEEE Transactions on Pattern Analysis and Machine Intelligence, 22*(10), 1168–1171. doi:10.1109/34.879796

Shen, T. W. (2005). *Biometrics identity verification based on electrocardiogram (ECG)* (PhD dissertation). University of Wisconsin.

Sidlauskas, D. P., & Tamer, S. (2008). Hand geometry recognition. In *Handbook of Biometrics* (pp. 91–107). Boston, MA: Springer. doi:10.1007/978-0-387-71041-9_5

Sumathi, S., & Malini, R. R. (2010, April). Face recognition system to enhance E Health. In *E-Health Networking, Digital Ecosystems and Technologies (EDT), 2010 International Conference on* (Vol. 1, pp. 195-198). IEEE.

Tabatabaee, H., Milani-Fard, A., & Jafariani, H. (2006, April). A novel human identifier system using retina image and fuzzy clustering approach. In *Proceedings of the 2nd IEEE International Conference on Information and Communication Technologies* (pp. 1031-1036). IEEE.

Zhang, D., Liu, Z., & Yan, J. Q. (2010). Dynamic tongueprint: A novel biometrics identifier. *Pattern Recognition, 43*(3), 1071–1082. doi:10.1016/j.patcog.2009.09.002

Zhang, D., Liu, Z., Yan, J. Q., & Shi, P. F. (2007, August). Tongue-print: a novel biometrics pattern. In *International Conference on Biometrics* (pp. 1174-1183). Springer.

Zhang, G. H., Poon, C. C., & Zhang, Y. T. (2009, November). A biometrics based security solution for encryption and authentication in tele-healthcare systems. In *Applied Sciences in Biomedical and Communication Technologies, 2009. ISABEL 2009. 2nd International Symposium on* (pp. 1-4). IEEE.

## KEY TERMS AND DEFINITIONS

**Biometrics Identity:** Biometrics identity refers to biometrics traits which are used to identify a person.

**Biometrics Identity Management:** Identity management is also known as identity and access management (IAM) which is used to ensure that resources are accessed only by the right people, at the right time and for the right reasons in the field of computer security and business discipline.

**Feature Extraction:** Feature extraction transforms an input image into a set of features.

**Matching:** Matching compares the test sample with the training samples.

**Multi-Biometrics System:** A multi-biometrics system integrates information from multiple biometrics traits, algorithms, sensors, and other components to make a recognition procedure more secure.

**Preprocessing:** Preprocessing dispels artifacts from the sensor to enhance the quality of the input biometrics sample (e.g., removing background noise).

**Similarity Score:** Similarity score is the score generated at the matching stage of a biometrics system.

**Verification:** Verification is the act of verifying an identity what he/she claims (1:1 matching).

*This research was previously published in Design and Implementation of Healthcare Biometric Systems; pages 1-28, copyright year 2019 by Medical Information Science Reference (an imprint of IGI Global).*

# Chapter 4
# Cyber–Physical Security in Healthcare

**Vasiliki Mantzana**
 https://orcid.org/0000-0003-0008-477X
*Center for Security Studies (KEMEA), Greece*

**Eleni Darra**
*Center for Security Studies (KEMEA), Greece*

**Ilias Gkotsis**
 https://orcid.org/0000-0003-2228-1387
*Center for Security Studies (KEMEA), Greece*

## ABSTRACT

*The healthcare sector has been considered a part of critical infrastructure (CI) of society and has faced numerous physical-cyber threats that affect citizens' lives and habits, increase their fears, and influence hospital services provisions. The two most recent ransomware campaigns, WannaCry and Petya, have both managed to infect victims' systems by exploiting existing unpatched vulnerabilities. It is critical to develop an integrated approach in order to fight against combination of physical and cyber threats. In this chapter, key results of the SAFECARE project (H2020-GA787005), which aims is to provide solutions that will improve physical and cyber security, to prevent and detect complex attacks, to promote incident responses and mitigate impacts, will be presented. More specifically, healthcare critical asset vulnerabilities; cyber-physical threats that can affect them; architecture solutions, as well as, some indicative scenarios that will be validated during the project will be presented.*

## INTRODUCTION

Critical infrastructure (CI) is an asset or system which is essential for the maintenance of vital societal functions. The damage to a CI, its destruction or disruption by natural disasters, terrorism, criminal activity or malicious behavior, may have a significant negative impact for the security of the EU and

DOI: 10.4018/978-1-6684-6311-6.ch004

the well-being of its citizens. Over the last decade, healthcare sector has been considered as a CI and the most vulnerable one, facing numerous physical-cyber threats that affect citizens' lives and habits, increase their fears and influence hospital services provision. Healthcare sector as a CI is safeguarding people, services, systems and physical infrastructure providing vital operation to the health services.

Health sector is responsible for delivering services that improve, maintain or restore the health of individuals and their communities (World Health Organisation, 2019). These services are large and complex, affect and get affected by multiple interacting actors, such as doctors, nurses, patients, citizens, medical suppliers, health insurance providers etc., with different backgrounds, knowledge, organizational beliefs, interests and culture. Health systems could provide services that are personal and non-personal. Personal health services can be therapeutic or rehabilitative and are delivered to patients and citizens individually. Non-personal health services are actions applied to individuals or collectives and might refer to health education (Peters, Kandola, Elmendorf, & Chellaraj, 1999).

Health services are widely relying on information systems (IS) to optimize organization and costs, whereas ethics and privacy constraints severely restrict security controls and thus increase vulnerability.

Threats in the healthcare sector can result in economic damage, human casualties, property destruction, and hospital assets functionality disruption that can produce cascading effects and harm patients' and citizens' confidence. Today, healthcare landscape is facing major threats, which cannot be analyzed as physical or cyber independently, and therefore it is critical to develop an integrated approach in order to fight against such combination of threats. Cyber-physical attacks are the results of the exploitable vulnerabilities that need to be considered by hospitals.

In this chapter, we will focus on a framework related to the enhancement of Hospitals' security and resilience, and respective solutions that will improve physical and cyber security to prevent and detect complex attacks, to promote incident responses and mitigate the impacts, based on the work implemented and further foreseen under SAFECARE project (H2020-GA787005),. In these terms, we will initially analyze the normative literature on CI and healthcare sector security and safety challenges and protection. In doing this, we will present healthcare critical assets' vulnerabilities and describe cyber-physical threats that can affect them (as they have been identified in SAFECARE). In addition, SAFECARE architecture solution will be presented, including a cyber-physical security system and proposed strategies that can boost their protection; avoid threats' cascading effects; enhance internal and external stakeholders' communication and response; mitigate impacts; and maintain healthcare services secure and available to citizens. Finally, some representative scenarios that will be validated during the project will be analyzed.

## BACKGROUND

### Critical Infrastructures

Europe has a long-standing history of approaches to improve CI protection. Past terrorist attacks fostered the development and adoption of the European Programme on critical infrastructure protection (EPCIP). The EPCIP provides systematic, network-based guidelines for member states to identify Critical Infrastructure assets (Izuakor & White, 2016) The EPCIP comprises the following pillars (European Commission, 2006): (a) means for its implementation (e.g., EPCIP action plan, CIWIN), (b) support for member states concerning National CIP, (c) contingency planning, (d) external dimension (exchange of information with non-EU countries), (e) EU security research program on "prevention, preparedness and consequence management of terrorism and other security related risks" and (f) financial measures.

The Directive 2008/114/EC functions as the main instrument of the EPCIP. Firstly, it provides definitions of CIs and ECIs. According to the Directive, ECIs are: "Assets, systems or parts thereof located in EU member states, which are essential for vital societal functions [...] the disruption or destruction of which would have a significant impact on at least two EU member states" (European Commission, 2008). The directive provides concrete support for three phases of EPCIP. The phase of identification includes specific criteria to identify CIs: (a) sectoral criteria and (b) CI definition, (c) transboundary elements and (d) cross-cutting criteria. The phase of designation includes all steps to negotiate and to decide on the criticality of any specific infrastructure: (a) notification of affected member states, (b) bilateral discussions and agreements and (c) final decision by the 'hosting country'. Finally, it provides two instruments that really contribute to the protection of infrastructures: (a) OSP (obligatory unless similar regulations are in place) and (b) liaison officer as contact point between the ECI owner/operator and relevant member state authorities.

CIs are complex and they are turning into cyber-physical infrastructures because information and communication technologies (ICT) are important in the context of infrastructure management. Today, most of organizations are susceptible to cyber threats because they are increasingly exposed to the internet and to the external world. Technological trends like Internet of Things (IoT), Industry 4.0 are driving this augmented connectivity. Nowadays, most CIs are controlled by industrial control systems (ICS) that need to be frequently updated during maintenance campaigns. Since the beginning of 21st century, Critical Infrastructures have faced multiple cyber-attacks.

## Healthcare Sector Challenges, Incidents and Protection

According to WHO definition "Hospitals complement and amplify the effectiveness of many parts of the health system, providing continuous availability of services for acute and complex conditions" (World Health Organisation, 2019). They are an essential element to health systems as they support care coordination and integration and play a key role in supporting other health-care providers, such as primary health care, community outreach and home-based services. They also often provide a setting for education of doctors, nurses and other health-care professionals and are a critical base for clinical research.

Any physical or cyber incident that causes loss of infrastructure or massive patient surge, such as natural disasters, terrorist acts, or chemical, biological, radiological, nuclear, or explosive hazards could affect the health care services provision and could cause overwhelming pressure to the affected health systems. Hospitals not only provide care services; but they are also the last shelters for disaster victims seeking care and represent an icon of social security, connectivity and community trust (World Health Organization, 2015). Thus, in this context, it is fundamental for a hospital to remain resilient; maintain the level of provided care; and be able to scale up its service delivery in any given emergency situation.

Healthcare sector is one of the most targeted sectors; 81% of 223 organizations surveyed, and >110 million patients in the US had their data compromised in 2015 alone (KPMG, 2015), with only 50% of providers thinking that they could protect themselves from cyberattacks (KPMG, 2015). It has been reported that between 2009 and 2018 there have been 2.546 healthcare data breaches involving more than 500 records and resulting in theft/exposure of 189,945,874 records (HIPAA, 2018). In the healthcare sector, hacking and malware (including ransomware) are the leading attack type of health data breaches

(HIPAA, 2018). These data breaches result in large financial losses, but also in loss of reputation and reduced patient safety. Some known data breaches in healthcare sector are the following:

- 2017 WannaCry attack infected more than 300,000 computers across the world demanding that users pay bitcoin ransoms. Despite this attack was not specifically directed at healthcare organizations, other ransomware has specifically targeted the healthcare sector and, according to US media, the Presbyterian Medical Centre shut down for 10 days until it paid a $17,000 ransom (Perlroth & Sanger, 2017).

- Medical Device Hijack (Medjack) is another known attack that injects malware into unprotected medical devices to move laterally across the hospital network (Hei, 2013); Between the first detection of Medjack in 2015 and now, there have been many variations of the attack with several hospitals' medical devices, including x-ray equipment, picture archive and communications systems (PACS) and blood gas analyzers (BGA), etc., having been attacked. The attacker establishes a backdoor within the medical device, and almost any form of manipulation of the unencrypted data stored and flowing through the device is possible.

- It was reported in the press that in January 2019 hackers performed a ransom attack in a heart specialist clinic in Melbourne, where the hackers hit patient files (Martin, 2019). As a result, staff was unable to access some patient files for more than three weeks. The Clinic could have mitigated the impact, if data was properly and fully backed and if they were investing consistently in IT security.

- A billing company based in USA, which operates the online payment system used by a network of 44 hospitals in USA, discovered that some of its databases that contained 2,652,537 patients' records, had been compromised in 2018. Upon discovery of the breach, access to data was terminated and forensic specialists were hired to review the incident, secure affected databases and improve security controls (HIPAA, 2018).

- 128,400 records were affected by a sophisticated phishing incident that happened at New York oncology and hematology clinic. More specifically, fourteen employee email accounts clicked on phishing emails, which exposed health information in the email accounts. The clinic hired forensic specialists to assess the breach and types of data affected. Moreover, improvements to data security following the incident included active monitoring of affected systems, regular password resets, additional employee training and new email protocols (HIPAA, 2018).

- A woman opened fire at a flat opposite a Catholic Hospital and then inside the hospital in the south-western town of Lorrach in Baden-Wuerttemberg, Germany, killing at least three, including one child, and wounding several patients before police shot her dead (The Times, 2010).

- A UK A&E registrar was held hostage by a patient brandishing a pair of steel surgical scissors in a cubicle, she did not panic. Moments earlier, she had gone in to check on the young patient, who was having a mental health episode after taking drugs, and had closed the door behind her. Unfortunately, the patient had managed to hide a pair of scissors, which she pulled out before backing the doctor into a corner. The police were eventually called, and restrained the patient (The Guardian, 2019).

- While a nurse was examining a female patient, the accompanying Roma (gypsies) group attacked her and slammed her on the face. The incident happened at the Salamina Island Health Center, Greece (POEDIN, 2018).

- General Hospital of Larnaka, Cyprus: A 27-year-old patient physically attacked a male and a female doctor examining his leg at the Emergency Department (OFFSITE, 2017).

It is prevalent that healthcare organizations have several assets that are essential for their operation and should be protected. ENISA identified assets and presented them in a report namely "Smart Hospitals: Security and Resilience for Smart Health Service and Infrastructures" (ENISA, 2016). Assets that can be attacked are the buildings and facilities, data, interconnected clinical Information Systems, mobile client devices, networking equipment, identification systems, networked medical devices and remote care systems.

The two most critical hospital's assets are the patients' health and their records (ENISA, 2016). The first one can be affected in many ways, for example, turning off a critical medical device can cause a serious injury to a patient. Patient records contains valuable information, as Personal Identifiable Information (PII) and Protected Health Information (PHI) that can be the most lucrative information for attackers. It has been reported that healthcare data is substantially more valuable than any other data, as the value for a full set of medical credentials can be over $1000 (Sulleyman, 2017). Data held within health organizations also has political value. For example, World Anti-Doping Agency was attacked and athletes' records had been made public (BBC, 2017).

It is prevalent, that healthcare organizations and their assets suffer from vulnerabilities that attackers can exploit to damage the environment and cause disruptions. These vulnerabilities can be either cyber (application & OS, control gaps and design flaws, unpatched devices, unprotected networks, weak credentials, lack of cyber threat prevention and detection, lack of smart sensors etc.) or physical (lack of access management, video monitoring, fire detection, smart sensors, security agents, policy, collaboration with police and firefighters, etc.).

Hackers have different goals, as they might wish to cause damage, obtain a ransom, cause the interruption of service, or collect data to prepare future impacting attacks. Therefore, the adversary' motivation should be considered while protecting a system. The attacks can be roughly divided in two categories:

- Untargeted attacks that do not have a specific target and the attacker chooses the targets that maximize their gain/cost ratio.
- Targeted attacks that have a specific target and the attacker knows what he/she wants and will do everything necessary to achieve his/her goal.

To develop an efficient and effective protection system it is important to consider both aforementioned types of attacks and understand the profile and sophistication of attackers. The table below, extracted from ISE's report, summarizes the profile and motivation of healthcare organizations attackers (Independent Security Evaluators, 2016). These assets can be also attacked in different ways, such as cyber (social engineering, spear phishing, malware, RATs, DDoS, vulnerability exploits), physically (intrusion, aggression, material destruction, bombing, manmade fire etc.) and/or from natural hazards (flood, earthquake, storm).

As such, health structures are pointed out as potential targets, which highlight the need to enhance the protection of these Critical Infrastructures. Healthcare organizations can take practical steps to protect themselves and reduce the effects of an attack, such as to strengthen resilience, as resilient organizations are less likely to be attacked and suffer less harm when attacks occur. For example, on Papworth Hospital in 2016, a ransomware attack took place just after the daily backup, so no data were lost. Moreover, Hospitals and healthcare organizations should not only invest on cyber perimeter security, but must also adopt technologies that support limiting damages in case of an attack (e.g. network segregation, data encryption, etc.) (INFOSEC, 2019). In addition to cyber protection measures, hospitals should

*Figure 1. Profile and motivation of healthcare organizations attacker (Independent Security Evaluators, 2016)*

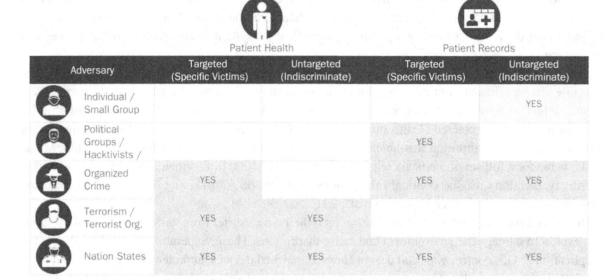

| | Patient Health | | Patient Records | |
|---|---|---|---|---|
| Adversary | Targeted (Specific Victims) | Untargeted (Indiscriminate) | Targeted (Specific Victims) | Untargeted (Indiscriminate) |
| Individual / Small Group | | | | YES |
| Political Groups / Hacktivists / | | | YES | |
| Organized Crime | YES | | YES | YES |
| Terrorism / Terrorist Org. | YES | YES | | |
| Nation States | YES | YES | YES | YES |

also focus on physical protection and should ensure that the file cabinets and doors are properly locked when unattended; security cameras and other adequate physical security controls should be installed (INFOSEC, 2019). It is also crucial that healthcare staff (including researchers, administrators, front desk workers, medics, transcriptionists, handlers of medical claims to IT, and technical staffs) should be properly trained on physical and cyber security issues (Martin, 2017). Last but not least, healthcare organizations need to develop and adopt common healthcare security standards and adopt a clear security policy and response plan.

In tackling crisis management, which has been defined as "the developed capability of an organization to prepare for, anticipate, respond to and recover from crises" (British Standard Institute [BSI], 2014), the following steps have been identified and should be followed:

**Preparedness:** The aim is to prepare organizations and develop general capabilities that will enable them to deliver an appropriate response in any crisis. Preparedness refers to activities, programs, and systems developed before crisis that will enhance capabilities of individuals, businesses, communities, and governments to support the response to and recovery from future disasters.

**Response:** Response begins as soon as an event occurs and refers to the provision of search and rescue services, medical services, as well as repairing and to the restoration of communication and data systems during a crisis. A response plan can support the reduction of casualties, damage and recovery time.

**Recovery:** When crisis occurs, organizations must be able to carry on with their tasks in the midst of the crisis while simultaneously planning for how they will recover from the damage the crisis caused. Steps to return to normal operations and limit damage to organization and stakeholders continue after the incident or crisis (Deloitte, 2016).

**Mitigation:** Mitigation refers to the process of reducing or eliminating future loss of life and property and injuries resulting from hazards through short and long-term activities. Mitigation strategies may range in scope and size.

The efficient and timely identification of risks, threats and vulnerabilities of the healthcare sector infrastructures and services the disruption or destruction of which would have significant socio-economic and environmental impacts, unquestionably requires communication, coordination, and cooperation at national level as well, in order to deter, mitigate and neutralize any posed hazard and ensure the functionality, continuity and integrity of all affected assets and systems.

## Critical Infrastructure Related EU Projects

The European Commission has put continuous effort, through several initiatives and research and innovation funding tools, in order to support the needs of CI operators for security enhancement. For example, there have been several funded projects under the topic CIP-01-2016-2017: Prevention, detection, response and mitigation of the combination of physical and cyber threats to the critical infrastructure of Europe, of Horizon 2020 programme, as depicted below:

1. DEFENDER (http://defender-project.eu/)

Defending the European Energy Infrastructures (DEFENDER) project is a project that will adapt, integrate, upscale, deploy and validate a number of different technologies and operational blueprints. The project has a vision to develop a new approach to safeguard existing and future European CEI operation over cyber-physical-social threats, based on novel protective concepts for lifecycle assessment, resilience and self-healing offering "security by design", and advanced intruder inspection and incident mitigation systems.

2. SAURON (https://www.sauronproject.eu/)

Scalable multidimensional situation awareness solution for protecting European ports (SAURON) project proposes a holistic situation awareness concept as an integrated, scalable and yet installation-specific solution for protecting EU ports and its surroundings. This solution combines the more advanced physical features with the newest techniques in prevention, detection and mitigation of cyber-threats, including the synthetic cyber space understanding using new visualization techniques (immersive interfaces, cyber 3D models and so on). In addition, a Hybrid Situation Awareness (HSA) application capable of determining the potential consequences of any threat will show the potential cascading effect of a detected threat in the two different domains (physical and cyber).

3. STOP-IT (https://stop-it-project.eu/)

Strategic, Tactical, Operational Protection of water Infrastructure against cyber-physical Threats (STOP-IT) assembles a team of major Water Utilities, industrial technology developers, high tech SMEs and top EU R&D providers, to find solutions to protect critical water infrastructure against physical and cyber threats. The main aims of STOP-IT are: a) Identification of current and future water infrastructure risks; b) co-development of an all-hazards risk management framework for the physical and cyber protection of critical water infrastructures.

4.  RESISTO (http://www.resistoproject.eu/)

RESIlience enhancement and risk control platform for communication infraSTructure Operators (RESISTO) is an innovative solution for Communication Infrastructure providing holistic (cyber or physical) situation awareness and enhanced resilience. RESISTO will help Communications Infrastructures Operators to take the best countermeasures and reactive actions exploiting the combined use of risk and resilience preparatory analyses, detection and reaction technologies, applications and processes in the physical and cyber domains. RESISTO main objective is to improve risk control and resilience of modern Communication CIs, against a wide variety of cyber-physical threats, being those malicious attacks, natural disasters or even un-expected.

5.  FINSEC (https://www.finsec-project.eu/)

Integrated Framework for Predictive and Collaborative Security of Financial Infrastructures (FIN-SEC) will develop, demonstrate and bring to market an integrated, intelligent, collaborative and predictive approach to the security of critical infrastructures in the financial sector. To this end, FINSEC will introduce, implement and validate a novel reference architecture for integrated physical and cyber security of critical infrastructures, which will enable handling of dynamic, advanced and asymmetric attacks, while at the same time boosting financial organizations' compliance to security standards and regulations. As a result, FINSEC will provide a blueprint for the next generation security systems for the critical infrastructures of the financial sector.

Independently of the thematic aim of the projects, there is a common focus on state-of-the-art solutions and frameworks that will assist CI operators, owners and security managers to address key emerging cyber-physical challenges in full of threats and uncertainties environment.

## Physical and Cyber Security Solutions and Technologies

In the past decade, the security landscape has dramatically changed with the introduction of several new security technologies to deter, detect and react to more disparate attacks. Organizations are constantly introducing new technologies and upgrading existing ones in order to ensure the security of their most valuable assets such as people, infrastructure, and property. Typical systems include among others the following: (a) Fences/Walls, (b) Guards, (c) Building control, (d) Intrusion detection and access control, € Video surveillance, (f) Audio surveillance, (g) CBRNE sensors and (h) Physical Security Information Management (PSIM) systems.

As in physical protection, CI facilities may also be subject to Cyber-attacks, requiring additional Cyber-security measures. Most of them are meant to protect the CI against Information leakage/loss, prevent unauthorized access, and secure all communication in and out of the facilities. Typical systems include the following: (a) Data Protection, (b) Network Monitoring, (c) Intrusion Response Systems, (d) Endpoint Monitoring, (e) Authentication and Access Control, (f) Software Development based on privacy by design techniques, (g) IoT Sensors for Health and (h) Artificial Intelligence techniques.

## SAFECARE PROJECT

In this direction, SAFECARE project (H2020-GA787005) (SAFECARE project, 2018) aims to provide solutions that will improve physical and cyber security in a seamless and cost-effective way. It will promote new technologies and novel approaches to enhance threat prevention, threat detection, incident response and mitigation of impacts. The SAFECARE solution will also participate in increasing the compliance between security tools and European regulations about ethics and privacy for health services. In doing this, SAFECARE will design, test, validate and demonstrate innovative elements, which will optimize the protection of Critical Infrastructures under operational conditions. These elements are interactive, cooperative and complementary (reinforcing in some cases), aiming at maximizing the potential utilization of the individual elements.

SAFECARE deals with the protection of Critical Infrastructures such as hospitals and public health national agencies. These organizations participate daily to the safety and security of European citizens. Health services breakdown can have tremendous negative effects on public healthcare and public order. Referring to the crisis events that affected over forty hospitals in UK by May 2017, cyber-attacks represent now a major threat for health organizations that mainly rely on IT systems and e-health devices.

The main aim of SAFECARE project is to build up a solution in order to better apprehend the combination of physical and cyber security threats. Furthermore, the project will focus on end users' needs (e.g. hospitals and a public health national agency), the risk assessment as well as and the study of applicable regulations. At the lens of these initial results, partners will be in position to develop innovative approaches and improve prevention and detection capacities on both physical and cyber security grounds.

### Healthcare Organizations' Security Stakeholders

Healthcare organizations' security stakeholders are individuals or organizations that may contribute to be affected by or get involved in issues related to security planning, response or recovery from an emergency situation. Security stakeholders can be categorized according to their perceived proximity to the hospital into internal and external. Internal stakeholders are groups or individuals who work within the hospital, while external are individuals or groups outside the hospital, but who can affect or be affected by it. An indicative list of healthcare organizations' security stakeholders as well as their role are analyzed below.

### Internal Stakeholders

- **Data Protection Officer (DPO):** The primary role of the Data Protection Officer is to ensure that organization processes the personal data of its staff, customers, providers or any other individuals (also referred to as data subjects) in compliance with the applicable data protection rules.
- **Physical Security Manager / Security Personnel:** The main role of a hospital security manager is to (a) develop and implement security policies, protocols and procedures, (b) manage budget and expenses for security operations, (c) manage training of security officers and guards, (d) plan and coordinate security operations and staff when responding to emergencies and alarm, (e) investigate and resolve issues and (f) review reports on incidents and breaches etc. Some hospitals might also subcontract security services to external security companies in order to support the permanent security personnel (and that is why hereafter is considered as internal).

- **IT Security Manager / Security Personnel:** IT Security manager is responsible for leading and managing the activities of the Information Security Risk Assessment and Security Operations team. In doing this, s/he is responsible to (a) manage security issues related to implementation, installation, monitoring and service/support of healthcare IT infrastructure (e.g. networks, platforms, applications, devices etc.), (b) manage (develop, assess, update and enforce) security plans and policies in accordance with IT policies, standards, and compliance requirements, (c) respond to cyberattacks and mitigate cyber risks, (d) provide reports on security issues/threats, (e) train the IT personnel.

- **Technical Manager/ Technical Staff:** The technical staff can identify the sensible technical components for a health structure, such as energy, elevators, technical gas/fluid, temperature, air control systems or building management). They are also responsible to manage access rights, hospital IT behavior system, threats and security events and security personnel related to healthcare organizations infrastructures and processes.

- Security and safety teams are responsible for safeguarding the Hospital against physical attacks: (a) technical assets (e.g. gas, electricity, water), (b) hazardous materials (e.g. radioactive, diagnostic or therapeutic materials), (c) personnel and patients, (d) against natural disasters and fire-fighting. These teams are continuously trained and participate in tabletop and field exercises and simulations with patients, staff, fire brigade, volunteers etc.

- Crisis Management Team (CMT) "focuses on detecting the early signs of a crisis; identifying the problem; preparation of a crisis management plan; encouraging the employees to face problems; and solving the crisis" (Mikušová, 2019).

## External Stakeholders

- **Interconnected Critical Infrastructures and Related Organizations:** This category includes all types of CIs (as described identified in the EU Directive 114/2008 and the NIS Directive) and national policies), Member States NCP for the CIP and EU officials from different DGs related to CI resilience programs and regulatory work, and the scientific community. They also support incident management for physical and cyber threats and respond against respective security events

- **Law Enforcement Agencies (LEAs):** Their aim is to ensure peace and order as well as citizens' unhindered social development, a mission that includes general policing duties and to prevent and interdict crime.

- **Fire Service:** Its mission is to provide fire and rescue services for the citizens and their property. It operates during fires, forest fires, car accidents, other natural or man-made disasters (technological and other disasters, such as earthquakes, floods, chemical - biological - radiological - nuclear (CBRN) threats) and during rescue and assistance operations. It protects and safeguards property that has been destroyed or threatened by fires or other disasters, until handed over to police officers or its owners.

- Other healthcare control centers identified through the interviews conducted are the following: (a) Centre for Disease Control and Prevention; (b) National Health Operations Centre etc.

- General Secretariat for Civil Protection is the body responsible for promoting the country's civil protection relations with relevant international organizations and relevant civil protection agencies in other countries.

- Ministry of Health role in crisis management process is to support, coordinate and formulate crisis management process in healthcare organizations.

Finally, the combination of the aforementioned innovation elements will bring a significant improvement in protecting Critical Infrastructures. With the effective integration of relevant disciplines and project coordination, a successful global optimum solution will be developed to demonstrate improved systemic security and management of the combination of physical and cyber threats.

## Healthcare Organizations' Critical Assets

Hospitals can be characterized as complex healthcare providing units that due to their dependency on interconnected internal and external support systems could potentially become highly vulnerable. Their continuing functionality depends on several factors varying from critical systems and vital equipment to essential clinical services and human recourses management as well. Within the scope of the project, a solid basis of understanding was created as to which aspects within a hospital determine its performance and therefore can be seen as critical assets.

An asset is a broad term that describes every entity of a system (Kersten & Klett, 2017). If an organization (like a hospital) can be described as a system (network) of processes (edges) and their inputs and outputs (nodes), an asset can be a process as well as an object as well as a bigger construct that is system emergent like organizational factors, e.g. culture. It appears that all aspects of a healthcare organization are assets.

Although all assets can be critical for a certain desired outcome, not every asset actually does. This means that it is necessary to define which outcomes are desired for a hospital in order to be able to evaluate the criticality of the assets (Bundesamt für Sicherheit in der Informationstechnik, 2013). Since these outcomes equal the objectives of a hospital, the assets are evaluated according to their impact on the following objectives (Bundesamt für Bevölkerungsschutz und Katastrophenhilfe, 2008):

- Preservation (= prevention of failure) of vital departments and restoration of functionality as quickly as possible respectively,
- Limitation of economic damage and restoration of efficiency and
- Securing (= prevention of endangerment) of human life.

The list below although not exhaustive, represents an attempt to identify all those elements that can be characterized as critical assets in health infrastructures:

- Specialist personnel: employees, persons with special functions, etc.
- Buildings and terrain: main and ancillary buildings, technical buildings, traffic areas, storage areas, open spaces, delivery, escape routes, etc.
- General technical plants and appliances: power supply, gas supply, district heating, water supply, wastewater disposal, kitchen, transport and traffic (including vehicles and supply of operating resources), access control, fire alarm system, building automation, etc.
- Special technical plants and special equipment: medical devices for diagnosis and treatment, laboratory apparatus, sterilizers, laundry inventory, etc.

- IT: networking equipment, telephone system, copy machines, software, software to monitor medical devices, firmware, entry points (wireless technologies, domain controller, old legacy protocols), etc.
- Data and records: patient data, billing data, company information, contracts, etc.
- Operating resources: medicinal products, medical consumables, laundry supply, sterile supply, food supply, etc.

Despite this categorization, to define the cyber-physical scenarios of threat (that will be validated during the project), it was necessary to consider a new set of categories, based in the assets categorization presented in the ENISA report (ENISA, 2016). The new assets categories are the following:

- **Specialist personnel:** employees, persons with special functions, etc.
- **Buildings and Facilities:** Main and ancillary buildings, technical buildings, power and climate regulation systems, temperature sensors, medical gas supply, room operation, automated door lock system, etc.
- **Identification Systems:** Tags, bracelets, badges, biometric scanners, CCTV (video surveillance) with recognition/authentication capabilities, RFID services, etc.
- **Networked Medical Devices:** Mobile devices (e.g. glucose measuring devices), wearable external devices (e.g. portable insulin pumps), implantable devices (e.g. cardiac pacemakers), stationary devices (e.g. computed tomography (CT) scanners), support devices (e.g. assistive robots), etc.
- **Networking Equipment:** Transmission media, network interface cards, network devices (e.g. hubs, switches, routers, etc.), telephone system, etc.
- **Interconnected Clinical Information Systems:** Hospital Information System (HIS), Laboratory Information System (LIS), Radiology information systems (RIS), Pharmacy Information System (PIS), Picture Archiving and Communication System (PACS), pathology information system blood bank system, etc.
- **Mobile Client Devices:** Mobile clients (e.g. laptops, tablets, smartphones), mobile applications for smartphone and tablets, alarm and emergency communication applications for mobile devices, etc.
- **Remote Care System Assets:** Medical equipment for tele-monitoring and tele-diagnosis, medical equipment for distribution of drugs and telehealth equipment (cameras, sensors, telehealth computer system for patients to register their physiological measurements themselves, etc.)
- **Data and Records**: Clinical and administrative patient data, financial, organizational and other hospital data, research data, staff data, vendor details, tracking logs, etc.
- **Operating Resources:** Medicinal products, medical consumables, laundry supply, sterile supply, food supply, etc.

In identifying an analytical list of hospitals critical assets, SAFECARE partners worked on focus groups, where participants were asked to name asset, justify their importance, and assign each asset to the business objectives over which it has an influence. Finally, the assets were assigned to the predefined categories.

## Vulnerabilities and Threats

To design new solutions that will improve the physical and cyber security in healthcare sector, it is very important to be aware of the physical and cyber vulnerabilities in health infrastructures, how they facilitate malicious actions, and how they may increase the likelihood and impact of human errors and system failures. It is also crucial to have a clear understanding of actual security strategies and controls implemented at health targeted infrastructures (medical devices, ICT and network infrastructures, e-health services, Information Systems, etc.).

The most common vulnerabilities in Critical Infrastructures are:

- **Legacy Software**: Usually critical systems run on legacy software that lack sufficient user and system authentication, data authenticity verification, or data integrity checking features that allow attackers uncontrolled access to systems.
- **Default Configuration**: Out-of-box systems with default or simple passwords and baseline configurations make it easy for attackers to enumerate and compromise the systems.
- **Lack of Encryption**: Legacy controllers (e.g. SCADA controllers) and industrial protocols lack the ability to encrypt communication. Attackers use sniffing software to discover username and passwords.
- **Remote Access Policies**: Systems like SCADA are connected to unaudited dial-up lines or remote-access servers, giving attackers convenient backdoor access to the OT network as well as the corporate LAN.
- **Policies and Procedures**: Security gaps are created when IT and OT personnel differ in their approach to securing industrial controls. Different sides should work together to create a unified security policy that protects both IT and OT technology.
- **Lack of Employee Awareness and Education**: Employees are a weakest link in privacy and security; companies cannot rely on annual training to solve the problem. It is crucial to make continuous improvements in cybersecurity knowledge and behavior to ensure that employees know their responsibilities and also foster an organizational culture of information security compliance, improving the mitigation of cyber-physical attacks.

As can be observed in the previous list, vulnerabilities are not identified only within information systems, they can also be found in organizational governance. External relationships, namely, dependencies on energy sources, supply chains, information technologies, and telecommunications providers can also be a source of vulnerabilities.

In addition, ENISA identified and defined the following threat taxonomy for smart hospitals (ENISA, 2016):

- Malicious actions, usual correlated with the adversarial threats, are deliberate acts by a person or an organization. It is important to distinguish malicious actions from other deliberate actions that bypass policies and procedures without malicious intent. A person carrying out a malicious action may be an external or an internal from the perspective of the affected organization. All the critical threats typically recognized and performed by the attacker in this case are malware attacks, hijacking, medical device tampering, social engineering attacks, device and data theft, skimming and denial of service attacks. The protection from these attacks is of particular significance as they can lead to unavailability of the hospital's systems.

- Human errors occur during the configuration or operation of devices or information systems, or the execution of processes. Human errors are often related to inadequate processes or insufficient training. Major examples include the medical system configuration error, the absence of audit logs to allow for appropriate control, unauthorized access control or lack of processes, non-compliance especially in the Bring Your Own Device (BYOD) paradigm, physician and/or patient errors. All human errors are highly pertinent to smart hospitals particularly due to the patient's data involved in the process.

- System failures are highly relevant in the healthcare context, particularly due to the increasing complexity and dynamics of the systems. Some examples of system failures include the software failures, inadequate firmware, device failure or simply limited/reduced capability, network components failure, insufficient maintenance which may leave operational issues undetected and unresolved, overload can lead to unavailability of a system or service, communication between IoT and non-IoT.

- Supply chain failure is outside the direct control of the affected organization as it typically affects or falls under the responsibility of a third party. As hospitals are increasingly dependent on third parties, third-party failures may have far-reaching consequences for them. Examples of third parties a failure of which would have an adverse impact on smart hospital operation include cloud service providers, medical device manufacturer, network providers

- Natural phenomena may also be the cause of incidents, particularly due to their disruptive or destructive impact, particularly on healthcare facilities and ICT infrastructure. Moreover, natural phenomena may impact the provision of remote patient care services even if their impact is not targeted to or impacting the hospital itself (e.g. if the metro-level network infrastructure is disrupted due to an earthquake). Examples may include earthquakes, floods and fires.

It is worth mentioning that there are different types of threat actors as well as attack vectors in hospitals. Each of these threat actors have different attack surfaces available within smart hospitals. The threat actors could include insider threats (staff with malicious intent), malicious patients and guests, remote attackers and other environmental or accidental equipment/software failure causes. The attack vectors they can affect the hospitals could be physical interaction with IT assets, wireless communication with IT assets, wired communication with IT assets and the interaction with staff.

## Solution Architecture

- Physical security solutions
- Cyber security solutions
- Integrated cyber-physical security solutions

The physical security solutions and the cyber security solutions consist of smart modules and efficient integrated technologies to respectively improve physical security and cyber security. More specifically, physical security solutions embed integrated intelligent video monitoring and interconnect building monitoring systems as well as management systems. While cyber security solutions correspond to cyber monitoring systems as well as threat detection systems related to IT, BMS and e-health systems.

Both physical security solutions and cyber security solutions are interconnected thanks to the integrated cyber-physical security solutions. The integrated cyber-physical security solutions consist of intelligent modules to integrate different data sources and better take into account the combination of physical and cyber security threats.

The following systems make up the physical security solutions (SAFECARE project, 2018):

- **Suspicious Behaviour Detection System:** The suspicious behavior detection system will capture video streams from surveillance cameras. It will perform near real-time analysis and it will trigger security alerts in case of crowding, loitering in restricted areas and suspicious activities on integrated devices.
- **Intrusion and Fire Detection System:** By interconnecting video monitoring system with existing access management and fire detection systems, it will be possible to notably extend threat detection capacities and reduce number of false positive incidents.
- **Data Collection System:** The system collects data from physical subsystems (such as ICS, SCADA, smart building sensors); sends fire detection events to the intrusion and fire detection system and to the Building Threat Monitoring System (BTMS).
- **Mobile alerting system.** The mobile alerting system will be used by local security agents providing the ability to quickly report specific categories of security threats or impacts correlated to a specific failure point. It will send notifications which consist of all the information needed to manage the security threat (e.g. location, emergency procedure, video etc.) The notifications will be sent to all the users according to their profile.
- **Building Threat Monitoring System:** The Building Threat Monitoring System is the basis for interaction of the physical security components with the rest of the architecture.

The following systems make up the cyber security solutions:

- **IT Threat Detection System:** The objective of the IT threat detection system is to detect the exploit of vulnerabilities in critical health infrastructure by monitoring the network traffic and analysing IT events (such as software logs) provided by the IT infrastructure.
- **BMS Threat Detection System:** A threat detection system will increase security protection and situational awareness by passively monitoring network traffic between the building management system and the building control sub-systems (e.g., lighting, power, medical devices, and lift). When threats are detected by the BMS threat detection system, the system generates security events.
- **Advanced File Analysis System:** The objective of the advanced file analysis system is to detect the malwares in critical health infrastructure by performing an in-depth analysis of files. The advanced file analysis system performs a static analysis to look for malicious code into the files and a dynamic analysis to check file behaviour in a sandboxing environment.
- **E-Health Devices Security Analytics:** E-Health device security analytics is a cybersecurity solution that is specialized to security monitoring, threat detection and reporting in healthcare critical infrastructures. The security analytics solution collects log data from medical devices, performs analytics to derive meaningful security data, and generates security insights, aggregated statistics and alerts upon detecting anomalous or suspicious security events.

*Figure 2. SAFECARE architecture and interconnections (SAFECARE project, 2018)*

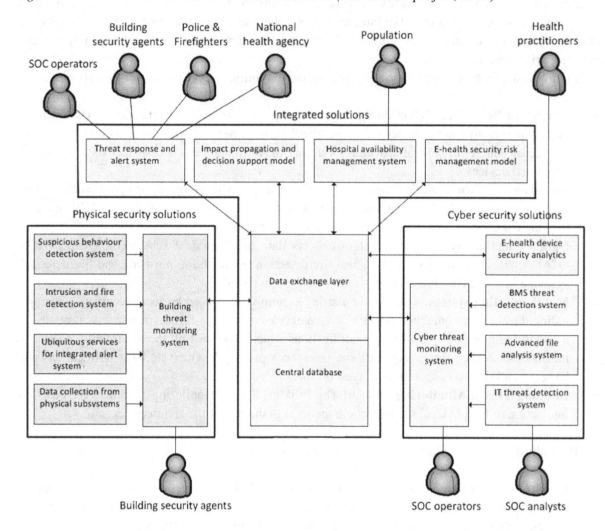

- **Cyber Threat Monitoring System:** The objective of the cyber threat monitoring system is to collect and centralize (a) security events and (b) potential impacts, organize the information and provide user-friendly interfaces to SOC operators so that they can visualize the threats and have an overview of the impacted assets.

The following systems make up the integrated cyber-physical security solutions:

- **Data Exchange Layer:** The data exchange layer triggers notifications to the other components when new physical and cyber incident (coming from the building threat monitoring system and the cyber threat monitoring system) or new impacts (coming from the impact propagation model) are sent.
- **Central Database**: Data centralization in a single database constitutes the pillar stone in order to build added-value indicators. Cross connecting data expands the capacity to create either more

consistent results or innovative results. The architecture of the database will take into account confidentiality, ethics and privacy constraints.

- **Impact Propagation and Decision Support Model:** The objectives of the Impact propagation model and decision support model are to (a) combine physical and cyber incidents that occur on assets, (b) infer cascading effects as impacts that could potentially affect the same or related assets and (c) alert other modules about the potential impacts and severity.
- **Threat Response and Alert System:** The threat response and alert system, once excited, will parse the "impact" data retrieved and run the corresponding response plan that will mainly consist in sending notification and alerts to internal and external practitioners. Notifications may include sending alerts to the Mobile alerting system.
- **Hospital Availability Management System (HAMS):** The Hospital Availability Management System will use the central database to get and store information about hospital assets and resources (e.g. department name and status, services, beds and staff availability, etc.).
- **E-health Security Risk Management:** E-health security risk management model goal is to effectively quantify the impact of security events in a uniform way for medical devices (e.g. visualize complex events by detailing how actors have obtained access to defined assets and what the potential risk outcome is for the related activity).

## Scenarios Design and Description

To develop a secure and reliable protection system it is important to identify and formalize relevant use-cases and complex attack scenarios against Critical Infrastructures. These scenarios should exploit combined physical and cyber threats in the context of cascading attacks, and how they can impact and destabilize health services and will be simulated in the hospitals of Marseille, Turin and Amsterdam, involving security and health practitioners.

To define cyber-physical scenarios of threat, Expression of Needs and Identification of Security Objectives / Expression des Besoins et Identification des Objectifs de Sécurité (EBIOS) security risk assessment methodology was used. EBIOS was developed by the French Central Information Systems Security Division and is used to assess and treat risks related to Information Systems security (ISS). It can also be used to communicate this information within the organization and to partners, and therefore assists in the ISS risk management process since it is compliant with major IT security standards (National Cybersecurity Agency of France (ANSSI), 2018).

EBIOS uses a progressive risk management approach: it starts in the major missions of the object under study (highest level) and goes to the business functions and techniques (lowest level), studying possible risk scenarios. It aims to obtain a synergy between compliance and scenarios, positioning these two complementary concepts in the best way, i.e., where they bring the highest value. The compliance approach is used to determine the security base of the scenarios, particularly to develop targeted or sophisticated scenarios. This assumes that accidental and environmental risks are treated a priori by the compliance approach. Thus, scenario risk assessment focuses on intentional threats (National Cybersecurity Agency of France (ANSSI), 2018).

In the following paragraphs, some of the most representative scenarios of threat identified will be described:

*Figure 3. Digital risk management pyramid (National Cybersecurity Agency of France (ANSSI), 2018)*

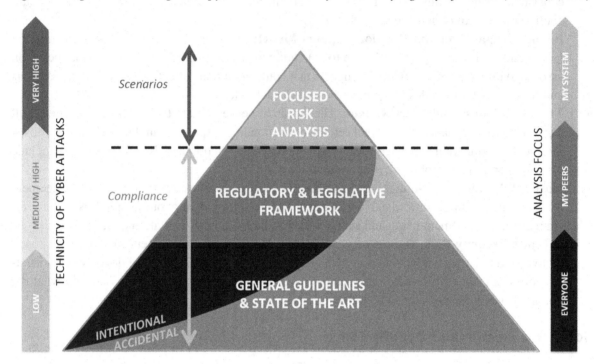

## Scenario 1. Cyber-Physical Attack Targeting Power Supply of the Hospital

In the first scenario the aim of the attack is to cause damage in the power supply of the hospital to precipitate an energy breakdown. The attacker can be an external person who conducts the attack to have some gain (hacker) or an employee who has malicious intentions or makes a mistake. To get the necessary information to carry out the attack, the attacker can use social engineering, internet research, on-site visits, etc. Social engineering refers not only to person-to-person interaction but also to network interaction using, for example, social networks (Facebook, LinkedIn, etc.), or even phishing emails. All the information collected is used by the attacker for physical or cyber access to the PLC. This can be done through network scalation privileges or impersonating a PLC maintainer, for example.

## Scenario 2. Cyber-Physical Attack to Steal Patient Data in the Hospital

Attackers are triggered by the strong possibility to acquire or even modify the patients' data. They can sell it with a big profit on the black market, ask for a ransom or even use it to damage the reputation of the hospital. The attacker can enter in the computer room stealing the data, damage the computer room or any other asset by triggering the fire alarm in order to take advantage of the confusion caused during the evacuation of the hospital

## Scenario 3. Cyber-Physical Attack Targeting the Population, IT Systems and Medical Devices in the Hospital, and Patient Data Base

The aim of an attacker is to access, extort, sabotage or even intimidate valuable information from different sources including both service and clinical functionalities. The idea of the attack is to trigger the fire alarm in order to take advantage of the confusion caused during the evacuation of the hospital to enter in the computer room (a restricted area). In this way, the attacker can steal the data, damage the computer room or any other hospital asset, and take advantage of these actions. This type of intrusion in the hospital could be due to the fact that the IT defenses of the hospital were extremely difficult to overcome, and the data were of extreme value dictating a manual steal of hardware or connection with hardware from the inside.

## Scenario 4. Cyber-Physical Attack Targeting the Air-Cooling System of the Hospital

As air cooling system is critical for the hospital environment, it can be attractive target for attackers. It is imperative to ensure good air quality and aseptic conditions to provide a safer environment for patients and staff. Using this attack vector, an attacker can not only disturb inpatients, but also cause serious damages to healthcare infrastructures, e.g. surgery rooms.

## Scenario 5. Shooting, Explosive or Sabotage in Critical Places (Visible or Invisible)

Healthcare facilities, because of their importance in society, are a target of terrorist attacks harming hospital critical facilities planting a bomb. Usually, the main purpose of these attacks is to provoke a state of terror in people, but many other collateral problems arise. This is also applicable to other bad intention persons or groups like ideological activists, pathological evil-doer or even people looking for revenge.

## Scenario 6: Theft at Hospital Equipment, Access to Hospital Network and IT Systems

It is known that many attacks are carried out from someone that works inside the healthcare institution. For example, for some reason an institution physician might want to erase some of the stored data referring to a medical operation. The physician may just want to hide some error, but the impact of his/her action on patient's safety can be very high.

## FUTURE RESEARCH DIRECTIONS

Over a 36-month time frame, the SAFECARE consortium will design, test, validate and demonstrate innovative elements which will optimize the protection of Critical Infrastructures under operational conditions. These elements are interactive, cooperative and complementary (reinforcing in some cases), aiming at maximizing the potential utilization of the individual elements. The consortium will also engage with leading hospitals, national public health agencies and security forces across Europe to ensure that SAFECAREs global solution is flexible, scalable and adaptable to the operational needs of various hospitals across Europe, and meet the requirements of newly-emerging technologies and standards. Based on these, the SAFECARE project will produce additionally the following key results:

- A cyber threat detection system to improve Advanced Persistent Threat and zero-day attacks detection on Information Technology and Building Management Systems;
- A physical threat detection system using advanced video monitoring techniques and data cross-connection with other building monitoring sensors;
- An analytics and risk management tool to improve threat prevention on medical devices;
- A central database of cyber and physical incidents validated by security experts of the domain;
- A threat response system implementing cyber-physical defence strategies and automated notifications;
- A threat mitigation system to better manage hospitals availability and inform the population;
- A modular and scalable solution implementing standard communication protocols;
- An operational and cost-effective solution co-designed with health and security practitioners;
- Three demonstrators in Turin, Marseille and Amsterdam to test solutions in operational conditions;
- An analysis of the demonstrations to validate the approach and measure key performance indicators;
- Guidelines to enhance risk management plans and technological best practices in health services;
- Dissemination throughout health-user community to enhance awareness against multi-faced threats;
- Dissemination throughout scientific community and standardization bodies in order to support the establishment of certification mechanisms;
- A business plan to report economical perspectives of the industrial partners.

## CONCLUSION

The SAFECARE project has as a notable ambition to contribute to Europe's strategy in reducing the vulnerabilities of Critical Infrastructure and increasing their resilience. Furthermore, it aims at contributing to some of the key initiatives undertaken by the Commission such as the European Programme for Critical Infrastructure Protection and the Critical Infrastructure Warning Information Network (CIWIN). The project will also participate in increasing the compliance between security tools and European regulations about ethics and privacy for health services. In terms of results, the project's main ambition is to bring a holistic approach that will consider both physical and cyber security. It will promote new technological uses and novel techniques to enhance prevention, detection, response and mitigation capacities against security threats. The project aims to demonstrate its results with a project pilot that will take place in Marseille with security practitioners, police and other local stakeholders. SAFECARE aims to contribute significantly towards the creation of new knowledge and the expansion of current knowledge and state-of-the-art in healthcare organizations' security and safety.

## ACKNOWLEDGMENT

The work presented in this paper has been conducted in the framework of SAFECARE project, which has received funding from the European Union's H2020 research and innovation programme under grant agreement no. 787002.

## REFERENCES

BBC. (2017). Who was hit by the NHS cyber-attack? Retrieved from https://www.bbc.com/news/health-39904851

BBC. (2017). Wiggins and Froome medical records released by Russian hackers. Retrieved from http://www.bbc.co.uk/news/world-37369705

British Standard Institute (BSI). (2014). *BS11200: Crisis Management – guidance and good practice*. BSI.

Bundesamt für Bevölkerungsschutz und Katastrophenhilfe. (2008). *Schutz Kritischer Infrastruktur: Risikomanagement im Krankenhaus*. Retrieved from https://www.google.com/url?sa=t&rct=j&q=&esrc=s&source=web&cd=1&cad=rja&uact=8&ved=2ahUKEwiC9oTthv3kAhVDb1AKHUiECG8QF-jAAegQIAhAB&url=https%3A%2F%2Fwww.bbk.bund.de%2FDE%2FAufgabenundAusstattung%2FKritischeInfrastrukturen%2FPationenKritis%2FSchutz_KRITIS_Ri

Bundesamt für Sicherheit in der Informationstechnik. (2013). *Schutz Kritischer Infrastrukturen: Risikoanalyse Krankenhaus-IT. Bonn*. Retrieved from https://www.google.com/url?sa=t&rct=j&q=&esrc=s&source=web&cd=1&ved=2ahUKEwjrxtyQhv3kAhUQJlAKHTkcC3wQFjAAegQIABAC&url=https%3A%2F%2Fwww.bsi.bund.de%2FSharedDocs%2FDownloads%2FDE%2FBSI%2FPublikationen%2FBroschueren%2FRisikoanalyseKrankenhaus.pdf%3F__blob%3

Data Protection Authority. (2019). *Data Protection Authority*. Retrieved from https://www.dpa.gr/portal/page?_pageid=33,40911&_dad=portal&_schema=PORTAL

Deloitte. (2016). *Cyber crisis management: Readiness, response, and recovery*. Retrieved from https://www.google.com/url?sa=t&rct=j&q=&esrc=s&source=web&cd=16&cad=rja&uact=8&ved=2ahUKEwij0amRn_3lAhXISxUIHeu5AWAQFjAPegQICRAC&url=https%3A%2F%2Fwww2.deloitte.com%2Fcontent%2Fdam%2FDeloitte%2Fde%2FDocuments%2Frisk%2FDeloitte-Cyber-crisis-management-Rea

ENISA. (2016). *Good Practice Guide on Vulnerability Disclosure. From challenges to recommendations*. Retrieved from https://www.enisa.europa.eu/publications/vulnerability-disclosure

ENISA. (2016). *Securing Hospitals: A research study and blueprint. Independent Security Evaluators*. Retrieved from https://www.securityevaluators.com/wp-content/uploads/2017/07/securing_hospitals.pdf

ENISA. (2016). *Smart Hospitals: Security and Resilience for Smart Health Service and Infrastructures*. Retrieved from https://www.enisa.europa.eu/publications/cyber-security-and-resilience-for-smart-hospitals

ENISA. (2019). *Greek National Cyber Security Strategy*. Retrieved from https://www.enisa.europa.eu/topics/national-cyber-security-strategies/ncss-map/national-cyber-security-strategies-interactive-map/strategies/national-cyber-security-strategy-greece/view

EU. (2008). *Council Directive 2008/114/EC.* Retrieved from https://eur-lex.europa.eu/legal-content/EN/TXT/?uri=uriserv%3AOJ.L_.2008.345.01.0075.01.ENG

EU. (2013). *Decision No 1082/2013/EU of The European Parliament and of the Council of 22 October 2013 on serious cross-border threats to health and repealing Decision No 2119/98/EC.* Retrieved from https://ec.europa.eu/health/sites/health/files/preparedness_response

EU. (2016). *Directive (EU) 2016/1148 of The European Parliament and of the Council of 6 July 2016 concerning measures for a high common level of security of network and information systems across the Union.* Retrieved from https://eur-lex.europa.eu/legal-content/EN/TXT

EU. (2016). *Regulation (EU) 2016/679 of the European Parliament and of The Council of 27 April 2016 on the protection of natural persons with regard to the processing of personal data and on the free movement of such data, and repealing Directive 95/46/EC (GDPR).* Retrieved from https://eur-lex.europa.eu/legal-content/EN/TXT/PDF/?uri=CELEX:32016R0679&from=EN

EU. (2017). *Cybersecurity Act.* Retrieved from https://eur-lex.europa.eu/legal-content/EN/TXT/?uri=COM:2017:0477:FIN

EU. (2017). *Regulation (EU) 2017/746.* Retrieved from https://eur-lex.europa.eu/legal-content/EN/TXT/?uri=CELEX:32017R0746

EU. (n.d.). REGULATION (EU) 2017/745. Retrieved from https://eur-lex.europa.eu/legal-content/EN/TXT/?uri=CELEX:32017R0745

European Commission. (2006). *Communication from the Commission on a European Programme for Critical Infrastructure Protection.* Brussels.

European Commission. (2008). *Council Directive 2008/114/EC on the Identification and Designation of European Critical Infrastructures and the Assessment of the Need to Improve their Protection.* Brussels.

Healthcare and Public Health Sector Coordinating Councils. (2017). *Health Industry Cybersecurity Practices: managing threats and protecting patients.* Retrieved from https://www.phe.gov/Preparedness/planning/405d/Documents/HICP-Main-508.pdf

Hei, X. D. X. (2013). Conclusion and Future Directions. In *Security for Wireless Implantable Medical Devices.* SpringerBriefs in Computer Science. doi:10.1007/978-1-4614-7153-0_5

Hellenic National Defence General Staff. (2019). *Hellenic National Defence General Staff.* Retrieved from http://www.geetha.mil.gr/en/hndgs-en/history-en.html

HIPAA. (2018). Healthcare Data Breach Statistics. Retrieved from https://www.hipaajournal.com/healthcare-data-breach-statistics/

HIPAA. (2018). Largest Healthcare Data Breaches of 2018. Retrieved from https://www.hipaajournal.com/largest-healthcare-data-breaches-of-2018/

Independent Security Evaluators. (2016). *Securing Hospitals - A research study and blueprinT.* Retrieved from https://www.securityevaluators.com/wp-content/uploads/2017/07/securing_hospitals.pdf

INFOSEC. (2019). Hospital Security. Retrieved from https://resources.infosecinstitute.com/category/healthcare-information-security/security-awareness-for-healthcare-professionals/hospital-security/

Izuakor, C., & White, R. (2016). Critical Infrastructure Asset Identification: Policy, Methodology and Gap Analysis. In *Proceedings of the 10th International Conference on Critical Infrastructure Protection (ICCIP)*, (pp. 27-41). Academic Press. 10.1007/978-3-319-48737-3_2

Kersten H., Klett G. (2017). Business Continuity und IT-Notfall management.

KPMG. (2015). *Health care and cyber security: increasing threats require increased capabilities.* Retrieved from https://assets.kpmg/content/dam/kpmg/pdf/2015/09/cyber-health-care-survey-kpmg-2015.pdf

Martin, G. M. P. (2017). Cybersecurity and healthcare: How safe are we? *BMJ (Clinical Research Ed.)*, *358*(j3179). PMID:28684400

Martin, L. (2019). Hackers scramble patient files in Melbourne heart clinic cyber attack. *The Guardian*. Retrieved from https://www.theguardian.com/technology/2019/feb/21/hackers-scramble-patient-files-in-melbourne-heart-clinic-cyber-attack

Mikušová, M., & Horváthová, P. (2019). Prepared for a crisis? Basic elements of crisis management in an organisation. *Economic Research-Ekonomska Istraživanja*, *32*(1), 1844–1868. doi:10.1080/1331677X.2019.1640625

National Cybersecurity Agency of France (ANSSI). (2018). *EBIOS Risk Manager – The method.* Retrieved from https://www.ssi.gouv.fr/en/guide/ebios-risk-manager-the-method/

NIS. (2019). *NIS.* Retrieved from http://www.nis.gr/portal/page/portal/NIS/

OFFSITE. (2017). 27χρονος επιτέθηκε σε γιατρούς στο Νοσοκομείο Λάρνακας. Retrieved from https://www.offsite.com.cy/articles/eidiseis/topika/231890-27hronos-epitethike-se-giatroys-sto-nosokomeio-larnakas

Perlroth, N., & Sanger, D. E. (2017). *The New York Times.* Retrieved from https://www.nytimes.com/2017/05/12/world/europe/uk-national-health-service-cyberattack.html

Peters, D., Kandola, K., Elmendorf, A. E., & Chellaraj, G. (1999). *Health expenditures, services, and outcomes in Africa: basic data and cross-national comparisons, 1990-1996 (English).* Washington, D.C.: The World Bank. doi:10.1596/0-8213-4438-2

POEDIN. (2018). Κέντρα Υγείας σε Αποδιοργάνωση. *POEDIN.* Retrieved from https://www.poedhn.gr/deltia-typoy/item/3413-kentra-ygeias-se-apodiorganosi-viaiopragies-se-varos-iatrikoy-kai-nosileftikoy-prosopikoy--klopes-sto-kentro-ygeias-salaminas-epithesi-apo-omada-roma-se-giatro-tou-ky-lygouriou-pou-efimereve-sto-tep-tou-gnnafpl

SAFECARE project. (2018). *Grant Agreement Number 787005, European Commission H2020.* Retrieved from https://www.safecare-project.eu/

Solon, A. H. A. (2017). Petya ransomware cyber attack who what why how. *The Guardian*. Retrieved from https://www.theguardian.com/technology/2017/jun/27/petya-ransomware-cyber-attack-who-what-why-how

Sulleyman, A. (2017). *NHS cyber attack: Why stolen medical information is so much more valuable than financial data.* The Independent. Retrieved from https://www.independent.co.uk/life-style/gadgets-and-tech/news/nhs-cyber-attack-medical-data-records-stolen-why-so-valuable-to-sell-financial-a7733171.html

The Guardian. (2019). Violence in the NHS: staff face routine assault and intimidation. Retrieved from https://www.theguardian.com/society/2019/sep/04/violence-nhs-staff-face-routine-assault-intimidation

The Times. (2010). Woman kills 3 in hospital shooting spree. Retrieved from https://www.thetimes.co.uk/article/woman-kills-3-in-hospital-shooting-spree-n9q9nbhws9b

World Health Organisation. (2019). Hospitals. Retrieved from https://www.who.int/hospitals/en/

World Health Organisation. (2019). *Health Systems.* Retrieved from http://www.euro.who.int/en/health-topics/Health-systems/pages/health-systems

World Health Organization. (2015). *Hospital Safety Index: Guide for Evaluators.* Retrieved from https://www.google.com/url?sa=t&rct=j&q=&esrc=s&source=web&cd=1&cad=rja&uact=8&ved=2ahUKEwi_tdq7n__kAhVE2aQKHVZfBbkQFjAAegQIAxAC&url=https%3A%2F%2Fwww.who.int%2Fhac%2Ftechguidance%2Fhospital_safety_index_evaluators.pdf&usg=AOvVaw3Jb3x3xUgBh-IK84EtnKD8

## ADDITIONAL READING

Abouzakhar, N. S., Jones, A., & Angelopoulou, O. (2018). Internet of Things Security: A Review of Risks and Threats to Healthcare Sector. In *Proceedings of the IEEE International Conference on Internet of Things (iThings) and IEEE Green Computing and Communications (GreenCom) and IEEE Cyber, Physical and Social Computing (CPSCom) and IEEE Smart Data (SmartData). IEEE Press.*

Ahmed, Y., Naqvi, S., & Josephs, M. (2019). Cybersecurity Metrics for Enhanced Protection of Healthcare IT Systems. In *Proceedings of the 13th International Symposium on Medical Information and Communication Technology (ISMICT).* Academic Press. 10.1109/ISMICT.2019.8744003

Alcaraz, C., & Zeadally, Z. (2015). Critical infrastructure protection: Requirements and challenges for the 21st century. *International Journal of Critical Infrastructure Protection, 8,* 53–66. doi:10.1016/j.ijcip.2014.12.002

Baggett, R. K., & Simpkins, B. K. (2018). *Homeland Security and Critical Infrastructure Protection.* Praeger Security International.

ENISA. (2016). *Securing Hospitals: A research study and blueprint. Independent Security Evaluators.* Retrieved from https://www.securityevaluators.com/wp-content/uploads/2017/07/securing_hospitals.pdf

ENISA. (2016). *Smart Hospitals: Security and Resilience for Smart Health Service and Infrastructures.* Retrieved from https://www.enisa.europa.eu/publications/cyber-security-and-resilience-for-smart-hospitals

EU. (2016). *Directive (EU) 2016/1148 of The European Parliament and of the Council of 6 July 2016 concerning measures for a high common level of security of network and information systems across the Union.* Retrieved from https://eur-lex.europa.eu/legal-content/EN/TXT

EU. (2016). Regulation (EU) 2016/679 of the European Parliament and of The Council of 27 April 2016 on the protection of natural persons with regard to the processing of personal data and on the free movement of such data, and repealing Directive 95/46/EC (GDPR). Retrieved from https://eur-lex.europa.eu/legal-content/ EN/TXT/PDF/?uri=CELEX:32016R0679&from=EN

HIPAA. (2018). Largest Healthcare Data Breaches of 2018. Retrieved from https://www.hipaajournal.com/largest-healthcare-data-breaches-of-2018/

## KEY TERMS AND DEFINITIONS

**Asset:** Something of either tangible or intangible value that is worth protecting, including people, information, infrastructure, finances and reputation.

**Attack:** Attempt to destroy, expose, alter, disable, steal or gain unauthorized access to or make unauthorized use of an asset

**Cyber:** Relating to, within, or through the medium of the interconnected information infrastructure of interactions among persons, processes, data, and information systems.

**Cyber Incident:** A cyber event that: a) jeopardizes the cyber security of an information system or the information the system processes, stores or transmits; or b) violates the security policies, security procedures or acceptable use policies, whether resulting from malicious activity or not.

**Healthcare:** Healthcare is defined as the prevention and treatment of diseases through medical professional services.

**Hospital:** An institution providing medical and surgical treatment and nursing care for sick or injured people.

**Incident:** Situation that can be, or could lead to, a disruption, loss, emergency or crisis

**Prevention:** Measures that enable an organization to avoid, preclude or limit the impact of an undesirable event or potential disruption

**Threat:** Potential cause of an unwanted incident, which may result in harm to individuals, assets, a system or organization, the environment or the community.

**Vulnerability:** Weakness of an asset or control that can be exploited by one or more threats. The existence of a weakness, design, or implementation error that can lead to an unexpected, undesirable event compromising the security of the computer system, network, application, or protocol involved.

*This research was previously published in Safety and Security Issues in Technical Infrastructures; pages 63-87, copyright year 2020 by Information Science Reference (an imprint of IGI Global).*

# Chapter 5
# Applying Blockchain Technologies in Healthcare:
## A Scientometric Analysis

**Zehra Ozge Candereli**
*Izmir Katip Celebi University, Turkey*

**Serhat Burmaoglu**
https://orcid.org/0000-0002-5537-6887
*Izmir Katip Celebi University, Turkey*

**Levent B. Kidak**
*Izmir Katip Celebi University, Turkey*

**Dilek Ozdemir Gungor**
*Izmir Katip Celebi University, Turkey*

## ABSTRACT

*Recently, one of the inventive developments penetrating many industries is blockchain technology. In the era of globalization and digitalization, blockchain has garnered interest in various application fields from health data management to clinical trials. In this study, we aimed to explore blockchain applications in healthcare with an explorative perspective with a scientometrics analysis. With this analysis, the trends and evolutionary relations between health and blockchain technology were examined via the queries in the Web of Science database. In the analysis, the author keyword co-occurrences were used for demonstrating concept relationships. To understand the new emerging study field, VosViewer was used for network visualizations and CiteSpace free java-based software was used for scientometrics analysis. As a result, it can be implied that the main focus areas of the studies on blockchain are solving payment systems, digital identity, and privacy and security issues in healthcare field.*

DOI: 10.4018/978-1-6684-6311-6.ch005

## INTRODUCTION

When innovation in healthcare is considered, economic wealth and better public health appear as two of the most prominent topics. As the access to care improves and technological innovation brings new perspectives in the medical field, new driving forces such as public expectations, more strict food and drug security measures, improved traceability and précised medicine increase come to the stage. The demand-side drivers force the health system to transform classical approaches into innovative ways to confront these demands in a cost-effective, appropriate and compatible manner (Petre, 2017a).

From a holistic perspective, healthcare is a complex ecosystem which brings together different services such as promotion, diagnosis, treatment, and rehabilitation. All these services are provided by different parties e.g. hospital, clinics, public sector, private sector, pharmaceutical and medical equipment manufacturers, private/public insurance facilities. As a result, patient healthcare data are scattered and fragmented among different parties of the healthcare system which makes data exchange and collaboration between institutions hard in current healthcare systems. However, patients need to secure and share their data whenever and wherever it is necessary. Due to the importance and sensitive nature of health data, their management is cumbersome in this context (Pilkington, 2017; Dubovitskaya et al., 2017; Szewczyk, 2017).

In many countries, paternalistic government policies prevent individuals from having access to their own health data. Individuals do not have full control of their health record. Current centralized structures of Electronic Health Records (EHR) are subject to hacking, strict security regulations, and excessive overhead costs (Simic et al., 2017; Swan, 2015: 56; McFarlane et al, 2017).

On the other hand, there are advancements in ICT enable cost-effective, technology-based, personalized solutions in the healthcare industry. Wearable devices, e-health, m-health, telehealth are all launched as the use of ICT and ICT based-products such as sensors, internet of things (IoT), cloud systems, remote monitoring system have become financially feasible. Therefore, these developments help patients track their vitals and health parameters while accumulating data in enormous amounts. Patient data acquired by many different devices, providers, and systems cause privacy, security concerns as well as issues related to big data. Therefore, healthcare services (paradigm) are shifting from a centralized, hospital-oriented model toward a distributed patient-centric model.

Rising expectations from healthcare-service providers necessitate improvements in operational efficiency in the healthcare industry and the use of data from various structured and unstructured resources is the key to success. Although a "killer app" does not seem possible in the near future, blockchain technology has the potential to overcome the aforementioned issues (COCIR, 2017).

Satoshi Nakamoto introduced blockchain technology, without mentioning its name explicitly (Mattila, 2016), in 2008 with a white paper in which Bitcoin is proposed as an electronic payment system based on a decentralized peer-to-peer network, without any need for intermediation. Shortly, blockchain is a protocol and widely acknowledged as a major breakthrough in fault-tolerant distributed computing, following decades of research in this field. As it was proposed, the first field of application was the finance sector. Yet blockchain is considered as a promising technology which has the potential to make significant improvements in different industries such including healthcare.

Because of these considerations, in this study, blockchain and healthcare relationship is analyzed with scientometrics. The study is outlined as follows. In the second section blockchain literature is reviewed and the technology is explained. Then, in the third section the literature related to blockchain and healthcare studies are reviewed. The fourth section describes the research methodology and in fifth section is presented findings. The final section discusses the possible effects of blockchain technology on healthcare.

## REVIEW OF BLOCKCHAIN LITERATURE

Globalization has found its true meaning with the developments in network technologies and the Internet. In this age, digital platforms changing the business models and whole society by enabling connected structure via cloud-based systems (Kushida et al., 2011; Pon et al., 2014; van Alstyne et al. 2016). Big data approach has been applied to these digital platforms and unprecedented solutions revealed from the data mountains. This perspective can enable a light-weight financial system, inter-organizational record-keeping, and multiparty data aggregation (Greenspan, 2016).

One of these technologies is blockchain, which is accepted today as a general purpose technology (GPT) like steam engine, electricity, and the Internet (Catalini and Gans, 2016). GPTs typically lead to subsequent innovation and productivity gains across multiple industry verticals, sustaining new technological paradigms and economic growth for multiple years (Bresnahan and Trajtenberg, 1995; Helpman and Trajtenberg, 1998; Rosenberg and Trajtenberg, 2001; Moser and Nicholas, 2004; Basu and Fernald, 2007). According to Naughton (2016), blockchain technology will be the most important information technology invention of our age.

Briefly, blockchain can be defined as a distributed ledger that contains all transaction executed in the Bitcoin network. This technology is described with three words as (i) disintermediated, (ii) censorship-resistant, and (iii) tamper-proof (Seppala et al., 2016). The ledger network is open and participants do not need to trust each other to interact. All transactions are verified and recorded by the nodes of the network through cryptographic algorithms, without supervisors, central authority, human intervention, and any other third-party organizations.

The reliability of the network is provided by the majority of nodes, even if some of them may be dishonest or malicious. For making human intervention or controlling authority unnecessary, a verification process is performed through a mathematical mechanism, called 'proof-of-work'. Proof-of-work systems run by "mining[1]", which does not serve for the purpose of verifying transactions, but for building a credible commitment against an attack. Consensus about the true state of a distributed ledger therefore emerges and becomes stronger as time (and blocks) go by. If a bad actor wanted to reverse a past transaction it would have to spend a disproportionate amount of resources to do so. This is the result of the bad actor not only having to outpace the growth rate of the legitimate chain, but also of having to re-compute all blocks after the one that is being manipulated.

Since the network always takes the longest valid chain as the true state of the ledger (i.e. as the "consensus"), the task of altering a past block of transactions and imposing it on the rest of the network becomes increasingly difficult as the chain is extended. As a result, in proof-of-work systems, a blockchain is only as secure as the amount of computing power dedicated to mining it. This generates economies of scale and a positive feedback loop between network effects and security: as more participants use a crypto-currency, the value of the underlying token increases (because the currency becomes more useful), which in turn attracts more miners (due to higher rewards), ultimately increasing the security of the ledger.

The main idea of the blockchain protocol is decentralization and permisionless attendance. However, there are different blockchains as permissioned like private, public etc. The steps of the Blockchain protocol is demonstrated in Figure 1.

*Figure 1. Blockchain process*
*(Source: https://blockgeeks.com/wp-content/uploads/2016/09/infographics0517-01-1.png)*

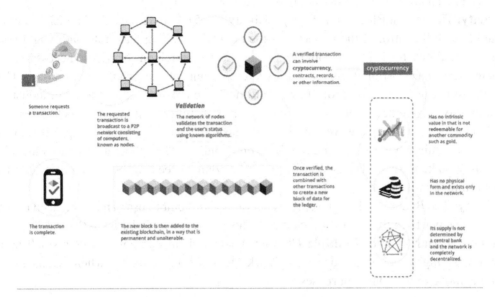

It is clear with the explanation of blockgeeks.com that blockchain process is paperless, disintermediated, unaltered, reliable and free. These characteristics make this system more popular especially for reducing transaction costs at first. These costs include the cost of verification and the cost of networking (Catalini and Gans, 2016). By using the blockchain protocol, for the first time in history, value could be reliably transferred between two distant, untrusting parties without the need of a costly intermediary.

However, the Blockchain technology has also some technical challenges and limitations that have been identified. Swan (2015) presents seven technical challenges and limitations for the adaptation of Blockchain technology in the future:

- **Throughput:** The potential throughput of issues in the Bitcoin network is currently between 4 to 7 transactions per second (tps), Ethereum 20 tps and these are limited when compared to VISA (56.000 tps) and PayPal (193 tps).
- **Latency:** To create sufficient security for a Bitcoin transaction block, it takes currently roughly 10 minutes to complete one transaction. To achieve efficiency in security, more time has to be spent on a block, because it has to outweigh the cost of double spending[2] attacks. Bitcoin protects against double spending by verifying each transaction added to the block chain, to ensure that the inputs for the transaction have not been spent previously. This makes latency a big issue in blockchain currently. Making a block and confirming the transaction should happen in seconds, while maintaining its security. To complete a transaction e.g. in VISA takes only a few seconds, which is a huge advantage compared to Blockchain.
- **Size and Bandwidth:** At the moment, the size of a blockchain in the Bitcoin network is over 100GB (http://www.coinfox.info/news/6700-bitcoin-blockchain-size-reaches-100-gb). When the throughput increases to the levels of VISA, blockchain could grow 214PB in each year. The Bitcoin community assumes that the size of one block is 1MB, and a new block is created every ten minutes. Therefore, there is a limitation in the number of transactions that can be handled (on

an average of 500 transactions in one block). If the Blockchain needs to control more transactions, the size and bandwidth issues have to be solved.

- **Security:** The current Blockchain has a possibility of a 51% attack. In a 51% attack, a single entity would have full control of the majority of the network's mining hash-rate and would be able to manipulate Blockchain. To overcome this issue, more research on security is necessary.
- **Wasted Resources:** Mining Bitcoin wastes huge amounts of energy ($15million/day). The waste in Bitcoin is caused by the Proof-of-Work effort. There are some alternatives in industry fields, such as Proof-of-Stake. With Proof-of-Work, the probability of mining a block depends on the work done by the miner. However, in Proof-of-Stake, the resource that is compared is the amount of Bitcoin a miner holds. For example, someone holding 1% of the Bitcoin can mine 1% of the "Proof-of-Stake blocks". The issue with wasted resources needs to be solved to enable more efficient mining in Blockchain.
- **Usability:** The Bitcoin API for developing services is difficult to use. There is a need to develop a more developer-friendly API for Blockchain. This could resemble REST APIs.
- **Versioning, Hard Forks, Multiple Chains:** A small chain that consists of a small number of nodes has a higher possibility of a 51% attack. An issue also emerges when chains are split for administrative or versioning purposes.

Beyond these limitations, according to Yli-Huumo et al. (2016), scalability is also an issue that needs to be solved for future needs. Therefore, to identify and understand the current status of research conducted on blockchain, it is important to gather all relevant research. It is then possible to evaluate what challenges and questions have been tackled and answered, and what the most problematic issues in blockchain are at the moment.

Due to the fact that the maturity of blockchain technology is still relatively low, the technological know-how is mainly concentrated to a small group of blockchain users in the World. However, in a decade the Blockchain platform has been approved with its bespoken characteristics. Hence, the idea behind it is to make the technology more widespread. It can be envisioned that the perspective will have potential to be improved with these common applications. For today there are many application areas of Blockchain, and here one of them is mentioned.

As an irreversible and tamper-proof public records repository for documents, contracts, properties, and assets, the Blockchain can be used to embed information and instructions, with a wide range of applications from private to public (Atzori, 2015). The most popular application is *smart contracts* which can be described as tamper- proof, self-executing and automatically enforceable. Based on Mattilla et al. (2017) American cryptographer Nick Szabo published an article in which he outlined the concept of smart contracts first in 1994. However, because of the immature technology and ICT infrastructure at that time, the idea could not find a way for application. Beyond Szabo's smart contract definition, today smart contracts are accepted as a set of promises in a digital form including protocols within which the parties perform on these promises. The Blockchain technology enables smart contracts to be programmed and embedded to the system easily. Moreover, it can be envisioned that these smart contract systems may be improved with self-execution and self-enforcement to be fully automatized in autonomous organizations. With these improvements in smart contracts it is envisioned to reach Decentralized Autonomous Organization/Corporations/ Societies (DAOs/DACs/DASs). In this concept, self-sufficient agents derived from artificial intelligence are capable of executing tasks without human involvement, for which the Blockchain can provide additional functionality. DAOs operate independently of their developers. In their structure, humans are moved from the center of the organization to its outskirts, as the system is used to organize human activity algorithmically. An open organization based on smart contracts may solve the problem of bad leadership or issues with the transparency of the organization. However, if left unregulated and ungoverned, errors in the programming code may prove to be very harmful or even dangerous. The DAO is still in the development stage and so it reveals new types of risks. The organizational character of the DAO in itself raises the question of, for instance, the distribution of liability for damages within such new types of applications. In addition, it involves ties to the question of determining the correct legal entity in economic activity based on new models of co-operation. Hence, developing technology is not only adequate for making the application common, but also social side should be handled with a holistic perspective.

Because of these evolutionary improvements in Blockchain, Swan (2015) described the technology as "fundamental for forward progress in society as Magna Carta or the Rosetta Stone" (Swan, 2015, p. 16). Again, based on Mattila (2016), the Blockchain technology is shifting society in two aspects. Firstly, it enables directly and reliable transactions of any assets over the Internet between any parties by providing censorship-resistant, disintermediated, tamper-proof digital platforms (Mattila & Seppälä, 2015; Mattila, 2016). Secondly, for enterprise- and industry- level systems, blockchain technology is providing efficiency gains on top of existing structures by removing the constant need for actively inter-mediated data-synchronization and concurrency control by a trusted third party (Mattila, 2016; Mattila et al., 2016). Therefore, the blockchain platform can be described as more democratic and equal for all nodes in the network. The main idea is accepting all parties sharing the same platform without having privileges and no third-party will provide other ones these privileges. Hence, the blockchain technology can enable all the participants to produce a platform together in a distributed manner, without having to trust each other in almost any capacity (Seppälä & Mattila, 2016; Mattila, 2016).

The deployment of blockchain technology in the healthcare industry will be undoubtedly disruptive. However, due to characteristics of the healthcare ecosystem, it is not expected to serve as a magic bullet to solve every emerging problem. Instead, it will be an evolutionary journey for blockchain-based healthcare systems or applications (Das, 2017). As it has the potential to transform healthcare delivery by enforcing patient-centric systems and improving security, privacy and interoperability; in time it may turn into a technical standard that enables individuals, healthcare providers, healthcare entities and medical researchers to securely share electronic health data (Rabah, 2017; Linn and Koo, 2016).

## BOUNDARIES BETWEEN HEALTHCARE AND BLOCKCHAIN LITERATURE

COCIR (2017) revealed an illustrative Healthcare Blockchain Ecosystem and projected potential applications based on blockchain as supply chain management, drug verification, secure exchange of data for reimbursement, control over personal EHR, and management of clinical trials. Capgemini (2017) examined the issue from a holistic perspective and asserted that blockchain applications could benefit the healthcare ecosystem as a whole conceptually. In addition, the elimination of third-party entities and middlemen would reduce administrative costs and increase efficiencies in processing of claims. Distributed ledger and built-in authentication controls would lower the risk of data theft and fraud. Capgemini (2017) concluded that this would foster higher levels of trust in electronic transactions, which would spur electronic payments and thereby reduce payment (accounts receivable) timelines. Furthermore, these studies accepted the use of blockchain technology in the healthcare field promising and disruptive.

According to Frost and Sullivan Report (2017) cited by Das (2017), the potential uses of blockchain in healthcare from the data management perspective were classified. The report demonstrated the use of five general blockchain-based healthcare which are as follows: clinic health data exchange and interoperability, claims adjudication and billing management, drug supply chain and provenance, pharma clinical trials and population health research, cybersecurity, and healthcare IoT. They are believed to indicate more outsanding opportunities, but their uses are employed at various levels by different health systems and countries. Moreover, in order to create globally integrated applications and build collaboration among different industry/parties; standards, and frameworks have to be established.

While use cases e.g. blockchain-based EMR and healthcare data management have the potential to eliminate the burden and cost of health data reconciliation and facilitate interoperability, other use cases e.g., claim adjudication, billing management, drug supply chain, clinical trails have the potential to reveal new economic benefits, effective solutions and quality healthcare services by disintermediating high-cost gatekeepers and automating transactional services across healthcare workflows (Frost and Sullivan, 2017).

However, Hölbl et al. (2018) indicated that blockchain technology in healthcare is mainly applied for healthcare data management including data sharing, health records and access control and rarely used for supply chain management, audit trail management and other scenarios, like drug prescription management and auditing (Hölbl et al., 2018).

After reviewing the literature, the potential use cases of blockchain in healthcare are decided to group in five fields of application. Following sub-headings are the group names and groups explained below.

## Healthcare Data Management

One of the most prominent topics in blockchain and healthcare relation is healthcare data management including data storage, exchange and sharing e.g. blockchain-based EMR. According to McFarlane et al. (2017), current electronic medical record (EMR) systems can not meet effective patient-provider relationship and deliver a limited capability of exchange of information among parties. The new healthcare paradigm requires effective and optimal care delivery to produce better care outcomes for patients. These needs force healthcare providers to be able to effectively coordinate and collaborate with other health care organizations and subsidiary health organizations such as laboratories and pharmacies in care delivery. They proposed a "Patientory Blockchain Network" which empowers patients, clinicians, and healthcare organizations to access, store and transfer information safely, thus improving care coordination while ensuring data security since it adheres to HIPAA compliance requirement (McFarlane et al., 2017; www.patientory.com).

Azaria et al. (2016) also proposed that "MedRec" prototype was decentralized health record management system facilitate data sharing, authentication and auditability. They suggested that it was integrated with existing data storage infrastructure and thus provided patients a detailed, immutable history and access control healthcare data via smart contracts. Dubovitskaya et al. (2017) also proposed blockchain based EMR prototype relating oncology patients. They designed a permission blockchain to manage and share clinical data with consent and authorization.

Another one of the blockchain-based and EMR-related implementation was collaboration between Guardtime which was data security firm and the Estonian eHealth Foundation. All citizens were provided a national eID card which links their EMR data with their blockchain-based identity. Every update and access to healthcare records via immutable, time-stamped data logs were registered in the blockchain and a "keyless signature" was returned and stored next to the record. These signatures have served as an electronic timestamp which could prove when changes were made, while the blockchain independently has verified who made them. In doing so, government has secured and managed the health records of over a million Estonians because the system facilitates improved access to vital information for health professionals, while simultaneously guaranteeing patient confidentiality and the integrity of their files (Angraal, 2017).

For medical data exchange among cloud service providers which was trustless parties, Xia et al. (2017) proposed MeDShare which was blockchain-based data sharing system. The system relies on smart contracts and access control mechanisms to effectively monitor data and also detect and cancel unauthorized access and tampering. In this way, cloud service providers could provide secure data sharing, data provenance and auditing on medical data with each other. Brennan (2017) asserted that Healthcoin encourage people for healthy life and diabetes prevention. Based on Brennan's proposal, Healthcoin allowed to individuals, suppliers, insurers and goverments across the globe to manage people's lifestyle change by offering exercising, eating right, better mental health as well as biomakers like weight, heart rate, sugar level etc. to a database run on the blockhain. Healthcoin's algorithm then could calculate the changes or improvement in the patient's health, accordingly, they earned a certain amount of Healthcoins could be used to decrease insurance cost, recognize achievement. In addition, patients could choose to share the information with friends, doctors, goverment or public health organization using it for research (Brennan, 2017).

Healthcare Data Gateway (HDG) which is a smart App proposed by Yue et al. (2016) has ensured that people manage personal healthcare data via blockchain storage system. Thus, patients could share their health data in secure way because private blockchain cloud-based application has notable features such as "purpose-centric access control" which provides patients to control their own data and "secure multi-party computation" without violating privacy with third party for patient data processing.

Several researchers also suggested that diverse blockchain-based healthcare data management scenarios such as e-health solutions (Liu, 2017; Dias et al., 2018), electronic prescriptions (Seitz et al., 2017), mobile health applications (Liang et al., 2017), healthcare data in cloud (Al Omar et al., 2019).

As a result, blockchain technology with immutable, cryptographically secured, time-stamped log features enable precise, real-time and longitudinal health data for all healthcare stakeholders.

## Claims Adjudication and Billing Management

For maintaining of healthcare delivery, claims data apart from health data has been substantial input especially in revenue cycle. Governments have the right to speak about how services are billed and money is collected but in current patient billing management systems are complex and related to the transparency and trust because claims data flows through different organizations and incline to manipulation by parties and so this result in fraudulent, excessive billing or billing for non-performed services (Rabah, 2017; Yip, 2017).

It can be assertedt that, blockchain based systems, which have the features like smart contract and verifiable ledger of all service and payment activities, can create more effective solutions via notary function for reducing healthcare billing-related issues. Thus, blockchain can help reduce fraud, extra payment, the need for intermediaries, administrative costs and waiting time for providers and payers (Randall et al., 2017; Das, 2017).

Yip (2017) stated that decentralizing system based blockchain can be alternative payment model. Based on Yip (2017)'s findings, it can be said that, blockchain will provide to add and update claim data much faster than current system and even payers and Bitcoin may be connected to private blockchains and thus patients can pay from a single point for the healthcare services they receive from multiple parties.

Culver (2016) proposed that smart contract, an agreement between provider and patient or government, can enable near real-time automating the majority of claim adjudication and payment processing activities. Thus, complex and ambiguous agreements will be turned into clear and transparent smart contracts and this will trigger to cut down administrative cost, transaction time and middleman.

Partnered with Capital One, Gem Health developed *GemOS* which is a blockchain-based ecosystem for exchanging claim data between and within organizations. It formed global identifiers to trace data and these identifiers connect to each other and record the location of data of a person and organization on a blockchain, along with the necessary consents and sharing policies (Allison, 2017).

## Drug Supply Chain Integrity and Provenance

Clauson et al. (2018) stated that supply chain manangement in healthcare is quite important because of its directly affects on patient life and outcomes. Healthcare delivery consists of many different inputs and drug supply chain is big part in terms of both quantity and cost and thus vulnerable to fraudulent attacks. It is well known that drug supply chains contain multiple countries, organizations, and products which have various legal, trade and regulatory enforcement. This nature of the chain makes it difficult to guarantee the chemical components of drugs. With the globalization of the pharmaceutical supply chain, drug counterfeiting is a major problem in this industry and public health. Many companies and blockchain start-ups try to find out blockchain based solutions such as simulation models, and prototyping for drug supply chain (Mackey and Nayyar, 2017; Clauson et al., 2018).

Blockchain based system has potential to create formal registry to track products and components by adding to immutable and timestamped log at every step of process (from manufacture to end user). Furthermore, adding the functionalities such as private keys and smart contract, system could provide transparency, trustworthy, authenticity, proof of ownership of the drug source (Das, 2017; Angraal, 2017; Engelhardt, 2017).

However, according to Mackey et al. (2019), the blockchain-based drug supply chain develops slowly when compared to other industries (e.g., food supply). Since there are no common global policies and regulatory standards, blockchain-based solutions need a consortium on which the concerned parties compromise. Thus, governance can be ensured on who will participate in the chain and how the data will be verified.

The MediLedger Project is a collaborative approach among cross-industry partnerships which have same standards. By forming a consortium, it aims to tackle serialization and other business problems (www.mediledger.com). Similarly, Hyperledger which is blockchain network cross-industry is backed by Linux Foundation and commenced a project for fighting counterfeit medicine. By using tracking and timestamp features of blockchain technology, it could make easy to determine when and where a drug was produced (Taylor, 2016).

## Pharma Clinical Trails, Biomedical Research and Population Health Research

Clinical trials are composed of multiple stakeholders, an essential part of which is patient, similar to the drug supply chain and so they have the same challenges like regulatory standards (Mackey et al., 2019). Furthermore, in clinical trials, reproducibility, data sharing, personal data privacy concerns, patient enrollment as well as missing data, endpoint switching, data dredging, and selective publication are a big problem and crucial safety issues for patients. Besides, these challenges result in knowledge gaps for healthcare stakeholders and health policymakers (Benchoufi and Ravaud, 2017; Nugent et al., 2016). Therefore, these issues affect research outcomes and quality because trials could take a long time and outcomes are important for the future of drugs and human health. The use of distributed ledger and time-stamped immutable records will provide traceability and guarantee patients' privacy (Dubovitskaya et al., 2017).

Moreover, using smart contracts can act as trusted administrators which are able to improve the transparency and accountability of data reporting during clinical trials, by immutably capturing all aspects of data including trial registration, protocol, subject registration, consent, clinical measurements, survey, tests, and statistic, etc. This can reduce waste, reporting errors and accusations of data manipulation or selective reporting. (Nugent et al., 2016; Petre, 2017b; Cocir, 2017).

In terms of biomedical research, healthcare data are obtained from different resources such as hospital, patient-related data including consent data, health plan data, genomic, laboratory, etc., clinical trial data, drug supply chain data, and internet of medical things like wearable devices, sensors, etc. In this manner, all data need to authenticity, integrity, provenance, and privacy. Thanks to the features of blockchain, they could be securely stored, time-stamped, current, and transparent (Kuo et al., 2017).

Blockchain-based solutions can improve trust among researchers, suppliers, patients, and other communities and this could help trigger collaboration among them. Therefore, researches can increase in medical field like precision medicine and population health because blockchain technology enable secure way to an ample set of standardized non-patient identifiable information in real-time from different ethnic and socio-economic backgrounds and various geographical environments. Particularly, real-time access to data could allow providers/ researchers to enhance care coordination in emergency case and quickly determine and interfere with environmental conditions in public health like epidemics (Linn and Koo, 2016).

Irving and Holden (2016) presented proof of concept study, they used a copy of the clinicaltrials. gov study protocol based on previously reported prespecified endpoints and planned analyses. By using public and private key produced from the protocol, they incorporated a transaction into the blockchain and so they provided a time-stamped record. As a result, the transaction was completed in a short time and it was low cost. Besides, they confirmed the authenticity of the original protocol and independently verifiable method to audit.

Many researchers also proposed blockchain-based solutions including MedRec (Ekblaw et al., 2016), Healthbank (Mettler, 2016) for clinical and biomedical research.

## Cyber Security and Healthcare IoT

Recently, not only current systems have ineligible health IT security infrastructure but also cyber attacks on health data and medical devices are increasing. Thus, they might be exposed to numerous breaches and cyber attacks by external hackers and internal attackers at organizational and individual level. Moreover, as health information technologies improve, current health IT security infrastructure has difficulty in supporting these technologies such as connected health, internet of medical things (IoMT) including wearable devices, sensors, etc., remote patient monitoring, and cloud-based device (Rabah, 2017). This gap increases privacy and security concerns about the transfer and logging of data transactions.

According to Berg Insight Report (2018), the number of remotely monitored patients around world was 16.5 million in 2017 and the market acceptance continues to grow. The number estimated to reach 83.4 million by 2023.

However, due to the characteristics of health data, both their security and privacy need to be ensured in the best way and their accessibility need to be ensured to provide quality healthcare. As mentioned above, blockchain-enable solutions have the potential to cope with the challenges e.g. interoperability, security, privacy and reliability (Brodersen et al., 2016; Rabah, 2017; Deloitte, 2018; Hölbl et al., 2018; Griggs et al., 2018).

Concerning this, Dwivedi et al. (2019) indicated that "the inability to delete and change information from blocks makes blockchain technology the best technology for the healthcare system." They suggested a combination of the private key, public key, blockchain, and other lightweight cryptographic primitives like Ring signature in order to reduce security and privacy concerns about IoT which has resource constraints.

Griggs et al. (2018) proposed a private blockchain based on the Ethereum protocol for enabling secure analysis and management of medical sensor like remote patient monitoring. They used smart contracts integrated with Wireless Body Area Networks (WBAN) systems like smart devices to provide real-time patiens monitoring and medical interventions by sending notifications to patients and healthcare providers in a HIPAA compliant manner.

Angeletti et al. (2017) stated that in the era of Internet of Things (IoT) when internet-based services uncontrollably grow, a huge amount of data, also called big data flow, consistently from different devices and so we need privacy-preserving applications where people maintain control of their own data. They presented a digital health application for using IoT data in clinical trials. In recruiting phase, in order to select desired patient profile meeting criteria, a clinical research institute need accurate data and trusted devices, but in terms of participants, they need privacy of their health data. Thus, they proposed IoT such as wearable devices are equipped with a tamper-proof memory space where the manufacturer places a private key. On the other hand, personal health data are not shared publicly until an individual is enrolled.

## The Challenges to Blockchain-Based Solutions

On the other hand, blockchain technology has technical, organizational and behavioral economic challenges and limitations before it has been used in healthcare industry. The maturity of blockchain technology is still relatively low. During the deployment of blockchain technology, the healthcare industry will face both technical challenges such as interoperability, scalability, throughput, latency, size and bandwidth, security, wasted resources, etc., and some organizational and behavioral economic challenges, for instance, adoption and incentives for participation, costs of operating blockchain technology and regulatory consideration etc. (Swan, 2015; Krawiec et al., 2016; Siyal et al., 2018; Gordon and Catalini, 2018; Katuwal et al., 2018). The challenges and their explanations are summarized in Table 1.

Current implementations of blockchain technology in healthcare are either prototyping stage or development phase, and they have the immature infrastructure. Therefore, it needs more research, experimental implementations, and investments for evaluating its effect on services and outcomes.

*Table 1. Challenges of blockchain in healthcare*

| Blockchain challenges | |
|---|---|
| Technical | • The number of transactions in healthcare sector is enormous and it needs high-volume and high-frequency transactions of clinical data but blockchain e.g. permissionless blockchain faces volume and storage constraints.<br>• At the same time, a blockchain consumes significant computing power to process transactions. The cost of computing power is derived from the volume and size of transactions submitted through the network.<br>• For blockchain-based solutions to operate effectively, stakeholders e.g. healthcare providers, patient, and insurance must be willing to cooperate and set standards about what data is stored on or off the blockchain, what size and format is offered etc., especially cross-border sharing of data.<br>• Likewise, it needs technically access control policies and synchronization mechanisms to operate in complex and diverse communication systems e.g. IoT devices.<br>• Although blockchain implementations are pseudonymous, namely, identity is typically obscured behind a public key, it can not ensure transactional privacy for each public key and so the value of transactions are publicly visible |
| Organizational | • Because it is a novel technology, blockchain has an uncertain cost of operations for healthcare sector,<br>• A network of co-operation of multiple stakeholders (nodes) must be found to provide the computing power necessary to generate blocks after a transaction is produced. Thus it needs incentives e.g. financial, operational for participation,<br>• For integration with multiple parties, healthcare policy makers should be executively collaboration and make regulatory framework as to patient's privacy like HIPAA. |
| Behavioral | • Patient-controlled data can be risky e.g. losting key,<br>• Blockchain is still in progress stage and so it confronts social challenges e.g. cultural shift, social acceptance and so it need to be users education, incentive etc. |

## METHODOLOGY AND DATA

In this study, we aimed to explore blockchain applications in healthcare with explorative perspective by using scientific publications indexed in WoS. Author keyword co-occurrences was used for demonstrating concept relationships. We believe that demonstrating big picture by using science visualization techniques will give opportunity to understand the new emerging study field and contribute existing literature. CiteSpace, free java-based software, was used for scientometrics analysis and VosViewer was used for network visualizations.

It is clear that WoS is not a health-focused index like PUBMED and MEDLINE but its coverage and metadata are accepted as powerful than others. Mongeon and Paul-Hus (2016) compared databases based upon journal coverage and found that for comparative research evaluation, databases should be carefully used due to their biases. Moreover, they did not conclude that one database was superior to the other in terms of journal coverage.

A number of free and commercial software tools are available to carry out the mapping study. Each has its strengths and weaknesses based on different characteristics to carry out science mapping analysis. Cobo et al. (2011)'s study can be reviewed for further comparative information about these tools. Among those, the present study used Citespace II (Chen 2006) software, which takes a set of bibliographic records as its input and models the intellectual structure of the underlying domain in terms of a synthesized network based upon a time series of networks derived from each year's publications. As CiteSpace is easy to use and has some favorable features, it was chosen for the purpose of the present study. Some of the visuals were generated by using VosViewer (van Eck and Waltman, 2007) free Java-based software.

*Figure 2. Timeline view of keyword co-occurrence network*

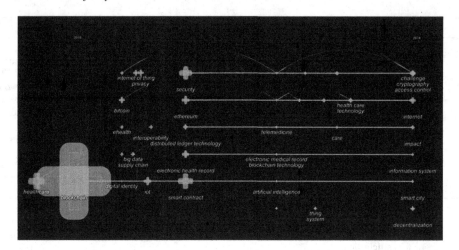

## ANALYSIS AND FINDINGS

Blockchain publications were retrieved by using lexical search query as "TS=((("blockchain" OR "distributed ledger" OR "cryptocurrenc*") AND ("health" OR "healthcare")) OR TI=(("blockchain" OR "distributed ledger" OR "cryptocurrenc*") AND ("health" OR "healthcare")))" in WoS. TS refers to topic sentence and TI refers to Title. 198 publications were reached with this query and after preprocessing data were analyzed.

First analysis was performed by using author keywords. Co-occurrence analysis was applied. Keyword co-occurrence analysis has been applied in several domains for understanding the dynamics of a scientific field. Keywords were clustered based on co-occurrences. As proposed by Chen and Song (2017), clusters were considered the embodiment of an underlying specialty. Therefore, all clusters represented various aspects of the analyzed domain. Cluster members were scrutinized in each cluster by identifying structural and temporal metrics of research impact and evolutionary significance. Timeline view of these clusters demonstrated in Figure 2.

In Figure 2, every vertical line represents different cluster and other arcs represent links between different keywords in clusters. Top to down order of clusters only refer to the higher number of members in the cluster. Plus signs represent frequency of usage of keywords. When the order of clusters considered from top to down, first cluster was labeled as "thing security" and its focus was mostly on privacy and security issues. It is clear that these issues were the critical challenges for medical informatics. Second cluster was labeled as "current research topics" based on titles of the clustered articles. In these cluster, payment systems mostly discussed in healthcare by using cryptocurrencies like Ethereum or Bitcoin. In third cluster, internet-based applications of healthcare were discussed and their distributed aspects were scrutinized. Electronic medical records were discussed in fourth cluster and trust aspect of blockchain platforms were examined. Fifth cluster was including blockchain applications and its some extensions like smart contracts. Last cluster was connection of health system and smart city concept.

It can be asserted that there were not many articles and focused terms to be called as emergent in analyzed dataset. However, mean publication year was seen as 2017 and focus of articles were about

*Figure 3. Country collaboration network map*

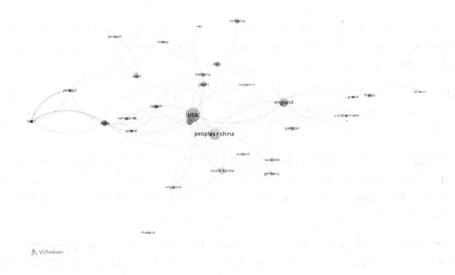

overcoming health challenges. Therefore, it can be implied that studies on blockchain will make contribution especially for solving payment system, digital identity, privacy, and security issues.

After analyzing keyword co-occurrences, it can be beneficial to see the country collaborations on the same subject. Country collaboration network map was prepared by using Vos Viewer (van Eck and Waltman, 2007) as demonstrated in Figure 3.

As can be seen in Figure 3, there were 9 clusters which were colored differently. USA, China, England, and South Korea published more articles than others when the size of circles considered. As in keyword co-occurrences network analysis, because of the low number of publications it is not easy to demonstrate some hot points in Figure 2. However, German-Chinese collaboration, USA-Japan collaboration, European network, and England-Pakistan-UAE collaboration may seem interesting.

## CONCLUSION

In this study, blockchain technology has been reviewed to understand whether it can be a cure for these challenges in healthcare. Even, blockchain technology is not mature, there were many studies in many fields which were promising. In this chapter, we tried to review real cases and visualize cognitive space of intersection of health and blockchain concepts. Finally, it can be asserted that healthcare system has important challenges regarding privacy, security and interoperability.

We identified six clusters in author keyword co-ocurrences network map. However, we couldn't identify emerging concepts with high frequency because of low number of publications in the field. We envisioned that privacy and security issues might be the first focus of blockchain studies in healthcare. Then, interoperability and payment systems will be integrated by establishing operating standards of blockchain technology in health field.

For further studies, focus issues that we emphasized with this study should be examined in detail and *Scopus, PUBMED and MEDLINE data should be combined with WoS data by eliminating duplicate problem.*

## REFERENCES

Al Omar, A., Bhuiyan, M. Z. A., Basu, A., Kiyomoto, S., & Rahman, M. S. (2019). Privacy-friendly platform for healthcare data in cloud based on blockchain environment. *Future Generation Computer Systems*, *95*, 511–521. doi:10.1016/j.future.2018.12.044

Allison, I. (2017). Gem shows off first blockchain application for health claims. International Business Times. Retrieved from https://www.ibtimes.co.uk/gem-shows-off-first-blockchain-application-health-claims-1622574

Angeletti, F., Chatzigiannakis, I., & Vitaletti, A. (2017, September). The role of blockchain and IoT in recruiting participants for digital clinical trials. In *Proceedings of the 2017 25th International Conference on Software, Telecommunications and Computer Networks (SoftCOM)* (pp. 1-5). IEEE. 10.23919/SOFTCOM.2017.8115590

Angraal, S., Krumholz, H. M., & Schulz, W. L. (2017). Blockchain technology: Applications in health care. *Circulation: Cardiovascular Quality and Outcomes*, *10*(9), e003800. doi:10.1161/CIRCOUTCOMES.117.003800 PMID:28912202

Azaria, A., Ekblaw, T. V., & Lippman, A. (2016). MedRec: Using Blockchain for Medical Data Access and Permission Management. In *Proceedings of the 2016 2nd International Conference on Open and Big Data (OBD)* (pp. 25-30). Academic Press. 10.1109/OBD.2016.11

Benchoufi, M., & Ravaud, P. (2017). Blockchain technology for improving clinical research quality. *Trials*, *18*(1), 335. doi:10.118613063-017-2035-z PMID:28724395

Brennan, B. (2017). Healthcoin – blockchain-enabled platform for diabetes prevention. *Blockchain Healthcare Review*. Retrieved from https://blockchainhealthcarereview.com/healthcoin-blockchain-enabled-platform-for-diabetes-prevention/

Brodersen, C., Kalis, B., Leong, C., Mitchell, E., Pupo, E., Truscott, A., & Accenture, L. (2016). *Blockchain: Securing a New Health Interoperability Experience*. Accenture LLP.

Capgemini. (2017). Blockchain: A healthcare endustry review. Retrieved from https://www.capgemini.com/wp-content/uploads/2017/07/blockchain-a_healthcare_industry_view_2017_web.pdf)

Chen, C. M. (2006). Citespace II: Detecting and visualizing emerging trends and transient patterns in scientific literature. *Journal of the American Society for Information Science and Technology*, *57*(3), 359–377. doi:10.1002/asi.20317

Clauson, K. A., Breeden, E. A., Davidson, C., & Mackey, T. K. (2018). *Leveraging blockchain technology to enhance supply chain management in healthcare. Blockchain in Healthcare Today*. doi:10.30953/bhty.v1.20

Cobo, M. J., Lopez-Herrera, A. G., Herrera-Viedma, E., & Herrera, F. (2011). Science mapping software tools: Review, analysis, and cooperative study among tools. *Journal of the American Society for Information Science and Technology*, *62*(7), 1382–1402. doi:10.1002/asi.21525

Cocir. (2017) Beyond the hype of blockchain in healthcare. Retrieved from http://www.cocir.org/uploads/media/17069_COC_Blockchain_paper_web.pdf

Culver, K. (2016). Blockchain Technologies: A whitepaper discussing how the claims process can be improved. In *Proceedings of the ONC/NIST Use of Blockchain for Healthcare and Research Workshop.* ONC/NIST.

Das, R. (2017). Does Blockchain Have A Place In Healthcare? *Pharma&Healthcare.* Retrieved from https://www.forbes.com/sites/reenitadas/2017/05/08/does-blockchain-have-a-place-in-healthcare/#552cb0c91c31

Deloitte. (2018). Blockchain to blockchains in life sciences and health care-What broader integration is making possible today. Retrieved from https://www2.deloitte.com/content/dam/Deloitte/us/Documents/life-sciences-health-care/us-lshc-tech-trends2-blockchain.pdf

Dias, J. P., Reis, L., Ferreira, H. S., & Martins, Â. (2018). Blockchain for access control in e-health scenarios.

Dubovitskaya, A., Xu, Z., Ryu, S., Schumacher, M., & Wang, F. (2017). Secure and Trustable Electronic Medical Records Sharing using Blockchain. In *Proceedings of the AMIA 2017 Annual Symposium Proceedings.* Academic Press.

Dwivedi, A. D., Srivastava, G., Dhar, S., & Singh, R. (2019). A decentralized privacy-preserving healthcare blockchain for iot. *Sensors (Basel), 19*(2), 326. doi:10.339019020326 PMID:30650612

Engelhardt, M. A. (2017). Hitching Healthcare to the Chain: An Introduction to Blockchain Technology in the Healthcare Sector. *Technology Innovation Management Review., 7*(10), 22–34. doi:10.22215/timreview/1111

Frost and Sullivan. (2017). Blockchain Technology in Global Healthcare, 2017–2025. Retrieved from http://www.frost.com/sublib/display-report.do?searchQuery=blockchain&id=K1DB-01-00-00-00&bdata=aHR0cHM6Ly93d3cuZnJvc3QuY29tL3NyY2gvY2F0YWxvZy1zZWFyY2guZG8%2FcGFnZVNppemU9MTImcXVlcnlUZXh0PWJsb2NrY2hhaW4mbWFya2V0Q29kZXM9SEMmZmlsdGVyU3dpdGNoNoPWZhbHNlQH5AU2VhcmNooIFJlc3VsdHNAfkAxNTE1MjU0MDg1NDk3

Gordon, W. J., & Catalini, C. (2018). Blockchain technology for healthcare: Facilitating the transition to patient-driven interoperability. *Computational and Structural Biotechnology Journal, 16*, 224–230. doi:10.1016/j.csbj.2018.06.003 PMID:30069284

Griggs, K. N., Ossipova, O., Kohlios, C. P., Baccarini, A. N., Howson, E. A., & Hayajneh, T. (2018). Healthcare Blockchain System Using Smart Contracts for Secure Automated Remote Patient Monitoring. *Journal of Medical Systems, 42*(7), 130. doi:10.100710916-018-0982-x PMID:29876661

Hölbl, M., Kompara, M., Kamišalić, A., & Nemec Zlatolas, L. (2018). A systematic review of the use of blockchain in healthcare. *Symmetry, 10*(10), 470. doi:10.3390ym10100470

IBM. (2016). Blockchain: The Chain of Trust and its Potential to Transform Healthcare – Our Point of View. Retrieved from https://www.healthit.gov/sites/default/files/8-31-blockchain-ibm_ideation-challenge_aug8.pdf

Irving, G., & Holden, J. (2016). How blockchain-timestamped protocols could improve the trustworthiness of medical science. *F1000 Research*, 5. PMID:27239273

Katuwal, G. J., Pandey, S., Hennessey, M., & Lamichhane, B. (2018). Applications of Blockchain in Healthcare: Current Landscape & Challenges.

Krawiec, R. J., Housman, D., White, M., Filipova, M., Quarre, F., Barr, D., . . . Tsai, L. (2016, August). Blockchain: Opportunities for health care. In *Proc. NIST Workshop Blockchain Healthcare* (pp. 1-16). Academic Press.

Kuo, T. T., Kim, H. E., & Ohno-Machado, L. (2017). Blockchain distributed ledger technologies for biomedical and health care applications. *Journal of the American Medical Informatics Association*, *24*(6), 1211–1220. doi:10.1093/jamia/ocx068 PMID:29016974

Liang, X., Zhao, J., Shetty, S., Liu, J., & Li, D. (2017, October). Integrating blockchain for data sharing and collaboration in mobile healthcare applications. In *Proceedings of the 2017 IEEE 28th Annual International Symposium on Personal, Indoor, and Mobile Radio Communications (PIMRC)* (pp. 1-5). IEEE. 10.1109/PIMRC.2017.8292361

Linn, L., & Koo, M. (2016). Blockchain for health data and its potential use in health it and health care related research. In *Proceedings of the ONC/NIST Use of Blockchain for Healthcare and Research Workshop*. ONC/NIST.

Liu, W., Zhu, S. S., Mundie, T., & Krieger, U. (2017, October). Advanced block-chain architecture for e-health systems. In *Proceedings of the 2017 IEEE 19th International Conference on e-Health Networking, Applications and Services (Healthcom)* (pp. 1-6). IEEE. Retrieved from https://www.iim.ftn.uns.ac.rs/is17/papers/28.pdf

Mackey, T. K., Kuo, T. T., Gummadi, B., Clauson, K. A., Church, G., Grishin, D., ... Palombini, M. (2019). 'Fit-for-purpose?'–challenges and opportunities for applications of blockchain technology in the future of healthcare. *BMC Medicine*, *17*(1), 68. doi:10.118612916-019-1296-7 PMID:30914045

Mackey, T. K., & Nayyar, G. A. (2017). A review of existing and emerging digital technologies to combat the global trade in fake medicines. *Expert Opinion on Drug Safety*, *16*(5), 587–602. doi:10.1080/14740338.2017.1313227 PMID:28349715

McFarlane, C., Beer, M., Brown, J., & Prendergast, N. (2017). Patientory: A Healthcare Peer-to-Peer EMR Storage Network v1. 0. Retrieved from https://patientory.com/patientory_whitepaper.pdf

Mediledger. (n.d.). Retrieved from https://www.mediledger.com/

Mettler, M. (2016). Blockchain technology in healthcare: The revolution starts here. In *Proceedings of the 2016 IEEE 18th International Conference on e-Health Networking, Applications and Services (Healthcom)*. IEEE.

Mongeon, P., & Paul-Hus, A. (2016). The journal coverage of web of science and scopus: A comparative analysis. *Scientometrics*, *106*(1), 213–228. doi:2-015-1765-5. doi:10.1007/s1119

Nugent, T., Upton, D., & Cimpoesu, M. (2016). Improving data transparency in clinical trials using blockchain smart contracts. *F1000 Research*, *5*, 2541. doi:10.12688/f1000research.9756.1 PMID:28357041

Petre, A. (2017a). Leveraging Sustainable Innovation in Healthcare. Retrieved from http://www.ancapetre. com/leveraging-sustainable-innovation-healthcare

Petre, A. (2017b). Blockchain use cases in healthcare. Retrieved from https://www.linkedin.com/pulse/ blockchain-use-cases-healthcare-anca-petre

Pilkington, M. (2017). Can Blockchain Improve Healthcare Management? Consumer Medical Electronics and the IoMT. doi:10.2139/ssrn.3025393

Rabah, K. (2017). Challenges & Opportunities for Blockchain Powered Healthcare Systems: A Review. *Mara Research Journal of Medicine & Health Sciences*, *1*(1), 45–52.

Randall, D., Goel, P., & Abujamra, R. (2017). Blockchain Applications and Use Cases in Health Information Technology. *J Health Med Informat*, *8*(276), 2.

Report, B. I. (2018) mHealth and Home Monitoring. Retrieved from http://www.berginsight.com

Seitz, J., & Wickramasinghe, N. (2017). Blockchain technology in e-health: The case of electronic prescriptions in Germany. In *Proceedings of the XVII International Scientific Conference on Industrial Systems*. Academic Press.

Simic, M., Sladic, G., & Milosaljevic, B. (2017). A Case Study IoT and Blockchain powered Healthcare. In *Proceedings of the 8th PSU-UNS International Conference on Engineering and Technology (ICET-2017)*. Academic Press.

Siyal, A., Junejo, A., Zawish, M., Ahmed, K., Khalil, A., & Soursou, G. (2019). Applications of Blockchain Technology in Medicine and Healthcare: Challenges and Future Perspectives. *Cryptography*, *3*(1), 3. doi:10.3390/cryptography3010003

Swan, M. (2015). *Blockchain Blueprint for a New Economy*. USA: O'Reilly Media.

Szewczyk, P. (2017). *Potential applications of the blockchain technology in helthcare*. Zeszyty Naukowe. Organizacja i Zarządzanie/Politechnika Śląska.

Taylor, P. (2016). Applying blockchain technology to medicine traceability. Retrieved from https://www. securingindustry.com/pharmaceuticals/applying-blockchain-technology-to-medicine-traceability/s40/ a2766/#.XLt6tOgzY2y

Van Eck, N. J., & Waltman, L. (2007). Bibliometric mapping of the computational intelligence field. *International Journal of Uncertainty Fuzziness and Knowledge-Based Systems*, *15*(5), 625–645. Available: 488507004911 doi:10.1142/S0218

Xia, Q. I., Sifah, E. B., Asamoah, K. O., Gao, J., Du, X., & Guizani, M. (2017). MeDShare: Trust-less medical data sharing among cloud service providers via blockchain. *IEEE Access*, *5*, 14757–14767. doi:10.1109/ACCESS.2017.2730843

Yip, K. (2017). Blockchain & alternate payment models. In *Proceedings of the ONC/NIST Use of Blockchain for Healthcare and Research Workshop*. ONC/NIST.

Yue, X., Wang, H., Jin, D., Li, M., & Jiang, W. (2016). Healthcare data gateways: Found healthcare intelligence on blockchain with novel privacy risk control. *Journal of Medical Systems*, *40*(10), 218. doi:10.100710916-016-0574-6 PMID:27565509

## ENDNOTE

[1] Mining: Nodes in the network compete to solve a mathematical puzzle that requires the consumption of computing power. Once the puzzle solved the new block of transactions is accepted by the network and committed to the Blockchain. The network nodes which is called miners rewarded with newly generated coins.

[2] Double-spending is the result of successful spending of money more than once.

*This research was previously published in Multidimensional Perspectives and Global Analysis of Universal Health Coverage; pages 69-92, copyright year 2020 by Medical Information Science Reference (an imprint of IGI Global).*

# Chapter 6
# Multi–Keyword Searchable Encryption for E–Health System With Multiple Data Writers and Readers

**Dhruti P. Sharma**

*Sarvajanik College of Engineering and Technology, India*

**Devesh C. Jinwala**

(iD) https://orcid.org/0000-0003-4830-1702

*S. V. National Institute of Technology, India*

## ABSTRACT

*E-health is a cloud-based system to store and share medical data with the stakeholders. From a security perspective, the stored data are in encrypted form that could further be searched by the stakeholders through searchable encryption (SE). Practically, an e-health system with support of multiple stakeholders (that may work as either data owner [writer] or user [reader]) along with the provision of multi-keyword search is desirable. However, the existing SE schemes either support multi-keyword search in multi-reader setting or offer multi-writer, multi-reader mechanism along with single-keyword search only. This chapter proposes a multi-keyword SE for an e-health system in multi-writer multi-reader setting. With this scheme, any registered writer could share data with any registered reader with optimal storage-computational overhead on writer. The proposed scheme offers conjunctive search with optimal search complexity at server. It also ensures security to medical records and privacy of keywords. The theoretical and empirical analysis demonstrates the effectiveness of the proposed work.*

## INTRODUCTION

Since the last decade, several countries are moving towards digitization of medical records to improve data availability, data accessibility, data interoperability and data exchange (Akinyele et al., 2011; Löhr

DOI: 10.4018/978-1-6684-6311-6.ch006

et al., 2010). Such digitized medical data would be effectively used in several applications concerning maintenance of health records in terms of EHR (electronic health record)(Rau et al., 2010; Schabetsberger et al., 2006), accounting and billing (Macdonald, 1986), medical research (Sunyaev et al., 2009). In practice, to offer ubiquitous access of data in cost effective manner, the exiting E-Health systems store medical data onto third party cloud server. Since such storage outsourcing may introduce risks of data leakage and security breach, most e-health systems offload encrypted data onto cloud server and subsequently use Searchable Encryption(SE) to search across the stored encrypted data. SE offers two significant features besides data privacy - (1) The data can be shared by the data owners (writers) to data readers and the reader has capability to query the shared data, (2) Query keywords and search operation would be secured in such a way that the service provider will be unable to access the unauthorized medical data stored over it(R. Zhang et al., 2017). There exist several different types of searchable encryptions based on - the cryptographic key(s) used for construction of ciphertext and search token, the structure of the search index used to compute ciphertexts, the number of keywords used to query data, the number of data writers and readers existed in system. Different E-Health systems require different searchable encryption schemes. Considering the number of writers/readers, the authors identify 4 different types of E-Health systems and suggest their suitable SE schemes - (1) When the outsourced data is created and accessed by the same user, then a Symmetric Searchable Encryption (SSE) could be used. For example, a hospital wants to maintain staff payroll, then an authorized accountant could store data onto could server and then would be able to search data from any location, (2) When a single data writer shares data with a single data reader, then any Public Key Searchable Encryption (PKSE) (Baek et al., 2008a; Boneh et al., 2004; Boneh & Waters, 2007) can utilize. Example, a patient shares his medical history with a doctor, (3) When a single data writer shares data with multiple data readers, then any multi-user searchable encryption scheme (Bao et al., 2008; Huang et al., 2016; Y. H. Hwang & Lee, 2007a; Kiayias et al., 2016; Lai et al., 2013; Wang et al., 2016; Ye et al., 2016; Y. Zhang et al., 2016)could be used. For example, a hospital wants to share the information about doctors currently working in that hospital with all registered patients, (4) When multiple data writers want to share data with multiple data readers, then either writer-managed multi-user SE(Bao et al., 2008; Huang et al., 2016; Y. H. Hwang & Lee, 2007b; J. Li & Chen, 2013) or trusted authority based multi-user SE could be used (M.-S. Hwang et al., 2014; Jingzhang et al., 2018; Kiayias et al., 2016; J. Li & Chen, 2013; Lv et al., 2014; Wang et al., 2016; Xu et al., 2019; Ye et al., 2016; Y. Zhang et al., 2016). An example of such E-Health system will be discussed in the Section **Problem Definition**.

Additionally, the existing SE schemes either offer search for a single keyword (Baek et al., 2008b; Boneh et al., 2004) or for multiple keywords (Ballard et al., 2005; Boneh & Waters, 2007; Byun et al., 2006; Z. Chen et al., 2012; Ding et al., 2012; M.-S. Hwang et al., 2014; Y. H. Hwang & Lee, 2007a; B. Zhang & Zhang, 2011)based on number of keywords allowed in search query. In practice, an E-Health system offering multi-keyword search by the stakeholders(viz. hospitals, pharmacy, insurance company etc.) is more desirable.

## Problem Definition

Let us consider a scenario of an E-Health system depicted in Figure 1. The system has multiple data owners viz. Doctors, Patients, Hospitals etc. Concerning security, the data collected from data owners are in encrypted form and stored at the centralized data repository. Assume that the collected data are analyzed by several data users. For example, a doctor located at remote place accesses patients' current record to treat him remotely, a data analyst sitting at analysis centre analyzes several medical records to generate report on health analysis report. In addition, a patient wants to perform search for cancer specialist or an insurance company wants to investigate hospital data for mediclaim disbursement. To perform all such tasks, extraction of the desired data from central data collection is indeed essential.Such extraction requires *'search over encrypted data'* since stored data are in encrypted form. In general, one could say that for an E-Health system that includes several potential data generators and data users, any public key searchable scheme with multi-reader, multi-writer capability could be used for effective data analysis.

*Figure 1. Scenario of an E-Health System*

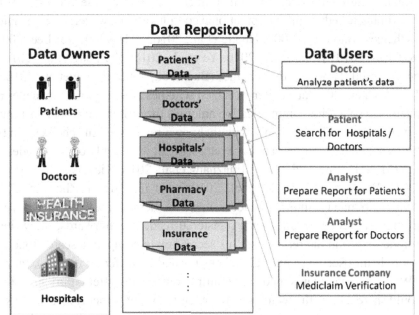

Additionally, let us consider some search queries generated by data users (Table 1). Taking the quoted texts in each query as keywords, it is determined that the search based on multiple keywords (in terms of conjunction (AND)) is required to be performed.

*Table 1. Potential Search Queries*

| Data Users | Query |
|---|---|
| Patient | 1. Find Cancer Specialists in Delhi.<br>***Query**= 'Cancer Specialist' AND 'Delhi'*<br>2. Find Cancer hospitals in Delhi.<br>***Query**='Cancer' AND 'Hospital' AND 'Delhi'* |
| Doctor | 1. List blood Pressure data of patient P1 on 26th April 2018.<br>***Query**='Patient' AND 'P1' AND 'Blood-Pressure'* |
| Data Analyst | 1. Find female patients suffering with breast cancer in Chennai.<br>***Query**='Patient' AND 'Female' AND 'Brest-Cancer' AND'Chennai'* |

From the above discussion, the authors infer that a public key searchable encryption supporting multiple writers/readers along with multi-keyword search would be more effective in design of such E-Health system.

## RELATED WORK

In typical public key searchable encryption (PKSE), since the writer generates searchable ciphertext by employing the public key of reader, his computational overhead would be O(D · W · R) where D=total number of documents required to share, W=total number of keywords to search and R=total number of readers in system. Aiming to reduce the computational complexity of a writer, several multi-user searchable encryption schemes (Bao et al., 2008; Huang et al., 2016; Y. H. Hwang & Lee, 2007a; Kiayias et al., 2016; J. Li & Chen, 2013; Wang et al., 2016; Ye et al., 2016; Y. Zhang et al., 2016)in public key setting have been proposed. However, the schemes (Bao et al., 2008; Huang et al., 2016; Y. H. Hwang & Lee, 2007a; J. Li & Chen, 2013)are writer-managed schemes where a writer manages multiple readers existed in system and so a prior communication amongst the writer and readers is utmost important. Consequently, a writer could share data only with theknown readers. Such schemes can be extended to multi-writer settings where each writer can share data with any randomly chosen readers. On the other hand, the schemes (M.-S. Hwang et al., 2014; Jingzhang et al., 2018; Kiayias et al., 2016; J. Li & Chen, 2013; Lv et al., 2014; Wang et al., 2016; Xu et al., 2019; Ye et al., 2016; Y. Zhang et al., 2016)employs Trusted Authority(TA) to manage multiple readers. In such schemes, TA first computes a master public key. He also prepares the secret keys for each registered readers. Afterwards, the writer uses master key to generate ciphertexts and the reader uses his secret key to compute a search token. Though each ciphertext in these schemes serves to multiple tokens (issued by different readers), they place optimal overhead (O(D ·W)) on the writer in supporting multiple readers in system. Furthermore, any writer in these schemes could share data with any unknown reader. However, support to a single keyword search is the major limitation of these schemes. On the other hand, the recent TA-based schemes (Sharma & Jinwala, 2017; Xu et al., 2019)support multiple writers/readers along with multi-keyword search. However, in these schemes, the TA is responsible to compute a search token for each reader based on the query keywords issued by the reader. Thus, the leakage of query keywords to TA is a major issue in these schemes. To overcome the issue, Sharma et al. have proposed a TA-based multi-writer, multi-reader conjunctive keyword searchable scheme (Sharma & Jinwala, n.d.)where each reader computes a search token from the search query (of keywords) using his private key issued by TA. However, all such TA-based schemes (Sharma & Jinwala, n.d., 2017; Xu et al., 2019)suffer from the lack of control on writers since any writer knowing master public key can compute searchable ciphertexts.

In the context of E-Health System, there exist several works offering security to medical records exchanged between entities viz. doctors, patients, hospitals etc. One of such work has been offered by Yu et al. (Yu et al., 2012)where a forward secure digital signature is employed to sign EMR (electronic medical record) shared between entities. With such signature, the authors ensure the validity of the old EMR record in case of signature key update. To exchange electronic patient record across different hospitals (potentially having heterogeneous record management system), Chen et al.(T.-L. Chen et al., 2012) have given a mobile agent based secure scheme for EMR. In this scheme, the authors employs Lagrange interpolation based key management scheme to propose a specialized program (mobile agent) that provides an efficient as well as secure access control for medical records in cross-hospital system.

Furthermore, the schemes (Akinyele et al., 2011; Liu et al., 2015)offer secure sharing of medical records among data provider and multiple data readers. Both of these schemes employ CPABE based access control mechanism (Goyal et al., 2006)that enables data readers possessing appropriate attributes to access medical records. A scheme (Eom et al., 2016) discusses an attribute based encryption where a patient being data provider can control accessing of his data to health service provider (i.e. doctor, nurse etc). However, none of these schemes (Akinyele et al., 2011; Eom et al., 2016; Liu et al., 2015)provide search across encrypted medical data. To offer solution, researchers have used searchable encryption to encrypt electronic health records. One of such solutions is given in(Wu et al., 2016) where authors have proposed a searchable encryptionhaving secure channel architecture. Additionally, this scheme offers support to more than one writers and readers in system. However, the computational complexity for a writer is linear to the total number of readers. Besides this, the scheme(Wu et al., 2016)provides a single keyword search only. Furthermore, the recent schemes (Jingzhang et al., 2018; H. Li et al., 2017; Xu et al., 2019)also offer SE for encrypted medical data in multi-reader setting. All these schemes employ the notion of attribute based encryption to control shared data access by multiple readers. In addition, the scheme (Jingzhang et al., 2018)provides attribute update capability whereas (H. Li et al., 2017; Xu et al., 2019)offer search across dynamic database using inverted index search structure. However, in scheme (Xu et al., 2019), database update (insertion/deletion of record) is performed by the centralized TA and hence introduces additional communication overhead between data provider and TA. Such overhead degrades the effectiveness of (Xu et al., 2019)as compared to (H. Li et al., 2017)where data provider himself could update database.

The more recent mechanism for secure sharing of sensitive data collected via smart devices viz. smart pacer, smart band,smart pulse rate monitor, smart glucometer among patients and doctors is proposed in [Swarna2020]. A prime objective of this mechanism is to define Deep Neural Network based Intrusion Detection System to prevent different cyberattacks potentially been performed by attackers on medical data before it reaches to the intended user (doctor). Furthermore, the workpresented in [] is targeted for the emerging field of preventive medicine. The authors in [] proposed two new approaches - variance ranking (attribute selection technique) and ranked order similarity (similarity measurement technique). With this approaches, they work over imbalanced medical dataset and compute minority target class which is especially used for predicting processes in preventive medicine.

Exploring the current literature, it is observed thatthere doesn't exists any PKSE scheme for encrypted medical records with inclusion of multi keyword search capability for the controlled multi-writer multi-reader settings with optimal computational complexity on the data owners (writers).

## CONTRIBUTIONS

In this work, the authors propose a PKSE scheme for E-Health system - **Multi-Keyword Searchable Encryption in Multi-Writer Multi-Reader Setting (MKSE-MWMRS)** that securely shares medical records amongst multiple data writers and data readers. The scheme puts optimal ciphertext computational overhead (that is independent of the number of readers) on writer and optimal ciphertext storage overhead on server. Furthermore, it enables readers to search across the shared data for the chosen query of keywords. The following are the major contributions:

1.  **Controlled multi-writer multi-reader settings**With the proposed scheme, registration is mandatory for each stakeholder (viz. Patient, Doctor, Hospital, Pharmacy etc.) of E-Health system. A stakeholder wishing to share data is registered as Writer whereas a stakeholder wishing to access data is registered as Reader. With registration, each writer (resp. reader) gets a write (resp. read) secret key from the trusted authority. The scheme offers a controlled environment where only the registered writer (possessing a write secret key) can upload data and registered reader (possessing a read secret key) can search data.

2.  **Multi-keyword search** The proposed scheme offers a computationally efficient search algorithm that takes a search token as input. Such token is computed from the chosen query of multiple keywords in conjunctive relation.

3.  **Search Keyword Privacy** In the proposed scheme each searchable ciphertext includes an encrypted payload message and the set of encrypted keywords. The keywords are encrypted using the proposed randomized encryption algorithm that uses write secret key and a random element. Thus, no two ciphertexts are same even if they computed from the same set of keywords. Hence, the storage server possessing a search token would not be able to find the association of keywords with payload unless having write secret key. Such keyword privacy offers security against chosen keyword attack potentially be performed by the server.

4.  **Medical Record Privacy**In the proposed scheme, to offer privacy, a symmetric cipher is used to encrypt each medical record. The symmetric key used to encrypt such record is chosen by each writer separately. Furthermore, to enable a reader to decrypt the record, the writer sends the encrypted form of the chosen symmetric key along with searchable ciphertext. The proposed encryption algorithm defines the way to encrypt the chosen symmetric key besides the way to encrypt keywords. Apparently, no adversary without having symmetric key would be able to decrypt the medical record and hence the proposed scheme offers record privacy.

## PRELIMINARIES

### Bilinear Map

Let $G_1$ and $G_2$ are groups of the prime order p. For $G_1$, assume P is any arbitrary generator. Assume the DLP (Discrete Logarithm Problem) i.e. the standard harness assumption (Pohlig & Hellman, 1978) is hard in $G_1$ as well as in $G_2$. A mapping e: $G_1 \times G_1 \rightarrow G_2$ satisfying the following properties is called **Cryptographic Bilinear Map**(Dutta et al., 2004).

1.  **Bilinearity**$\forall P,Q \in G_1$ and $(a,b) \in Z_p$, $e(aP, bQ) = e(P, Q)^{ab}$.
2.  **Non-degeneracy**$e(P, P) \neq 1$. i.e. if P is a generator of $G_1$, then $e(P, P)$ is a generator of $G_2$ with order p.
3.  **Computability**An efficient algorithm which could compute a pairing e(P, Q) is always existed for all $P, Q \in G_1$.

## Assumption

**Decisional Diffie-Hellman (DDH) Assumption**Assume Gis a finite cyclic subgroups with order p for an elliptic curve. Assume P is a generator of G. Then DDH problem for the given input tuple (P, aP, bP, cP, abP) is to differentiate the tuple (P, aP, bP, abP) from (P, aP, bP,cP). Here a,b,c $\in Z_p$ are random elements. The advantage for an Acan be defined as

$$Adv_A^{DDH} (\lambda) = |\,Pr[A(aP, bP, abP)=1] - Pr[A(aP, bP, cP)=1]\,|$$

Here, $\lambda$is a security parameter. The DDH assumption holds if the advantage $Adv_A^{DDH}(\lambda)$ is negligible.

## FORMAL DEFINITION & SECURITY MODEL

This section describes asystem model, proposed algorithms and a security model.

## System Model

A system model for the proposed MKSE-MWMRS (Figure 2) includes four entities:

1.  **Trusted Authority (TA)** An entity that computes a master public-private key pair as well as system's global parameters. It also performs registration for writers and readers. As a part of registration, it issues a write secret key to the writer and a read secret key to the reader. Additionally, it is responsible to maintain the lists of registered writers and readers onto storage server.
2.  **Writer (WR)** An entity that outsources encrypted medical record(s) to cloud server for providing convenient and reliable data access by the registered readers of the E-Health system. To enable search across encrypted data, it associates a set of encrypted keywords with each medical record. The keywords are encrypted using a write secret key issued by TA.
3.  **Reader (RD)** An entity that generates a search token from the chosen query of keywords in conjunctive form. A token includes a set of query keywords encrypted using read secret key. By issuing a search token, the reader enables the server to search across available medical record(s).
4.  **Cloud Server(CS)** An entity that offers storage for encrypted medical records along and their associated set of keywords. On receiving a search token from the reader, it performs search across the stored sets of keywords and forwards the encrypted medical record to the reader if search is successful. On unsuccessful search, it returns null to the reader.

## Proposed Algorithms

The proposed MKSE-MWMRS provides the following polynomial time algorithms. The notations used are as in Table 2.

1.  **Sys_Init($\lambda$,n)** Executed by TA

*Figure 2. System Model*

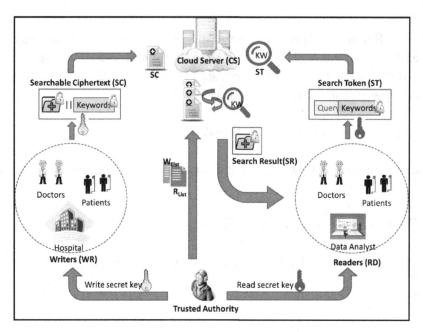

From security parameter λ, the ***System Initialization*** algorithm firstly defines a keyword space K for n keyword fields. It also considers any standard symmetric cipher for encryption of original medical

*Table 2. List of Notations*

| Symbol | Description |
|---|---|
| K | Keyword Space |
| GP | Global parameter |
| (MPK, MSK) | Master Public Key, Master Secret Key |
| $ID_r$, $ID_w$ | Unique Identifierfor a reader and a writer |
| $W_{sc}$, $W_{sr}$ | Write secret key, Write server key |
| $R_{sc}$, $R_{sr}$ | Read secret key, Read server key |
| $W_{List}$, $R_{List}$ | Listsshowing registered Writers and Readers |
| M | Medical record in plaintext |
| $\ell$ | Total Keywords in query |
| SC | Searchable ciphertext |
| n | Total Keywords in ciphertext |
| K | $K=\{k_1, k_2, ..., k_n\}$, a set of keywords in ciphertext |
| K' | $K'=\{k_1, k_2, ..., k_\ell\}$, a set of query keywords where $\ell <= n$ |
| Q | A conjunctive query Q comprises of two sets {K',P'} where K' is as mentioned above and $P'=\{p_1, p_2, ..., p_\ell\}$ is a set of positions of query keywords in ciphertext. |
| $ST_Q$ | Search Token computed from query Q |
| $SR_Q$ | Search Result for query Q |

records. TA then generates the global parameter GP and a master key pair (MPK, MSK). It also generates the lists of registered writers and readers as $W_{List}$ and $R_{List}$ respectively. TA sends these lists with the initial empty value to CS.

2. **WR_Reg(ID$_w$,GP, MSK)** Executed by TA

The TA uses *Writer Registration* algorithm to register a new data writer possessing ID$_w$. The algorithm uses MSK to compute a write secret key $W_{sc}$ for the registered writer and the associated server side key $W_{sr}$. For each new registered writer, TA updates $W_{List}$ at CS.

3. **RD_Reg(ID$_r$,GP,MSK)** Executed by TA

The TA uses *Reader Registration* algorithm to register a new reader possessing ID$_r$. The algorithm uses MSK to compute a read secret key $R_{sc}$ for the registered reader and the associated server side key $R_{sr}$. For each new registered reader, TA updates $R_{List}$ at CS.

4. **Encryption(ID$_w$,GP, MPK, W$_{sc}$,K, M)** Executed by WR possessing ID$_w$

The *Encryption* algorithm first computes encrypted input medical record M'=Enc$_{key}$(M). Here, 'Enc' is any predefined symmetric cipher with key. The algorithm then encrypts 'key' using $W_{sc}$ and generates encrypted key 'key''. It also computes a ciphertext C by encrypting keywords in list K={$k_1$,$k_2$,...,$k_n$} using (GP,MPK,$W_{sc}$). Finally, it outputs a searchable ciphertext SC=(C,M',key',ID$_w$).

5. **SC_Store(SC,W$_{List}$)** Executed by CS

The *Ciphertext Store* algorithm first checks the authenticity of the received SC using available $W_{List}$. The algorithm stores SC only if it comes from the authenticated writer.

6. **TokGen(ID$_r$, GP, R$_{sc}$, Q)** Executed by RD possessing ID$_r$

The *Token Generation* algorithm generates a search token ST$_Q$ for input query Q=(K',P') by encrypting keywords in query using (GP,R$_{sc}$). Here, K'={$k'_1$,$k'_2$,...,$k'_\ell$} is a set of query keywords and P'={$p_1$, $p_2$,..., $p_\ell$} shows their positions in ciphertext.

7. **Search(GP,SC, ST$_Q$,R$_{sr}$,R$_{List}$)** Executed by CS

The *Search* algorithm first checks the authenticity of the received ST$_Q$ using available $R_{List}$. If token is from genuine reader, then the algorithm performs conjunctive search by applying ST$_Q$ on ciphertext C of SC using $R_{sr}$. For the successful search, the algorithm returns SR$_Q$=(M',key'). Otherwise, it returns SR$_Q$=⊥.

8. **WR_Dereg(ID$_w$,W$_{List}$)** Executed by TA

The **Writer Deregistration** algorithm revokes the writer WR (having $ID_w$) by removing its entry from $W_{List}$. It then updates $W_{List}$ at CS.

9.  **RD_Dereg($ID_r$, $R_{List}$)** Executed by TA

The **Reader Deregistration** algorithm revokes the reader RD (having $ID_r$) by removing its entry from $R_{List}$. It then updates $R_{List}$ at CS.

10.  **Decryption($SR_Q$, $R_{sc}$)** Executed by RD

The **Decryption** algorithm first decrypts encrypted key key' using $R_{sc}$. It then applies the predefined symmetric cipher with key onto M' to generate original medical record M.

**Assumptions:** (i) There exist secure communication channels amongst entities, (ii) The CS is a semi-honest server which is curious to learn plaintext keywords from the set of encrypted keywords and token, (iii) TA assigns a unique identifier$ID_r$ to each reader and $ID_w$ to each data writer after physical document verification.

## Security Model

The assumption for the proposed cloud storage based E-Health System is that the trusted authority as well as the registered writers and readers are honest entities and they follow the proposed algorithms. Besides this, assume that the server is semi-honest who honestly follows the algorithms but curious to acquire the underlined meaning of the stored medical records. Consequently the server could attempt to get information available within an encrypted record by decrypting it. The server could also try to identify the keywords from the available searchable ciphertexts and tokens that include list of encrypted keywords. Against this adversary, the authors proposes semantic security (aka. indistinguishability of ciphertext against chosen keyword attack (IND-CKA)) following the security game ICLR (Indistinguishability of Ciphertext from Limited Random) (Golle et al., 2004; M.-S. Hwang et al., 2014; Lee et al., 2013).

## Game ICLR

Assume **A** is a polynomial bounded adversary and **B** is a challenger algorithm. In ICLR game, when **A** issues a set K of 'n' keywords and a subset T⊆{1,2,...,n}, **B** responses with two encrypted keyword sets that are associated with T in the way that **A** can't differentiate the encrypted keyword sets created with T. Hence **A** can't deduce keywords from the other keyword sets. The phases defined for the proposed game are as follows:

1.  **Setup Phase** Initially, **B** runs the algorithm **Sys_Init()** and generates the system's global public parameter GP as well as a master key pair (MPK, MSK). It also registers writers and readers by running the appropriate **WR_Reg()** or **RD_Reg()**. Accordingly, each registered writer has given a write secret key $W_{sc}$ and each reader has given a read secret key $R_{sc}$. The corresponding server side keys i.e. $W_{sr}$ and $R_{sr}$ are also given to **A**.

2.  **Query Phase** After system setup, an adversary **A** adaptively requests **B** for ciphertext and token for the chosen sets of keywords $k_i$ and the chosen query $Q_i$. In response to the ciphertext

query for K keywords, **B** executes SC←Encryption($\text{ID}_w$,GP,MPK,$W_{sc}$,K,M) and sends SC to **A**. Furthermore, in response to search token query for the conjunctive query keywords Q, **B** executes $\text{ST}_Q$←TokGen($\text{ID}_r$,GP,$R_{sc}$,Q) and sends $\text{ST}_Q$ to **A**. In addition, **A** may ask for ciphertexts and tokens for the chosen sets of keywords in this phase repeatedly.

3. **Challenge Phase** In this phase, **A** takes the keyword set K, a subset T⊆{1,2,...,n} and σ ∈T in the way that no token given in **Query Phase** are distinguishing the sets generated by Rand(K,T) and Rand(K,T–{σ}). Here, Rand(K,T) generates a set K where keywords indexed by T (i.e. the set {$k_i$ | i ∈T}) are replaced by random values. **A** then sends (K,T,σ) to challenger **B**. In response, **B** generates two keyword sets $K_0$=Rand(K,T–{σ}) and $K_1$=Rand(K,T). Further, **B** randomly selects b∈{0,1} and returns a challenge ciphertext SC←Encryption($\text{ID}_w$,GP,MPK,$W_{sc}$,$K_b$,M) to **A.**

4. **Repeat Query Phase** Here, **A** can again query for ciphertexts and tokens for the chosen sets of keywords. However, the restriction is that **A** can't make request for the token that is distinguishing for $K_0$ and $K_1$.

5. **Guess Phase** From the available tokens, and challenge ciphertext, **A** tries to guess a bit b'∈{0,1}. Apparently, he could win ICLR game for b'=b.

The following is the advantage (ε) for adversary **A** in winning the ICLR

$$\text{Adv}_A(\lambda) = |\text{Pr}[b' = b] - \tfrac{1}{2}| \geq \epsilon$$

For the negligible advantage ε, the proposed MKSE-MWMRS is IND-CKA secure.

## DETAILS OF MKSE-MWMRS

This section presents the formal construction of MKSE-MWMRS along with the security proof for medical record as well as for encrypted keywords.

### Construction

MKSE-MWMRS works in 5 stages: *System Initialization, Registration and Deregistration, Record Storage, Record Search, Record Retrieval.*

### System Initialization

The Trusted Authority (TA) sets up a system by running the following system initialization algorithm.

**Sys_Init(λ,n)** Following this algorithm, TA takes security parameter λ to generate two bilinear group $G_1$ and $G_2$ of the same prime order p with P be the generator of $G_1$. Then TA takes a bilinear map e:$G_1$× $G_1$→$G_2$ and a hash function H:{0,1}*→$Z_p$*. It defines a keyword space K of n keyword fields where position of each field is prefixed. TA also considers a standard symmetric cipher SYMM(Set(),Enc(),Dec(),key) where Set(),Enc() and Dec() are the algorithms as SGP← Set(), M'←$\text{Enc}_{key}$(M) and M←$\text{Dec}_{key}$(M'). Here SGP is the global parameter for SYMM.

Further, TA selects random elements $\alpha$, $\beta$, $\gamma \in Z_p^*$ and computes $PK_1 = \alpha P$, $PK_2 = \beta P$ and $PK_3 = \gamma P$. It then sets the global parameter as $GP = \{G_1, G_2, e, P, H, n, K, SGP\}$, a master public key as $MPK = \{PK_1, PK_2\}$, a master secret key as $MSK = \{\alpha, \beta\}$ and an encryption element $E = \{PK_3\}$.

Additionally, TA prepares $W_{List}$ and $R_{List}$ with two fields i.e. $W_{List} = \{ID_w, W_{sr}\}$ and $R_{List} = \{ID_r, R_{sr}\}$. It then stores both lists with initial empty fields i.e. $W_{List} = \{\perp, \perp\}$, $R_{List} = \{\perp, \perp\}$ onto CS.

## Registration and Deregistration

The TA manages all writers and readers by registering them on demand. TA can also revoke the registered writers and readers by deregistering them. The algorithms for registration and deregistration are as follows:

**WR_Reg($ID_w$, GP, MSK, E)** To register a new writer possessing $ID_w$, TA first selects $w \in Z_p^*$ at random. Using input (GP, MSK, E), he sets a write secret key as $W_{sc} = \{w, E\}$ and the corresponding server side key as $W_{sr} = \{wP\}$. TA then issues $W_{sc}$ to writer and updates $W_{List}$ on CS by setting $W_{List} = W_{List} \cup \{ID_w, W_{sr}\}$.

**RD_Reg($ID_r$, GP, MSK, E)** To register a new reader possessing $ID_r$, TA first selects $u \in Z_p^*$ at random. Using input (GP, MSK), he sets a read secret key as $R_{sc} = \{u_1 = k, u_2 = (\beta - u)P, E\}$ and the corresponding server side key as $R_{sr} = \{u\}$. TA then issues $R_{sc}$ to reader and updates $R_{List}$ on CS by setting $R_{List} = R_{List} \cup \{ID_r, R_{sr}\}$.

**WR_Dereg($ID_w$, $W_{List}$)** To revoke a registered writer possessing $ID_w$, TA updates a local $W_{List}$ as $W_{List} = W_{List} - \{ID_w, W_{sr}\}$. He then replaces the old $W_{List}$ at CS with this new $W_{List}$.

**RD_Dereg($ID_r$, $R_{List}$)** To revoke a registered reader possessing $ID_r$, TA updates a local $R_{List}$ as $R_{List} = R_{List} - \{ID_r, R_{sr}\}$. He then replaces the old $R_{List}$ at CS with this new $R_{List}$.

## Record Storage

In this stage, a registered writer WR constructs a searchable ciphertext SC and forwards it to storage server CS. Further, CS checks the authenticity of the received ciphertext and stores it if valid. The algorithm for ciphertext construction i.e. *Encryption()* and for ciphertext storage i.e. *SC_Store()* are as follows.

**Encryption ($ID_w$, GP, MPK, $W_{sc}$, K, M)** A writer possessing $ID_w$ first selects a symmetric **key** for the cipher SYMM and computes encrypted medical record $M' = E_{key}(M)$. He then encrypts **key** using an encryption element $E \in W_{sc}$ as key' = key $\oplus E$. Further, from an input list of keywords $K = \{k_1, k_2, ..., k_n\}$, the writer WR computes a ciphertext $C = \{C_{1i}, C_2\}$. Here, $C_{1i} = r(H(k_i)PK_1 + PK_2) + wP$ and $C_2 = rP$ for a random $r \in Z_p^*$ and $1 \leq i \leq n$. Finally, WR offloads the searchable ciphertext as $SC = \{C, M', key', ID_w\}$ onto CS.

**SC_Store(SC, $W_{List}$)** Following this algorithm, CS first checks the authenticity of each input SC by verifying the entry of $ID_w \in SC$ in the available list $W_{List}$. If $ID_w \in W_{List}$, then CS updates SC by replacing $C_{1i} = C_{1i} - W_{sr}$ for $1 \leq i \leq n$. He then stores this updated SC onto storage space. On the other hand, if $ID_w \notin W_{List}$, then CS rejects the input SC.

## Record Search

To search a medical record, a registered reader first computes a search token and issues it to CS. On receiving a token, CS first checks the authenticity of token. If token is sent by the registered reader, then CS uses this token to perform conjunctive search on the available SC. The algorithm for computation of a search token i.e. *TokGen()* and its application on SC to perform search i.e. *Search()* are as follows.

**TokGen(ID$_r$,GP,R$_{sc}$,Q)** Any registered reader possessing ID$_r$ and the corresponding R$_{sc}$ can compute a search token from the chosen conjunctive query Q=(K',P'). Here, K'={k'$_1$,k'$_2$,...,k'$_\ell$}is a set of query keywords and P'={p$_1$,p$_2$,...,p$_\ell$} shows their positions in ciphertext. Such a search token is ST$_Q$={ST$_1$,ST$_2$,P',ID$_r$} where ST$_1$=t($\sum$(H(k'$_j$)u$_1$P + u$_2$)) for p$_1 \leq$j$\leq$p$_\ell$and ST$_2$ = tP for a random t $\in$Z$_p$*. The reader RD then sends ST$_Q$ to CS to perform search across available SCs.

**Search(GP,SC,ST$_Q$,R$_{sr}$,R$_{List}$)**For the input search token ST$_Q$, the CS first checks its authenticity by verifying the entry of ID$_r \in$ST$_Q$ in the available list R$_{List}$. If ID$_r \in$R$_{List}$, then CS computes C'=$\sum$C$_{1i}$ and T'=ST$_1$-($\ell$R$_{sr}$ST$_2$) where $\ell$=|P'|. He then perform search by checking the equality

$$e(C',ST_2) = e(T',C_2) \tag{1}$$

If the above Eq. (1) holds, the CS returns the search result SR$_Q$=(M',key'), else it returns SR$_Q$=$\perp$.

## Record Retrieval

Once the receiver RD gets the search result SR$_Q$=(M',key') from CS, he retrieves the original medical record by using *Decryption( )* algorithm as follows

**Decryption(SR$_Q$,R$_{sc}$)** The RD first decrypts key' using E$\in$R$_{sc}$ as key=key'$\oplus$E. He then generates the plaintext medical record as M=Dec$_{key}$(M').

## Correctness Analysis

The authors demonstrates that the correctly generated search token can search across correctly generated ciphertext. The proof for the correctness of the equality Eq. (1) is as follows.

For a valid ST$_Q$, the proposed *Search( )* algorithm computes

C' = $\sum$ C$_{1i}$for p$_1 \leq$ i $\leq$p$_\ell$

= r(H(k$_{p1}$)$\alpha$P + $\beta$P) + r(H(k$_{p2}$)$\alpha$P + $\beta$P) + ... + r(H(k$_{p\ell}$)$\alpha$P + $\beta$P)

= rP($\sum$(H(k$_i$)$\alpha$) + ($\ell\beta$)) for p$_1 \leq$ i $\leq$p$_\ell$

T' = ST$_1$ - ($\ell$R$_{sr}$T$_2$)

= t($\sum$(H(k'$_j$)u$_1$P + u$_2$)) - ($\ell$R$_{sr}$T$_2$) for p$_1 \leq$ j $\leq$p$_\ell$

= t($\sum$(H(k'$_j$)$\alpha$P + ($\beta$-u)P)) - ($\ell$utP)

= t($\sum$(H(k'$_j$)$\alpha$P)) + ($\ell$t$\beta$P) - ($\ell$tuP) - ($\ell$utP)

= t($\sum$(H(k'$_j$)$\alpha$P) + ($\ell\beta$P))

= tP($\sum$(H(k'$_j$)$\alpha$) + ($\ell\beta$))

The equality is then checked i.e. e(C',ST$_2$) = e(T',C$_2$) where

e(C',ST$_2$) = e(rP($\sum$(H(k$_i$)$\alpha$) + ($\ell\beta$)),tP) for p$_1 \leq$ i $\leq$p$_\ell$

= e(P,P)$^{(rt(\sum(H(ki)\alpha) + (\ell\beta))}$ (2)

e(T',C$_2$)= e(tP((H(k'$_j$)$\alpha$) + ($\ell\beta$)),rP) p$_1 \leq$ j $\leq$p$_\ell$

= e(P,P)$^{(rt(\sum(H(kj)\alpha) + (\ell\beta))}$ (3)

From Eq. (2) and (3), L.H.S. = R.H.S if (k$_i$=k'$_j$ and i=j).

## Security Analysis

The authors here analyze security of MKSE-MWMRS. The security proof for the medical records is given in **Theorem 1** whereas security for the corresponding keywords is described **Theorem 2**. With Theorem 1, the authors prove that the adversary including storage server would not be able to get plaintext from the encrypted medical records and thus security of medical records is proved. With Theorem 2, the authors prove that the cloud server with available search tokens and challenge ciphertext would not be able to learn keywords in plaintext under DDH assumption and so the security for ciphertexts against chosen keyword attack (IND-CKA) has been proved.

**Theorem 1:** A medical record in the proposed MKSE-MWMRS is secure.

*Proof*: In the proposed scheme, the TA during system initialization phase chooses any standard symmetric cipher SYMM=(*Set(), Enc(), Dec()*) to encrypt/decrypt a medical record M. In addition, it publishes the global parameter of such a symmteric cipher SGP with system's global parameter GP. As a result, SGP is available to each registered writer and reader. As discussed in the proposed *Encryption()*, a writer first selects a secret key '**key**' and computes an encrypted medical record as M' $\leftarrow$ Enc$_{key}$(M). Subsequently, he secures the selected '**key**' by encrypting it as key'=key$\oplus$ E where E is the encryption element issued by TA only to the registered writers and readers. The writer then sends (key',M') along with encrypted keywords as a searchable ciphertext SC to the cloud server CS for further storage.

For any adversary **A** (including CS) in such a scheme, to learn a plaintext record M from the available SC, it is indeed necessary to get decryption (symmetric) key 'key'. However, 'key' available within SC is already encrypted by writer using E. Such an encryption component E is actually been generated by TA using secret element $\gamma$. Thus, the probability of **A** to compute record M is equivalent to computing E. Since, E is only available to the registered reader and writer, no adversary would be able to learn M from the available (M',key') with negligible probability. Thus, it can be claimed that a medical record shared with the proposed MKSE-MWMRS is indeed secure.

**Theorem 2:** The MKSE-MWMRS is IND-CKA secure if DDH assumption holds.

*Proof*: Consider a polynomial time adversary **A** who makes maximum q(<p) token queries with a non-negligible advantage $\epsilon$ in solving DDH problem in G$_1$. Assume that there exist two bilinear groups G$_1$ and G$_2$ having same prime order p with P be the generator of G$_1$. For such a setup, there exist an algorithm **B**(simulator) as a challenger having an advantage $\epsilon$'to simulate the security game. Here $\epsilon$'=$\epsilon$/(nqe$^n$) where e is a base of natural logarithm.

Consider a tuple (aP, bP, cP) as DDH challenge in G$_1$ for **B** where a,b,c $\in Z_p$* are the randomly selected elements. The aim of **B** is to differentiate cP=abP from the random element of G$_1$. To do so, **B** uniformly selects a position z that is independent of position $\sigma$ selected by **A** during *Challenge Phase* of the game ICLR. The simulation for ICLR can be as follows:

1. **Setup Phase** In this phase, TA selects random elements $\alpha$, $\beta$, $\gamma \in Z_p$* and computes PK$_1$= $\alpha$P, PK$_2$=$\beta$P and PK$_3$=$\gamma$P. It then sets the Global Parameter GP={G$_1$,G$_2$,e,P,H,n,K},Master Public Key MSK={PK$_1$, PK$_2$}, Master Secret Key as MSK={$\alpha$,$\beta$} and Encryption element E={PK$_3$}. Afterwards, TA publishes (GP, MPK). Thus, **A** and **B** have (GP,MPK). TA also provides W$_{sc}$={w,E} and R$_{sc}$={u$_1$=k,u$_2$=($\beta$ - u)P,E} to **B** for random element w,u $\in Z_p$*. In addition, TA sends the server side keys W$_{sr}$={wP} and R$_{sr}$={u} to **A**.

2. **Query Phase** Here, **A** adaptively requests **B** for the ciphertexts for the chosen sets of keywords K$_i$ and tokens for queries Q$_i$ where $1 \leq i \leq q$.

As a ciphertext query, **A** sends a keyword set $K=\{k_1,k_2,...,k_n\}$ to **B**. In response, **B** executes *Encryption(ID_w,GP,MPK,W_sc,K,M)* as follows:

For every keyword $k_i \in K$ where $1 \leq i \leq n$, **B** randomly selects $\gamma_i \in Z_p^*$, $r \in Z_p^*$ and computes $C=\{C_{1i},C_2\}$ $_{\{1 \leq i \leq n\}}$. Here, $C_{11}=r(\gamma_1 PK_1 + PK_2)+(wP)$, $C_{12}=r(\gamma_2 PK_1 + PK_2)+(wP)$, $C_{1z}=br(\gamma_z PK_1+ PK_2 +(wP))$, ..., $C_{1n}=r(\gamma_n PK_1 + PK_2)+(wP)$, and $C_2=rP$. Finally, **B** sends C to **A**. Furthermore, **A** collects multiple such ciphertexts $C_i$ of the chosen $K_i$ where $1 \leq i \leq q$. For each available ciphertext, **A** checks authenticity and stores only valid ciphertexts by running *SC_Store()* algorithm. Note that the given theorem concerns only keywords security, and thus the other parameters of searchable ciphertext are ignored here.

To get a search token, **A** sends a token query $Q=(K',P')$ where $K'=\{k'_{p1},k'_{p2},...,k'_{p\ell}\}$ and $P'=\{p_1,p_2,...,p_\ell\}$ to **B**. In response **B** executes *TokGen(ID_r,GP,R_sc,Q)* as follows:

**B** randomly selects $t \in Z_p^*$ and computes $ST_1=(t \cdot (\sum(H(k'_j)u_1 P + u_2))$ for $p_1 \leq j \leq p_\ell$, $ST_2=tP$. **B** then sends $ST_Q$ to **A**. Furthermore, **A** collects multiple such tokens $ST_{Qi}$ for different queries $Q_i$ for $1 \leq i \leq q$.

3. **Challenge Phase** In this phase, **A** issues a tuple $(K,T, \sigma)$ to simulator **B** with $\sigma \in T$ and $T \subseteq \{1,n\}$.

In response **B** checks the selected z. If $z \neq \sigma$, **B** issues a random guess as a response of DDH challenge. This implies that **B** sends challenge ciphertext $C_0$ with random values for all keywords in $K_i$.

If $z=\sigma$, **B** sends $C_1$ with encrypted keywords computed as follows

**B** first sets $C_{1\sigma}^*=c(\gamma_\sigma PK_1+PK_2)$. Then for $i \neq \sigma$, $i \in T$, it sets $C_{1i}^*=\ell_i'$ where $\ell_i' \in Z_p^*$. Furthermore, for $i \neq \sigma$, $i \notin T$, **B** sets $C_{1i}^*=a(\gamma_i PK_1 + PK_2)$. Besides these, it computes $C_2^*=aP$.

Finally, **B** sends **A** the challenge ciphertext $(C_{1i}^*,C_2^*)$ where $1 \leq i \leq n$. **A** then wins the security game if $z = \sigma$. Note that the received ciphertext is encryption of keywords $k_i$ for every $i \notin T$. On the other hand, the received ciphertext is an encrypted form of $w_\sigma$ for position $\sigma$ where $c=ab$. The ciphertexts for the elements at the other positions are random values.

4. **Repeat Query Phase** In this phase, **A** asks for ciphertexts for various keyword sets. He also asks for tokens for different chosen queries. **B** responses in the similar way as there in *Query Phase*. The constraint here is **A** can't issue the above queries for a location $\sigma$.

5. **Guess Phase** Finally, from the available tokens, and challenge ciphertext, **A** guesses a bit $b' \in \{0,1\}$. If $b' =1$, **B** outputs 'Yes', and (aP,bP,cP) is considered as a DDH tuple. So, for $z=\sigma$, a proof showing (aP,bP,cP) as DDH tuple is as follows.

As know, *Search()* includes the equality check

$$e(C',ST_2) = e(T',C_2) \tag{4}$$

where

$$e(C',ST_2) =e(br(\gamma_z PK_1+PK_2), tP)$$

$$= e(br(\gamma_z \alpha P+\beta P), tP)$$

$$= e(P,P)^{(brt(\gamma z)\alpha+\beta)} \tag{5}$$

$e(T',C_2) = e(t\,(H(k_z)\alpha P + \beta P),\, rP)$

$$= e(P, P)^{(rt(H(kz)\alpha+\beta))} \qquad (6)$$

Using challenge ciphertext,

$e(C',ST_2) = e(c(\gamma_\sigma PK_1 + PK_2),\, tP)$

$= e(c(\gamma_\sigma \alpha P + \beta P),\, tP)$

$$= e(P,P)^{(ct(\gamma\sigma)\alpha+\beta)} \qquad (7)$$

$e(T',C_2) = e(t\,(H(k_z)\alpha P + \beta P),\, aP)$

$$= e(P, P)^{at\,(H(kz)\alpha+\beta)} \qquad (8)$$

From the above Eq. (5), (6), (7), (8)

$e(P,P)^{(brt(\gamma z)\alpha+\beta)}/e(P,P)^{(rt\,(H(kz)\alpha+\beta))} = e(P,P)^{(ct\,(\gamma\sigma)\alpha+\beta)}/e(P,P)^{at\,(H(kz)\alpha+\beta)}$

$e(P,P)^{(brt(\gamma z)\alpha+\beta)} \cdot e(P,P)^{at(H(kz)\alpha+\beta)} = e(P,P)^{(ct(\gamma\sigma)\alpha+\beta)} \cdot e(P,P)^{(rt(H(kz)\alpha+\beta))}$

$e(P,P)^{(abt(\gamma z)\alpha+\beta)} \cdot e(P,P)^{rt(H(kz)\alpha+\beta)} = e(P,P)^{(ct(\gamma\sigma)\alpha+\beta)} \cdot e(P,P)^{(rt\,(H(kz)\alpha+\beta))}$

$e(P,P)^{(abt(\gamma z)\alpha+\beta)} = e(P, P)^{(ct(\gamma\sigma)\alpha+\beta)}$

$$ab = c \qquad (9)$$

Furthermore, the given challenge (aP,bP,cP) can't be proved as DDH tuple in case of b'=0 since the challenge ciphertext includes random element at position *i* and so the Eq. (9) can't confirm.

The simulations for **B**'sthe advantage are: (i)S1 where **B**responses with the token queries for n keyword sent by **A** and (ii) S2 where **B** is not aborting in a challenge phase.

The probability of S1 and S2(for large enough q) is defined as

$Pr[S1]=1/e^n$ and $Pr[S2]=1/(nq)$

Thus, advantage for **B**to solve DDH problem is $\epsilon' = \epsilon \cdot Pr[S1 \cap S2] = \epsilon/(nqe^n)$.

As per the propositions discussed in(Golle et al., 2004), if an adversary with non-negligible advantage in winning ICC(Indistinguishability of Ciphertext from Ciphertext) game is available, then there exists an another adversary with the non-negligible advantage in winning ICLR game. However, **B**'s advantage is $\epsilon/(nqe^n) \in [0, 1/2(nqe^n)]$ which is negligible. Thus, the MKSE-MWMRS is at least $(1-1/2\,(nqe^n))$ secure in ICLR game providing DDH assumption holds. This proves **Theorem 2**.

*Table 3. Comparative Analysis*

| Analysis Parameters | | (Wu et al., 2016) | (Jingzhang et al., 2018) | (Sharma & Jinwala, n.d.) | MKSE-MWMRS |
|---|---|---|---|---|---|
| **Characteristics** | **Type of Search** | Single-Keyword | Multi-Keyword (Exact) | Multi-Keyword (Conjunctive) | Multi-Keyword (Conjunctive) |
| | **Controlled MWMR** | No | Yes | No | Yes |
| | **Record Encryption/ Decryption** | Yes | Yes | No | Yes |
| **Storage Overhead** | **On Cloud Server** | $(1+n+R)G_1+G_2$ | $(3+2A)G_1+G_2$ | $(1+n)G_1+C$ | $(2+n)G_1+C$ |
| **Computational Overhead** | **On Writer (during Encryption())** | $(2+n+R)E+P+$ Enc | $(5+3A)E+P+$ Enc | $(1+2n)M+$ Enc | $(3+2n)M+$ Enc |
| | **On Reader (during TokGen())** | $2E$ | $(8+2A)E$ | $(1+\ell)M$ | $(1+\ell)M$ |
| | **On Server (during Search())** | $2nP$ | $(3+2A)P+AE$ | $1M+2P$ | $1M+2P$ |
| | **On Reader (during Decryption()** | $1E+1P+$Dec | $(1+2A)P+$Dec | - | $1X+$Dec |

**n**: Total keywords in ciphertext, $\ell$: Total keywords in a query, **R**: Total readers in system, **A**: Number of attributes in policyused in CPABE ciphertext, **C**: Size of ciphertextoutput by symmetric encryption, $G_1$, $G_2$: Element Size for bilinear groups$G_1$ and $G_2$, **P**: Pairing, **E**: Exponentiatio, **X**: Ex-OR,**M**: Scalar Multiplication, (**Enc, Dec**): Computationaloverhead incurred by Encryption and Decryption algorithm of the used symmetric cipher

## PERFORMANCE ANALYSIS

The performance analysis of MKSE-MWMRS as compared to the existing multi-writer, multi-reader searchable schemes especially designed for secure sharing of medical records(Jingzhang et al., 2018; Sharma & Jinwala, n.d.; Wu et al., 2016) is given in this section.

### Theoretical Comparison

The theoretical comparison of MKSE-MWMRS with the schemes(Jingzhang et al., 2018; Sharma & Jinwala, n.d.; Wu et al., 2016) is given in Table 3. Focusing on the characteristics offered by each of the listed schemes, it could be determine that though the scheme (Jingzhang et al., 2018)provides multi-keyword search similar to the proposed MKSE-MWMRS, it can search for the exact set of keywords only. On the other hand, though the scheme (Sharma & Jinwala, n.d.)performs conjunctive keyword search, it doesn't offer controlled environment for multiple writers and readers as that in MKSE-MWM. More precisely, in (Sharma & Jinwala, n.d.)any data owner knowing public key can write ciphertexts onto the storage server. With such an uncontrolled environment, the storage server could be overloaded by malicious writers. Furthermore, the scheme (Sharma & Jinwala, n.d.)doesn't discuss encryption/decryption mechanism to securely share medical records.

In addition, Table 3demonstrates the storage overhead (ciphertext size) on the server for the scheme (Wu et al., 2016)which is O(n+R) where n=total number of keywords in ciphertext and R=total number of readers in system. Such scheme is impractical in comparison with MKSE-MWMRS and (Sharma &

*Table 4. Simulation Parameters*

| Parameter | Simulation Values |
|---|---|
| n | {10,25, 50, 75, 100} |
| $\ell$ | {10,20,30,40,50} |
| R | {100, 200, 300, 400, 500} |

Jinwala, n.d.)where storage overhead is optimal (independent from R) i.e. O(n). On the other hand, the storage complexity for the scheme (Jingzhang et al., 2018) is O(|A|) where |A|=total number of attributes involved in policy associated with CPABE ciphertext. Though the scheme offers optimal overhead, the size ofA affects the storage overhead. More precisely, increasing the size of A offers strong access control whereas setting |A|=1, any reader possessing only a single attribute satisfying access policy would be able to get ciphertexts from the server.

Furthermore, the ciphertext computational overhead suffered by the writers in the proposed MKSE-MWMRS is optimal i.e. O(n) as compared to the schemes- (Wu et al., 2016) with complexity O(n+R) and(Jingzhang et al., 2018)with complexity O(A). Such optimal complexity makes the proposed scheme more acceptable in practical applications. In addition, the scheme(Wu et al., 2016)puts constant overhead O(1) on reader during token generation. However, with such an overhead, the reader could generate a token for a single keyword search. On the other side, though the scheme (Jingzhang et al., 2018)generates a token for multi-keyword search with overhead O(A), the server with such a token can search for the exact match of keyword sets. For the proposed scheme, a reader could construct a token with computational complexity O($\ell$)same as the scheme (Sharma & Jinwala, n.d.). However, the server receiving such a token would be able to perform conjunctive search. Furthermore, with the proposed scheme, the server could perform conjunctive search across available ciphertexts with constant computational complexity O(1). With such optimal search complexity, the proposed scheme performs much more better than the scheme (Wu et al., 2016) with search overhead O(n) and the scheme (Jingzhang et al., 2018) with overhead in O(A). Additionally, from Table 3 one woulddetermine that the result processing cost besides actual decryption in proposed scheme is optimal (involving only one EX-OR operation). With such a cost, MKSE-MWMRS performs record decryption faster than the schemes(Jingzhang et al., 2018; Wu et al., 2016) involving exponentiation and pairing operations besides actual decryption.

## EXPERIMENTAL EVALUATION

For empirical analysis, the authors simulate the proposed MKSE-MWMRS as well as the existing schemes (Jingzhang et al., 2018; Sharma & Jinwala, n.d.; Wu et al., 2016) on Windows 7 machine having 32-bit, Pentium Core 2 Duo,2.10 GHz CPU. The implementation is done through Java language with JPBC (java pairing based cryptographic) library (De Caro & Iovino, 2011). To build the cryptographic environment, an elliptic curve of*Type A*having160-bit group order and 512-bit field order from JPBC is used.

Since there does not exist any public EHR dataset, the Enron email dataset (Cohen, 2009)is used as test dataset. The randomly chosen emails from this dataset are used as M to simulate the algorithms. Furthermore from javax.crypto package, the standard AES algorithm (128-bit key) is usedfor encryption/decryption of payload message M. Additionally, a keyword space K of size n=100 keyword fields relevant to the Email system is prepared. The experimental results are demonstrated with respect to three parameters: the number of keywords in ciphertext (n), number of Keywords in a query ($\ell$), and the number of readers in the system (R). The simulation is performed at least 10 times for different values of each of these parameters (Table4) and the average value is considered as the final result. The simulation results for *Encryption(), TokGen(),Search()* algorithms are shown in Figure3, 4, 5respectively. Note that to simulate the scheme (Jingzhang et al., 2018), the authors consider the number of attributes A=10 for average case analysis.

*Figure 3. Simulation Results: Encryption()*

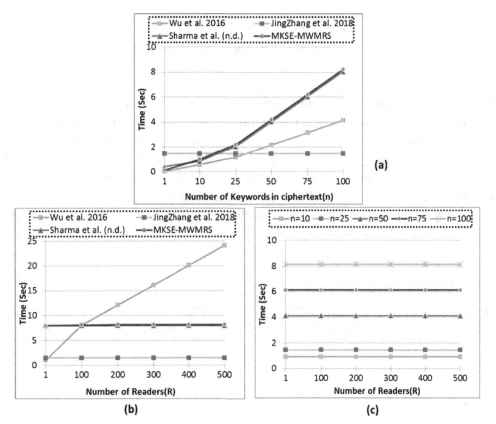

(a)

(b)

(c)

The results in Figure 3(a) show that the encryption costinMKSE-MWMRSis linearly proportional to **n** as that in the other MWMR schemes (Sharma & Jinwala, n.d.; Wu et al., 2016). However, the provision of the controlled multi-writer multi-reader support makes the proposed *Encryption()* algorithm slower than the encryption algorithms of(Sharma & Jinwala, n.d.; Wu et al., 2016). On the other hand, though the scheme (Jingzhang et al., 2018)reflects efficiency with constant encryption cost on writer, the computed ciphertext can't support conjunctive keyword search which is more desirable in real-life applications. Additionally, Figure 3 (b) shows that the *Encryption()*is not affected by the existence of multiple readers in system. The scheme (Wu et al., 2016) on the other hand offers multi-reader support with the computational overhead linear to **R** on the writer. Besides this, the Figure 3 (c) represents that

*Figure 4. Simulation results: TokGen()*

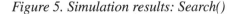

though the encryption complexity is constant even in case of more than one reader, the increasing values of keywords(n) in ciphertextindeed affects the performance of *Encryption()* algorithm.

The results in Figure 4 show that the computational complexity of the proposed *TokGen()* algorithm is linear to the keywords in query, unlike the schemes (Jingzhang et al., 2018; Wu et al., 2016). However, with this overhead, the proposed algorithm generates a search token for the given conjunctive query that ultimately supports conjunctive search. The other remarkable point is that with the almost same token generation cost as that in (Sharma & Jinwala, n.d.), the proposed scheme offers the controlled environment for multiple readers and writers in system.

*Figure 5. Simulation results: Search()*

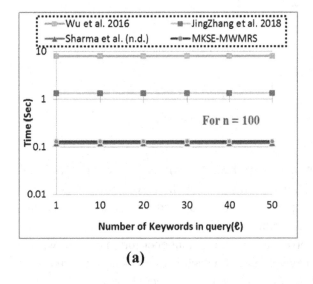

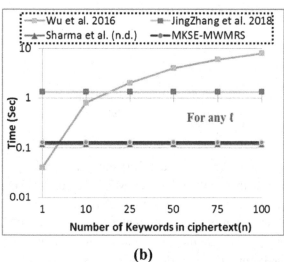

(a)　　　　　　　　　　　　　　　　(b)

The Figure 5 (a) demonstrates that the computation cost for the *Search()* is constant regardless of the number of keywords in query as that in (Jingzhang et al., 2018; Sharma & Jinwala, n.d.; Wu et al.,

2016). More specifically, the proposed scheme provides conjunctive search with reduced computational overhead on server in comparison to the overhead incurred by the schemes(Jingzhang et al., 2018; Wu et al., 2016) and so it is more practical.

Furthermore, Figure 5 (b) shows that efficiency of *Search()* is never affected by the number of keywords in ciphertexts(n). However, it indeed degrades the search performance of (Wu et al., 2016).

Finally, it could be infer that that with the almost same computational overhead as in (Sharma & Jinwala, n.d.), MKSE-MWMRS offers controlled multi-reader, multi-writer settings where only the registered writer can share medical records and registered reader can search for the records.

*Figure 6. Simulation results: Decrypt()*

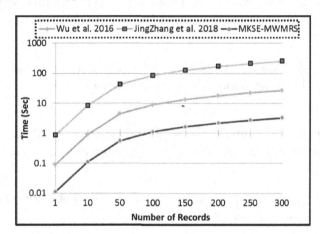

Furthermore, as shown in Figure6, the decryption cost incurred by the proposed *Decryption()*is much less than the schemes supporting record decryption(Jingzhang et al., 2018; Wu et al., 2016). Hence, the proposed solution is more suitable for the environment where readers have resource constrained devices.

## CONCLUSION

The authors in this work define a multi-keyword public key searchable encryption (MKSE-MWMRS) especially for Medical Records. Precisely, the MKSE-MWMRS is a practical approach for E-Health system with multi-writer,multi-reader settings. In the proposed work, the registered data writer can securely share medical records with the registered data readers. For such a data sharing, the proposed scheme incurs optimal computational burden on writers and optimal storage overhead on the cloud server. Furthermore, each registered reader can easily search for records based on the conjunctive query of the chosen keywords. With the security analysis, it is proved that the proposed scheme ensures medical record security as well as searchable ciphertext security against chosen keyword attack. With the extensive performance analysis, including theoretical comparisons and experimental evaluation, the authors show the efficiency of MKSE-MWMRS in terms of storage and computationalcomplexity as compared to the existing searchable schemes designed for medical data. Since the proposed work offers cost-effective solution, it would indeed be acceptable by the real-word E-Health applications.

# REFERENCES

Akinyele, J. A., Pagano, M. W., Green, M. D., Lehmann, C. U., Peterson, Z. N. J., & Rubin, A. D. (2011). Securing electronic medical records using attribute-based encryption on mobile devices. *Proceedings of the 1st ACM Workshop on Security and Privacy in Smartphones and Mobile Devices*, 75–86. 10.1145/2046614.2046628

Baek, J., Safavi-Naini, R., & Susilo, W. (2008a). Public key encryption with keyword search revisited. *Computational Science and Its ...*, 1–15. Retrieved from https://link.springer.com/chapter/10.1007/978-3-540-69839-5_96

Baek, J., Safavi-Naini, R., & Susilo, W. (2008b). Public key encryption with keyword search revisited. In *Computational Science and Its Applications—ICCSA 2008* (pp. 1249–1259). Springer. doi:10.1007/978-3-540-69839-5_96

Ballard, L., Kamara, S., & Monrose, F. (2005). Achieving efficient conjunctive keyword searches over encrypted data. In *Information and Communications Security* (pp. 414–426). Springer. doi:10.1007/11602897_35

Bao, F., Deng, R. H., Ding, X., & Yang, Y. (2008). Private query on encrypted data in multi-user settings. *International Conference on Information Security Practice and Experience*, 71–85. 10.1007/978-3-540-79104-1_6

Boneh, D., Di Crescenzo, G., Ostrovsky, R., & Persiano, G. (2004). Public key encryption with keyword search. *Advances in Cryptology-Eurocrypt*, *2004*, 506–522.

Boneh, D., & Waters, B. (2007). Conjunctive, subset, and range queries on encrypted data. In *Theory of cryptography* (pp. 535–554). Springer. doi:10.1007/978-3-540-70936-7_29

Byun, J. W., Lee, D. H., & Lim, J. (2006). Efficient conjunctive keyword search on encrypted data storage system. *European Public Key Infrastructure Workshop*, 184–196. 10.1007/11774716_15

Chen, T.-L., Chung, Y.-F., & Lin, F. Y. S. (2012). A study on agent-based secure scheme for electronic medical record system. *Journal of Medical Systems*, *36*(3), 1345–1357. doi:10.100710916-010-9595-8 PMID:20857325

Chen, Z., Wu, C., Wang, D., & Li, S. (2012). Conjunctive keywords searchable encryption with efficient pairing, constant ciphertext and short trapdoor. *Pacific-Asia Workshop on Intelligence and Security Informatics*, 176–189.

Cohen, W. W. (2009). *Enron email dataset*. Academic Press.

De Caro, A., & Iovino, V. (2011). jPBC: Java pairing based cryptography. *Proceedings of the 16th IEEE Symposium on Computers and Communications, ISCC 2011*, 850–855. 10.1109/ISCC.2011.5983948

Ding, M., Gao, F., Jin, Z., & Zhang, H. (2012). An efficient public key encryption with conjunctive keyword search scheme based on pairings. *2012 3rd IEEE International Conference on Network Infrastructure and Digital Content*, 526–530.

Dutta, R., Barua, R., & Sarkar, P. (2004). Pairing-based cryptography: A survey. *Cryptology Research Group, Stat-Math and Applied Statistics Unit, 203.*

Eom, J., Lee, D. H., & Lee, K. (2016). Patient-controlled attribute-based encryption for secure electronic health records system. *Journal of Medical Systems, 40*(12), 253. doi:10.100710916-016-0621-3 PMID:27714562

Golle, P., Staddon, J., & Waters, B. (2004). Secure conjunctive keyword search over encrypted data. *Applied Cryptography and Network Security*, 31–45.

Goyal, V., Pandey, O., Sahai, A., & Waters, B. (2006). Attribute-based encryption for fine-grained access control of encrypted data. *Proceedings of the 13th ACM Conference on Computer and Communications Security - CCS '06*, 89. 10.1145/1180405.1180418

Huang, H., Du, J., Wang, H., & Wang, R. (2016). A Multi-keyword Multi-user Searchable Encryption Scheme Based on Cloud Storage. *Trustcom/BigDataSE/I SPA, 2016 IEEE*, 1937–1943.

Hwang, M.-S., Hsu, S.-T., & Lee, C.-C. (2014). A new public key encryption with conjunctive field keyword search scheme. *Information Technology and Control, 43*(3), 277–288. doi:10.5755/j01.itc.43.3.6429

Hwang, Y. H., & Lee, P. J. (2007). Public key encryption with conjunctive keyword search and its extension to a multi-user system. In *Pairing-Based Cryptography—Pairing 2007* (pp. 2–22). Springer. doi:10.1007/978-3-540-73489-5_2

Jingzhang, S., Chunjie, C., & Hui, L. (2018). Searchable Encryption Scheme Based on CPABE with Attribute Update in a Cloud Medical Environment. *International Conference on Cloud Computing and Security*, 265–276. 10.1007/978-3-030-00012-7_25

Kiayias, A., Oksuz, O., Russell, A., Tang, Q., & Wang, B. (2016). Efficient encrypted keyword search for multi-user data sharing. *European Symposium on Research in Computer Security*, 173–195. 10.1007/978-3-319-45744-4_9

Lai, J., Zhou, X., Deng, R. H., Li, Y., & Chen, K. (2013). Expressive search on encrypted data. *Proceedings of the 8th ACM SIGSAC Symposium on Information, Computer and Communications Security*, 243–252.

Lee, C.-C., Hsu, S.-T., Hwang, M.-S., & ... (2013). A Study of Conjunctive Keyword Searchable Schemes. *International Journal of Network Security, 15*(5), 321–330.

Li, H., Yang, Y., Dai, Y., Bai, J., Yu, S., & Xiang, Y. (2017). *Achieving secure and efficient dynamic searchable symmetric encryption over medical cloud data. IEEE Transactions on Cloud Computing.*

Li, J., & Chen, X. (2013). Efficient multi-user keyword search over encrypted data in cloud computing. *Computer Information, 32*(4), 723–738.

Liu, J., Huang, X., & Liu, J. K. (2015). Secure sharing of personal health records in cloud computing: Ciphertext-policy attribute-based signcryption. *Future Generation Computer Systems, 52*, 67–76. doi:10.1016/j.future.2014.10.014

Löhr, H., Sadeghi, A.-R., & Winandy, M. (2010). Securing the e-health cloud. *Proceedings of the 1st Acm International Health Informatics Symposium*, 220–229. 10.1145/1882992.1883024

Lv, Z., Zhang, M., & Feng, D. (2014). Multi-user searchable encryption with efficient access control for cloud storage. *2014 IEEE 6th International Conference on Cloud Computing Technology and Science*, 366–373.

Macdonald, A. J. R. (1986). An introduction to medical manipulation. *Pain, 24*(1), 124. doi:10.1016/0304-3959(86)90035-7

Pohlig, S., & Hellman, M. (1978). An improved algorithm for computing logarithms over GF (p) and its cryptographic significance (Corresp.). *IEEE Transactions on Information Theory, 24*(1), 106–110. doi:10.1109/TIT.1978.1055817

Rau, H.-H., Hsu, C.-Y., Lee, Y.-L., Chen, W., & Jian, W.-S. (2010). Developing electronic health records in Taiwan. *IT Professional, 12*(2), 17–25. doi:10.1109/MITP.2010.53

Schabetsberger, T., Ammenwerth, E., Andreatta, S., Gratl, G., Haux, R., Lechleitner, G., Schindelwig, K., Stark, C., Vogl, R., Wilhelmy, I., & Wozak, F. (2006). From a paper-based transmission of discharge summaries to electronic communication in health care regions. *International Journal of Medical Informatics, 75*(3-4), 209–215. doi:10.1016/j.ijmedinf.2005.07.018 PMID:16112892

Sharma, D., & Jinwala, D. C. (2017). Multi-User Searchable Encryption with Token Freshness Verification (MUSE-TFV). *Security and Communication Networks, 2017*, 16. doi:10.1155/2017/6435138

Sharma, D., & Jinwala, D. C. (n.d.). Multi-Writer Multi-Reader Conjunctive Keyword Searchable Encryption. *International Journal of Information and Computer Security*.

Sunyaev, A., Kaletsch, A., Mauro, C., & Krcmar, H. (2009). Security Analysis of the German Electronic Health Card's Peripheral Parts. *ICEIS*, (3), 19–26. doi:10.5220/0001854000190026

Wang, S., Zhang, X., & Zhang, Y. (2016). Efficiently Multi-User Searchable Encryption Scheme with Attribute Revocation and Grant for Cloud Storage. *PLoS One, 11*(11), e0167157. doi:10.1371/journal.pone.0167157 PMID:27898703

Wu, Y., Lu, X., Su, J., & Chen, P. (2016). An efficient searchable encryption against keyword guessing attacks for sharable electronic medical records in cloud-based system. *Journal of Medical Systems, 40*(12), 258. doi:10.100710916-016-0609-z PMID:27722976

Xu, L., Xu, C., Liu, J. K., Zuo, C., & Zhang, P. (2019). Building a dynamic searchable encrypted medical database for multi-client. *Information Sciences*.

Ye, J., Wang, J., Zhao, J., Shen, J., & Li, K.-C. (2016). Fine-grained searchable encryption in multi-user setting. *Soft Computing*, 1–12.

Yu, Y.-C., Huang, T.-Y., & Hou, T.-W. (2012). Forward secure digital signature for electronic medical records. *Journal of Medical Systems, 36*(2), 399–406. doi:10.100710916-010-9484-1 PMID:20703711

Zhang, B., & Zhang, F. (2011). An efficient public key encryption with conjunctive-subset keywords search. *Journal of Network and Computer Applications, 34*(1), 262–267. doi:10.1016/j.jnca.2010.07.007

Zhang, R., Xue, R., & Liu, L. (2017). Searchable encryption for healthcare clouds: A survey. *IEEE Transactions on Services Computing, 11*(6), 978–996. doi:10.1109/TSC.2017.2762296

Zhang, Y., Liu, L., & Wang, S. (2016). Multi-User and Keyword-Based Searchable Encryption Scheme. *Computational Intelligence and Security (CIS), 2016 12th International Conference on*, 223–227.

*This research was previously published in Implementing Data Analytics and Architectures for Next Generation Wireless Communications; pages 107-131, copyright year 2022 by Information Science Reference (an imprint of IGI Global).*

Chapter 7

# Internet of Things (IOT) in Healthcare – Smart Health and Surveillance, Architectures, Security Analysis and Data Transfer:
## A Review

**Parthasarathy Panchatcharam**
*VIT University, Vellore, India*

**Vivekanandan S.**
*VIT University, Vellore, India*

## ABSTRACT

*Wellbeing is fundament requirement. What's more, it is human appropriate to get quality health care. These days, India is confronting numerous medical problems in light of fewer assets. This survey article displays the idea of solving health issues by utilizing a recent innovation, the Internet of Things (IOT). The Internet of Things with their developing interdisciplinary applications has changed our lives. Smart health care being one such IoT application interfaces brilliant gadgets, machines, patients, specialists, and sensors to the web. At long last, the difficulties and prospects of the improvement of IoT-based medicinal service frameworks are talked about in detail. This review additionally summarizes the security and protection worries of IoT, administrations and application of IoT and smart healthcare services that have changed the customary medicinal services framework by making healthcare administration more proficient through their applications.*

DOI: 10.4018/978-1-6684-6311-6.ch007

## 1. INTRODUCTION

Healthcare is essential component that human require. It is vital for individual the development of individual and additionally for the development of society. So, physical and mental wellness is imperative as it plays vital move for advancement. Presently a Global medical problem is real concern. Meaning of healthcare as indicated by World Health Organization (WHO) is - "A state of complete mental, physical and social prosperity and not just nonappearance of illness and sickness" (http://www.medicalnewstoday. com/articles/150999.php) . Particularly nation like India which has second rank in population (http:// www.sunrom.com/p/heart-beat-sensor-digitalpulse-Out), medical problem impact their development and improvement. It significantly impacts the population of India. There are many narratives and account ailments which are significant medical problems.

Significant concern - The second significant concern is poor sanitation. As per one study of WHO, just 30% of individuals of India gets quality medicinal services. We have major illnesses like: Malaria, Cancer, Blood glucose, Chronicle ailment, Hepatitis, AIDS/HIV, arthritis and Typhoid (2009 World Health Organization Health Profile). Additionally, individuals live in towns cannot get appropriate human services as we have huge hole amongst country and urban zone. India faces high weight of illness in view of absence of natural sanitation and safe other natural issues, poor living conditions, and restricted access to preventive and therapeutic healthcare administrations (http://www.indiatimes.com/health/buzz/ healthcare-what-are-the-biggest-problems-forindian).

The idea of Internet of Things involves the utilization of hardware gadgets that catch or screen information and are associated with the private or open cloud, empowering them to naturally trigger certain occasions (http://www.indiatimes.com/health/buzz/healthcare-what-are-the-biggest-problems-forindian). It empowers regular gadgets to speak with each other or potentially with people, enables protest sense and control frequently is alluded to as the Internet of Things (IoT). It is an exceedingly unique and profoundly circulated organized framework, made out of countless articles.

IoT is an idea mirroring an associated set of anybody, anything, whenever, wherever, any administration, and any system. The IoT is a megatrend in cutting edge advances that can affect the entire business range and can be thought of as the interconnection of extraordinarily identifiable brilliant articles and gadgets inside the present web framework with broadened benefits. Advantages commonly incorporate the propelled availability of these devices, frameworks, and administrations that goes past machine to-machine (M2M) scenarios (Höller et al., 2014). In this manner, presenting mechanization is possible in about each field. The IoT gives proper answers for an extensive variety of utilizations, for example, smart cities, traffic blockage; squander administration, auxiliary wellbeing, security, crisis administrations, logistics, retails, mechanical control, and human services. The intrigued reader is alluded to (Korteum, Kawsar, Fitton, & Sundramoorthy, 2010l Romer, Ostermaier, Mattern, Fahrmair, & Kellerer, 2010) for a more profound comprehension of the IoT. Medicinal care and human services speak to a standout amongst the most alluring application territories for the IoT (Guinard, Trifa, & Wilde, 2010). The IoT can possibly offer ascent to numerous restorative applications, for example, remote health monitoring, work out schedules, constant illnesses, and elderly care. Consistence with treatment and medicine at home and by social insurance suppliers is another imperative potential application. Subsequently, different therapeutic gadgets, sensors, and indicative and imaging gadgets can be seen as savvy gadgets or articles constituting a center piece of the IoT.

IoT-based healthcare systems are relied upon to lessen costs, increment the personal satisfaction, and enhance the client's involvement. From the point of view of healthcare providers, the IoT can possibly decrease gadget downtime through remote arrangement. What's more, the IoT can effectively recognize ideal circumstances for renewing supplies for different gadgets for their smooth and nonstop operation. Further, the IoT accommodates the productive booking of restricted assets by guaranteeing their best utilize and administration of more patients (Tan & Wang, 2010).

Up-to-date healthcare networks driven by remote advancements are relied upon to help endless maladies, earlier analysis, ongoing observing, and medicinal crises. Portals, restorative servers, and wellbeing databases assume fundamental parts in making wellbeing records and conveying on-request wellbeing administrations to approved partners. Over the most recent couple of years, this field has pulled in wide consideration from scientists to address the capability of the IoT in the human services field by thinking about different down to earth challenges. As an outcome, there are presently various applications, administrations, and models in the field. Research inclines in IoT-based medicinal services incorporate system models and stages, new administrations and applications, interoperability, and security, among others. Also, strategies and rules have been created for conveying the IoT innovation in the medicinal field in numerous nations and associations over the world. Be that as it may, the IoT stays in its earliest stages in the healthcare field. At this stage, an exhaustive comprehension of IoT in the healthcare setting is relied upon to be valuable for different partners inspired by additionally inquire about. This article provides various issues in IoT-based healthcare research and reveals different issues that must be routed to change medicinal services advancements through the IoT development. In such manner, this paper contributes by Classifying existing IoT-based medicinal services arrange considers into three patterns and displaying a synopsis of every innovation (Pang, 2013; Vasanth & Sbert, 2014).

Various advances have been made in medicinal services observing and control (Ashton, 2009), interoperability and security (Brock, 2001), unavoidable healthcare (Schreier, 2010; Doukas & Maglogiannis, 2012), and medication connection checking (Jara, Alcolea, Zamora, Skarmeta, & A;saedy, 2010), and so forth. These accomplishments have exhibited the adequacy and promising fate of IoT-based social insurance framework. In spite of the existent achievement, uncertainty and specialized test still exist with respect to the subject of how to quickly and systematically set up and additionally send a shrewd IoT-based social insurance framework that includes huge information administration. Going for expanding the abilities of IoT in medicinal services frameworks, an ever-increasing number of scientists and associations have been de-voted to the improvement of IoT-based advancements for therapeutic applications (Sundmaeker, Guillemin, Friess, & Woelfflé, 2010; Bui & Zorzi, 2011). The motivation of this paper is to summarize the history and headway of best in class considers in IoT-based healthcare frameworks, and to give a methodical survey of empowering advancements and smart healthcare devices in IoT. Specifically, the usage procedures and systems enveloping cosmology-based asset administration, learning administration and enormous information administration, and soon have been examined in light of our comprehension.

## 2. SMART HEALTH CARE SYSTEM

The smart health care system encounters the experiences the keen wellbeing ailment of smart health disease surveillance. Ordered of this reconnaissance are essentially smart IOT devices and smart spine gadgets. This conclusively serves the mechanisms of cloud computing and principle servers at the clinics. Individual Survey and a global reaction took after by general wellbeing by World Health Organization (WHO) that has declared plans to set up the Disease Intelligence Unit that will work autonomously. The

*Figure 1. General architecture of IoT - smart healthcare system*

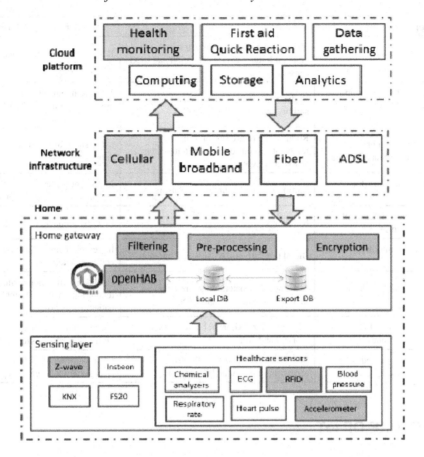

patterns and investigation have achieved the backbone network that is the common need of today. Smart diseases surveillance is extraordinary novel and advancement to accelerate the current procedure of reconnaissance to achieve the most astounding objectives of exactness and ongoing real-time database. Smart disease observation is an epidemiological practice by which episode and spreading can be checked. Primary part is to foresee and to see to limit mischief to the lives. Present day correspondence innovation incorporates association like WHO and communities for disease prevention that now can report with improved and propelled application like smart grid and smart devices like heart rate monitoring, biochip, transponders for bio-medical applications, etc. (Savali & Vaibhavi, 2017).

With a particular true objective to comprehend a system which joins a couple of IoT conventions in the lower layer and proficiently transmits data pieces of information to the remote servers, the paper proposed a plan called IoT-based Remote Health Monitoring (IReHMo). The general architecture of IReHMo involves five layers, to be specific detecting layer, home gateway, network framework, distributed/cloud computing and application layer, as depicted in Figure 1. Table 1 shows a comparison of existing healthcare systems.

*Table 1. Comparison of existing healthcare systems (Sreekanth & Nitha, 2016)*

| Approach | Sensors | Services and Technologies |
|---|---|---|
| An IoT-Aware Architecture for Smart healthcare Systems | Temperature sensor, barometric pressure, ambient light, 3-axis acceleration and ECG sensor | Remote monitoring, management of emergency situation |
| Medical Monitoring And its Application related to Cloud System Based On Internet Of Things | Body sensor, environment sensor and activity sensor | Medical monitoring and managing in hospital systems, PSOSAA algorithm for medical monitoring |
| Applying Internet Of Things For Personalized Healthcare In Smart Homes | Room temperature sensor, room temperature controller, body temperature sensor and light sensor | IoT system for smart homes, layered approach |
| Context Aware intelligent Wallet for Healthcare | Motion sensors, environment sensors | Intelligent wallet for supervised monitoring of individuals, layered approach |
| The Appliance Pervasive of Internet of things in healthcare systems | RFID tags | Medical products with tagged patients |
| A Medical Healthcare Monitoring System Using WSN | Blood pressure sensor, heart rate monitor | Increases coverage of services, decreases end to end delay |
| Body Sensor Networks For Mobile Health Monitoring | ECG, accelerometer, blood pressure monitor, weight scale and GPS | Cardiac rhythm monitoring, cardiac rehabilitation, COPD problems, discharged patient monitoring |
| Around The Clock Personalized Heart Monitoring Using Smart Phones | ECG monitor, oximeter, blood pressure monitor and GPS | Alarms and warnings for patient, system high risk cardiac patients |
| AMON: A Wearable sensor based Monitoring And Alert System | SPO sensor, ECG sensor, BP sensor, acceleration sensor and BT sensor | Wrist worn medical device, monitoring and alert system for cardiac/repertory patients |

# 3. ARCHITECTURE OF IoT

There is no single accord on design for IoT, which is concurred all around. Distinctive structures have been proposed by various scientists.

*Figure 2. Architecture of IoT (A - three layers) (B - five layers)*

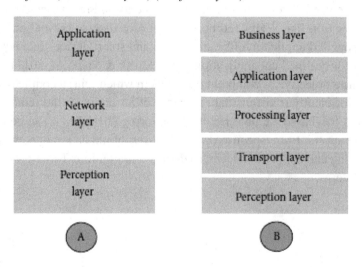

## 3.1. Two Types of Various Layered Architectures

The most fundamental design is three-layer architecture (Vermesan, Friess, & Guillemin, 2011; Mashal et al., 2015; Said & Masud, 2013; Wu et al., 2010) as appeared in Figure 2. It was presented in the beginning times of research around there. It has three layers, to be specific, the perception, network, and application layers.

The perception layer consists of sensors for detecting and assembling data about the environment. It detects some physical parameters or recognizes other smart objects in the environment. The network layer is in-charge of interfacing with other smart things. Its highlights are additionally utilized for transmitting and preparing sensor information. The application layer is responsible for conveying application particular services to the clients. It characterizes different applications in which the Internet of Things can be conveyed, for instance, smart homes, smart cities, and smart health.

The three-layer architecture characterizes the fundamental thought of the Internet of Things, yet it isn't adequate for investigate on IoT in light of the fact that examination frequently concentrates on better parts of the Internet of Things. That is the reason; we have numerous more layered structures proposed in the literature. One is the five-layer architecture, which also incorporates the processing and business layers (Vermesan, Friess, & Guillemin, 2011; Mashal et al., 2015; Said & Masud, 2013; Wu et al., 2010). The five layers are perception, transport, processing, application, and business layers (see Figure 2). The part of the perception and application layers is the same as the architecture with three layers. We layout the capacity of the staying three layers:

1.  The transport layer exchanges the sensor data from the perception layer to the processing layer and other way around through networks such as wireless, 3G, LAN, Bluetooth, RFID, and NFC;
2.  The processing layer is also known as the middleware layer. It stores, dissects, and forms tremendous measures of information that originates from the transport layer. It can oversee and give an assorted arrangement of administrations to the lower layers. It utilizes numerous advances, for example, databases, distributed computing, and huge information handling modules;
3.  The business layer deals with the entire IoT framework, including applications, business and benefit models, and clients' protection. The business layer is out of the extent of this paper. Subsequently, we don't talk about it further.

Another design proposed by Ning and Wang (2011) is enlivened by the layers of handling in the human cerebrum. It is enlivened by the insight and capacity of people to think, feel, recollect, decide, and respond to the physical condition. It is constituted of three sections. In the first place is the human cerebrum, which is comparable to the preparing and information administration unit or the server farm. Second is the spinal cord, which is similar to the dispersed system of information handling hubs and brilliant entryways. Third is the system of nerves, which relates to the systems administration parts and sensors.

## 3.2. Fog and Cloud Based Architectures

Let us now a chance to talk about two sorts of frameworks structures: cloud and fog computing (see the reference architectures in Weyrich and Ebert (2016)). Specifically, we have been somewhat unclear about the idea of information created by IoT devices, and the idea of information preparing. In some frame-

*Figure 3. Fog architecture of a smart IoT gateway*

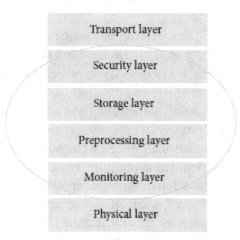

work structures the information preparing is done in a substantial unified manner by cloud PCs. Such a cloud driven design keeps the cloud at the middle, applications above it, and the system of keen things underneath it (Gubbi, Buyya, Marusic, & Palaniswami, 2013). Cloud computing is given supremacy since it gives incredible adaptability and versatility.

Recently, there is a move towards another framework design, to be specific, fog computing (Bonomi, Milito, Natarajan, & Zhu, 2014; Bonomi, Milito, Zhu, & Addepalli, 2012; Stojmenovic & Wen, 2014), where the sensors and network gateways complete a piece of the information preparing and analytics. Fog architecture (Aazam & Huh, 2014) presents a layered approach appeared in Figure 3. The monitoring layer monitors power, resources, responses, and services. The pre-processing layer performs analytics of sensor data, filtering and processing. The temporary storage layer provides storage functionalities such as data replication, distribution, and storage. Finally, the security layer performs data integrity, privacy, encryption and decryption. Monitoring and pre-processing are done on the edge of the network before sending information to the cloud. Often the terms "fog computing" and "edge computing" are used interchangeably. The last term originates before the previous and is interpreted to be more non-specific.

As far as the framework architecture, the building chart isn't considerably unique in relation to Figure 3. Accordingly, we don't depict edge figuring independently. At long last, the qualification between convention structures and system architectures isn't exceptionally crisp. Often the conventions and the framework are co-designed. We might utilize the non-specific 5-layer IoT convention stack (engineering outline exhibited in Figure 3) for both the mist and cloud structures (Atzori, Iera, & Morabito, 2011).

## 4. HEALTH SURVEILLANCE

The smart Medic-care services framework experiences the smart health disease surveillance. Arranged of this reconnaissance are mainly smart IOT devices and smart backbone devices. This indisputably serves the components of distributed computing and principle servers at the doctor's facilities. Individual Survey and a worldwide reaction took after by general wellbeing by World Health Organization (WHO) that has declared plans to set up the Disease Intelligence Unit that will work freely. The trends

*Figure 4. Logical structure of smart healthcare (Stojmenovic & Wen, 2014)*

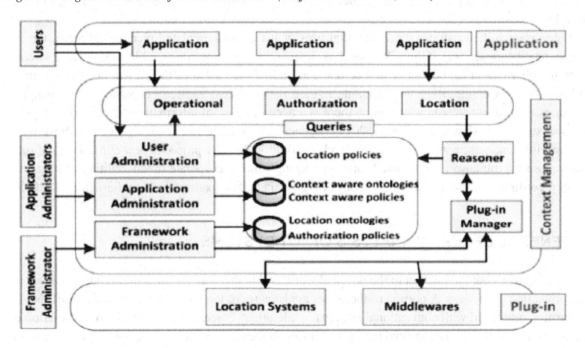

and investigation have achieved the backbone network that is the prevalent need of today. Smart diseases observation is extreme novel and advancement to accelerate the current procedure of reconnaissance to achieve the most noteworthy objectives of precision and real-time database. Main role is to predict and to observe to minimise harm to the lives. Current correspondence innovation incorporates association like world healthcare association WHO and spots for illness control that now can report with overhauled and pushed application like "smart grid" and smart devices like heart observing, biochip, transponders, and so forth (Mathew, Amreen, Pooja, & Verma, 2015).

Figure demonstrates the LOGICAL STRUCTURE to build up an approach to get to the data from convenient stage based on therapeutic work force and authoritative personnel. Each client can permit getting to of this incorporated data relying on its score move through this stage (Kumbi, Naik, Katti, & Kotin, 2017).

In late decades, the fast developing of maturing populace has been a test to worldwide social healthcare frameworks. Numerous nations have been dynamic in experiencing clinic rebuilding through streamlining restorative assets and expanding the utilization of home social insurance IoT now has been perceived as an upheaval in ICT and is relied upon to be connected to numerous modern divisions including healthcare.

Priti et.al. presents an IoT-based wise home-driven social healthcare platform (I-Home framework), which consistently interfaces savvy sensors connected to human body for physiological observing and wise pharmaceutical bundling for every day solution administration Bedmuttha, Jain, Thigale, Gargori, & Patil, 2017). Geng yang et.al, display an IoT-based canny home-driven healthcare platform which consistently associates smart sensors for physiological checking and keen pharmaceutical bundling for day by day drug administration (Geng et al., n.d.). Now a day's bio-patch's mechanical and electrical unwavering quality by overlaying a thin plastic protection layer over the fix to secure the conductive follows and investigating new application situations for this health IoT stage are open issues to take a shot at. This article depicts how the Internet of things is upsetting human services (Natrajan, Prasath, & Kokila, 2016).

Late research demonstrates more potential uses of IoT in data escalated mechanical areas, for example, healthcare services (Gipsa, Varghese, & Jose, n.d.). It can be conceivable to join LCD screens on to the pharmaceutical box that could be made as an interface between the patient and the specialist to have a video meeting. Raga lavima et. al., in their paper discuss ZigBee's capability of exchanging sensor esteems adequately however when there is a need of constant information transmission ZigBee flops in such cases (Lavima & Sarma, 2015). Reducing examining rate takes care of the above issue however influences the nature of signs. Researchers additionally have proposed new clinical uses of such innovations for frameworks of remote health monitoring which incorporate functionalities for long haul status recording, and restorative access to physiological data of the patient (Hassanalieragh et al., 2015).

## 5. GENERAL SECURITY ANALYSIS OF IOT SYSTEMS

The IoT stretches out the Internet to the physical world and in this way postures numerous new security and protection challenges. A portion of the issues are because of the inborn attributes of the IoT and its disparities contrasted with conventional systems, while others emerge because of the reconciliation of the IoT and the Internet. As appeared in Figure 2 different foes may come in at various focuses to assault IoT Systems (Liu, Zhao, Li, Zhang, & Trappe, 2017). To ensure against those assaults, it is essential to look at the security issues as per the data streams and potential ill-disposed purposes of control. In Figure 5 we diagram four security and protection/privacy issues.

### 5.1. Authentication and Physical Threats

Profoundly circulated organizations of countless devices, for example, RFID labels and remote sensors, will generally be deployed in public areas without any protection, which makes the hard to oversee and defenceless against physical assaults. For instance, an illegitimate sensor may enroll itself guaranteeing that it is at one area while it is really at an alternate area. This presents the test of validating IoT devices, which includes perceiving the devices and checking its relationship with a right topological address.

Security issues are extremely basic for medicinal services field. These issues have been conquered utilizing a solid confirmation instrument. The proposed solid validation system essentially relies upon CoAP with ECC calculations. Proposed strategy fit the necessities of IoT obliged devises. Little ECC key has lessened the figuring necessities while giving a capable encryption superior to different kinds of cryptography. The principle challenges those analysts confront isn't just to propose new confirmation instruments, yet additionally to propose a validation that backings different IoT devices. The techniques for validation that work for cell phones will likewise be utilized to confirm watches, indoor regulator, and extensive variety of sensors and microchips (Koreshoff, Robertson, & Leong, 2013; Kulkarni & Sathe, 2014). Two principle kinds of device personality security arrangements have been proposed: physical protection solution and cryptography-based verification arrangement. Physical assurance approach is intended to shield gadget from being harmed or assaulted in the level of physical layer by applying physical ideas (Govinda & Saravanaguru, 2016; Mahalle, Babar, Prasad, & Prasad, 2010; Toma, Simperl, & Hench, 2009; Gubbi, Buyya, Marusic, & Palaniswarmi, 2013). Customary network verification strategies and methodologies require high assets in regard to handling (Madakam, Ramaswamy, & Tripathi, 2015).

*Figure 5. Potential threats for the IoT systems (Liu, Zhao, Li, Zhang, & Trappe, 2017)*

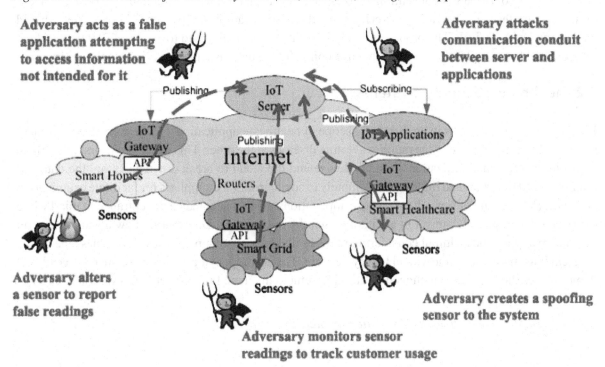

IoT is viewed as a compelled asset condition where preparing and energy resources are constrained. A light weight authentication approach with robust security highlights is required to save vitality and fit processing capacities (Suresh, Daniel, Parthasarathy, & Aswathy, 2014; Zhang et al., 2014).

Diverse calculations have been proposed to provide authentication to IoT devices. In Yang, Hao and Zhang (2013) an upgraded common confirmation display has been proposed for IoT condition. They proposed some improvements to the algorithm of authentication of Challenge-reaction based RFID confirmation convention for circulated database condition (Rhee, Kwak, Kim, & Won, 2005). They made it more appropriate to IoT control framework condition. Their approach has three fundamental advances: include reinforcement devices for every terminal, gadgets utilized for controlling, adding screen gadgets to take after and screen terminal gadgets lastly include a push in alert instrument for disturbing for any failed authentication process.

In Porambage, Schmitt, Kumar, Gurtoy, and Ylianttila, (2014) Wireless Sensor Networks in Distributed IoT Applications with two-stage Authentication Protocol has been proposed. This convention is a certificate-based verification approach, two stage validations permit both IoT device and the control station to confirm and perceive each other, a safe association is set up and information is exchanged safely. They utilized protocol supports resource limitation of sensor hubs and contemplates organize adaptability and heterogeneity. Declaration specialist (CA) has been accustomed to issuing endorsements. Existing hubs can move and change their area after they get their own authentication. CA can approve sensors character and speak with different substances of the system. In Kalra and Sood (2015) Secure authentication scheme have been proposed for IoT and cloud servers which basically relies upon Elliptic Curve Cryptography (ECC) based calculations which underpins better security arrangements when it is contrasted and other Public Key Cryptography (PKC) calculations (Batina et al., 2007) in view of its little key size. This confirmation convention utilizes EEC for installed devices which utilize HTTP convention. Utilizing the treats of HTTP to verify shrewd gadgets is a novel approach. These gadgets should be designed with TCP/IP. The proposed validation convention is intended to utilize HTTP treats which are executed to fit implanted gadgets that have compelled situations and controlled by cloud servers.

## 5.2. Healthcare Security Systems

IoT plays a noteworthy part in an expansive scope of healthcare applications, from overseeing ceaseless sicknesses toward one side of the range to averting diseases at the other. This expects sensors to assemble physiological data and utilizations passage device and the cloud to break down and store the data and after that send the examined information remotely to social insurance suppliers for facilitate examination and audit (Vermesan & Friess, 2014). These applications won't just enhance the entrance to mind while expanding the nature of care yet in addition lessen the cost of care. Distributing new advancements in healthcare applications without considering security makes persistent protection defenceless the physiological information of an individual is very delicate. The accompanying Figure 6 (Kumar & Lee, 2012) demonstrates the healthcare architecture utilizing remote medicinal sensor network (WMSN).

*Figure 6. Healthcare architecture for patient monitoring*

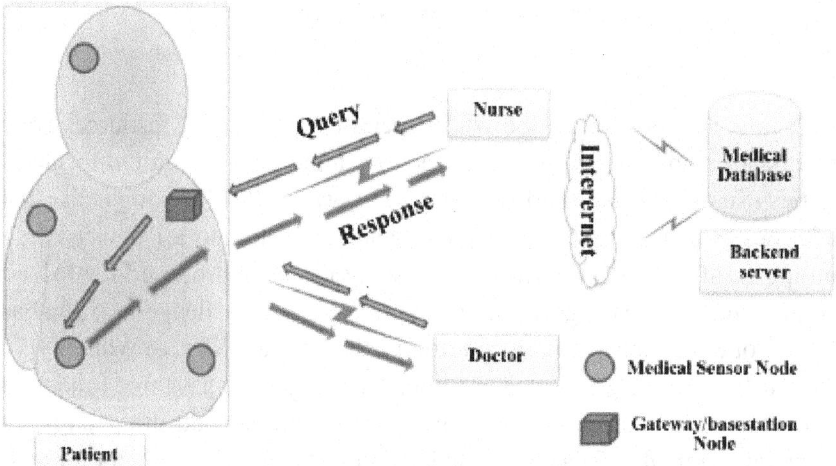

## 5.3. Security Requirements in IoT Healthcare

So far as the research work has been done, the security and protection of the patient are of significant concern. The security requirements appeared in Figure 7 should be satisfied to guarantee the security in IoT human services. Likewise, because of need in satisfying these security prerequisites, certain difficulties or issues appeared in Figure 8 force enormous issues (Islam, Kabir, Kwak, Kwak, & Hossain, 2015; Sharma & Sunanda, 2017).

Brilliant IoT devices are computationally compelled because of low-speed processors. These gadgets are intended for compelled conditions performing cost in-productive operations and for expanding their

*Figure 7. Security requirements in IoT Healthcare (Sharma & Sunanda, 2017)*

adequacy, security arrangement limiting asset utilization and boosting security is the need of hour. The brilliant devices utilized as a part of IoT healthcare, for example, circulatory strain sensor, temperature sensor, so on, have constrained battery power and in this manner spare power by actuating rest mode when no perusing should be accounted for. Other security issues identified with versatility and adaptability should be tended to (Islam, Kabir, Kwak, Kwak, & Hossain, 2015).

## 6. EFFICIENT DATA TRANSFER METHODS

The fast advancement of present-day Information and Communication Technologies (ICTs) as of late and their presentation into individuals' day by day lives around the world, has prompted new circumstances at all levels of the social condition. In healthcare specifically, sensors and information joins offer potential for steady checking of patient's side effects and needs, continuously, empowering doctors to analyze and screen medical issues wherever the patient is, either at home or outside. To manage these overheads, novel measurements, and techniques are acquainted in an endeavour with augment the capabilities and augment acknowledgment/use gave by the Internet of Things (Mitton & Simplot-Ryl, 2011).

The wide development of the idea of Internet of Things is feasible because of the development of the related technologies, for example, Bluetooth, Radio Frequency Identification (RFID) (Mitton & Simplot-Ryl, 2011) and Near Field Communication (NFC). These advances are quickly presented in the

*Figure 8. Security challenges in IoT Healthcare (Sharma & Sunanda, 2017)*

accompanying passages for the non-authority reader who needs to get comfortable with the technologies identified with the IoT.

These days, maturity, low cost, and solid help from the business group makes it perfect for the vision of IoT. RSN (RFID Sensor Networks), which comprise of RFID readers and RFID sensor hubs, stretch out RFID to incorporate detecting and bring the benefits of little, modest and seemingly perpetual RFID labels to remote sensor systems (Buettner & Greenstein, 2008).

The appearance of NFC innovation, which improves cell phones with RFID capacities, for example, going about as a smartcard or RFID tag, and also perusing smartcards and RFID labels takes the perpetual availability marvel an essential above and beyond: NFC empowered cell phones associate a totally new gathering of clients to regular things and, as such, expand the part of cell phones by new types of communication between people and objects (Welbourne et al., 2009).

## 6.1. Available Architectures

Mobile communication, SMS, GPRS and Wi–Fi/ADSL technology, which are as of now the overwhelming ones and are relied upon to stay critical in years to come also. In our scenario, a user may have any kind of fitness device, empowered with Bluetooth, WI–Fi, NFC, RFID or some other sort of innovation that takes into account information enlistment and correspondence with a cell phone or a PC. Some sort of suitable portable or web application trades information with a web benefit, and relying upon the innovation utilized for the information exchange, three discrete models emerge, which are quickly depicted underneath (Paschou, Sakkopoulos, Sourla, & Tsakalidi, 2013).

*Figure 9. SMS based transfer architecture (Paschou, Sakkopoulos, Sourla, & Tsakalidi, 2013)*

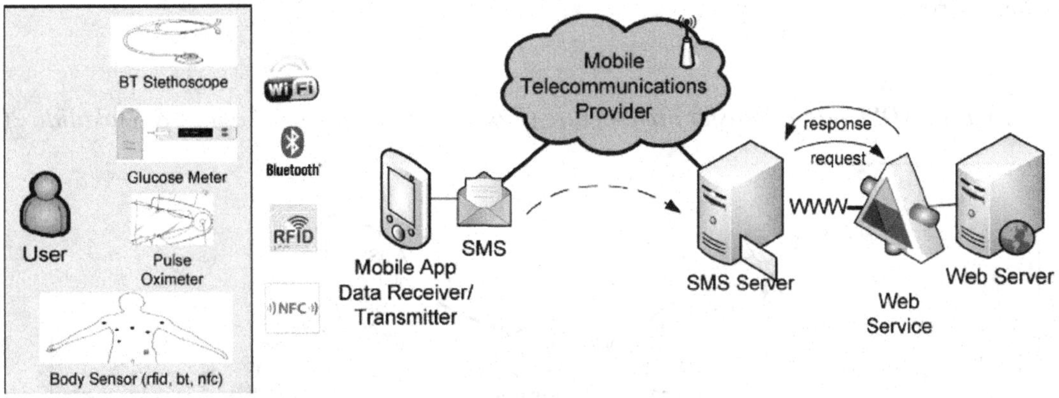

In the first architectural approach (Figure 1), the mobile application sends information to a web benefit utilizing at least one SMS. The SMS server gets the SMSs sent through the Mobile media communications Provider and changes their substance to a demand to the web benefit.

In the second architectural approach (Figure 2), the portable mobile application is associated with the web through its Mobile Telecommunications Provider, utilizing GPRS innovation. After the association is set up, the application sends information straightforwardly to the web benefit.

*Figure 10. 3G/GPRS based transfer architecture (Paschou, Sakkopoulos, Sourla, & Tsakalidi, 2013)*

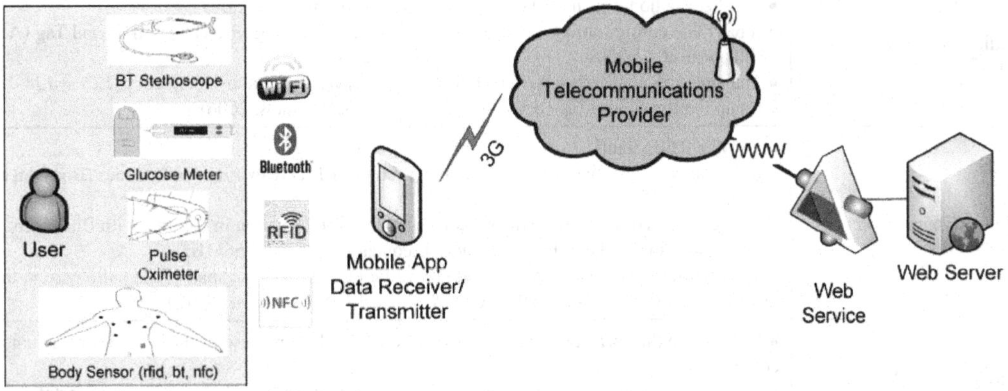

In the third compositional approach (Figure 11), the portable application abuses the built-up ADSL web association and the presence of a remote switch. Information's are sent to the remote switch utilizing Wi-Fi innovation and afterward are sent to the web benefit through the ADSL Internet Provider.

## 6.2. Intricate Technologies

Different innovations are involves implementing the idea of IOT. In article we will provides a overview of some technologies includes Radio frequency Identification (RFID) Near Field Communication

(NFC) Machine-to-Machine Communication (M2M) Vehicle-to-Vehicle Communication (V2V) (Shah & Yaqoob, 2016).

*Figure 11. Wi–Fi/ADSL based transfer architecture (Paschou, Sakkopoulos, Sourla, & Tsakalidi, 2013)*

*Table 2. Overview of different technologies*

| Technologies | Descriptions |
|---|---|
| RFID (Radio frequency identification) | • It utilizes radio frequency electromagnetic fields to send the data.<br>• It has three configurations namely Passive Reader Active Tag (PRAT), (ARPT) and Tag (ARAT). (Welbourne et al., 2009)<br>• Transmission may shows up in different frequency bands from low frequency (LF) at 124-135 KHz up to ultra- high frequency (UHF) at 860-960 MHz (Juels, 2006) |
| Near Field Communication | • It is like RFID setup.<br>• NFC can be made client arranged by integration of RFID reader into cell phones (Booysen et al., 2012).<br>• No paring is required before the genuine sending of information in contrast with Bluetooth<br>• NFC works inside the unlicensed Radio Frequency band of 13.56MHz<br>• The typical range of NFC is 20m and generally it relies upon the span of the radio wire in the gadget (Burlington & Vacca, 2009; Cerf & Delal, 1974; Chen et al., 2012) |
| Machine to Machine (M2M) | • It alludes to the correspondences between PCs, installed processors, shrewd sensors, actuators and cell phones (Dye, 2008)<br>• It has applications in various parts like human services, savvy robots, digital transportation frameworks (CTS), producing frameworks, keen home advances, and shrewd lattices |
| Vehicle-to-Vehicle Communications (V2V) | • V2V communications involve a vehicle, which goes about as a hub in a system and correspondence is finished by the utilization of different sensors associated in a specially appointed system<br>• There is no any fixed topology in V2V.<br>• Vehicles communicate with each other within the range of 1000m (Lawton, 2004).<br>• As per structural perspective, it focuses mainly on routing protocols that are Physical layer (PHY), Medium Access Control MAC layer, and broadcasting (Booysen, Zeadally, Rooyen, & Van, 2011) |

*Table 3. Comparison between IOT healthcare services and applications (Islam, Kwak, Kabir, Hossan, & Kwak, 2015)*

| IoT Healthcare Services | IoT Healthcare Applications |
|---|---|
| • There is no standard definition of IoT services. Services are used to develop applications.<br>• It is a developer-centric.<br>• General services and protocols required for IoT frameworks may require slight adjustments for their legitimate working in healthcare situations. (Include notification services, resource sharing services, internet services, cross-connectivity protocols for heterogeneous devices, and link protocols for major connectivity.) | • Applications are directly used by users and patients.<br>• It is user-centric.<br>• The next subsections address various IoT-based healthcare applications, including both single- and clustered-condition applications. |

## 7. IoT HEALTHCARE SERVICES AND APPLICATIONS

IoT-based healthcare frameworks can be connected to a various cluster of fields, including nurture paediatric and elderly patients, the supervision of long-term disease, and the administration of private healthcare and wellness, among others. For a superior comprehension of this broad point, this paper comprehensively orders the discourse in two angles: services and applications.

Applications are further divided into two groups: single- and clustered-condition applications. Figure 12 illustrates this categorization Note that this grouping structure is encircled in light of the present accessible healthcare solutions using the IoT. This list innately unique in nature and can be effectively upgraded by including extra services with particular highlights and various applications. This section presents each of the administrations and applications appeared in the figure (Islam, Kwak, Kabir, Hossan, & Kwak, 2015).

## 8. CONCLUSION

In this article, we have considered the impact that the worldview Internet of Things may have in Health Informatics area and how it can be utilized to profit patients and also any other individual identified with the field of healthcare. This paper reviews differing parts of IoT-based healthcare services and presents different healthcare network architectures, about efficient data transfer, security issues, stages that help access to the IoT backbone. In addition, the paper provides detailed survey about general security analysis of IoT system. For more profound experiences into industry inclines and empowering advances, the paper offers a wide view on how later and continuous advances in sensors, devices, web applications, and different advances have spurred reasonable healthcare devices and associated health administrations and applications to vastly extend the capability of IoT-based medicinal services administrations for further improvements. To better understand IoT healthcare security, the paper considers various security requirements and challenges. The discussion on several important cost-effective data transmission and its architecture also described. In whole, the results of this overview are relied upon to be valuable for specialists, engineers, healthcare experts working in the zone of the IoT and medicinal/healthcare services advancements.

*Figure 12 IOT in healthcare – services and applications (Islam, Kwak, Kabir, Hossan, & Kwak, 2015)*

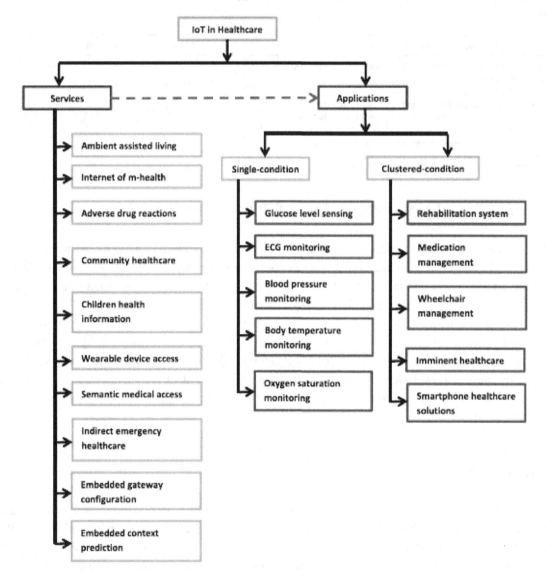

## REFERENCES

Aazam, M., & Huh, E.-N. (2014). Fog computing and smart gateway based communication for cloud of things. In *Proceedings of the 2nd IEEE International Conference on Future Internet of Things and Cloud (FiCloud '14)*, Barcelona, Spain (pp. 464–470). 10.1109/FiCloud.2014.83

Alex, G., Varghese, B., Jose, J. G., & Abraham, A. (2016). A Modern Health Care System Using IoT and Android. *International Journal on Computer Science and Engineering*, 8(4).

Ashton, K. (2009). That 'internet of things' thing. *RFiD J.*, 27(7), 97–114.

Atzori, L., Iera, A., & Morabito, G. (2011). SIoT: Giving a social structure to the internet of things. *IEEE Communications Letters*, *15*(11), 1193–1195. doi:10.1109/LCOMM.2011.090911.111340

Batina, L., Guajardo, J., Kerins, T., Mentens, N., Tuyls, P., & Verbauwhede, I. (2007). Public-key cryptography for RFID-tags. In *Pervasive Computing and Communications Workshops*. PerCom Workshops. doi:10.1109/PERCOMW.2007.98

Bedmuttha, P., Jain, N., Thigale, Y., & Gargori, S. (2017, April). A Health-Iot Platform Based On The Biosensor And Intelligent Medicine Box. *International Journal Of Computer Science And Mobile Computing*, *6*(4), 433–438.

Bonomi, F., Milito, R., Natarajan, P., & Zhu, J. (2014). Fog computing: a platform for internet of things and analytics. In *Big Data and Internet of Things: A RoadMap for Smart Environments* (pp. 169–186). Berlin, Germany: Springer. doi:10.1007/978-3-319-05029-4_7

Bonomi, F., Milito, R., Zhu, J., & Addepalli, S. (2012). Fog computing and its role in the internet of things. In *Proceedings of the 1st ACM MCC Workshop on Mobile Cloud Computing* (pp. 13–16). 10.1145/2342509.2342513

Booysen, M. J., Zeadally, S., & Van Rooyen, G. J. (2011). Survey of media access control protocols for vehicular ad hoc networks. *IET Communications*, *5*(11), 1619–1631. doi:10.1049/ietcom.2011.0085

Brock, D. L. (n.d.). The electronic product code.

Buettner, M., Greenstein, B., Sample, A., Smith, J. R., & Wetherall, D. (2008, October). Revisiting smart dust with RFID sensor networks. In *Proceedings of the 7th ACM Workshop on Hot Topics in Networks (HotNets-VII)*.

Bui, N., & Zorzi, M. (2011). Health care applications: a solution based on the internet of things. In *Proceedings of the 4th International Symposium on Applied Sciences in Biomedical and Communication Technologies*. ACM. 10.1145/2093698.2093829

Welbourne, E., Battle, L., Cole, G., Gould, K., Rector, K., Raymer, S., ... & Borriello, G. (2009). Building the internet of things using RFID internet experience. *IEEE Internet Computing*, *13*, 48–55. doi:10.1109/MIC.2009.52

Cerf, V., Dalal, Y., & Sunshine, C. (1974). Specification of internet transmission control program (No. RFC 675).

Doukas, C., & Maglogiannis, I. (2012). Bringing iot and cloud computing towards pervasive healthcare. In *Proceedings of the Sixth International Conference on Innovative Mobile and Internet Services in Ubiquitous Computing (IMIS)* (pp. 922–926). IEEE. 10.1109/IMIS.2012.26

Govinda, K., & Saravanaguru, R. (2016). Review on IOT Technologies. *International Journal of Applied Engineering Research*, *11*, 2848–2853.

Gubbi, J., Buyya, R., Marusic, S., & Palaniswami, M. (2013). Internet of Things (IoT): A vision, architectural elements, and future directions. *Future Generation Computer Systems*, *29*(7), 1645–1660. doi:10.1016/j.future.2013.01.010

Gubbi, J., Buyya, R., Marusic, S., & Palaniswami, M. (2013). Internet of Things (IoT): A vision, architectural elements, and future directions. *Future Generation Computer Systems*, *29*(7), 1645–1660. doi:10.1016/j.future.2013.01.010

Guinard, D., Trifa, V., & Wilde, E. (2010, November). A resource oriented architecture for the web of things. In 2010 Internet of Things (IOT) (pp. 1-8). IEEE.

Hassanalieragh, M., Page, A., Soyata, T., Sharma, G., Aktas, M., Mateos, G., . . . Andreescu, S. (2015, June). Health monitoring and management using Internet-of-Things (IoT) sensing with cloud-based processing: Opportunities and challenges. In 2015 IEEE international conference on services computing (SCC) (pp. 285-292). IEEE.

Höller, J., Tsiatsis, V., Mulligan, C., Karnouskos, S., Avesand, S., & Boyle, D. (2014). *From Machine-to-Machine to the Internet of Things: Introduction to a New Age of Intelligence*. Amsterdam, The Netherlands: Elsevier.

India Times. (n.d.). What are the biggest problems for India. Retrieved from http://www.indiatimes.com/health/buzz/healthcare-what-are-the-biggest-problems-forindian

Islam, S. R., Kwak, D., Kabir, M. H., Hossain, M., & Kwak, K. S. (2015). The internet of things for health care: A comprehensive survey. *IEEE Access : Practical Innovations, Open Solutions*, *3*, 678–708. doi:10.1109/ACCESS.2015.2437951

Islam, S. R., Kwak, D., Kabir, M. H., Hossain, M., & Kwak, K. S. (2015). The internet of things for health care: A comprehensive survey. *IEEE Access : Practical Innovations, Open Solutions*, *3*, 678–708. doi:10.1109/ACCESS.2015.2437951

Jara, A. J., Alcolea, A. F., Zamora, M. A., Skarmeta, A. G., & Alsaedy, M. (2010, November). Drugs interaction checker based on IoT. In 2010 Internet of Things (IOT) (pp. 1-8). IEEE.

John, R. V. (2009). *Computer and information security handbook*. Morgan Kaufmann.

Juels, A. (2006). RFID security and privacy: A research survey. *IEEE Journal on Selected Areas in Communications*, *24*(2), 381–394.

Kalra, S., & Sood, S. K. (2015). Secure authentication scheme for IoT and cloud servers. *Pervasive and Mobile Computing*, *24*, 210–223. doi:10.1016/j.pmcj.2015.08.001

Koreshoff, T. L., Robertson, T., & Leong, T. W. (2013). Internet of things: a review of literature and products. In *Proceedings of the 25th Australian Computer-Human Interaction Conference: Augmentation, Application, Innovation, Collaboration* (pp. 335-344). 10.1145/2541016.2541048

Kortuem, G., Kawsar, F., Sundramoorthy, V., & Fitton, D. (2010). Smart objects as building blocks for the internet of things. *IEEE Internet Computing*, *14*(1), 44–51.

Kulkarni, A., & Sathe, S. (2014). Healthcare applications of the Internet of Things: A Review. *International Journal of Computer Science and Information Technologies*, *5*, 6229–6232.

Kumar, P., & Lee, H.-J. (2012). Security Issues in Healthcare Applications Using Wireless Medical Sensor Networks: A Survey. *Sensors (Basel)*, *12*(1), 55–91. doi:10.3390120100055 PMID:22368458

Lavima, P. R., & Sarma, G. S. (2015). An IoT based intelligent medicine box. *International Journal of Computer Science and Mobile Computing*, *4*(10), 186–191.

Lawton, G. (2004). Machine-to-machine technology gears up for growth. *Computer*, *37*(9), 12–15.

Liu, X., Zhao, M., Li, S., Zhang, F., & Trappe, W. (2017). Security Framework for the Internet of Things in the Future Internet Architecture. *Future Internet*, *9*(3), 27. doi:10.3390/fi9030027

Chen, M., Wan, J., & Li, F. (2012). Machine-to-machine communications: Architecture, standards and applications. *Transactions on Internet and Information Systems (Seoul)*, *6*(2), 480–497.

Booysen, M. J., Gilmore, J. S., Zeadally, S., & Van Rooyen, G. J. (2012). Machine-to-machine communications in vehicular networks. *Transactions on Internet and Information Systems (Seoul)*, *6*(2), 529–546. doi:10.3837/tiss.2012.02.005

Madakam, S., Ramaswamy, R., & Tripathi, S. (2015). Internet of Things (IoT): A literature review. *Journal of Computer and Communications*, *3*(05), 164–173. doi:10.4236/jcc.2015.35021

Mahalle, P., Babar, S., Prasad, N. R., & Prasad, R. (2010). Identity management framework towards internet of things (IoT): Roadmap and key challenges. In *International Conference on Network Security and Applications* (pp. 430-439). 10.1007/978-3-642-14478-3_43

Mashal, I., Alsaryrah, O., Chung, T.-Y., Yang, C.-Z., Kuo, W.-H., & Agrawal, D. P. (2015). Choices for interaction with things on Internet and underlying issues. *Ad Hoc Networks*, *28*, 68–90. doi:10.1016/j.adhoc.2014.12.006

Mathew, A., FAS, A., Pooja, H. N., & Verma, A. (2015). Smart Disease Surveillance Based on Internet of Things (IoT). *International Journal of Advanced Research in Computer and Communication Engineering*, *4*(5), 180–183.

Mitton, N., & Simplot-Ryl, D. (2011). From the internet of things to the internet of the physical world. *Comptes Rendus Physique*, *12*(7), 669–674. doi:10.1016/j.crhy.2011.06.006

MobileIn. (n.d.). Machine-to-machine communications. Retrieved from www.mobilein.com/m2m.htm

Natarajan, K., Prasath, B., & Kokila, P. (2016). Smart health care system using internet of things. *Journal of Network Communications and Emerging Technologies*, *6*(3).

Ning, H., & Wang, Z. (2011). Future internet of things architecture: Like mankind neural system or social organization framework? *IEEE Communications Letters*, *15*(4), 461–463. doi:10.1109/LCOMM.2011.022411.110120

Nordqvist, C. (2017). Health: What does good health really mean. Medical News Today. Retrieved from http://www.medicalnewstoday.com/articles/150999.php

Pang, Z. (2013). *Technologies and Architectures of the Internet-of-Things (IoT) for Health and Wellbeing* [Doctoral dissertation]. KTH Royal Institute of Technology.

Paschou, M., Sakkopoulos, E., Sourla, E., & Tsakalidi, A. (2013). Health Internet of Things: Metrics and methods for efficient data transfer. *Simulation Modelling Practice and Theory*, *34*, 186–199. doi:10.1016/j.simpat.2012.08.002

Porambage, P., Schmitt, C., Kumar, P., Gurtov, A., & Ylianttila, M. (2014). Two-phase authentication protocol for wireless sensor networks in distributed IoT applications. In *2014 Wireless Communications and Networking Conference (WCNC)* (pp. 2728-2733). IEEE.10.1109/WCNC.2014.6952860

Rhee, K., Kwak, J., Kim, S., & Won, D. (2005). Challenge-response based RFID authentication protocol for distributed database environment. In Security in Pervasive Computing (pp. 70-84). Springer.

Romer, K., Ostermaier, B., Mattern, F., Fahrmair, M., & Kellerer, W. (2010, November). Real-time search for real-world entities: A survey. *Proceedings of the IEEE*, *98*(11), 1887–1902. doi:10.1109/JPROC.2010.2062470

Said, O., & Masud, M. (2013). Towards internet of things: Survey and future vision. *International Journal of Computer Networks*, *5*(1), 1–17.

Sayali, S. & Vaibhavi, P. (2017, January). A Survey Paper on Internet of Things based Healthcare System. *IARJSET*, *4*, 4.

Schreier, G. (2010). *Pervasive Healthcare via The Internet of Medical Things*. Graz, Austria: Austrian Institute of Technology GmbH.

Shah, S. H., & Yaqoob, I. (2016, August). A survey: Internet of Things (IOT) technologies, applications and challenges. In 2016 IEEE Smart Energy Grid Engineering (SEGE) (pp. 381-385). IEEE.

Sharma, C. & Sunanda. (2017). Survey on Smart Healthcare: An Application of IoT. *International Journal on Emerging Technologies*, *8*(1), 330–333.

Shinde, S. P., & Phalle, V. N. (2017). A Survey Paper on Internet of Things Based Healthcare System. *Internet of Things and Cloud Computing*, *4*(4). doi:10.11648/j.iotcc.s.2017050501.11

Sreekanth, K. U., & Nitha, K. P. (2016, February). A Study on Health Care in Internet of Things. *International Journal on Recent and Innovation Trends in Computing and Communication*, *4*(2).

Stojmenovic, I., & Wen, S. (2014). The fog computing paradigm: scenarios and security issues. In *Proceedings of the Federated Conference on Computer Science and Information Systems (Fed-CSIS '14)*, Warsaw, Poland (pp. 1–8). IEEE. 10.15439/2014F503

Sundmaeker, H., Guillemin, P., Friess, P., & Woelfflé, S. (2010). Vision and challenges for realising the Internet of Things. *Cluster of European Research Projects on the Internet of Things. European Commission*, *3*(3), 34–36.

Sunrom. (n.d.). Heart beat sensor digital pulse out. Retrieved from http://www.sunrom.com/p/heart-beat-sensor-digitalpulse-Out

Suresh, P., Daniel, J. V., Parthasarathy, V., & Aswathy, R. (2014). A state of the art review on the Internet of Things (IoT) history, technology and fields of deployment. In *2014 International Conference on Science Engineering and Management Research (ICSEMR)* (pp. 1-8).

Tan, L., & Wang, N. (2010). Future Internet: The Internet of Things. In *Proc. 3rd Int. Conf. Adv. Comput. Theory Eng. (ICACTE)* (Vol. 5, pp. 376-380).

Toma, I., Simperl, E., & Hench, G. (2009). A joint roadmap for semantic technologies and the internet of things. In *Proceedings of the Third STI Roadmapping Workshop*, Crete, Greece.

Vasanth, K., & Sbert, J. (2013). Creating solutions for health through technology innovation. *Texas Instruments*. Retrieved from http://www.ti.com/lit/wp/sszy006/sszy006.pdf

Vermesan, O., & Friess, P. (2014). *Internet of Things Applications—From Research and Innovation to Market Deployment*. River Publishers.

Vermesan, O., Friess, P., Guillemin, P., Gusmeroli, S., Sundmaeker, H., Bassi, A., ... & Doody, P. (2011). Internet of things strategic research roadmap. *Internet of Things-Global Technological and Societal Trends*, (1), 9-52.

Welbourne, E., Battle, L., Cole, G., Gould, K., Rector, K., Raymer, S., ... Borriello, G. (2009). Building the internet of things using RFID: The RFID ecosystem experience. *IEEE Internet Computing*, *13*(3).

Weyrich, M., & Ebert, C. (2016). Reference architectures for the internet of things. *IEEE Software*, *33*(1), 112–116. doi:10.1109/MS.2016.20

Wu, M., Lu, T.-J., Ling, F.-Y., Sun, J., & Du, H.-Y. (2010). Research on the architecture of internet of things. In *Proceedings of the 3rd International Conference on Advanced Computer Theory and Engineering (ICACTE '10)*, Chengdu, China (Vol. 5, pp. 484-487). IEEE.

Yang, G., Xie, L., Mäntysalo, M., Zhou, X., Pang, Z., Da Xu, L., ... Zheng, L. R. (2014). A health-IoT platform based on the integration of intelligent packaging, unobtrusive bio-sensor, and intelligent medicine box. *IEEE Transactions on Industrial Informatics*, *10*(4), 2180–2191.

Yang, J., Pang, H., & Zhang, X. (2013). Enhanced mutual authentication model of IoT. *Journal of China Universities of Posts and Telecommunications*, *20*, 69–74. doi:10.1016/S1005-8885(13)60218-6

Zhang, Z.-K., Cho, M. C. Y., Wang, C.-W., Hsu, C.-W., Chen, C.-K., & Shieh, S. (2014). IoT security: ongoing challenges and research opportunities. In *2014 IEEE 7th International Conference on Service-Oriented Computing and Applications* (pp. 230-234).

*This research was previously published in the International Journal of Software Innovation (IJSI), 7(2); pages 21-40, copyright year 2019 by IGI Publishing (an imprint of IGI Global).*

# Chapter 8
# Healthcare IoT Architectures, Technologies, Applications, and Issues:
## A Deep Insight

**Karthick G. S.**
*Bharathiar University, India*

**Pankajavalli P. B.**
*Bharathiar University, India*

## ABSTRACT

*The internet of things (IoT) revolution is improving the proficiency of human healthcare infrastructures, and this chapter analyzes the applications of IoT in healthcare systems with diversified aspects such as topological arrangement of medical devices, layered architecture, and platform services. This chapter focuses on advancements in IoT-based healthcare in order to identify the communication and sensing technologies enabling the smart healthcare systems. The transformation of healthcare from doctor-centric to patient-centric with the diversified applications of IoT is discussed in detail. In addition, this chapter examines the various issues to be emphasized on designing an effective IoT-based healthcare system. It also explores security in healthcare systems and the possible security threats that may be vulnerable to the security essentials. Finally, this chapter summarizes the procedure of applying machine learning techniques on healthcare streaming data which provides intelligence to the systems.*

## INTRODUCTION: OVERVIEW OF INTERNET OF THINGS

The idea of the IoT was originated and devised with the context of Radio Frequency Identification (RFID), which is used for tracking the objects in various domains like logistics and supply chain management. For example, Automated Teller Machines (ATMs) are interconnected to the bank network, which enables the payments with ATM cards at the point of sales depots. ATM uses the machine-to-machine (M2M)

DOI: 10.4018/978-1-6684-6311-6.ch008

networks and these established a basement for IoT through network connected systems and data. The probability of connecting the objects to the network provides tagging, tracking and reading of data from objects that goes hand in hand with greater efforts which would become a promising technology of this era called as IoT.

IoT was first coined by Kevin Ashton in 1999 and developed in analogous to Wireless Sensor Networks (WSN) (Rose et al., 2015). The term IoT refers to the physical devices that are interconnected to gather and share the data with each other via communication technology and cloud computing enables to collect, record and to analyze the data stream more accurately within short span of time. The term "Things" in IoT specifies variety of devices includes sensors, automobiles, buildings, industries, human beings, animals, plants any type of goods. WSNs are assumed to rely on wireless communication technologies whereas IoT does not assumed to rely on specific communication technology. The characteristics of wireless sensors like tiny, rugged, inexpensive and low powered renovated the IoT, facilitates the smallest objects can be integrated with different environments. IoT can be considered as an upcoming evolution of the internet which uses many existing features including machine-to-machine communication (M2M), radio frequency identification (RFID) and sensors.

IoT is defined as an ever growing technology through which computing devices, mechanical and digital machines, physical objects, animals or human beings are interconnected via communication medium provides the ability to exchange information and automate the tasks without human-interaction.

IoT is being labeled by different applications, protocols, standards and architectures. IoT is not just a technology but certainly comprising of different things like data analytics, actuators, hubs, artificial intelligence, communication, wide range of sensors, IoT nodes, gateways, networks, cloud computing, edge computing, processing, optimization, IoT platforms and so on. Connecting the physical things through networks and data stream processing increases the potentiality of IoT by adding intelligence to the systems. The common technologies driving the IoT applications are depicted in the Figure 1.

As IoT can be considered as a fully dependent on the potentials of sensors and other technologies, IoT devices must possess three basic qualities such as:

- **Sensable:** IoT devices must be able to sense and aggregate the data. For example, in healthcare field aggregating the blood glucose, pulse rate and body temperature data via sensors. The data aggregated must be self-directed.
- **Communicable:** The data aggregated must be transmitted to data centers or other devices upon specific conditions via communication medium (i.e. Wireless Technologies).
- **Actionable:** The data aggregation itself doesn't make any sense or change behavior. It must exhibit some actions. For example, if a patient's pulse rate or blood level exceeds its normal range, the IoT system must automatically send an alert message to the healthcare providers for further interventions.

## INTERNET OF THINGS IN HEALTHCARE

The aim of IoT is to connect devices, information and human beings together with respect to local and global scenario. In the sky of various domain, the healthcare is the fastest domain which adopting it's infrastructure to the IoT. The application of sensory capabilities to all the medical devices, gives a pathway and transforming facilities for the whole bionetwork of doctors, patients, medical equipment's and pharmacies. The available infrastructure in hospitals for providing medical services to the patients becomes insufficient and flourishing technologies induced the medical sector to draft or reshape the way of servicing and managing medical units with the support of the IoT. The medical applications and hospitals are connected together through IoT, which allows doctors, patients and supporting staff to make use of advancements in medical sector efficiently. Mobile-based health technology use smart phone as an interface for caregivers and patients which lead to offer digitized medical care. Since this platform promptly supports digitized medical care, enables caregivers to provide better intervention and patients can have faster recovery. Digitization of the chronic disease management is highly empowered by IoT-enabled medical devices which include drug delivery systems, uninterrupted glucose monitoring system and other important physiological vital signs monitoring system.

*Figure 1. Technologies driving IoT*

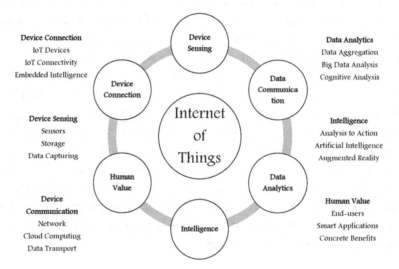

The recent researches in IoT has opened a wide opportunities for caregivers with reduced medical expenses and also it increases the quality of service. In traditional healthcare systems, disease predictions may subject to error prone. Whereas IoT uses different sensors which highly facilitated with cross-device connectivity allows aggregating, maintaining and analyzing the real-time patient data, reduces the chance of erroneous disease prediction. IoT acquired the attention of elderly patients, individual patients suffering from chronic diseases and also the patients in need of constant medical intervention.

The uprising technologies of IoT changing the lives of humans with the advanced solutions that provides the following benefits:

- Real-time aggregating, sharing and analyzing of patients data from healthcare systems.
- The quality of medical services will increase based on the accurate data.
- Reachability of healthcare providers becomes simple and easier.
- Healthcare providers can monitor their patients regularly via remote monitoring medical systems.
- Providing alert mechanism to send emergency messages to family members and healthcare providers on patient's emergency situations.

- Caregivers can access and analyze their patient information without any geographical restrictions.
- Providing highly-personalized and controlled data storage for individual users.

The IoT plays a major role in variety of healthcare applications ranging from monitoring chronic diseases to preventing diseases. The application of IoT in healthcare is a five step process as in Figure 2, through which the healthcare providers operates more efficiently for patient betterment.

*Figure 2. HIoT Five Step Process Model*

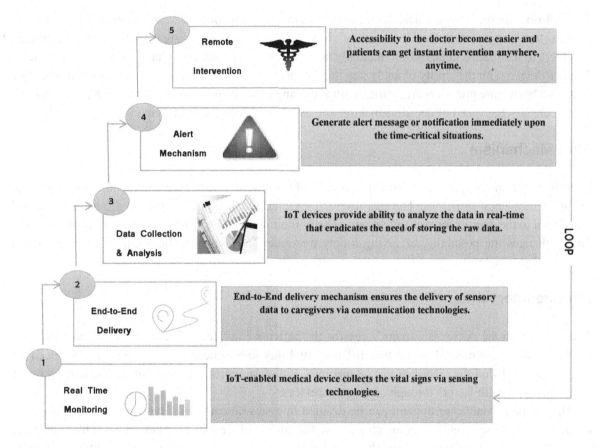

## Real-Time Monitoring

The Real-time IoT-enabled medical device collects the health data such as blood glucose, pressure, body temperature, ECG and respiratory rate. The smart medical devices make use of the communication technologies or smart phones for communicating the gathered data to cloud storage and then the authorized persons like healthcare providers, doctors or clinical assistants are allowed to access the patient's data irrespective of their place, time or device.

## End-to-End Delivery

The effective end-to-end delivery mechanism provides high mobility solutions with respect to interoperability, device-to-device communication and data exchange. Some of the connectivity protocols like Bluetooth, Wi-Fi, ZigBee modified the way of spotting illness and health disorders. This constantly reduces the cost involved in network setup and increases the efficient use of resources.

## Data Collection and Analysis

The real-time IoT-enabled medical device generates huge volume of data within a short span of time, is hard to store and maintain locally in case of cloud unavailability. It is a great challenge for healthcare providers to maintain and analyze it manually, as they receive the data generated from various devices. The IoT device with the ability of analyzing the data in real-time eradicates the need of storing the raw data. The healthcare providers are availed with accessing of analyzed reports and visual representations. Thus increases the speed of decision-making and avoid the occurrences of manual errors.

## Alert Mechanism

Providing alert notification is considered as crucial event which saves the life of humans during the medical emergency situations. The real-time IoT-enabled medical device gathers the health data and transfers it to the doctors for real-time monitoring of their health status irrespective of location and time. Thus enhances the possibility of giving timely treatment and improves the accuracy of intervention made by doctors.

## Remote Intervention

Accessibility to the doctor is a major issue for the patients who are in emergency condition and who needs an immediate medical assistance. IoT adds mobility to healthcare domain; physicians can check the patients and find the disorders instantaneously. It also supports automatic drug distribution based on the instant health factors through connected devices.

The drifts in healthcare domain can be divided into several categories with respect to supporting technologies like sensing, communication, analytics and intelligence. This congregates the consumer devices and healthcare devices. Recently smartphones are being designed to provide healthcare support via incorporated medical sensors and that can be called as Mobile-Health (M-Health). M-Health make use of smartphone applications and wireless communication technologies for public health monitoring and interventions. The IoT has been applied in various ways for improving the medical intelligence as showed in Table 1.

## HIoT DESIGN ANATOMY

The IoT collects a huge amount of information from healthcare devices (i.e., medical equipment, sensors) which are connected to the network platform. The idea behind in connecting the clinical devices to the network platform is to give accessibility and controllability features; hence it becomes uniquely

*Table 1. IoT in Human Healthcare*

| Nature of Applicability | Use Case |
|---|---|
| Remote Patient Monitoring | Remote Patient Monitoring enables the remote investigation of patient vital sign with the help of sensory technologies. This can be highly adoptable for chronic disease management like hypertension, diabetes, coronary heart diseases and kidney diseases. |
| Mobile-Health | Mobile-Health application is entirely depending upon the mobile app interface for monitoring and delivery of interventions. |
| Assisting-Medical devices | The devices are mainly used in tracking of patient activities, assisting surgeries and smart medical equipment's enables the doctor to give assistance. |
| Virtual Intervention | Virtual Intervention allows the healthcare providers to give medicine delivery, virtual therapy and consultation with the help of connected devices and multimedia solutions. |
| Rehabilitation System | The main aim of rehabilitation system is to provide clinical monitoring for persons who are physically challenged and independent elder patients. This system will be mostly in the form of wearable's which records the vital signs of elderly patients and give intimation or alerts to the concern healthcare providers in case of finding any abnormalities. |

identifiable clinical devices. In addition, patients are exclusively monitored via smartphones and embedded devices which also uses the network as it constituents. Designing of such system is acting as a back bone for transmitting and delivering of medical data. Healthcare Internet of Things (HIoT) design has been analyzed into three different categories which includes HIoT network topology, HIoT architecture and HIoT platform as shown in Figure 3.

*Figure 3. HIoT Network Design Anatomy*

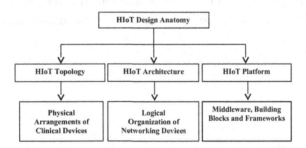

## HIoT Network Topology

HIoT Network Topology depicts how the medical devices are organized in a network and also defines the layout for establishing communication between clinical sensors, actuators and gateways. Building the IoT-based healthcare system without network topology is merely difficult to design an efficient system. The factors to be considered on selecting the suitable network topology and protocols for IoT-enable system are power consumption, cost, reliable and communication. These factors can be carefully handled by analyzing the characteristics, abilities and performance of the network topologies include: latency, throughput, fault tolerance, scalability, range and number of hops.

The HIoT uses the network topologies based on the networking standards and this can be divided into three different topologies as shown in Figure 4.

*Figure 4. HIoT Topologies*

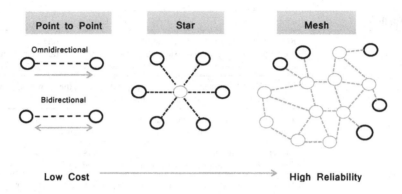

## Point-to-Point Topology

A point-to-point topology establishes a link between any two networking nodes or devices. This topology is much simpler and cost effective that exhibits the one-to-one relationship between two devices. As point-to-point topology is limited to lay a communication between two devices, it does not provide scalability and the capability of ranging is also limited to one hop. In HIoT, the sensor nodes collects real-time medical data gets directly transmitted to the network or gateway via a short range communication medium such as Bluetooth or WLAN as shown in Figure 5 (Patel et al., 2012). The point-to-point topology can able to take two forms either omnidirectional or bidirectional according to the use case. The healthcare systems which use omnidirectional form can only transfer the data to its gateway and such system cannot receive any data from other side. In bidirectional form, the data can be transmitted to the gateway and also the intervention can be delivered to the patients using the same medium i.e. via gateway to the node.

*Figure 5. HIoT Point-to-Point Topology*

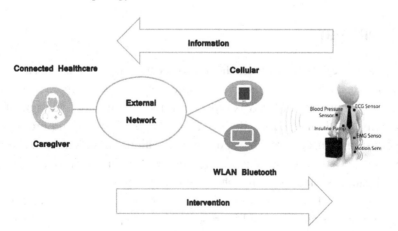

## Star Topology

A star topology is composed of one central control node called hub (gateway), through which all other nodes (sensor nodes) in the network are connected. The central control node behaves like a relay for all other nodes, thus all the sensor nodes send and receive the data via central control node only. In star topology, the hub can be internal which widely uses the Wi-Fi network or external which uses public network. The start topology results in providing high throughput, consistency, reliable and low latency communication. The finding of faulty nodes will be easier, by means of isolation of distinct nodes in the network. On the other side, star topology suffers from drawbacks such as limitation in range of transmission and in case of central control node failure, and then the entire network loses the communication with gateway.

Most of the IoT-enabled health monitoring systems is composed of medical sensor nodes, gateways, data center and healthcare providers. The vital signs of various patients made available to the doctors or caregivers for providing medical intervention from remote location any time. The star topological scenario is highly suitable for this kind of application as shown in Figure 6. The individual patient data gets transmitted to the gateway via internal network i.e. Wi-Fi. Generally gateway acts as a central control node through which various patient's medical data is being transmitted to the data center (Amir et al., 2018).

*Figure 6. HIoT Star Topology*

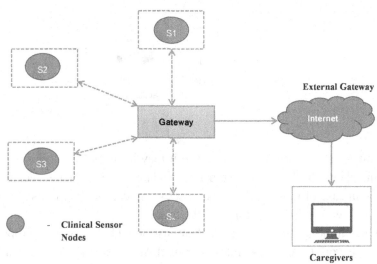

## Mesh Topology

A mesh topology provides a high reliable network which composed of three different kinds of nodes: gateway node, distinct sensor nodes and router/sensor nodes. Like star topology, gateway allows the sensed data to reach the external world (i.e. data center). The distinct sensor nodes simply broadcast the data to the gateway whereas router/sensor nodes not only broadcast its own data but also it acts as a relay for other sensor nodes. In mesh network data reaches the gateway by passing through multiple router/sensor nodes. The complexity factor of mesh topology is high when compared to point-to-point and star

*Figure 7. HIoT Mesh Topology*

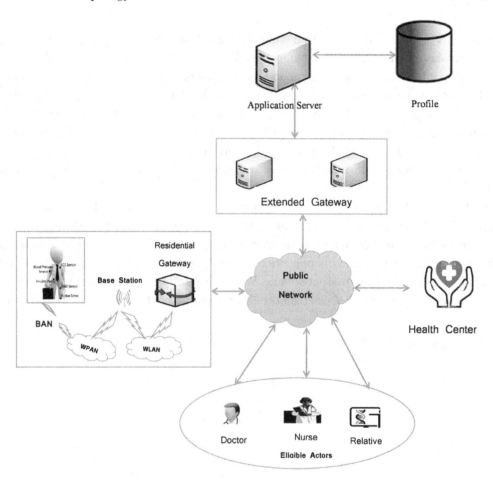

topologies. It also suffers from high latency because it may have multiple hops to reach the gateway. This topology permits the multiple nodes to transmit the data simultaneously even under heavy traffic. Unlike star topology, in case of failure in any router/sensor node, the data transfer doesn't get affected because alternate nodes are available to carry out the task.

An IoT-enabled health monitoring system can be constructed based on mesh topology, which comprises of Body Area Network (BAN), a Wireless Personal Area Network (WPAN), a WLAN, extended gateway, application server and healthcare center as shown in Figure 7. The Body Gateway (BG) gathers the data from BAN which contains medical sensors and then forwards the data to the Base Station (BS) via WPAN. The BS forwards the data to the Residential Gateway (RG) through WLAN and RG is responsible for connecting BS with the public network. The healthcare providers can make use of data aggregated at health center for giving remedies to their patients (Fengou et al., 2012). There is an extended gateway that provides secured framework for accessing the patient profile database via application server.

*Figure 8. HIoT Architecture*

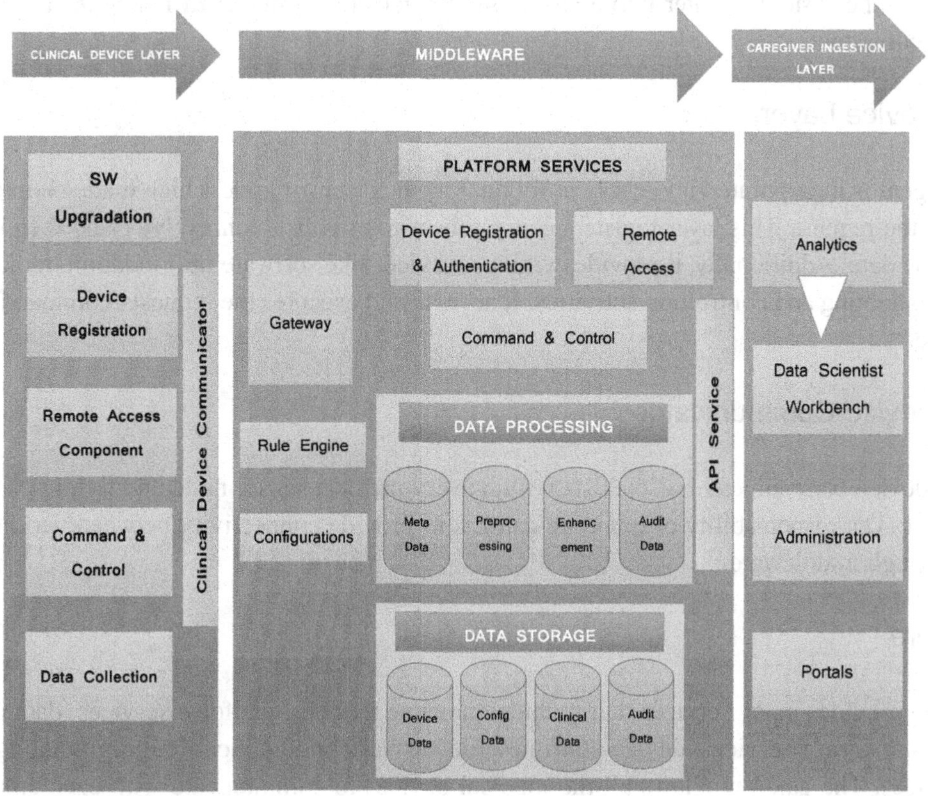

## HIoT Architecture

HIoT must concentrate on providing healthcare to the patients without any geographical limitations and also it must continuously monitor their medical data for preventing them from life time risks. This can be achieved by developing an IoT-enabled healthcare system, which incorporates five major constituents such as: sensors, network infrastructure, cloud computing, data analytics and healthcare providers. With respect to these components, HIoT architecture has been designed in Figure 8. This architecture has its own characteristic features which include:

- **Constancy:** HIoT systems are capable of providing real-time monitoring, this architecture constantly make a request to sensor nodes for trustworthy data collection. .
- **Continuity:** This provides interoperability support for communication system thus helps the network to maintain continuity in communication among end-users, nodes and links.
- **Confidentiality:** This architecture provides a scalable and secured storage in cloud which can save the real-time data and while accessing it allows the user to handle data confidentially.
- **Usability:** Data analytics is a heart of this architecture because it converts dynamic medical data into useful information which helps healthcare providers to make better decisions.

Developing HIoT systems must bind the four features together, in case of missing any one of the feature allows the system to enter into a valueless and defected system. HIoT architecture is made of four major components:

## Clinical Device Layer

A device agent is incorporated into every individual medical sensor node which made them capable of processing the request. This layer registers every sensor to establish connectivity and then it can able to collect the data. Additionally, it provides various services like software up-gradation, remote accessing, troubleshooting and controlling activities. It accepts and executes the requests/commands from the middleware.

## Clinical Device Communicator

A clinical device communicator also exists within every medical sensor node and tightly coupled with device agent. The responsibility of communicator is to provide connectivity between various medical devices through middleware.

## Middleware

Middleware provides many services that include: gateway services, platform services, data processing services, data storage services, device configuration services and application programming interface (API) services. The gateway allows all the medical devices to communicate with each other. A platform service handles the functionalities such as device registration, authentication, remote accessing, controlling the devices on the network and requests the device agent to act according to its commands. The data processing does four jobs (i.e. metadata, preprocessing, enhancement and audit trails) in order to generate a suitable datasets for analytics. Data storage services provides four separate storage spaces for storing device data, configuration data, clinical data and audit data, in order to avoid conflicts while accessing. The API service provides a platform for end-user to access the collected data. Another important component in middleware layer is rule engine, which is a software entity that allows devices to register and configure the infrastructure.

## Caregiver Ingestion Layer

The caregiver ingestion layer is where the end-users like physicians, nurses and pharmacists make use of information. This layer provides an opportunity to develop many applications based on the collected information. For example, a user interface can be created for every end-user with different access permissions and workbench can be designed for users to access the data and also facilitates the detection of diseases by means of analytical programs.

## HIoT Network Platforms

The HIoT platform is a set of entities used to maintain, control and monitor the medical devices by deploying self-regulating and secure communication between devices. The platform is an application which binds cloud services and the intelligent devices. It is also called as HIoT middleware; it serves as an inter-mediator for both application layer and hardware devices. HIoT platform is entirely different from other platforms with respect to the following features:

- **Elasticity:** HIoT platforms are capable of accepting any number of end devices as per the requirements of users.
- **Flexibility:** It provides a convenient API's for developing an IoT based systems, the developers may have flexibility over coding, integration, communicating schemas and security.
- **Security:** It gives security via encryption techniques for data in flow, data at rest. It is responsible for granting access on data and ownership. It also provides isolated cloud storage for storing sensitive data.
- **Interoperability:** HIoT platform allows the integration of any hardware and software which belongs to different manufacturers significantly.

The HIoT platform ensures integration of dissimilar hardware by using communication protocols, appropriate topology and necessary software. This platform has been designed with interfaces required for feeding the medical data into storage and then used for data analytics. The HIoT platform can proficiently adopt any kind of medical devices and can be integrated with the applications. HIoT platform depicted as four-tier structure which includes: medical things, connectivity, management services, data analytics and user interface. The management services is a core tier of this platform model which securely stores the collected data via encryption techniques, manages and controls the devices, provides tools for data processing and does the adoption of communication protocols. HIoT platform model is shown in the Figure 9.

## Medical Things

The medical things is the bottom most layer of HIoT platform which is analogous to the physical layer in the OSI network reference model. It consists of internet-connected physical devices like clinical sensors, medical devices, wearables and mobile applications. This can be referred as base-tier, as these medical things have ability to grasp the patient's physiological vital signs. The caregivers can monitor their patient's behavior using the data generated by these things and hence it can be otherwise called as Data Generator.

## Connectivity

Connectivity is the second-tier of HIoT platform model acts as heart of IoT-enable medical devices. Like human heart maintains the body alive by circulating the blood throughout the body, this tier provides a network connection for transmitting the medical data gathered in bottom most layer to the next higher level layer. To carry out the transmission four components are involved: Local Area Network (LAN) communication, cross-domain protocol gateway, agent gateway and internet communication protocols. LAN communication is responsible for transferring the data from medical things to the gateways. Some of the commonly used communication technologies are Bluetooth, ZigBee, 6LoWPAN, Wi-Fi, Z-Wave and Low Range (LoRa) will be discussed in next section. Cross-domain protocol gateway enables the embedded systems to transfer the information between the devices which are having dissimilar security

*Figure 9. HIoT Platform Model*

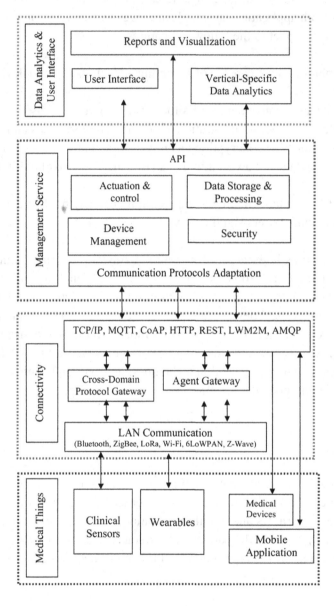

concerns. This ensures data confidentiality, data integrity and data availability without any security consequences. The agent gateway is responsible for establishing a relationship between LAN and distributed external systems. It is done by providing network policy and agent migration information. An internet communication protocol receives the medical data from gateway and forwards to the next higher layer for processing. Some of the protocols used in this case are TCP/IP, MQTT, AMQP, REST, HTTP and CoAP (*"Internet of Things Protocols and Standards", 2018*).

## Management Service

The management service is the core-tier of HIoT platform model which performs various operations such as protocol adaption, device management, security, data storage, data processing and APIs. All these functionalities have to take place at cloud infrastructure as it provides elastic resources based on usage patterns.

## Data Analytics and User Interface

This is the top most tier of HIoT platform model composed of many components such as user interface, visualization, reports, vertical-specific data analytics. User interface allows the end-users (doctors or caregivers) to make use of available portals (web-based or mobile-based) to visualize the patient's medical reports. The major component is vertical-specific data analytics that offers a group of intelligence specifically designed for medical analytic applications. This enables healthcare providers to drive a better decision and conclude where to emphasis the treatment.

# HIoT TECHNOLOGIES

Healthcare domain is constantly gaining the importance as much how the rate of population increases. The healthcare accessibility ratio of rural and semi-urban area is unknown. The aim of attaining the healthy population is always being a dream due to lack of technology. But now it has been made possible by improvements in sensors and communication technologies. With this great openings healthcare providers can be easily directly accessed by patients around the clock. In this section both sensor and communication technologies which improved the healthcare domain are discussed.

## Communication Technologies

Communication medium is a nervous system of HIoT through which medical data transfer takes place from one end to another end. Based on the applicability of medical things and geographical constraints communication technologies has been broadly classified into two types: Short-range communications and long range communications. Most of the IoT-based health monitoring system uses the two communication technologies. The medical data transmission in HIoT systems has two relays. The first relay is for medical things to communicate with gateway requires short-range communication medium. The data collected at gateway becomes useless; until extracting high-level information for decision making. For that next relay, uses long-range communication for forwarding the data to the storage location where the caregivers can access it. Many factors has to be analyzed while selecting the short and long-range communications.

## Short-range Communications

In IoT-based healthcare system, short-range communication technologies take part between medical things and internal gateways. This section discovers and compares the widely used short-range communication technologies in HIoT. In order to use short-range communications in healthcare systems it is necessary

*Table 2. Short-range Communication Technologies for HIoT*

| Parameters | Technologies | | | | |
|---|---|---|---|---|---|
| | Bluetooth | UWB | Wi-Fi | Z-Wave | ZigBee |
| Authentication | Shared Secret | CBC-MAC (CCM) | WPA2 (IEEE 802.11i) | AES-CBCMAC | CBC-MAC (Extension of CCM) |
| Battery Life | Days to Weeks | Hours to Days | Hours | 3 Years | Months to Years |
| Cost | Low | Low | High | Low | Low |
| Data Protection | 16-bit CRC | 32-bit CRC | 32-bit CRC | 8-Bit Checksum | 16-bit CRC |
| Data Rate | 1–24 Mb/s | 110 Mbits/s to 1.6 GBits/s | 1 Mb/s – 6.75 Gb/s | 250 kb/s | 250 Kbits/s |
| Encryption | E0 Stream Cipher | AES Block Cipher | RC4 Stream Cipher (WEP), AES Block Cipher | AES-OFB | AES Block Cipher |
| Energy Consumption | Medium | Low | High | Medium | Very Low |
| Frequency Band | 2.4 GHz | 3.1 to 10.6 GHz | 5-60 GHz | 908.4 MHz | 868/915 MHz, 2.4 GHz |
| Nodes | 8 | 128 | 32 | 232+ | 65,000 |
| Spreading | FHSS | DS-UWB, MB-OFDM | DSSS, CCK, OFDM | FSK | DSSS |
| Standard | IEEE 802.15.1 | IEEE 802.15.3 (Ratified) | IEEE 802.11 a/c/b/d/g/n | IEEE 802.11 | IEEE 802.15.4 |
| Topology | Mesh, Star, Tree | Star, P2P | Star, P2P | Mesh | P2P, Star, Tree and Mesh |
| Transmission Range | 8m – 10m | 4m – 20m | 20m - 100m | 100m | 10m – 300m |

to examine the communication factors affecting human body, transmission delay, reliability. While selecting long-range communications, factors to be analyzed are reliability, error correction mechanisms, latency, delay and confidentiality. The selection of short-range communication for healthcare systems must provide strong security mechanisms for ensuring the privacy of patient's data. The communication technology with low-latency is highly preferable for health-care or time-critical IoT applications, because it may alert doctors and ambulance services during medical emergencies. If data transmission is delayed, it leads the patients to enter into the life time risks and such kind of communication technologies is not preferable. Major studies (Jara et al., 2013) (Kalsnia et al., 2012) have merited the Wi-Fi, Bluetooth, Z-Wave, ZigBee and Ultra Wide Band (UWB) as most commonly used technologies in healthcare systems. Table 2 compares the various HIoT enabling short-range communication technologies with respect to distinct parameters.

## Long-Range Communications

A subset of long-range communication is low-power wide area networks (LPWAN) that are highly applicable for healthcare systems. Normally LPWAN ranges up to several kilometers which are extremely covers long distance than the coverage distance of Wi-Fi or Bluetooth. LPWAN used in healthcare devices such as remote health monitoring, rehabilitation systems operates around the clock to reduce the life time risk of patients because of interrupted connectivity. As per the study made, LPWAN is considered as a best long-range communication for transmitting data from gateway to the cloud storage for processing. Long-range communications must satisfy all the essentials as like short-range communications. In addition, high error correction mechanism is required to ensure that the data remains unaltered during transmission. Finally, availability is important feature required to transmit data at any time without any geographical restrictions. The most commonly used LPWANs are Worldwide Interoperability for Microwave Access (WiMAX), Cellular, Sigfox and LoRa. Table 3 provides the comparison of long-range communication used in HIoT with respect to their features.

*Table 3. Long-range Communication Technologies for HIoT*

| Parameters | Technologies | | | |
|---|---|---|---|---|
| | Sigfox | LoRa | Cellular | WiMAX |
| Authentication | AES Encrypted / 16 bit | CCM | High Security, back by major telecoms | CBC-MAC |
| Battery Life | 5-10 Years | Years | 1 day | Months to Years |
| Cost | Low | High | High | High |
| Data Protection | 128-bit CRC | 128-bit CRC | --- | 128-bit CRC |
| Data Rate | 100 bps | 0.3–50 Kb/s | High | 1 Mb/s–1 Gb/s (Fixed) |
| Encryption | No Network Encryption | AES Block Cipher | CMEA | 3DES, AES Block Cipher |
| Energy Consumption | Low | Very Low | High | Medium |
| Frequency Band | 868/915MHz | 868/900 MHz | 200KHz | 2-66 GHz |
| Nodes | 50000 | 120 | 5000/Gateway | 100 |
| Spreading | UNB(Ultra Narrow Band) | Chirp Spread Spectrum (CSS) | --- | OFDM |
| Standard | No | IEEE 802.15.4g | GSM, LTE | IEEE 802.16 |
| Topology | Star | Star-of-Stars | Star | Radio Access Network (RAN), Mesh |
| Transmission Range | <9.5 Kms | < 30 Kms | <35-200Kms | < 50 Kms |

## Sensing Technologies

Technical improvements in sensors converted the traditional healthcare systems into modernized healthcare systems with remote monitoring capability. Sensors are identified as a key component for caregivers to monitor their patient's vital signs. Nowadays sensors are made in the form of wearables like watch, pendant, wrist bands for the flexibility and comfort of the patient's. There are two types of sensors used widely in healthcare system: Non-invasive and Inertial sensors.

## Non-Invasive Sensors

A non-invasive sensor provides a new vision to change the former techniques available for monitoring the physiological factors. It is also called as unobtrusive sensing method which enables to take physiological data without the requirement of bio fluids. Wearable based health monitoring devices popularized with the wide improvements in the field of non-invasive sensors and biosensors. These sensors can be easily fitted into the things which are used in our day to day lives. Such kind of sensors provides accurate and consistent for diagnosing the patient's disease. This section is focused on fundamental non-invasive sensors which are used for monitoring the vital signs.

## Blood Pressure Sensor

Blood pressure is the rate at which blood is pumped in the arteries by the heart. This blood pressure sensor evaluates the rate of pressure into two variations – Systolic and Diastolic (pumping and relaxing). High Blood pressure (Hypertension) is considered as an important sign of heart disease and cardiovascular diseases.

## Body Temperature Sensor

Body temperature is a predominant factor for diagnosing hyperthermia, stroke and fever. These sensors give accuracy results based on proximity to the human body. Hence it has been widely integrated in wearable-based health monitoring systems.

## Electrocardiogram (ECG) Sensor

ECG sensor is commonly used medical test for monitoring the muscular functioning of the heart. It evaluates the abnormal cardiac rhythms and cardiac pathologies such as ischemia and palpitations. ECG sensors are capable of acquiring data even from the hand palms of the patient rather than heart.

## Electroencephalogram (EEG) Sensor

EEG sensor is monitors and records the activity of the brain from the sensor electrodes placed on the scalp. It can be carried out for predicting the abnormal brain activities, tumors, seizures, dizziness and sleeping disorders by using four waves such as alpha, beta, theta and delta waves. In IoT-based healthcare systems, EEG sensors are used for capturing the driver drowsiness and stress analysis (Li.G et al., 2015) (Ha et al., 2015).

## Blood Glucose Sensor

Blood glucose sensor contains electrochemical strips through which the glucose concentration in the blood can be assessed. Building a real-time blood glucose monitoring system can be highly useful for diabetes patients to manage their lift in blood glucose levels.

## GSR (Galvanic Skin Response) Sensor

GSR sensor evaluates the skin conductance which acts as a symptom psychological and physiological stimulation. Hence through the evaluation of skin conductance, the emotion can be identified. GSR predicts the emotions using two electrodes that can be placed on any two fingers. GSR sensor is useful in designing a healthcare system for monitoring stress levels, as our nervous system stimulates the sweat glands to secrete more sweat on strong emotions.

## Pulse Oximetry Sensors

$SpO_2$ sensor or pulse oximetry sensor examines the level of oxygen in the blood but it is not treated as a vital sign like blood pressure. It acts as a pointer of respiratory functions and helpful in diagnosing the hypoxia (reduced oxygen in tissues).

## Pulse Sensors

Pulse sensor measure the heart beat rate and it is the most commonly monitored vital signs to predict many health disorders include cardiac arrest, vasovagal syncope and pulmonary embolisms (Zenko.J et al., 2016). This sensor is capable of reading the pulse rate at various parts of our human body such as chest, fingers and earlobes. Even though it can be read from many part of the body, accuracy of reading is more important. While analyzing the accuracy factor, it has been found that reading the pulse from earlobe and finger which attains more accurate results. Placing the pulse sensors as wearables at ears and fingers are not comfortable and it can be worthy to be in the form of wrist bands.

## Respiratory Rate Sensors

Respiratory Sensor or airflow sensor calculates the inhale and exhale rates per minute and it acts as a vital sign for predicting the lung cancer, attacks, barriers in airway and tuberculosis. From the studies (Milici et al., 2017) (Varon et al., 2015), it is identified that the healthcare systems were developed for measuring respiratory rate, as it is considered to be an important factor for diagnosing many diseases.

## Inertial Sensors

An inertial sensors used in healthcare systems are based on micro-electro-mechanical system (MEMS) which measures the force applied, angular rate and magnetic fields around the body. This can be achieved by integrating three different inertial sensors such as accelerometer, magnetometer and gyroscope. Many healthcare systems have been developed for regular monitoring of patients physical activities (Rand et al., 2009) (Bonnie et al., 2013). Another important inertial sensor is body position sensor, which monitors the body postures like standing, sitting and so on to predict the future health issues.

## HIoT APPLICATIONS

The developing interdisciplinary applications in the field of IoT transformed the traditional way of living into smart living. Among various applications, healthcare is one of the growing technology, which provides doctors or caregivers on a pocket. It is not possible to eradicate the chronic disease in a while with the help of IoT. But the chronic diseases can be managed by doctors or caregivers with regular remote monitoring of their patients vital signs. The regular monitoring process is time consuming and costlier. IoT has changed the scenario like health check-ups from doctor-centric to patient-centric. All these have been accomplished with the applications of IoT in human healthcare domain. In this section, applications of HIoT are presented as two categories: Distributed Applications and Clustered Applications as shown in Figure 10. Distributed applications deals with the systems that focus on monitoring any single vital sign whereas clustered applications clubs two or more vital signs together.

### Blood Pressure Monitoring

J.Puustjarvi et al. designed a system for monitoring and controlling the blood pressure remotely via a communication layered between patient and data center (Puustjarvi et al., 2011). A similar system has been presented in (Guan, 2013). T.J.Xin et al. developed an intelligent blood pressure monitoring along with location tracking facility (Xin et al., 2013).

### Body Temperature Monitoring

Finding of common abnormalities like fever, hyperthermia and stroke is much simpler using body temperature. An IoT-enabled temperature monitoring system makes use of home-based communication to transmit collected data to remote data center is presented in (Jian et al., 2012). A TelosB mote system uses IPv6 communication between patients and caregivers for visualizing the changes in body temperature (Istepanian et al., 2011). Likewise, a system designed for recording the body temperature and uses RFID technology for sending recorded data to the storage (In Z.L, 2014).

### Blood Glucose Monitoring

Diabetes is one of a metabolic disease caused due to persistent high glucose level in blood. The real-time monitoring system uses temperature sensor and non-invasive blood glucose sensor for tracking the patient's temperature and blood glucose patterns. (Z.J. Guan, 2013) presented an IoT-based utility model for sensing the blood glucose which is composed of three elements such as blood glucose collector unit, processing unit and mobile device.

### ECG Monitoring

ECG is used for monitoring the activities of the heart via rhythms. (M.L.Liu et al., 2012) introduced a portable ECG monitoring system which consists of transmitter and receiver and this system identifies the cardiac problems using real-time ECG data.

*Figure 10. Classification of HIoT Applications*

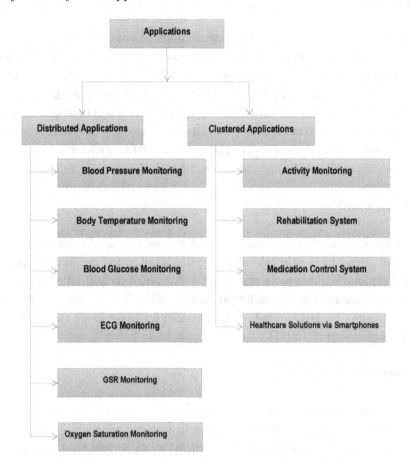

## GSR Monitoring

The internal and external stimuli are controlled and regulated by the sympathetic and parasympathetic nervous systems. The parasympathetic system of human body is known for preserving and restoring the energy level. The various vital signs like blood pressure, heart beat rate and sweat secretion has been driven by the sympathetic system. In many of the health monitoring system GSR is used for monitoring the stress and emotion level of humans (Critchley.H.D, 2012) (Bakker et al., 2011). A wearable-based GSR monitoring device is invented and reveals the psychophysiological conditions with low power consumption (P.Bonato, 2003) (Sano et al. 2013).

## Oxygen Saturation Monitoring

Oxygen Saturation Monitoring is used for evaluating the amount of oxygen present in blood. The abnormal level of oxygen in blood is a symptom for various health issues such as cardio-vascular, pulmonary diseases and anemia. A cost effective and low energy consuming pulse oximeter system is designed for monitoring the patient's oxygen level in blood (Larson et al. 2012) and also a wearable based system oxygen saturation monitoring device has been developed (Larson et al., 2011).

## Activity Monitoring

The musculoskeletal diseases and fall prediction in rehabilitation system can be arrived by regular monitoring of physical movements of body parts. (S.Mulro et al., 2003) study identified that the health conditions can be revealed by the patient's walking postures and patterns. Necessity arises for a system to observe the balancing and synchronization of body parts while walking. A wearable device is developed using three inertial sensors such as an accelerometer, a magnetometer and a gyroscope for observing the limb movements of a person (Bertolotti et al., 2016). A gait-event detection device developed for measuring the angular velocity and flexion angle of legs (Bejarano et al., 2015). This device is composed of inertial and magnetic sensors along with that an adaptive algorithm has been integrated to predict the gait-event.

## Rehabilitation System

The rehabilitation restores the life of differently abled persons and aged persons who all are living independently. The adoption of IoT in rehabilitation systems renovated the life of independent persons. From the studies it is identified that more number of IoT-enabled rehabilitation system has been introduced which includes rehabilitation system for prisons (Lin.D.Y, 2013), system for hemiplegic patient's (Guangnan, Z., & Penghui, L., 2012) rehabilitation system for smart city (Yue-Hong et al., 2014) and for childhood autism (Liang et al., 2011).

## Medication Control System

Healthcare domain is constantly considered as a time-critical domain in which all activities have to be carried out at a right time. Likewise delaying in the medication creates a serious health issues and cause financial losses. To avoid such kind of delay in medication, an IoT-enabled medication management system is developed with intelligence (Pang et al., 2014). This gathers patient's vital signs via wearable sensors and diagnoses the disease for suggesting medicines. A similar system is also designed using an RFID tag which enables caregivers to prescribe medicines remotely (Laranjo et al., 2012).

## Healthcare Solutions via Smartphones

The smartphone users are relatively high and it drives the healthcare domain to new platform where timely alerts will be possible during emergency situations. Nowadays smartphones are integrated with sensors that collect the data from smartphone users and forward it to the caregivers for real-time monitoring. Many healthcare apps are developed for diagnosing the health conditions like pulmonary disease, cough, respiratory problems, heart rate, blood pressure, oxygen saturation and diabetes.

## ISSUES IN DESIGNING OF HIoT SYSTEMS

The HIoT have a significant social impact and shaping the networking strategies. Recent years many research activities are taking part towards the designing of architectures and standards but enormous amount of deployment issues to be solved globally to provide consistency and quality in treatments. The most common design issues to be considered while developing HIoT system will be discussed in this section.

## Battery Life

As discussed in the section, HIoT aims to provide healthcare solutions without geographical restrictions. HIoT tends to deploy the sensors nodes at every users environment for collecting vital signs. During deployment an important issue must be carefully blended is that the battery life. The communication technologies, protocols and hardware used in the system have a direct impact on battery life. Every nodes like wearables are battery powered, which will never throw any problem in case of limited number of nodes. When it grows to millions of nodes it would increase the expenses for battery replacements. The only solution to this problem is energy harvesting which includes solar cells and piezoelectric elements.

## Data Transmission Vulnerability

The regulatory bodies must ensure the security of individual's health information which is exchanged among the connected devices and stored in a centric-location. The strong access control mechanisms are not enough but every healthcare regulatory body must ensure that the patient's personal data is stored in an encrypted format. The healthcare regulatory body doesn't have any control over end-devices to ensure data security during transmission. This vulnerability increases it severity when new devices are included to the network.

## Multiple Protocols and Devices Integration

When connecting the diversified devices together in a network is another barrier for implementing the IoT in healthcare. The issue arises when multiple devices are connected to share information with each other effectively is a problem. This is due to the systems connected in the network belongs to various manufacturers doesn't have any set of communication protocols and standards. The medical devices connected in IoT healthcare network suffers from lack of uniformity and thus affects the scalability.

## Accuracy

The process of gathering and aggregating data via healthcare systems is useful for extracting the high level information and insights which provides better treatment to patients. The extraction of insights from large amount of healthcare data requires refined analytical programs. In particular, recognizing and categorizing valid insights becomes a critical task for caregivers when amount of data increases. This may reduce accuracy and the quality of decision made.

## HIoT SECURITY AND PRIVACY ISSUES

The security in HIoT is a pain and an untidiness which annoying the journey of human between life and death. HIoT poses more risk while comparing it with other kinds of IoT smart applications. Because the connected system contains the individuals personal identical information attracts the intruders. They try to compromise the network or medical things to gain access into those medical records. In order to address the security issues, a healthcare system must comply on three crucial factors such as:

- Warranting whether the healthcare system ensures availability, accessibility and consistency (A2C),
- Adopting strong authentication and authorization mechanism, and
- Ensuring system reliability.

Figure 11 presents a Tetrahedron Security Level Model, which depicts the HIoT vulnerability with respect to users, process, things, and tools i.e. platform and applications. The medical things in HIoT are likely to suffer in the process of securing the sensors, network components, communication protocols and application platform. HIoT composed of diversified components and expandable in nature, increases the vulnerability towards human resources as represented at users node. The severity of vulnerability at process and tool nodes is relatively low when comparing it with other nodes i.e. things and users.

In this section, crucial HIoT security issues will be discussed into two factors: HIoT Security Essentials and HIoT Security Threats.

## HIoT Security Essentials

The security needs for HIoT systems are analogous to the security essential standards of traditional communication circumstances. In order to attain secure HIoT systems, it becomes necessary to focus on security essentials which are specified below:

## Authentication

The medical devices connected together in a network must ensure the identity of all other devices to certify the participating device is valid or not. Upon the successful verification each other's identity, both the participating devices can exchange information.

## Authorization

The process of authorization allows the nodes in the network to gain access on the resources and services provided by HIoT systems. It also validates the user's access level on data while they are trying to access the medical data.

## Availability

As HIoT is a time-critical application, it must allow caregivers to monitor their patient's vital signs and provide medical intervention without geographical restrictions. If availability is breached then the healthcare systems becomes useless.

## Confidentiality

Confidentiality is a basic security requirement in HIoT systems, as it designed to sense and store medical information. The system must restrict the unauthorized users to access the medical data. To ensure the confidentiality data center must deploy encryption mechanisms.

*Figure 11. Tetrahedron Security Level Model*

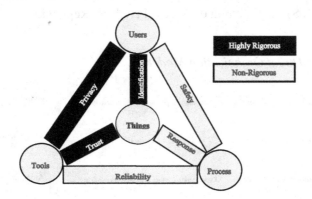

## Data Reliability

Every healthcare system is capable of collecting the medical data continuously and forwards it to the data center for real-time monitoring. Hence the data center content is being updated around the clock; the system must ensure that the data received at data center are very recent.

## Fault Tolerance

The healthcare system must comply to work with dynamic environment for delivering the uninterrupted services even under mobility issues and component failures.

## Data Integrity

The data integrity is a mechanism of ensuring that the medical information received at data center is reliable and not modified by malicious insiders during transmission. If the system is made to work on the environment without encryption mechanism, then it is not sure that the medical information received is original as sent by transmitter. With the tampered information, the decision made by caregivers becomes worthless. Hence data integrity must be ensured to avoid tampering of data on transmission.

## Non-Repudiation

Non-repudiation serves as an evidence of legitimacy and source of all medical information transmitted. This guarantees that the message sent or received cannot be further denied even by sender or receiver.

## HIoT Security Threats

The vulnerability factors are growing parallel to increase rate of security threats with respect to HIoT devices and networks. Such threats may initiate from inside and outside of the HIoT network. When the threat originates from healthcare devices within a network, then the severity of attack is more. Figure 12 presents a HIoT Security Threat Organization Model where identified healthcare system threats are related with respect to the security essentials. The identified healthcare system threats are: Data Leakage, Denial of Service (DoS), Exploitation of Access Privilege, Repudiation, Spoofing and Tampering.

*Figure 12. HIoT Security Threat Organization Model*

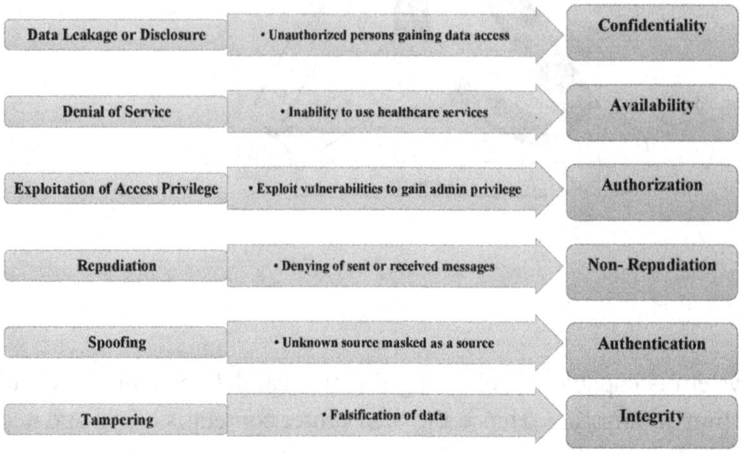

| Data Leakage or Disclosure | • Unauthorized persons gaining data access | Confidentiality |
| Denial of Service | • Inability to use healthcare services | Availability |
| Exploitation of Access Privilege | • Exploit vulnerabilities to gain admin privilege | Authorization |
| Repudiation | • Denying of sent or received messages | Non- Repudiation |
| Spoofing | • Unknown source masked as a source | Authentication |
| Tampering | • Falsification of data | Integrity |

## MACHINE LEARNING FOR HIoT

Machine learning is an intelligence paradigm that enables the system to build a model based on the patterns identified from the raw data and automatically uses that model to make predictions on new data as shown in Figure 13. HIoT device generate the volume of data, which grows when the number of devices increases. Intelligent analysis and processing of medical data is the key factor for developing smart medical applications. To make the HIoT system intelligent, two important techniques must be bonded together that are: streaming data and machine learning. It is necessary to understand the needs of integrating IoT, streaming data and machine learning which brings benefits to healthcare domain. HIoT systems monitor the vital signs and when it is combined with machine learning algorithm, doctors can apply smart treatment to their patients. It improves the quality of chronic disease management at lower costs.

*Figure 13. Overview of Machine Learning*

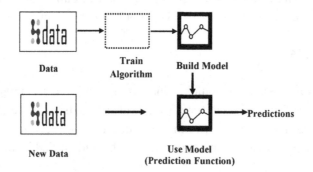

*Figure 14. Application of Machine Learning Algorithm on Streaming Data*

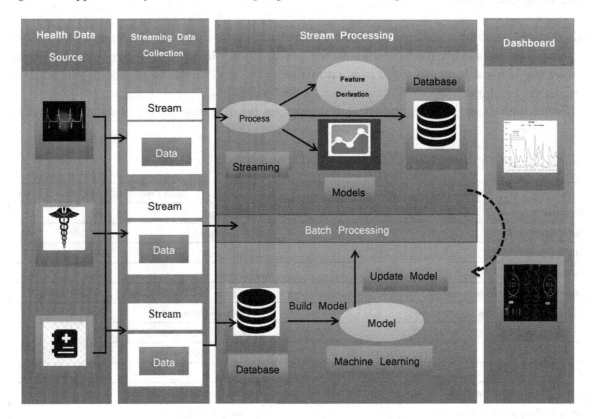

The process of applying streaming medical data with machine learning algorithms is presented in the Figure 14. It consists of four components that are: Health Data Source, Streaming Data Collection, Processing and Dashboard. Health Data Source is the first component which supplies a stream of data from the healthcare systems. Streaming data collection is the assembling unit where all the sensory medical data are organized. In order to make predictions on streaming health data, it is required to build an offline model. The next step is processing, which is composed of two entities: Batch Processing where an offline model is being build and Stream Processing where predictions are made based on streaming data.

In batch processing, historical medical data is used for constructing an offline-model which exhibits the normal behavior. Such model is built by applying the appropriate machine learning algorithms machine learning algorithms commonly used on streaming data are listed in Table 4). After formulation of normal behavior model, it can be validated against real-time systems to identify the variations in streaming data. Such variations are termed as anomalies.

## Anomaly Detection

The anomaly detection is the basic operation which identifies the similarities in the input data. It first establishes the normal behavior pattern and then a comparison will be made with observed behavior. If there any abnormal patterns found from normal behavior, an alert will be generated. It is a part of unsupervised learning.

Healthcare systems are real-time systems, it generates the data continuously and such data will be

*Table 4. Commonly used Machine Learning Algorithms on Streaming Data*

| Machine Learning Algorithm | Data Processing Tasks |
|---|---|
| K-Nearest Neighbors | Classification |
| Naive Bayes | Classification |
| Support Vector Machine | Classification |
| Linear Regression | Regression |
| Support Vector Regression | Regression |
| Classification and Regression Trees | Classification/Regression |
| Random Forests | Classification/Regression |
| Bagging | Classification/Regression |
| K-Means | Clustering |
| Canonical Correlation Analysis | Feature extraction |
| One-class Support Vector Machines | Anomaly detection |

considered as a stream which is called as window. The window comprised of last few time slot data logs. The collected data logs are analyzed to build another model for predicting the abnormality in health. This model is applied to the streaming data (online) and abnormality patterns obtained upon the observed sequence. If there any abnormal patterns recognized, an alert notification is generated at dashboard region where caregivers can visualize their patient's status. Thus the machine learning algorithm made every healthcare system as intelligent system.

## CONCLUSION

The HIoT design taxonomy is a primary element and acts as a backbone for facilitating the transmission and reception of medical data. The vision on wireless communication technology is available for building a healthcare system is expected to facilitate the selection of suitable technology. Recent advancements in sensing technologies and applications of IoT in healthcare systems expand the potential of IoT services for future developments. The perception on designing an effective healthcare system highlighting the major issues to be solved for providing consistent and quality in treatments. The current state of the art presented towards the security issues, discloses the various research problems under security aspects. Exploring the application of machine learning algorithm on real-time streaming data significantly improves the intelligence of healthcare systems. This chapter anticipated the major constituents of intelligent healthcare systems and promotes the universal deployment of IoT in healthcare.

## REFERENCES

Amir, Rahmani, Gia, Negash, Anzanpour, Azimi, Jiang, & Liljeberg. (2018). Exploiting smart e-Health gateways at the edge of healthcare Internet-of-Things: A fog computing approach. *Future Generation Computer Systems, 2*(78), 641–658.

Bakker, J., Pechenizkiy, M., & Sidorova, N. (2011). What's your current stress level? Detection of stress patterns from GSR sensor data. *IEEE 11th International Conference on Data Mining Workshops,* 573-580.

Bejarano, N. C., Ambrosini, E., Pedrocchi, A., Ferrigno, G., Monticone, M., & Ferrante, S. A. (2015). Novel Adaptive, Real-Time Algorithm to Detect Gait Events from Wearable Sensors. *IEEE Transactions on Neural Systems and Rehabilitation Engineering, 23*(3), 413–422. doi:10.1109/TNSRE.2014.2337914 PMID:25069118

Bertolotti, G. M., Cristiani, A. M., Colagiorgio, P., Romano, F., Bassani, E., Caramia, N., & Ramat, S. A. (2016). Wearable and Modular Inertial Unit for Measuring Limb Movements and Balance Control Abilities. *IEEE Sensors Journal, 16*(3), 790–797. doi:10.1109/JSEN.2015.2489381

Bonato, P. (2003). Wearable sensors/systems and their impact on biomedical engineering. *IEEE Engineering in Medicine and Biology Magazine, 22*(3), 18–20. doi:10.1109/MEMB.2003.1213622 PMID:12845812

Bonnie, S., Basia, B., Kevin, C., Catherine, W., Jeff Coppersmith, J. H., & Rehabil Dev, J. (2013). *Bodies in motion: monitoring daily activity and exercise with motion sensors in people with chronic pulmonary diseases.* Academic Press. doi: .0045 doi:10.1682/JRRD.2003.10

Critchley, H. D. (2002). Book Review: Electro dermal Responses: What Happens in the Brain? *The Neuroscientist, 8*(2), 132–142. doi:10.1177/107385840200800209 PMID:11954558

Fengou, Mantas, Lymberopoulos, Komnios, Fengos, Lazarou, & Nikolaos. (2012). A New Framework Architecture for Next Generation e-Health Services. *IEEE Transactions on Information Technology in Biomedicine.*

Guan, Z. J. (2013). *Internet-of-Things human body data blood pressure collecting and transmitting device.* Chinese Patent 202 821 362 U.

Guan, Z. J. (2013). *Somatic data blood glucose collection transmission device for Internet of Things.* Chinese Patent 202 838653 U.

Guangnan, Z., & Penghui, L. (2012). *IoT (Internet of Things) control system facing rehabilitation training of hemiplegic patients.* Chinese Patent 202 587045 U.

Ha. (2015). A wearable EEG-HEG-HRV multi model system with simultaneous monitoring of tES for mental health management. *IEEE Transactions on Biomedical Circuits and Systems, 9*(6), 758–766. PMID:26742142

In, Z. L. (2014). *Patient body temperature monitoring system and device based on Internet of Things.* Chinese Patent 103 577688 A.

Internet of Things Protocols and Standards. (n.d.). Retrieved from https://www.cse.wustl.edu/~jain/cse570-15/ftp/iot_prot

Istepanian, R. S. H., Hu, S., Philip, N. Y., & Sungoor, A. (2011). The potential of Internet of m-health Things 'm-IoT' for non-invasive glucose level sensing. *Proc. IEEE Annu.*

Jara, A. J., Zamora-Izquierdo, M. A., & Skarmeta, A. F. (2013). Interconnection framework for m-Health and remote monitoring based on the Internet of Things. *IEEE Journal on Selected Areas in Communications, 31*(9), 47–65. doi:10.1109/JSAC.2013.SUP.0513005

Jian, Z., Zhanli, W., & Zhuang, M. (2012). *Temperature measurement system and method based on home gateway.* Chinese Patent 102811 185A.

Klasnia, P., & Pratt, W. (2012). Healthcare in the pocket: Mapping the space of mobile-phone health interventions. *Journal of Biomedical Informatics, 45*(1), 184–198. doi:10.1016/j.jbi.2011.08.017 PMID:21925288

Laranjo, Macedo, Santos, & Alexandre. (2012). Internet of Things for Medication Control: Service Implementation and Testing. *Elsevier Procedia Technology, 5,* 777-786.

Larson, E. C., Goel, M., Boriello, G., Heltshe, S., Rosenfeld, M., & Patel, S. N. (2012). Spiro Smart: Using a microphone to measure lung function on a mobile phone. *Proc. ACM Int. Conf. Ubiquitous Comput.,* 280-289.

Larson, E. C., Lee, T., Liu, S., Rosenfeld, M., & Patel, S. N. (2011). Accurate and privacy preserving cough sensing using a low-cost microphone. *Proc. ACM Int. Conf. Ubiquitous Comput.,* 375-384.

Li, G., Lee, B. L., & Chung, W. Y. (2015). Smart watch-based wearable EEG system for driver drowsiness detection. *IEEE Sensors Journal, 15*(12), 7169–7180. doi:10.1109/JSEN.2015.2473679

Liang, S., Zilong, Y., Hai, S., & Trinidad, M. (2011). *Childhood autism language training system and Internet-of-Things-based centralized training center.* Chinese Patent 102 184661 A.

Lin, D. Y. (2013). *Integrated Internet of Things application system for prison.* Chinese Patent 102 867236 A.

Liu, M. L., Tao, L., & Yan, Z. (2012). *Internet of Things-based electro cardio-gram monitoring system.* Chinese Patent 102 764118 A.

Milici, S., Lorenzo, J., Lazaro, A., Villarino, R., & Jirbau, D. (2017). Wireless breathing sensor based on wearable modulated frequency selective surface. *IEEE Sensors Journal, 17*(5), 1285–1292. doi:10.1109/JSEN.2016.2645766

Mulro, S., Gronley, J., & Weiss, W. (2003). Use of cluster analysis for gait pattern classification of patients in the early and late recovery phases following stroke. *Gait & Posture, 18*(1), 114–125. doi:10.1016/S0966-6362(02)00165-0 PMID:12855307

Pang, Z., Tian, J., & Chen, Q. (2014). Intelligent packaging and intelligent medicine box for medication management towards the Internet-of-Things. *16th International Conference on Advanced Communication Technology*, 352-360. 10.1109/ICACT.2014.6779193

Patel, S., Park, H., Bonato, P., Chan, L., & Rodgers, M. (2012). A Review of Wearable Sensors and Systems with Applications in Rehabilitation. *Journal of Neuro Engineering and Rehabilitation, 20*(9).

Puustjarvi, J., & Puustjarvi, L. (2011). Automating remote monitoring and information therapy: An opportunity to practice telemedicine in developing countries. *Proc. IST-Africa Conf.*, 1-9.

Rand, D., Eng, J. J., Tang, P. F., Jeng, J. S., & Hung, C. (2009). How active are people with stroke? use of accelerometers to assess physical activity. *Stroke, 40*, 163–168. doi:10.1161/STROKEAHA.108.523621

Rose, K., Eldridge, S., & Chapin, L. (2015). *The Internet of Things (IoT): An Overview –Understanding the Issues and Challenges of a More Connected World*. Internet Society.

Sano, A., Picard, & R. W. (2013). Stress Recognition Using Wearable Sensors and Mobile Phones. *Proceedings of the 2013 Humaine Association Conference on Affective Computing and Intelligent Interaction, 671-676.* 10.1109/ACII.2013.117

Varon, C., Caicedo, A., Testelmans, D., Buyse, B., & Van Huffel, S. (2015). A novel algorithm for the automatic detection of sleep apnea from single-lead ECG. *IEEE Transactions on Biomedical Engineering, 62*(9), 2269–2278. doi:10.1109/TBME.2015.2422378 PMID:25879836

Xin, T. J., Min, B., & Jie, J. (2013). *Carry-on blood pressure/pulse rate/blood oxygen monitoring location intelligent terminal based on Internet of Things*. Chinese Patent 202 875315 U.

Yue-Hong, Y., Wu, F., Jie, F. Y., Jian, L., Chao, X., & Yi, Z. (2014). *Remote medical rehabilitation system in smart city*. Chinese Patent 103488 880 A.

Zenko, J., Kos, M., & Kramberger, I. (2016). Pulse rate variability and blood oxidation content identification using miniature wearable wrist device. *Proc. Int. Conf. Syst. Signals Image Process (IWSSIP)*, 1-4.

## ADDITIONAL READING

Ahmed, M. U., Begum, S., & Raad, W. (Eds.). (2017). *Internet of Things Technologies for HealthCare*. Västerås, Sweden: Springer Publisher.

Bouchard, B. (Ed.). (2017). *Smart Technologies in Healthcare*. CRC Press Publisher. doi:10.1201/9781315145686

Fengou, A., Mantas, G., Lymberopoulos, D., Komninos, N., Fengos, S., & Lazarou, N. (2013). A New Framework Architecture for Next Generation e-Health Services. *IEEE Journal of Biomedical and Health Informatics, 1*(17), 9–18. doi:10.1109/TITB.2012.2224876 PMID:23086531

Guarda, T., Augusto, M. F., Barrionuevo, O., & Pinto, F. M. (2017). Internet of Things in Pervasive Healthcare Systems. In J. M. Machado, A. Abelha, M. F. Santos, & F. Portela (Eds.), *Next Generation Mobile and Pervasive Healthcare Solutions* (pp. 21–31). IGI Publishers.

Krohn, R., Metcalf, D., & Salber, P. (Eds.). (2017). *Connected Health: Improving Care, Safety, and Efficiency with Wearables and IoT Solution*. CRC Press Publisher.

Kvedar, J. C. (Ed.). (2015). *The Internet of Healthy Things*. Internet of Healthy Things Publisher.

*This research was previously published in Intelligent Systems for Healthcare Management and Delivery; pages 235-265, copyright year 2019 by Medical Information Science Reference (an imprint of IGI Global).*

# Chapter 9
# IoT–Based Smart and Secure Health Monitoring System

**Parul Verma**
*Amity University, Lucknow, India*

**Brijesh Khandelwal**
*Amity University, Raipur, India*

## ABSTRACT

*IoT is not a new keyword. The latest gradations in the technology are now leaving no stone unturned to make IoT a part of every domain. Be it education, agriculture, transportation, business, or healthcare, every domain is now ready to exploit the benefits of IoT. By end-to-end connectivity and simultaneous monitoring and reporting, it is improving the efficiency of the healthcare systems and thus improving the health of patients. The chapter focuses on how IoT can be integrated with healthcare systems and draw maximum benefits from its ubiquitous presence. The chapter also covers various security concerns of an IoT-based healthcare system and their suggested solutions to overcome those concerns.*

## INTRODUCTION

According to Kevin Ashton, as published in RFID journal in year 2009, almost a decade after his introduction to phrase IoT, the IoT can be better understood in its reality in a way where, without taking human assistance, if all possible data can be gathered with the help of computers, and making it possible to know all about everything by tracking, recording, and sensing etc. Such mechanism would certainly reduce the cost, loss, and waste too. By counting, tracking, sensing things would be in a condition at all time to know about their good time for replacement, repairing, and recalling etc. S. Sinha (2018)

*It is high time; we need to understand computers can be empowered to be capable of getting things done as per the requirement generated by gathering information. The computers or devices would be able to sense in possible ways viz., hear, see, smell, touch, etc. and confirms the actions' initiation accordingly.*

DOI: 10.4018/978-1-6684-6311-6.ch009

If we conclude Ashton words, it means that making our devices and the users smart by simply sharing each and every whereabouts by the help of connecting devices and make information available for processing. This is possible only by connecting all such devices by some means in order to share data and information.

The IoT is a huge pool of interconnected devices, sensors, vehicles, embedded software and many other things. Such things are connected seamlessly using wired/wire-less connection media. Each such device/sensor/thing is treated as a node which can be configured by itself. This globally connected network of things/nodes works on infrastructure that is dynamic in nature and well supported by the communication technologies like - GSM– Wi-Fi, RFID, GPRS etc. Verma P. et. al. (2017)

IoT is not limited to a particular domain. It is vast and its usage is also versatile. Its usage can be justified in various domains like HealthCare systems, Transportation, Education, Energy Management, Agriculture and Business to name a few. IoT has been used in versatile domain and had justified its role in each domain. The use of IoT is no more restricted to only few domains. Nowadays if we turn around we can see use of IoT in every domain in some or other way. The chapter will discuss about the usage of IoT in Health Care Systems and its security concerns.

## IoT and Health Care Systems in Current Scenario

In Health Care Systems earlier there was AI which was supposed to help doctors and patients to communicate in a better way. Doctors and Patients are connected through a device which helps in better diagnosis by doctors. AI enabled Chatbots communicate to the patients and suggest primary medical help to them.

IoT is one step ahead to all what AI enabled bots had offered. Healthcare IoT can be understood as a coupled mechanism of software applications and medical instruments capable to communicating with numerous healthcare/ medical IT systems. The objective of IoT is to ascertain a better health in a record time in the competitive environment, IoT in healthcare unites patients and healthcare support providers via software and technologies. The Internet of Things for healthcare industry is an example of technology that enables physicians/ medical practitioners to experience healthier relationships with patients and eventually it nurture patients' involvements and establishing their trust in this mechanism.

Various researchers had worked and showed that remote health monitoring is not a dream now. IoT has shown promising results in many other fields by remote monitoring and data collection and processing. Similarly IoT can be used for the similar purpose of health monitoring of individuals and reporting their health status to the caretaker parties like doctors, health care centers or emergency services.

Such remote monitoring systems are quite helpful for non-critical patients where doctors or health centers can guide them by getting updated status of their health based on various parameters. These systems can be a boon to the elderly people where people living in the rural areas have critical issue of reachability to the doctors or hospitals.

The vision of Smart Health Care System is to cater the solutions for following two needful areas-

1.  Improvised disease management systems which may result for better experience of patients
2.  Reducing the healthcare associated costs so that it's affordable for wider demographics of patients

As per the recent literature published the global growth of Internet of Things (IoT) in the world's healthcare market is expected to be $158.07 billion in year 2022 as compared to $41.22 billion in year 2017 with a Compound Annual Growth Rate of 30.80%. This projected phenomenal growth is significant and perhaps that is why pharmaceutical products are now being meticulously planned, manufactured in good volume and quality and also been used, stored and consumed by the good variety of demographics. S Sivagami & D Revathy (2016)

Remote monitoring and controlling of IoT enabled healthcare devices/ machines have been emerged as most demanding technologies in the health care sector. IoT based system is considered as one of the sought for technology which has empowered physicians not only to deliver superlative care to their patients but also guarantees safe and healthy patients. Eventually, it has resulted in reinforcement of patients' satisfaction. Now, patients are finding it more convenient to get convenient engagement with physicians and to have easy interactions with doctors/ practioners. IoT enabled healthcare systems have made things more efficient. In addition to this, overstay in hospitals and re-admissions like bottlenecks of prevailing systems have also been checked and reduced. IoT enabled healthcare devices and systems as a whole resulted into reducing healthcare costs extensively and improving treatment results.

IoT is no doubt benefitting the way the whole network of Health and Care industry works. The benefits are manifolds and there are various application areas where IoT is directly or indirectly impacting the way traditional health care systems works. Monitoring systems helps doctors in many ways by early symptoms predictions and also sometimes emergency situations can also be predicted. IoT devices are playing quite promising role in patient care and offers lot of opportunities for the present health care systems. These devices are vulnerable to various security threats and the risk factor for such devices is comparably high in health care zone than consumer zone. Patients share their health related data through multiple devices to the centralized health care system. The data is being used by hospital management at various levels, hence the security of such data is crucial and since the IoT devices are quite vulnerable the chances of data breach is also higher.

## IoT based Health Care Monitoring Systems and Devices

Besides other industries healthcare is the one which has adopted IoT and its benefits at the first step. Integration of IoT with various health devices is giving promising results. The effectiveness these devices bring high value of health care especially in elderly patients suffering from some chronic disease and require regular attention. An estimation says that IoT healthcare solutions are a new buzz and by 2025 the total spend amount will reach to $1 trillion.

## KAA

Kaa is one of the leading enterprises based on IoT platform. It allows Original Equipment Management (OEM) and healthcare systems to implement cross device communication connectivity and also implement latest and smart features in medical devices and health care system. Kaa functionality can be integrated with the hardware and software devices produced by Healthcare companies in order to meet their IoT objectives in very less expenses.

Kaa had made a strong impact on scalability and flexibility of IoT based health care solutions. The flexibility feature lets you expand the size of Kaa cluster, so that as many number of devices can be supported with the assurance of optimal performance. The use risk of downtime can be minimized by available deployment of Kaa. Security is of the prime importance in IoT health care devices. The best part of Kaa is that it makes use of modern security protocols like TLS supports it in secure data exchange between devices.

## OpenAPS

Dana Lewis and her husband Scott Leibrand had hacked two health devices based on IoT . The devices hacked by them were Insulin pump and Continuous Glucose Monitor (CGM). They developed their own software which utilizes the data from CGM and modified the quantity of insulin delivered by Dana Lewis insulin pump. In Austin, during OSCon it was observed that more than 50 people are using Open Source Software for the modifications in their own health device. Western PA (2018)

## Cancer Treatment through Activity Trackers

This IoT device is of great importance in treatment of cancer patients. The Memorial Sloan Kettering Cancer Center (MSK) and cloud research firm Medidata are collecting data from task trackers in order to collect information regarding the living style of patients that are being gone under treatment for multiple myeloma. Patients are supposed to wear this activity tracker prior to their treatment for one week and later on for months till the treatment carry on. Digital Intelligence (2016)

The tracker logged down all information regarding the activities of patients like activity level, exhaustion and hunger etc, all such information is saved to Medidata's Patient Cloud ePRO app on their own mobile phones. The analysis of data collected through these activity trackers and wearables are being analyzed by various techniques and on the basis of results treatment can be upgraded in many circumstances. The device help in planning strategically treatment of the patients where after effects of a particular therapy can be monitored for further planning of their treatment.

## Monitoring Inhalers

The IoT technology is gone far away in health care and they are used not only in spotting disease, besides that it also helps doctor in keeping the precise record of whether patients are following their specified treatment plan or not. The other side of this technology is that patients get reminders through mobile apps attached to the devices to check their devotion level towards treatment.

The pharmaceutical company Novartis along with Propeller Health and Qualcomm are trying to create connected inhaler. This can be used successfully for the patients of protracted disruptive pulmonic disease. Propeller's technology has been linked through sensors to its digital platform which records and conveys useful information.

## 1.2.5 Proteous Discover

Ingestible sensors are an example of digital medicine. It has been introduced by Proteus Digital Health. A study by WHO in 2003 shows that almost 50% of the prescribed medicines are not eaten as they should be. Proteus system is one of the solutions to decrease this percentage.

Proteous discover comprises of ingestible sensors, a small wearable sensor patch, an application on a mobile device and a provider portal. The application is claimed to give an ever seen in-sight of the patient's health parameters. It also reports about the medication effectiveness status which leads to take meaningful decisions regarding treatment of patient.

## Google Smart Lens

Google has developed smart lens technology which is being used successfully by Alcon which is a part of Novartis. Smart lens comprises of in-built non-intrusive device. The glucose level of the patients is measured through their tears and the lens will further transfer the data to a mobile device.

## AutoBed

It is quite painful to wait outside the emergency rooms. Sometimes it takes hours to complete. Mt. Sinai Medical Center in New York City used IoT devices to reduce the wait times for their emergency patients by 50%. They used AutoBed program which tries to solve the problem of hospital by managing the available beds.

AutoBed is an algorithm which utilizes the recommendation for the nurses who admit patients and the data produced in real time about the availability of hospital beds to find out the best possible match as per the requirements of the patient to be admitted. The nurses keep data in the form of electronic medical record which is vast that included data on gender too. The real time data is collected using devices like radio-frequency identification tags, infrared to name a few. The AutoBed is capable of monitoring 1200 beds on the basis of fifteen various parameters and can process eighty requests for bed.

## Telehealth

Telehealth is a new wave in health care domain. Patients living in a remote area or elderly patients need not to visit hospital at a preliminary stage of illness. Telehealth is a solution for such patients. It is one of the most popular applications of IoT based health care systems. Telehealth facilitates long distance patient and clinician in many ways like contacting and care, advising patient, reminders to the patient and doctors too, educating patients, monitoring health of patient and remote admissions as well.

It helps in reducing number of visits to the hospital and also improves patient's quality of life by avoiding travel for them. Some patients have limited mobility and depend largely on public transportation; Telehealth can be one of the solutions for them.

## Philips-e-Alert

The hospitals now require next-gen hardware and software. There are many devices in hospital whose improper working can be a huge risk for the patient's life. One of them is MRI system. Such equipment's are susceptible to various risks be it power breakdown or system failure- each one of them can be matter of life or death. A new IoT based device called e-Alert developed by Philips aims to resolve such issues.

e-Alert is a smart device which does not wait for causality to occur rather than it follows preemptive approach by monitoring medical hardware and it also alerts hospital staff members in prior if any such device reports problem. Recently Philips revealed this new product with the collaborative effort with OpenMarket.

## Drug Monitoring

The advancement of technology is all set to touch new benchmarks in healthcare. It seems science fiction that upcoming pills will be sensitized by microscopic sensors which can transmit information to the external device connected to them in order to ensure prescribed dosage of a medicine.

The information passed to the external device can be useful in ensuring that patients are taking prescribed medication and in proper dosage and also suggesting new medications. Patients can also access that data through app and have a check on their performance and improvements.

## Health Net Connect

The basic aim of HealthNet connect is to improve the accessibility of healthcare and also decrease cost for healthcare. The health net connect Telehealth resource provide a combined package of workflows, use-cases, process, education and technology to various sectors like schools, enterprises, hospitals, health care centers to name a few, whoever are keen in providing distant health care.

IoT is been a big help for many revolutionary treatments of chronic diseases. There is a combination of devices and technology that are helping in curing chronic diseases. Utilities like Fitbit use the IoT to monitor personal health — such information can be shared with a doctor to help solving chronic issues. Very recently Health Net Connect started a program for diabetes management to improve the clinical treatment and reducing cost of treatment for patients. Their program got success and they produced exciting results.

## LITERATURE REVIEW

Recent advancements in IoT technology has opened up various opportunities for health care systems. Latest Biosensors and other IoT based medical devices are capable of monitoring various health related parameters and are setting new benchmarks in this field. This section will discuss work of various contributors in this field.

Bui N. and Zorzi M. (2011) mentioned that IoT can be the key enabler for health care applications working in a distributed manner. A. A. N. Shirehjini, A. Yassine et. al. 2012 also used passive RFID for locating equipment in hospitals. Li et. al. 2012 proposed a secured data access framework for patients to access their PHR (Patient Health Record) which are stored on servers.

A. Redondi,M. Chirico et. al. 2013 proposed the successful usage of WSN for various healthcare applications in nursing institutes. Caro De N. and Colitti W. (2013) They focused on CoAP and MQTT protocols which are light weight in nature and compared their quantitative and qualitative performance.

C. Occhiuzzi, C. Vallese et. al. (2014) developed RFID based system called NIGHT-Care. The system is supposed to monitor health status of disabled and elderly people during night.

D. De Donno, L. Catarinucci in 2014 proposed REMA which is used for monitoring and tracking of patients. In the 6LoWPAN standard and smart mobile communication techniques are combined to monitor the health condition of patients and provide several effective healthcare services. More in detail, the proposed solution makes use of WSN devices to measure photo plethysmo gram (PPG) signals and deliver them to a server through the Internet.

Donno De D., Catarinucci L., and. Tarricone L (2014) combined the standard 6LoWPAN and mobile communication technique to provide efficient healthcare services for the health monitoring of the patients.

Bezawada et al. 2015 proposed PASS (Pattern Aware Secure Search) which used the concept of symmetric key based approach for secure encrypted searching of health data in cloud environment. Khoi Manh N. and Ahlund C. (2015) discussed various issues related to network like low band width consumption, remote health monitoring and many more. They suggested IReHMo architecture which is capable of combining many automation sensors with IoT healthcare devices at the sensing layer level.

Li et. al. 2016 also proposed WBAN (Wireless Body Area Network) which uses secure key management and authentication scheme. All health data items generated from WBAN will be encrypted before transmission. Lounis et. al. 2016 proposed an architecture for wireless network for cloud based health care systems. They introduced a secured access control architecture which depends on CP-ABE (Ciphertext-Attribute Based Encrytpion).

Liao Y. (2016) proposed a precise I2O (in to out) human body path loss model which rely on a safe heterogeneous human body model. Mio et. al. 2016 developed multi keyword search based on various attributes. Their approach is used to search encrypted data of patient's health record.

Hu et. al. 2017 proposed a secure IoT based health monitoring system for elderly people which uses cloud computing. The system utilizes digital certificate, envelope, time-stamp and asymmetric encryption technology for the transmission of related health data in the system.

Salunke P. and Nerkar R. (2017) proposed a system which is valuable for elder people who have limitations for arriving to healthcare facilities and also for doctors who are puzzled because of patient load. Lu and Li 2018 introduced k-anonymity algorithm to maintain the security of the wearable health devices.

Various researchers have worked in the area of secure health care systems. Many of them have provided secure solutions for the processing and accessing of electronic health data in health care systems.

## ARCHITECTURE OF IOT BASED HEALTH CARE SYSTEM

The complete architecture of Health Care System based on IoT can be divided into various layers. The overall architecture can be viewed as a four layered system where each and every layer had a different role to support the functioning of this system.

### Innermost Layer (Wearable and Monitoring Devices)

The innermost layer of the architecture is wearable or monitoring devices. The whole Health Care System initiates its working from this layer itself. These devices are an integral part of the system and are used to monitor any significant changes in a regular pattern and issue an alert message in case of any imperfection in a pattern. There are various wearable and monitoring devices nowadays present in the market. All such devices are helping the end user in some or other way. Devices like *Wearables, Activity Tracking, Weight Loss, Consultation with Virtual Doctor, Hydration Tool, BioSensors, Sensiotec Virtual Medical Assistant, Freestyle Libre Flash, Health Patch are quite handy to the end users.*

## Machine to Machine Data Transfer Layer

Next to innermost layer is a Data Transfer Layer. This layer requires a device named Multi Service IoT gateway. The purpose of this device is to amalgamate protocols for networking, and to help in managing storage and edging analytics on the data, and also smooth the progress of data flow between edging devices and the cloud in a secure manner.

IoT enabled systems are quiet complex with versatile devices and consumers of data as well. There is a need to unify various dissimilar devices over the network environment such as sensors, actuators, measuring devices, smart machines, automated human/machine interfaces, and the legacy systems for making data communications amongst consumers easy and comfortable.

There are various businesses which are looking forward to adopt IoT and its robustness but they don't have that technical expertise to implement it. Implementing an IoT infrastructure needs skilled professionals on protocols that can write TCP/IP stacks, operating system kernels or many other algorithms required. Besides that integration of the devices with the back-office business information system also requires expert professionals. In short, they need help to create a functional IoT system.

## The Multi-Service Gateway Approach

Enterprises require such expertise to solve the complexity of the IoT system. Complexity of IoT systems can be solved by using a multi-service gateway approach. This is done by the integration of disparate which will ensure claimed better decision making by having access to essential and valuable data.

In a nutshell, with the multi-service gateway approach:

- Several related business relevant jobs are tackled and consolidated technically.
- Data delivery to destination point uses an open protocol efficiently segregating the data consumers and the data providers
- IT centric IoT enabled device application development by making use of a programmed framework to implement application layer business logic in smart edge devices having different protocols using gateways.

The Multi-service gateway is used for the complex systems and is used as an integration device for two different environments. It simplifies the working of the complex systems by using cloud environment for the integration purpose. These gateways can tackle bi-directional communication. The customers are capable of connecting their devices, actuators and sensors to the various enterprises with the help of Multi-Service Gateway. The gateway supports real time management of the data and the customers have their control on devices that are part of the field.

## Third Layer (M2M Integration)

Next layer is of M2M integration. In such system sensors or devices monitor themselves and keep a track of each and every communication taken place. Hence removing the human intervention is avoided. Patient's vital signs drop can also be taken as good example where a device connected to the devices' cloud (private or public) may control vital oxygen and cater care additionally till healthcare experts reach on the spot of concern. With M2M based technology, the patient or consumers don't even have to be in the healthcare units to get any such care. Instead, all this can be delivered effectively to the patient at his/ her home. M2M integration is a new paradigm which supports the IoT systems whether it is a data transfer through wearable. In broader way one can say that M2M is a technology which integrates disparate networked devices and help them in communication and performing action without human intervention.

Following claimed actions/ tasks must be performed by an effective and efficient M2M integrated platform-

- Firstly, it should work like an operating system for the IoT, capable of ensuring transfer of device's data irrespective of programming language and operating system .
- Secondly, it should offer the possible means to carry out effective thorough management of the devices in the concerned field
- And thirdly, it should flawlessly put together with the organizational computational world, using best practices of information technology approaches at the same time implementing optimal M2M based technologies. Andres R. (2013)

The basic aim of M2M technology is to assemble data received from sensors, devices, actuators and then transmit it to a public networks using public access methods like mobile network of Ethernet. M2M is quite different from SCADA(Supervisory Control and Data Acquisition is a control system architecture that uses computers, networked data communications and graphical user interfaces for high-level process supervisory management) or other remote monitoring tools as they use cost effective means of data transmission. The major constituents of M2M based systems incorporate sensors, RFID systems, cellular communications connection along with a software program which performs automatic computing which helps the particular device to understand data and statistics to go with decisions.

The popular M2M communication is telemetry in which there is an automated communication process to collect data from some remote location and transmit it to receiving equipment for monitoring. In early days of telemetry telephone line were used and later on it started using radio waves for the transmission of performance dimensions congregated from sensing gadgets from remote areas. The revolution in wireless and radio technology has increased and extended the working domain of telemetry with engineering technologies and science to electric meters and various connected devices through IoT. There are several ways the M2M is enhancing telemedicine, helping providers offer a quality of care that's potentially better than many in-person treatment modalities. Rouse M.(2018)

The perfect M2M based integration platform is more or less middleware that behaves like a governing platform or operating system for the Internet of Things. It is an in-between system of disseminated units and the software applications that make use of the data arriving from these IoT enabled devices. Any established communication amongst devices should be a two-way communication in nature, and should allow these kinds of software applications to manage the devices where ever required. The M2M based system must ensure the relocation of device's data irrespective of language, and governing operating system. It must finally provide accommodation for the complicated nature of M2M based projects.

## Uppermost Layer

The uppermost layer can be considered as output layer or response layer. In IoT based health care system output may be in the form of some alert message or some reports. The uppermost layer will receive data

*Figure 1. Architecture of IoT based healthcare systems*

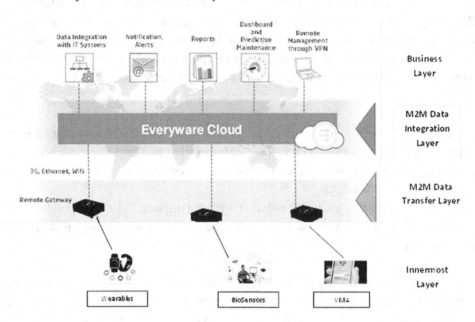

through M2M integration and will be analyzed and processed based on some previous history or patterns. On the basis of such processing, alerts or reports must be delivered to the end users.

For example in a health care system patient's will be notified on a particular day by their wearable devices for their appointment with the doctor. The device will also notify for the medicine schedule of the patient. Old age patients are highly benefitted as they most of the time they do not remember to take their medicines on time and also their appointments with their doctors. In such cases these health care systems are really a boon for them. M2M integration provides range of benefits like social connectivity, health and fitness monitoring and tracking to name a few. Figure 1 shows the architecture of IoT based healthcare system.

## SECURITY ASPECTS OF IOT BASED HEALTH CARE SYSTEMS

Security of IoT data is a critical issue from the collection point at the device level to the destination point. IT fraternity has a great concern as there are no such defined security standards for IoT based health care systems hence high risk factors are associated to IoT device and possibility of data breaches is high. The diversity of the various endpoints and absence of proper tools to manage them is a big challenge for the security team. The devices from different vendors require different methods for updation which puts a significant burden on IT teams who deals with security.

FDA took a step in defining common security standards for all medical devices FDA released a draft of "Postmarket Management of Cybersecurity in Medical Devices". Draft addresses various guidelines which manufacturers need to follow to address security risks associated to the IoT devices.

The more and more devices are getting connected in various hospitals and health care systems. Hospitals and health care centers must pay attention and should be very cautious about the security of these devices. The hospital management should be proactive and should implement full proof plan to secure the devices and protect them from any threat.

"There are so many benefits that come with these new connected devices," mentioned by Mike Nelson, vice president of a healthcare solutions at DigiCert, a security certification company in Lehi, Utah. "But they also present some new risks and vulnerabilities that as an industry we haven't, firmly dealt with to this point". Those risks include possible harm to the patient's safety and health, loss of PHI (Patient Health Information) and unauthorized access to devices, Nelson said. Lee K. (2016)

## Security Vulnerabilities in Health Care Devices and Systems

IoT health applications might be seen in hospitals or medical centres, in the home, or while on the move (tying into some aspect of a person's location through GPS tracking). Following are the diversified applications of IoT in Health Care Systems and their security vulnerabilities –

## Wearables

There are numerous such type of devices available in the market and are used to monitor daily activities and their effects on human being. These devices store the metrics of various data like heartbeat, blood pressure, glucose level of the person. Such devices have their own specific features and way of collecting data. In general all such devices are used to track calorie burn and route used while running exercises through GPS. There is no proper security check on such data which is generated through these devices. GPS reveals the physical location of the person using wearable devices. Besides that other health related data can also be spoofed. For example suppose a fitness tracker display's a person's current heart rate and urges them to move quicker in order to increase their rate and burn more calories – an attacker able to spoof the heart rate (to be lower than the actual value) might be able to put a victim into an exercise state that increases their heart rate to dangerous or lethal levels.

## Health Care Monitoring and Communication

Remote patient monitoring is one of the biggest advantage of IoT based health care systems. The people who live in remote areas or not physically fit to visit health care stations often can be monitored by the health care systems staff from remote locations. They can monitor their sugar levels, heart rate etc. and can give primary medication and suggestions. Inside hospitals also patients are allowed to roam here and there with the sensors connected to it. These sensors keep on updating health related data to the central location. These systems are in general support Bi-directional communications which allows to direct patients in the hospitals to report back at their times of medication also calling remote patients and advising them in adverse situations. However there is serious threat of unavailability of the concerned. The attackers can disrupt this bi-directional communication and this will pose a serious situation for the patients at remote areas as well as in the hospitals.

## Drug Supply System

There are some IoT based health care system equipment's which works autonomously. These systems used to assess health status of a patient in a real time and after analysis disperse medication. For example – a remote, immobile patient might suffer from diabetes and require periodic insulin depending on blood sugar levels. Some connected devices might automatically monitor blood sugar levels and automatically inject insulin when necessary. However there can be very serious implications, if such systems are being attacked and can be a threat for the health of the patients and insufficient doses or overdoses of medication can be really deadly for the patients.

## Health Implant Devices

A pacemaker which is a kind of implant device is quite common in health monitoring devices. With the improvement in technology the device is also upgraded its Wi-Fi enabled version. Such wireless version of pacemakers allows monitoring of health related data which can be used for diagnosis. The serious security threat associated to such devices. Any person who wishes to harm any patient can send dangerous commands and can stops or malfunction the working of such devices and can put patient in a serious situation.

## e-Calling

In April 2018 e-calling is made mandatory for all the new cars in Europe. It is basically an innovative initiative which is meant to provide quick assistance to the cars involved in accident or crashing. When any eCall equipped vehicle crashes and automatic call goes to the nearest health centre in order to provide them first hand medical assistance to the victims of vehicle crash. In case passengers are seriously injured and are not able to speak then too minimum set of data is sent to the nearest emergency health centre. However any attacker can spoof the data sent to the emergency health centre and this will mislead the team to some other location where there is no causality.

## Health Drones

Health Drones are also called as Air Ambulance. People living in remote areas who require urgent medical aid can be served using these Health Drones. It's already more than one year since the first trials of AirMule which can airlift two people and autonomously man oeuvre itself in locations where helicopters would not be able to manoeuvre and land. Attackers can make these drones unavailable or can hijack them and can make its illegal use.

## General Security Vulnerabilities In Iot Devices

The IoT devices are quite vulnerable and hence chances of data spoofing, breaching and threat for the people is higher. There are numerous reasons behind the vulnerability of IoT devices. The reasons behind their vulnerabilities are quite many –

- IoT devices are the products which are commonly released and do not undergo regressive security testing phase.
- Some IoT health devices are quite small and also have limited capabilities. Like small chipsets of memory are not able to support larger upper limit of encryption. Hence it makes the device vulnerable as it gets quite easier to exploit the smaller upper limits of encryption.

- Due to small upper limits of small devices they are more vulnerable for attacks. In devices like implanted pacemaker or an insulin pump the installation of updates is not an easy task because the responsibility of update installation cannot be identified among manufacturers, vendors or hospital/medical centers.
- Communication is the core aspect of IoT health devices and in case communication is disrupted the patient's health is at the risk. The small size of these devices also hinders implementation of any backup feature. In any case if device goes out of the network channel by no means it can report it to the healthcare system that it is out of action.

## RECOMMENDATIONS FOR SECURE IOT BASED HEALTH CARE SYSTEMS

### Recommended Consumer/Patient Actions

To minimize the risk, consumers/patients should take following actions:

- Consumers should not buy devices from unknown or less popular vendors. The devices should be bought from the reputable manufacturers which are globally known.
- Consumers should take care while selecting passwords so that it cannot be hacked. Consumers should read the license terms and conditions related to security properly in order to avoid any kind of legal issues in future.
- In case the health device is issued by the hospital or health care center, consumers must ensure about the security of device.
- Consumers should be careful while using IoT health devices online through mobile or computers.

### Recommended Manufacturer Actions

The manufacturer of IoT devices should also take measures to improve the safety and security of devices. Following are the recommended actions for IoT health device manufacturers:

- A **Privacy Impact Assessment (PIA)** is a technique of identification and taking actions against the prospective security and privacy risks in new projects. PIA helps manufacturers to design effective and efficient process in order to reduce security risks. Many devices in spite of processing data transfer it to some Apps. In that case the data security of the particular app should be assessed.
- The implementation of Secure Software Development Lifecycle by manufacturers. This means implementing security at the time of designing of products is mandatory. Besides that not only implementing security but the testing and validation of security is also obligatory throughout the lifecycle of a product.
- The post product release phase of an S-SDLC is of great importance. The device should be engaged in rigorous security testing in this phase.
- Manufactures should try to implement standard security measure in order to maintain consistency.

## Recommendations for IoT Devices Infrastructure

At infrastructure level following are the recommendations for security of health care systems-

### Encryption of Data

Patient's health related data is of high importance hence it is advisable to use encryption techniques to encrypt useful data. Sensors and other biomedical devices used in IoT based health care systems have limited processing capabilities. The complicated encryption algorithm which demands for high computational power cannot be a solution. Hence the demand is to have a balanced security protocols to manage between data and the computational energy.

### Authorized Access

Another way of making healthcare systems secure is by authorized access of various devices involved in the system. Every authorized user should have a certified key. Strong key management is an important aspect of cryptosystem. ABE (Attribute Based Encryption) is considered as the scalable option for such cryptosystems for flexible access management. Various technologies are being used at Access Control level- like ABE and CP-ABE (Ciphertext-Policy Attribute Based Encryption)

### Trusted Third Party Authorization

The data stored on cloud servers by health care systems can be compromised by modification and deletion of data by unauthorized users. For security purpose trusted third party is introduced in the system to provide unbiased auditing results.

### Searching Secure Data

In health care systems sensitive data of patients should be encrypted and data search should be avoided in a plain text manner. Hence the need of encrypted cloud search is raised. Few popularly used encryption techniques for data search are SSE (Searchable Symmetric Encryption) and PEKS (Public-key encryption) with keyword search. Following are the secure data search technology – Symmetric Key, APKS and CP-ABE

### Anonymity of Data

Patient's data can be divided into explicit identifiers (personal details like – id, name, phone no.), quasi-identifiers (details lie – Age, date of birth etc) and privacy attributes (patient's health related data). Nowadays k-anonymity and l-diversity are the techniques used to maintain anonymity of the data in health care systems W Sun et. al. 2018

## Authentication Layer

The authentication layer is required to be added for the correct identification of these connected medical devices. The data encryption is also required so that chances of data breaches should be minimized. The device that is sending data also needs to be authenticated. The authenticated users should only be able to send commands to the device.

## Digital Certificate

Another way of securing these health devices is to provide authentication and authorization by issuing them a digital certificate. There should be one control and monitoring software to manage all such devices in a particular health care system. The system can then be configured to accept signals only from the authentic and authorized devices which are able to produce authentication certificate. This way a protected and secure network channel is established between the server and medical device. Some metadata information can be added to these digital certificates with the specification of the people allowed to handle certain device.

## SOLUTIONS FOR SECURE IOT BASED HEALTH CARE SYSTEMS

HIMSS (Healthcare Information and Management Systems Society) focuses on the security of new technologies especially IoT devices security, related to health care system. The machine data is harnessed in order to ensure the security of the various critical systems in health care centers. The success of healthcare systems depends largely on their ability of harnessing machine data. The more intelligently systems harness this data it will result in better focus on care delivery systems.

Conventionally organizations assets and processes should be HIPAA-complaint, but the current scenario is that the healthcare industry is exploded with variety of IoT medical devices and you have patients roaming wearing health care devices hence it is getting difficult to manage all those devices and make them HIPAA-complaint.

The latest HITECH Act issues notification to the individuals to ensure that their health device is following security norms and information is transmitted in encrypted form. This helped in forming the updated HIPAA Breach Notification Rule to send notifications to the individuals who are in significant risk position in terms of finance, health or any other risk. The rule mentioned that notification should not be delayed and in any case it should not be late than 60 days after breach is discovered. (Hipa Journal)

Researchers mentioned that basic authentication of health care devices is must. This will limit the device access and firmware of the device is verified and proper scrutiny of communication among devices is being done. Secured booting of a device also ensures that device configuration is not tampered.

Hence the need of innovative security measures is required for such systems. CodeBlue is a prevalent healthcare project which has been developed at Harvard Sensor Network Lab. It has been deployed in hospital emergency care where various medical sensors are placed on various parts of patient's body. However the authors of CodeBlue admit lack of expected security and also explained its necessity. D. Malan et al (2004)

Following are the solutions suggested for the IoT based health care systems –

## Secure REST(Representational State Transfer) API and OAuth

API's have significant roles in implementing secure health care systems. These API allow you to connect customers and application in a secure manner. Since APIs connect various devices in the IoT framework in the health care system hence it is necessary to deploy flexible and scalable API management. REST is basically a concept which is being used most popularly in the modern web as it uses JSON and XML for data transfer over HTTP.

REST is a suggested model for IoT based applications as each and every device can make its state available and can use standard methods to create, read and update that data. To fulfill the goal of IoT framework we need REST API for every device involved in a system. REST allows flowing data over internet protocols and also managing authorization.

Security integration with REST API makes it robust. REST API can be secured in many ways by using basic auth or OAuth but it should be stateless in nature. The authorization and authentication should be done for each API request on the server by authentication credentials rather than using cookies or sessions.

OAuth 2.0 is an open standard for authorization and authentication which does not provide any authentication protocol it provides a framework for authenticating decisions and mechanisms. Following are the major components of OAuth –

Resource Owner – It controls the data which is being exposed by the API.
Authorization Server – It issues, controls and revokes tokens in the OAuth system. It is also called as
    Security Token Service (STS)
Client – It is the application or a website or any other system that is requesting for data.
Resource Server – It exposes and stores/sends the data. It is basically an API.

OAuth follows implicit flow by delegating access to the resources. Client sends its request to the Authorization Server which request for authentic user-id and password which is further passed to the Authentication Server for its approval or denial. After its approval now client can request to access resource from Resource Server.

OAuth uses various security tokens like JWT tokens, CWT tokens, WS- Security tokens, legacy tokens to name a few. JWT stands for JSON web token which is a security token used for the secure deployment of various standard applications. The contents of JWT are secured by making use of JWS (JSON web signature) and JWE (JSON web encryption). However JWT is considered inefficient for IoT based systems which basically use low power radio technologies. To remove these anomalies CWT is being introduced known as Consent Web Token. The basic role of CWT is transmission of secure claims between two different parties. CWT uses a cryptographic key for signing the consents given by the users. The key guarantees the origin and validity of the consent. CWT grants security by using signatures to assure integrity. But it does not create a secure token themselves.

OAuth allows the secure communication and data exchange in client-server applications. The basic purpose of OAuth framework is to enable secure authorization on top of the transport layer.

## MQTT (Message Queue Telemetry Transport)

It is popularly being used by IoT based applications. It is basically a light weighted message protocol which uses PUB/SUB operations for message transfers between client and servers. This protocol is considered ideal for IoT based health applications because it is smaller in size, uses low power, packets used in message passing are smaller in size and quite easy to implement. MQTT allows multiple clients to connect with broker at the same time for two basic purposes –

- Subscribe for a particular topic and then receiving updates on it.
- Publish messages related to a particular topic.

MQTT exchanges all information in the form of plain text which can be accessed and readable easily. Hence it is the utmost requirement to make MQTT secure and this can happen by following these steps-

- Using a private key (CA key)
- Using this private key produce a certificate (CA cert)
- Produce a certificate for Mosquitto MQTT server using private key
- Finally configuring Mosquitto MQTT so that it can use those certificates.

MQTT protocol is preferred over HTTP protocol because of fewer payloads of data; publish/subscribe architecture which uses small message size hence making it ideal for small size memory devices.

## LoraWAN

It is Long range, low power Wide Area Network designed specifically for the IoT setup. It emphasizes on smart, secure and seamless bidirectional communication between various things connected. It uses varied frequency channels and data rates for end to end communication between devices. The data rates ranges from .3 to 50 kbps, hence various communication channels do not interfere with each other. It creates virtual channels to increase the capacity of the gateway. It uses Adaptive Data Rate (ADR) plan to improve the capacity of network and battery life of the devices. Adaptive data-rate lets LoRa Server control the data-rate and power of the device, so that it uses less airtime and less power to transmit the data.

LoRa is a secure way of connecting to the devices end to end. It addresses the security issue by providing encryption at various levels like network, application and device by making use of unique network key (EUI64), application key(EUI64) and a unique device specific key (EUI128). Each device is authenticated by a 128 bit AES key and a global unique identifier EUI-64. The security of LoRa is also strengthening by the use of AES cryptographic primitive along with CMAC2 for integrity and CTR3 for encryption.

It could be exploited well by the medical devices. The devices that record and send signals or reports to the health care system like hospital bed, blood glucose sensor, scale that reports your weight to name a few can utilize LoRaWAN as it utilizes wide spectrum of data rates and it is a complete solution for sending noiseless and secure data without any obstructions.

## Symphony Link

Link Labs (2016,2017). It is an alternative synchronous protocol which uses LoRa at its physical layer. All messages send through Symphony Link are acknowledged and all messages can be of longer length. Though it is a secure and robust protocol but It is not energy efficient as lot of energy is consumed in

*Figure 2. Architecture of IoT Base Health Care System Using Smart E-Gateway*

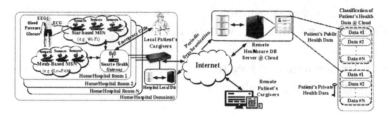

synchronizing nodes frequently with the network. The increased power consumption and lack of deployment are the main limiting factors in using Symphony Link for healthcare purposes.

## DTLS (Datagram Transport Security Layer)

E. Rescorla and N. Modadugu have suggested that end-to-end security protocols are one of the solutions for implementing security in health care systems. Datagram Transport Layer Security (DTLS) is considered as most relevant protocols in this regard. It is based on Transport layer security protocol and provides security which is equivalent to it. It is basically designed for the security of data between two communication ends. E. Rescorla and N. Modadugu (2012)

## E-Health Gateway

It is proposed by R. Mueller et al (2007) which was called SwissGate used for the optimization of sensor networks. They employed their proposed gateway on home automation systems. In the year 2015, Rahmani et.al. (2015) proposed a smart e-health gateway called UT-GATE which provides intelligence to the ubiquitous healthcare systems. The proposed gateways work as a temporary storage of users and sensors information (like local database). This database is further utilized for various data interpretation techniques and facilitates intelligence to the system hence making it smart gateway.

These intelligent gateways are supposed to provide preliminary results and hence reduce the repeated communication between the cloud servers for performing data aggregation and compression techniques. In this way, remote cloud computers will just provide premium services which are often computationally intensive and require to access to the central database.

## SEA – Smart Gateway

Sanaz Rahimi Moosavi et. al. (2015) suggested the secured architecture for healthcare systems which includes following major components –

- **Medical Sensor Network (MSN):** The network is supposed to collect contextual signal from the medical sensors on the body of the patients or may be by biomedical devices kept in the rooms of the patients. The network is capable of ubiquitous identification, intelligent sensing and also communicating the signals received. These signals are further transmitted to the smart gateways via wireless or wired communication protocols such as Wi-Fi, SPI, Serial or Bluetooth.

*Figure 3. BSN-Care secured framework*

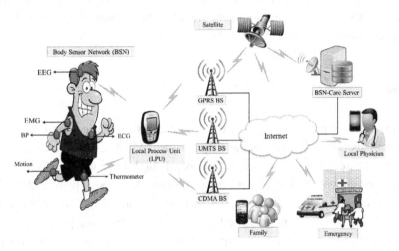

- **Smart e-Health Gateway:** The purpose of this gateway is to work as a bridge between MSN and the Internet or local switch. It supports various communication protocols. The main function of this gateway is to receive data from various sub-networks and perform versatile activities like data filtering, aggregation, protocol conversion and dimensionality reduction.
- **Back-End System:** Rest of the part makes back-end system which comprises of a switch, cloud platform for broadcasting, datawarehouse, big analytic server and hospital database. The role of back-end system is to synchronize with the remote healthcare server.
- **Web Client:** The GUI's at client are meant for data visualization. Lot of data is collected regarding health of patients and also contextual information. The collected health data can be used by analyst and researches for drawing various inferences.

## BSN (Body Sensor Network)

Gope P. et. al. (2016) proposed BSN –Care which is Body Sensor Network based secure health care system. They implement security measures at two places Network Security and Data Security. They used Lightweight Anonymous Authentication Protocol for the security of network and for Data Security is managed by using OCB (Offset Codeback) authenticated encryption mode. Figure 3 shows their Secure BSN network.

## ECC(Eliptic Curve Cryptography) Model

Amjad Ali Almar et. al. (2016) proposed an identification authentication protocol which is based on eliptic curve cryptography (ECC) to avoid the vulnerabilities of RFID based systems. Most of the IoT based system deployment is based on RFID as it consists of most robust features in comparison of other peer technologies. However the technology is prone to various security issues due to wireless communication media. Almar along with ECC also used ECDH (elliptic curve Diffie–Hellman) key agreement protocol to implement security measures for IoT deployment.

The researchers have tried to overcome the hurdle of security in IoT based healthcare systems. Many of them as discussed above have given solutions for implementation of secure IoT based health care system and got success also. However there is still a long road to go ahead.

## CONCLUSION

Health care systems are most promising area of IoT applications. IoT based health care systems deal with personal data of patients hence security is the major aspect. Most of the communication in IoT based health care systems is wireless in nature hence it demands high level of security. The researchers have worked in this area and shown great concern. Many solutions have been provided as already discussed in the chapter. The security of data, authorization and access control are major concerns in health IoT. Various parties are being involved in IoT based health care systems like patients, doctors, health care staffs, manufacturers etc. hence the need of secure and robust data communication is of high importance.

*This research was previously published in the Handbook of Research on the Internet of Things Applications in Robotics and Automation; pages 265-286, copyright year 2020 by Engineering Science Reference (an imprint of IGI Global).*

## REFERENCES

*A Comprehensive Look at Low Power, Wide Area Networks for 'Internet of Things' Engineers and Decision Makers.* (2016). Annapolis, MD: Link Labs.

Alamr, Kausar, Kim, & Seo. (2016). A secure ECC-based RFID mutual authentication protocol for internet of things. *Journal of Super Computing, 1.*

Andres, R. (2013). *M2M integration platforms enable complex IoT systems.* Received December 1, 2013, from http://www.embedded-computing.com/embedded-computing-design/m2m-integration-platforms-enable-complex-iot-systems

Bezawada, B., Liu, A. X., Jayaraman, B., Wang, A. L., & Li, R. (2015). Privacy Preserving String Matching for Cloud Computing. *Proceedings of the 35th IEEE International Conference onDistributed Computing Systems, ICDCS '15*, 609–618. 10.1109/ICDCS.2015.68

Bui, N., & Zorzi, M. (2011). Health Care Applications: A Solution Based on The Internet of Things. Department of Information Engineering, University of Padova Via Gradenigo. doi:10.1145/2093698.2093829

Caro De, N., & Colitti, W. (2013). *Comparison of two lightweight protocols for smartphone -based sensing.* Department of ETRO-IRIS Vrije University Brussels. doi:10.1109/SCVT.2013.6735994

De Donno, D., Catarinucci, L., & Tarricone, L. (2014, July). RAMSES: RFID augmented module for smart environmental sensing. *IEEE Transactions on Instrumentation and Measurement, 63*(7), 1701–1708. doi:10.1109/TIM.2014.2298692

Digital Intelligence Blog. (2016). *Wearable's impact on cancer patient's quality of life to be tested.* Received July, 26 2016 From http://www.pmlive.com/blogs/digital_intelligence/archive/2016/july/ wearables_impact_on_cancer_patients_quality_of_life_to_be_tested

Donno De, D., Catarinucci, L., & Tarricone, L. (2014, April). A battery-assisted sensor-enhanced RFID tag enabling heterogeneous wireless sensor networks. *IEEE Sensors Journal, 14*(4), 1048–1055. doi:10.1109/JSEN.2013.2293177

Gope, P., & Hwang, T. (2016). BSN-Care: A Secure IoT-Based Modern Healthcare System Using Body Sensor Network. *IEEE Sensors Journal, 16*(5), 1368–1376. doi:10.1109/JSEN.2015.2502401

Hipa Journal. (n.d.). *Healthcare Data Security.* Retrieved from https://www.hipaajournal.com/category/ healthcare-data-security/page/6/

Hu, Chen, Fan, & Wang. (2017). An intelligent and secure health monitoring scheme using IoT sensor based on cloud computing. *Journal of Sensors.*

Khoi, M. N., & Ahlund, C. (2015). *IReHMo: An Efficient IoT Based Remote Health Monitoring System for Smart Regions.* Department of Computer Science, Electrical and Space Engineering Lulea University of Technology Skelleftea.

Lee, K. (2016). *Healthcare IoT security issues: Risks and what to do about them.* Retrieved from https:// internetofthingsagenda.techtarget.com/

Li, C. (n.d.). *Introduction and overview of Biosensors and Electrochemistry.* Retrieved from http:// nanohub.org/resources/2261/download/nanobiotechnology_and_biosensors.pdf

Li, C.-T., Lee, C.-C., & Weng, C.-Y. (2016). A secure cloud-assisted wireless body area network in mobile emergency medical care system. Journal of Medical Systems, 40(5), 1–15. doi:10.100710916-016-0474-9

Li, M., Yu, S., Zheng, Y., Ren, K., & Lou, W. (2012). Scalable and secure sharing of personal health records in cloud computing using attributebased encryption. *IEEE Transactions on Parallel and Distributed Systems, 24*(1), 131–143. doi:10.1109/TPDS.2012.97

Liao, Y., & Leeson, S. M. (2016). *Analysis of In -to-Out Wireless Body Area Network Systems: Towards QoS-Aware Health Internet of Things Applications.* School of Engineering, University of Warwick.

Liu, F., & Li, T. (2018). A clustering k-anonymity privacy-preserving method for wearable IoT devices. *Security and Communication Networks, 2018,* 1–8. doi:10.1155/2018/1635081

Lounis, A., Hadjidj, A., Bouabdallah, A., & Challal, Y. (2016). Healing on the cloud: Secure cloud architecture for medical wireless sensor networks. *Future Generation Computer Systems, 55,* 266–277. doi:10.1016/j.future.2015.01.009

Malan, D. (2004). CodeBlue: An Ad hoc sensor Network Infrastructure for Emergency Medical Care. WIBSN'04.

Mathews, K. (2018). *6 Exciting IoT Use Cases in Healthcare.* Received May 03, 2018 From https:// www.iotforall.com/exciting-iot-use-cases-in-healthcare/

Miao, Y., Ma, J., Liu, X., Wei, F., Liu, Z., & Wang, X. A. (2016). m2-ABKS: Attribute-based multi-keyword search over encrypted personal health records in multi-owner setting. *Journal of Medical Systems*, *40*(11), 246. doi:10.100710916-016-0617-z PMID:27696175

Moosavi, Gia, Rahmani, Nigussie, Virtanen, Isoaho, & Tenhunen. (2015). SEA: A Secure and Efficient Authentication and Authorization Architecture for IoT-Based Healthcare Using Smart Gateways. *Proceedings of 6th International Conference on Ambient Systems, Networks and Technologies (ANT 2015)*.

Mueller, R. (2007). Demo: A Generic Platform for Sensor Network Applications. MASS'07, 1–3. doi:10.1109/MOBHOC.2007.4428693

Occhiuzzi, C., Vallese, C., Amendola, S., Manzari, S., & Marrocco, G. (2014). NIGHT-care: A passive RFID system for remote monitoring and control of overnight living environment. *Procedia Computer Science*, *32*, 190–197. doi:10.1016/j.procs.2014.05.414

Rahmani, A. (2015). Smart e-Health Gateway: Bringing Intelligence to IoT-Based Ubiquitous Healthcare Systems. CCNC'15.

Redondi, A., Chirico, M., Borsani, L., Cesana, M., & Tagliasacchi, M. (2013). An integrated system based on wireless sensor networks for patient monitoring, localization, and tracking. *Ad Hoc Networks*, *11*(1), 39–53. doi:10.1016/j.adhoc.2012.04.006

Rescorla, E., & Modadugu, N. (2012). Datagram Transport Layer Security (DTLS) Version 1.2. RFC 5238.

Rouse, M. (2018). *IoT analytics guide: Understanding Internet of Things Data*. Received May 2018, from https://internetofthingsagenda.techtarget.com/definition/machine-to-machine-M2M

Salunke, P., & Nerkar, R. (2017). IoT Driven Healthcare System for Remote Monitoring of Patients. Department of E&TC, SITRC.

Sebastian, S. (2018). *How to protect against IoT security threats in healthcare*. Received December 13 2018 from https://www.cabotsolutions.com/how-to-protect-against-iot-security-threats-in-healthcare www.cabotsolutions.com

Shen, W. (2011). Smart Border Routers for eHealthCare Wireless Sensor Networks. WiCOM'11, 1–4. doi:10.1109/wicom.2011.6040606

Shirehjini, A. A. N., Yassine, A., & Shirmohammadi, S. (2012, November). Equipment location in hospitals using RFID-based positioning system. *IEEE Transactions on Information Technology in Biomedicine*, *16*(6), 1058–1069. doi:10.1109/TITB.2012.2204896 PMID:24218700

Sinha, S. (2018). *Introduction to Internet of Things: IoT Tutorial with IoT Application*. Retrieved December 24, 2018, from https://www.edureka.co/blog/iot-tutorial/

Sivagami, S., & Revathy, D. (2016). Smart Healhcare System implemented using IoT. *International Journal of Contemporary Research in Computer Science and Technology*, *2*(3), 641–646.

Sun, W., Cai, Z., Li, Y., Liu, F., Fang, S., & Wang, G. (2018). Security and Privacy in the Medical Internet of Things: A Review. *Security and Communication Networks*, *2018*, 1–9.

Symphony Link vs. LoRaWAN. (2017). Link Labs. Available: https://www.link-labs.com/whitepaper-symphony-link-vs-lorawan

Verma, P., Rajnish, R., & Fatima, S. (2017). Challenges: Wearable Computing for Internet of Things. *International Journal of Science and Research, 6*(4), 1306-1311.

Western PA Healthcare News Team. (2018). *The Market vs. technologists: Treating type one Diabetes.* Received November 21, 2018, from https://www.wphealthcarenews.com/?s=OpenAps

# Chapter 10
# Advanced Cyber Security and Internet of Things for Digital Transformations of the Indian Healthcare Sector

**Jonika Lamba**
*The NorthCap University, Gurugram, India*

**Esha Jain**
https://orcid.org/0000-0002-0152-8566
*The NorthCap University, Gurugram, India*

## ABSTRACT

*Cybersecurity is not just about fortification of data. It has wide implications such as maintaining safety, privacy, integrity, and trust of the patients in the healthcare sector. This study methodically reviews the need for cybersecurity amid digital transformation with the help of emerging technologies and focuses on the application and incorporation of blockchain and the internet of things (IoT) to ensure cybersecurity in the well-being of the business. It was found in the study that worldwide, advanced technology has been used in managing the flow of data and information, India should focus on maintaining the same IT-enabled infrastructure to reduce causalities in the nation and on the other hand improve administration, privacy, and security in the hospital sector. Depending on the network system, resource allocation, and mobile devices, there is a need to prioritize the resources and efforts in the era of digitalization.*

## INTRODUCTION

As per available reports spending of the Indian government on healthcare is estimated to be 1.5% of the total GDP which is low as far as the population of the nation is considered. The spending of the government in the healthcare sector is too low in comparison to other nations. The healthcare sector theaters a pivotal part in the accomplishment and prosperity of a nation, so the government should devote

DOI: 10.4018/978-1-6684-6311-6.ch010

considerable resources to the upliftment of the living conditions of people. The government has taken various steps to improve the present condition of the healthcare sector by framing policies such as the National Health Policy 2017 focused on plummeting infant mortality rate and providing access to good quality healthcare services to the people of the nation. The current situation in the country is alarming and the COVID-19 pandemic had forced nations to rethink the present health care infrastructure as the government alone will not be able to cope up with the present situation (Jain & Lamba, 2020). It need support from the big industrialists to fasten the process of developing the infrastructure for the COVID-19 patients. The time has come where a nation can sustain only based on investment in the well-being care sector due to drastic changes in the environment, pollution level, and modern living habits. The well-being care sector is one of the most important pillars of the Indian economy as it supports the rest of the sectors in smooth functioning.

A healthy nation will be able to face any pandemic and will emerge out of being a winner in the period of disguise. The health care sector is one of the most important pillars of the Indian economy as it supports the rest of the sectors in smooth functioning. A healthy nation will be able to face any pandemic and will emerge out of being a winner in the period of disguise. With the advancement in information and technology, every sector has get influenced to some extent. The need for data management and organization has paved the way for evolving know-hows such as Blockchain and the Internet of Things (IoT) (Miraz et al., 2020; Aich et al., 2019). Blockchain is the technology that integrates healthcare and data. The distinguishing features of blockchain such as transparency, data attribution, accurate and reliable reporting and data analytics help in resolving rigorous data management issues in clinical trials (Omar et al., 2020; Rathee, 2020; Fekih & Lahami, 2020; Fekih et al., 2020). The healthcare sector shown tremendous improvement such as patient retention, data integrity, privacy and regulatory compliances due to adoption of blockchain advanced application. The peculiarities of advanced technology such as Blockchain and how it improved the operations in the healthcare domain with the assistance of its key features and innovative applications. The major risks and opportunities related to technology adoption have also been discussed in the study.

The impact of COVID 19 on the economy of different countries has been studied and it was analyzed that COVID 19 had seriously impacted the healthcare sector (Attia et al. 2019; McGhin et al., 2019; Epiphaniou et al. 2019; Hasselgren et al., 2020). The use of advanced tools and applications such as Artificial Intelligence (AI), Internet of Things (IoT), Unmanned Aerial Vehicles (UAVs) and Blockchain etc., helps in reducing the influence of contagion on the environment (Chamola et al., 2020).

The Healthcare sector is the most important domain of a nation's prosperity. Data and health integration can solve many difficult problems in the healthcare sector. It facilitates exchange and dealings in the database that can be shared across authorized operators. It is peer-to-peer disseminated ledger know-how. It consists of majorly three components which are namely distributed network, shared record, and digital transaction. Blockchain technology ensures that no one can change any information or record and that can be done with the permission of all authorized operators in the system. Blockchain is the most used technology to assemble scattered data and at the critical time, it serves its purpose at best (Abdellatif et al., 2020; Ray et al., 2020). This technology has brought many changes in the well-being sector and in the way, data is managed in the hospital industry. The availability of crucial data at the right point in time has saved many lives (Alladi et al., 2019). Looking at the outdated healthcare infrastructure, emerging technologies have raised the expectations from blockchain and the Internet of Things (Hussein et al., 2019). Emerging technologies such as the Internet of Things (IoT), blockchain, artificial intelligence, machine learning, and big data all together have brought a drastic change in data compilation and management (Abdullah & Jones, 2019). These technologies help in maintaining the confidentiality of patients and provide access to a secure platform for the exchange of information. Step by step implementation of these evolving technologies will brighten the future of the healthcare sector in the long run. Maintaining the privacy of patients and the exchange of transactions between hospitals lead to the proper treatment of patients with less time frame. This helps in the organization of patients' records such as their chronicles related to laboratory tests, patient history of ailment, surgery records, medicine ledger, disease registries, and lab results, etc. With the help of master keys patients, records can be grasped in a quick manner that will facilitate the management of data on the other hand. Block-chain technology has the budding to renovate the hospital sector and bring revolutionary changes which will be beneficial for both patients and hospitals. Though it is quite costly to integrate with the existing infrastructure it is expected that its benefits will outweigh outlays in the extended run. It will also have a promising future in supply change management and claim settlement. Evolving technologies such as big data, the internet of things (IoT), blockchain, and machine learning will together have the potential to bring digital transformation in every sphere of the healthcare industry. Blockchain technology can renovate medical trials, SCM, remedy supply administration, and avert frauds in the healthcare business (Kumar & Mallick, 2018; Akram et al., 2020).

## REVIEW OF LITERATURE

*Martin et al. (2017)* stated that digital transformation in the healthcare sector has huge potential for improving the level of services for the patients. The cyber security threats such as ransomware highlighted the significance of the cyber security to ensure safety of patient records. Due to the inherent limitations of healthcare sector, this sector encounters the largest cyber risk in its security position. The healthcare sector is the soft and easy target for the attackers due to loopholes in its security mechanism and it offers plenty of valuable data.

*Pilkington (2017)* examined the requirement of distributed ledger technology in the hospital and medicine segment after encountering the problems with private and public enterprises for retrieving data related to patients. The distributed ledger technology has acknowledged the remarkable role for the organization and compilation of electronic health records (Bell et al., 2018). The study aroused the fast-mounting demand for medical equipment by the consumers and figure out the role of public-private relationships for designing blockchain technologies for the health care sector.

*Rose (2017)* stated that online medicine ordering i.e., telemedicine is not a new concept in the nation but the outburst of COVID 19 has made this mobile health concept very much popular. The concept of mhealth has led to wider integration of hospitals and patients and resulted in wider reach and participation (Celesti et al., 2020). The chapter focused on the alarming usage of electronic media and health apps in the period of novel coronavirus which will help to overcome the fear of infection due to physical interaction between people (Kalla et al., 2020; Ahmad et al., 2021). The study explored the upsurge in the concept of mhealth and what are its developments, and what kind of opportunities are being offered by this emerging concept in the medical industry. The challenges and threats posed by this concept were also covered by the study.

*Teoh & Mahmood (2017)* stated that the digital economy is possible with the help of cyber security. The cyber space is becoming very challenging and there are new advancements with each passing day. This calls for the enactment of National cybersecurity strategy (NCSS) to protect the digital economy in the phase of drastic online transformation (Brunetti et al., 2020). The adoption of NCSS is not mandatory but it will help in continuous growth and prosperity in the online world.

*Rabah (2018)* said that data is the new blood in the economy. Data management is required in every field whether it is healthcare, manufacturing, retail, food, transport, service, operational and agriculture, etc. and demand for professionals in big data is also increasing day by day. It played a crucial role in identifying the needs of consumers and supplying requisite goods at the best price to remain ahead of their competitors. Developing knowledges such as the, blockchain, artificial intelligence, Internet of Things (IoT), machine learning, and big data all together have brought a drastic change in data compilation and management. This will lead to a promising industrial revolution. The study focused on the implementation of evolving technology in healthcare and any other domains it answered many questions related to the application of technology in the fast-changing era of digitalization. Data is the basis of evolving artificial intelligence and helps in the growth of every sector of the economy.

*Attia et al. (2019)* focused on security architecture in the field of IoT and blockchain for reviewing the healthcare applications. Various appropriate examples have been used to validate this framework at design level. In advanced technology framework, devices are connected and information needs to be placed in a highly secure environment.

*Abraham et al. (2019)* examined that Healthcare sector is most vulnerable to cyber security. The cyber risk due to malware, ransomware, hacking and phishing, etc,. pose serious threats in the operation of healthcare sector. The United States (US) healthcare domain found that due to excessive legality and discordant systems, application of cyber security has become difficult. The governance, securities laws, compliance regulations futher complicate the challenge of cyber security into the system.

*Dai et al. (2019)* dicussed about the opportunities and challenges of IoT in the technology driven environment. There are number of loopholes noticed in the IoT applications such as privacy, security, decentralization and deprived interoperability. The study also discussed how blockchain adoption helped in overcoming the challenges caused by IoT.

*Epiphaniou et al. (2019)* explored the peculiarities of advanced technology such as Blockchain and how it improved the operations in the healthcare domain with the assistance of its key features and innovative applications. The major risks and opportunities related to technology adoption have also been discussed in the study.

*Meske et al. (2019)* examined the possibilities of online shoving in medical clinics and reasoned that computerized poking in medical clinics can decidedly impact the utilization of innovation, new worth creation, the difference in structures, and subsequently monetary elements of advanced change, supporting guardians as well as overseers.

*Ricciardi et al. (2019)* found that the influence of the digitalization process has been thoughtful, and it is projected to be more thoughtful in nearby future (Jain & Lamba, 2021). The study evaluated whether health care services contributed in a significant manner to the goals of health care processes and systems. Optimally decision should be taken at which level digital services should be introduced based on the evidence from the medical industry.

*Alam (2020)* emphasized how blockchain can be fruitful in the mobile health (mhealth) of patients. Patients nowadays are more knowledgeable and need to know all information related to their health on a real-time basis and this would empower them. The blockchain phenomena will boost mobile health and its applications and usage. The combination of the Internet of Things (IoT) and blockchain will provide a unique identification number to the connected device in the framework including mobile and medical devices. This will be helpful for the patients to monitor their health and reduce the cost of physically visiting the hospitals. In a nutshell, the adoption of emerging advancements in the field of technology will provide relief and comfort to effectively monitor patient's health problems and it will also benefit the doctors and hospital staff to perform their duties while maintaining integrity in the system.

*Chamola et al. (2020)* inspected the impression of COVID 19 on the budget of diverse countries and it also analyzed that COVID 19 had seriously impacted the healthcare sector. The use of advanced tools and applications such as, Internet of Things (IoT), Unmanned Aerial Vehicles (UAVs), Artificial Intelligence (AI) and Distributed expertise etc., helps in reducing the influence of pandemic on the economy.

*El-Gazzar & Stendal (2020)* studied the advantages and challenges faced by the health care sector with the application of blockchain technology and how the innovation in the information and technology sector enhanced the exchange of patient-sensitive data and empowered the patients and found that adoption of this distributed ledger technology may raise the problems of the health care sector instead of solving them. It was found that there is a requirement of using more cases to understand the sharing of information with the health care domain (Khezr et al., 2019).

*Fekih & Lahami (2020)* examined that blockchain technology applications in the medicine and well-being domain. The research in this sector is emerging rapidly. The advanced technology is used for patient monitoring, reviewing drug supply chain and sharing the electronic medicinal histories. The study also focused on the limitations of blockchain also.

*Mathy et al. (2020)* studied the influence of digitalization on the supply chain of the hospital industry. The digitalization of the supply chain had raised concerns for decision-makers in the healthcare sector. These are usually valued with techniques such as return on investments, Health technology assessments (HTA), etc. The introduction of ADS (automated dispensing system) in French hospital central pharmacy with a posteriori evaluation from the opinion of hospitals. It has led to hidden cost assuagement which does not generate any cash flow i.e., financial flow and it has not been valued. When they are given weightage, the results changed dramatically, as the profitability changes from negative to positive. Importance should be given to these hidden costs and gains as they had a drastic impact on the evaluation of the organization's impact.

*Moro Visconti & Morea (2020)* explored the influence of making digital the smart hospital project financing (PF) promoted by pay-for-performance (P4P) inducements. Electronic stages facilitate the exchange of information between different agents. Submission to healthcare public-private firms (PPPs) has importantly led to the steadiness of electronic stages with the well-being problems and the intricacy of the shareholder's interface. Digital savings can be very useful for all the stakeholders and it has proved beneficial in the digitalization of supply chains and is significantly contributing towards a patient-centric approach. Digitalization of the medicine sector will be beneficial for surveillance of infectious disease, supplement massive healthcare intervention, provide timely and accurate data, and helps in the decongestion of hospitals during the COVID 19 period.

*Omar et al. (2020)* explored the prospects in the well-being domain wide the applications of Blockchain technology. The distinguishing features of blockchain such as transparency, data attribution, accurate and reliable reporting and data analytics help in resolving rigorous data management issues in clinical trials. The healthcare sector shown tremendous improvement such as patient retention, data integrity, privacy and regulatory compliances due to adoption of blockchain advanced application.

*Ratthe (2020)* discussed about the wide applications of IoT such as healthcare, agriculture, public safety, smart phones and smart homes. The IoT is now considered as IoE "Internet of Everything". It has undertaken a drastic revolution in the field of advanced technology. It has a promising future ahead.

*Singh & Singh (2020)* studied the integration of blockchain and the Internet of Things (IoT) in the agriculture and healthcare sector predominantly. With emerging advancements and innovations these technologies will transform the food and healthcare industry (Kumar et al., 2018). It was discovered that 20% of papers are accessible in agriculture and 14% obtainable in the hospital sector that integrated blockchain with AI and IoT. It will help in managing healthcare and nutrition stock chain administration (Farouk et al., 2020).

*Srivastava et al. (2020)* The technology of the Internet of Things (IoT) has increased the usage of blockchain applications in the well-being sector. The aim is to reap maximum benefits from the request of blockchain in the well-being domain. The sphere of blockchain has reached many sectors besides the financial sector, the chapter focused on IoT applications specifically in the well-being sector by making use of distributed ledger expertise (Clauson et al., 2018). This is a challenging area of research as per today's scenario and the chapter dealt with positive attributes of this technology and what will be its future implications has been discussed in detail in the study. The author emphasized exploring this new horizon and IoT integration with the blockchain.

*Tripathi et al. (2020)* found that blockchain helped to overcome the failure of privacy and security-related issues. The study explored the technical and communal hurdles while adopting Smart Healthcare Systems (SRS) by exploring the views of experts and operators and observed the role of blockchain as the remarkable to facilitate the security and veracity of the system (Mistry et al., 2020).

*Caldarelli et al. (2021)* intended to inspect and overwhelmed the barricades to the extensive acceptance of blockchain technology and reinforced the impression that the blockchain explanation could be an appreciated add-on in maintainable supply chains. However, a high thoughtful knowledge of technology and widespread statement with patrons is obligatory for fruitful incorporation.

*Foster et al (2021)* stated the remarkable advancement in the field of technology and how it is going to decide the survival and growth in the wake of digitalization in the future. The technologies have been become agile such as blockchain, Machine learning, IoT, Virtual Reality have fostered the digital transactions in the country. These tools are going to decide the which sector will flourish in the 2021. Innovations and research in education industry are shaping the future of the nation.

*Kamble et al. (2021)* acknowledged intrant heaviness, companion willingness, apparent practicality, and seeming comfort of use as the most persuading aspects for blockchain acceptance.

*Mathivathanan et al. (2021)* recognized the espousal barricades and showed that the absence of commercial consciousness and acquaintance with distributed expertise on what it can deliver for upcoming supply chains, are the greatest powerful barricades that obstruct blockchain espousal. These barricades delay and influence trades choice to create a blockchain-enabled supply chain and that other barricades act as subordinate and related variable star in the implementation procedure.

*Sharma & Joshi (2021)* recognized barricades in the direction of the implementation of distributed technology in Indian hospital and well-being industry and recommended that low-slung consciousness linked to permissible subjects and little provision from upper level of organization have supreme pouring control.

## OBJECTIVE OF THE STUDY

The aim of the study is as follows:

## Primary Objectives

- To study the need for cyber-security amid digital transformation with the aid of emerging technologies.
- To study the application and combination of blockchain and the Internet of Things (IoT) for ensuring cyber-security in the healthcare industry.

## Secondary Objectives

- To study the various innovations in the healthcare sector concerning technology adoption.
- To study the worldwide applications and developments of blockchain in the well-being domain.
- To study measures to mitigate cyber risk in wake of digitalization.

## RESEARCH METHODOLOGY

This article methodically reviews the present literature published in peer-reviewed journals related to the application of blockchain and the Internet of Things (IoT) in the healthcare industry to overcome cyber risk in the period of digitalization. The information gathered in this study has been taken from authentic sources of secondary data collection including past studies. The study is a descriptive analysis of need for cyber-security amid digital transformation with the support of emerging technologies and the integration of blockchain and the Internet of Things (IoT) in the hospital sector and also throw some light on the worldwide applications of blockchain in the healthcare domain to ensure security and integrity in the phase of digital transformation.

## USE OF DIGITAL TECHNOLOGY IN HEALTHCARE SECTOR

Technology has become the most important need of every sector. The technologies in the healthcare domain have wide applications from hospital administration applications to surgery and cancer research to eradicate the flaws in the system and make the patient experience with the hospital as pleasant as possible and improve overall efficacy in the well-being business (Jain, 2020).

### Administrative

The use of IoT and blockchain has organized the administrative work in hospitals. The AI applications help in calculating the waiting time for a patient and also ask preliminary questions which makes it easier for the doctors and professionals to pact with patients in an operative manner. This has led to the more efficient and effective functioning of hospitals in the country.

### Surgical Treatment

The use of machine learning, and robotics has been widely used in surgical procedures. During the COVID-19 period (Chamola et al., 2020) robotics has helped a lot in discharging services to patients and eradicate the chances of catching an infection. Robots are assisting doctors from minor surgeries to open-heart operations. Healthtech had a bright future ahead and the pandemic situation made the need for further advancement in the field of robotics. Augmented Reality (AR) is also helping doctors in explaining concepts to patients more clearly.

## Medicine Development

Medicine and drug development is an important area of research and this has become all the way more vital due to the emergence of a pandemic. Healthcare and pharmaceutical companies are using artificial intelligence and paving new methods of drug development. It has simplified the process of drug development and reduce the period as well leading to the optimal drug. The patients and drug suitability can be checked via artificial intelligence.

## Fitness

A healthy body is a must for keeping other things workable. There has been advancement in the number of applications that guide people on how to keep themselves healthy including wearables to keep a record of several steps in a day, sleep schedule measurement, weight reducing tips, etc.

## Fault Reduction and Diagnostics

Early detection of disease can save millions of lives so the integration of Healthtech in the field of diagnosis is of paramount importance. Integration of technology in the field of genetics, pathology, diagnosis fields helped in the early detection of deadly diseases such as cancers and provided solutions with accuracy to treat can patients.

## Psychological Well-Being

In today's era keeping your mind healthy is of paramount importance in one's life. Due to the continuously changing environment and increasing competition, it has become vital to pay attention to mental health. Disease such as depression, PTSD, Alzheimer's, etc. are arousing so there is a need to tackle these problems by inventing telemedicine apps where patients can access counselors online and exposure therapies can also be helpful to revive patients from depression.

## APPLICATIONS OF DIGITAL TECNOLOGY IN THE HEALTHCARE SECTOR

- **Eradicating Centralization:** With the emergence of blockchain in technological advancement things changed drastically, earlier only authorized representatives had access to the repository of patient information but the introduction of blockchain led to decentralization where every user can access the information available on digital or cloud platform without any authorization and hurdles.
- **Enhanced data security and confidentiality:** The usage of blockchain leads to the removal of concerns related to data security and privacy concerns as they transform the exchange process,

now information is accessible in an encrypted format only which is difficult to decode. Moreover, the use of master and primary keys leads to the chronological arrangement of data and enhanced the security of patient records and details.

- **Control over patient records and ownership:** The patient's consent should be taken before using their treatment records. Using blockchain technology patients can monitor where data has been used and what are replications of that. The patients possess the ultimate control over their records and should not part on their privacy at any cost.
- **The atmosphere of Trust:** The step-by-step adoption of blockchain in the health care sector ensures the integrity of the system while sharing information. The uncluttered and see-through features of blockchain boost the trust and help various stakeholders of the health care sector in the implementation of numerous applications of data compilation, arrangement, retrieval, and management.
- **Claim Verification:** The use of blockchain in the healthcare domain has simplified the process of claim adjudication as it will make the process of verifying documents of patients much easier and reliable.
- **Data Accessibility:** The data stored on multiple nodes in the blockchain is easily available on the available to all the entitled users and their chances of data theft or loss are also minimal due to the security framework developed by blockchain and IoT technology and there will no corruption on part of data accessibility.

## NEED FOR CYBERSECURITY IN PHASE OF DIGITAL TRANSFORMATION

The pace of digitalization in the market today calls for security issues as well, the emerging cyber-crimes such as hacking of websites, bank frauds, ATM card fraud, Call center fraud and Napster case etc., arose the fear of cyber threat in the business (Srivastava et al., 2020). The benefits offered by digitalization are numerous but challenges also need to be addressed on an immediate basis. In data driven society security of information needs to be maintained, to secure trust of public in technology. Recently the data of Dominos company related to credit card information of customers have been leaked which possess the threat to personal information of the customers. The advanced research in cyber security is providing tools and mechanism to control the menace of digital frauds. There have been several laws enacted at national and international level to control the menace of frauds by technocrats. The advancement in the IT sector is commendable but it offers certain challenges and threats also. These applications include Augmented Reality (AR), Big Data, Blockchain, Robotics and Virtual Reality and many more. There is a need for controlling cyber risk by strict application of security measures in the system and appointment of Chief Information Security Officer to maintain the safety of dealings in the business. The malicious activities need to be curbed to better use the leading advancement in the information technology sector. It need to be focused that no digital transformation should be taken without understanding its security implications. The Healthcare sector is a data enrich sector which is more lucrative to cyber attackers to impede the security of the system.

## CYBER SECURITY ROADMAP

- **Consider Cyber Security Risk:** Recognize core and assignment perilous roles and formulate an reservior of susceptible assets and allot a risk influence score to each susceptible asset.
- **Escalating cybersecurity risk and measures:** Evaluate the adverse consequences linked with diverse outbreak set-ups. Then estimate the outlay of suggested risk reduction measures such as prevention, recognition and retrieval and use of erudite analytics to guess the likelihood of adverse consequences and allied outlay.
- **Collaborating cybersecurity activities and results:** Upsurge transparency about cybersecurity strategy and measures. Adapt communications and attain a certain level of shared understanding and accord on inferences of cybersecurity events.

## EMERGING MEDICAL DEVICES IN THE ERA OF DIGITALIZATION

The upsurge of digitization has taken over the world. All the evolving technologies like Cloud-based solutions, the Internet of Things (IoT) and Artificial Intelligence (AI), and many others are serving individuals animate a healthier and relaxed lifespan. The service division has been promoted a lot from digitization especially in the health care industry.

**Patient-Generated Health Data (PGHD):** It is a healthcare mobile application that provides information related to symptoms, lifestyle, the healing process, disease, treatment history, habits, and many more. It provides a critical analysis of the patient's disease history and helps in reducing the number of visits to a clinic.

**Wearable Devices:** Digital wearable devices always provide continuous nursing of health. It provides facilities such as quality of sleep, heart rate, steps walked, and more. They are widely used in the North American region.

**Communication Channels:** The recent developments in communication technology helps in keeping updated on all details related to their treatment such as instant messaging, emergency calls (SOS Signals), real-time video calls, and many more. By incorporating all these facilities in a mobile application companies are planning to offer real-time sustenance to patients in the time of need.

**Geolocation:** It is one of the distinguishing features of every mobile health application. It allows patients to locate nearby hospitals' addresses, clinics, and medical stores. It also has a provision in case of emergency when the patient is unable to locate his current location then he can make emergency calls. During the COVID 19 phase, it helps to locate COVID hot spots during the pandemic phase. It helps in fighting against the deadly virus. For instance, the government of the nation has developed an app named "Aarogya Setu" that uses geolocation and Bluetooth data to aware the users in the case of COVID 19 patients adjacent.

**Contact Tracing:** To combat the spread of this deadly virus infection and the practice of returning to a new world of normal requires the use of contact tracing. It helps in silent tracking of the COVID 19 patients and alerts the people promptly regarding any of their contacts who tested positive of this deadly disease.

**Internet of Things (IoT):** It has provided significant assistance in the era of digitalization; it helps in the collection of data from the connected devices and transmits it to the health care service provider. It can be vigilant for the doctors as they will be informed if anything wrong happens to a patient or any values crosses the threshold limits. The problem of depression has been well monitored by the usage of these technologies.

**Cloud-based Solutions:** EMR (Electronic Medical Records) have been integrated with EHR (Electronic Health Records) with cloud-based solutions that allow easy access to the patient treatment history, their recovery process, medical bills, insurance plans, and many more. With the emergence of cloud-based solutions and infrastructure, hospitals and healthcare companies promise to render better services at a relative lessor cost.

# ELEMENTS OF ADVANCED BLOCKCHAIN TECHNOLOGY

- **Distributed Ledger Technology:** Blockchain is a record of all transactions in a peer-to-peer system. It is a dispersed ledger technology that ensures that everyone in the network has access to the information without any delay.
- **Encryption of Information:** The use of blockchain ensures that information is encrypted and leads to secure transfer of information. In short, it maintains the integrity and security of the data.
- **No need for Third Party:** All the authorized users in the system can directly share information amongst themselves that reduces the need for any third-party organization to authenticate the dealings.
- **Smart Contracts:** It permitted the agreement on additional business logic and automatic enforcement of the expected behavior of dealings or assets embodied in blockchain technology.

## CYBER THREATS IN THE DIGITAL TRANSFORMATION OF HEALTHCARE SECTOR

- **Ransomware:** With the help of this malware the wrongdoers are trying to stop users from accessing their systems or data and even to delete their files unless a fees is paid to attackers.
- **Information theft for Impact:** Now a days there is common practice of stealing the data and information just for the sake of publicity stunts such as in case of high profile people, politicians and celebrities their health data is used for publicity purpose.
- **Stealing data for financial gains:** The attackers steal the information such personal information including names, address, credit card details, etc to use them for unethical monetary gains.
- **Denial of Service attacks:** It often used by attacker to cause disruption in the network by blocking the network with artificial requests, blackmail and activism.
- **Phishing:** It is a common fraud technique where a link is send over email and the victim by clicking on the link gives the way to intruder to access his/her system. Due to this victim faces huge financial loss.
- **Malevolent attacks:** These types of attacks can lead to complete or partial loss od data related to customers, accounts and financial dealings leading to serious regulatory desecrations.

## WORLDWIDE ADVANCED TECHONLOGY APPLICATIONS IN HEALTHCARE SECTOR

### Factom

It is widely used in information technology and enterprise system in Austin, Texas. It develops products that assist the healthcare sector to store data related to patients on the organization's blockchain that is available to hospital staff and operators only. Only authorized people can access the information stored in the Factom security chip. It laboring blockchain distributed technology for data handling and store information in a secured manner digitally.

### Medicalchain

It is widely used in maintaining health records electronically and blockchain assists that only in London, England. It ensures the privacy of patients as outsiders cannot access the patient's confidential information and doctors, professionals and laboratories can access information from a record origin as well. With the help of blockchain, they can maintain the information from the origin and protect the confidentiality of patients.

### Guardtime

It is used in cybersecurity in Irvine, California. It is being applied in the healthcare sector for cybersecurity applications. It is very much helpful for government and healthcare companies to integrate blockchain with cybersecurity applications.

### Simplyvital Health

This company is using decentralized technology in the healthcare domain in Watertown, Massachusetts. It provides an open database where pertinent information is stored and made available to health care professionals for further research in the healthcare industry. Patients' information can be accessed in a time-effective manner and information can be shared for obtaining coordination.

### Coral Health Research and Discovery

It employs blockchain to speed up the process of administration, care process and automate other health operations queries and improve the resulting information. It led to smart contracts between patients and professionals in the medical industry.

### Robomed

This company does the task of gathering information related to patients with the help of AI and share the information gathered with healthcare benefactors. It is put up in Moscow, Russia, and used blockchain technology to securely access and share information with professionals and healthcare operators only.

## Patientory

It focused on maintaining the confidentiality of patient's data in Atlanta. Georgia. It provided end-to-end encryption of data and information. All patient's information has been placed under one roof from where all doctors, professionals, surgeons can retrieve the information as per their requirement by employing blockchain technology.

## RECENT DEVELOPMENTS IN BLOCKCHAIN TECHNOLOGY

- **Blockchain As a Service (BaaS):** This trend has been made famous more in 2020 as blockchain has been integrated with start-up ventures. The users can make their online products with the assistance of blockchain. These products can take the form of decentralized applications and smart contracts, all the more it offers services that don't require blockchain infrastructure. Companies such as Microsoft and Amazon making blockchain applications need of the hour to remain competitive.
- **Coalesced Blockchain Transfers to the Center Phase:** It is one of the latest and demanding trends in blockchain technology. The case used has been increased with the help of federated blockchain. It led to decentralization where diverse authorities can control nodes of blockchain. It has sped up the processing speed and will provide a more customized outlook.
- **High Demand of Stablecoins:** To stabilize the volatility in the cryptocurrencies blockchain stable coins will be in high demand in the year 2021.
- **Blockchain Networks:** These networks have fastened the process of exchange of data and sharing of information from one network to another integrated via blockchain.
- **Lucrative to Government Organizations:** Government agencies are required to monitor a huge volume of data, blockchain applications will reduce the burden of storage by providing a separate database for a specific activity. The adoption of distributed ledger technology will improve the functioning of government departments.
- **Blockchain integration with Artificial Intelligence:** The combination of blockchain and artificial intelligence can boost the machine learning concept and blockchain can make AI more understandable and comprehensive. It can trace why conclusions are reached in machine learning and enhance the application domain of emergent technology.

## MEASURES TO MITIGATE CYBER RISK IN WAKE OF DIGITALIZATION

Depending on the nature of business, complexity of dealings and usage of network, the measures should the adopted to prevent cyber risk in light of digitalization in the economy.

- Identification of the risk at the initial phase helps in prevention of a big problem from originating. Depending on the network system, allocation of resources and mobile devices, there is a need to prioritize the resources and effort in wake of digitalization.

- The practice of restricting the permission to access the system is one of the common ways to mitigate cyber risk. Use of passwords and proper administration will help in achievement of cyber security in the system.
- Encryption devices makes sure that data that is private and confidential is not available to people outside the organization domain.
- Use of proper software and firewall applications serve the purpose of cyber security in digital transactions.
- Periodic monitoring of the system also helps in maintaining security of the system in the network and often ensure smooth functioning of the system as well. The information security manager should be alert all the time to ensure the integrity and trust in the system.
- A proper response strategy also helps in overcoming the severity of cyber-attacks. The strategy helps in fetching legal remedies and reduces the monetary impact of unwanted dealings in the system.
- There is need for timely backup and customized training for ensuring reliability and integrity at all stages of organization.
- The vetting needs to be done for cloud service providers to ensure compliance with auditing standards such as SAS 70 and FIPS 200.
- Deploying AI automated structures that proactively notice and prevent outbreaks on web and devices.
- A risk management regimes needs to be set up and embedded into cybersecurity of the business dealings

## MAJOR FINDINGS OF THE STUDY

- The introduction of advanced tehnology in digital world led to decentralization where every user can access the information available on digital or cloud platforms without any authorization and hurdles.
- The digital transformation led to smart contracts between patients and professionals in the medical industry.
- Cybersecurity ensures the privacy of patients as outsiders cannot access the patient's confidential information and doctors, professionals and laboratories can access information from a record origin as well.
- Digital wearable devices always provide continuous nursing of health. It provides facilities such as quality of sleep, heart rate, steps walked, and more.
- The step-by-step adoption of blockchain in the well-being sector ensures the integrity of the system while sharing information. The uncluttered and see-through features of blockchain boost the trust and help various stakeholders of the health care sector in the implementation of numerous applications of data compilation, arrangement, retrieval, and management.
- Emerging technologies such as the Internet of Things (IoT), blockchain, artificial intelligence, machine learning, and big data all together have brought a drastic change in data compilation and management. These technologies help in maintaining the confidentiality of patients and provide access to a secure platform for the exchange of information.

- Internet of Things (IoT) has provided significant assistance in the era of digitalization; it helps in the collection of data from the connected devices and transmits it to the health care service provider.
- Government agencies are required to monitor a huge volume of data, blockchain applications will reduce the burden of storage by providing a separate database for a specific activity.
- It is very much helpful for government and healthcare companies to integrate blockchain with cybersecurity applications.
- It is highly recommended to maintain adequate documentation on the technical standards followed and aspired to be followed by the businesses and that need to be driven by adequate policy and top managerial employees. It further suggested that top and senior management should be guided by a competent and professional Chief Inforamtion Security Officer.
- Identification of the risk at the initial phase helps in prevention of a big problem from originating. Depending on the network system, allocation of resources and mobile devices, there is a need to prioritize the resources and effort in wake of digitalization.
- The use of blockchain in the healthcare domain has simplified the process of claim adjudication as it will make the process of verifying documents of patients much easier and reliable.
- The use of master and primary keys leads to the chronological arrangement of data and enhanced the security of patient records and details.

## SOLUTIONS AND RECOMMENDATIONS

The healthcare sector is very soft target of the malicous attackers so security needs to be fostered at every level of business transactions. It is highly recommended to maintain adequate documentation on the technical standards followed and aspired to be followed by the businesses and that need to be driven by adequate policy and top managerial employees. It further suggested that top and senior management should be guided by a competent and professional Chief Inforamtion Security Officer. The information security manager should be alert all the time to ensure the integrity and trust in the system.he following security measures should be pracrices such as use of proper software and firewall applications that serve the purpose of cyber security in digital transactions and continous monitoring of the system also helps in maintaining security of the system in the network and often ensure smooth functioning of the system as well. A proper response strategy also helps in overcoming the severity of cyber-attacks. The strategy helps in fetching legal remedies and reduces the monetary impact of unwanted dealings in the system. There is need for timely backup and customized training for ensuring reliability and integrity at all stages of organization.

## FUTURE RESEARCH DIRECTIONS

The cybercrime is a universal challenge, the present study mainly discussed about the cyber security threats, measures and digital advancement in the healthcare sector. There is scope for other sectors to analyse the cyber security impications in the era of digitalization. The effective cybersecurity must become an vital part of healthcare domain and further guidelines and compliance actions should be subject of imminent research tactics.

# CONCLUSION

Cybersecurity is not just about protection of data it has wide implications such as maintaining safety, privacy, integrity, trust of the patients in the healthcare sector. The need for data management and organization has paved ways for advanced technologies such as Blockchain and the Internet of Things (IoT). The Healthcare sector is the most important domain of a nation's prosperity. Data and health integration can solve many difficult problems in the healthcare sector. It facilitates exchange and dealings in the database that can be shared across authorized operators. Advanced technology such as Blockchain is peer-to-peer disseminated ledger know-how. It consists of majorly three components which are namely distributed network, shared record, and digital transaction. The healthcare industry has undergone various reforms since the evolution of blockchain and Internet of Things (IoT) technology came into the picture. The emergence of these techniques has led to a drastic improvement in the field of Hospital administration, Medicine development, Surgery, Mental Health, and cybersecurity, etc. During the COVID 19 phase, the most affected sector was healthcare where technological advancement was much needed. Robotics helped the nations to face this pandemic with strength.

The technologies in the healthcare domain have wide applications from hospital administration to surgery and cancer research to eradicate the flaws in the system and make the patient experience with the hospital as pleasant as possible and improve overall efficiency in the healthcare industry. Emerging technologies such as the Internet of Things (IoT), blockchain, artificial intelligence, machine learning, and big data all together have brought a drastic change in data compilation and management. This will lead to a promising industrial revolution. The study focused on the implementation of evolving technology in the healthcare sector. Worldwide, blockchain technology has been used in managing the flow of data and information and ensuring security in the system, India should focus on maintaining the same blockchain-enabled infrastructure to reduce causalities in the nation. The adoption of these techniques has led to the secure transfer of information and helped in maintaining the confidentiality of patient's health records.

*"Healthcare is an important sector of Indian Economy. Both government and technocrats should work together in the best possible manner by exploiting emerging technologies so that it leads to improvement of healthcare services and the well-being of the nation."*

# ACKNOWLEDGMENT

This study received no explicit grant from any funding agency in the public, commercial, or not-for-profit divisions.

# REFERENCES

Abdellatif, A. A., Al-Marridi, A. Z., Mohamed, A., Erbad, A., Chiasserini, C. F., & Refaey, A. (2020). Health: Toward secure, blockchain-enabled healthcare systems. *IEEE Network*, *34*(4), 312–319. doi:10.1109/MNET.011.1900553

Abdullah, T., & Jones, A. (2019, January). eHealth: challenges far integrating blockchain within health-care. In *2019 IEEE 12th International Conference on Global Security, Safety and Sustainability (ICGS3)* (pp. 1-9). IEEE.

Abraham, C., Chatterjee, D., & Sims, R. R. (2019). Muddling through cybersecurity: Insights from the US healthcare industry. *Business Horizons*, *62*(4), 539–548. doi:10.1016/j.bushor.2019.03.010

Ahmad, R. W., Salah, K., Jayaraman, R., Yaqoob, I., Ellahham, S., & Omar, M. (2021). The role of blockchain technology in telehealth and telemedicine. *International Journal of Medical Informatics*, *148*, 104399. doi:10.1016/j.ijmedinf.2021.104399 PMID:33540131

Aich, S., Chakraborty, S., Sain, M., Lee, H. I., & Kim, H. C. (2019, February). A review on benefits of IoT integrated blockchain-based supply chain management implementations across different sectors with case study. In *2019 21st international conference on advanced communication technology (ICACT)* (pp. 138-141). IEEE. 10.23919/ICACT.2019.8701910

Akram, S. V., Malik, P. K., Singh, R., Anita, G., & Tanwar, S. (2020). Adoption of blockchain technology in various realms: Opportunities and challenges. *Security and Privacy*, *3*(5), e109. doi:10.1002py2.109

Alam, T. (2020). mHealth Communication Framework using blockchain and IoT Technologies. *International Journal of Scientific & Technology Research*, *9*(6).

Alladi, T., Chamola, V., Parizi, R. M., & Choo, K. K. R. (2019). Blockchain applications for industry 4.0 and industrial IoT: A review. *IEEE Access: Practical Innovations, Open Solutions*, *7*, 176935–176951. doi:10.1109/ACCESS.2019.2956748

Attia, O., Khoufi, I., Laouiti, A., & Adjih, C. (2019, June). An IoT-blockchain architecture based on hyperledger framework for health care monitoring application. In *NTMS 2019-10th IFIP International Conference on New Technologies, Mobility and Security* (pp. 1-5). IEEE Computer Society.

Bell, L., Buchanan, W. J., Cameron, J., & Lo, O. (2018). Applications of blockchain within healthcare. *Blockchain in Healthcare Today, 1*(8).

Brunetti, F., Matt, D. T., Bonfanti, A., De Longhi, A., Pedrini, G., & Orzes, G. (2020). Digital transformation challenges: Strategies emerging from a multi-stakeholder approach. *The TQM Journal*, *32*(4), 697–724. doi:10.1108/TQM-12-2019-0309

Caldarelli, G., Zardini, A., & Rossignoli, C. (2021). Blockchain adoption in the fashion sustainable supply chain: Pragmatically addressing barriers. *Journal of Organizational Change Management*, *34*(2), 507–524. doi:10.1108/JOCM-09-2020-0299

Celesti, A., Ruggeri, A., Fazio, M., Galletta, A., Villari, M., & Romano, A. (2020). Blockchain-based healthcare workflow for tele-medical laboratory in federated hospital IoT clouds. *Sensors (Basel)*, *20*(9), 2590. doi:10.339020092590 PMID:32370129

Chamola, V., Hassija, V., Gupta, V., & Guizani, M. (2020). A comprehensive review of the COVID-19 pandemic and the role of IoT, drones, AI, blockchain, and 5G in managing its impact. *IEEE Access: Practical Innovations, Open Solutions*, *8*, 90225–90265. doi:10.1109/ACCESS.2020.2992341

Clauson, K. A., Breeden, E. A., Davidson, C., & Mackey, T. K. (2018). Leveraging blockchain technology to enhance supply chain management in healthcare: an exploration of challenges and opportunities in the health supply chain. *Blockchain in Healthcare Today, 1*(3), 1-12.

Dai, H. N., Zheng, Z., & Zhang, Y. (2019). Blockchain for Internet of Things: A survey. *IEEE Internet of Things Journal, 6*(5), 8076–8094. doi:10.1109/JIOT.2019.2920987

El-Gazzar, R., & Stendal, K. (2020). Blockchain in health care: Hope or hype? *Journal of Medical Internet Research, 22*(7), e17199. doi:10.2196/17199 PMID:32673219

Epiphaniou, G., Daly, H., & Al-Khateeb, H. (2019). Blockchain and healthcare. In *Blockchain and Clinical Trial* (pp. 1–29). Springer. doi:10.1007/978-3-030-11289-9_1

Farouk, A., Alahmadi, A., Ghose, S., & Mashatan, A. (2020). Blockchain platform for industrial healthcare: Vision and future opportunities. *Computer Communications, 154*, 223–235. doi:10.1016/j.comcom.2020.02.058

Fekih, R. B., & Lahami, M. (2020, June). Application of blockchain technology in healthcare: a comprehensive study. In *International Conference on Smart Homes and Health Telematics* (pp. 268-276). Springer.

Foster, I., Lopresti, D., Gropp, B., Hill, M., & Schuman, K. (2021). *A National Discovery Cloud: Preparing the US for Global Competitiveness in the New Era of 21st Century Digital Transformation.* arXiv preprint arXiv:2104.06953.

Hasselgren, A., Kralevska, K., Gligoroski, D., Pedersen, S. A., & Faxvaag, A. (2020). Blockchain in healthcare and health sciences—A scoping review. *International Journal of Medical Informatics, 134*, 104040. doi:10.1016/j.ijmedinf.2019.104040 PMID:31865055

Hussein, A. H. (2019). Internet of things (IOT): Research challenges and future applications. *International Journal of Advanced Computer Science and Applications, 10*(6), 77–82. doi:10.14569/IJACSA.2019.0100611

Jain, E. (2020). Digital Employability Skills and Training Needs for the Indian Healthcare Industry. In *Opportunities and Challenges in Digital Healthcare Innovation* (pp. 113–130). IGI Global. doi:10.4018/978-1-7998-3274-4.ch007

Jain, E., & Lamba, J. (2020). Covid-19: Economic Hardship and Financial Distress in Indian Economy. *International Journal of Disaster Recovery and Business Continuity, 11*(3), 3081–3092.

Jain, E., & Lamba, J. (2021). Management and Digitalization Strategy for Transforming Education Sector: An Emerging Gateway Persuaded by COVID-19. In Emerging Challenges, Solutions, and Best Practices for Digital Enterprise Transformation (pp. 69-83). IGI Global.

Kalla, A., Hewa, T., Mishra, R. A., Ylianttila, M., & Liyanage, M. (2020). The role of blockchain to fight against COVID-19. *IEEE Engineering Management Review, 48*(3), 85–96. doi:10.1109/EMR.2020.3014052

Kamble, S. S., Gunasekaran, A., Kumar, V., Belhadi, A., & Foropon, C. (2021). A machine learning based approach for predicting blockchain adoption in supply Chain. *Technological Forecasting and Social Change, 163*, 120465. doi:10.1016/j.techfore.2020.120465

Khezr, S., Moniruzzaman, M., Yassine, A., & Benlamri, R. (2019). Blockchain technology in healthcare: A comprehensive review and directions for future research. *Applied Sciences (Basel, Switzerland), 9*(9), 1736. doi:10.3390/app9091736

Kumar, N. M., & Mallick, P. K. (2018). Blockchain technology for security issues and challenges in IoT. *Procedia Computer Science, 132*, 1815–1823. doi:10.1016/j.procs.2018.05.140

Kumar, T., Ramani, V., Ahmad, I., Braeken, A., Harjula, E., & Ylianttila, M. (2018, September). Blockchain utilization in healthcare: Key requirements and challenges. In *2018 IEEE 20th International Conference on e-Health Networking, Applications and Services (Healthcom)* (pp. 1-7). IEEE.

Martin, G., Martin, P., Hankin, C., Darzi, A., & Kinross, J. (2017). Cybersecurity and healthcare: How safe are we? *BMJ (Clinical Research Ed.), 358*. doi:10.1136/bmj.j3179 PMID:28684400

Mathivathanan, D., Mathiyazhagan, K., Rana, N. P., Khorana, S., & Dwivedi, Y. K. (2021). Barriers to the adoption of blockchain technology in business supply chains: A total interpretive structural modelling (TISM) approach. *International Journal of Production Research*, 1–22.

Mathy, C., Pascal, C., Fizesan, M., Boin, C., Délèze, N., & Aujoulat, O. (2020, July). Automated hospital pharmacy supply chain and the evaluation of organisational impacts and costs. In Supply chain forum: An international journal (Vol. 21, No. 3, pp. 206-218). Taylor & Francis.

McGhin, T., Choo, K. K. R., Liu, C. Z., & He, D. (2019). Blockchain in healthcare applications: Research challenges and opportunities. *Journal of Network and Computer Applications, 135*, 62–75. doi:10.1016/j.jnca.2019.02.027

Meske, C., Amojo, I., Poncette, A. S., & Balzer, F. (2019, July). The Potential Role of Digital Nudging in the Digital Transformation of the Healthcare Industry. In *International Conference on Human-Computer Interaction* (pp. 323-336). Springer. 10.1007/978-3-030-23538-3_25

Miraz, M. H. (2020). Blockchain of things (BCoT): The fusion of blockchain and IoT technologies. In *Advanced Applications of Blockchain Technology* (pp. 141–159). Springer. doi:10.1007/978-981-13-8775-3_7

Mistry, I., Tanwar, S., Tyagi, S., & Kumar, N. (2020). Blockchain for 5G-enabled IoT for industrial automation: A systematic review, solutions, and challenges. *Mechanical Systems and Signal Processing, 135*, 106382. doi:10.1016/j.ymssp.2019.106382

Moro Visconti, R., & Morea, D. (2020). Healthcare digitalization and pay-for-performance incentives in smart hospital project financing. *International Journal of Environmental Research and Public Health, 17*(7), 2318. doi:10.3390/ijerph17072318 PMID:32235517

Omar, I. A., Jayaraman, R., Salah, K., Yaqoob, I., & Ellahham, S. (2020). Applications of blockchain technology in clinical trials: Review and open challenges. *Arabian Journal for Science and Engineering*, 1–15.

Pilkington, M. (2017). Can blockchain improve healthcare management? Consumer medical electronics and the IoMT. *Consumer Medical Electronics and the IoMT.*

Rabah, K. (2018). Convergence of AI, IoT, big data and blockchain: a review. *The Lake Institute Journal, 1*(1), 1-18.

Rathee, G., Sharma, A., Saini, H., Kumar, R., & Iqbal, R. (2019). A hybrid framework for multimedia data processing in IoT-healthcare using blockchain technology. *Multimedia Tools and Applications*, 1–23. doi:10.100711042-019-07835-3

Rathee, P. (2020). Introduction to Blockchain and IoT. In *Advanced Applications of Blockchain Technology* (pp. 1–14). Springer. doi:10.1007/978-981-13-8775-3_1

Ray, P. P., Dash, D., Salah, K., & Kumar, N. (2020). Blockchain for IoT-based healthcare: Background, consensus, platforms, and use cases. *IEEE Systems Journal.* Advance online publication. doi:10.1109/JSYST.2020.2963840

Ricciardi, W., Pita Barros, P., Bourek, A., Brouwer, W., Kelsey, T., Lehtonen, L., Anastasy, C., Barros, P., Barry, M., Bourek, A., Brouwer, W., De Maeseneer, J., Kringos, D., Lehtonen, L., McKee, M., Murauskiene, L., Nuti, S., Ricciardi, W., Siciliani, L., & Wild, C. (2019). How to govern the digital transformation of health services. *European Journal of Public Health, 29*(Supplement_3), 7–12. doi:10.1093/eurpub/ckz165 PMID:31738442

Rose, K. J. (2017). Mobile Health: Telemedicine's Latest Wave but This Time It's for Real. In L. Menvielle, A. F. Audrain-Pontevia, & W. Menvielle (Eds.), *The Digitization of Healthcare.* Palgrave Macmillan. doi:10.1057/978-1-349-95173-4_9

Sharma, M., & Joshi, S. (2021). Barriers to blockchain adoption in health-care industry: an Indian perspective. *Journal of Global Operations and Strategic Sourcing.*

Singh, P., & Singh, N. (2020). Blockchain With IoT and AI: A Review of Agriculture and Healthcare. *International Journal of Applied Evolutionary Computation, 11*(4), 13–27. doi:10.4018/IJAEC.2020100102

Srivastava, A., Jain, P., Hazela, B., Asthana, P., & Rizvi, S. W. A. (2021). Application of Fog Computing, Internet of Things, and Blockchain Technology in Healthcare Industry. In *Fog Computing for Healthcare 4.0 Environments* (pp. 563–591). Springer. doi:10.1007/978-3-030-46197-3_22

Srivastava, G., Parizi, R. M., & Dehghantanha, A. (2020). The future of blockchain technology in healthcare internet of things security. *Blockchain Cybersecurity, Trust and Privacy*, 161-184.

Teoh, C. S., & Mahmood, A. K. (2017, July). National cyber security strategies for digital economy. In *2017 International Conference on Research and Innovation in Information Systems (ICRIIS)* (pp. 1-6). IEEE. 10.1109/ICRIIS.2017.8002519

Tripathi, G., Ahad, M. A., & Paiva, S. (2020, March). S2HS-A blockchain based approach for smart healthcare system. In Healthcare (Vol. 8, No. 1, p. 100391). Elsevier.

# Chapter 11
# Healthcare Security Assessment in the Big Data Era:
## Lessons From Turkey

**Ionica Oncioiu**
*Titu Maiorescu University, Romania*

**Oana Claudia Ionescu**
*Titu Maiorescu University, Romania*

## ABSTRACT

*By its nature, the improvement of the individual's health is a service that involves a rigorous sharing of data in real time. Integrating innovative advances in technologies into the healthcare system by organizations from Turkey is a challenge, an approach to the economic and social boundary, and an attempt to balance consumer-oriented actions. This chapter aims to contribute to the decrease of the shortcomings that exist in the healthcare security assessment by focusing on data mining for public institutions and organizations in Turkey.*

## INTRODUCTION

The transition from the industrial society to the information society, technologically-oriented developments also contributed to the increase of the importance of knowledge by accelerating the production, storage, processing and sharing of the data (Frese & Fay, 2001). The rapid progress in information technology has brought many changes, from the daily life of people to the work processes of public and private sector organizations, from the provision of public services such as health and education to the emergence of new areas of expertise and professions (Pettigrew, Woodman & Cameron, 2001).

The use of information in administrative processes, adaptation to information and communication technologies is seen as an element that provides comparative advantage of competition among countries as well as between countries (Mikalef & Pateli, 2017). For this reason, investments for organizations

DOI: 10.4018/978-1-6684-6311-6.ch011

and for information and communication technologies for countries have become a strategic priority (Grimson, Grimson & Hasselbring, 2000).

Today, traditional hardware and software it is now possible to store, process, share and analyze large volumes of data, which are costly to be stored and analyzed by their solutions, thanks to developing information technologies, hardware and software solutions (Şener & Yiğit, 2017). In the 1990s, states and public organizations changed the procedures and procedures, using public facilities and facilities, as well as traditional means, introduced public goods and services, developed and implemented public policies (Ibbs & Kwak, 2000).

At the same time, data mining is a relatively new phenomenon for governments and the public sector, with an advanced implementation network in sectors such as banking, marketing, information, telecommunications and healthcare (Ericksen & Dyer, 2005).

The process of adaptation of the healthcare security assessment to information technology, starting with the state of affairs, now faces new challenges in Turkey such as social media and Web 2.0, open source software, large data, machine learning and open data (Yiğit, 2017).

Many field data mining applications are often found, such as risk analysis and irregularity detection, customer acquisition, credit card fraud detection, customer loss determination, fraud detection, line density estimates, medical diagnosis and appropriate treatment processes (Low & Chen, 2012). The large amount of data and data mining to government programs in Turkey, are included in development plans and policy documents such as the top national action plans (Bolman & Deal, 1999).

It is understood that this area is very dynamic and evolving. Nevertheless, it seems that public services and policies are limited to specific areas such as health. The first question that needs to be answered is "What should the purpose of health policy be?" It is not enough to define the goal as simply "providing each patient with treatment". Because protecting healthy people from diseases and accidents is as important and necessary as being treated. For this reason, this chapter aims to contribute to the decrease shortcomings that exist in the healthcare security assessment by focusing on data mining for public institutions and organizations in Turkey.

In this context, the objective of government policy in Turkey, development plans and action plans as senior policy papers with the strategic plans of the ministries big analyzed using content analysis method data and data mining on public policies and services. Thus, examples of good practice developed especially in the ministries have been identified.

## BACKGROUND

The presentation of public services and the decision to implement public policies have been reshaped since the 1980s with the wave of administrative reform (Ozcan, 2008).

As a result of adopting the private sector in the organizational structure and processes, a similar relation is established between the public organizations and the citizen with the market mechanisms and the innovative service methods are started to be applied. Living change accounted for public administrators and to increase public organizations' productivity.

At the same time, the provision of organizational decentralization has led public administrators to be held responsible for their performance targets and the restructuring of public organizations (Narcı, Ozcan, Sahin, Tarcan & Narcı, 2015).

Professional governance, open performance standards and criteria in the public sector, focus on control of output, recruitment, application of private sector management techniques, productivity and discipline in resource use are the basic principles of the wave of reforms, called new public administration (Crowley, Gold, Bandi & Goel, 2016).

International organizations such as the World Bank and the International Monetary Fund have recommended and encouraged operator reforms, public administration has spread on a global scale (Liu, Zhang, Keil & Chen, 2010). In the 1990s, developments in information and communication technologies became a new wave of reform in the public sector.

In fact, the rapid progress in technology has become a driving force for change in both private and public sector management. Innovations such as the use of information and communication systems such as computer systems, the Internet and new databases have been the prerequisite for inclusion in the public sector, called e-government.

In the US, one of the countries in which YKI emerged, at the beginning of the 2000s, President Bush pursued a policy of making more use of information technologies to reduce costs through productivity growth. In the UK, the use of information and communication technologies, the Labor government, which came to power in 1999 has been one of its main objectives. Discussions within the European Union in this period also focused on efficiency, efficiency and service delivery rather than the democratic potential of new information and communication technologies (Hadad, Hadad & Simon-Tuval, 2013).

With the widespread use of other developed and developing countries, e-government applications have gained an international character and spread all over the world (Bukachi & Pakenham-Walsh, 2007). In this period, public organizations have been adapting applications such as e-mail, web site management, online transaction and now web based services have become an integral part of the state.

The e-government has been the forerunner of the transformation of individual-state relations in the first quarter of the 21st century (Bostan, 016). Services provided under the e-government, shared data and realized transactions significantly increased the amount of data in circulation. In this period, the development of technologies such as smartphones and tablet computers and the widespread use of the internet have changed the expectations from the state.

Technologies such as customized forum pages, chat rooms, and group emailing have increased the opportunities for mass and private communication (Andreassen et al., 2007). In conjunction with Web 2.0 technologies, which are called next-generation Internet applications, in which an average user can share their participation and knowledge, the Internet has become able to contribute to any content and re-publish existing content, transforming from the static internet structure into a dynamic structure involving collaboration between social networks and users.

Social media tools based on Web 2.0 technologies have steadily increased in number since the early 2000s, and private sector and public organizations have remained indifferent to developments in this area (Pelone, F., Kringos, D.S, Romaniello, Archibugi, Salsiri & Ricciardi, 2015). Public organizations have begun to use corporate social media accounts mainly for information sharing, reporting, interaction and partly for participation and cooperation. Thus, the possibility of public services to be offered more effectively and quickly, citizens to take public decisions and to form politics has been improved.

Following a memorandum issued by President Obama in the United States in 2009, open government and open data policies have emerged that are based on transparency, participation and collaboration and advocate the incorporation of digital transformation possibilities into governance processes (Varabyova & Müller, 2016).

While openness in management is not a new concept, the difference from the previous ones is that it is more holistic enough to include transparency, participation and cooperation and is also used more effectively with the integration of tools such as information technology, the internet and social media.

This goal of open administration also differentiates it from classical e-government applications that prioritize online transaction and service provision. With the influence of international organizations such as the Open Government Partnership established in 2011, open management has become a widespread policy among a large number of countries in a short period of time (Mikalef & Pateli, 2017). Innovations that support the development of open administration include open data and open source software

Open data has helped national and local governments to ensure that users have access to a wide range of data in an easy-to-use format. The widespread use of open source software provides the necessary facilities for processing and analyzing large amounts of data, as well as programs that can be used for data access allowing them to be redesigned accordingly.

In recent years, we can say that we are faced with a new challenge with the development of technologies that can collect and process large amounts of data thanks to the widespread use of the internet and networks.

At present, there are applications called Industry 4.0 in the delivery of certain public services, in the management of production processes of factories and in the delivery of some private sector services (Girginer, Kose & Uckun, 2015). Innovations such as the integration of machine sensors, software, cloud computing and storage systems have opened up the opportunity to use the results obtained from interrogating large data sets as a way to perform organizational operational processes as a feedback.

Thus, the machines and the things we use, such as cars, refrigerators, factory robots, analyze what they collect while performing their functions, solve problems quickly, and develops an advanced personalized product and service mentality.

The impact of the learning of machines and the transformation of goods in terms of public utilities and politics, which are expressed in terms of internet, is not yet extensively addressed (Pettigrew, Woodman & Cameron, 2001). The in-depth study of all these developments is beyond the limits of this chapter. However, it is thought that this study will contribute to the related by evaluating the data mining issue, which has a critical role in processing large data, and the effects of data mining on public services.

On the other hand, data generated by means such as health data, shopping data, stock market and financial data, social media data, public transaction data, private sector data and personal use of the internet are quite large in size, and thanks to developing information technology, hardware and software solutions databases and cloud computing resources.

Hidden data cannot be analyzed by human ability using conventional methods have reached their size (Low & Chen, 2012). For this reason, it is necessary to analyze using special software and programs. This includes the Google-developed GFS file system and the MapReduce programming technique, and the Hadoop ecosystem to run applications that can be used to process large amounts of data on simple servers.

It is an open source infrastructure developed in Java that brings together a distributed file system called Hadoop Distributed File System (HDFS) and MapReduce features (Hasselbring, 2000). Hadoop is software that consists of HDFS and MapReduce components. As a result of that it has become possible to process collected data by using appropriate software, algorithms and technologies on large data, to determine the relationship between them, to determine the coexistence and to remove the patterns.

Anyway, today, besides statistics, data analysis and management are also used by those working in science branches such as information systems (Şener & Yiğit, 2017). In addition, experts examine social problems by integrating text mining techniques, a kind of data mining, into their research processes. Unstructured data is collected in databases and transformed into structured data, stored in tabular format in a specific format.

Data mining studies are carried out with the aim of identifying and predicting data through the structured data contained in the institution's databases and data warehouses. Large data, on the other hand, are often indicative of a non-structural dataset that results from the merging of multiple, unrelated datasets. The processing of this data requires confidential information to be collected over a limited time and to be resolved by means of large database specific coding techniques.

## CHALLENGES AND DESIGN CONSIDERATIONS OF THE HEALTHCARE SECURITY ASSESSMENT IN TURKEY

During the Seljuk and Ottoman periods, health services were mostly offered through foundations (Briggs, Cruickshank & Paliadelis, 2012). However, it was not possible for the whole community to benefit from these services because the services were progressing with palace and soldiers.

Private medicine was also developed in the direction of the conditions. Until the end of the 19th century, those who were financially competent were treated by private physicians in their homes and received care (Aytekin, 2011).

The first hospital equipped with the help of the government of the Turkish geography in which we live is accepted as Gülhane. There is no well-equipped health facility up to this turnaround.

However, when the Gülhane Military Hospital was compared with the western hospitals of its era, it was far behind both equipment and information level (Briggs, Cruickshank & Paliadelis, 2012). Together with the publicity of the Republic, health has been one of the primary issues and has been one of the first ministries established.

Over time, the world began to blow, the welfare state and social state currents and Turkey also have the understanding that influenza health care is guaranteed by the state is born. Health services that were socialized in 1960 began to weaken in the face of liberal trends that began to develop in the 1980s and had to change (Du, Wang, Chen, Chou & Zhu, 2014).

In particular, the medical education given here by German teachers is of great importance for Turkish medicine. The training given by Rieder was, in theory, a practical training course, but only at that time. A team of medical information has been discovered a long time ago by Westerners, Rieder still not known and it is taught geography in Turkey have been identified and demonstrated by physicians (Gülsevin & Türkan, 2012). With the establishment of the Ministry, the central organization and the provincial organization have been restructured. Ministry of Health, as the first task; determining the priorities of health services, increasing the achievements in the field of health and allocating resources according to the determined criteria.

A government body and a health directorate have been established for the implementation of preventive health services in line with the identified basic mission (Gemmel, Vandaele & Tambeur, 2001). Treatment services are planned to be performed by municipalities and special administrations, and it is envisaged that poor patients will be treated free of charge by government agencies and other organizations.

In 2003, the Health Transformation Program has brought the country's health system to a completely different position, as well as the first phase of changes in health perceptions (Pan, Johnston, Walker, Adler-Milstein, Bates & Middleton, 2005). The changes that have taken place in Social Insurance Institution premiums and the start of dominance of the public private partnership in the market point to bigger changes in our health care system.

As a result, it has been seen that physicians who make a living with their work in the medical examination have been away from providing preventive services. The health centers suffering from the loss of doctors and nurses were reinstated with the Full Day Law issued in 1978, but remained physicians without any remedy (Škrinjar, Bosilj-Vukšić, & Indihar-Štemberger, 2008).

With the adoption of the Law on the Socialization of Health Services No. 224 in 1961, it was aimed to provide health services in a continuous, widespread and integrated manner to meet the needs of the public (Narcı, Ozcan, Sahin, Tarcan & Narcı, 2015). In accordance with this purpose; health centers, health centers, district and provincial hospitals were opened and a structuring integrated into the province was carried out gradually in the presentation of health services.

In addition to these objectives, the General Health Insurance (GSS), Draft Law, which was enacted in October 2008, was prepared at these times but was not presented to the Council of Ministers. Second Five-Year Development Plan coming to the fore again with the GSS in 1969, Turkey has not been adopted by the Grand National Assembly (SB 2007). The State Planning Organization (DPT) established a master plan on health services in 1990. In the process of evaluating health reforms, the first and second National Health Conferences were held (Uçkun, Girginer, Köse & Şahin, 2016).

The 'Green Card' application, which was enacted in 1992 with the Law No. 3861, providing free public health services for low-income groups with no power to meet health care needs. Health reform studies in general; such as the collection of the social security institution under a single umbrella, the establishment of the GSS, the separation of health care service provision and financing functions, the effective restructuring of the Ministry of Health through supervision and planning tasks, prioritization of preventive health services, autonomy of hospitals, contains basic topics (Ozcan, 2008).

The main targets for health in the scope of Everyone's Health under the Urgent Action plan announced on 16 November 2002 (Celik & Esmeray, 2014) are as follows: functional and administrative restructuring of the Ministry of Health; all citizens to be covered by universal health insurance; the gathering of health institutions under one roof; giving importance to mother and child health; the financial and administrative autonomy of the hospitals; the transition to the practice of family medicine; prevalence of preventive medicine; elimination of the lack of health personnel living in priority regions in development; encouragement of private sector to invest in health field; all the public institutions to the lower levels of authority transfer; the e-transformation project in the field of health is the passing of a dream.

Moreover, Health Transformation Program announced by the Ministry of Health in December 2003 will design the future health system by considering project and reform studies from past to present and plan to make the necessary changes for the transition to this system. This program is structured to address the health sector in all its dimensions and consists of components and subcomponents. Each component is associated with one other component and is basically constructed on three main legs. Bağ-Kur, Retirement Fund and Social Insurance Institution (SSI) programs, which cover different working groups with the province GSS program, are collected under the single insurance institution umbrella in 2006 (Beylik, Kayral & Naldöken, 2015).

In the Ministry of Health hospitals, 'Performance Based Payment System' has been passed on to the requests for health services in the scope of access to health services. In all policies implemented under the SDP, health service provision is increase of to keep the increase in health expenditures in balance and to ensure effective use of resources allocated for health services (Yiğit, 2017).

The model of the Family Physician, proposed by the World Bank in its 2003 document, for the Turkish health system, constitutes the second basic pillar of health reform (Beylik, Kayral & Naldöken, 2015). According to family medicine model, family physicians will provide services in the framework of the practice system by contracting with the General Health Insurance. However, due to the failure of the General Health Insurance system to be fully implemented, family medicine is financed by the MoH (Bayraktutan, Arslan & Bal, 2010). It is envisaged that the financing of family physicians will be provided through agreement after the General Health Insurance system is fully implemented. It is not possible for the citizens who do not regularly pay their premiums to benefit from the family medicine system. The most important feature of the planned family medicine system that is planned to be implemented is that it is a mandatory step in the referral chain.

In the family medicine system, physicians are transformed into entrepreneurs who earn money according to market conditions rather than public element. Family physicians are able to choose their own staff and provide the requirements outside the medical service through subcontracting firms (Akyuz, Yıldırım, Balaban, 2015).

When the Health Transformation Program is examined, it is observed that the provision of services to entrepreneurs, that is to leave the private sector, is aimed to be placed on the health insurance side of the public (Bal, 2013).

This area is a major precedent when it is examined specifically in the context of family medicine, in its current form in the UK, Clinical Commissioning Groups (CCGs), formerly known as Primary Care Trusts. CCGs are family physicians contracted with the National Health Service (NHS). The financing of health services in the UK is actually covered not by general taxation but by health-specific taxation. (Lee, Yang & Chen, 2016).

In the third basic footing of the Health Transformation Program, the Law on the Law No. 663 and the Public Hospital Unions (KHB) reform described in the Official Gazette dated 02/11/2011 take place. The reform goal is to reorganize the second and third level treatment institutions affiliated to the Ministry of Health as 'autonomous' under the roof of public hospital associations (Dogan & Gencan, 2014).

According to Article 30 of the Decree Law No. 663, Turkey Kamu Hospitals Institution establishes second and third level health institutions and public hospital associations at provincial level in order to use resources effectively and efficiently (Sebetci & Uysal, 2017).

Although access to health services for individuals is facilitated after the health transformation program, there are differences between regions in terms of the supply of health services and it is observed that injustice is not remedied. A comparison between regions in terms of the number of beds per 10,000 people is located well below the average of the Southeastern Anatolia Region of Turkey and Istanbul (Bal & Bilge, 2013). Therefore, it is seen that physicians and bed numbers are not done in proportion to the population in the supply of health services.

At the same time, the projects of city hospitals, which are being carried out by public private partnership, have begun to take place in our lives. It is certain that these investments, which have come to fruition with very high investments, will also affect the insurance structure. It is unlikely that the Turkish Health System will be kept away from the changes that are taking place in the world for sustainability.

## RESULTS

The environment in which health organizations are operating today is constantly changing, requiring a thorough knowledge of changes, factors of influence, and future developments. The shift from product orientation to market orientation towards the consumer has forced health organizations to adopt ways of knowing it.

In Turkey, health services are strongly influenced by the changes that take place as a result of the health system reform, which aims to decentralize the health system by increasing the role of local authorities, professional associations, funding institutions and the community (Bircan, 2011). The measures taken have had various consequences both on the supply and the way of financing as well as on the demand. Thus, at the level of the supply and financing system, the development and consolidation of the privatization process, the development of integrated health services (primary care, ambulatory, hospital and emergency care), the creation of a combined financing model, from public resources and private and the introduction of private health insurance. That is why, at the level of health systems, we are discussing the directions for reforming them, due to the fiscal pressures that have accentuated over the years. Emphasis is placed on finding new sources of funding, on efficient management and on finding alternative ways of organizing services.

## SOLUTIONS AND RECOMMENDATIONS

From the perspective of change, the complex problems of the Healthcare security assessment face cannot be analysed objectively and continuously within the current tasks (Alamin & Yassin, 2015). The lack of success of many advertising campaigns and the negative effect they generated were considered failures of marketing in health services. Thus, medical staff and consumers considered the publicity made by hospitals to be useless. The skepticism of marketing merits, especially promotion, has led to organizations in the field experiencing serious financial withdrawals during this period. In addition, hospitals were seeking to reduce their costs, and marketing spending was an easy target to operate. As a result, budgets for such activities were cut off, and marketing staff was fired. For some organizations, marketing activities have not been completely eliminated, and they are often embedded in strategic and development plans. In addition, this has enabled marketers to reevaluate that field and focus on developing basic concepts that can be used when marketing is back in place in these organizations. As a result of the diversification of the offered health services, the researches have also increased marketing on the health service consumer.

Governments undoubtedly want to raise their level of health. It is possible to see this interesting in every government's program and in the statements of every politician and manager. Those with political decision-making authority would prefer not to give priority to health, but to other issues, among the many jobs required to be done. Politicians, like everyone, care about their health or their relatives when they are sick. They do not even think that one day they will get sick and find the service they need. The first thing to do is to find the way to influence governments, not academic debates.

## CONCLUSION

In order to explain the behavior of the healthcare consumer, it is not enough just to study the behavior of the healthcare consumer, but also the relationship between medical staff - especially the doctor - and the consumer as the main determinant of his behavior and consumption. The significance of this relationship is extremely important for health services because the creation and delivery of services and their quality depend to a large extent on the relationship between the two. Medical staff can help improve this relationship by constantly informing the consumer through a realistic picture of the illness and the judicious use of the possibilities and resources available to the consumer.

Because the medical sector is a highly conditioned technology, it presents some challenges for health service providers in terms of developing and implementing marketing strategies. First of all, it is necessary to continue monitoring of the environment and developments in the field, because the technological breakthroughs lead to the improvement of the quality of the services rendered and to the diversification of the offer, as well as an advantage over the competitors.

New waves of technological change often allow participants from different levels to enter the market. For example, in hospitals, technology has spread to such an extent that procedures that once were only carried out in large hospitals or university institutes can now be achieved in many smaller hospitals or even at the level of medical offices.

In Turkey, the supply of health services is heavily influenced by the changes that take place as a result of the reform of the health care system, which involves the transition from the integrated, centralized, tax-based, government-controlled and state-controlled system to the social security system - decentralized and pluralistic, based on contractual links between health care homes (service buyers) and providers of these services.

## REFERENCES

Akyuz, K. C., Yıldırım, I., & Balaban, Y. (2015). Measuring efficiencies of the firms in paper sector by using data envelopment analysis. *International Journal of Economic and Administrative Studies*, *14*, 23–38.

Alamin, T. H. M., & Yassin, A. A. (2015). Measuring hospitals efficiency using data envelopment analysis tool: Study on governmental hospitals services at Ministry of Health–Khartoum State. *International Journal of Science and Research*, *4*(2), 1586–1592.

Andreassen, H. K., Bujnowska-Fedak, M. M., Chronaki, C. E., Duritru, R. C., Pudele, I., Santana, S., ... Wynn, R. (2007). European citizens' use of E-health services: A study of seven countries. *BMC Public Health*, *7*(53), 1–14. PMID:17425798

Aytekin, S. (2011). The performance measurement of the health hospitals with low bed occupancy rates: An application of data envelopment analysis. *Uludag Journal of Economy and Society*, *30*(1), 113–138.

Bal, V. (2013). Data envelopment analysis and medical image archiving and communication systems to investigate the effects of the performance of public hospitals. *Journal of Suleyman Demirel University Institute of Social Sciences*, *17*, 31–50.

Bal, V., & Bilge, H. (2013). Efficiency measurement with data envelopment analysis in education and research hospitals. *Manas Journal of Social Studies*, *2*(2), 1–14.

Bayraktutan, Y., Arslan, I., & Bal, V. (2010). The evaluation of the effects of health information systems to the performance of hospitals by data enveloping analysis: An application in the thoracic medicine hospitals. *Gaziantep Medical Journal*, *16*(3), 13–18.

Beylik, U., Kayral, İ. H., & Naldöken, Ü. (2015). Public hospital unions' performance analysis in terms of health care services efficiency. *Cumhuriyet University the Journal of Social Sciences*, *39*(2), 203–224.

Bircan, H. (2011). Measurement of the efficiency of village clinics in the Sivas by data envelopment Analysis. *Cumhuriyet University Journal of Economics and Administrative Sciences*, *12*(1), 331–347.

Bolman, L. G., & Deal, T. E. (1999). 4 Steps to keeping change efforts heading in the right direction. *Journal for Quality and Participation*, *22*(3), 6–11.

Bostan, I. (2016). Investigating the Effectiveness of Programs on Health Financing Based on Audit Procedures. *Iranian Journal of Public Health*, *45*(8), 1074–1079. PMID:27928534

Briggs, D., Cruickshank, M., & Paliadelis, P. (2012). Health managers and health reform. *Journal of Management & Organization*, *18*(5), 641–658. doi:10.1017/S1833367200000584

Bukachi, F., & Pakenham-Walsh, N. (2007). Information technology for health in developing countries. *Chest Journal*, *132*(5), 1624–1630. doi:10.1378/chest.07-1760 PMID:17998362

Celik, T., & Esmeray, A. (2014). Measurement of cost efficiency in private hospitals in Kayseri using by data envelopment analysis. *International Journal of Alanya Faculty of Business*, *6*(2), 45–54.

Dogan, N. O., & Gencan, S. (2014). Performance assessment using DEA/AHP integrated method: An application on public hospitals in Ankara. *Gazi Universitesi Iktisadi ve Idari Bilimler Fakultesi Dergisi*, *16*(2), 88–112.

Du, J., Wang, J., Chen, Y., Chou, S. Y., & Zhu, J. (2014). Incorporating health outcomes in Pennsylvania Hospital efficiency: An additive super efficiency DEA approach. *Annals of Operations Research*, *221*(1), 161–172. doi:10.100710479-011-0838-y

Ericksen, J., & Dyer, L. (2005). Toward a strategic human resource management model of high reliability organization performance. *International Journal of Human Resource Management*, *16*(6), 907–925. doi:10.1080/09585190500120731

Frese, M., & Fay, D. (2001). Personal initiative: An active performance concept for work in the 21st century. *Research in Organizational Behavior*, *23*, 133–187. doi:10.1016/S0191-3085(01)23005-6

Gemmel, P., Vandaele, D., & Tambeur, W. (2001). Hospital Process Orientation (HPO): The development of a measurement tool. *Total Quality Management & Business Excellence*, *19*(12), 1207–1217. doi:10.1080/14783360802351488

Grimson, J., Grimson, W., & Hasselbring, W. (2000). The system integration challenge in health care. *Communications of the ACM*, *43*(6), 49–55. doi:10.1145/336460.336474

Gülsevin, G., & Türkan, A. H. (2012). Evaluation of efficiencies of hospitals in Afyonkarahisar using data envelopment analysis. *Afyon Kocatepe University Journal of Sciences*, *20*, 1–8.

Hadad, S., Hadad, Y., & Simon-Tuval, T. (2013). Determinants of healthcare system's efficiency in OECD countries. *The European Journal of Health Economics*, *14*(2), 253–265. doi:10.100710198-011-0366-3 PMID:22146798

Hasselbring, W. (2000). Information system integration. *Communications of the ACM*, *43*(6), 33–38. doi:10.1145/336460.336472

Ibbs, C. W., & Kwak, Y. H. (2000). Assessing project management maturity. *Project Management Journal*, *31*(1), 32–43. doi:10.1177/875697280003100106

Lee, Y. H., Yang, C. C., & Chen, T. T. (2016). Barriers to incident-reporting behavior among nursing staff: A study based on the theory of planned behavior. *Journal of Management & Organization*, *22*(1), 1–18. doi:10.1017/jmo.2015.8

Liu, S., Zhang, J., Keil, M., & Chen, T. (2010). Comparing senior executive and project manager perceptions of IT project risk: A Chinese Delphi study. *Information Systems Journal*, *20*(4), 319–355. doi:10.1111/j.1365-2575.2009.00333.x

Low, C., & Chen, Y. H. (2012). Criteria for the evaluation of a cloud-based hospital information system outsourcing provider. *Journal of Medical Systems*, *36*(6), 3543–3553. doi:10.100710916-012-9829-z PMID:22366976

Ozcan, Y. A. (2008). *Healthcare benchmarking and performance evaluation an assessment using data envelopment analysis (DEA)*. Springer.

Pan, E., Johnston, D., Walker, J., Adler-Milstein, J., Bates, D. W., & Middleton, B. (2005). *The Value of Healthcare Information Exchange and Interoperability*. Chicago: Health Information Management and Systems Society.

Pelone, F., Kringos, D. S., Romaniello, A., Archibugi, M., Salsiri, C., & Ricciardi, W. (2015). Primary care efficiency measurement using data envelopment analysis: A systematic review. *Journal of Medical Systems*, *39*(1), 1–14. doi:10.100710916-014-0156-4 PMID:25486892

Pettigrew, A. M., Woodman, R. W., & Cameron, K. S. (2001). Studying organizational change and development: Challenges for future research. *Academy of Management Journal*, *44*(4), 697–713.

Sebetci, Ö., & Uysal, İ. (2017). The Efficiency of Clinical Departments in Medical Faculty Hospitals: A Case Study Based on Data Envelopment Analysis. *International Journal on Computer Science and Engineering*, *5*(7), 1–8.

Škrinjar, R., Bosilj-Vukšić, V., & Indihar-Štemberger, M. (2008). The impact of business process orientation on financial and non-financial performance. *Business Process Management Journal*, *14*(5), 738–754. doi:10.1108/14637150810903084

Uçkun, N., Girginer, N., Köse, T., & Şahin, Ü. (2016). Analysis efficiency of public hospitals of metropolitan municipalities in Turkey. *International Journal of Innovative Research in Education*, *3*(2), 102–108.

Varabyova, Y., & Müller, J. M. (2016). The efficiency of health care production in OECD countries: A systematic review and meta-analysis of cross-country comparisons. *Health Policy (Amsterdam)*, *120*(3), 252–263. doi:10.1016/j.healthpol.2015.12.005 PMID:26819140

Yiğit, V. (2017). Technical Efficiency of Physicians In Performance Based Supplementary Payment System: Application In A University Hospital. *Electronic Journal of Social Sciences*, *16*(62), 854–866.

## ADDITIONAL READING

Crowley, K., Gold, R., Bandi, S., & Goel, A. (2016). *The Public Health Information Technology Maturity Index: An approach to evaluating the adoption and use of public health information technology*. School of Public Health, University of Maryland.

Girginer, N., Kose, T., & Uckun, N. (2015). Efficiency analysis of surgical services by combined use of data envelopment analysis and gray relational analysis. *Journal of Medical Systems*, *39*(5), 1–9. doi:10.100710916-015-0238-y PMID:25764507

Mikalef, P., & Pateli, A. (2017). Information technology-enabled dynamic capabilities and their indirect effect on competitive performance: Findings from PLS-SEM and fsQCA. *Journal of Business Research*, *70*, 1–16. doi:10.1016/j.jbusres.2016.09.004

Narcı, H. O., Ozcan, Y. A., Sahin, I., Tarcan, M., & Narcı, M. (2015). An examination of competition and efficiency for hospital industry in Turkey. *Health Care Management Science*, *18*(4), 407–418. doi:10.100710729-014-9315-x PMID:25515038

Şener, M., & Yiğit, V. (2017). Technical Efficiency of Health Systems: A Research on the OECD Countries. *Journal of Süleyman Demirel University Institute of Social Sciences*, *26*, 266–290.

*This research was previously published in Network Security and Its Impact on Business Strategy; pages 60-71, copyright year 2019 by Business Science Reference (an imprint of IGI Global).*

# Section 2
# Securing Medical Devices

# Chapter 12
# Cyber Security in Health:
## Standard Protocols for IoT and Supervisory Control Systems

**Bruno J. Santos**
*Instituto Federal de São Paulo, Brazil*

**Rachel P. Tabacow**
*Instituto Federal de São Paulo, Brazil*

**Marcelo Barboza**
*Instituto Federal de São Paulo, Brazil & Escola Politécnica da Universidade de São Paulo, Brazil*

**Tarcisio F. Leão**
*Instituto Federal de São Paulo, Brazil*

**Eduardo G. P. Bock**
https://orcid.org/0000-0003-3962-9052
*Instituto Federal de São Paulo, Brazil*

## ABSTRACT

*Cyber security in Healthcare is a growing concern. Since it has been a proliferation of IoT devices, data breaches from the healthcare industry are increasing the concern about how cyber security can protect data from connected medical devices. Recent years have seen numerous hacking and IT security incidents. Many healthcare organizations are facing problems to defend their networks from cybercriminals. In the current digital era, the physical world has a cyber-representation. Both the real and virtual worlds are connected in areas, such as informatics and manufacturing. Health 4.0 (H4.0) refers to a group of initiatives aiming to improve medical care for patients, hospitals, researchers, and medical device suppliers. Increasing collaboration in terms of medical equipment, artificial organs, and biosensors is a way to facilitate H4.0. As a result, cyber security budgets have increased, new technology has been purchased, and healthcare organizations are improving at blocking attacks and keeping their networks secure.*

DOI: 10.4018/978-1-6684-6311-6.ch012

# INTRODUCTION

In contemporary society, information is one of the most valuable resources. It does not matter if it is an eastern or western society, information is fundamental in the decision-making process or in the creation of new products and in competitiveness in the healthcare industry. Information enables successful treatments to be distance replicated independently and it turns possible to minimize human errors. New healthcare treatment techniques are created and assimilated with this information. As a valuable asset data is highly protected, redoubling precautions because it is critical in relation to patients' lives. Digital cyber security operates with the objective of protecting this information, privacy and well-being of patients, minimizing risks, establishing controls and establishing an information security policy (Castells, 1997).

Cyber security in Healthcare is a growing concern for further steps towards technological growth of society, especially when it comes to digital threats and data protection. Since there is a proliferation of Internet of Things (IoT) devices, healthcare industry is increasing the concern about how cyber security can protect data from connected medical devices. The United States designed a law to provide privacy standards and to protect medical records that took effect on April 14, 2003. This law also complies with other health information provided by patients, usage and disclosure with health insurance companies, hospitals and even doctors. According to Health Insurance Portability and Accountability Act (HIPAA), last years have seen numerous hacking and information technology (IT) security incidents. Many healthcare organizations are facing problems to defend their network of cybercriminals not just in US but in the whole world. The General Data Protection Regulation (GDPR) is a European Union Regulation accepted on April 27, 2016 (Scholl et al., 2008; Torres, Campos, Martins, & Bock, 2019).

Cybercrime emerged in the late 1970s as the computer IT industry took shape. Even in 2015, healthcare suffered cyberattacks and industry data were compromised in more than 113 million records. More patient records were exposed or stolen in 2015 than in previous 6 years combined (Scholl et al., 2008; Von Solms & Van Niekerk, 2013). Data breaches are growing and cybercriminals are developing sophisticated tools to attack, to gain access to data and to hold data and networks. This book chapter aims to cover the best technologies and academic background to protect healthcare industry with effective policies, standards and procedures (Baheti & Gill, 2011; Bock et al., 2017; Zhou, Thieret, Watzlaf, DeAlmeida, & Parmanto, 2019).

# BACKGROUND

An increase in attacks and invasions on medical devices has caused regulators to take notice; Food and Drugs Administration (FDA) issued a safety communication in June 2013 entitled "Cybersecurity for Medical Devices and Hospital Networks". The working group, involving representatives of the FDA, the Office of the National Coordinator for Health Information Technology, and the Federal Communications Commission, has released a report calling for increased private-sector involvement and a risk-based regulatory framework. But the problem is that they did not define the framework, and burdensome with regulation could greatly increase emerging threats. Cyberattack is a clear and present threat in healthcare; thus it is time to organize, convene, and focus in protection of patient data. Since technology has unquestionably improved healthcare, it is mandatory to ensure that the promised benefits continue to be delivered safely (Baheti & Gill, 2011).

An important related topic is Telehealth, an approach that aims to provide high quality health services to people who cannot easily access these services. When it comes to cyber threats and frequently reported health data breaches, many people may be hesitant to use Telehealth-based services. The HIPAA protocol includes comprehensive details that are not always specific to telehealth and is therefore difficult for telehealth professionals to use (Zhou et al., 2019).

The term Industry 4.0 first appeared in Germany in 2011 proposing the beginning of the 4th Industrial Revolution by the combination of technology and intelligent data processing. Due to exponential advance of computers processing capacity, the immense amount of digitized information in networks requires new strategies of industrial innovation and security (Cavalheiro et al., 2011b; Santos et al., 2018).

Industry 4.0 is consolidated by complementing industrial information technology and industrial automation technologies such as: Wireless, Radio Frequency Identification (RFID), Service Oriented Architecture (SOA), Cognitive Computing and Cloud (Perakslis, 2014; Santos et al., 2018). The main pillars of Industry 4.0 are: capacity for decision making and modification of production processes in real time; virtualization of the productive process; decentralization of decision-making processes; modularity in subunits of productive system and interoperability with communication capacity between cyber-physical systems, sensors, actuators and humans. One of the main sectors impacted by Industry 4.0 is the healthcare industry with the common term Health 4.0 (Coventry & Branley, 2018; Tabacow, Bock, & Nakamoto, 2018).

## STANDARD PROTOCOLS FOR IOT

The Reconfigurable Platform of Assistive Technology (RPAT) was built based on Computer Integrated Manufacturing (CIM) approach. RPAT can be essentially considered, for all intents and purposes, as a case study presented here, illustrative, didactic and an exploratory experimental research. Even though it is not exactly a production process, RPAT adopts a local driver integration and real-time demand supervision system for all operating system resources and information, for data use, computing, and automation.

The concept of CIM emerged in 1973 as a suggestion for the development of industrial enterprises, proposing an optimization not by increasing the enterprise efficiency in context, but as interdependent, information-driven manner. According to the CIM concept, the main obstacle to the exercise of development functions is the lack of integration between departments, activities, and systems. The global state and greater capacity and adaptability merged into a coordinated, rapid and flexible manner, according to the characteristics of two information sources:

- **External:** Orders and changes or the market/customers.
- **Internal:** The anticipated and unexpected events from the company and the shop floor.

Systems control tools do not use the Distributed Hierarchical Control System (DHCS) concept. As control actions are carried out by the combination of decision-making machines, they are geographically distributed, autonomous and self-contained, by the combination of advanced, work for the implementation of the global control task.

The CIM Hierarchical Structure is the total set of functions that are implemented by a distributed control system, which presents the high level of performance and action index. Thus, actions can be applied at various hierarchical levels, having the specific temporary and temporal characteristics of each level.

A structure of the CIM is made by four levels: machine, cell, sector and factory, where each level is organized hierarchically as shown in Figure 1.

The CIM structure was adapted to the reality of RPAT, being modeled as:

1. **Machine**: Area of operation of local controllers, based on the command and acquisition system of actuators and sensors.
2. **Cell:** Organization of local controllers operations, aiming at a responsive flow of commands.
3. **Sector:** Responsible for the intelligent control of RPAT, based on cognition of operation data, specialist diagnosis and patient treatment evolution.
4. **Factory:** Responsible for RPAT's customization capability for the clinical application of a specific patient even though RPAT comes from an industrial production process.

## Industry 4.0 and Health 4.0

Health 4.0 is characterized by high connectivity of devices and equipment, so digital security has become a key element with the expansion of communication networks (Perakslis, 2014). In a Health 4.0 scenario, there is the integration of industry, hospitals, patients and IoT devices, through an intelligent central. Alternatively, systems can count with Artificial Intelligence algorithms, Big Data processing and cloud computing services. A key to ensuring security is access protection. From protecting physical and logical access to devices, the healthcare industry can establish monitoring services and policies to minimize threats (Cavalheiro et al., 2011b).

The security policies are based on the three pillars of prevention procedures: integrity, availability and confidentiality. Integrity guarantees that information has not been unduly altered or unauthorized. If information tampering occurs, it is important to have mechanisms that signal such occurrence. Availability is the guarantee that information will be available whenever necessary. Confidentiality is the certainty that access to information will be made only by those who have the right. It is important to emphasize that the objective is not to deny access to information, but to prevent information from becoming available to undue persons, while ensuring that those who are authorized can access it (Kruse, Frederick, Jacobson, & Monticone, 2017; Perakslis, 2014).

## IoT and Collaborative Control Theory

The IoT, or as it may be called, Web of Things (WoT), is a concept that has gained fame and recognition in modern western society. However, while many people can already see the impacts of an interconnected network of smart products connected to the internet, there are several steps that are still being defined in the history of civilization.

One of the points being discussed is the concept of sustainable mobility. Sustainable mobility is one of the main goals of an Intelligent City. Thus, the development of intelligent transport and parking systems is a key aspect in achieving this goal. Among many facilities and benefits to society, security is also an aspect that can guarantee police tracking, speed control policies and fines.

One of the impacts to be measured is the transformation of conventional markets impacting the way people hire and provide services. The business impact of intelligent equipment connected to large databases goes beyond simply connecting people and objects through gadgets.

*Figure 1. A structure of CIM and its four levels: machine, cell, sector and factory*

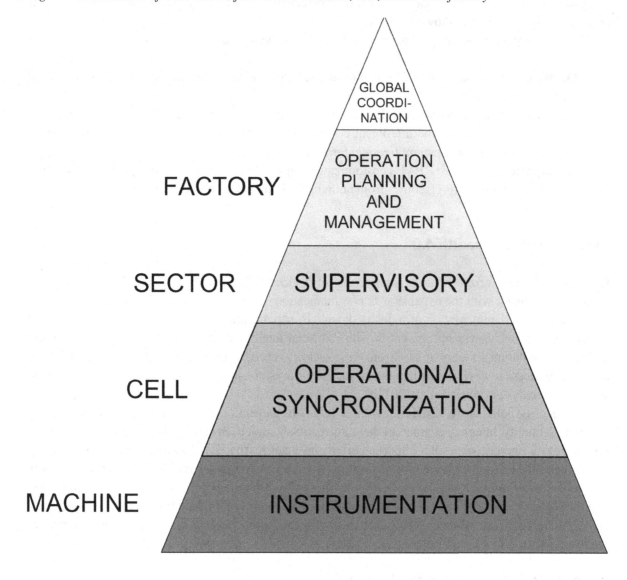

But, as discussed since the beginning of this chapter, a very relevant aspect is the increase in security vulnerabilities and the difficulty of attesting the cyber security linked to the use of IoT, its technical and ethical challenges.

Thus, several IoT protocols focus on the use of security and reciprocity concepts for the protection of critical data. The most commonly used protocols today are: IEEE 802.15.4; IPv6 over Low-Power Wireless Personal Area Networks (6LoWPAN) and Routing Protocol for Low-Power and Lossy Networks (RPL); Message Queuing Telemetry Transport (MQTT); Constrained Application Protocol (CoAP); Data Distribution Service (DDS) and other proprietary protocols.

A discussion regarding future trends in health equipment, artificial organs and biosensors is required for collaborations aiming to improve medical care for patients, change the business practices of hospitals and create new insight for researchers and medical device manufacturers (Sousa Sobrinho et al., 2018).

In fact, in some industries, this practice, which is called digital and cyber convergence, has already been established, and the IoT is the main technology used. IoT is the basis of Industry 4.0 (I4.0) in manufacturing and digital convergence in informatics. These technologies can be studied under collaborative control theory (CCT) ("Cyber crime timeline," n.d.).

Collaboration enables the improvement of any natural or artificial system (Sannino, De Falco, & De Pietro, 2019). Collaboration can be achieved by sharing information, resources, and responsibilities by distributing agents to plan, create and analyze activities required to achieve individual and common goals ("Cyber crime timeline," n.d.).

Based on the Industry 4.0 concept, Health 4.0 (H4.0) has been derived according to the health domain. H4.0 has been established based on collaboration control theory (Sousa Sobrinho et al., 2018).

## RPAT Operational Flow Chart

In RPAT, linear actuators are driven by local controllers with acquisition and actuation routines following the operating commands of a supervisory controller incorporated in Health 4.0. In addition, local controllers are responsible for the sensors' data acquisition such as temperature, humidity, RPAT slope and others. For satisfactory operation of RPAT, controllers should have efficient and organized priority communication. RPAT's communication architecture was validated in virtual environment where local controllers interpreted a series of analog inputs, simulating possible sensors (Temperature, Humidity, Load, Applied Force, Motor Rotation, Ultrasonic) and sent status flags (operations, assistance or safety operations in extreme cases) to the supervisory controller.

In supervisory controller, flags were first authenticated by a Structured Query Language (SQL) database, and through the compiled compare and actuation routine, sent actuation flags to the local controller. In the local controller, the actuation flags were interpreted and proportionally triggered the actuators (heating, vibration, movement, platform elevation and physiotherapy routines). During actuation, state data was sent to the supervisory controller, which in turn stored the data in memory and sent it to Big Data, which was simulated by server programs. The structure of RPAT counts with linear actuators, where their association allows the maintenance of RPAT in three different positions:

- Horizontal Execution: Aiming to assist the patient and the physiotherapist in the physiotherapy session.
- Verticalized Execution: Aiming to aid in blood circulation.
- Mixed Execution: Aiming to assist in the transition of a patient with limited movement.

RPAT operations flowcharts are presented at hardware (Figure 2), software (Figure 3), and data (Figure 4) levels.

Figure 2 shows the RPAT operational hardware flowchart and what happens in each predetermined state. In the "zero" state, it can be seen that RPAT is flat like a table or a bed in Physiotherapy Clinic. The state "one" represents the tipping for patient reception. In state "two", RPAT adapts to the curvature of the patient's spine opening option, in state "three" for physiotherapy or recreation.

Figure 3 represents the Human Machine Interface and the operational flowchart. As soon as the zero state routine is started, there is a choice of A (Artificial Intelligence) or B (Cloud Storage), when the decision making impacts on actuators and sensors interacting for each following states (one, two or

*Figure 2. RPAT hardware operational flowchart showing states and positions*

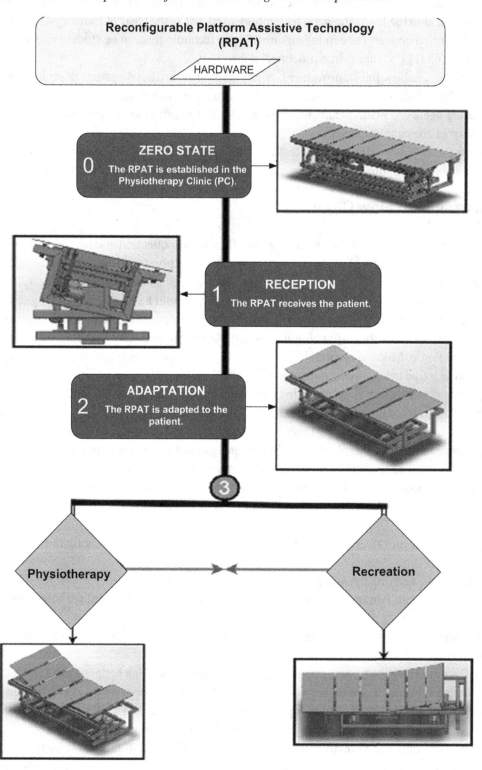

*Figure 3. RPAT software interface and operational flowchart*

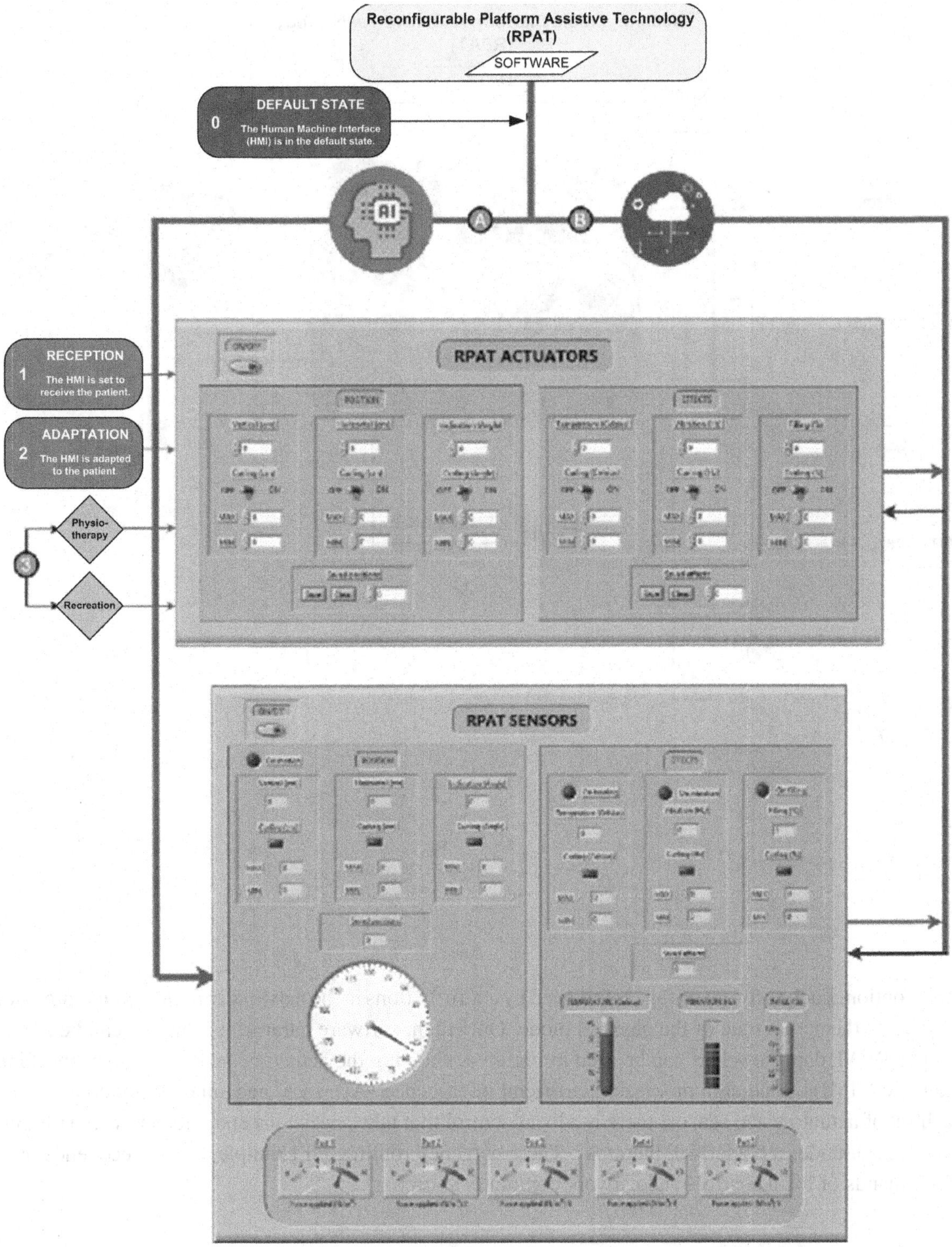

*Figure 4. RPAT data flowchart showing actuators, sensors, HMI, cloud, AI, local and supervisory control*

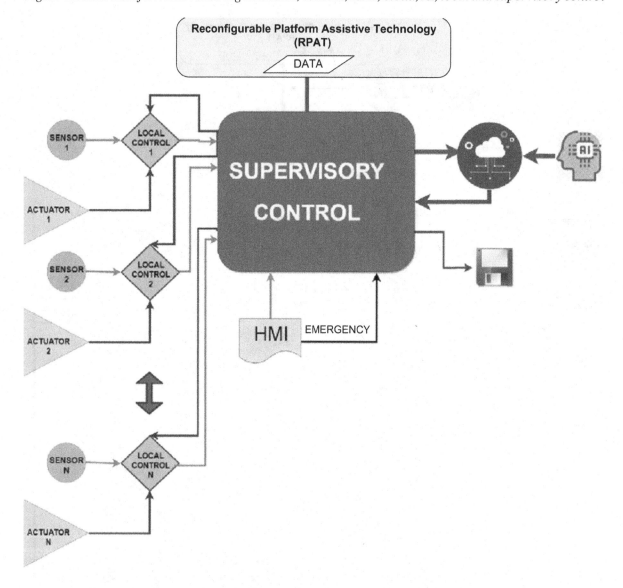

three) option. Each software change is followed by confirmations in the network communication protocol to validate the actual state of the physical mode. Only then, software parameters changes can be made.

The RPAT data flowchart can be seen in Figure 4, showing the actuators, sensors, human-machine interface (HMI), cloud data processing, artificial intelligence (AI), local and supervisory control. For each set of actuators and sensors there is a local control that takes decisions and interacts with supervisory control under a predefined hierarchy. The emergency routine, for example, takes precedence over the demands of local controls and network communication.

*Figure 5. Control architecture and Supervisory Control System based on three layers applied in Reconfigurable Platform of Assistive Technology (adapted from Bock et al., 2017)*

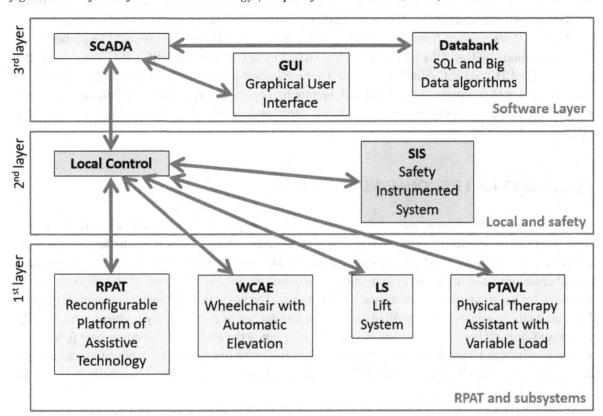

## RAMI 4.0 and Supervisory Control Systems

The most commonly used reference architecture model during the third industrial revolution was ISA 95 (Araki et al., 2018). This model is also known as the automation pyramid. The ISA 95 model is hierarchical and centralized in such a way that it is proposed that each layer only communicates with its neighboring layers (Araki et al., 2018; Lu, Morris, & Frechette, 2016; Otto, Campos, De Souza, Martins, & Bock, 2018; Zezulka, Marcon, Vesely, & Sajdl, 2016).

The concept of a Supervisory Control and Data Acquisition (SCADA) does apply with graphics and batch processing parallel with Safety Instrumented System (SIS) as it can be seen in the example illustrated in Figure 5.

In this application, RPAT was modeled with Collaborative Control Theory in order to allow IoT devices hierarchy and assured cyber security. In this case, security and safety are comprised by SIS interaction.

Data acquisition and future implementation algorithms are shown in the third layer (at the top) of Figure 5. First layer is composed by the main RPAT and the three other peripheral subsystems. Each system has its own drivers and controls. Second layer is mainly an adaptation for the Local Control physically management of events with SIS.

In the fourth industrial revolution, to deploy an autonomous, distributed production system that narrows the relationship between real and virtual world, ISA 95 reference architecture is no longer sufficient.

Therefore, Reference Architectural Model for Industry 4.0 (RAMI 4.0) was created (Araki et al., 2017; Leão et al., 2014; Otto et al., 2018; Zezulka et al., 2016). RAMI 4.0 is a reference architecture model for industry 4.0. This model was first presented at the Hannover Fair in 2015 (Adolphs et al., 2015).

RAMI 4.0 was created from the following standards adopted by the International Organization for Standardization (ISO) and the International Electrotechnical Commission (IEC): ISO/IEC 62264, IEC 62541, IEC 61512 and IEC 62890. It proposed a three-dimensional model to provide a basic reference architecture for I4.0 systems. Thus, CIM architecture for healthcare systems can be built from ISO/IEC standards to identify cyber threats at various levels (Bock et al., 2011b; Kagermann, Wahlster, & Helbig, 2013; Uebelhart et al., 2013).

## SOLUTIONS AND RECOMMENDATIONS

As can be seen in this chapter, while IoT technologies play important roles in people's daily lives, their incorporation into health systems may leave them vulnerable to threats. This is due to the fact that medical devices are connected and provide easy access. In addition, outdated systems and lack of emphasis on cyber security can make the system and the network unsafe. As the focus of this work is to seek solutions for improving patient safety and health, it should be noted that IoT health technologies contain large amounts of valuable and sensitive data. Other attacks can be motivated by political gains, even by the cyber war itself between countries. An attack can result in the loss of critical equipment functioning within hospitals and intensive care units. The escalation of ransomware attacks in hospitals can paralyze entire health systems (Bock et al., 2011a; Bock et al., 2011c; Bock et al., 2008; Cavalheiro et al., 2011a; Fonseca et al., 2008; Leão et al., 2012).

Critical health systems can be protected by the technologies presented here, and thus, when attacked, human lives will not be at risk.

It is mentioned in the introduction that this work is focused and delimited on the application of standard protocols for IoT and Supervisory Control Systems in 4.0 Health, as we consider that the focus is on applying a technology to control systems without extending the problem to the creation or programming of codes for cyber threats in security systems. The healthcare industry is an attractive target for criminals and digital threats for two key reasons, it is a rich source of valuable data and its defenses are currently weak. Cyber security breaches include health information theft and ransomware attacks in hospitals and may include attacks on deployed medical devices. Therefore, the technological advancement of systems based on safe protocols is fundamental for patient safety (Henriksen, Burkow, Johnsen, & Vognild, 2013; Lutes, 2000; Uwizeyemungu, Poba-Nzaou, & Cantinotti, 2019).

## FUTURE RESEARCH DIRECTIONS

Due to the emergence and consolidation of HIPAA, a lot of research work has been done in the field of cyber security in health. Various forms of threats and protections are constantly appearing and evolving, thus making an incessant technological race. Nevertheless, as proposed in this work, a very delicate and subtle theme is the practical use in embedded equipments and IoT devices, which may be implantable. With the methodology proposed in RPAT, a solid foundation has been consolidated for deployment of secure systems according to what is expected for future developments in Industry 4.0. Although not all forms of cyber threats have been addressed, the adopted protocols allow the platform to deploy different security mechanisms and update them over time.

## CONCLUSION

In the quest for greater independence for people with disabilities and to improve the results of long-term therapies within the hospital or home, assistive technologies are increasingly being studied and developed. In them, more and more automations are present, being essential the development of a supervisory system that is responsible for the control of the various local control systems and their integration with the cyber security in health.

Some lessons can be drawn from what has been exposed in this chapter. Among the main threats to the health of patients it can be included the rapid technological advance and the evolution of security policies. As the healthcare IT infrastructure faces new technology and security protocols, the industry is a major target for stealing medical information. While examples have been illustrated here and reports have been made of security and government efforts to reduce the prevalence of cyberattacks, the health sector is lagging behind other leading industries in protecting vital data.

Healthcare must continually adapt to changing cyber security trends and threats, such as ransomware, where critical infrastructure is tapped and valuable patient data is extracted for the benefit of the intruder. It is imperative that time and funding need to be invested in researching data safety models, as well as maintaining and ensuring the protection of healthcare technology and the confidentiality of patients' information from unauthorized access (Kruse et al., 2017). In future works, more emphasis will be placed on power consumption issues as this is an important factor IoT handling devices.

With the presentation of these facts, the concern has further increased with the identification of health technology security weaknesses by the 'White Hacker' (the hacker who assumes the doctor's credential). This suggests that remote manipulation of medical devices, such as artificial hearts and insulin pumps, is an unnerving possibility for the possibility of killing a person from a distance.

Cyber security is an essential part of maintaining patient safety, privacy and trust. More money and effort should be invested to ensure the safety of healthcare technologies and patient information. Security should be designed from product design to avoid future cyber attack issues. Cyber security praxis must become part of the patient care culture (Coventry & Branley, 2018).

Internet of Things in parallel with Assistive Technologies can promote greater independence for people with disabilities and improve long-term therapies results inside the hospital. The proposed control architecture for Cyber Security in Health based on protocols (as illustrated in Figure 1) also allows big data analysis, a potential source for clinical discoveries in future. Cloud computing can provide the infrastructure for IoT integrating monitoring devices, storage devices, analytics tools, visualization platforms and client delivery. Since Cyber Security remains one of the most important issues that baffle the development and applications of IoT, a taylor-made designed SIS methodology is a promising part in Supervisory Systems Architecture.

## ACKNOWLEDGMENT

This research was supported by Brazilian Funding Agencies: Coordination for the Improvement of Higher Education Personnel [grant number CAPES PGPTA 88887.123938/2014-00]; National Council for Scientific and Technological Development [grant number CNPq 310085/2015-2]; and The São Paulo Research Foundation [grant number FAPESP PIPE/PITCHGOV 2017/25233-9].

## REFERENCES

Adolphs, P., Bedenbender, H., Dirzus, D., Ehlich, M., Epple, U., Hankel, M., . . . Wollschlaeger, M. (2015). *Referenzarchitekturmodell Industrie 4.0 (RAMI4.0)* [*Reference architecture model Industrie 4.0 (RAMI 4.0)*] (Status Report). Frankfurt am Main, Germany: ZVEI & Düsseldorf, Germany: VDI. Retrieved October 30, 2019, from https://www.zvei.org/fileadmin/user_upload/Themen/Industrie_4.0/ Das_Referenzarchitekturmodell_RAMI_4.0_und_die_Industrie_4.0-Komponente/pdf/Statusreport-Referenzmodelle-2015-v10.pdf

Araki, S. Y., Florentino, P., Bock, E., Saito, M., Hernandes, M., & Fuentes, L. ... De Arruda, A. C. F. (2018). Automatic elevation system of a wheelchair. In J. C. M. Carvalho, D. Martins, R. Simoni, & H. Simas (Eds.), Mechanisms and Machine Science: Vol. 54. Multibody mechatronic systems. (pp. 474-484). Cham, Switzerland: Springer International Publishing.

Araki, S. Y., Florentino, P., Saito, M., Hernandes, M., Bock, E., & Fuentes, L., ... De Arruda, A. C. F. (2017). Computational modelling of an automatic wheelchair lift system for assistive technology. In *Proceedings of the 3rd International Conference on Control, Automation and Robotics (ICCAR)* (pp. 448-452). New York: IEEE. 10.1109/ICCAR.2017.7942736

Baheti, R., & Gill, H. (2011). Cyber-physical systems. In T. Samad, & A.M. Annaswamy (Eds.), The impact of control technology, 161-166. New York: IEEE Control Systems Society.

Bock, E., Andrade, A., Dinkhuysen, J., Arruda, C., Fonseca, J., Leme, J., ... Nosé, Y. (2011a). Introductory tests to in vivo evaluation: Magnetic coupling influence in motor controller. *ASAIO Journal (American Society for Artificial Internal Organs)*, *57*(5), 462–465. doi:10.1097/MAT.0b013e31823005dc PMID:21841468

Bock, E., Antunes, P., Leão, T., Uebelhart, B., Fonseca, J., Leme, J., ... Arruda, C. (2011b). Implantable centrifugal blood pump with dual impeller and double pivot bearing system: Electromechanical actuator, prototyping, and anatomical studies. *Artificial Organs*, *35*(5), 437–442. doi:10.1111/j.1525-1594.2011.01260.x PMID:21595708

Bock, E., Antunes, P., Uebelhart, B., Leão, T., Fonseca, J., & Cavalheiro, A. ... Arruda, C. (2011c). Design, manufacturing and tests of an implantable centrifugal blood pump. In L. M. Camarinha-Matos (Ed.), IFIP Advances in Information and Communication Technology: Vol. 349. Technological innovation for sustainability – DoCEIS 2011 (pp. 410-417). Berlin, Germany: Springer.

Bock, E., Araki, S., Souza, R., Ronei, D., Hernandes, M., & Frantz, J., ... Campos, A. (2017). Integrated supervisory system to control a reconfigurable platform of assistive technology. In *Proceedings of the 3rd International Conference on Control, Automation, and Robotics (ICCAR)* (pp. 444-447). New York: IEEE. 10.1109/ICCAR.2017.7942735

Bock, E., Ribeiro, A., Silva, M., Antunes, P., Fonseca, J., Legendre, D., ... Andrade, A. (2008). New centrifugal blood pump with dual impeller and double pivot bearing system: Wear evaluation in bearing system, performance tests, and preliminary hemolysis tests. *Artificial Organs*, *32*(4), 329–333. doi:10.1111/j.1525-1594.2008.00550.x PMID:18370949

Castells, M. (1997). *End of millennium: The information age: Economy, society and culture.* Cambridge, MA: Blackwell Publishers.

Cavalheiro, A., & Santos, Fo. D., Andrade, A., Cardoso, J. R., Bock, E., Fonseca, J., & Miyagi, P. E. (2011a). Design of supervisory control system for ventricular assist device. In L. M. Camarinha-Matos (Ed.), IFIP Advances in Information and Communication Technology: Vol. 349. Technological innovation for sustainability – DoCEIS 2011 (pp. 375-382). Berlin, Germany: Springer.

Cavalheiro, A. C. M., Santos Fo, D. J., Andrade, A., Cardoso, J. R., Horikawa, O., Bock, E., & Fonseca, J. (2011b). Specification of supervisory control systems for ventricular assist devices. *Artificial Organs*, *35*(5), 465–470. doi:10.1111/j.1525-1594.2011.01267.x PMID:21595713

Coventry, L., & Branley, D. (2018). Cybersecurity in healthcare: A narrative review of trends, threats and ways forward. *Maturitas*, *113*, 48–52. doi:10.1016/j.maturitas.2018.04.008 PMID:29903648

Cyber crime timeline. (n.d.). CW Jobs. Retrieved October 30, 2019, from https://www.cwjobs.co.uk/careers-advice/it-glossary/cyber-crime-timeline

Fonseca, J., Andrade, A., Nicolosi, D. E. C., Biscegli, J. F., Legendre, D., Bock, E., & Lucchi, J. C. (2008). A new technique to control brushless motor for blood pump application. *Artificial Organs*, *32*(4), 355–359. doi:10.1111/j.1525-1594.2008.00554.x PMID:18370953

Henriksen, E., Burkow, T. M., Johnsen, E., & Vognild, L. K. (2013). Privacy and information security risks in a technology platform for home-based chronic disease rehabilitation and education. *BMC Medical Informatics and Decision Making*, *13*(1), 85. doi:10.1186/1472-6947-13-85 PMID:23937965

Kagermann, H., Wahlster, W., & Helbig, J. (2013). *Recommendations for implementing the strategic initiative INDUSTRIE 4.0 securing the future of German manufacturing industry (Final Report of the Industrie 4.0 Working Group).* Berlin, Germany: Forschungsunion.

Kruse, C. S., Frederick, B., Jacobson, T., & Monticone, D. K. (2017). Cybersecurity in healthcare: A systematic review of modern threats and trends. *Technology and Health Care*, *25*(1), 1–10. doi:10.3233/THC-161263 PMID:27689562

Leão, T., Fonseca, J., Bock, E., Sá, R., Utiyama, B., & Drigo, E., ... Andrade, A. (2014). Speed control of the implantable centrifugal blood pump to avoid aortic valve stenosis: Simulation and implementation. In *Proceedings of the 5th RAS/EMBS International Conference on Biomedical Robotics and Biomechatronics* (pp. 82-86). New York: IEEE. 10.1109/BIOROB.2014.6913756

Leão, T. F., Bock, E., Fonseca, J., Andrade, A., Cavalheiro, A., & Uebelhart, B., ... Campo, A. (2012). Modeling study of an implantable centrifugal blood pump actuator with redundant sensorless control. In *Proceedings of the 44th Southeastern Symposium on System Theory (SSST)* (pp. 174-178) New York: IEEE. 10.1109/SSST.2012.6195148

Lu, Y., Morris, K. C., & Frechette, S. P. (2016). Current standards landscape for smart manufacturing systems (NIST Interagency/Internal Report [NISTIR] 8107). Gaithersburg, MD: U.S. National Institute of Standards and Technology.

Lutes, M. (2000). Privacy and security compliance in the E-healthcare marketplace. *Healthcare Financial Management, 54*(3), 48–50. PMID:10847915

Otto, T. B., Campos, A., De Souza, M. A., Martins, D., & Bock, E. (2018). Online posture feedback system aiming at human comfort. In F. Rebelo, & M. Soares (Eds.), Advances in Intelligent Systems and Computing: Vol. 777. Advances in ergonomics in design (pp. 924-935). Cham, Switzerland: Springer. doi:10.1007/978-3-319-60582-1_93

Perakslis, E. D. (2014). Cybersecurity in health care. *The New England Journal of Medicine, 371*(5), 395–397. doi:10.1056/NEJMp1404358 PMID:25075831

Sannino, G., De Falco, I., & De Pietro, G. (2019). A continuous non-invasive arterial pressure (CNAP) approach for Health 4.0 systems. *IEEE Transactions on Industrial Informatics, 15*(1), 498–506. doi:10.1109/TII.2018.2832081

Santos, B., Leão, T., Tabacow, R., Souza, J., Campos, A., & Martins, D. ... Bock, E. (2018). Controle de uma plataforma reconfigurável de tecnologia assistiva incorporada a Saúde 4.0 [Control of a reconfigurable platform of assistive technology incorporated to Health 4.0]. In F. O. Medola, & L. C. Paschoarelli (Eds.), Tecnologia assistiva – Pesquisa e conhecimento II (pp. 93-102). Bauru, Brazil: Canal 6 Editora.

Scholl, M., Stine, K., Hash, J., Bowen, P., Johnson, A., Smith, C. D., & Steinberg, D. I. (2008). *An introductory resource guide for implementing the health insurance portability and accountability act (HIPAA) security rule (NIST Special Publication 800-66 Rev. 1)*. Gaithersburg, MD: U.S. National Institute of Standards and Technology. doi:10.6028/NIST.SP.800-66r1

Sobrinho, J. R. S., Legaspe, E., Drigo, E., Dias, J. C., Dias, J. C., Barboza, M., ... & Santos Filho, D. J. (2018, May). Supervisory control system associated with the development of device thrombosis in VAD. In L. M. Camarinha-Matos, K. O. Adu-Kankam, & M. Julashokri (Eds.), IFIP Advances in Information and Communication Technology: Vol. 521. Technological innovation for resilient systems (pp. 90-97). Cham, Switzerland: Springer International Publishing.

Tabacow, R. P., Bock, E. G. P., & Nakamoto, F. Y. (2018). Modelagem em Redes de Petri do sistema de controle local da plataforma de tecnologia assistive [Modeling in Petri Nets of the local control system of the assistive technology platform]. *The Academic Society Journal, 2*(3), 173–178. doi:10.32640/tasj.2018.3.173

Torres, E. C., Campos, A. A., Martins, D., & Bock, E. (2019). Robotic system for active-passive strength therapy. In T. Ahram, W. Karwowski, & R. Taiar (Eds.), Advances in Intelligent Systems and Computing: Vol. 876. Human systems engineering and design (pp. 987-993). Cham, Switzerland: Springer International Publishing. doi:10.1007/978-3-030-02053-8_150

Uebelhart, B., Da Silva, B. U., Fonseca, J., Bock, E., Leme, J., Da Silva, C., ... Andrade, A. (2013). Study of a centrifugal blood pump in a mock loop system. *Artificial Organs, 37*(11), 946–949. doi:10.1111/aor.12228 PMID:24237361

Uwizeyemungu, S., Poba-Nzaou, P., & Cantinotti, M. (2019). European hospitals' transition toward fully electronic-based systems: Do information technology security and privacy practices follow? *JMIR Medical Informatics, 7*(1), e11211, 1-32.

Von Solms, R., & Van Niekerk, J. (2013). From information security to cyber security. *Computers & Security, 38*, 97–102. doi:10.1016/j.cose.2013.04.004

Zezulka, F., Marcon, P., Vesely, I., & Sajdl, O. (2016). Industry 4.0–An introduction in the phenomenon. *IFAC-PapersOnLine, 49*(25), 8–12. doi:10.1016/j.ifacol.2016.12.002

Zhou, L., Thieret, R., Watzlaf, V., DeAlmeida, D., & Parmanto, B. (2019). A telehealth privacy and security self-assessment questionnaire for telehealth providers: Development and validation. *International Journal of Telerehabilitation, 11*(1), 3–14. doi:10.5195/ijt.2019.6276 PMID:31341542

## ADDITIONAL READING

Dubgorn, A., Kalinina, O., Lyovina, A., & Rotar, O. (2018). Foundation architecture of telemedicine system services based on Health 4.0 concept. In *SHS Web of Conferences, 44* (00032, pp. 1-10). EDP Sciences.

Ferrer-Roca, O., & Méndez, D. G. (2012). Health 4.0 in the i2i Era. *International Journal of Reliable and Quality E-Healthcare, 1*(1), 43–57. doi:10.4018/ijrqeh.2012010105

Health Insurance Portability and Accountability Act (HIPAA) compliance checklist. (2018-2019). *HIPAA Journal*. Retrieved October 30, 2019, from https://www.hipaajournal.com/hipaa-checklist-download/

Moghaddam, M., & Nof, S. Y. (2018). Collaborative service-component integration in cloud manufacturing. *International Journal of Production Research, 56*(1-2), 677–691. doi:10.1080/00207543.2017.1374574

U.S. Department of Health & Human Services. *Cyber security guidance material*. (n.d.). Retrieved October 30, 2019 from, https://www.hhs.gov/hipaa/for-professionals/security/guidance/cybersecurity/index.html

U.S. Department of Health & Human Services. (n.d.). *Ransomware guidance – fact sheet*: Ransomware *and HIPAA*. Retrieved October 30, 2019, from https://www.hhs.gov/sites/default/files/RansomwareFactSheet.pdf?language=es

U.S. National Institute of Standards and Technology. (2018). *Framework for improving critical infrastructure cybersecurity* (Version 1.1). Retrieved October 30, 2019, from https://nvlpubs.nist.gov/nistpubs/CSWP/NIST.CSWP.04162018.pdf

Zhong, H., Levalle, R. R., Moghaddam, M., & Nof, S. Y. (2015). Collaborative intelligence - definition and measured impacts on internetworked e-work. *Management and Production Engineering Review, 6*(1), 67–78. doi:10.1515/mper-2015-0009

## KEY TERMS AND DEFINITIONS

**Artificial Intelligence (AI):** An area of computer science that emphasizes the creation of intelligent machines that work and react like humans.

**Big Data:** Extremely large data sets that may be analyzed computationally to reveal patterns, trends, and associations, especially relating to human behavior and interactions.

**Collaborative Control Theory (CCT):** A collection of principles and models for supporting the effective design of collaborative e-Work systems.

**Computer Integrated Manufacturing (CIM):** The manufacturing approach of using computers to control entire production process. This integration allows individual processes to exchange information with each other and initiate actions.

**Distributed Hierarchical Control System (DHCS):** A form of control system in which a set of devices and governing software are arranged in a hierarchical tree.

**Food and Drugs Administration (FDA):** The American agency is separated into divisions that oversee a majority of the organization's obligations involving food, drugs, cosmetics, animal food, dietary supplements, medical devices, biological goods, and blood products.

**Health 4.0 (H4.0):** Since Industry 4.0 extends further the IoT model with the inclusion of robotics and automation, H4.0 is the application of the I4.0 paradigm to the healthcare sector.

**Health Insurance Portability and Accountability Act (HIPAA):** The Health Insurance Portability and Accountability Act of 1996 (HIPAA) is an American federal law that requires employers to protect employee medical records as confidential. HIPAA includes regulations that cover how employers must protect employees' medical privacy rights and the privacy of their health information.

**Internet of Things (IoT):** A system of interrelated computing devices, mechanical and digital machines, objects, animals or people that are provided with unique identifiers (UIDs) and the ability to transfer data over a network without requiring human-to-human or human-to-computer interaction.

**Radio Frequency Identification (RFID):** A form of wireless communication that incorporates the use of electromagnetic or electrostatic coupling in the radio frequency portion of the electromagnetic spectrum to uniquely identify an object, animal or person.

*This research was previously published in Cyber Security of Industrial Control Systems in the Future Internet Environment; pages 313-329, copyright year 2020 by Information Science Reference (an imprint of IGI Global).*

# Chapter 13
# Medical Device Security

**Md Abdullah Al Momin**
*University of Louisiana at Lafayette, USA*

## ABSTRACT

*Implantable medical devices (IMDs) are miniaturized computer systems used to monitor and treat various medical conditions. Examples of IMDs include insulin pumps, artificial pacemakers, neuro-stimulators, and implantable cardiac defibrillators. These devices have adopted wireless communication to help facilitate the care they provide for patients by allowing easier transferal of data or remote control of machine operations. However, with such adoption has come exposure to various security risks and issues that must be addressed due to the close relation of patient health and IMD performance. With patient lives on the line, these security risks pose increasingly real problems. This chapter hopes to provide an overview of these security risks, their proposed solutions, and the limitations on IMD systems which make solving these issues nontrivial. Later, the chapter will analyze the security issues and the history of vulnerabilities in pacemakers to illustrate the theoretical topics by considering a specific device.*

## INTRODUCTION

Implantable Medical Devices (IMDs) are miniaturized computer systems used to monitor and treat various medical conditions. Examples of IMDs include insulin pumps, artificial pacemakers, neuro-stimulator, and implantable cardiac defibrillators. These devices have adopted wireless communication to help facilitate the care they provide for patients by allowing easier transferal of data or remote control of machine operations. However, with such adoption has come exposure to various security risks and issues that must be addressed due to the close relation of patient health and IMD performance.

Because IMDs are implanted inside the human body, there exist several limitations on these devices. For example, size, battery power, computational power, and inadaptability are issues associated with the physical devices themselves that prove troublesome for implementing security measures. Along with this, there also exist situational limitations or limitations related to the use of these devices, which also cause problems for security. Such as requirements of availability and desires for unobtrusive operation.

It has been shown before that IMDs are incredibly vulnerable to malicious attacks by outside agents. Rios and Butts et al. evaluated the security protocols on pacemaker devices in 2017 and found over 80

DOI: 10.4018/978-1-6684-6311-6.ch013

thousand security vulnerabilities. Radcliffe et al., 2011 displayed his ability to remotely gain complete control over an audience member's insulin pump during a conference. These security risks often exist because manufacturers are reluctant to include security measures to avoid bugs or problems which would slow down production or regulatory approval and ultimately beat their competition to the market.

In response to these attacks, a body of research has been done on methods with which to secure IMDs and IMD systems despite the restrictions in place. These solutions primarily involve controlling access to the IMD through the use of authentication, key generation, or key distribution, managing communication with an IMD, detecting unauthorized or malicious attacks, and keeping them from influencing the IMD.

With patient lives on the line, these security risks pose ever increasingly real problems. This chapter hopes to provide an overview of these security risks, their proposed solutions, and the limitations on IMD systems which make solving these issues nontrivial. Later, the chapter will analyze the security issues and the history of vulnerabilities in pacemakers to illustrate the theoretical topics by considering a specific device.

## LIMITATION AND RESTRICTIONS

Because of the implantable nature of IMDs, there exist several restrictions which limit the ability of IMDs to perform traditional or even adequate security measures. Chief among these is that the devices must be small enough to be implanted in a human body without the body rejecting them. This size restriction is one of the causes of a limitation in the amount of computational power available to the device. Along with this size restriction, should computational power increase to the point of unrestricted usage, there is also the idea of the heat produced by these computations causing harm to the body with which it is implanted.

Because these devices are implanted using invasive surgeries, they are designed with longevity in mind. The idea is to limit the number of times throughout the patient's life to replace or adjust the device. This is one of the reasons that wireless modules have become so pervasive in IMDs recently, as they allow modification of parameters and collection of data without the use of invasive surgeries. However, one method that wireless communication cannot improve is battery life. Because these devices are designed with longevity in mind, they are given batteries that, with appropriate usage, would last a decade or more. The idea of recharging a battery inside an IMD comes with a series of problems and issues in and of itself, namely the element of the battery heating up during power conference. This restriction on battery life also affects computational power, as heavy computational activities can wear down an IMDs battery, leading to unwanted surgeries and a lower quality of life for the patient. The size limitations mentioned earlier also put a subsequent limitation on battery size and lifetime, which further affects computational availability. With these things in mind, it is easy to see how the usage of IMDs informs its physical properties, which in turn inform the limitations placed on it. These limitations are interconnected, with each affecting another in some way.

Additionally, with new security schemes and solutions being introduced regularly, backward compatibility is essential. Similar to the idea behind long battery life, invasive surgeries are almost universally unwanted. Because of this, new security mechanisms should take into consideration backward compatibility with older models already implanted. Though this is not a necessary limitation, should large-scale vulnerabilities be found, such as the outdated libraries of (Rios and Butts et al.), patients with old IMDs would need to consider undergoing surgery to update their model or be at risk of attack.

Along with physical limitations imposed by usage, there are also limitations on IMDs due to other factors. As Zheng et al. interestingly point out, one crucial factor when designing security systems for IMDs is psychological acceptance of the proposed methodology. As we will see later, the one proposed solution for security measures is wearable external devices or WEDs. Because these devices must be kept track of and worn at all times to provide adequate security, there is a psychological toll taken from the patient who must carry this burden. Similarly, there should be an effort to limit the intrusiveness of security solutions in a patient's life. Patients may be likely to forsake practical security solutions but will get in the way of everyday living. This is, of course, the purpose of IMDs in the first place: to make day-to-day life more tolerable to patients. In the same vein, security solutions should not get impaired by the functionality of the device. This ties in with limited computational power, but the primary responsibility of IMDs is to provide medical assistance to patients. Any security scheme that degrades an IMDs ability to do so should not be considered applicable.

Lastly, there exists an additional tradeoff to consider when developing security solutions for IMDs. We have already discussed the tradeoff of limited resources vs. security, but the tradeoff of security vs. accessibility comes with this. In the event of an emergency, the nearest medical professional or first responders are the ones to treat the patient. In such a situation, any security mechanism must not deny access to the medical professional seeing the patient. Techniques such as key distribution or authorization can act as burdens in this situation and possibly lead to server consequences, even death. The main trouble with such a system lies in determining when an emergency occurs and distinguishing between a legitimate medical professional and a malicious attacker in both normal situations and emergencies. Proposed solutions that are too lenient are liable to be abused by malicious attackers, and too strict solutions are liable to refuse access to first responders in the event of an emergency.

## CLASSIFICATION OF ATTACKS

Traditionally, attacks on IMDs are classified into two categories: passive attacks and active attacks. Passive attacks primarily include eavesdropping attacks, which listen in on the communication between IMDs and programmers. Considering the limitations discussed earlier, many IMDs do not implement any form of encryption when communicating with other devices, either by design or necessity. This fault in security, along with things such as lack of authentication or access control mechanisms, can lead to the attacker discovering not only who among a crowd has an IMD, but also potentially disclose information such as the device's make, model, and the patient name, age, current condition, ID, and health records (Hei et al., 2013). Valuable information can be inferred using passive attacks, such as the device's relationship with the patient, the device's capacities, or the device's settings. For example, it has been shown that with an oscilloscope and software radio, an attacker could obtain personal information using an ICD along with information on the ICD itself (Halperin et al., 2008). This information can potentially be used to calculate a plan of attack to use against the patient.

While these attacks are dangerous in their own right, their true potential lies when used in conjunction with active attacks. Active attacks are malicious attacks that modify, impersonate, or replay messages between IMDs and programmers, with the end goal of performing some action or set of activities that would detriment the patient. These attacks are much more frequent and dangerous than passive attacks, but passive attacks are often used as a forefront to active attacks, to get their foot in the door, so to speak. Active attacks can include Man-In-The-Middle attacks, DoS or battery draining attacks, performing unauthorized or potentially harmful actions, jamming communication between the device and the programmer, holding the device ransom, or completely shutting off the device. Though the range of possible actions included under the tag of active attack is broad, all of these attacks have the potential to be devastating or even fatal to the patient. (Halperin et al., 2008).

## CLASSIFICATION OF PROPOSED SOLUTIONS

Solutions proposed to counter attacks on IMDs are as varied as IMDs and the patients who trust their health. However, most of these proposed solutions share some commonalities, allowing them to fit into broad classifications. Most proposed solutions to security issues in wireless IMD systems fall into the following categories: Key Management, Communication Control through Proxy, Attack Detection/ Reaction, and general Access Control/Authentication. These classifications are intentionally broad, as there are many different techniques presented in the literature, with many other methods designed around overcoming the many limitations of IMDs. You may notice that the first two categories could potentially fall under the umbrella of access control. Though potentially arbitrary, this distinction is intentional, as these are two of the more heavily researched areas among the proposed solutions and deserve to be explored independently.

## COMMUNICATION CONTROL

External devices typically handle control of communication between IMDsand programmers. These WEDs are well known throughout wireless medical device security literature. These devices are the IMDGuard, IMDShield, and Cloaker. The IMDGuard intercepts all communication with the IMD and acts as a man in the middle. ECG signals are used to authenticate the IMD and IMDGuard. The IMD-Shield offers one-way confidentiality by way of jamming. The IMDShield will jam the IMD's frequency to communicate, blocking all traffic to the device. The Shield knows the method for jamming, so it can reverse the technique to retrieve messages from the IMD and transfer them to a caregiver. Lastly, we have the Cloaker. The Cloaker is simple in that it blocks all communication to the IMD except to an authorized caregiver. While the cloaker is active, nothing can communicate with the IMD except the authorized caregiver, but simply removing the Cloaker allows full access in the event of an emergency.

## ATTACK DETECTION AND REACTION

The main solution proposed for detecting and responding to a malicious attack comes from (Hei et al., 2011) in the form of a machine learning technique that uses patient access models that contain various dimensions of access, such as access location and time, day, etc. The patient's cell phone is used to offload storage and computation, preventing the use of precious resources on the IMD. When the IMD attempts to interface with a programmer, it will send a verification message to the patient's phone. The patient's phone will run a classification algorithm to determine if access is malicious or not. If the phone decides the access is normal, then the IMD continues with the access as planned. Should the phone determine that the access is abnormal or malicious, it will send a blocking command to the IMD, which will then go to sleep, saving power and rejecting any access attempt. Lastly, if the phone is unsure of the validity of the access request, it will prompt the user to intervene, trusting their judgment.

Another technique is presented in MedMon, which can detect adversarial attacks that deviate from legitimate transmissions by some measurable physical characteristic such as signal strength, time of arrival, or angle of arrival. Upon receiving a new command, MedMon will compare this new data with the records of historical data to decide whether there exists some anomaly. Upon detection, MedMon can either respond passively by alerting the patient or actively by jamming transmissions.

## GENERAL ACCESS CONTROL

There exist a small section of techniques that do not fall under the categories listed above. They primarily deal with proximity-based solutions, but unlike the ones described earlier, they do not share keys. Examples include magnetic field solutions, such as a magnetic switch within the IMD which a powerful magnet can trigger to switch on the device's wireless communication module. These techniques have some shortcomings. Because they can be activated by any strong magnet, not just the ones intended for such use, and is less secure than other options. The last example includes Near Field Communication, or NFC, technology. In this method, a smartphone is given a key at IMD insertion and cannot be regenerated. A use case for this technique involves an in-vivo NFC chip additionally implanted in the patient, which is used to communicate with the smartphone. Because NFC technology draws power from the reader, it requires no power from the IMD. However, in the event of a lost phone, the data stored on the IMD becomes irretrievable. This technique also does not qualify as a key sharing technique because the key is shared once and can never be shared again, so sharing keys is not a part of the technique's normal operation.

## CASE STUDIES: INTRODUCTION ON PACEMAKERS

With thousands of pacemakers implanted into people a year, and millions already in circulation, ensuring the security of medically implanted pacemakers is paramount to the long-term survival and longevity of the people that rely on them. With a pacemaker, someone who has a debilitating heart problem can live a long and fulfilling life and can even be alerted to complications or issues quickly, possibly before they are even aware of difficulties, thanks to in-home monitoring technology. However, these life-saving devices create a unique problem: Their livelihood, safety, and even their own lives are only as secure as the measures put in place to protect against malicious intent. This chapter aims to analyze the different attack vectors, attack symptoms, known security issues, and other vulnerabilities of implanted pacemakers in patients.

## HOW PACEMAKERS WORKS

To fully understand how a hacker could interfere with a pacemaker, one must understand how the pacemaker functions, communicates, and interfaces with other technology. The purpose of a pacemaker is to treat arrhythmia in the heart, which is any irregularity of the heartbeat. This is detected by the electrodes surgically placed in one to three of the heart's chambers. These electrodes are where a pacemaker will assist the patient by sending an electric jolt into the heart's muscular tissue, forcing a contraction. The electrodes are attached to a pulse generator via wires placed in the patient's veins. The pulse generator creates the electric pulse by pulling on power from the battery within its system. The device must be replaced approximately every ten years, as the battery is not rechargeable internally without serious danger to a patient. There are non-implantable pacemakers, but they limit the patient's maneuverability and freedom, often do not come with network-enabled features and are traditionally seen as a temporary solution.

Many of the newest models of pacemakers come packed with networking functions, known as "telemetry," that can allow medical personnel to both access the data from the pacemaker on-demand and wirelessly reconfigure the rate of impulse and capabilities of the device (Halperin et al., 2008).

## ATTACK VECTORS

*Figure 1. Network vectors for attacks*

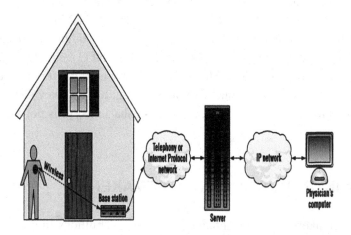

As shown in Figure 1 from (Halperin et al., 2008) and mentioned previously, major pacemaker manufacturers can now acquire data from implanted devices and relay it to a central repository over either a Wi-Fi signal or a dial-up connection. This data repository is available to medical professionals via a website utilizing SSL protocols. The visible connections in the diagram are our attack vectors for this communication system. The attack vectors are the user's device to the network, the user's home network to the data repository, the data repository to the user's network, and the user's network to the user's device. This chapter primarily focuses on the network communications between the user and their surrounding network.

## THE DANGER OF IMPROPER SECURITY

The most important and terrifying type of hack that a hacker can perform concerning Implanted Medical Devices (IMDs) like pacemakers is the attack on the user and the device itself. If one needs an example, they would only need to Google "Barnaby Jack", a renowned gray hat hacker. At conferences in 2011 and 2012, Barnaby Jack was able to show that he could hack into any pacemaker with an RF communication. The hack would cause the device to either withhold therapy that the device would deliver, which would cause extreme discomfort or pain or directly deliver a potentially lethal 830-volt shock to a person's heart (Sen et al., 2020). He was able to accomplish this by having the devices disclose their serial and model numbers and alter the transmitter's code while simultaneously extracting data that would identify that person and their medical healthcare provider, as often crucial medical information stored on these devices is not encrypted. The encryption of this data is usually handled by either the base station that is associated with the device or via a cellular device before the upload to the network. Barnaby Jack also stated in an interview that this type of attack could be turned into a worm-based style attack. This worm-based style attack can then be broadcasted to any internet-connected pacemaker, allowing nearly anyone with a pacemaker to become a victim of a large-scale cyber-attack suddenly, held hostage by the devices keeping them alive.

## NETWORK TO HOSPITAL

The tradeoff between allowing emergency system access to healthcare providers and ensuring that the device avoids unauthorized access is a significant issue in pacemaker protection (Pinisetty et al., 2018). The comprehensive survey discusses certain tradeoffs for cyber-physical systems (CPS), such as a pacemaker (a cyber-component) regulating the rhythmic beating of the human heart (a physical system). This can be referred to as an "Internet of Bodies" network. People are becoming increasingly reliant on IMDs such as pacemakers, insulin pumps, etc. being able to communicate with external devices such as smartwatches, cellular devices, and each other for ease of use and quick, reliable access data. (Sen et al., 2020). Cyber-security in IMDs is hampered by three major issues (Puat et al., 2020): Most embedded devices lack the memory and processing power needed to support cryptographic security, encryption, and access control. Doctors and patients value convenience and accessibility over protection. The ability to control embedded devices remotely is a good function, but it also renders them vulnerable. Power versus security: Most embedded medical devices lack the memory, processing power, or battery life needed to support cryptographic protection (Puat et al., 2020), encryption, or access control. Using HTTPS instead of HTTP (a method of encrypting web traffic to prevent eavesdropping) is an example. Cryptography suites (the algorithms and keys used to prove identity and keep transmissions secret) are designed for computers, and they require complex mathematical operations that are beyond the capabilities of small, low-cost IoT devices. Moving cryptography into dedicated hardware chips is an emerging solution, but this increases the cost.

- **Convenience vs. Security:** Doctors and patients do not anticipate having to log into these medical devices regularly. The prospect of remembering usernames, passwords, and encryption keys are incompatible with how they want to use them. Likewise, no one anticipates having to log into their toaster or refrigerator. Fortunately, the pervasiveness of mobile phones and their use as interfaces to "smart" IoT computers are altering users' expectations. Often, communications between devices in the body of things happen through either a Radio Frequency (RF) connection or a Bluetooth Low Energy (BLE) connection. BLE can easily be used to connect to a smartphone or other external device, which then can be sent to the patient monitoring system in the hospital if required (Heydari et al., 2020). BLE connection's greatest strength is a low-energy communication type that is easily discoverable and accessible. However, this is also the greatest weakness, as those with the knowledge on how to exploit this connection can efficiently utilize it in an unethical and dangerous way.

- **Remote Monitoring vs. Security:** When surgical implants need to be removed or replaced, they pose an immediate medical risk. As a result, remote monitoring is unquestionably a lifesaving technology for patients who are using these devices. Patients are no longer dependent on the low battery "buzz" sound, and doctors may easily upgrade the device's software if it malfunctions. Regrettably, this remote control feature introduces a whole new level of danger. Others will upgrade the program remotely if your doctor can.

Cyber security Attacks (Kaschel et al., 2019) are divided into two categories. Attacks that aren't focused on a particular objective but instead terminate and disable items are known as blind attacks. Targeted attacks aim to ruin everything by focusing on specific individual details. Targeted attacks are a form of intentional attack. If the information is not encrypted, an attacker may insert false data or steal it during the communication phase. In addition, the attacker may install malicious software on the computers.

## USER TO NETWORK ATTACK

A modern pacemaker will gather information about a patient and send it over Wi-Fi to an access point or medical equipment used during hospital visits. The data is sent to remote servers by the access point systems (Pinisetty et al., 2018), which collect information about the patient's health when they are at home. Patients with mobility issues can benefit from pacemakers that can send data over the internet. However, the communications protocols to send data to remote servers are very simple and vulnerable to hacking. As healthcare facilities increasingly rely on devices that communicate with each other, hospital medical record systems, and the internet, concerns about the vulnerability of medical devices such as pacemakers, ICDs, insulin pumps, defibrillators, fetal monitors, and scanners are growing. Using brute-force attacks and hard-coded logins, these are simple to break. Failures may include disclosing sensitive patient information, mishandling, inadequate supervision, gaining access to the equipment system, changing computer scheduled tasks, causing battery swings, or even delivering unwanted stimuli or disabling alarms.

The most common method of attack is to use Wi-Fi communication to avoid having to be close to the victim (Longras et al., 2020). With the ease with which backdoors can be installed in hospital networks and with medical devices linked to the same network, several systems can be compromised with malware, including the likelihood of twenty-four insulin pumps and pacemaker failures that can be controlled remotely.

A forced authentication attack, also known as a resource exhaustion attack, is a denial of service attack (DoS). IMDs that communicate wirelessly with external readers or monitors are vulnerable to this attack. When an external reader tries to bind to an IMD, the first move is for the IMD and the reader to authenticate each other (Longras et al., 2020). If the authentication fails, the reader's contact with the IMD will be terminated. However, the authentication process necessitates IMD communications, which consume a significant amount of power. If an unauthorized reader tries to connect to an IMD multiple times, the IMD will perform multiple authentications, consuming a substantial amount of the necessary battery power.

Furthermore, this form of attack produces many security logs, which causes IMD storage to become overburdened. This type of attack can be repeated nearly infinitely while in range of the signal and attacks two resources of the IMD simultaneously, causing a pacemaker that may not need to be replaced for almost a decade to need to be surgically repaired and replaced in a matter of weeks. (Hei et al., 2010). When contact is blocked, and interference is made, this form of DoS occurs. By repeatedly sending true or false messages, the attacker exploits machine resources. This is Radio Jamming. Man-in-the-middle attack: To gain access to confidential health information (Longras et al., 2020), the intruder listens without interrupting or changing the conversation. Another scenario is for an intruder to intercept data or code from a medical device when radio frequencies are working and then transmit the altered data to the monitor or warning system. Replay Attack: The intersection and representation of the medical device or monitoring system, represented by a network attack in which real data is manipulated, are also part of this attack. Such an attack may be used to avoid receiving care, for example, by mucking up the order in which packets arrive at IMD or, even worse, by sending the same message to medical equipment and the monitoring system repeatedly. Code Injection: When an intruder modifies the source code on a medical device, monitor, or even a potential warning system to perform an undefined function, such as changing the pacemaker program to deliver electric shocks regularly, this is known as a medical device compromise.

## COUNTER MEASURES

Many of these attacks, however, have had proposed alterations and system changes occur as a result. Many new security ideas, such as having an application that creates a trusted connection jam the emitted BLE signal from the pacemaker to make the device more secure and less targetable from Bluetooth-based attacks. (Heydari et al., 2020). Security methods have been recommended that utilize a patient's daily schedules and times and necessary locations for access to determine if the attempt to authorize should be allowed or is likely an attack (Hei et al., 2010). This would help reduce the number of requests the pacemaker would have to handle in an RD attack. The following security properties must be considered to secure patients who use IMDs. Authentication: Before conducting any procedure, the identities of the communicating parties must be verified. The lack of proper authentication in the case of IMDs may be used to launch an elevation of privileges attack (EoP). Authorization Both users' use and management should be clearly stated and tracked. Only those with the appropriate privileges may perform each procedure. Reprogramming the IMD, for example, requires the collaboration of a doctor and a technician. Availability the service provided by the IMD must be accessible at all times. Because of the vital role that IMDs perform, their availability is a must. Active jamming can be used to block the radio channel, making the IMD inoperable. The intruder may also overload the system with network traffic, preventing access and draining the battery. Non-Repudiation In the access log, the system must record and validate all user activities. No log-in is used in current IMDs due to memory limitations. If logging is used, an alarm may be set off to notify the user if a malicious incident occurs. To hide their tracks, attackers will try to remove access logs. The device should be able to detect and prevent parameter manipulation and protect against tampering and reverse engineering. During transmission, IMD data may be intercepted and changed. The IMD could also allow malicious input, which could carry out attacks such as code injection. The lack of integrity checking allows data stored on the IMD memory to be altered. Confidentiality Only approved parties should have access to data. Since the various components of the IMDs (Tabasum et al., 2018) interact over the network, they are vulnerable to eavesdropping. Private patient data will be exposed if the data is not encrypted, putting the patients' privacy at risk. Possession (or control) to avoid unauthorized control, coercion, or intervention, protect the design (Tabasum et al., 2018), installation, service, and maintenance of systems and associated processes. Before being deployed, IMDs are subjected to extensive security monitoring. However, the systems must be modified to combat emerging security threats (Tabasum et al., 2018). The framework is protected from malicious updates by allowing changes in a highly restricted and validated environment.

- **Anomaly Detector:** If an attack is detected, the patient can be notified (for example, via a warning mechanism), or the system can be made unavailable by turning off the communications (or jamming the channel) while the medical functions continue to operate. The use of the wireless communication channel makes it difficult to avoid these types of attacks (Kaschel et al., 2019). The reader's communication with the IMD begins with the IMD authenticating the reader. The contact is disrupted if the reader fails the authentication stage. Failure to authenticate may use up resources in the IMD, which can be abused by an opponent who, for example, tries to connect with the IMD repeatedly. The result would be a classic Denial-of-Service (DoS) attack, in which the battery level would be significantly reduced, and memory/storage would be impacted. Some registers are used to store security values, including session tokens and logs in each authentication. This type of attack is known as a Resource Depletion (RD) attack since it focuses on wasting the IMD's resources. They are straightforward to enforce, and the effects can be very harmful, as sending dummy requests can reduce the battery life of the IMD from many years to a few weeks.

- **Access Control:** Unauthorized and improper use of the IMD functions was prevented by access control mechanisms (Kaschel et al., 2019). Before performing a specific action (e.g., entry, reading, reprogramming, etc.), the requester's rights are assessed to determine whether or not it is allowed to perform that action. Permitted and prohibited operations, in particular, are regulated by access control policies that define who may do what, depending on the context in which the access request is made. Access control is completely compatible with other security measures such as cryptographic protocols to secure the communication channel. Furthermore, access control typically necessitates prior authentication because decisions about whether or not an operation is allowed are taken based on the requester's identity, which must be identified beforehand.

- **Cryptographic Measures:** Cryptography-based security solutions (Kaschel et al., 2019), (Tabasum et al., 2018) are heavily reliant on cryptographic primitives, which fall into three categories. Hash functions and one-way permutations are examples of unkeyed primitives. We may differentiate between symmetric-key and public-key primitives in keyed cryptographic tools. A hidden key is exchanged between the trusted entities in symmetric-key primitives. Symmetric key ciphers solutions (Kaschel et al., 2019), (Tabasum et al., 2018) (block and stream ciphers), message authentication codes (MACs), pseudorandom sequences, and identification primitives are among the primitives in this group. Asymmetric-key primitives, on the other hand, include public-key ciphers and signatures. Two keys are used in this form of an algorithm, one of which is public, and the other must be kept secret. However, the main disadvantage of this approach is its high energy consumption.

- **Biometric Access:** Using biometrics to access the IMD (Tabasum et al., 2018), (Hei et al., 2011), such as fingerprints, iris, and speech, will alleviate the urgent access restriction. A two-level access control system is proposed (Hei et al., 2011). The first level uses the patients' fingerprints, iris color, and height as biometrics, and the second level uses an effective iris authentication scheme. Thus, in an emergency, medical personnel can access data using the patient's biometrics, which does not require anything from the patient. It also eliminates the need for the patient to recall passwords or bring authentication tokens.

## SECURITY WITH RUNTIME VERIFICATIONS

Pacemaker security threats are life-threatening, turning a life-saving system into a possible killer. Existing pacemaker monitoring solutions necessitate wireless contact with the device. This adds to the security risks, mainly when encryption and key distribution are complex. We suggest a monitoring system that does not rely on contact with the pacemaker or any other external device. The monitor is a wearable system that uses an individual's ECG to detect events of interest. The cardiologist programs the system with strong pacemaker timing values. We believe that no wireless protocol is used to link this device to any other device, including the pacemaker. We adapt a timed automata runtime verification method to build a monitor that detects anomalous events in real-time. An alarm is heard to warn the patient if any anomaly is observed. Approaches to runtime verification (RV) (Pinisetty et al., 2018) are concerned with monitoring and verifying if a device's run under inspection satisfies or violates a particular desired property. Since RV is only concerned with runs of the machine, which is called a black-box, it is an excellent match for pacemaker security. As a result, there will be no need to modify the current pacemaker, and no new wireless protocols or key distribution will be needed. There will be no extra certification costs as well. RV is a lightweight, formally based verification approach. One of the key focuses of formally based RV approaches is to produce RV monitors from a formal high-level specification of a collection of properties. The system's execution is unaffected by RV monitors. They are used to check whether a system's stored performance (offline verification) or its current live execution (online confirmation) meets the desired correctness property. An externally wearable system that continuously tracks the body's ECG signals using runtime verification techniques to verify essential safety properties specified for heart-pacemaker operation, adding an extra layer of protection and safety.

The RV (Pinisetty et al., 2018) monitor (externally worn device) is expected to have more power and computational resources than the pacemaker and measure ECG signals. The pacemaker is supposed to stay inside the body for a long time after it is implanted. The doctor programs it with the assistance of a programming unit (outside controller) with a direct connection before being implanted. If the pacemaker has to be reprogrammed after implantation, it should be done wirelessly. Doctors may use the programming unit to communicate with the pacemaker via radio frequency transmission to change running parameters (timers), change operating modes, or retrieve stored data. The doctor will consult with the patient to determine the right pacemaker for them. The doctor sets the pacing mode (e.g., DDD), the threshold voltage value of the pacing pulse, the pacemaker's sensitivity, and, most importantly, the timers such as AVI and AEI when programming. If a hacker gains access to the pacemaker, they can attempt to alter either of these timers.

*Figure 2. Wearable devices*

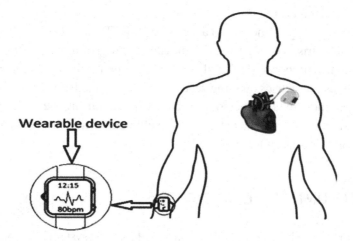

- **An External Device:** After the pacemaker is implanted, the patient receives the wearable unit (Pinisetty et al., 2018), (Tabasum et al., 2018). Any computing device with an ECG sensor and an accelerometer, such as a smartwatch, may be used as this external wearable device. The doctor also sets the timing values for the external wearable system. Both of the values of the set timers are stored in the memory of the wearable computer. It also knows the normal heart rate at which the pacemaker is set to pace (for example, 60–120 BPM) and the pacing pulses' characteristics such as voltage, current, and impedance. In addition, the software includes an accelerometer that tracks the user's movement.

The diagram above depicts a general explanation of how external devices function. End-system requests (Tabasum et al., 2018) are routed via an external device rather than directly to the IMD. The external computer is in charge of authenticating all incoming requests and safeguarding the IMD against various attacks. The external unit can be recharged and has fewer size restrictions than the IMD. In an emergency, medical personnel may remove the external monitor and communicate with the IMD directly. However, the patient must still be near the external system, which is a disadvantage of this approach. This approach is also appropriate if the IMD is already implanted in the patient's body and protection is needed later.

*Figure 3. External device*

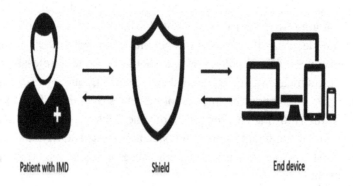

## CONCLUSION

In this chapter, the description of the restrictions placed on security mechanisms for IMDs, including the purpose or reasons for such restrictions is discussed in detail. As well as some manner of classification for both security attacks and security solutions are also discussed. Attacks can be split into the categories of passive and active attacks. At the same time, solutions can be classified as either key management, communication control, attack detection and reaction, or general access control techniques. This chapter also addressed the security of medical device communications, focusing on the security of communications with other systems, such as the monitoring system, which is critical because it affects people's health, if not their lives. As a result, it's critical to put "security" first. Finally, a number of flaws in these systems and potential attack types and how to mitigate them are analyzed.

## REFERENCES

Halperin, D., Heydt-Benjamin, T. S., Fu, K., Kohno, T., & Maisel, W. H. (2008). Security and privacy for implantable medical devices. *IEEE Pervasive Computing*, 7(1), 30–39. doi:10.1109/MPRV.2008.16

Halperin, D., Heydt-Benjamin, T. S., Ransford, B., Clark, S. S., Defend, B., Morgan, W., ... Maisel, W. H. (2008). Pacemakers and Implantable Cardiac Defibrillators: Software Radio Attacks and Zero-Power Defenses. *2008 IEEE Symposium on Security and Privacy*. 10.1109/SP.2008.31

Hei, X., & Du, X. (2011). Biometric-based two-level secure access control for Implantable Medical Devices during emergencies. *2011 Proceedings IEEE INFOCOM*. 10.1109/INFCOM.2011.5935179

Hei, X., & Du, X. (2011). Biometric-based two-level secure access control for Implantable Medical Devices during emergencies. *Proceedings - IEEE INFOCOM*, 346–350. doi:10.1109/INFCOM.2011.5935179

Hei, X., & Du, X. (2013). IMD Access Control during Emergencies. *SpringerBriefs in Computer Science Security for Wireless Implantable Medical Devices*, 19-35. doi:10.1007/978-1-4614-7153-0_4

Hei, X., Du, X., Wu, J., & Hu, F. (2010). Defending Resource Depletion Attacks on Implantable Medical Devices. *2010 IEEE Global Telecommunications Conference GLOBECOM 2010*. 10.1109/GLOCOM.2010.5685228

Hei, X., Du, X., Wu, J., & Hu, F. (2010, December). *Defending resource depletion attacks on implantable medical devices. In 2010 IEEE global telecommunications conference GLOBECOM 2010*. IEEE.

Heydari, V. (2020). A New Security Framework for Remote Patient Monitoring Devices. *2020 International Symposium on Networks, Computers and Communications (ISNCC)*, 1-4. 10.1109/ISNCC49221.2020.9297214

Kaschel, H., & Ahumada, C. (2019). Security Mechanism to Protect the Privacy and Security of Patients Who have cardiovascular Diseases (ECG). *2019 IEEE CHILEAN Conference on Electrical, Electronics Engineering, Information and Communication Technologies (CHILECON)*, 1-7. doi: 10.1109/CHILECON47746.2019.8987984

Longras, A., Oliveira, H., & Paiva, S. (2020). Security Vulnerabilities on Implantable Medical Devices. *2020 15th Iberian Conference on Information Systems and Technologies (CISTI)*, 1-4. doi: 10.23919/CISTI49556.2020.9141043

Pacemakers. (n.d.). *National Heart Lung and Blood Institute*. Available: https://www.nhlbi.nih.gov/healthtopics/pacemakers

Pinisetty, S., Roop, P. S., Sawant, V., & Schneider, G. (2018). Security of Pacemakers using Runtime Verification. *2018 16th ACM/IEEE International Conference on Formal Methods and Models for System Design (MEMOCODE)*, 1-11. doi: 10.1109/MEMCOD.2018.8556922

Puat, H. A. M., & Abd Rahman, N. A. (2020, December). IoMT: A Review of Pacemaker Vulnerabilities and Security Strategy. *Journal of Physics: Conference Series, 1712*(1), 012009.

Radcliffe, J. (2011). Hacking medical devices for fun and insulin: Breaking the human SCADA system. Black Hat Conference presentation slides.

Rios, B., & Butts, J. (2017). *Security evaluation of the implantable cardiac device ecosystem architecture and implementation interdependencies*. Available: http://blog.whitescope.io/2017/05/understanding-pacemaker-systems.html

Rostami, M., Burleson, W., Koushanfar, F., & Juels, A. (2013). Balancing security and utility in medical devices? *Proceedings of the 50th Annual Design Automation Conference on - DAC 13*. 10.1145/2463209.2488750

Rostami, M., Juels, A., & Koushanfar, F. (2013). Heart-to-heart (H2H). *Proceedings of the 2013 ACM SIGSAC Conference on Computer & Communications Security - CCS 13*. 10.1145/2508859.2516658

Sen, Maity, & Das. (2020). The body is the network: To safeguard sensitive data, turn flesh and tissue into a secure wireless channel. *IEEE Spectrum, 57*(12), 44-49. doi:10.1109/MSPEC.2020.9271808

Tabasum, A., Safi, Z., AlKhater, W., & Shikfa, A. (2018). Cybersecurity Issues in Implanted Medical Devices. *2018 International Conference on Computer and Applications (ICCA)*, 1-9. doi: 10.1109/COMAPP.2018.8460454

Zheng, G., Zhang, G., Yang, W., Valli, C., Shankaran, R., & Orgun, M. A. (2017). From WannaCry to WannaDie: Security trade-offs and design for implantable medical devices. *2017 17th International Symposium on Communications and Information Technologies (ISCIT)*. 10.1109/ISCIT.2017.8261228

*This research was previously published in Security, Data Analytics, and Energy-Aware Solutions in the IoT; pages 173-191, copyright year 2022 by Engineering Science Reference (an imprint of IGI Global).*

# Chapter 14
# Quantum Cryptography for Securing IoT–Based Healthcare Systems

**Anand Sharma**

(iD) https://orcid.org/0000-0002-9995-6226

*Mody University of Science and Technology, Lakshmangarh, India*

**Alekha Parimal Bhatt**

*Capgemini IT India Pvt. Ltd., India*

## ABSTRACT

*IoT-based healthcare is especially susceptible as many IoT devices are developed without keeping in mind the security issue. In addition, such smart devices may be connected to global networks to access anytime, anywhere. There are some security challenges like mobility, computational limitation, scalability, communication media, dynamic topology, and above all the data confidentiality in storage or in transmission. There are some security protocols and methodology which is used in IoT-based healthcare systems like steganography, AES cryptosystems, and RSA cryptographic techniques. Therefore, it is necessary to use quantum cryptography system to make sure the security, privacy, and integrity of the patient's data received and transmitted from IoT-based healthcare systems. Quantum cryptography is a very fascinating domain in cyber security that utilizes quantum mechanics to extend a cryptosystem that is supposed to be the unbreakable secure system.*

## 1. INTRODUCTION

The proliferation of physical objects connecting to the Internet leads to a novel paradigm called "Internet of Things (IoT)."

The Internet of things is an emerging global Internet-based information infrastructure in which associated physical objects furnished with sensors, actuators, and processors communicate with one another to serve an important purpose. The 'thing' in Internet of Things can alluded as an individual or any device

DOI: 10.4018/978-1-6684-6311-6.ch014

that has been relegated an IP address. The Internet of Things (IoT) is characterized as a paradigm which is presently situated as the true stage for ubiquitous sensing and customized service delivery. Internet of Things has been characterized by various authors, yet at the most crucial level it tends to be depicted as a network of devices connecting with one another by means of machine to machine (M2M) communication, empowering collection and exchange of data. It guarantees another data foundation wherein all items around us are associated with the Internet, having the ability to communicate with each other with minimal conscious interventions (Guo, Zhang, Yu et al, 2013). By its computing and networking capabilities, today the Internet has contacted pretty much every edge of the globe and is influencing human life in incomprehensible manners.

The Internet of Things (IoT) is being used in pretty much every part of life today, despite the fact that this reality is frequently obscure and not publicized. The fuse of IoT into regular procedures will keep on expanding. IoT permits individuals and devices to interface at whenever, and anyplace, with anything and anybody, in a perfect world are associated with a network to facilitate worldwide exchange to accomplish complex errands that require a high level of insight and intelligence and delivery of intelligent and relevant services (Perera et al., 2013). These IoT devices are outfitted with actuators, sensors, handsets, processors, transceivers and storage units. The IoT infrastructure comprises of heterogeneous, addressable and readable virtual and physical objects that can convey over internet, where every unit is skillful to produce or consume intelligent services. Lately, scientific advancement is estimated by smart sensor device that are introduced in the virtual and physical domain of IoT to go about as or for the benefit of individuals. With this innovative and progressive extension, it is presently workable for our day by day objects to know about our needs: what we like or need and when and where we need them.

Rather than an official meaning of IoT in 2016, NIST published an article titled "Networks of 'Things" to quantify the shortfall of having an ordinary IoT definition (Voas, 2016). In that article, five natives were introduced for any network of "things." The primitives are sensors, aggregators, communication channels, *e*-Utilities and decision trigger.

## A. Working of IoT

In a classical IoT system devices and services are the key component where they are establishing connection among them and change as per the requirement. In and IoT System first the data have been collected from device then it will be preprocessed and communicated for the intelligent decision or servie.

- Data Collection: The data is collected by actuators and sensor devices, which helps in communicating the physical world. There are a number of sensors are available for example The accelerometer - for motion sensing, gyroscope – for orientation, thermometer- for temperature, camera – for visual capturing, barometer- for atmospheric pressure, magnetometer – for magnetic fields detection, proximity sensor - for calculation of distance, chemical sensors- for chemical and biochemical substances
- Data Preprocessing: The data collected by the actuators and sensor devices then preprocessed at the specific sensor or some different proximate device. Sensors have to be process intelligently to derive valuable inferences from it.
- Data Communicaton: Now, after the processing of collected data, some intelligent action is required on the source inferences. The character of actions may be diverse. For making intelligent decision the processed information can be send to other smart devices or some server. The IoT

sensors' communication is mostly wireless since they are usually installed at different geographically locations. There are various methodologies by which the sensors are communicating for example Wireless Sensor Networks Near Field Communication, Bluetooth Low Energy, Zigbee, Low Power WiFi and so on.

## B. Layered Architecture

As the IoT is collection of various heterogeneous device connected to each other, the connections and working of these devices is defined by the layered architecture. There are no single and final consensuses are available on layered architecture. There are many architecture have been proposed by many researches but the classical architecture is three-layered architecture (Mashal et al., 2015).

- Perception Layer: It is a physical, known as a device layer which is used for sensing and producing information. It works like people's ears, eyes and nose. It senses some physical parameters and has the responsibility for identifying other smart. The sensors are selected based on application requirement.
- Network layer: it is like transmission layer which is responsible to connect other smart things, devices, and network servers to each other. It acts like a bridge between application layer and perception layer. Its features are also used for processing and transmitting the data collected from the physical objects through sensors.
- Application Layer: It is responsible for the application service delivery to the user in which IoT has deployed. The application and services may be changeable for every application because services are depended on the sensors' collected information.

## C. Integration with Big Data and Cloud Computing

As it has been seen in nearly all of the cases, a large generated data are mentioning the requirement of the big data system for storage, analysis and building intelligent services. And for the large storage and communication it is required to be associated with cloud computing. The layered architecture of the IoT gives communication among devices, network infrastructure and cloud infrastructure. Cloud computing and big data helps IoT for advance analytics and monitoring of IoT devices. In a cloud and big data enabled IoT infrastructure, applications can be deployed to process and analyze the collected data rapidly and make intelligent decisions instantly. Cloud computing working as a workplace for IoT and big data where IoT is the producing the data and big data is analyzing it for intelligent decisions. The union of the inter-disciplinary IoT, big data and cloud computing influence new possibilities of decision support system.

## D. Healthcare Systems

Healthcare nowadays is costlier than ever, the population is on a rise and also new diseases are seen every few months. With the introduction of IoT integration with healthcare systems, now these facilities are lighter on the pockets and more accessible. The combining of IoT with healthcare systems has revolutionized the way our healthcare works. Healthcare services are now very easily accessible to each and every one, and also quality of life has improved significantly.

For countries like Africa with low access to medical facilities and sparse distribution of doctors, eHealth systems prove to be a boon.

Various advancements like real time monitoring of body vitals like blood pressure, sugar levels, heart rate, etc. to identify any risk factors, remote medical assistance, alerts reduce the cost of routine checkups significantly and help healthcare workers make informed decisions.

Where on one side eHealth systems have many benefits, technologies are usually prone to malicious attacks. There have been numerous incidents where IoT systems have been attacked and data have been stolen. Data security is a huge risk. As IoT devices transmit data in real time, cyber criminals can hack into the systems to steal the data like patient's ID and medical records and later use them to buy drugs and sell in a black market.

## 2. APPLICATIONS OF IoT

Along with the incredible enlargement in the variety and number of sensors connected to the Internet, the IoT has been emerging into Smart Home, smart cities, Smart vehicular networks, healthcare, Smart grid, agriculture, and other enterprises. Internet of Things is a technology trend that is on a sharp rise these days.

There are a huge number of areas and domains where intelligent applications and services have been developed. There are several applications of IoT in various different sectors. Some examples are given here:

### A. Home Automation

*The* IoT applications have emerged in Smart homes. The sensors and communication technologies are making the home smarter. In smart home different sensors have been deployed which automate the application as per the users' requirement for automated and intelligent services. Turning OFF / ON any electronic gadget, intelligently and automatically is the best example of it. It also helps in automating the daily routine tasks. By using motion sensor it can provide security to the user. Temperature sensors and fire sensor can also be deployed for home automation.

Smart Home concept refers to the automation of different household appliances and devices. An example can be Air Conditioning system which can be controlled through SMS, when an SMS indicating ON is sent to the AC it turns on, similar for turning it off. Another example is smart lighting systems which can adjust the brightness, color intensity, etc. of the lights according to the weather, mood, etc.

### B. Smart City

A city can be a smart city by deploying the IoT applications and services like smart transportation system- in which the traffic lights can be managed by sensors and their intelligent processing, smart parking system- in which the free space for parking is checked while entering, Smart Water Systems- to deal with water scarcity and intelligent distribution of water and waste management-monitoring of environment.

In traffic management smart cameras are installed on the traffic signals which can detect if someone is violating the traffic rules (like exceeding the speed limit, or travelling without helmet on 2-wheeler vehicle), capture their image, and search up the particular person's details using the license plate and he/she has to pay the due fine. This method accommodates for the absence of traffic inspectors on the traffic signals.

## C. Smart Grid

The IoT enabled power grids are getting intelligent and smart enough to make the power system as smart grid. To make the generation, transmission, distribution and conservation smarter the smart grid utilized the intelligence at each and every step.

## D. Supply Chain

IoT helps to abridge real life procedure in enterprises, commerce and their managerial systems (Ferreira et al., 2010). The goods like raw materials, packaged product and intermediate product in the supply chain can be easily tracked by the IoT enabled tracking systems from the place of manufacture industries to the distributor.

## E. Human Life and Entertainment

Entertainment plays a key role in people's life. There are many application and services that keep tracking the human activities. "Opportunistic IoT" (Guo, Zhang, Wang et al, 2013) refers to data sharing among gadhets based on availability and movement of contacts. Personal gadgets like wearables, mobile phones and tablets have sensing and transmission capabilities. Individuals' can search and communicate among themselves. "Circle Sense" (Liang & Cao, 2013) is an application, utilizing various types of sensors data to detect the social activities of individual. There is another IoT based technology "Affective computing" (Picard & Picard, 1997), which recognizes, stimulates, understands and responds to the human beings emotions "Logmusic" (Lee & Cho, 2014), is an entertainment application, which recommends music depending upon the time, weather and location.

## F. Smart Agriculture and Environment

Some parameters such as humidity, soil information and temperature are imperative for agricultural development. Farmers are using sensors to measure such parameters in the field.

Greenhouses Production (Zhao et al., 2010) is an service of IoT in agriculture for automated irrigation. Environmental parameters like humidity, temperature, and soil information, are collected in run time and forwarded to a application server for analysis. The intelligent results are then utilized to get better yield and crop quality.

## G. Baby Monitors

Baby monitoring systems are very essential these days where both the parents are working. This system is integrated with camera, voice module, and artificial intelligence which can monitor the baby's surroundings and can alert the parents on the mobile application of something is not right.

## H. Wearables

Wearables are very trending application of IoT. These are devices that are mostly integrated with watches (smart watches) or are standalone as fitness bands. These devices are capable to measuring and monitoring parameters like heart rate, step counts, calories burnt, etc. Also, these devices can be paired with smart phones to control the smart phones from smart watches.

## I. Healthcare

IoT devices can be integrated with healthcare services to make them more fast and accessible. Examples can be devices that continuously transmit high risk patient data to the hospitals. This can be very important in monitoring the health of patients that suffer from heart diseases, hypertension or other chronic illness. If the device senses that the patient's body vitals are below a certain level, it can trigger an alert to the relatives and call an emergency service like ambulance. Also data collection can be done for research and analysis.

## J. Smart Cars

Smart cars refer to the cars that have a wide-ranging network of many sensors, embedded software, and antennas. These help in making decisions regarding speed, accuracy, and avoid accidents on the road. Also, these cars are further being developed into autonomous vehicles where there will be no human intervention required to drive the car.

## 3. IoT IN HEALTHCARE

Healthcare is an indispensable part of human life. Regrettably, the gradually increase in populace and the associated increase in sickness is introduced noteworthy sprain on healthcare systems. Obviously, a resolution is necessary to decrease the strain on healthcare systems at the same time providing high-quality treatment and care to patients. Research in this area has shown that the IoT has a prospective resolution to lessen the pressures on healthcare systems. In this section, the IoT in healthcare system is highlighted and explored.

## A. IoT Sensors for Healthcare

The IoT has been recognized as a key module of a healthcare system founded on such developments of sensors or devices which can sense, assess and monitor the various medical parameters in the body (Bui & Zorzi, 2011). These IoT enabled healthcare sensors can aspire at a patient's health monitoring when they are away from hospital. Afterward, they can present real time data to the doctor, patient, or the relatives. Mc Grath and Scanaill (McGrath & Scanaill, 2013) have shown the variety of sensors that can be used for monitoring. There are various wearable sensor devices available which are ready with medical sensors that are competent of sensing diverse parameters like the pulse, heart rate, body temperature, blood pressure and respiration (Pantelopoulos & Bourbakis, 2010).

- Pulse Sensors

Possibly the usual read imperative sign, pulse can be utilizes to detect a huge assortment of crisis circumstances, like pulmonary embolisms, cardiac arrest, and vasovagal syncope. Pulse sensor has been broadly researched, for both the purposes, medical and fitness tracking.

- Blood Pressure

BP (Blood pressure) is often measured beside the other medical parameters. a known risk factor of high BP is hypertension for cardiovascular disease, including heart attack.

- Body Temperature Sensors

The next vital sign is body heat temperature, which might be utilized to identify fevers, heat stroke, hypothermia and so on. As, body temperature is a helpful diagnostics measure that would be incorporated in a IoT based healthcare system.

- Respiratory Rate Sensors

Next important sense is respiratory rate, the breaths count per minute. Because to the significance of respiration, many researchers have developed various sensors. Monitoring respiration might aid in the recognition of circumstances like asthma attacks, apnea episodes, tuberculosis, lung cancer and so on.

- Pulse Oximetry Sensors

It sense the oxygen level in the blood. Like blood oxygen, blood pressure level is not a fundamental sign, but does provide an indication of respiratory system and can aid in diagnostics of hypoxia conditions.

- Neural Sensors

It is used for sensing signals from neurons in the brain to understand the brain state and train it for improved concentration and focus. The neurons electronically communicate and generate electric field, which can be measured as frequencies. Further, based on the frequency, waves may be classified into alpha, beta, gamma, theta, and delta waves. The brain is wandering in thoughts or calm, can be detected based on brain wave. This is called as neurofeedback (Gruzelier, 2014), which can be taken in real time and can be utilized to train the brain to mange stress, focus, and encompass better mental health.

## B. IoT Sensor to aid

- Hearables

Hearables are hearing aid devices which have completely changed the way people who suffer from hearing loss relate with the outside world. It has the provisions to filter, even out and append layers to real-world sounds so that the people with hearing loss can get real life hearing experience.

- Ingestible sensors

These are special pills which have sensors embedded in them. When these pills are ingested, they can monitor our body from the inside. It can monitor whether the patient has taken the medicine and what effects the medicine is having in the patient's body. It is a boon for patients with ailments like diabetes, blood pressure, heart diseases.

- Mood elevating devices

These are mood improving devices which help in enhancing our mood. These devices can be worn over our head and they can send soothing currents to our brain which can help in releasing of calming chemicals thereby elevating the mood.

- Medical assistance through drones

Drones can be used for emergency services. First aid kits can be delivered through drones at any specified location in minimum time.

- Computer vision

This technology helps the visually impaired people to move around while detecting and helping them avoid the obstacles.

- Body vitals charting

These devices are implants on the patient's body and they can monitor parameters like blood pressure, heart rate, sugar levels, etc. This helps the medical professionals by saving a lot of time. It can also help the patient by saving their visits to the doctor just to get these vitals measured. The doctors can get routine updates and can prescribe the medicines to the patients accordingly. Also, when the patient is showing some danger signs the doctor can initiate emergency procedures and send ambulance for the patient to reach the hospital on time.

## C. IoT Solutions for Healthcare

The IoT has the potential and plays an important role to transform healthcare systems in a variety of healthcare applications, from supervision of chronic diseases, preventing disease to make hospital network smarter. The IoT based healthcare systems includes clinics, hospitals and other care amenities which sense, collect, and use data by combining the major business and technical trends of automation, mobility and data analytics to get better patient care delivery. The data collected from these IoT based healthcare devices and sensors can then be analyzed by the health care organization for the following purposes.

- Enhanced patient care

Patients who requires close attention could be closely monitored by offering novel or improve care services and delivery using IoT-driven sensing. The medical sensors collect various parameters and utilize cloud server to store and analyze the information and revert intelligent decision to health-worker for further care.

- Personalized patient care

By Learning more about patients' preferences and requirements concurrently enhance the quality of personalized care and experience care through steady attention.

- Optimize patient care

The collected data can be utilized to develop new solutions and services that improve efficiency and reduces the operating cost by eliminating the requirement for a health-worker to vigorously engage in data collection and analysis

- Remote monitoring

There are individuals' who don't have access to healthcare may suffer. But tinny, powerful IoT sensors are making it possible to those individuals'. These systems can be utilized to capture patient medical data, analyze the data and then share it with health-worker who can give proper medical recommendations.

- Early prevention / intervention

Healthy people could take advantage of IoT- based healthcare system by monitoring their daily health parameters and activities. For example, a senior citizen who is living alone, can detect an interruption in everyday activity or fall and report it to family members or emergency responders. For other example, an athlete such as a biker or hiker could benefit from such a solution at any age.

- Make hospital networks smarter

by actively monitoring the significant infrastructure, deployment of information technology and automating the healthcare system the hospital network can be made smarter.

## 4. IoT DEPLOYMENT ISSUES IN HEALTHCARE SYSTEMS

IoT develops an inter-connected environment of heterogeneous objects and platforms by dealing both physical and virtual world together. This section covers the challenges which has been faced while IoT deployment in healthcare systems. (Chaqfeh & Mohamed, 2012; Razzaque et al., 2016).

## A. Interoperability and Compatibility

As IoT is being considered a collection of heterogeneous device and platforms, there is an issue regarding interoperability. The deployment of different software and hardware component may not work properly. It is depended on whether the correct component has been chosen, the component has the proper reliability and the specification and infrastructure of the system.

## B. Scalability

This concern started from an expectation that a huge amount of devices are communicated as a part of the system. The services to connect all of them are frequently comparatively economical and therefore make a chance to functionality inflate. That makes complexity to increase gradually, causing intricacy for checking and performance.

## C. Measurement

By the lack of IoT measures and metrics it is difficult to deploy IoT-based healthcare system. Measures and metrics are the key factors. There are only few measures and metrics available to integrators and adopters.

## D. Synchronization

This concern generated by the distributed computing behavior of IoT systems. The distributed computing system has different activity and computations happening concurrently. In healthcare system there can be huge activities and computations occurring simultaneously, and those activities and computations must require some synchronization.

## E. Excessive Data

The anxiety is irresistible amounts of data that get produced, collected and processed in a system. It is essential to analyze all data to make an intelligent decision. Mostly IoT systems have a rapidly and dynamic workflow. There is a possibility to have huge inputs sources such as sensor devices, peripheral databases, the clouds, and other outside subsystems. The likelihood of not providing the integrity of huge data is a big concern.

## F. Design Complexity

IoT based healthcare faces a foremost measure because of design complexity for both its network as well as applications. The applications or services must be with lesser complexity and must not need additional knowledge for activities by its users.

## 5. SECURITY IN IoT BASED HEALTHCARE SYSTEMS

With the beginning IoT applications are typically related to individuals' personal life. In IoT based healthcare systems, the exchange of medical data and information becomes a daily routine. Due to the advancement, security and privacy are major concern for all types of IoT applications (Sharma et al., 2017). For example, medical data might be theft, deleted, tampered, or insecurely transmitted, permitting it to be used by adverse parties. Therefore, security and integrity of the medically sensetive data issues need to be addressed in all such IoT systems. This can be achieved by classical cryptography approach depending on the requirements and needs of an application. The system should have been developed with theses cryptographically mechanisms to guarantee the issues and integrity of patient's data, along with user authentication and access control mechanism. Security management of internal threats and policing are also required as security mechanism (Kamm¨uller et al., 2017).

### A. Vulnerabilities in IoT Based Healthcare Systems

Like classical information security, IoT security is not a small problem, it requires the mechanism to counter this problem. Utilization of different applicability and difference in deployment mode, the privacy and security are of extremely required. As an alternative, it should be predictable that the security issue of IoT is based upon standardization. Mostly the threats occur because of insufficient mechanism of security feature. Some vulnerability is there that stay undetected due to the inattention of security mechanism (Li et al., 2016). These Vulnerabilities are explored on the basis of attack mode and assessment of application, hardware, protocol, organization or software (Amit et al., 2013).

- Insecure protocols
- Insecure infrastructure
- Inefficient data encryption and transport
- Common managing interface
- Firmware insecurity
- XSS (Cross-site scripting)
- Unauthenticated scans
- Process isolation
- User policies and patching

These are some example by the exploration on loopholes and vulnerabilities at the different level of IoT-based healthcare systems.

### B. Security Frameworks for IoT Based Healthcare Systems

Here in this section the various security frameworks have been explored.(Park & Shin, 2017) (Ma et al., 2018).

- Encryption and Hashed Based Security

As the classical information security there must be some mechanism to provide the security in IoT system. In the system the information is travelling through insecure channels also, for that purpose some encryption and hash function based mechanism is required to secure information from the attackers.

- Access Control and Authorization-based Mechanisms

As the IoT has a huge number of sensors and devices. These sensors require an identity for authorization and accessibility to communicate among themselves. Consequently, support and security of those devices is subjected to the management of personal data as well particular services This type of mechanism provides securing the users by limiting the control over the usability of components and services. The strength of this mechanism depends upon the novelty of architecture were the devices dependent on other devices to connect and communicate.

- Secure Authentication-based Framework

Authentication of the devices and users is of extremely important and crucial. All the services and data are to be given to authenticated users only. The authentication guarantees the safety of authenticated and legitimate users by giving a safe communication mode.

- Risk-Assessment-based Adaptive Framework

A framework that is obliging to decrease the security challenges is a Risk-Assessment-based Adaptive Framework. It observes the complete system with regular intervals to identification of potential conflicting and to find changes through detection modeling. These frameworks guesses the attack type to pre-identify any potential risks and predicts the loss in leveraging services.

- Services-based Framework

Security of a network has been affected by the service type. Some of the services require light-frameworks while others require quick processing frameworks

- Reputation and Anomaly Detection Based Mechanism

To detect the misbehavior of user and Identification of false users or services, in an IoT system, collaboration of nodes mechanism is proposed. It is accountability of security mechanism to identify communities and users by the maintenance of reputation table and the watchdog mechanism. such a classified mechanism are executed by inspection the correctness of a user or device against the predefined policies of precise operations.

In this section a number of security mechanisms have been explored but due to the advancement in computing power at the adversary side, these security mechanisms are easily breakable. For this reason, It is required that the deployment of IoT system is done in ultra-reliable formations. Further, such cryptographic protocols are required by which the security implications, assessment, and threat modeling can be done against adversary during the functioning of IoT devices. For that purpose the quantum cryptography is deployed in IoT based healthcare system.

## C. Security Breaches in IoT Based Healthcare Systems

These days, the networks are globally extended and information is sent from many devices to many other. Information exchange has increased significantly. Important data and information are now being stored in devices and are transmitted through various channels to various locations.

As information plays such a fundamental role, the computer systems are being targeted by the cyber criminals to either steal the crucial information or to disturb the significant information system for some personal gain. Information channels are also being targeted the same way.

Classical cryptographic algorithms provide a set of techniques to make sure that the malicious intentions of the cyber criminals are disillusioned and in turn ensure that the actual end users have access to all the information in an uninterrupted manner. Here in this section the authors discuss the ways in which security can be compromised in healthcare systems working with IoT systems/devices.

There have been numerous security breaches when IoT devices are used in healthcare systems. The main reasons why IoT devices are so vulnerable to these breaches are:

- IoT devices are developed on obsolete software and old versions of operating systems that make them more prone to attack.
- IoT devices are more progressively storing and collecting large amounts of data due to which they are an attractive and easy target for cyber criminals.
- IoT devices act as a straightforward entry point for attackers wanting to move across across an IT network and get access to more critical information. Another way the systems can be attacked is by shutting them down altogether causing a heavy loss to the organization.

Healthcare data security breaches often render highly critical information, from personally identifiable information such as ID numbers, names, and patients' medical histories.

The IoT devices used in healthcare operate on very low resources, low power, limited computational memory and the security mechanisms have to be integrated within these limitations which are a tough task and hence complexity has increased.

These days medical equipments like MRI machines, Sonography machines are connected to a network to transfer the reports and images. Cyber criminals can hack the systems easily or attack the systems with ransom ware as these systems generally use older, less secure versions of operating systems. Medical equipments combined with IoT are the most vulnerable devices for cyber attacks as compared to all the other IoT devices.

The healthcare devices in the previous section can be hacked as:

- Hearables can be hacked to transmit wrong signals which could lead to distress to the person wearing them.
- If ingestible sensors are attacked that may lead to very bad consequences as it may lead to triggering wrong medicines at the wrong position inside the body.
- Medical drones can be hacked to change the route so that emergency help doesn't reach the patient in time
- Body vitals charting devices can be hacked and the transmitted information can be intercepted and used for wrongful purposes.

D. Classical Cryptography Techniques and their Disadvantages

- Steganography

Steganography is a cryptographic technique which is used to hide the content by embedding it in something else giving the notion that no content is present at all. In an image various parameters like pixel values, brightness, and filter settings can be changed in order to encode some information in it. The person seeing the image can never make out that there is some hidden information in the image.

In medical systems, electronic patient records can be embedded in images and stored/transferred with a good level of security.

Loophole in Steganography: cyber criminals can intercept the images and replace them with malicious images which when accessed by anyone can infect their device with virus or ransomware. Cyber criminals will put more prominence on making it tough to detect and trace the malware back to its origin.

- DES (Data Encryption Standard) Algorithm

DES is a symmetric block cipher cryptographic approach. The data blocks are encrypted in size of 64 bits. The encryption and decryption key has 56 bit. Initially the key consists of 64 bits but every 8th bit is removed (not used by encryption algorithm) making it 56 bits long. The algorithm works as: initially the 64 bit plaintext goes through a preliminary permutation that shuffles the bits to produce the permitted output. Output of the final round is of 64 bits that are a function of input plain text and key. The left and right halves of input are swapped to produce another output. Finally this output is passed through inverse permutation (used before) to get a 64 bit cipher text. After that for each round, a subkey Ri is created by combination of left circular shift and permutation. Data block size is 64 bit; the rounds will be 16. Hence, it will use dissimilar subkeys for each round. And the number of subkeys will be 16.

Loophole in DES algorithm: It is possible to break this algorithm with rigorous brute force attack on modern processors using parallel processing capabilities, so this algorithm is not used anymore for any crucial systems.

- AES (Advanced Encryption Standard) Algorithm

AES algorithm is a replacement of the DES algorithm. It is also a symmetric block cipher cryptographic algorithm. The data blocks are encrypted in size of 128 bits. Keys can be of 128, or 192, or 256 bits. AES treats 128 bits plaintext as 16 bytes data blocks. Number of rounds depends upon the size of key: 128 bits, 10 rounds; 192 bits, 14 rounds; 256 bits, 14 rounds.

The algorithm works as:

The 16 bytes of input is substituted according to a fixed table. The output is a matrix of size 4x4. Each row is then shifted to left: don't shift the first row, shift 2nd row by 1, shift 3rd row by 2, shift 4th row by 3. Now columns are mixed using a mathematical function which takes one column as input and outputs a transformed column. Now the 128 bits (16 bytes) are XORed with 128 bits of key. The process is repeated for the required number of rounds.

Loophole in AES algorithm: It uses algebraic structures that are too simple and every block is encrypted in the same fashion. This can be a very big advantage for a hacker if he/she decodes the pattern of encryption.

- RSA (Rivest–Shamir–Adleman) Algorithm

RSA algorithm is an asymmetric cryptographic algorithm. It consists of two keys: private key and public key. The public key is given to everyone whereas the private key is kept with the client who decrypts the message. The public key consists of 2 numbers in which one is a multiplication of a very large prime numbers. The private key is also determined from the same 2 prime numbers. The only way these keys can be compromised is if someone can factor the large number. The strength of encryption increases exponentially with the size of numbers.

Loophole in RSA algorithm: the basic loophole in this algorithm is that the security can be compromised if the numbers are factorized and prime numbers are determined. But if the numbers are very large it can be a very cumbersome task for a classical computer. So RSA is considered to be very secure. But we will see in further topics how this loophole can be exploited to break this secure crypto algorithm.

## 6. QUANTUM CRYPTOGRAPHY

Cryptography is known as a scientific approach of secret message sharing. It is used to develop and execute techniques of private message sharing between two parties along with the presence of a third party. Further the Quantum cryptography (QC) is one of the most vigorous cryptographic approaches consists on the sharing of a common secret key by using the polarization of photon with a secure channel between the parties; QC is depended upon consistent and fundamental of quantum mechanics principles. The method shows that the level of security is depending upon complexity of the key and the protection of the used channel and not the complexity of the algorithm's process. QC concerned in 20$^{th}$ century, is depended on quantum mechanics principle and on the principle of photon polarization and Heisenberg Uncertainty principle.

Heisenberg's uncertainty principle says that it is nearly not possible to measure the quantum state without disturbing the system. That can only be measured in a specific measurement time and with a particular polarization. This concept is a key factor in opposing the adversary attempt in a system which is QC enabled.

The second important principle of QC is photon polarization. It describes that the photon particle can be oriented or polarized in a particular direction so that a filter can detect the said photon in a particular polarization else it will be destroyed.

In QC, 'qubit' is known as a bit of quantum information(Bhatt et al., 2018). In QC the photon is characterize based upon the polarization plane, ranging from 0° to 180°with horizontal and vertical orientation.

The QC was developed by C. H. Bennet and G.Brassard in 1984 as fraction of a study between information and physics(Bennett & Brassard, 1984). It is the unstoppable photons associated with Heisenberg Uncertainty principle that makes QC a tempting option for guarantee the security of data.

QC does not send or receive any message signal in its place it is only utilized to generate and for distribution of key. The key generation is depending upon the how and how much photon have been received by a recipient [25

The way the private key cryptosystems work is based on sharing of private keys between the sending and receiving parties so that the message can be encrypted and decrypted correctly. Let the sending party be 'A' and receiving party be 'B'. 'A' encode the message with a private key and sends the message to

'B'. Now, 'B' will need the private key 'A' used in order to decrypt the message. Here comes the main issue: how to exchange the keys so that they are not intercepted by a malicious eavesdropper and used to read the message? Here, the concept of Quantum Cryptography comes into use. Let's see how:

We have been using classical computers everyday for our daily tasks and experiencing its benefits in several ways. However, there are some challenges that are beyond the scope of classical computers to solve as they don't have enough computing power and resources. So, to solve some of those problems, we can use Quantum Computers.

Our classical computers rely on 0 and 1 bits to store and maneuver data and information, whereas Quantum computers use Quantum bits (or, Qubits) derived from the quantum mechanical laws to work with data.

Qubits can be in a coherent superposition of multiple states simultaneously. And the superposition can be broken in 0 or 1 if measured.

Quantum Cryptography is a field of cryptography that uses the laws of Quantum mechanics to develop a system that has the maximum security. No one can intercept the system without getting noticed by either of the parties involved in the transfer of secure data. This property of Quantum mechanics is based on several facts such as:

- The particles are uncertain in nature and exist as a superposition of two or more valid states.
- Photons are generated randomly in one of two quantum states.
- Quantum property can never be measured without disturbing or changing it.
- Only some of the properties of a particle can be cloned, not the whole particle.

Quantum Entanglement is another property which plays an important role in Quantum Cryptography. Entanglement of particles describes a relationship among their primary properties. Quantum Entanglement occurs when two particles become inseparably linked and whatever changes happen to one particle immediately affects the other particle regardless of the distance they are separated by. Entanglement is broken when entangles particles decohere through interaction with environment like measurement through outside interception. This property can help us detect if anyone is maliciously intercepting the network.

Quantum cryptographic systems also use the well known Heisenberg Uncertainty Principle which says that measuring a Quantum system disturbs it and gives incomplete information about the system. This in turn alerts the users of some kind of eavesdropping on the communication channel.

One of the most common cryptographic algorithms today (RSA algorithm) uses the property of prime factorization of large numbers to derive the keys. Factorizing large numbers is a very cumbersome and time taking task for the classical computers which can very easily be accomplished by the quantum computers using the Shor's algorithm.

## A. Shor's Algorithm

Shor's algorithm is a quantum approach for factoring a large number N. It has $O((\log N)^3)$ time complexity and $O(\log N)$ space complexity.

Current cryptographic algorithms like RSA work on a basic principle where the key is a multiplication of 2 very large prime numbers. No classical algorithm exists yet which can solve the factorization of large numbers in polynomial time. So currently RSA is believed to be unbreakable.

Shor's algorithm is probabilistic in nature. It generates the accurate answer with a good probability and repetition of the algorithm improves the performance.

It works on 3 principles:

- Modular arithmetic
- Parallelism in Quantum computers
- Quantum Fourier Transform (QFT)

## 7. QUANTUM KEY DISTRIBUTION

Quantum Key Distribution is secure method of communication which is based on the laws of Quantum mechanics. Using QKD, the parties involved in information exchange can produce a random private key which is only known to them, and use that for encryption and decryption of messages to be transferred.

There are various QKD protocol developed by the researchers. Some are using single state polarization and some are entangled photon to generate the secret key. Because of the need of channel's security to keep the channel secure from attackers, the QKD with BB84 protocol is utilized. The QKD approach can transmit over 144 Km trough free space when it is executed in 5G-IoT [26]. Additionally, this protocol includes two various kinds of channels which can be utilized in a 5G wireless communication [27]: the main sort is the Quantum channel and its job is the exchange of the regular polarization of light's key, and the second sort is the ordinary channel which empowers the communication between the two parties and the exchange of the encoded data.

Subsequently, the QKD doesn't avoid Man in the middle attack, so the adversary can use spoofing to mask himself as an authorized collector at that point can peruse the traded information, however with the deployment of some authentication techniques, for example, counter based it can be prevented [28].

An important quantum phenomenon that QKD uses is the ability to detect the eavesdropper due to disturbance in quantum system because of the measurement of the photons. It also uses the phenomenon of Quantum Entanglement and Quantum Superposition to transfer the information securely over a communication channel.

Quantum Entanglement is the phenomenon where the particles have a relationship between their fundamental properties. They are governed by the same wave function and the changes occurring in one particle are reflected in a complementary (opposite in nature) way to the other particle.

Quantum Superposition is a phenomenon where two or more Quantum states can be added to produce a new Quantum state that will be valid. Conversely, every Quantum state can be represented as a superposition of two or more valid and distinct Quantum states.

Let us assume two parties: Alice and Bob. Let Alice be the sender and Bob be the receiver. In QKD the information is usually encoded in single photons.

The protocol described below was developed by Charles Bennett and Gilles Brassard in 1984 and hence this protocol is famously known as the BB84 protocol.

Alice can choose to encode the bit sequences in one of the following polarizations: horizontal polarization, vertical polarization, +45° or -45°. The horizontal and vertical polarizations are called as rectilinear schemes, the +45° and -45° polarizations are called as diagonal schemes. The horizontal and +45° represents the binary bit 1 and the vertical and -45° represents the binary bit 0. Here, when an external attempt to intercept is made the photon polarizations change resulting in change in the final measurements, so intruder is detected.

Alice uses the four polarizations randomly while sending the photon stream to Bob. The photons reach Bob and he then uses either rectilinear (+) or diagonal (X) bases to read the polarizations of the photons. Bob doesn't know the bases Alice used and hence he randomly guesses any one of the beam splitters- rectilinear or diagonal. Now after all the photos have been sent Bob tells Alice (thorugh a public channel) which bases he has used for photon measurement and Alice compares them with the bases she used while sending the photons. The photons measured by Bob using the wrong base are discarded and the other ones are kept and these photons become the key for communication. Finally Alice and Bob cross check their keys by adding the bits; both should either get an odd calculation or even calculation.

This key can only be used once. Hence it is called one-time-pad (OTP).

Now if there was any eavesdropper in Alice and Bob's communication, he would have measured the photons and once measured the photon states will have changed. One can never read/measure a photon and just forward it without any changes without being detected, so Alice and Bob will know that security has been compromised.

The mechanism described above can be depicted as follows:

*Table 1. Quantum Key Distribution Protocol*

| Alice's bit sequence | 1 | 0 | 1 | 1 | 0 | 0 | 1 | 1 | 0 | 0 | 1 | 1 | 1 | 0 |
|---|---|---|---|---|---|---|---|---|---|---|---|---|---|---|
| Bob's detection | + | X | + | + | X | X | + | + | X | + | X | X | + | + |
| Bob's measurements | 1 | 0 | 0 | 1 | 0 | 0 | 1 | 1 | 0 | 0 | 0 | 1 | 0 | 0 |
| Key | 1 | - - | - - | 1 | 0 | 0 | - - | 1 | 0 | 0 | - - | 1 | - - | 0 |

There is another very famous Quantum Cryptography protocol developed by Artur Ekert in 1991 known as the E91 protocol. This protocol uses the entangled photon pairs to secure the communication channel. The entangled pairs of photons are created and distributed between Alice and Bob such that both of them get either of the photon from the entangled pair. When Alice and Bob measure the photons with vertical or horizontal bases they get the same answers with 100 percent probability. Also when they both use complementary bases they will get the same answers with the same 100 percent probability. But the results are random and Alice can never make out whether Bob has vertical polarization or horizontal polarization. When the eavesdropper tries to intercept and measure the photons the polarization gets disturbed and this can be detected by Alice and Bob. So this is also a secure protocol that will prevent interception in communication channel.

## 8. QC IN IOT-BASED HEALTHCARE SYSTEMS

IoT based healthcare has many applications as already discussed in the previous sections. Healthcare is a very critical field of application where very important data are transmitted from one device to the other[29]. Unfortunately this is the field with the least secure connections and networks. If cyber criminals get hold of these data records they can exploit them in various different malicious ways. If a patient's health record gets leaked to a cyber criminal it can lead to identity theft, insurance fraud, wrongful acquisition of drugs and selling in black market, etc. So it is very important to protect these data.

As we saw in previous sections that classical cryptography is not 100 percent secure and unbreakable. Quantum cryptography can break the classical algorithms quite easily and all the secure data can be leaked easily[30]. So, to prevent this from happening we can apply the Quantum cryptography protocols in the medical devices and equipments.

Devices like body vitals tracking devices, ingestible sensor pills, etc. are required to be safe guarded against attacks.

Take an example of body vitals tracking device: This device continuously monitors the body parameters like heart rate, blood pressure, sugar levels, etc. and transmits the data continuously to the hospital. If it was intercepted, the eavesdropper can read all the data being transmitted and can change the data which may either lead to a fatal condition not being reported or the doctor prescribing a wrong dose of medication which could eventually be fatal for the patient.

Also, hospital equipments like Sonography machines are now enabled with technologies which can transfer the captured images to a computer for faster record processing. If this transfer is intercepted, the eavesdropper can access the crucial medical images and use them for insurance frauds or for his/her own benefit in a wrong way.

So it is increasingly important to secure the transmissions from these devices.

The authors' proposed method is to integrate the healthcare devices with quantum cryptography protocols [31].

The devices can implement the BB84 protocol explained in the previous section and establish a secure channel for communication.

Let us take the example of hospital equipment like Sonography machine. When the machine wants to transfer the images and data records to the computer, the machine can encrypt the data or photons using either the horizontal, vertical, +45° or -45° polarizers and send the data to the computer. The computer can then randomly choose either rectilinear beam splitter or diagonal beam splitter. Then the coinciding photons between the machine and the computer are kept as the secret key for communication. This way the communication can be secure[32].

Another example is of body vitals tracking device. Usually the device communicates with a smart phone application which in turn transfers the data to the medical center (in some cases there can be direct communication from device to the medical center, but let us consider the mentioned scenario here). So here, 2 channels are required to be secured: one from device to the smart phone and other from the smart phone to the medical center receiver, as interception can happen at any of the channels. Now the smart phone works as both the transmitter and receiver so it has to perform both the actions. First the device establishes a secure key with the smart phone according to the BB84 protocol and sends the body vitals' data. Then the smart phone establishes a secure connection with the medical center receiver according to the BB84 protocol and forwards the data.

Next example is of the ingestible sensor pills. These are the pills that go into the patient's body and monitor if the patient is taking regular medication and if the medication is working properly in the body. This pill is currently not approved for human use but soon it will be out for human consumption. This pill will then use a three layer communication: it will transmit the data to a wearable patch (because it is difficult to integrate the support for communication with a smart phone in a small sized pill), which will transmit the data to smart phone, which will finally transmit the data to the medical center receiver. So now there will be three paths for communication and three paths will need to be secured. The wearable patch as well as the smart phone will now act as both senders and receivers. The BB84 protocol will be followed between the pill and the wearable patch, the wearable patch and the smart phone, and the smart phone and the medical center receiver.

These are some ways in which Quantum cryptography can be used in healthcare devices. Thus crucial medical records can be secured.

## 9. ADVANTAGES OF QC IN IoT-BASED HEALTHCARE SYSTEMS

The QC is theoretical unbreakable approach which can secure the medical data in the IoT-based health-care system. To enable secure IoT-based healthcare system, all devices, users, applications and services within the system are QC enabled.

In adding together to IoT containment, QC security mechanism provide layered security across multiple levels of the network. At the lower physical perception layer the device and user are kept secure by QC as it is can be used for authentication and authorization purpose. That means only limited persons those are authentic and authorized to access the data is permitted to use the medical data.

Next at the network layer, QC protected the medical data while transmission by provide the secure channel. It protect network from adversary, potential back doors, embedded malware and vulnerabilities.

Further at the application layer the QC protocols provide the security by identifying malicious user, activity, and services, detection of anomaly, limiting bandwidth and blocking the unwanted user and achieve QoS[33].

With the application of Quantum cryptography in eHealth systems we can achieve many benefits. First and the most important benefit is that communication will become secure and non-interceptable. As the communication will be secured, the data and information being transmitted will be 100 percent correct which can help the patients in getting correct treatment; it can help the doctors better understand the patient's condition and ailment and help them recommend proper treatment and medications. Also, when the data is used for research and analysis it will yield better results and help in the growth of our medical systems so that we can be ready for any diseases that might attack in the future.

We can take an example of the most recent pandemic which started in the late 2019: Sars-Cov-2 or Covid-19. Tracking device can be installed on some of the infected patients of all age groups which can help the medical professionals and researchers in understanding the way the virus works inside the human body and behavioral patterns can be deduced from this data. Tracking devices can also be placed on the recovered patients and analysis can be done on how their bodies react after the deadly virus is removed and many important conclusions can be derived about the nature of the virus.

We can say that as the classical cryptographic algorithms work on the basis of assumptions that are computationally unproven they are not said to be completely secure whereas Quantum cryptography uses the laws of Quantum mechanics and Physics, so it is much more reliable and secure than classical algorithms.

The QC gives the overall security to IoT-based healthcare system. The followings are some additional measures which QC provides along with the security of sensitive data.

- Data Integrity

The QC is capable to provide the data integrity in IoT-based healthcare system. Data integrity is very much essential regarding the medical data because bases on this data only the intelligent medical decision are taken.

The integrity and quality data involves lots of parameters like, accuracy, availability, fidelity, and confidence that the data cannot be tampered or corrupted with. These concerns are taken care by QC in IoT-based healthcare system.

- Reliability

Reliability is a key concern for IoT–based healthcare systems. It ensure that the system is working perfectly for any given context and environment. QC gives guarantee for reliability by ensuring secure information of the context and environment.

- Certification

QC provides the certification without any conflict. QC resolves the problem regarding the selection of certificate provider. With the satisfactory answers to these questions, it is improbable that QC can offer the certification that is required by IoT adopters.

- Credential management

By keeping the credentials like sensitive data and keys which are essential for secure communication, safe and secure, QC provide the credential management mechanism. The security and privacy of devices against network-based vulnerability is ensured by credential management.

## 10. CHALLENGES OF QC IN IoT-BASED HEALTHCARE SYSTEMS

There are a few challenges when Quantum cryptography is considered. First is that a commercially usable quantum computer has not yet been designed, so these algorithms cannot be applied to the IoT devices as of now. And integrating the quantum components on such small scale devices can take some time. Quantum computers are very difficult to build and program. Hence they have a high error rate such as noise and faults.

In future developments, we can expect some new protocols and algorithms for the quantum computers so that the error rates are reduced and commercial quantum computers can become a reality.

Quantum computing in future can be very much useful in developing vaccines for new found diseases within days. Presently the vaccine making procedure can take years because the molecules are made in the laboratory and then tested against various parameters. Molecules are made without any predictions beforehand. And we can only know the results after the tests. After the testing too, it is not possible to predict the future complications these molecules could create. With the help of quantum computing we can simulate the molecules with the help of already present databases and the data collected from tracking of patients (as mentioned in the previous section). Vaccines can be made within a number of days along with almost all the predictions of the future complications.

## 11. CONCLUSION AND FUTURE WORK

The most awaited IoT uprising in healthcare system is already in progress, as shown in this work. These mechanism and techniques is just the tip of the recognizable iceberg, as new circumstances and situations continue to appear to measure the urgent requirement of accessible and affordable, care. In the intervening time, It has been seeing that the IoT approaches of automation and security mechanism continue to be recognized.

IoT security mechanism especially in healthcare application should support the huge data storage and computations because of data generated by the various devices are huge. This is, unfortunately, not always feasible. However, there are some IoT devices which have sufficient capabilities, like for storing, processing and communicating capabilities. The important patient data records, medical images, details, etc. are to be protected the most. Because if these things are leaked any malicious cyber criminal can take wrong advantage like faking medical records for medicines, insurance frauds, blackmailing the owner/organization for money in return for the sensitive medical records, creating fatal conditions for a patient, etc. To avoid this we need to secure the communication channels so that they are not intercepted in between the transfer of data. The problem that were recognized are also somewhat prejudiced by the outlook of the healthcare data since information was produced by them to take the intelligent medical decision. Approaches for IoT-based healthcare data security offer an exciting research field producing solutions that harmonize security mechanism and protocols for application and services.

Classical cryptographic algorithms are not powerful enough to prevent the systems against the attacks. The algorithms may seem secure now but they are just based on the unproven solvability of the logic by the classical computers.

When the authors talk about Quantum Cryptography, they mention how easily classical cryptography can be broken by the quantum cryptography protocols. Also, the authors discuss how the IoT devices in the healthcare sector can be secured with the help of applying the quantum cryptography algorithms in the IoT devices. This way the devices can be secured 100 percent against any interception in the networks.

For example, in the post-quantum era, that is vulnerable against cryptoanalysis done by quantum computer, security would have a key issue because all the classical cryptographic approaches will be replaced by quantum cryptography. Even the exchange and distribution of cryptographic keys for wireless communication would be based on QC.

By exploring various approaches and techniques to secure IoT data, it has been concluded that QC is very much appropriate for the IoT-based healthcare system. Applying QC in IoT will further enter in to all significant application of connected smart environment. In near future, IoT applications will be pervasive and the security issue of that application will be measured by QC. Under such critical secure setting, QC is supposed to be ubiquitous.

## REFERENCES

Amit, Y., Hay, R., Saltzman, R., & Sharabani, A. (2013). *Pinpointing security vulnerabilities in computer software applications.* US Patent 8,510,842.

Bennett, C. H., & Brassard, G. (1984). *Quantum cryptography: Public key distribution and coin tossing. IEEE Intl. Conf. Computers, Systems and Signal Processing.*

Bhatia & Sumbaly. (2014). *Framework For Wireless Network Security Using Quantum Cryptography.* Academic Press.

Bhatt, A. P., Babuta, T., & Sharma, A. (2018, February). Quantum information processing and communication: Asian perspective. *Intl. Journal of Computer and Mathematical Sciences, 7*(2), 616–621.

Bhatt, A. P., & Sharma, A. (2019, September). Quantum Cryptography for Internet of Things Security. *Journal of Electronic Science and Technology, 17*(3), 213–220.

Bui, N., & Zorzi, M. (2011). Health care applications: a solution based on the internet of things. In *Proceedings of the 4th International Symposium on Applied Sciences in Biomedical and Communication Technologies (ISABEL '11).* ACM. 10.1145/2093698.2093829

Chaqfeh, M. A., & Mohamed, N. (2012). Challenges in middleware solutions for the internet of things. *Proceedings of the 13th International Conference on Collaboration Technologies and Systems (CTS '12),* 21–26. 10.1109/CTS.2012.6261022

Chen, C. Y., Zeng, G.-J., Lin, F. J., Chou, Y. H., & Chao, H.-C. (2015, October). Quantum Cryptography and Its Applications over the Internet. *IEEE Network, 29*(5), 64–69. doi:10.1109/MNET.2015.7293307

Chen, S., Xu, H., Liu, D., Hu, B., & Wang, H. (2014, April). A Vision of IoT: Applications, Challenges, and Opportunities with China Perspective. *IEEE Internet of Things Journal, 1*(4), 349–359. doi:10.1109/JIOT.2014.2337336

Ferreira, P., Martinho, R., & Domingos, D. (2010). Iot-aware business processes for logistics: limitations of current approaches. *Proceedings of the Inforum Conference, 3,* 612–613.

Gruzelier, J. H. (2014). EEG-neurofeedback for optimising performance. I: A review of cognitive and affective outcome in healthy participants. *Neuroscience and Biobehavioral Reviews, 44,* 124–141. doi:10.1016/j.neubiorev.2013.09.015 PMID:24125857

Guo, B., Zhang, D., Wang, Z., Yu, Z., & Zhou, X. (2013). Opportunistic IoT: Exploring the harmonious interaction between human and the internet of things. *Journal of Network and Computer Applications, 36*(6), 1531–1539. doi:10.1016/j.jnca.2012.12.028

Guo, B., Zhang, D., Yu, Z., Liang, Y., Wang, Z., & Zhou, X. (2013). From the internet of things to embedded intelligence. *World Wide Web (Bussum), 16*(4), 399–420. doi:10.100711280-012-0188-y

Kamm¨uller, F., Kerber, M., & Probst, C. W. (2017). Insider threats and auctions: Formalization, mechanized proof, and code generation. *Journal of Wireless Mobile Networks, Ubiquitous Computing and Dependable Applications, 8*(1), 44–78.

Khan, S., Abdullah, J., Khan, N., Julahi, A. A., & Tarmizi, S. (2017). *Quantum-Elliptic curve Cryptography for Multihop Communication in 5G Networks. IJCSNS International Journal of Computer Science and Network Security.*

Lee, M., & Cho, J.-D. (2014). Logmusic: context-based social music recommendation service on mobile device. In *Proceedings of the ACM International Joint Conference on Pervasive and Ubiquitous Computing (UbiComp '14)* (pp. 95–98). 10.1145/2638728.2638749

Li, J., Li, J., Xie, D., & Cai, Z. (2016). Secure auditing and deduplicating data in cloud. *IEEE Transactions on Computers*, *65*(8), 2386–2396. doi:10.1109/TC.2015.2389960

Liang, G., & Cao, J. (2013). CircleSense: a pervasive computing systemfor recognizing social activities. In *Proceedings of the 11th IEEE International Conference on Pervasive Computing and Communications (PerCom '13)* (pp. 201–206). IEEE.

Ma, C., Kulshrestha, S., Shi, W., Okada, Y., & Bose, R. (2018). E-learning material development framework supporting vr/ar based on linked data for iot security education. In *International Conference on Emerging Internetworking, Data & Web Technologies* (pp. 479–491). Springer. 10.1007/978-3-319-75928-9_43

Mashal, I., Alsaryrah, O., Chung, T.-Y., Yang, C.-Z., Kuo, W.-H., & Agrawal, D. P. (2015). Choices for interaction with things on Internet and underlying issues. *Ad Hoc Networks*, *28*, 68–90. doi:10.1016/j.adhoc.2014.12.006

McGrath, M. J., & Scanaill, C. N. (2013). *Body-worn, ambient, and consumer sensing for health applications. In Sensor Technologies.* Springer.

Pantelopoulos, A., & Bourbakis, N. G. (2010). A survey on wearable sensor-based systems for health monitoring and prognosis. *IEEE Transactions on Systems, Man and Cybernetics. Part C, Applications and Reviews*, *40*(1), 1–12. doi:10.1109/TSMCC.2009.2032660

Park, K. C., & Shin, D.-H. (2017). Security assessment framework for iot service. *Telecommunication Systems*, *64*(1), 193–209. doi:10.100711235-016-0168-0

Perera, C., Zaslavsky, A., Christen, P., & Georgakopoulos, D. (2013). Context aware computing for the internet of things: A survey. *IEEE Communications Surveys and Tutorials*, *16*(1), 414–454. doi:10.1109/SURV.2013.042313.00197

Picard, R. W., & Picard, R. (1997). *Affective Computing* (Vol. 252). MIT Press.

Razzaque, M. A., Milojevic-Jevric, M., Palade, A., & Cla, S. (2016). Middleware for internet of things: A survey. *IEEE Internet of Things Journal*, *3*(1), 70–95. doi:10.1109/JIOT.2015.2498900

Sharma, A., Ojha, V., & Goar, V. (2010, May). Security aspect of quantum key distribution. *International Journal of Computers and Applications*, *2*(2), 58–62. doi:10.5120/625-885

Sharma, V., Lee, K., Kwon, S., Kim, J., Park, H., Yim, K., & Lee, S.-Y. (2017). *A consensus framework for reliability and mitigation of zero-day attacks in iot* (Vol. 2017). Security and Communication Networks.

Spiller, T. P. (1996, December). Quantum Information Processing: Cryptography, Computation, and Teleportation. *Proceedings of the IEEE*, *84*(12), 1719–1746. doi:10.1109/5.546399

Sufyan. (n.d.). *Defeating Man-in-the-Middle Attack in Quantum Key Distribution*. Academic Press.

Voas, J. (2016). *Networks of Things, NIST Special Publication (SP) 800-183*. National Institute of Standards and Technology.

Xu, F., Curty, M., Qi, B., & Lo, H. (2015, March). Measurement-Device-Independent Quantum Cryptography. *IEEE Journal of Selected Topics in Quantum Electronics*, *21*(3).

Zhao, J.-C., Zhang, J.-F., Feng, Y., & Guo, J.-X. (2010). The study and application of the IOT technology in agriculture. *Proceedings of the 3rd IEEE International Conference on Computer Science and Information Technology (ICCSIT '10)*, 462–465.

# Chapter 15
# Constructive Solutions for Security and Privacy Issues at the Edge:
## Securing Edge Framework – A Healthcare Application Use Case

**Indra Priyadharshini S.**
*R. M. K. College of Engineering and Technology, India*

**Pradheeba Ulaganathan**
*R. M. K. College of Engineering and Technology, India*

**Vigilson Prem M.**
*R. M. D. Engineering College, India*

**Yuvaraj B. R.**
*Anna University, India*

## EXECUTIVE SUMMARY

*The evolution in computing strategies has shown wonders in reducing the reachability issue among different end devices. After centralized approaches, decentralized approaches started to take action, but with the latency in data pre-processing, computing very simple requests was the same as for the larger computations. Now it's time to have a simple decentralized environment called edge that is created very near to the end device. This makes edge location friendly and time friendly to different kinds of devices like smart, sensor, grid, etc. In this chapter, some of the serious and non-discussed security issues and privacy issues available on edge are explained neatly, and for a few of the problems, some solutions are also recommended. At last, a separate case study of edge computing challenges in healthcare is also explored, and solutions to those issues concerning that domain are shown.*

DOI: 10.4018/978-1-6684-6311-6.ch015

## INTRODUCTION

Edge is only the augmentation of the fog. Edge computing has the accompanying attributes: it ranges to contiguous physical areas; upholds online examination; the administration is given by savvy, yet not ground-breaking gadgets; underpins different interchanges arranges, and is circulated computing The objectives of the edge computing worldview are to diminish the information volume and traffic to fog workers, decline inertness, and improve nature of administration (QoS). Edge computing comprises 3 fundamental parts, (an) IoT nodes, (b) edge nodes, and (c) back-end fog. The principle parts of layer 1 are the IoT gadgets and correspondence joins between them. These gadgets are answerable for detecting and acting in the earth by producing occasions and sending them to higher layers. Layer 2 involves the switches, switches, entryways, and gadgets that encourage the associations between gadgets at the edge of the system and the Internet. This layer mirrors the great definition proposed for Edge computing. At present, the Edge infrastructure idea may likewise remember the gadgets for layer 3. Layer 3 contains the infrastructure for customary Fog computing (elite workers, and server farms with immense capacity and processing limits) (Ren et al., 2019)

Another captivating zone where the modernization has pushed its foundations is IoT. IoT is getting expanding coordinated into our everyday lives. Contemplating this IoT can be utilized to give a skilled and sorted out way to deal with and improve the healthcare of humankind. By utilizing these smart articles, they can be coordinated into healthcare to offer wise types of assistance for far off observing the wellbeing and prosperity of patients. By utilizing this it could help manage staff deficiencies and reaction times inside healthcare. As IoT has the attribute of pervasiveness the frameworks associated with healthcare (medication, apparatuses, and people) can permit the ceaseless observing and the board of these substances. Along these lines, the expense and nature of the healthcare offered can be improved via robotizing processes that were recently directed by people. How IoT and Edge go connected at the hip?

Edge computing gives calculation, stockpiling, and systems administration administrations between end gadgets (Things) and customary fog computing server farms. Edge computing stage is ordinarily situated at the edge of the system; here and there the expression "edge" is utilized reciprocally with the expression "edge". It gives low inertness, area mindfulness and improves Quality of Service (QoS) and Quality of Experience (QoE) for healthcare administrations by diminishing idleness and expanding its consistency when contrasted with the fog. Despite edge computing being a promising new turn of events, to serve IoT Things and applications effectively, there are various explorations provokes that should be thought of. Inside edge computing which can comprise of different gadgets in the system (switches, switches, and so on.) and end gadgets or potentially things (smartphones, wearable gadgets, and virtual sensor nodes that could be utilized inside healthcare frameworks)? Consequently having the option to gather, configuration, and process this heterogeneous information just as the capacity of correspondence among various gadgets is as yet an open examination challenge.

Considering that edge devices work at the edge of networks, edge faces new security also, security challenges on the head of those inherited from fog computing. Assault vectors, for example, man-in-the-middle have the potential to become an ordinary assault in Edge computing. Edge computing is a promising answer for help data fusion, filtering, and investigation in e-healthcare systems since it extends data computing from fog to the edge of a network and is more intelligent and powerful than e-healthcare devices. Without appropriate security and protection protections for underlying connected health systems, providers and patients need trust in the arrangements. News about the absence of security of IoT devices and unethical practices of some companies that gather and abuse personal data from owners of connected devices have made consumers care about the technology and more proactive in protecting personal data. Even when the IoT health care system itself isn't compromised, the care receivers can be the casualties of overzealous enterprises that have questionable use of patient data with potential legal ramifications, as medical data in numerous countries is protected by law.

In the customary edge-assisted data sharing scheme the edge node is integrated to process and re-encrypt the shared data for efficient medical examination. Privacy leakage and security threats may happen during data partaking in edge-assisted e-healthcare systems. Initially, personal privacy may be disclosed during data sharing. Unauthorized users may access the shared data collected from patients. For example, some corrupt pharmaceutical companies may analyze the health data and get patients' health status to spread advertisements and medication advancements. The shared health data might be tampered with during data transmission from data collection to storage. For instance, the blood glucose of patients might be altered when it is delivered to healthcare centers, leading to incorrect healthcare treatments. To protect the shared data against privacy leakage, unauthorized data access, and data tampering, Ciphertext-Policy Attribute-Based Encryption (CP-ABE)(Tang et al., 2019) is widely proposed for health data sharing through the fog, because it can uphold multiple data accessing standards with data confidentiality preservation. Patients define access policies to encrypt their shared data and send the ciphertext to the fog server. Data users access the shared data and decrypt the ciphertext just if their attributes fulfill access policies. But the same level of protection can't be given to the edge side, as they are different devices in nature. Some of the popular research articles give solutions to general issues like data accumulation, latency, preliminary security for transferring data, etc., However, the accompanying issues despite everything remain unaddressed. (1) How would we pre-process health data on the edge node for efficient data use? (2) How would patients be able to retrieve and decrypt their health data after the edge node encrypts them? (3) How would we be able to guarantee patient privacy when the shared data are re-encrypted? by the semi-trusted edge node? (4) How would we prevent unauthorized data access if the edge node collides with other entities for the shared plaintext?

With these brief introductions, this chapter is organized as follows: the immediate next topic briefs the reason for the evolution of edge computing from fog (along with issues in fog), then a general architecture of edge with obligatory working details, attacks &threats, Cryptographic techniques, authentication and access control policies and a case study of edge based healthcare framework with specific security issues, solutions and recommendations is explained.

## NECESSITY OF EDGE COMPUTING – FROM THE PERSPECTIVE OF SECURITY AND PRIVACY

Before getting into the necessity of Edge, one ought to get into the real difference between fog and Edge. Some of the key features which make both of these computing ends differently are, Fog architecture is centralized and comprises large data centers that can be located the world over, a thousand miles from client devices. Edge architecture is distributed and comprises a large number of little nodes located as close to client devices as could be expected under the circumstances. Edge goes about as a mediator between data centers and hardware(Ren et al., 2017), and hence it is closer to end-users. On the off chance that there is no edge layer, the fog communicates with devices directly, which is time-expending. In fog computing, data processing takes place in remote data centers. Edge processing and storage are done on the edge of the network close to the source of data, which is critical for real-time control. Fog is more powerful than an edge regarding computing capabilities and storage limits. The fog comprises a few large server nodes. Edge includes a huge number of little nodes. Edge performs momentary edge examination due to moment responsiveness, while the fog focuses on long haul deep investigation due to slower responsiveness. Edge provides low latency; fog — high latency.

A fog system collapses without an Internet connection. Edge computing uses different conventions and standards, so the danger of failure is a lot of lower. Edge is a more secure system than the fog due to its distributed architecture(Dimitrievski et al., 2019). Like Fog systems, an Edge system is composed of IaaS, PaaS, and SaaS respectively, alongside the expansion of Data services. The Edge IaaS stage is created utilizing Cisco IOx API, which includes a Linux and CISCO IOS networking operating system. Any device, for example, switches, routers, servers, and even cameras can become an Edge node that has computing, storage, and network connectivity. Edge nodes collaborate among themselves with either a Peer-to-Peer network, Master-Slave architecture, or by framing a Cluster. The Cisco IOx APIs enable Edge applications(Wang et al., 2014) to communicate with IoT devices and Fog systems by any user-defined convention. It provides simplified management of utilizations, automates policy enforcement, and supports multiple development environments and programming languages. The data service decides the suitable place (Fog or Edge) for data examination identifies which data. Numerous researchers are embracing a security-centric or secure by design reasoning for creating such distributed systems. Yet, this viewpoint is still in its outset and needs a comprehensive understanding of the security threats and challenges confronting an Edge infrastructure. This chapter provides a systematic review of Edge stage applications, determines their possible security holes, analyses existing security arrangements, and then advances a rundown of comprehensive security arrangements that can eliminate numerous potential security flaws of Edge-based systems.

Fog Security Alliance(Waters & Encryption, 2011) has identified five basic security issues and these issues directly sway the distributed, shared, and on-demand nature of fog computing. Being a virtualized environment like Fog, the Edge stage can likewise be affected by the same threats however there are very solid security mechanisms that could easily get integrated with edge architecture.

1. Authentication and Trust issues
2. Privacy
3. Security
4. Fog Servers
5. Energy consumption

Details about the above sorts of threats are explained in (Curtis, 2020). However, the betterment over the fog stage can be discussed as follows. The accompanying rundown details three such technologies, including some of their key differences with Edge systems. Edge Computing performs localized processing on the device utilizing Programmable Automation Controllers (PAC), which can handle data processing, storage, and correspondence. It poses an advantage over Edge computing as it reduces the purposes of failure and makes each device more independent. However, the same feature makes it hard to manage and accumulate data on large scale networks. Foglet is a middle piece of the 3-tier hierarchy "mobile device - foglet - fog". There are four significant attributes of Foglet: entirely self-overseeing possesses enough compute power, low end-to-end latency, and expands on standard Fog technology. Foglet differs from fog computing as application virtualization isn't suitable for the environment, consumes more resources, and can't work in offline mode. A miniaturized scale data center is a little and completely useful data center containing multiple servers and is capable of provisioning numerous virtual machines. Numerous technologies, including Edge computing, can benefit from Microdata centers as it reduces latency, enhances reliability, is relatively portable, has underlying security conventions(Yang et al., 2015), saves bandwidth utilization by compression, and can accommodate numerous new services. So on the whole the accompanying attributes make the edge it gets different from the fog and makes it better than the above.

An Edge framework will have moderately small registering assets (memory, preparing, and capacity) when contrasted with a Fog framework, notwithstanding, the assets can be expanded on-request; They can process data generated from a diverse set of devices; They can be both dense and sparsely distributed based on the geographical area; They uphold Machine-to-Machine correspondence and wireless connectivity; an Edge system can be installed on low specification devices like switches and IP cameras, and One of their principal uses is currently for mobile and portable devices. On the whole, these are the main differences between fog and edge because of which edge has become flexible to most of the devices. So it's time to learn some problems that are available with edge and to know some common solutions to those problems.

## GENERAL EDGE ARCHITECTURE

The physical distance to the Cloud and the available resources inside the infrastructure increases the latency and reduce the Quality of Service (QoS). One of the recent standards in this area to solve issues of Cloud Computing is Edge Computing. Even though there are several naming for Edge computing, for example, Fog Computing and Cloudlets, inside this paper, just the term Edge Computing will be used. Figure 1 shows how the layered architecture can be the plot in between Cloud, Fog, and Edge Computing. Edge Computing combines multiple technologies, for example, Cloud Computing, Grid Computing, and IoT. It includes an extra tier between the Cloud and the end-devices and moves computational power to the end-device as close as could be expected under the circumstances. This means that, in the need of more computational resources by the end-device or a system, the errand can be offloaded to an Edge Server instead of the Cloud. Edge Computing is expected to reduce the latency and increase the QoS for errands which can't be handled by these devices. These undertakings are normally computationally heavy, for example, enormous data processing, video processing, computerized reasoning, or time-sensitive. On the off chance that the calculation must be done in real-time, usage of Cloud is not feasible since Cloud and Internet offer just best-effort service and delivery. Devices with limited computing limits may likewise have basic deadlines for their essential errand. In these circumstances, the errand can be offloaded to an Edge Server utilizing the same imperatives and can be accomplished at this level. Depending on the outcome of the undertaking, the system reacts to the result, e.g., sends the data back to the end-device. The Edge Servers can likewise offload the errands to other Edge Servers by considering the available resources, network, and calculation delays. One of the principle objectives of Edge Computing is to reduce latency and to keep the QoS as high as could reasonably be expected. Edge Computing intends to solve the issues of Cloud Computing or IoT by including an extra tier between the IoT devices and back-end infrastructure for computing and correspondence purposes. As this tier additionally have intermediate components for the primary gathering, investigation, calculation of the data. These intermediate components are called Edge Servers. Edge Server is definitely not a complete replacement of the Cloud with respect to its functionalities. Even though its available resources are

*Figure 1. Layered Architecture of Edge with Fog and Cloud Layers*

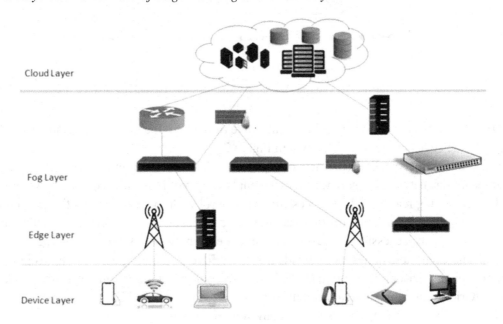

higher than the end-devices, they are lower than the Cloud. Instead, exceptionally repeated errands, or undertakings that require in time response are preferred to be executed in an Edge Server. The proposed architecture for Edge Computing comprises of Cloud Tier, Edge Tier, and Device Tier. In the Device Tier, there are end-user devices. The green squares in the Edge Tier are Edge Servers. These servers gather, aggregate, analyze, and process the data before offloading them to the Cloud Tier or send back to the devices. The end devices can be in the same physical area, or in different areas as depicted in the figure. When an end-device needs to communicate with the Cloud, first, the request is sent to then, if the Edge Server is capable of completing the assignment without anyone else, it naturally handles the data and responds to the end-device with the result. If not, the data is offloaded to another server in the same tier provided that it exists. Otherwise, the data is offloaded to the Cloud. Edge Computing is a worldview which uses Cloud Computing technologies and gives more responsibilities to the Edge tier. These responsibilities are namely, computing offload data reserving/storage, data processing, service appropriation, IoT management, security, and privacy protection. Edge Computing is a worldview which uses Cloud Computing technologies and gives more responsibilities to the Edge tier. These responsibilities are namely, computing offload data reserving/storage, data processing, service appropriation, IoT management, security, and privacy protection Without restricting the Cloud Computing features, Edge Computing needs to have the accompanying requirements, some of which are likewise defined for Cloud Computing: Interoperability, Scalability, Extensibility, Abstraction, Time sensitiveness, Security & Privacy, Reliability

Edge arrangements are typically multi-layered disseminated models incorporating and adjusting the remaining task at hand between the Edge layer, the Edge cloud or Edge organization, and the Enterprise layer(Li et al., 2018). Moreover, when we talk about the Edge, there are the Edge gadgets and the neighborhood Edge workers. It should be noted that Edge processing structures are an extension of IoT (Internet of Things) models and use terms like OT for operational innovation. The change and union of

*Figure 2. Edge Computing Device Hierarchy*

IT and OT advancements can convey colossal incentive throughout the following decade. Brief flow of computing in the edge environment is shown in Figure 2.

From a systematic perspective, edge networks provide a distributed computing system with hierarchical geography. Edge networks target meeting stringent latency requirements, reducing power utilization of end devices, giving real-time data processing and control with localized computing resources, and decreasing the burden of backhaul traffic to centralized data centers. And of course, excellent network security, reliability, and accessibility must be inherent in edge networks. Edge Computing utilizes wide scope of advancements and unites them. Inside this area, Edge Computing uses numerous innovations, for example, remote sensor organizations (WSN), portable information securing, versatile mark examination, Fog/Grid Computing, disseminated information activities, distant Cloud administrations, and so forth. Also, it consolidates the accompanying conventions and terms:

1)  **5G correspondence**: It is the fifth era remote framework that focuses on the higher limit, lower power utilization, and lower dormancy contrasted with the past ages. Because of the expanded measure of information between the information, 5G is required to understand traffic issues that emerged with the expanded number of associated gadgets.

2)  **PLC conventions**: Object Linking and Embedding for Process Control Unified Architecture (OPC-UA) is a convention created for mechanical computerization. Because of its transparency and strength, it is broadly utilized by ventures in the region of oil and gas, drug, advanced mechanics, and assembling.

3)  **Message line specialist**: MQTT and TCP/IP are famous message conventions of savvy sensors and IoT gadgets. Supporting these message intermediaries, Edge Computing expands the gadget check that it interfaces. For the issue of MQTT security, AMQP is helpful in the correspondence with Cloud Computing worker.

4)  **Event processor**: After messages of IoT show up in the Edge worker, occasion processor investigations those messages and makes semantic occasions utilizing pre-characterized rules. EsperNet, Apache Spark, and Flink are a few models for this empowering influence.

5)  **Virtualisation**: Cloud administrations are conveyed as virtual machines on a Cloud worker or bunches. Utilizing virtual machines permit running different examples of working frameworks (OS) on a similar worker.

6)  **Hypervisor**: As well as a virtual machine, execution assessment and information dealing with are required and acknowledged by the hypervisor to control virtual machines in the host PC.

7)  **OpenStack**: Managing numerous assets could be testing. OpenStack is a Cloud working framework that makes a difference control of pools of processing and capacity assets quiet through a control board and observing devices.

8)  **AI stage**: Rule-based motor and Machine learning stage upholds information investigation in neighborhood level. As expressed in

Segment III-A, this is very critical to arrive at one of the objectives of Edge Computing which is to assemble, break down, and play out the first sifting of the information.

9)  **Docker**: Virtual machines work with establishment of working frameworks. In contrast to virtual machines, Docker is a Container as a Service (CaaS), which can utilize a solitary shared working framework and run programming in detached condition. It just requires the libraries of the product which makes it a lightweight framework without agonizing over where the product is conveyed.

That is about the prologue to edge design with every minor detail. We should save this one as the base for comprehension for investigating the security issues and their proposals which can be application explicit.

## GENERAL ISSUES IN EDGE ARCHITECTURE

### Web Advancement

What's more, edge nodes can recognize users based on MAC addresses or cookies, track user requests, cache files, determine nearby network conditions. It is additionally possible to embed feedback contents inside a web page to measure the user browser's rendering speed. The feedback content reports directly to the Edge nodes and illuminates the user's graphical resolution, current area reception (if wireless), and network congestion. In another comparable paper, Edge computing altogether reduced the response time of a Fog-based temperature prediction system. Due to Edge systems, the prediction latency was decreased from 5 to 1.5 s, web-page show latency from 8 to 3 s and internet traffic throughput from 75 to 10 Kbps. Utilizing Edge stages for upgrading web-services will likewise introduce web security issues. For example, if user input isn't properly validated, the application becomes vulnerable to the code injection assaults, SQL injection, where SQL code provided by the user is consequently executed resulting in the potential for unauthorized data access and change. This could result in the compromise of the entire Edge system's database or the sending of modified data to a central server. Additionally, due to insecure web APIs, assaults like a session and cookie hijacking (acting as a legitimate user), insecure direct object references for illegal data access, pernicious re-directions, and drive-by assaults could force an Edge stage to expose itself and the attached users.

### Reconnaissance Video Transfer Preparing

A video data stream generated by camera sensors is sent to the respective Edge nodes, where it is stored and processed. The privacy of the stream ought to be maintained as it contains sound and visual data, which are transmitted to heterogeneous clients. Here, not exclusively is the security of Edge node is significant, yet the network and all end-user devices involved in the transmission ought to likewise be considered, especially against APTs. On the off chance that an Edge stage or network contains any bugs due to the absence of diligence, the critical video stream may be viewed, altered, and even destroyed. It is significant that the Edge node ensures a secure connection between all imparting devices and protects multi-media content by obscurity techniques, fine-grained access control, generating a new connection for the video stream, selective encryption, and restricting the number of connections.

## Sparing Energy in Edge Computing

This specific application encourages the use of Edge stages in putting away and processing specific (user-defined) sorts of the (private) data locally in the Edge nodes, reducing the correspondence cost and delay. However, the presence of such private data places the Edge stage in a sensitive position(Merlino et al., 2019). As previously mentioned there are numerous threats, which are capable of bargaining the CIA of data, for example, noxious insiders can read, alter, and delete data. These issues can be resolved using encryption, authentication (uniquely approving and verifying each user), data characterization based on sensitivity, checking, and data coverage.

## Catastrophe Reaction and Antagonistic Situations

Disaster recovery is a sensitive area whereby Edge systems and connected devices are supposed to work in extreme circumstances. In this case, the integrity and accessibility of the system are more significant than confidentiality. Wireless security conventions can do checksum (detect data errors), encrypt packets with negligible resources, and arrange fine-grained access control to carefully validate users (terminating unwanted connections(Glikson et al., 2017)). Furthermore, in case of emergency and key management to prevent losing decryption keys, these mechanisms ought to be considered to retain accessibility and integrity without trading off the overall performance of the system.

## SECURITY AND PRIVACY ISSUES IN EDGE COMPUTING:

Edge Computing facilitates the shift of storage and computation jobs from execution in cloud environments to the edge of the network. But this comfort comes with the confront questions in Privacy and security. The integration of emerging technologies such as Cloud or Edge computing, IoT, Artificial Intelligence, Machine Learning, Big Data Analytics is bringing enormous outcomes in various domains like Finance, Health, Education, E-commerce, etc., (Alabdulatif et al., 2019) The characteristics of Edge computing gives an easy way for lightweight devices to efficiently perform the complex processing tasks in the network edge itself. The Healthcare industry is also undergoing a huge paradigm shift from its traditional working model to digital services. The rapid advancement of this digitization of health records, IoT devices, and edge computing all together is transforming the healthcare industry.

The wide use of smart IoT devices, attached to networking technologies these days have improved less expensive and more reasonable medical systems. IoT has become a significant factor in the development of these health frameworks, giving (cheap cost) sensors to monitor the status of patient life. Health Frameworks based on Edge computing consists of sensitive patient data which has to be protected from unauthorized access (Alabdulatif et al., 2019). The electronic health records stored should be anonymous in such a way that the patient's identity should not be revealed, as the privacy of the patients has to be preserved. Sensitive patient health records should maintain the integrity and must be available with no delay. Hence security and privacy of outsourced patient's sensitive data is a challenging problem in the health frameworks built on Edge Computing.

## Where to Enforce Security?

Security procedures are not confined to the basic networking level and can likewise be significant at much higher abstractions, for instance, at the service provisioning level. As services become more distributed, data such as service type and interface, device hostname, and possession might be viewed as delicate and require protection. Huge consideration has been devoted to the design of protocols for private (as in privacy-preserving) service discovery over the network (Khan et al., 2017). Unfortunately, a significant number of these conventions were proposed as of late and have not been completely investigated concerning security, performance, or simplicity of deployment, which adds up to interesting research challenges.

1) **Cloud Data Center – Top Layer**:

It is important to indicate that, all edge paradigms might be supported by many infrastructures like centralized cloud service and the administration frameworks, core infrastructures are managed by similar third party providers such as mobile network operators. This would raise tremendous difficulties, for example, privacy leakage, data altering; denial of service attacks and service control, given these core infrastructures might be semi-trusted or totally untrusted. This results in challenges of privacy disclosure and damage to data integrity.

2) Distributed Edge Nodes:

As previously mentioned, edge computing understands the interconnection of IoT devices and sensors by the combination of various communications, for example, mobile core network, wireless network, and the Internet, which raise many network security difficulties of these communication infrastructures. By utilizing the servers at the edge of the network, the conventional network attacks, such as denial of service (DOS) and distributed denial of service (DDOS) attacks, can be restricted efficiently. Such attacks will just upset the vicinity of the edge networks and have very little impact on the core network; additionally, the DOS or DDOS attacks happening in core networks may not truly interfere with the security of the edge data centers..

3) IoT Devices on the Edge:

In edge computing, the edge devices dynamically played as an active participant in the distributed edge network at different layers, so that even a small loophole in the security aspect of edge devices may lead to dangerous outcomes for the whole edge ecosystem. For example, any devices controlled by an adversary can endeavor to agitate the services with a mixture of false information or intrude the system with some malicious actions. Likewise, malicious devices can control services in some particular circumstances, where the malicious enemies have captured the control advantage of one of these devices.

## ATTACKS & THREATS

The following list shows the predominant threats and attacks that are encountered by the edge computing frameworks in various application domains (Xiao et al., 2019). These types of threats are usually

*Figure 3. DDoS attack on Edge Server*

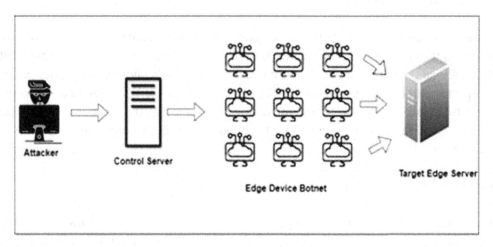

caused because of the weak framework design or flaws in the design, security misconfigurations and errors due to the implementation.The protective mechanisms deals with detection of such loopholes in the system which acts as an entry point for the attacks or preventing the attacks from happening through blocking the unusual activities.

1)    Distributed Denial of Service Attacks (DDoS)

DDoS is the attack which disturbs the services given by a single or set of servers by using botnets i.e. by compromising a cluster of edge devices and sending continuous requests to the server. This attack is a dangerous attack as it blocks the service of authorised users through bogus requests pretending as legitimate requests. A conventional DDos attack happens when the attacker continuously sends many request packets to the server from the compromised devices in the distributed network. The server's hardware resources gets exhausted servicing these bogus requests persistently thereby leaving the legitimate requests unserviced. DDos attacks are more troublesome in case of edge servers because they are computationally less capable to defend themselves when compared to cloud servers. These bogus requests might confuse the edge server to decide that all its communication channels and hardware resources are busy. Edge servers provide services to the edge devices connected to them. In general, these edge devices are weak with respect to security because they have limited hardware resources and multiplatform software. Attackers utilize this and attack the edge devices first and then they use these compromised edge devices to attack the edge server. A notorious example is the 'Mirai' botnet where the attacker compromised 65000 IOT devices and these devices are used to initiate a DDoS attack to attack the servers like Kerbs and Dyn.

The Figure 3 depicts an example DDoS attack on Edge Server. DDoS attacks can be categorized into flooding attacks and zero day attacks.

a.    Flooding Attacks:

This attack is a common type of DDoS attack which stops or limits the service of a server by flooding huge numbers of bogus or malicious packets. The different kinds of flooding attacks are as follows,

i.    i) UDP Flooding:
ii.   The attacker persistently floods many UDP packets to the victim edge server resulting in the failure of the victim edge server where it can't service the legitimate UDP packets and leads to disturbed UDP services from the edge server.
iii.  ii) CMP Flooding:
iv.   This attack makes use of ICMP protocol and sends a huge number of ICMP request packets continuously not even bothering about the reply messages. This makes the victim edge server suffer on the two way communication channel receiving the ICMP echo request and sending the reply messages which slowly turns the server incapable.
v.    iii) SYN Flooding:
vi.   The three way handshake protocol of TCP is utilized by this attack. The attacker sends a lot of SYN requests with spoofed IP addresses continuously and the victim servers respond with SYN+ACK messages to the spoofed IP addresses, waiting for the reply ACK messages which would never come from the spoofed IP addresses.
vii.  iv) Ping of Death (PoD):
viii. This attack exploits the maximum size of an IP packet which is 65535 bytes. The attacker creates an intended IP packet with malicious content which is more than the maximum number of bytes. so the IP packet is splitted into fragments. These segmented packets are again reassembled at the edge server again. If an attacker keeps on sending such large packets, the victim edge server is kept busy and all its resources are utilized in the fragmentation and reassembly process.
ix.   v) HTTP Flooding Attack:
x.    This type of attack generates many standard requests like HTTP GET, PUT, POST and sends them as legitimate requests to the target edge server. This results in the choking of edge server as it becomes busy serving bogus requests and it runs out of computational resources to resolve the real legitimate requests.
      vi)   Slowloris Attack:

In this type of attack, the attacker initiates a number of incomplete HTTP connections resulting in keeping the target server maintaining these partial HTTP connections in parallel till it reaches the maximum pool size after which the server crashes. Incomplete HTTP connections are created by sending only the HTTP headers and not the subsequent messages.

b.    **Zero-day DDoS attacks**:

This attack is usually launched by an experienced attacker where he finds an unknown vulnerability in the application code or operating system running on the target server. This unknown vulnerability found is called zero-day vulnerability, which is exploited and attack is made with a relevant payload causing serious damage in memory or computing ability leading to server crash. These attacks cause serious damage and it is difficult to detect and defend because it utilizes the zero-day vulnerability which is not known before.
      2) Side Channel Attacks:

The escape characters are not filtered in SQL queries when it is processed in database management systems. Attackers make use of this loophole and attempt to do SQL injection attacks resulting in loss of data confidentiality and integrity. In addition, a more serious problem is that attackers can inject malicious scripts or malwares through SQL select statements. Consider this scenario, when an edge server gets service from other cloud servers or edge servers, it visits them as a client and accesses the services. If an attacker tries to perform an XSS attack now, it is a client side attack which injects malicious javascript codes into the code executed by the target server. The client is the edge server which gets the service and the target server is the edge or cloud server which provides the service. Unlike conventional client-server systems, XSS attacks can happen in edge servers in edge computing model.

The technique of compromising security and privacy through publicly available information is called side channel attacks. This kind of public information which need not be privacy-sensitive is called side channel information.Such side channel information related to secret private data must be protected. Side channel attacks are more prevalent in edge computing systems. Because there are lot of side channels in edge computing systems like communication paths, power consumption by edge devices, /proc file system used by smartphones, sensors etc., Consider the following scenario, when an attacker compromises an edge framework by collecting particular side channel information (for example, accessing the data from /proc file of mobile phones) and the obtained information is given as input to particular machine learning models, a lot of sensitive inferences can be obtained as output.

a) Communication Channel attacks:

Utilizing the communication channels in the edge computing system is the easiest way to initiate the attack and also an effective way to steal the sensitive information. Because the attacker need not be an edge device or an edge server to monitor the communication channel, he can be any malicious node on the network who passively sits and eavesdrops the communication channel to pull out the sensitive information from it. Communication channel attacks can be categorized into two kinds i) Analyzing the packet streams in channel and ii) Analyzing the wave signals in channel.

b) Attacks based on Power Consumption:

Attacks based on the analysis of power consumption of various devices on the edge system reveals the information about the devices itself through the power consumption profiles.The consumption of power is based on the strength of computations of a process. so this might give a lead to explore its relationship with sensitive data. This attack can be categorized into i) attacks based on power consumption measured by meters ii) attacks based on power consumption measured by oscilloscopes.

i) Attacks based on power consumption measured by meters:

Nowadays smart electric meters are available which precisely calculates the power consumption of households. In the era of IoT and Cloud, smart homes are implemented where everything is connected. Therefore analysing the power consumption data of smart home appliances, sensitive activities at home can be detected.

ii) Attacks based on power consumption measured by oscilloscopes:

In embedded systems, security is achieved by implementing the cryptographic algorithms in a chip. The power consumption of a hardware device can be measured by an instrument called an oscillator. Researchers have proved that the key to break the algorithm can be guessed by analysing the power consumption of hardware. however such power analysis attacks can be done only when the attacker is able to access the target device physically or gets access to the target device through some malicious applications.

c) Attacks based on smartphone communication channels:

Smartphones play a key role in edge based systems. In addition to IoT devices, smartphones also act as edge devices in the system. They are more advanced than IoT devices as well as more prone to attacking. Attacks on smartphones can be done in two ways.i) attacks on the /proc file system and ii) attacks on the sensors embedded in smartphones

3) Malware Injection Attacks

The process of injecting malicious code or malwares into computers is termed as malware injection attacks. The conventional computer networks have strong attack defence systems to enforce security and maintain data integrity like firewalls, Intrusion Detection Systems etc., But edge based systems have less computational power devices and minimally configured edge servers. so they may not have strong defence mechanisms and are prone to these injection attacks. Figure 4 shows the architecture of malware injection attacks in edge computing systems.

*Figure 4. Malware Injection attacks in Edge systems*

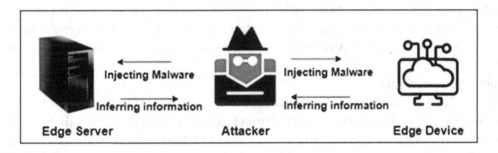

As shown in the architecture diagram above, the malwares are injected to both edge server and edge devices to steal sensitive information.

i) Injection on Edge Server

In edge based frameworks, injection attacks primarily focus on the edge servers. Popular injection attacks which gets placed in OWASP top 10 releases include XSS - cross site scripting, CSRF- Cross-site Request Forgery and XML based attacks. SQL injection attacks utilizes the loophole of SQL's nature of not filtering the escape characters in the user constructed sql queries. Authorized users may construct sql queries with columns they are allowed to access but the attacker constructs SQL queries inserting escape characters like quotation marks and tries to access the unauthorized data.

XSS attacks tries to include malicious client side scripts in the web data content which is automatically executed by the server. CSRF is a similar attack where an edge server is tricked to execute malicious code through web applications. When edge based frameworks use Simple Object Access Protocol (SOAP) for communication, XML based attacks can be easily deployed because SOAP exchanges messages in XML format.

ii) Injection on Edge Device

IoT devices are lightweight and heterogeneous in nature of both hardware and firmware. If any zero-day vulnerabilities are found by attackers in firmware, malwares can be injected to gain the command and control of edge devices.

## CRYPTOGRAPHIC TECHNIQUES TO ENFORCE SECURITY

In the edge computing paradigm, the edge devices are more reliable and have incredible performance than cloud computing terminals, they are data owners, yet in addition they also play the job of data producers. For an edge user, the advantages from edge thing are as per the following: processing offload, caching the data, storage ability and processing, decreased maintenance cost, minimal transmission consumption and response time, and also the distributed request and service delivery from edge things, brings about a more elevated level of utilization of resources, and along these lines, forces little power cost to service providers (Alabdulatif et al., 2019). Despite the fact that the edge computing model has many advantages contrasted with conventional cloud computing model, there are still security concerns that developed as a hitch to acquisition of edge computing model.

1) Symmetric key Encryption

Symmetric encryption algorithms can be grouped into stream ciphers and block ciphers where the plain text bits are encoded individually in stream ciphers and using blocks of bits in block ciphers. Despite the fact that block ciphers require more hardware and memory, their performance is commonly better than stream ciphers since they have a permutation stage and also a substitution stage. As recommended by Shannon, plaintext must be prepared by two primary substitution and permutation stages to achieve the confusion and diffusion properties.

2) Public Key Encryption

Symmetric key encryption or public key encryption is utilized to solve the issue of key circulation. In Asymmetric keys, two keys are utilized; private and public keys. Public key is utilized for encryption and private key is utilized for decryption (E.g. RSA and Digital Signatures). Since users will in general utilize two keys: public key, which is known to the public and private key which is known uniquely to the user[ 2]. There is no requirement for conveying them preceding transmission. In any case, public key encryption depends on mathematical functions, computationally intensive and isn't exceptionally effective for small mobile devices. (Curtis, 2020). Asymmetric encryption strategies are very nearly 1000 times more slow than Symmetric methods, since they require more computational processing power.

3) Attribute Based Encryption

Attribute-based encryption (ABE) is a basic cryptographic technique to control the decryption capacity of the data owner over the encrypted data. An attribute-based access control framework comprises two elements: 1) Trusted authority (TA) who is responsible for distributing attribute keys and dealing with users' attribute set, 2) The user incorporates the message sender and the recipient which relate to the data owner and user. The basic Attribute-Based Encryption (fuzzy IBE) as a modification of IBE scheme in which the identities are replaced with a set of attributes. In ABE algorithm, the attributes of the user is mapped as $Z*p$ by the hash functions, which the ciphertext and private keys are identified with the attributes. Two types of ABE are i) Key Policy based ABE (KP-ABE) and ii) Cipher Text based ABE (CP-ABE).

4) Identity based Encryption

Identity-Based Encryption (IBE) is a public key encryption methodology where a public key is a random string, for example, an email address or a phone number (Patonico et al., 2019). The respective private key in the pair must be produced by a Private Key Generator (PKG) who knows about a master secret. Utilizing this development, anybody can encode messages or validated signatures without prior key distribution past the spread of public boundaries and the public key "strings." This is valuable where the arrangement of a conventional authentication authority-based PKI is badly designed or infeasible, as IBE-based frameworks don't need certificate manager, eliminating the requirement for certificate searches and complex certificate revocation schemes. The main focus of Identity-Based Cryptography is that private keys must be received from the PKG. How one safely and productively acquires this private key is essential to the security of the framework. For instance, how the PKG concludes who has to be given the private key related to an email address is pivotal to maintain the integrity of the system. Another thought is cost: key generation can be computationally costly.

5) Proxy Re-encryption

Proxy Re-encryption (PRE) is the ciphertext switching protocol which converts the ciphertext of one key into ciphertexts of another key by using a proxy element. In other words, a proxy is made to convert the ciphertext encrypted by the data owner's public key into a ciphertext as if it is encrypted by data user's public key with the help of encryption key and also there is an assurance that the proxy may not be able to decrypt the ciphertext. So the PRE scheme is popularly used in cloud based applications for performing data forwarding, data distribution, and data exchange operation in multiuser environments.

6) Homomorphic Encryption

Homomorphic encryption, otherwise called privacy homomorphism, is a cryptography method that permits users to work the ciphertext to perform arbitrary mathematical operations. This means, when we perform one basic mathematical operation, say addition, on the ciphertexts and, at that point when you decrypt, this decryption result is the same as the outcome that we legitimately perform addition on the plaintext. The benefit of this particular encryption form is that the user can perform any operation on the encrypted data with explicit conditions, the encryption strategies with these benefits can improve the effectiveness of data processing, guarantee the protected transmission of data, and also can get the correct decryption results. From this unique computing feature, the homomorphic encryption technique can be broadly utilized in data encryption, preserving the privacy, encrypted querying, and secure multi-party computation, The different types of Homomorphic encryption are as follows,

a.  Full Homomorphic Encryption
b.  Partial Homomorphic Encryption
c.  Somewhat Homomorphic Encryption

7) Searchable Encryption

It is desirable to store data on data storage servers, for example, mail servers and file servers in encrypted form to decrease security and privacy dangers. In any case, this normally infers one needs to forfeit usefulness for security. For instance, if a customer wishes to recover just reports containing certain words, it was not recently realized how to let the data storage server perform the search and answer the question without loss of data classification''. The most immediate arrangements are as per the following: 1) One technique is to download all the ciphertext data to the nearby and decryption, at that point search in plaintext with keywords, however this activity will likewise download the superfluous records that don't contain the specific keywords which may cause the asset squandering of network and storage. Moreover, the decryption and searching activity of superfluous records will cost the enormous computational overhead, and this technique isn't reasonable for low broadband network situations. 2) Another outrageous arrangement is sending the private key and keywords to the storage server, at that point decode the encrypted archives and search on the server. An undeniable downside to this methodology is that the user's private data is re-presented to the server which will be a genuine danger to

*Figure 5. Entities in Access Control Policies*

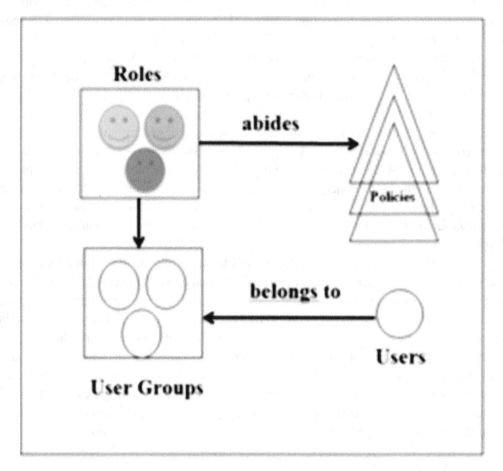

data security and individual privacy. Two types of searchable encryption are 1) Symmetric searchable encryption and 2) asymmetric searchable encryption.

## AUTHENTICATION POLICIES AND ACCESS CONTROL SCHEMES

Access control policies identify authority, that is, power which has been authentically acquired, and to how authority is designated. Access control is related to guarantee that subjects and processes in a system access resources in a controlled and approved way (Moffett, 1994). Resources, for example, files and directories must be shielded from unapproved access and access authorization must be allocated distinctly by subjects or managers with authority to do such tasks. The Figure 5 shown below describes the entities participating in the Access Control Policies.

1)    Attribute based Access Control

Attribute-based control policies (ABAC) is one of the transcendent innovative technologies to control information access in cloud computing, which can be all around applied to the distributed architecture and accomplished fine-grained data access control by setting up the decoding ability based on a user's attributes.

2)    Role-based Access Control

Role Based Access Control (RBAC) can give an adaptable access control and privilege management by users-to-roles and roles-to-objects authority mapping mechanism which implies the RBAC can manage the access of users to resources and applications dependent on recognizing roles and actions of users in the framework(Osborn et al., 2000).

3)    Discretionary Access Control

Discretionary access control policies allow users to assign rights to objects through building rules by subjects. Subjects have the control to decide who can access objects. DAC model is followed by major operating systems to implement file systems (Li & Tripunitara, 2005). For example, sample.txt rwxr-xr-x indicates the owner of sample.txt can read, write and execute the file, the other user groups can execute and read the file but could not write it.

4)    Mandatory Access Control

Mandatory access control (MAC) assigns privileges based on a tree -like structured hierarchical model (Ausanka-Crues, 2001). All users in the system are assigned with a security clearance level. All object resources are assigned with the security label in the hierarchical model. Users can access a resource in the same security level or below level in the hierarchy.

## CASE STUDY: HEALTHCARE FRAMEWORK BASED ON EDGE COMPUTING

## Introduction

Another use of Edge computing in healthcare includes Electrocardiogram (ECG) feature extraction to diagnose heart diseases. This involves medical sensors communicating data to an Edge layer that stores data in distributed databases, extract ECG features, and giving a graphical interface to show results in real-time.. The detection of a person having a stroke is of key importance as the speed of medical intervention is a life basic. Two fall detection systems have been implemented utilizing the Edge stage, named U-FALL and FAST. The two systems distribute computational errands between Edge and Fog stages to provide an efficient and scalable arrangement, which is essential as it considers a fast detection and notice of a patient fall. Patient health records contain sensitive data and there are multiple focuses in any Edge stage where they can be compromised, for example, by exploiting any system and application vulnerability, unauthorized data access while in storage or during transmission, malignant insiders threat, and while offering data to other systems. Medical sensors are constantly communicating data to Edge stages, through either wired or wireless connection. It is quite possible to compromise patient privacy, data integrity, and system accessibility by exploiting sensors and their underlying correspondence network. Wireless sensors for the most part work in open, unattended, and hostile environments. This ease-of-access can increase the chances of assaults like DoS, report disturbance, and selective sending assaults. What's more, if the Edge node manages sensitive data and needs access control mechanisms, it may leak the data due to account hijacking, unintended access, and other vulnerable purposes of entry. To stay away from such issues, exacting policies ought to be enforced to keep up a significant level of control utilizing multifaceted or shared authentication, private networks, and fractional (selective) encryption.

## Requirements of the Edge based HealthCare Framework

The requirements (Zhang et al., 2018) of healthcare framework build using edge computing is as shown in the Figure 6 below.

*Figure 6. Security Requirements*

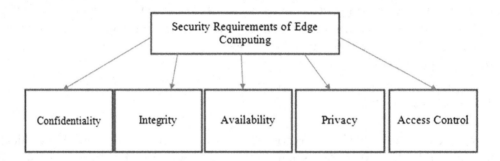

1)  Confidentiality

The basic need of any healthcare framework is to ensure that the EHRs of patients are only accessed by the EHR owner and authorised users, if any. EHRs must not be accessed by unauthorized users when it is being processed or stored in the edge or cloud data centers. In edge computing, the sensitive health data of patients is moved to the edge server and its ownership and control are isolated, which makes users lose their physical authority over the outsourced health data. Moreover, the sensitive health data in the edge servers are prone to data loss, breach of EHRs (Electronic Health Records), illegitimate data access or alterations (for example duplicating or removing the health records, and disclosure or distribution of health records). To address these dangers, a proper data confidentiality scheme has to be prepared to ensure the security of health data moved in the edge servers, which implies the patient's sensitive data has to be encrypted before moving it to the edge servers. At present, to maintain the confidentiality and to secure the patient data, the traditional method is to encrypt the sensitive data, and then it is outsourced to edge servers, after which it is uploaded to the data centers and can be decrypted by any legitimate user on demand.

2)  Integrity

This requirement ensures the correctness of the patient's data stored in the edge or cloud. If the integrity of the EHR is not maintained, it may lead to serious problems. Assume if the vital signs of the patient are altered by an intruder, it may result in critical issues even causing the loss of the patient's life. Data integrity is a significant issue for the security of edge computing since the patient's data is moved to the edge servers while the data integrity is questionable during this transit. This leads to the process that the data owners must check the integrity and accessibility of outsourced data to ensure that there are no undetected modifications of data by any illegitimate users or systems. With respect to edge computing, data integrity must be concentrated on the following factors, batch auditing, dynamic auditing, privacy preserving and low complexity.

3)    Availability

Health data stored in the system should be made available to the authorised users on demand for quick diagnosis. To maintain the purpose of automated healthcare services the immediate availability of EHRs is very much essential for quick diagnosis of diseases. The shorter the delay in response time and the reliable maintenance makes the automation of healthcare systems more popular.

4)    Privacy

Privacy is one of the significant difficulties in other computing standards as the patients' sensitive data and personal data are moved from edge devices to the remote servers. In edge computing, privacy issues are an important issue because there are various honest but curious adversaries, for example, edge data centres, infrastructure service providers, other service providers and even some users. These attackers are generally approved entities whose main objective is to acquire sensitive data that can be utilized in different selfish manners. In this circumstance, it is unacceptable to expect to know whether a service provider is trustworthy in such an open ecosystem with various trust spaces. For instance in smart grid, a considerable amount of private data of a family can be revealed from reading the smart meters or some other IoT gadgets, it implies that regardless of the house is empty or not, if the smart meters were controlled by an adversary, the user's privacy is completely leaked. Specifically, the leakage of private data, for example, data, identification, can lead to dangerous situations.

5)    Access Control

Due to the outsourcing characteristic of edge computing, if there are no proficient authentication policies in that place, any malicious user without an authorized access can misuse the resources in edge or cloud data centers. This presents a major security challenge for the protected access control framework; for instance, the virtualization asset of edge servers can be accessed, misused, and altered by edge devices if they hold any specific privileges. Furthermore, in the distributed edge computing paradigm, there are numerous trust areas by various infrastructures cohabiting in one edge ecosystem, so it is important to build up the fine-grained access control framework in each trust domain. But most of the conventional access control mechanism usually focuses on one trust domain, and not on multiple trust domains in edge computing. There are many cryptography based solutions and policies to enforce access control in edge computing paradigms.

*Figure 7. Healthcare Framework with Edge Computing*

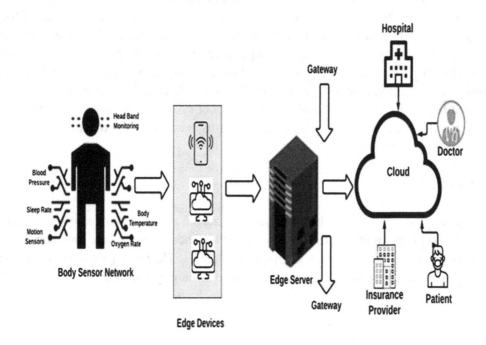

## Architecture of the Edge based HealthCare Framework

Here we are representing a sample framework for depicting Healthcare networks with computational ends. Figure 7 shows the flow of processing the healthcare data right from the sensor till the higher end.

The following scenario in a health cloud environment which uses Proxy Reencryption(PRE) scheme is explained below.

1) Doctor encrypts the EHR of a Patient or the sensor data of patients using his Public Key $PU_A$ - Ciphertext C1 is moved to cloud
2) Re-encryption key is generated to give access to an insurance agent. Doctor generates the re-encryption key encrypting his/her Public Key $PU_A$ with the Insurance agent's public key $PU_B$ and the encryption key $RK_{A->B}$ is transmitted to the cloud.
3) The cloud service provider may act as a proxy and it re-encrypts the Ciphertext C1 with $RK_{A->B}$ - Ciphertext C2
4) The Insurance agent decrypts the re-encrypted ciphertext with his private key $PR_B$.

The above procedure clearly shows that the intruder or adverse enemy can't decrypt the encrypted text. The disadvantage is that the semi-trusted proxy not only transfers the ciphertext from doctor to insurance agent but also vice-versa, which means it can reversibly converts the ciphertext of insurance agent to doctor without the permission of insurance agent by exploiting the discrete logarithm properties. Another issue with the PRE scheme is that both doctor and proxy can collude and try to deduce the private key of the insurance agent. To solve these problems variants of this scheme are introduced namely Identity based PRE, Conditional PRE etc.

## Security Requirements in Edge based HealthCare Framework

Even however each Edge deployment has a different set of security requirements, applications, and sensitivity, the accompanying subsections provide comprehensive, efficient, and applicable security requirements for healthcare systems. They can likewise be used as generic best practice guidelines while developing the Edge software, so the security is enabled from inside the stage. Some of the working arrangements are,

## Data Encryption

The data needs to be secured before (at rest in source area), during (moving through the network) and after (at rest in destination area) correspondence among IoT devices, the Edge network, and the Fog stage.

## Preventing Cache Assaults

Edge stages maintained for the Cache management system are prone to software cache-based side-channel assaults, for example, exposing cryptographic keys, which may lead toward leaking sensitive data.

## Network Checking

Edge systems that are consistently handling private data (e.g. generated by IoT devices) from end-user to Fog stage and vice versa, should screen and detect abnormal action in a network through automated enforcement of correspondence security rules and policies.

## Malware Protection

Edge systems ought to protect themselves against both new and existing malware-based assaults, which can happen as infection, Trojan, rootkit, spyware, and worms to keep away from unwanted infection and serious damage.

## Wireless Security

The internal and external wireless interchanges of the Edge stage with end-user devices need to minimize packet sniffing, rouge access focuses, and comparative challenges by implementing both encryption and authentication procedures. In Secured vehicular networks, to increase street safety and real-time utilization of vehicular networks(Freedman, 2003), they ought to protect themselves from internal and external security threats.

## Secured Multi-tenancy

Edge computing should enable profoundly constrained access control on both data and network, alongside reasonable resource assignment mechanisms to protect confidentiality and integrity inside a multi-user environment.

## Backup and Recovery

Depending upon the sort of utilization, Edge stages ought to have a data backup and recovery modules. Such a system should reflect copies of data on location, off-site, or both on a regular premise. It will benefit the two customers and friends to keep the operations running from utilizing previous backups, limiting service interruptions.

## Security with Performance

A balanced trade-off between the level of usefulness and integrated security is fundamental for Edge network performance. It will enable completely featured applications meanwhile protecting the CIA of data and networks against internal and external threats.

## Security Solutions Recommendations for Edge Based HealthCare Framework

### Privacy Safeguarding in Edge Figuring

With regards to medical care, the primary examination gets into safeguarding protection in sensor-edge networks comprises of the accompanying summed up steps to make sure about wellbeing sensor information between end-client gadget and Edge organization: They gather sensor information and concentrate highlights. Fluffing of information by embeddings Gaussian commotion in information at a specific degree of difference to bring down the opportunity of listening in and sniffing assaults; Segregation by parting information into squares and rearranging them to maintain a strategic distance from Man-in-the-Middle (MITM) assaults; Implementing Public Key Infrastructure for encoding every information square; and Transmit isolated information to Edge hub, where information bundles are unscrambled and re-requested. The framework additionally incorporates a component decrease capacity for limiting information correspondence with Edge hubs to help limit hazard. This work is of criticalness as it focussed on safeguarding individual and basic information during transmission. A method can be improved by choosing an encryption and key administration calculation, focussing on those that assume a significant part in keeping up the security of information. Anyway, the necessary computational overheads for performing broad information control (fluffing, isolation, encryption, unscrambling and requesting, reordering) when the correspondence must be investigated before its gets into the real usage of the situation. This could be of essentialness when planning and creating an Edge framework as the necessary calculation overheads probably won't be accessible. Another significant perspective to see here is that sensors send information persistently, perhaps over longer timeframes, stickand the proposed security structure may over-burden or even accident the fundamental Edge framework. That is the place the heap adjusting calculations must be work.

## Alleviating Insider Information Burglary

One path for shielding information from malignant insiders any delicate gadget organization, for example, medical services utilizing parts of Edge and Cloud figuring would consolidates conduct profiling and fake ways to deal with alleviate security dangers. On the off chance that any profile shows anomalous conduct, for example, the expansion of getting to various archives at uncommon occasions, the framework will label the entrance as dubious and square the individual client. Fake is a disinformation assault that incorporates counterfeit reports, honeyfiles, honeypots and different sorts of goading information that can be utilized to distinguish, befuddle and get the malevolent insider. This examination space is huge as it exhibits likely adjusting and alleviation strategies to shield against information burglary. All the more explicitly, One can show that the proposed strategy can accurately distinguish unusual conduct with a normal exactness more noteworthy than 90%. For instance, an examination is performed with a restricted measure of information. All the more explicitly, eighteen understudies from a solitary college over the term of four days. Consequently, the outcomes regarding exactness they guarantee may not reproducible or widespread. Their procedure can be improved by expanding the populace size and running the trial over longer stretch of time(Stolfo et al., 2012). Moreover, the computational prerequisites of such a methodology are not referenced. The paper gives no subtleties on the amount of information that is put away, just as the CPU time and memory required during investigation. Such conduct profiling methods are regularly acted in a conventional customer worker engineering where calculation assets are openly accessible. It isn't clear how this strategy can be executed on an Edge hub without having unfriendly effects on center usefulness. The method can be additionally improved through fundamentally breaking down and choosing achievable machines learning procedures and preparing information required for conduct profiling. This conveys more significance because of the presence of an enormous number of patients and records. The conduct profiling, checking and client coordinating cycle would not apply any weight on Cloud assets and forestall real information burglary without uncovering any patient touchy information. As an additional advantage, these tasks will happen on-premise and execute generally quicker because of low transmission capacity idleness.

## Strategy Driven Secure Administration of Assets

The following famous issue in medical care is strategy the board system for the assets of Edge registering to upgrade secure collaboration, sharing and interoperability among client mentioned assets. The framework is separated into five significant modules:

1) Policy Decision Engine (PDE) for making a move dependent on pre-characterized strategy rules;
2) Application Administrator (AA) to oversee Edge multi-occupancy;
3) Policy Resolver (PR) for characteristic based validation;
4) Policy Repository (PRep) holding rules and approaches; and
5) Policy Enforcer (PE) to distinguish any inconsistencies in strategy execution.

AA is answerable for characterizing rules and arrangements (put away in PRep) while thinking about different occupants, applications, information sharing and correspondence administrations. At the point when a specific assistance demand is produced using a client, it is sent to a PR that recognizes the client dependent on explicit arrangement of traits and access benefits against a mentioned asset. The client ascribes and their separate authorizations are put away in an information base. PDE takes client data from the PR, separates rules from the PRep, dissect them and authorize through the PE. The eXtensible Access Control Markup Language (XACML) is utilized to make rules and the OpenAZ system for building PDE. Regardless of being in an underlying stage, this strategy structure can possibly turn into a vital piece of constant circulated frameworks in future, where there is a solid requirement for access, personality and asset the executives capacities. Notwithstanding, this structure is restricted to just those frameworks, which can distribute devoted assets inside Edge stages for the greater part of calculations required by different modules to execute the system. Edge stages ought to be fit for dealing with profoundly time-delicate applications, be that as it may, the proposed approval cycle may take more time to decide. Another imperfection in their strategy is that the arrangement itself is characteristically powerless against DoS assaults because of the intricate confirmation measure in PR and PDE. On the off chance that an aggressor sets up a lot of associations all the while, rehashes the 'approval cycle's in a similar association ceaselessly or reacts to the validation convention in a low and moderate way, the Edge assets will get depleted and delivered inaccessible for the proposed clients. In any case, these security concerns can be decreased by building an exhibition model that is gathering estimations of memory, CPU and plate use and occasionally contrasting and assessed values. In the event that the framework recognizes an oddity, the client would be diverted to the Shark Tank group, which is basically an intermediary to intently screen the client however can give full application capacities.

## Verification in Edge Stage

Shaky validation conventions between Edge stages And medical care gadgets have been recognized as a fundamental security worry of Edge registering. The case is that that the IoT gadgets, particularly in keen lattices, are inclined to information altering and satirizing assaults and can be forestalled with the assistance of a Public Key Infrastructure (PKI), Diffie-Hellman key trade, Intrusion discovery strategies and observing for changed info esteems. Moreover, effect of MITM assault on Edge processing by dispatching a Stealth assault on video call among 3G and the WLAN clients inside an Edge network didn't cause any noticeable change in memory and CPU utilization of Edge hub, henceforth it is very hard to distinguish what's more, relieve. The proposal is that the danger of such assaults can be forestalled by making sure about correspondence channels between the Edge stage and the client of medical services gadgets to execute validation plans. In view of the present status of validation in wellbeing system Edge stage, they are missing thorough verification and secure correspondence conventions according to their determination and prerequisites. In an Edge stage both security and execution factors are considered related, and systems, for example, the encryption procedures known as completely homomorphic and Fan-Vercauteren to some degree homomorphic can be utilized to make sure about the information. These plans comprises of a half and half of symmetric and public-key encryption calculations, just as different variations of quality based encryption. As homomorphic encryption grants ordinary activities over the records information without decoding the information, the decrease in key dissemination will keep up the protection of information. A framework can perform information collection dependent on the homomorphicPaillier cryptosystem. As the homomorphic capacity of encryption makes it workable for neighborhood network passages to play out a procedure on figure text without decoding, it decreases the confirmation cost (regarding preparing power) while keeping up the mystery of information.

## Utilizing Advance Encryption Standard (AES)

Some examination may infer that AES is a reasonable encryption calculation for a gigantic information collection in medical services where Edge stage assumes a significant job. Different measurements have been considered for the presentation assessment: client load against CPU time and document size against encryption/unscrambling time and memory usage. Our case is that, encryption time will be almost the equivalent for cell phone and PC, any sort of fitbits and other computerized screens for persistent information which collects modest quantity of information, for example, 500 Kb, 5 Mb, and 10 Mb. In spite of the fact that, AES encryption is all around acknowledged and is attainable for Edge figuring, because of low equipment particulars and littler calculations, one can't contrast AES and some other accessible encryption calculation. What's more, the size of the encryption key assumes a significant function in reinforcing the encryption. Utilizing little example size probably won't give the profound knowledge to whether AES is an appropriate calculation for Edge organizations and capacity or not. So it is suggested that, distinctive measured information must be put for AES choice. Moreover, literary information, pictures or some other information configuration can be utilized for encryption/unscrambling measures. In addition, the Edge stage comprises of heterogeneous gadgets with various details and single calculation probably won't have the option to cover every conceivable situation. Encryption is now an extra assignment for the Edge stage and furthermore devours a lot of assets. The determination of encryption calculation (regardless of whether symmetric, hilter kilter or cross breed) ought to be acted as per supplier and foundation necessities.

## REFERENCES

Alabdulatif, A., Khalil, I., Yi, X., & Guizani, M. (2019). Secure Edge of Things for Smart Healthcare Surveillance Framework. *IEEE Access: Practical Innovations, Open Solutions*, *7*(c), 31010–31021. doi:10.1109/ACCESS.2019.2899323

Ausanka-Crues, R. (2001). *Methods for access control : Advances and limitations*. Harvey Mudd College.

Curtis. (2020). *What are the issues with fog computing*. https://www.yourtechdiet.com/blogs/fog-computing-issues/

Dimitrievski, A., Zdravevski, E., Lameski, P., & Trajkovik, V. (2019, September). Addressing Privacy and Security in Connected Health with Fog Computing. In *Proceedings of the 5th EAI International Conference on Smart Objects and Technologies for Social Good* (pp. 255-260). 10.1145/3342428.3342654

Freedman, A. (2003). Securing the Edge. *Queue*, *1*(1), 6-9.

Glikson, A., Nastic, S., & Dustdar, S. (2017, May). Deviceless edge computing: extending serverless computing to the edge of the network. In *Proceedings of the 10th ACM International Systems and Storage Conference* (pp. 1-1). 10.1145/3078468.3078497

Khan, S., Parkinson, S., & Qin, Y. (2017). Fog computing security: A review of current applications and security solutions. *Journal of Cloud Computing*, *6*(1), 19. Advance online publication. doi:10.118613677-017-0090-3

Li, C., Xue, Y., Wang, J., Zhang, W., & Li, T. (2018). Edge-oriented computing paradigms: A survey on architecture design and system management. [*ACM Computing Surveys*, *51*(2), 1–34. doi:10.1145/3154815

Li, N., & Tripunitara, M. V. (2005). On safety in discretionary access control. *Proceedings - IEEE Symposium on Security and Privacy*. 10.1109/SP.2005.14

Merlino, G., Dautov, R., Distefano, S., & Bruneo, D. (2019). Enabling workload engineering in edge, fog, and cloud computing through OpenStack-based middleware. *ACM Transactions on Internet Technology*, *19*(2), 1–22. doi:10.1145/3309705

Moffett, J. D. (1994). Specification of management policies and discretionary access control. *Network and Distributed Systems Management*, 455–479. http://scholar.google.com/scholar?hl=en&btnG=Search&q=intitle:The+Even+More+Irresistible+SROIQ#0%5Cnhttp://citeseerx.ist.psu.edu/viewdoc/download?doi=10.1.1.17.7145&amp;rep=rep1&amp;type=pdf

Osborn, S., Sandhu, R., & Munawer, Q. (2000). Configuring Role-Based Access Control to Enforce Mandatory and Discretionary Access Control Policies. *ACM Transactions on Information and System Security*, *3*(2), 85–106. Advance online publication. doi:10.1145/354876.354878

Patonico, S., Braeken, A., & Steenhaut, K. (2019). Identity-based and anonymous key agreement protocol for fog computing resistant in the Canetti–Krawczyk security model. *Wireless Networks*, 6. Advance online publication. doi:10.100711276-019-02084-6

Ren, J., Guo, H., Xu, C., & Zhang, Y. (2017). Serving at the edge: A scalable IoT architecture based on transparent computing. *IEEE Network*, *31*(5), 96–105. doi:10.1109/MNET.2017.1700030

Ren, J., Zhang, D., He, S., Zhang, Y., & Li, T. (2019). A Survey on End-Edge-Cloud Orchestrated Network Computing Paradigms: Transparent Computing, Mobile Edge Computing, Fog Computing, and Cloudlet. *ACM Computing Surveys*, *52*(6), 1–36. doi:10.1145/3362031

Stolfo, S. J., Salem, M. B., & Keromytis, A. D. (2012, May). Fog computing: Mitigating insider data theft attacks in the cloud. In *2012 IEEE symposium on security and privacy workshops* (pp. 125-128). IEEE.

Tang, W., Ren, J., Zhang, K., Zhang, D., Zhang, Y., & Shen, X. (2019). Efficient and privacy-preserving fog-assisted health data sharing scheme. *ACM Transactions on Intelligent Systems and Technology*, *10*(6), 1–23. doi:10.1145/3341104

Wang, X., Zhang, J., Schooler, E. M., & Ion, M. (2014, June). Performance evaluation of attribute-based encryption: Toward data privacy in the IoT. In *2014 IEEE International Conference on Communications (ICC)* (pp. 725-730). IEEE. 10.1109/ICC.2014.6883405

Waters, B., & Encryption, C. P. A. B. (2011). An Expressive, Efficient, and Provably Secure Realization. *Lecture Notes in Computer Science*, 6571.

Xiao, Y., Jia, Y., Liu, C., Cheng, X., Yu, J., & Lv, W. (2019). Edge Computing Security: State of the Art and Challenges. *Proceedings of the IEEE*, *107*(8), 1608–1631. Advance online publication. doi:10.1109/JPROC.2019.2918437

Yang, J. J., Li, J. Q., & Niu, Y. (2015). A hybrid solution for privacy preserving medical data sharing in the cloud environment. *Future Generation Computer Systems*, *43*, 74–86. doi:10.1016/j.future.2014.06.004

Zhang, J., Chen, B., Zhao, Y., Cheng, X., & Hu, F. (2018). Data Security and Privacy-Preserving in Edge Computing Paradigm: Survey and Open Issues. *IEEE Access, 6*(Idc), 18209–18237. doi:10.1109/ACCESS.2018.2820162

# Chapter 16
# Personalized Mobile eHealth Services for Secure User Access Through a Multi Feature Biometric Framework

**Georgios C. Manikis**
(iD) https://orcid.org/0000-0002-3396-0644
*Institute of Computer Science, Foundation for Research and Technology Hellas, Heraklion, Greece*

**Marios Spanakis**
(iD) https://orcid.org/0000-0003-2163-0653
*Institute of Computer Science, Foundation for Research and Technology Hellas, Heraklion, Greece*

**Emmanouil G. Spanakis**
*Institute of Computer Science, Foundation for Research and Technology Hellas, Heraklion, Greece*

## ABSTRACT

*Humans have various features that differentiates one person from another which can be used to identify an individual for security purposes. These biometrics can authenticate or verify a person's identity and can be sorted in two classes, physiological and behavioural. In this article, the authors present their results of experimentation on publicly available facial images and the efficiency of a prototype version of SpeechXRays, a multi-modal biometric system that uses audio-visual characteristics for user authentication in eHealth platforms. Using the privacy and security mechanism provided, based on audio and video biometrics, medical personnel are able to be verified and subsequently identified for two different eHealth applications. These verified persons are then able to access control, identification, workforce management or patient record storage. In this work, the authors argue how a biometric identification system can greatly benefit healthcare, due to the increased accuracy of identification procedures.*

DOI: 10.4018/978-1-6684-6311-6.ch016

## INTRODUCTION

Biometric authentication is the process of verification of a person's identity using a physical trait or a behavioural characteristic in order to accept the identity of the person and verify him/her as an authorized user (Jain et al., 2007; Li & Jain, 2009). From the technical perspective, biometric systems mainly rely on models derived from pattern recognition, where several characteristics from a person (e.g. voice, facial expression, fingerprint, etc.) are first transformed into a feature vector and then processed to deny or reject the verification and identification of a user. A major prerequisite in this process is the so-called training phase of the model composed of a pipeline in which: (i) captured biometric characteristics from specific users are stored in a database, and (ii) used for training the model based on that known content. Once training is performed accurately, the biometric system can be applied for verification and identification.

Verification process addresses biometric authentication of a specific user who claims an identity and desires to be recognized by the system (i.e. John Doe uses his magnetic ID card and his fingerprints, and requests access to building A). The system performs a one-to-one comparison between the biometrics of the user requesting access and his/ her corresponding characteristics retrieved from the database. A pattern recognition model estimates the level of similarity or matching score between the characteristics and allows access, in case this similarity metric shows a value above a predefined level of security. User identification is a more computationally complex process in which the biometric system searches all the available information stored in the database when a user requests access without providing any credentials. The system is responsible for answering questions such as "who is this person?", "is he-she enrolled in the database?" and conducts a one-to-many comparison to verify that the user is registered to the security protocol and has been granted access to the requested entrance. Biometric recognition systems extract the features from voice, face and compare them with templates stored in databases for verification of a person. If the system uses only a single trait it is characterized as a unimodal biometric system, whereas if two or more biometric traits are used to identify and authenticate a person, the system is called multi-modal (Larcher et al., 2012; Ross et al., 2006).

SpeechXRays biometric system is designed in order to develop and test in real-life environments a user recognition platform based on voice acoustics analysis and audio-visual identity verification (http://www.speechxrays.eu/). SpeechXRays provide a state-of-the-art, high accuracy and user-friendly solution allowing storage and analysis of biometric data for authentication. The system aims to apply in eHealth in order to authenticate users and provide different level of access to medical personnel, based on their rank in patient management (Spanakis et al., 2016; Chronaki et al., 2003; Kartakis et al., 2012). Security issues for eHealth system (Hristoskova et al., 2014; Spat et al., 2011) are usually centred on user authentication, data integrity, data confidentiality, and patient privacy protection. With SpeechXRays we aim to study how to address these by providing reliable and secure user authentication, compared to the traditional approaches. The eHealth pilot for SpeechXrays involves one hospital and all corresponding wards/ clinics aiming to enrol >400 medical users. In the context of the pilot study, the medical personnel will use the SpeechXrays in order to be authenticated as users of a medical application (OAcare). The OAcare application is a dynamic web application developed for patients and clinicians for the management of osteoarthritis (OA) (Maniadi et al., 2015). Recently an evaluation survey and preliminary results regarding functionality, efficiency and user-friendly environment were presented along with the acceptance of using the biometric system proposed from SpeechXRays for user authentication (Spanakis et al., 2016). On the other hand, in order the biometric system to be applied in a clinical environment it is essential to evaluate its performance regarding successful authentication of the user. The aim of this work is to present a methodological multi-feature biometric framework based on machine learning and feature selection techniques, addressing the needs of SpeechXRays. The proposed approach is a prototype and for feasibility reasons, currently is dealing with multi-feature extractions of facial characteristics due to larger variability that is observed in voice analysis (Cocioceanu et al., 2016a; Cocioceanu et al., 2016b). The biometric system is flexible in terms of adjusted decision thresholds that must be defined and adapted, based on the level of security and confidentiality of the medical data that the user attempts to access.

## BIOMETRIC SYSTEM ERRORS

A biometric verification system usually makes two types of errors: (i) mistaking biometric measurements from two different persons to be from the same person, and (ii) mistaking two biometric measurements from the same person to be from two different persons (Jain et al., 2004).

Errors of the first type are measured using FMR (false match rate) or FAR (false acceptance rate), whereas FNMR (false non-match rate) or FRR (false rejection rate) are frequently used to quantify errors of the second type.

There is a trade-off between FMR and FNMR in every biometric system. In fact, both FMR and FNMR are functions of the system threshold *t*; if *t* is decreased to make the system more tolerant to input variations and noise, then FMR increases. On the other hand, if *t* is raised to make the system more secure, then FNMR increases accordingly. The threshold at which FMR is equal to FNMR is known as the Equal Error Rate (EER). An illustrative representation of a biometric system performance is given from plots depicted in Figure 1.

It is possible to reduce the errors by trying to record more biometric characteristics for every user so that, in case of variations on a template, the other can be used. However, on the other hand, there are natural variations to biometric characteristics, which may not be erased but could be minimized through the appropriate equipment. Another possibility is to act on the threshold of the system. This threshold defines how much the biometric characteristics must be similar, in order to make a positive comparison. In other words, it measures the correspondence between characteristic to check and template stored in the database. By elevating the threshold, the risk that not authorized users can fool the system diminishes (FAR is reduced), but, on the other hand, it is more probable that some authorized users can sometimes be refused (FRR increases). Biometric system errors can occur due to various reasons such as:

- Sampling (imperfect imaging conditions)
- Changes in characteristics (i.e. bruises or voice changes due to illness)
- Ambient conditions (temperature humidity)
- User interaction with the sensor (i.e. distance)
- Sensors (different smartphones)

### Efficiency of Biometric System and Application in SpeechXRays Data

Detection theory is a fundamental tool in decision analysis. However, many decision functions both formal (e.g. likelihood ratio) and informal (e.g. maximum of function) evolve in a wide variety of applications. Detection (binary), same fibre or not, and classification methods form the basis of detection processors including modern machine learning algorithms. The major question that arises when investigating these

*Figure 1. Efficiency analysis of biometric systems (Subha, 2017)*

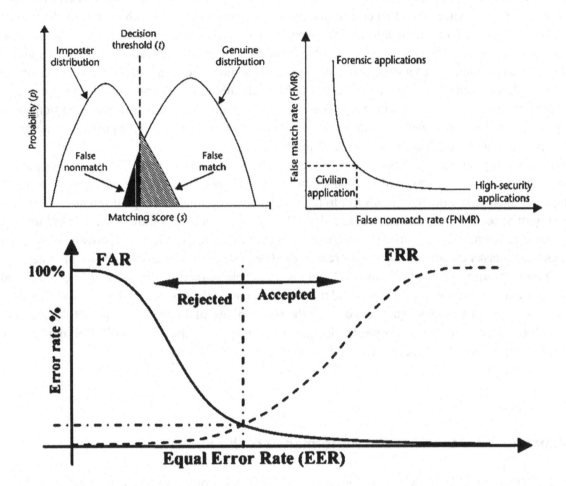

methods is their underlying performance on problems of interest. There exists a variety of metrics that can be applied to evaluate algorithm performance, ranging from confusion matrices to sophisticated statistical hypothesis tests. A complete separation implies perfect discrimination while complete overlap implies no discrimination. The classifier assigns a probability that the outcome is positive or negative depending on the threshold.

## SpeechXRays Description & Target eHealth Application

SpeechXRays aims to apply in real-life environments (i.e. medical units) as a user recognition platform based on audio-visual identity verification. SpeexhRays' scope is to bring superior anti-spoofing capabilities and integrate them into an existing healthcare service (Spanakis et al., 2017). The main advantage of the SpeechXRays system is that the user not only will be authenticated but also specific level of access level will be granted depending on security and confidentiality of the medical data that the user is attempting to access (e.g. nursing staff vs treating physicians).

The eHealth pilot for SpeechXrays involves one university hospital (University General Hospital of Heraklion, Crete, Greece) and all corresponding wards/ clinics aiming to enrol >400 medical users regarding audio-visual biometric information (speech, lip movement and face characteristics). The enrolment of the users and the biometric data record will be implemented according to the International and European standards of biometric data collection and handling and data will be stored in a template database, placed inside the hospital, which will fulfil all the necessary characteristics regarding security, privacy, usability and cost-efficiency. The medical specialists that will voluntarily participate in the pilot study will be informed and with an informed consent form to sign will be provided prior to the participation in the eHealth use case SpeechXRays trial.

Till today, a prototype application, for personal health supporting systems (Spanakis et al., 2016; Kondylakis et al., 2015), was used to conduct an evaluation survey and preliminary results from 18 volunteers (including 9 doctors) in respect to the acceptability of a biometric platform as the one proposed from SpeechXRays (Spanakis et al., 2016). These evaluation results shown that the platform is a functional, efficient and user-friendly environment (for both medical specialists and patients) since it can respond to all tasks utilizing all necessary resources. The system has a user-friendly, usable interface. Our previous work presented that almost 80% of the users believe that security is of great concern and especially in respect of the way of access and the method for authorization and authentication (Spanakis et al., 2017). All participants, when asked about the potential use of an integrated biometric system to the platform, such as the one proposed by SpeechXRays, responded that they would feel more secure and safer to use it in order to access sensitive, personal, medical information.

## METHODOLOGY

### Estimating the Generalization Performance of the System

The performance of the SpeechXRays biometric system in its implementation will be assessed using experimental protocols based on both unimodal and multimodal data. Data will be randomly separated into enrolment data and data used at the verification level in order to simulate a real case scenario. However, the estimation of the system performance can be influenced by the selection of data used for enrolment and verification, affecting a good generalization in performance. SpeechXRays biometric system will be applied to health domain applications, thus such model needs to demonstrate at first adequate verification capability on the data used for designing the system. Cross validation is a widely used procedure for estimating the generalization performance of pattern recognition systems in general, in a way to protect the decision of a system against over-fitting. Basic forms in cross-validation are the $k$-fold and the leave-one-out cross-validation.

In SpeechXRays audio and voice data will be first partitioned into $k$ equally (or nearly equally) sized folds. Subsequently $k$ iterations of enrolment and verification will be performed such that, within iterations, a different fold of the data is held-out for verification purposes while the remaining $k$-1 folds will be used as data for the enrolment phase. Finally, $k$-fold cross-validation will run several times, increasing the number of estimates, where data from the experimental protocol will be reshuffled and re-stratified before each run.

Security requirements such as confidentiality, integrity, authenticity, non-repudiation and availability are essential for computer and network-based systems. The following steps were performed by the

SpeechXRays biometric system to enroll the person: (i) acquire and store the appropriate data, (ii) verify the person by comparing the captured data against the database, and (iii) authenticate or revoke access based on the comparison/ classification of the biometric trait.

- Enrolment: capture, process and store speech and face biometric information of an individual as a biometric template in a database.
- Verification: compare the captured biometric sample with the stored biometric template of the individual to verify the identity is matching or not.
- Authentication: if matching, secure session is opened between two parties and if not, the access is denied.
- Revocation: revoke access based on security risk such as template leakage, spoofing attempts, etc.

In the context of SpeechXRays, the aforementioned steps are concluded in the pipeline below for achieving enrolment, verification, authentication, and revocation through the provided biometric system.

## Enrolment Phase

According to the eHealth scenario of the SpeechXRays, medical personnel will be advised to register the enrolment phase and provide speech and facial imaging data under different times, environment conditions (i.e. noisy background, low light, etc.), and facial expressions. The enrolment phase in the context of the pilot study is supervised by our research team in order to secure the optimum capture of the biometric features but it is aimed that the final version of SpeechXRays system will execute the enrolment phase by an automated interaction of the user with the system. This multimodal information will be extracted using the aforementioned feature extraction techniques for voice and face data, and stored individually as a biometric template to a database. This template will be linked to a specific token (i.e. identity, name, etc.) related to each medical personnel. Once the information gathering is finished, two separate unimodal biometric systems will be applied to the data in order to construct SpeechXRays biometric system. Through enrolment of the system, appropriate thresholds will be estimated and assigned specifically to the medical data with different levels of security/ sensitivity.

## Verification Phase

At the verification level, a medical specialist requires access to medical data classified with a specific security level degree. The user presents a token, facial and speech data, and the biometric feature template associated with the user is retrieved from the database. The system processes the given data, extracts the facial and speech features and compares them with the features stored at the database at the enrolment phase. The mathematical expression for the verification analysis of the feature vectors is given below:

$$\left(I, X_q\right) \in \begin{cases} W_T, & \text{if } S\left(X_q, X_1\right) \geq T_s \text{ or } D\left(X_q, X_1\right) \leq T_D \\ W_F, & \text{otherwise} \end{cases}$$

The input feature vector is given by $X_q$, the claimed identity is $I$, and $T_s$ and $T_d$ are the calculated thresholds based on the EER and the security level of the medical data to access. In case the similarity measure is based on distance similarity, $T_d$ is used. Otherwise, $T_s$ is applied to assess the similarity degree between the template and the provided data at the verification level. $D(X_q, X_I)$ is the similarity measure between the biometric template and the provided by the user facial and speech data. $W_T$ and $W_F$ reflect the genuine and impostor, respectively.

## Authentication/ Revocation Phase

The output of the comparison from the verification is an accept/reject decision according to the formula above. The user can proceed again to the verification process and depending on the security levels, assigned to the medical data a number of attempts can be made including the cases that require a secure connection from remote location (e.g. via tablet/ smartphone).

## Demonstration of the Context Dependent Tuning Framework of SpeechXRays

## SpeechXRays System - Experimental Protocol

Aiming to the SpeechXRays scope of using multimodal biometrics and according to project's developing procedure, initially, individual unimodal biometric analysis will be first applied to both speech and face data. The derived matching scores will be afterwards fused to conclude to the final decision at the verification phase. To this respect, in this work, a multi-feature approach of facial characteristics as a unimodal biometric system was implemented firstly using publicly available data from the ORL database (http://www.cl.cam.ac.uk/research/dtg/attarchive/facedatabase.html), composed of 400 facial images of size 112x92. Ten different images of each of 40 distinct subjects-persons were captured in different times, lightning, facial expressions (i.e. open/ closed eyes, smiling/ not smiling) and details (i.e. glasses/ no glasses). All the images were captured against a dark homogeneous background with faces in an upright position in frontal view, with a tolerance for some side movement.

Facial features were exported using the methodology described previously in (Shen et al., 2007; Kovesi et al., 1999). A Gabor filter bank was constructed comprising filters of 8 orientations and 5 scales and applied to the facial images. Multiple Gabor related features for each subject were derived from both magnitude and phase responses of the filter bank. Additionally, phase congruency techniques that have been proved to be robust against changes in lighting conditions were applied to all input images, and a high dimensional feature vector composed of 18,432 features was generated for each image. To reduce feature dimensionality, 4 different feature selection-ranking techniques of good simplicity and computational efficiency such as ReliefF (Kovesi, 1999), Feature Selection via Concave Minimization (Bradley & Mangasarian, 1998), Mutual Information, and Pairwise Correlations using Pearson's linear correlation coefficient were used in the analysis to rank all features in terms of their accuracy in distinguishing the given subjects. To avoid any overfitting issues during the design of the biometric system, the 500 most highly ranked imaging features from each feature selection method were further pre-processed linearly (Linear Discriminant Analysis and Principal Component Analysis) and non-linearly (Kernel Fisher Analysis and Kernel Principal Component Analysis), and imaging characteristics of all data were projected onto a lower dimensional space constructing linear and non-linear combinations respectively.

Finally, matching score calculations were performed using a nearest neighbour classifier and impostor and genuine distributions were calculated using the Euclidean distance measure.

Following an iterative process to assess the verification accuracy of the SpeechXRays biometric system, the entire data of each of the 40 distinct subjects was randomly partitioned into subsets act as enrolment and verification data respectively. Particularly, 80% of the images of each subject contributed to the enrolment phase of the biometric system, while the remaining 20% served as the set for verification. A 10-fold cross-validation was applied to the subset simulating the enrolment phase, to estimate the generalization performance of the system. To eliminate any bias when assessing the verification accuracy of the system, all pre-processing steps were tested during the cross-validating enrolment phase before applied to the remaining set for verification. To improve the readability of this manuscript, acronyms for ReliefF, Feature Selection via Concave Minimization, Mutual Information and Pairwise Correlations using Pearson's linear correlation coefficient were defined as RF, CM, MI and PC respectively. Accordingly, Linear Discriminant Analysis, Principal Component Analysis, Kernel Fisher Analysis and Kernel Principal Component Analysis were presented as LDA, PCA, KFA and KPCA.

## RESULTS AND DISCUSSION

### SpeechXRays Enrolment and Verification Phase

A quantitative representation of the identification accuracy of the biometric system at the enrolment phase is given in Table 1. All folds at the cross-validation process contributed equivalently to the estimation of the performance and an average value was calculated. To evaluate the performance of the system, results are given for EER, the automatically estimated threshold at EER, and pairs of FRR and FAR when triggering a score threshold in the DET curve. Pairwise correlations using PC in conjunction to LDA achieved the highest score among all combinations with a verification rate of 98.14%. Figure 2, and Figure 3 illustrate qualitatively the performance of the combination giving the best (PC+LDA) and worst (MI+KFA) verification rate at the enrolment phase, respectively. Figure 4 depicts the performance of the system using the best combination when applied to the subset of images used for verification. Additionally, the performance of the presented biometric system is given in table format in which the verification rate at the EER threshold achieves a score of 98.28% (Table 2).

ROC curve analysis was performed at the cross-validation phase in which verification accept rates were plotted against the associated false accept rates (top left of Figure 2 and 3). Relationship between FAR and FRR is graphically displayed in Figure 2 and Figure 3 (top right). DET curve analysis based on the relationship between the FAR and FRR measurements is also depicted in Figure 2 and Figure 3 (bottom right). Varying the system's threshold, thus adjusting a more or less secured level to SpeechXRays system, the operating point along the DET curve is moved. The error graphs of FAR and FRR, (bottom left of Figure 2 and Figure 3) were respectively defined as the probability that an unauthorized user is accepted as authorized, and that an authorized user is rejected as unauthorized for each fold acted as a set during verification. In any given subset through the cross-validation procedure the intersection point of these two graphs resulted to the EER.

The calculated value for EER was used to give automatically the threshold of the biometric system. The lower the EER the better the system performance is, as the total error rate, which is the sum of the

FAR and the FRR at the point of the EER decreases. A quantitative representation of the identification accuracy of the biometric system is given in Table 3, for indicative points in the DET curves.

*Table 1. Performance evaluation of the SpeechXRays biometric system at the enrolment phase using all possible combinations of pre-processing techniques*

| Feature Ranking | Dimensionality Reduction | EER threshold | EER | Verification Rate @ERR | FRR @ 0.01%FAR | FRR @ 0.1%FAR | FRR @ 1%FAR |
|---|---|---|---|---|---|---|---|
| RF | KFA | 0.254 | 27.16% | 72.92% | 99.55% | 83.66% | 70.31% |
| RF | KPCA | 0.345 | 17.37% | 82.64% | 83.62% | 73.17% | 53.17% |
| RF | LDA | 0.531 | 2.95% | 97.07% | 14.32% | 11.16% | 4.99% |
| RF | PCA | 0.420 | 13.95% | 86.04% | 62.47% | 54.80% | 39.93% |
| MI | KFA | 0.288 | 44.51% | 55.36% | 99.55% | 98.00% | 95.58% |
| MI | KPCA | 0.370 | 38.60% | 61.40% | 98.06% | 95.92% | 88.95% |
| MI | LDA | 0.441 | 36.17% | 63.87% | 95.02% | 90.30% | 81.39% |
| MI | PCA | 0.569 | 36.79% | 63.17% | 94.89% | 90.18% | 82.32% |
| CM | KFA | 0.265 | 29.98% | 70.13% | 99.55% | 86.04% | 75.67% |
| CM | KPCA | 0.376 | 22.70% | 77.32% | 91.16% | 80.25% | 63.32% |
| CM | LDA | 0.543 | 4.10% | 95.90% | 18.56% | 13.32% | 7.72% |
| CM | PCA | 0.500 | 17.78% | 82.23% | 75.14% | 66.73% | 48.17% |
| PC | KFA | 0.279 | 35.64% | 64.31% | 99.55% | 92.01% | 82.94% |
| PC | KPCA | 0.513 | 17.25% | 82.75% | 78.07% | 67.25% | 49.58% |
| **PC** | **LDA** | **0.527** | **1.85%** | **98.14%** | **12.14%** | **7.46%** | **3.49%** |
| PC | PCA | 0.560 | 15.29% | 84.71% | 71.85% | 58.86% | 43.24% |

## CONCLUSION

The efficiency of a biometric system is identified by the DET curve, which is a visual characterization of the trade-off between the FAR and the FRR. In this work, a methodological multi-feature biometric framework, part of which is also implemented in SpeechXRays, regarding various decision thresholds was presented. Although the presented methodology refers to multi-feature facial analysis, the approach is similar for voice authentication despite the fact that voice offers a greater level of variability and requires greater number of recordings for the FAR and ERR (Cocioceanu, 2016a; Cocioceanu, 2016b). This issue will be addressed in future works considering the results from the eHealth pilot study. In general, the presented methodological framework aims to apply in the context of SpeechXRays project on verifying medical personnel's authentication through DET curve analysis for the multimodal biometric system of SpeechXRays. Several pre-processing techniques were used in the analysis and their performance was assessed through a cross-validating verification framework to avoid overfitting and bias of the results. Based on provided unimodal datasets a demonstration of the context dependent tuning framework through DET curve analysis was described in order to test the verification rates based on different thresholds. SpeexhRays' scope is to bring superior anti-spoofing capabilities and integrate

*Figure 2. Curve analysis for MI and KFA combination at the enrolment phase based on: (top-left) ROC of verification rate vs FAR, (top-right) relationship between FAR and FRR, (bottom-left) error rates of FAR and FRR for different folds used and (bottom-right) DET of FRR vs FAR shown in percentages*

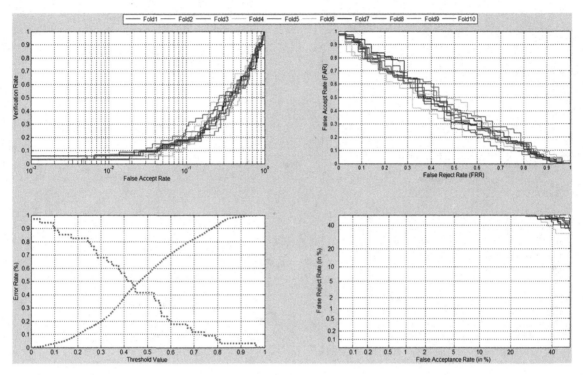

them into an existing healthcare service. Upcoming updates of the SpeechXRays biometric system will include more advanced feature ranking techniques and pattern recognition models for calculating the matching scores (i.e. Support Vector Machines) and multimodal datasets.

## ACKNOWLEDGMENT

This work is supported by the research project SpeechXRays which receives funding from the European Commission (EC) through Horizon 2020 Grant agreement No 653586.

*Figure 3. Curve analysis for PC and LDA combination at the enrolment phase based on: (top-left) ROC of verification rate vs FAR, (top-right) relationship between FAR and FRR, (bottom-left) Error rates of FAR and FRR for different folds used and (bottom-right) DET of FRR vs FAR shown in percentages*

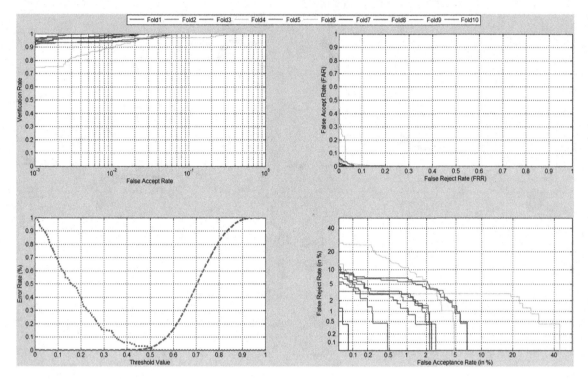

*Figure 4. Curve analysis for PC and LDA combination at the verification phase based on: (top-left) ROC of verification rate vs FAR, (top-right) relationship between FAR and FRR, (bottom-left) error rates of FAR and FRR for different folds used and (bottom-right) DET of FRR vs FAR shown in percentages*

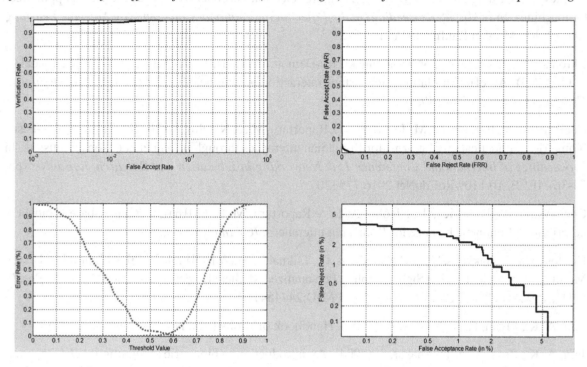

*Table 2. Performance evaluation of the SpeechXRays biometric system at the verification phase using PC and LDA combination yielding best verification score*

| Feature Ranking | Dimensionality Reduction | EER threshold | EER | Verification Rate @ERR | FRR @ 0.01%FAR | FRR @ 0.1%FAR | FRR @ 1%FAR |
|---|---|---|---|---|---|---|---|
| PC | LDA | 0.573 | 1.68% | 98.28% | 4.84% | 3.75% | 2.19% |

*Table 3. Verification rates of successful enters in the system for different EER for ORL dataset in SpeechXRays*

| Threshold | Verification Rate @ defined threshold |
|---|---|
| EER | 98.28% |
| EER – 10% EER (more strict) | 96.25% |
| EER – 20% EER (more strict) | 93.13% |
| EER – 30% EER (more strict) | 80.31% |
| EER – 50% EER (more strict) | 50.00% |
| EER + 10% EER (less strict) | 100.00% |

## REFERENCES

Bradley, S., & Mangasarian, O. L. (1998). Feature selection via concave minimization and support vector machines. In *ICML '98 Proceedings of the Fifteenth International Conference on Machine Learning* (pp. 82-90). Morgan Kaufmann Publishers.

Chronaki, C., Chiarugi, F., Mavrogiannaki, E., Demou, C., Lelis, P., Trypakis, D., ... Orphanoudakis, S. C. (2003). An eHealth platform for instant interaction among health professionals. *Proceedings of Computers in Cardiology*, *30*, 101–104.

Cocioceanu, A., Barbulescu, M., Ivanoaica, T., Raportaru, M., & Nicolin, A. (2016b). Testing voice-based biometrics authentication platforms for Romanian utterances through infrequent consonant clusters. In *Proceedings of International Conference 15th Networking in Education and Research, RoEduNet* (pp. 34-36). IEEE. 10.1109/RoEduNet.2016.7753205

Cocioceanu, A., Ivanoaica, T., Nicolin, A. I., & Raportaru, M. C. (2016a). Computer-based statistical description of phonetic balance for Romanian utterances. *ICT Innovations*, 59–67.

Hristoskova, A., Sakkalis, V., Zacharioudakis, G., Tsiknakis, M., & De Turck, F. (2014). Ontology-Driven Monitoring of Patient's Vital Signs Enabling Personalized Medical Detection and Alert. *Sensors (Basel)*, *14*(1), 1598–1628. doi:10.3390140101598 PMID:24445411

Jain, A. K., Flynn, P., & Ross, A. A. (2007). Handbook of Biometrics. NY: Springer-Verlag, Inc.

Jain, A. K., Ross, A., & Prabhakar, S. (2004). An introduction to biometric recognition. *IEEE Transactions on Circuits and Systems for Video Technology*, *14*(1), 4–20. doi:10.1109/TCSVT.2003.818349

Kartakis, S., Sakkalis, V., Tourlakis, P., Zacharioudakis, G., & Stephanidis, C. (2012). Enhancing Health Care Delivery through Ambient Intelligence Applications. *Sensors (Basel)*, *12*(9), 11435–11450. doi:10.3390120911435 PMID:23112664

Kondylakis, H., Spanakis, E. G., Sfakianakis, S. G., Sakkalis, V., Tsiknakis, M. N., Marias, K., . . . Dong, F. (2015). Digital Patient: Personalized and Translational Data Management through the MyHealthAvatar EU Project. In *2015 37th Annual International Conference of the IEEE Engineering in Medicine and Biology Society (EMBC)* (pp. 1397-1400). IEEE. 10.1109/EMBC.2015.7318630

Kovesi, P. (1999). *Image Features from Phase Congruency*.

Larcher, A., Lévy, C., Matrouf, D., Bonastre, J. F., Tresadern, P., & Cootes, T. (2012). Bi-Modal Person Recognition on a Mobile Phone: Using Mobile Phone Data. In *2012 IEEE International Conference on Multimedia and Expo Workshops* (pp. 635-640). doi:10.1109/ICMEW.2012.116

Li, S. Z., & Jain, A. K. (2009). *Encyclopedia of Biometrics*. Springer. doi:10.1007/978-0-387-73003-5

Maniadi, E., Spanakis, E. G., Karantanas, A., & Marias, K. (2015). A supportive environment for the long term management of knee osteoarthritis condition. In *Proceedings of the 5th EAI International Conference on Wireless Mobile Communication and Healthcare*. 10.4108/eai.22-12-2015.151108

Ross, A. A., Nandakumar, K., & Jain, A. (2006). *Handbook of Multibiometrics*. US: Springer.

Shen, L., Bai, L., & Fairhurst, M. (2007). Gabor wavelets and General Discriminant Analysis for face identification and verification. *Image and Vision Computing*, 25(5), 553–563. doi:10.1016/j.imavis.2006.05.002

Spanakis, E. G., Spanakis, M., Karantanas, A., & Marias, K. (2016). Secure access to patient's health records using SpeechXRays a mutli-channel biometrics platform for user authentication. In *Proceedings of Annual International Conference of the IEEE Engineering in Medicine and Biology Society* (pp. 2541-2544). 10.1109/EMBC.2016.7591248

Spanakis, M., Manikis, G., Porwal, S., & Spanakis, E. G. (2017). Developing a context-dependent tuning framework of multi-channel biometrics that combine audio-visual characteristics for secure access in eHealth platform for osteoarthritis management. In *Proceedings of 7th EAI International Conference on Wireless Mobile Communication and Healthcare.*

Spat, S., Höll, B., Beck, B., Chiarugi, F., Kontogiannis, V., Spanakis, E. G., ... Pieber, T. (2011). A mobile android-based application for in-hospital glucose management in compliance with the medical device directive for software. In *2nd International ICST Conference on Wireless Mobile Communication and Healthcare.*

Subha, R. (2017). Biometrics in Internet of Things (IoT) Security. *International Journal of Engineering Research and General Science*, 5(5).

*This research was previously published in the International Journal of Reliable and Quality E-Healthcare (IJRQEH), 8(1); pages 40-51, copyright year 2019 by IGI Publishing (an imprint of IGI Global).*

# Chapter 17
# "Sensitive but Essential Information":
## Policy Debates on Fitness Application Privacy and Data Security

**Alison Nicole Novak**
*Rowan University, USA*

## ABSTRACT

*As fitness trackers and applications grow popular, many actors involved in the development, use, and regulation of these devices expressed concerns of privacy and control of data gathered through these platforms. This chapter explores how government representatives, industry leaders, regulators, and politicians discursively constructed and critiqued data privacy in fitness applications in congressional contexts. Findings indicate the following discourses: (1) fitness trackers as indicative of larger data collection issues, (2) weighing the pros and cons of use, (3) military implications for fitness application data security, (4) consumers as responsible for their own data privacy, (5) organizations failing to keep pace with cyber security threats, and (6) the misuse of data collected in fitness applications for promotion/strategic communication uses.*

## INTRODUCTION

With the growth of fitness trackers, or fitness applications for mobile media, many actors involved in the development, use and regulation of these devices expressed increased attention to the privacy and control of data gathered through these platforms. Devices such as Fitbit and Apple Watch and applications such as Strava and PolarFlow provide users with customizable data warehouses to track daily information such as physical exercise, dietary intake, and vital signs. While this data provides users with insights into their own activity, members of the public, advocacy groups, and even government regulators and politicians voiced criticism of privacy implications and risks. In a September 2018 testimony before the Senate Commerce, Science and Transportation Committee, Senior Vice President of AT&T Len Cali

DOI: 10.4018/978-1-6684-6311-6.ch017

reflected that fitness trackers collect "sensitive but essential information" and "now there appears to be a growing need for a new and comprehensive federal privacy law" (Cali, 2018, 06:26).

This chapter explores how government representatives, industry leaders, regulators and politicians discursively constructed and critiqued data privacy in fitness applications in Congressional contexts. Since 2012, there were 341 mentions of "fitness applications" (or "apps") and "data privacy" in Congressional hearings, testimonies, and House sessions. These mentions are critical points of inquiry for researchers grappling with the ethics of regulation in data privacy. Mentions are archived through C-SPAN, which documents all Congressional activity (Browning & Browning, 2013). This analysis provides deeper understanding of the various perspectives on data privacy (including politicians, lobbyists, and regulators). Further, analysis of these mentions provides insight into future policies and developments in data privacy regulation.

To conduct this analysis, the 341 videos and corresponding transcripts are analyzed using a discursive approach. Using Gee's (2011) methodology, the analysis provides a set of discourses that exhaustively captures the characterization of data privacy in fitness applications by individuals who are charged with regulating it. Findings indicate the following discourses: (1) fitness trackers as indicative of larger data collection issues, (2) weighing the pros and cons, (3) military implications for fitness application data security, (4) consumers as responsible for their own data privacy, (5) organizations failing to keep pace with cyber security threats, and (6) the misuse of data collected in fitness applications for promotion/strategic communication uses. This chapter provides quotes and examples from the dataset to highlight discursive patterns and insights.

This study provides a comprehensive overview of the policy debates surrounding data privacy on fitness applications in Congress. This analysis holds three foci: (1) describe various regulatory perspectives on fitness applications and data privacy, (2) describe changes and the evolution of discourses from 2012-2019, and (3) reflect on the ethical arguments presented in Congressional debates and discussions. This chapter holds findings for those studying data privacy, the relationship of policy and ethics, and changes to policy debates over time.

## BACKGROUND

### Fitness Trackers, Data Privacy, and the Quantified Self

Barber, Carter, Harris and Reinerman-Jones (2017) note that fitness trackers have become an increasingly popular way for individuals to monitor and adjust their daily activities since the early 2000s.[1] Although fitness trackers evolved from much earlier models of pedometers and heart rate monitors, today's fitness trackers are capable of monitoring and helping diagnose health issues such as 24 hour sleep-wake rhythm disorders, eating disorders, and epilepsy. Although there is an ongoing debate amongst medical professionals about the accuracy of fitness tracker data and its use in diagnosis, Stiglbauer, Weber, and Batinic (2019) note that as the technology becomes more reliable, it is likely to play a larger role in medicine.

As the technological capabilities of fitness trackers has grown, so have public interest and adoption. Wurmser (2019) found that 56.7 million adult Americans or 22% of the population use a fitness tracker at least once per month. This number grew at approximately 3% per year and is expected to reach 25% of the American population by 2022 (Wurmser, 2019). In particular, young people are most likely to purchase a wearable fitness tracker with 38% of the 25-34-year-old demographic using a fitness tracker at least once per month (Wurmser, 2019). Lee and Lee (2018) argue that fitness trackers are most likely to be worn by people who are both aware of the technology and who have an interest in self-efficacy or health improvement. For those individuals, health and fitness trackers are considered an "assistance-technology" because they help achieve a goal of health, weight loss, or personal insight (Lee & Lee, 2018). Lupton (2016) documented the rise in popularity of fitness tracker in her book *The Quantified Self*. She argues that wearable fitness trackers build off the self-tracking culture which purports that an individual that knows their daily habits is in a better position to affect change. Fitness trackers turn individuals in "hybrid beings" that blend human and technological elements to create an optimal human experience (Lupton, 2016).

Fitness trackers are part of the "wearables" market, or devices that are worn on the physical body and connected to a smart device such as a phone or tablet (Asimakopoulous, Asimakopoulous, & Spillers, 2017). In recent years, sales of traditional fitness trackers, such as Fitbit, declined while sales of smartwatches that integrate fitness trackers with other technological capabilities increased (Liu, 2019). In 2018, Fitbit's stock plunged after the company announced that it barely broke-even due to the growing popularity of Apple's new smartwatch (*USA Today,* 2018). Since 2018, the smartwatch category grows increasingly popular, with market expectations of staying the most popular form of a wearable until at least 2022 (Allison, 2018).

One reason for the popularity of smartwatches reflects the many different services or applications that can be incorporated into the device. Quoting Ramon Llamos from analyst firm IDC, Allison (2018) notes:

*...developments within digital health will be at the heart of continued smartwatch growth. "Smartwatch operating systems will emphasize connection, not only between users but between wearers and other smart devices and systems. Expect further developments focusing on health with the smartwatch playing a critical role in tracking your health goals and detecting potential ailments," he said. (para. 5)*

For example, the 2019 edition of the Apple Watch (Apple's smartwatch) default setting monitors: heart rate and irregularities, steps, elevation, hydration, sleep amount and quality, fall detection, and caloric intake and expenditure. In addition, the smartwatch allows applications from a variety of third-party developers to track information such as: medicine intake, neurological disorders (ranging from migraines to depression), and menstrual cycles. On its website, Apple proudly boasts quotes from medical professionals who argue that the Apple Watch is helping doctors gain insight into patient lives because of the depth of information collected daily. One doctor reflected, "Apple is democratizing healthcare, providing on-demand access to accurate sensors and software that can help consumers develop real healthcare literacy and inform how daily choices impact their health" (Apple, 2019b, para. 14).

However, the amount of health information collected through fitness trackers and wearables like the Apple Watch has drawn concern from journalists, users, and regulators who are concerned over the security and privacy of data. In a 2019 *NPR* report on data privacy, Sydell (2019) reflected that major health systems, such as UC San Diego, cautions their patients to be informed "so that they're not inadvertently sharing information with third parties they would not want to have this information" (para. 15). Other reports, such as an investigation launched by the *Wall Street Journal,* found that third party healthcare applications were often responsible for selling user data (on everything from heart rates to menstrual cycles) to advertisers and to social network sites such as Facebook (Schechner & Secada, 2019). While both Apple and Facebook have updated their privacy standards to protect healthcare data from being sold to advertisers, some health systems are concerned that the practice may be ongoing without user knowledge (Sydell, 2019).

Beyond the intentional selling of data to advertisers, there are other concerns over the safety of healthcare data stored through fitness tracker applications. In 2018, MyFitnessPal, a popular third-party application owned by Under Armour, left the data (usernames, passwords, email addresses, and stored credit card information) of 150 million users exposed to hackers (Bonnington, 2018). Humer and Finkle (2018) reflect that while users are calmed because that particular hack did not include any specific healthcare data, hackers know that healthcare data is one of the most valuable assets on the black market: "Stolen health credentials can go for $10 each, about 10 or 20 times the value of a U.S. credit card number" (para. 11). In addition, attempted hacks on healthcare related applications rose by 40% since 2016, resulting in calls by advocacy groups and think tanks such as Ponemon Institute on data protection policy for urgent attention to the lack of regulations governing how applications collect, store, and protect user data (Humer & Finkle, 2018).

There are military implications for the vulnerability of fitness data as well. In 2018, the popular fitness tracking application Strava reported that it had accidentally revealed the secret locations of military bases around the world through accessible heat maps that display the most frequent walking and running pathways (Hern, 2018a). Strava quickly suggested that military personnel opt-out of the heat map feature (Hern, 2018b). Hern (2018a) reflected:

*In locations like Afghanistan, Djibouti and Syria, the users of Strava seem to be almost exclusively foreign military personnel, meaning that bases stand out brightly. In Helmand province, Afghanistan, for instance, the locations of forward operating bases can be clearly seen, glowing white against the black map. (para. 14)*

Months later, PolarFlow, another popular fitness application, revealed that it too accidentally shared not only the locations of military operations, but also associated personnel. A joint investigation from Bellingcat and De Correspondent found that any individual could track military operations through three steps:

*First, you manually navigate to any location using Google Maps. For interesting results, pick a war zone, a military base or a secret service headquarters (such locations can be easily found using Wikipedia). Then, click on activities performed in the area to see the attached profiles. Choose one of them and then see where that person has also been exercising. All over the world. On the same map. (Chopyk, 2018, para. 5)*

The firm estimated that the identity of 6,460 military personnel was revealed using this method (Chopyk, 2018).

As healthcare data grows increasingly valuable and fitness trackers grow increasingly popular, responses to incidents like MyFitnessPal, Strava, and PolarFlow call for the possibility of government and regulatory intervention. The following section outlines the limited current regulations facing the industry.

## The Wearable Industry and Government Regulation

Among the significant issues facing the development of fitness trackers and wearable technologies, privacy and data security remain critical. Lupton (2016) reports "In the United States, where many internationally popular apps are developed, there are no legal requirements that app developers provide privacy policy statements in their information for users" (p. 125). In the three years since her book, no additional legal requirements were set, although organizations like Apple now strongly encourage each app sold in its online store to at least address privacy in the end-user licensing agreement (Apple, 2019a). However, although policy statements are now recommended, there are no requirements or recommendations for how apps approach data security or the measures they need to take in order to protect consumer data.

Barcena, Weueest and Lau (2014) found that there are two main ways that hackers can gain access to user data on healthcare apps. First, data is vulnerable when it is transmitted from one location to another (i.e. from a personal device to the cloud). Second, databases or warehouses may be vulnerable (Barcena et al., 2014). Despite calls in 2015 from the Nuffield Council on Bioethics for stronger regulations that force third party developers to consider privacy and security throughout the design process, thus far, no US policies exist, and minimal progress was made throughout the European Union (Nunffield Council on Bioethics, 2019).

Nissenbaum (2011) and Tene and Polonetsky (2013) argue that a traditional barrier to new legislation comes from public failures to understand the threats posed by these apps. As a result there is little motivation for members of Congress to develop legislation that would protect users. In addition, organizations like Apple spend millions of dollars each year lobbying on privacy and data security issues to ensure policies that protect corporate interests (Hollister, 2019). When these efforts are combined with an onerous and bulky legislative system, it can be difficult to develop and pass policies that address current technological challenges (Punj, 2019). Galetsi, Katsaliaki, and Kumar (2019) found globally, most privacy policies take government actors three to five years to develop, propose, and convert into law, meaning that many reactionary policies that respond to current privacy threats or issues do not go into effect for years.

However, there is evidence that recent data security threats and incidents have propelled government representatives to act quickly to propose policies that would address growing concerns. In 2018, Deputy Defense Secretary Patrick M. Shanahan announced new policies that would prohibit US military personnel from using activity trackers using GPS technologies (Garamone, 2018). Army Colonel Robert Manning III reflected, "The rapidly evolving market of devices, applications and services with geolocation capabilities presents a significant risk to the Department of Defense personnel on and off duty, and to our military operations globally" (Garamone, 2018, para. 2). By the end of 2018, countries including France, Germany, China, and Australia similarly adopted policies banning the technology for deployed personnel.

Further, organizations such as the American Bar Association (ABA) have introduced task forces with official policy recommendations for wearable manufactures and fitness tracker developers. Notably, the ABA suggested the expansion of HIPAA (Health Insurance Portability and Accountability Act) that would include fitness tracker data that is given to healthcare professionals for medical assessment (Patterson & Monahan, 2017).

Currently, the United States Food and Drug Administration (FDA) has issued the only policy requirements for fitness trackers through the Federal, Food, Drug and Cosmetic Act. Policies issued in 2016 require manufacturers to determine whether a product is classified as a "general wellness product" or is designed to treat "a disease or condition" (Patterson & Monahan, 2017, para. 4). Products designed to treat a disease or condition require "pre-market review and post-market regulatory requirements" while "general wellness products" are outside the purview of current FDA policies (Patterson & Monahan, 2017, para. 4). Critics of the FDA's policies state that most trackers are now used for a hybrid of activities which may span both classifications (Sumra, 2018). Because devices such as the Apple Watch allow the use of third party apps which may fall into either classification, it is difficult for any product or device to identify its purpose, thus allowing products designed to treat a disease or condition to avoid regulation.

While outside the scope of Congress, the move of federal agencies and the military to more closely monitor fitness trackers and wearable technology has spurred additional journalistic and public attention to the issue. This has inspired members of Congress to consider these technologies and the recommendations made by the agencies. In summer 2019, Senators Amy Klobuchar (D-MN) and Lisa Murkowski (R-AK) introduced the Protecting Personal Health Data Act (S. 1842). The pair reflected that reading human-interest pieces about the consequences of data breaches caused them to look into the issue. The act would direct the Department of Health and Human Service to develop regulations of "security of health-related consumer devices, services, applications, and software" (Tonsager, Kraus, Ackerman, & Ponder, 2019, para. 1). As of October 2019, no companion bill was introduced in the House of Representatives and no date was scheduled for a floor debate.

On the state level, some states have proposed legislation that would regulate apps developed in their state. For example, California is:

*...considering a bill that would expand California's health privacy law to include any information in possession of or derived from a digital health feedback system, which is broadly defined to include sensors, devices, and internet platforms connected to those sensors or devices that receive information about an individual. (Tonsager et al., 2019, para. 2)*

Again, although this bill was introduced in 2019, no vote or debate is scheduled (Chau, 2019).

Internationally, several countries have implemented privacy regulations that impact fitness trackers. For example, in 2018 in the European Union, the EU's General Data Protection Regulations (GDPR) was enacted to enforce the "requiring the consent of subjects for data processing, anonymizing collected data to protect privacy, providing data breach notifications, safely handling the transfer of data across borders, and requiring certain companies to appoint a data protection officer to oversee GDPR compliance" (De Groot, 2019). Although GDPR impacts technologies beyond wearable devices and fitness trackers, many organizations have already made modifications to their international policies, which also apply to the USA. For example, in response to the new GDPR policies, Fitbit users "now have the right to access and export your personal information; to delete data or your account (which might take up to 90 days); as well as to object to Fitbit's use of your personal data for things like marketing" (Charara, 2018, para. 12). There is some evidence that developments in European policy may motivate policy changes by organizations on a global scale. In 2019, Fitbit released a statement that summarized how GDPR policies now impact how US citizens can control the use of private data: "All Fitbit users globally enjoy the same account settings and tools that enable our European users to exercise their rights. These settings and tools let our users access, export, edit, delete, object to, and control certain uses of their data" (Charara, 2018, para. 3).

Despite these developments in the regulation of data collected through fitness trackers, little is known about how US policy makers discuss these technologies and related privacy issues. With the implementation of policies from federal agencies, introduction of bills in Congress, and state law developments, more research examining how governmental representatives discursively construct these issues and technologies is important.

## Critical Media Industry Studies and C-SPAN

Havens and Lotz (2012) framework for media industries research from a "critical cultural" approach analyzes the cultural forms that make up the corporate, public, and regulatory "dimensions" (p. 24) of media. Ramanathan and Tan (2015) argue that to understand how a technological issue like privacy is understood by the public and manifests in everyday life, scholars should analyze the many ways that an issue is discursively constructed by various actors. A critical media industry analysis allows researchers to examine how those actors discuss, relate, and critique an issue like privacy and data security while considering the potential impact of such statements (Havens, Lotz & Tinic, 2009).

Previous research establishes the importance of examining privacy and data security within fitness trackers from the perspective of users, journalists, and international governing bodies (primarily the EU) (Kronemyer, 2018; Millington, 2016; Pinto & Yagnik, 2017). However, no published studies have examined how fitness trackers are invoked by US regulators, members of Congress, or within public policy debates. Importantly, how fitness trackers and corresponding issues of privacy and data security are constructed by members of Congress could provide insight into the direction of future regulations and policies. Critical media industry studies support this research endeavor because it reinforces a need to understand how regulatory bodies use and construct technology in the development of policy. Novak's (2016) chapter examining how government representatives constructed the role of Netflix in everyday life during Congressional debates foreshadowed the way that government regulators would approve and hinder the development of future streaming technologies. Insight into how members of Congress construct a technological device can help scholars understand and predict future regulatory policies and actions (Herbert, Lotz & Marshall, 2019).

Stewart (1988) argued that Congressional discussion and debate is important to understanding how journalists, organizations, and the public interpret and interact with new technologies. Lee and Lee (2018) note that the framing of the future of public policy, government action or regulation by members of Congress can impact the public's awareness and journalistic coverage of a new technology. Congressional discourses have a "direct impact on the public's view of a media platform as well as any policies or laws tied to a platform" (Novak, 2016, p. 99).

Previous research by Allen (1998) and Seceleanu and Papari (2013) suggests that Congressional speeches are unique because they must both introduce a technology and persuade the audience that current policies are inadequate at addressing problems produced by such technology. Throughout this process, the speaker helps construct the definition and application of a technology for the listener, all while aiming to motivate action. Using a critical media industry analysis perspective, interpreting how members of Congress construct such technologies can produce insight into future policy actions.

C-SPAN serves as a digital archive of all activities happening in Congress including speeches on the Congressional floor, testimony in front of committees, and Congressional sponsored conferences. Novak (2016) argues C-SPAN is an important "hybrid between the media, the political process" (p. 37) and the construction of technological policies. As guaranteed by Congress, C-SPAN has archived all recorded footage in digital databases since the 1990s. Popkin and Kabashima (2007) argue C-SPAN is an important part of the media landscape because of its unique ability to provide access and enhance transparency between Congressional representatives and the public. In addition, C-SPAN provides academics access to all transcripts since 1992, which, unlike the official Congressional record, cannot be modified by speakers to correct past claims or irregularities. In short, C-SPAN's database allows scholars to apply a critical media industry studies perspective and analyze how speakers construct new technologies and related policies.

## METHODOLOGICAL APPROACH

This analysis uses Gee's (2011) discursive analysis approach to understand how Congressional speakers make meaning of fitness trackers and associated issues such as privacy and data security. To collect data, the C-SPAN archives were searched for any transcript containing the phrase "fitness tracker" or "tracking." In total 341 videos and corresponding transcripts were collected for analysis including 130 hours of related C-SPAN coverage. Videos and corresponding transcripts were then read and a set of emergent discourses were then identified to exclusively and exhaustively represent the ways speakers constructed fitness trackers. After the set of discourses was identified, the researchers again read and analyzed the transcripts and videos, selecting examples of each discourse for inclusion in the findings section. For a step-by-step procedure, see Appendix. As a qualitative approach, this project emphasizes a quixotic reliability foundation that aims to provide evidence throughout the findings with quotes and examples.

To establish the discourses, Gee's (2011) 'meaning-making task' patterns were assessed for significance, practices, identities, relationships, politics, connections, and sign systems/knowledge. Previous scholarship uses this framework to investigate C-SPAN discourses because of its strength in identifying the many ways that a term can be invoked in speeches and testimony (Brown, 2018). For definitions and examples of each meaning making task, see Table 1 in the Appendix. This research procedure was adapted from Browning and Browning (2013), Brown (2018), and Oxley (2018).

### Discourse 1: Fitness Trackers as Indicative of Larger Data Issues

### Broad privacy issues

Most frequently, the term "fitness tracker" was used as an example of larger privacy and data issues. In these examples, "fitness trackers" were often included in a list of technologies or devices that the speaker perceived to have similar risks or properties. For example, Representative Brad Sherman (D-CA) reflected:

*From fitness trackers to smart watches to smart phones, most of us have at least one device that could be used to track us... But they could post a security risk. This is especially true for our diplomats overseas whose locations and travels can reveal sensitive information sources. Location information is a potential gold mine for our adversaries. (Sherman, 2018, 26:48)*

Here, Sherman links fitness trackers to smartwatches and smartphones as a way to explain the importance of regulating these devices and potential risks associated without regulation. By further connecting fitness trackers to the safety of diplomats, Sherman invokes a sense of urgency and salience in his argument that these devices require government regulation.

Similarly, Representative Jaoquin Castro (D-TX) linked fitness trackers to other safety threats facing members of the government abroad:

*As members of Congress, and especially those who conduct oversight of the US State Department, we must protect our diplomats who serve our nation from any threats, including fitness trackers, for example, that expose locations… As lawmakers, we have a responsibility to ensure these brave diplomats and development workers have the protections they deserve. (Castro, 2017, 5:45).*

By using the terminology "any threats, including fitness trackers," Castro illustrates a connection between the devices and other actions or items that may endanger individuals. While he does not specifically name other threats, by invoking them, he discursive constructs a relationship between fitness trackers and danger.

## Discourse 2: Weighing the Pros and Cons

Beyond constructing relationships between fitness trackers and threats, speakers also used fitness trackers to illustrate larger concepts, such as data privacy and security. For example, Len Cali, Global Public Policy Senior Vice President for AT&T, was called to testify before the Senate Commerce, Science and Transportation Committee on data privacy. During his speech, Cali used "fitness trackers" as an example technology that the company was working to make safer within a military context. He reflected, "when location information is publicly posted for military personnel by a fitness tracker…if personal identifiers are removed, location information could enhance a beneficial traffic mapping app" (19:12). Here, fitness trackers are used to introduce some of AT&T's new applications that are designed to address everyday common frustrations, such as commute traffic. While Cali acknowledges the risks associated with sharing private information through fitness trackers, he frames this information as a way to solve nearly universal daily frustrations. When probed by Senator John Thune (R-SD), Cali reflects that although privacy concerns are ongoing, the information revealed through fitness trackers is relatively low-risk, and the benefits outweigh the negatives.

This type of argument, that the benefits associated with fitness trackers outweigh other concerns over privacy and even safety of military personnel were frequent throughout the dataset, particularly when coming from organization representatives (such as Cali from AT&T). This type of consequentialist argument suggests that the positive information garnered from fitness trackers outweighs the consequences or risks associated with their use. Discursively, speakers invoked an ethical consequential argument when defending the use of fitness trackers as a type of cover-technology for other devices that may similarly share location and healthcare information. Like Castro's speech, which used fitness trackers as an example, speakers were quick to use fitness trackers as a way to discuss other technologies, without ever mentioning them by name.

In a speech on the Internet of Things, Vice President for the Center for Data Innovation and Director of Information Technology & Innovation Foundation Daniel Castro explained to a GovLoop training session that new fitness trackers were specifically designed for those with physical or neurological limitations, such as Parkinson's Disease. When describing the risks associated with privacy violations of fitness trackers, Castro reflected, "It increases their independence, it addresses a major health condition. So why does any of this [privacy concerns] really matter" (Castro, 2017, 1:02)? Again, Castro argues that the benefits for Parkinson's patients outweighs the negatives of privacy violations.

Importantly, within these examples, no speaker specifically outlined what these privacy risks or threats were, but instead vaguely referenced them as if the audience already comprehensively understood them. While fitness trackers were often linked to other technologies, the concept of privacy risks or threats was not further explained or linked to other issues. It was often invoked in a consequentialist argument, but not explained beyond vague references (or referring to privacy as "this" or "it"). Discursively, this may be a strategic aim to reinforce fitness trackers as positive or beneficial items within society by individuals with a vested interest in their success (like AT&T, who just launched its own tracker through its cellular service). However, individuals who are critical of fitness trackers were also vague about the privacy concerns, even when introducing or vocalizing support for the privacy risks. Representatives Sherman and Castro, who spoke favorably about a bill that would require the military to develop policies that would regulate soldiers' use of fitness trackers, failed to use their time to illustrate the risks associated with these devices, but instead emphasized how the trackers are part of larger concerns over smart devices. These concerns were not described, but instead invoked to motivate votes to support the bills.

## Discourse 3: Military Implications for Data Security

Outside of using fitness trackers as representative of other technologies and risks, speakers often reflected on the military's role in developing, using, and regulating this technology. In a 2018 hearing to confirm Lieutenant General Paul Nakasone, the nominee to be the next director of the National Security Agency (NSA) and commander of U.S. Cyber Command, Nakasone reflected that "devices like Fitbits" were growing threats to the military and would require eventual policies to regulate how data is collected and stored by members of the armed forces. He stipulates that these technologies are an opportunity for counterintelligence threats that are life-threatening for members of the military. Therefore, he supports a ban on fitness trackers that collect GPS information until these devices can be made secure and safe.

Speakers like Nakasone illustrate a common discursive construction of fitness trackers, that they are a threat to the armed forces because of unspecified future attacks. During a confirmation hearing for Navy Secretary nominee Richard Spencer in 2017, Spencer similarly argued that the risks associated with these devices outweigh their benefit to each individual, again, supporting a policy that bans them from the military. In both cases, the speakers failed to specify the associated risks, but instead vaguely emphasized the consequences before suggesting a ban that would diminish the problem.

This was consistent with other speeches and hearings involving members of the military including General Mattis in 2017. Risks and threats were generalized and vague, relying on the listener to guess the types of dangers associated with such fitness tracking. Despite the missing details about the threats, all military representatives were consistent in their belief that the only solution was to ban the devices until they can be made safe.

Speakers made suggestions about changes fitness tracking companies should make before the devices are safe for military personnel. Nakasone suggested that GPS tracking should be optional, allowing military personnel to decline that feature. Spencer suggested that fitness trackers should keep data locally, preventing the vulnerability of transferring data to a cloud or centralized location. Finally, Mattis suggested keeping profiles encrypted, preventing hackers from being able to associate data with an individual. These suggestions all allude that the responsibility of data security and privacy with respect to military users lies with the device manufacturers and app developers, not with the users. And, because these organizations failed to enact safety measures, it was the responsibility of the leaders of the armed forces to enact policies that blocked the threat. This was dramatically different from how non-military personnel described the use of fitness trackers and the individuals responsible for everyday user data security and privacy.

## Discourse 4: Consumers as Responsible for Data Privacy

Unlike the speeches by military leadership, users were prevalently considered responsible for their own data security and privacy. Most speakers reflected that consumers were unaware of the potential data security risks associated with devices, particularly emphasizing that this ignorance was dangerous and problematic. For example, Senator John Thune (SD-R) reflected:

*Right now, consumers do not understand what is being done with their data and current legislation does provide protection, but it's been outstripped by technological development. HIPAA protects medical information stored in the doctor's files and not the medical information collected by your Fitbit. (Thune, 2019, 7:11).*

As Thune notes, users are unaware of the policies that regulate their healthcare data even in regard to traditional doctor files, let alone in new fitness trackers. Through Thune's speech, he clearly employs users to be more aware of how apps and devices collect and store data, rather than asking the organizations to improve security measures or policies. This directly contrasts with the clear suggestions outlined by military leadership aimed at changes in organizational policy (outlined in the previous section).

This was echoed by Len Cali (Global Public Policy Senior Vice President for AT&T), when he said "consumers need to understand the rules of the road regardless of the company collecting their data or the technology used" (Cali, 2018, 06:26). Like Thune, Cali suggests that users must become more aware of how their data is collected and stored. However, unlike Thune, Cali represents AT&T, and organization with an interest in diminishing the responsibilities (and therefore the liability) of the organization.

In a 2017 speech by Representative David Schweikert (R-AZ), the speaker again suggested that users must be better informed on issues of privacy or security threats, or they shouldn't be surprised when their information is vulnerable to hacks. Schweikert further argues that users should seek out opportunities for education on the topic, such as through the privacy policies outlined on organizational websites to become more familiar.

In instances like these, speakers often alluded to other health-related technologies that could carry similar privacy and data security concerns. Two years later, Schweikert proposed that wearable technologies were the "tip of the iceberg" and other innovations, including a kazoo that you blow into to get a flu diagnosis and then can order medicine, could similarly require consumers to be aware of privacy and data security issues. Discursively, connecting fitness trackers with other futurist technologies positions the devices as important pieces of technology that require consumer literacy and responsibility. Again, this reinforces a consumer, not organizational, responsibility for managing data and privacy. This does not mean that speakers ignored organizational responsibility altogether, but instead this was a focus after a cyber security threat was identified.

## Discourse 5: Organizations Fail to Keep Pace with Threats

While most speeches focused on the role and responsibility of users in monitoring their own data, some speakers called out organizations for failing to proactively create policies and take steps against threats.

Senator Mark Warner (D-VA) reflected that organizations were increasingly risky when handling private information, which meant that the US was quickly falling behind in developing technologies that both address human needs while keeping users safe. He reflected, "increasingly, we are walking away from setting the standards" and allowing other regions, such as the EU to develop policies that impact US companies and users.

However, it wasn't just organizations failing to realize the threats associated with fitness trackers, Warner explained that it was the government that previously struggled to develop policies that would adapt and respond to growing threats. Because of vulnerabilities exposed by Strava and US military personnel, he reflected, "We are finally ready to have some overdue conversations in the privacy, data transparency and other critical issues related to social media." For Warner, the developments which left US military personnel vulnerable were motivating and illustrated larger problems with the lack of federal regulations on the topic. He even expands the notion of privacy to include other devices and platforms besides fitness trackers including social media.

Other speakers similarly reflected that Congress needed to provide more comprehensive policies and reflection on fitness trackers, including speakers from advocacy groups. CEO Consumer Technology Association Gary Shapiro said:

*We have a culture and constitution that values privacy...Google, Apple, Fitbit, Samsung.... Keep it clean, simple and honest as it goes. I don't think this is Rocket Science... The Government has to be involved to enforce some of the segments in the future (Shapiro, 2019, 04:51).*

Here, Shapiro suggests that it is the government's responsibility to motivate organizational change through the enforcement of policy.

Importantly, rather than propose actual legislation or policies, these speakers instead focused on illustrating its importance and constructing the role of the government in privacy. This was consistent across speakers of all backgrounds (military, Congress, advocacy groups, private corporations) and truly reflects the limitations of current policies on fitness trackers, data security and privacy. In short, most conversations discuss why policy and attention on the topic are important, but not what policies should be or address.

## Discourse 6: Data Collected for Promotion/Strategic Communication Uses

Finally, there were limited references to the potential risks associated with data vulnerability outside of the context of hacking. For most speakers, hacking private fitness tracking information was the strongest threat to users (especially military personnel). However, other speakers acknowledged that the selling of private data to third parties for use of promotional or strategic communication was also a threat and violation of privacy standards. In Galen Institute President Grace Marie-Turner's testimony, she noted that an ongoing risk to Medicare patients was their vulnerability when sharing medical information with third-party (non-doctor) offices who may later sell their data to advertisers or predatory companies. This threat, she reflected, "increases when introducing wearable technology." To Marie-Turner, these technologies collect even more data that Medicare patients may not be aware of. Unlike earlier arguments, here Marie-Turner explains that certain population segments may be prey to predatory organizations who can sell or use medical information for advertising purposes. Here, the threat is not hackers, but the strategic aims of predatory companies that sell user data to advertisers.

In his testimony on privacy rights in the US, Federal Trade Commission Chair Joseph Simons adds that over time, organizations learn how to manipulate user experiences without breaking laws. In short, organizations make the most of user provided data, learning how to make it profitable. As users trade privacy for the convenience of data storage and tracking data, organizations view this exchange as a valuable. However, Simons advises Congress that there need to be actionable policies created to ensure that third parties do not take advantage of this data in unethical or risky ways. Again, there Simons makes no official suggestions for policies, but reinforces that this is a growing issue that Congress should pay attention to.

## SOLUTIONS AND RECOMMENDATIONS

This discursive analysis describes the six ways that speakers construct fitness trackers and correlating issues such as privacy and data security. Based on these six discourses, several overall reflections and future research recommendations can be reached: (1) various regulatory perspectives on fitness applications and data privacy, (2) changes and the evolution of discourses from 2012-2019, and (3) the ethical arguments presented in Congressional debates and discussions.

First, when speakers described fitness trackers, they often did so as an example of a new technology that needs regulatory control to ensure its safe and effective use. Although there were no examples within the 341 videos where regulatory proposals were issued or bills were formally announced, nearly all speakers reflected that some future regulations were necessary. Even in instances where leadership from telecommunications organizations (such as AT&T) testified, there were still calls for regulation.

Importantly, there was also little consensus on who or what body should be responsible for developing and implementing regulations. Testimony from FTC leadership suggested that Congress should develop policy, while testimony from members of Congress suggested that the FTC or FDA should be charged. The only speakers who directly proposed changes (but not policies) in the handling of personal data collected through fitness trackers were military leadership, but even these members failed to call out one regulating body that should oversee regulation.

Importantly, the lack of specific proposals and disagreement over what bodies should regulate fitness trackers seemingly reinforce Galetsi et al. (2019) and Tene and Polonetsky's (2013) conclusions that new technologies are very difficult to regulate. In addition to their conclusion that technological regulation is very difficult because of a bulky and onerous system, these discourses suggest that Congressional representatives fail to propose specific changes that could produce regulation. In short, there is talk about fitness trackers and associated issues, there is consensus that regulation is necessary, but there are no examples of specific actions or policies that would allow the first two points to manifest beyond talk on the Congressional floor.

It is likely that the lack of specific recommendations or proposals reflects the relative newness of fitness trackers and the complex nature of associated issues such as data privacy and security. Nissenbaum (2011) notes that complicated technological challenges often garner great attention from the public, but have a difficult time motivating actual regulatory actions because of their complicated nature. It is likely that this phenomenon extends into the political sphere and on the Congressional floor. More research that considers the self-reflection of regulators may better explain the reasoning for a lack of proposals or specific policies.

However, the lack of specific policy proposals challenges the findings of Allen (1998) and Seceleanu and Papari (2013) who argue Congressional speeches must both inform and persuade. Throughout this dataset, speakers mostly informed listeners about the potential problems and prevalence of fitness trackers but did not seem to persuade listeners to adopt a specific stance, change actions, or even develop their own policies. Future research should consider whether these findings persist long-term, beyond 2019, or if future speeches later become more persuasive once specific policies are proposed or adopted.

Second, the dataset provides insight into how discourses have evolved since 2012. Most notably, the number of mentions of fitness trackers grew each year since 2012, which may reflect the growing popularity and prevalence of the devices (see Table 2 in the Appendix). The frequency of mentions and videos seems to correlate with Wurmser's (2019) growth of 3% per year in the number of Americans who regularly wear fitness trackers. Based on the market predictions of Lee and Lee (2018), if the popularity of smartwatches and wearable technologies continues to grow; it is possible that mentions by members of Congress may also continue to grow.

While more statistical research is necessary to confirm a correlation, the growth of fitness tracker popularity alongside the increasing frequency of the terminology in Congressional speeches suggests a relationship between the popularity of a subject and its attention by Congress. This also supports Nissenbaum (2011) and Tene and Polonetsky's (2013) arguments that public interest can motivate Congressional action (as disinterest motivates inaction). Again, while a specific examination of this topic is outside the scope of this study, the growth in the use of "fitness tracker" in speeches should support future research.

Additionally, when examining the discourses collectively, there is also evidence that developing events or issues motivated the attention and focus of speeches. For example, US Military leadership as well as members of Congress used the privacy violations of Strava and PolarFlow to illustrate how data collected by trackers could threaten the safety of the military. Speakers treated the Strava and PolarFlow incidents as case studies that illustrate the vulnerabilities of stored personal data as well as the uncertainty of how these devices could threaten lives or operations in the future. Galetsi et al.'s (2019) work on the development of reactionary policies for technology suggests that current events often serve as a springboard for political action because they galvanize the public and provide tangible evidence of threats that can be mitigated through policy. However, Galetsi et al. (2019) also note that reactionary policies can take years for development and implementation, meaning that initial speeches reflecting on these threats can come up to five years before actualized changes. Because the Strava and PolarFlow incidents only occurred in 2018, future work should examine if later reactionary policies were developed, thus supporting the three to five year development process outlined by Galetsi et al. (2019).

Finally, speakers tended to invoke only one ethical argument when reflecting on fitness trackers. The consequentialist argument, which suggests looking at the consequences of an action to determine its value, was invoked by Congressional representatives, military leadership, and telecommunications leadership. In these instances, speakers almost always identified the consequences of fitness trackers as threats to personal and public safety. However, these threats were rarely described beyond the invocation of current issues such as Strava and PolarFlow. In short, while many speakers used consequentialism to frame the reasons why regulatory policies were necessary, they were vague about the exact consequences. Importantly, these threats were both framed illegally through invoking of hackers, and legally through corporate business deals that sell information for personalized advertising. Although neither consequence was framed as better or worse than the other, both served as arguments for stronger regulations to minimize risks or threats.

However, not all consequences were framed negatively. There were instances where speakers discussed how the personal insight and health information gained through fitness trackers may outweigh any risks associated with privacy or data security. In these cases, Lupton's (2016) quantifiable self-argument was invoked by speakers who framed data as a type of power for individuals. Although safety and security were still important to these speakers, in these speeches, the information garnered outweighed these risks, thus prioritizing the quantifiable self. Future research should look at other ways that actors invoke the quantifiable self, such as through journalistic coverage of fitness trackers. It is likely that the consequentialist discourse emerges in other sets of data specifically as speakers grapple with the task of balancing the benefits of fitness trackers with the risks.

## FUTURE RESEARCH DIRECTIONS

Future studies should continue to examine how Congressional discourses evolve to characterize issues associated with fitness trackers, especially if (or) when formal policies are introduced, debated, enforced, or challenged. Further work should also examine how global policies impact and shape discourses and technological capabilities across national borders. As fitness trackers in various forms continue to grow popular and permeate global lifestyles, more attention to associated issues such as privacy and data security is necessary to ensure their safe use.

## CONCLUSION

As fitness trackers and applications continue to grow popular, regulators and members of Congress will be faced with additional challenges to data privacy and security. It is likely that incidents, such as the revealing of military intelligence, will appear and demand regulatory attention by developers, advocates, and the public. These discourses may continue to evolve as incidents occur, and future scholars should continue to study how members of Congress shift discourses to address future issues.

## ACKNOWLEDGMENT

This research received no specific grant from any funding agency in the public, commercial, or not-for-profit sectors.

## REFERENCES

Allen, J. (1998). Who shapes the future? Problem framings and the development of handheld computers. *ACM SIGCAS Computers and Society, 28*(2), 3–8. doi:10.1145/276758.276762

Allison, C. (2018, Dec. 19). Smartwatches will remain the most popular wearables into 2022. *Wearable.com.* Retrieved from: https://www.wareable.com/smartwatches/smartwatches-most-popular-wearable-2022-idc-6840

Apple. (2019a). App store review guidelines. *Apple.com*. Retrieved from https://developer.apple.com/app-store/review/guidelines. /

Apple. (2019b). Apple Watch: Helping your patients identify early warning sings. *Apple.com*. Retrieved from: https://www.apple.com/healthcare/apple-watch/

Asimakopoulos, S., Asimakopoulos, G., & Spillers, F. (2017). Motivation and user engagement in fitness tracking: Heuristics for mobile healthcare wearables. *Informatics*, *4*(1), 5. Advance online publication. doi:10.3390/informatics4010005

Barber, D., Carter, A., Harris, J., & Reinerman-Jones, L. (2017). *Feasibility of wearable fitness trackers for adapting multimodal communication*. doi:10.1007/978-3-319-58521-5_39

Barcena, M. B., Weueest, C., & Lau, H. (2014). *How safe is your quantified self?* Symantech.

Bonnington, C. (2018, March 29). The MyFitnessPal hack may affect 150 million people. it could've been even worse. *Slate*. Retrieved from https://slate.com/technology/2018/03/myfitnesspal-hack-under-armour-data-breach.html

Brown, N. E. (2018). Using C-SPAN to examine the political discourse of HIV/AIDS, 1985-1987. In R. Browning (Ed.), *The year in C-SPAN archives research* (Vol. 4). Purdue University Press.

Browning, R., & Browning, R. (2013). The C-SPAN video archives: A case study. *The American Archivist*, *77*(2), 425–443. doi:10.17723/aarc.77.2.b40251245102j258

Cali, L. (2018). AT&T response. *C-SPAN*. Retrieved from: https://www.c-span.org/video/?448484-2/us-house-meets-legislative-business&transcriptQuery=fitness&start=18134

Castro, J. (2017). Government use of the Internet of Things, Part 1. *C-SPAN*. Retrieved from: https://www.c-span.org/video/?327798-1/discussion-connected-government&start=1186

Charara, S. (2018, April 25). Your fitness app's privacy policy may be about to change – and that's a good thing. *Wearable.com*. Retrieved from https://www.wareable.com/wearable-tech/fitness-apps-privacy-policies-gdpr

Chau, M. (2019, Feb. 5). AB-384 Information privacy: digital health feedback systems. *Legislature of California*. Retrieved from https://leginfo.legislature.ca.gov/faces/billTextClient.xhtml?bill_id=201920200AB384

Chopyk, J. (2018). Another security breach. *Lawless Tech*. Retrieved from https://lawless.tech/another-security-breach-fitness-trackers-that-track-things-way-beyond-fitness

De Groot, J. (2019). What is the General Data Protection Regulation? Understanding & complying with GDPR requirements in 2019. *Digital Guardian*. Retrieved from https://digitalguardian.com/blog/what-gdpr-general-data-protection-regulation-understanding-and-complying-gdpr-data-protection

Edwards, L., Klein, B., Lee, D., Moss, G., & Philip, F. (2013). Framing the consumer: Copyright regulation and the public. *Convergence*. Retrieved from http://eprints.whiterose.ac.uk/76877/3/LeeDJ.pdf

Galetsi, P., Katsaliaki, K., & Kumar, S. (2020). Big data analytics in health sector: Theoretical framework, techniques and prospects. *International Journal of Information Management, 50*, 206–216. doi:10.1016/j.ijinfomgt.2019.05.003

Garamone, J. (2018, Aug. 6). New policy prohibits GPS tracking in deployed settings. *Department of Defense.* Retrieved from https://www.defense.gov/Newsroom/News/Article/Article/1594486/new-dod-policy-prohibits-gps-enabled-devices-in-deployed-settings/

Gee, J. P. (2011). *An introduction to discourse analysis: Theory and method* (3rd ed.). Routledge.

Gessert, D., & Schuetz, S. (2018). 1115 Using a fitness tracker to diagnose non-24-hour sleep-wake rhythm disorder. *Sleep, 41*(suppl1), A414–A414. doi:10.1093leep/zsy063.1114

Havens, T., Lotz, A., & Tinic, S. (2009). Critical media industry studies: A research approach. *Communication, Culture & Critique, 2*(2), 234–253. doi:10.1111/j.1753-9137.2009.01037.x

Havens, T., & Lotz, A. D. (2012). *Understanding media industries.* Oxford University Press.

Herbert, D., Lotz, A., & Marshall, L. (2019). Approaching media industries comparatively: A case study of streaming. *International Journal of Cultural Studies, 22*(3), 349–366. doi:10.1177/1367877918813245

Hern, A. (2018a, Jan 28). Fitness tracking app gives away location of secret US army bases. *The Guardian.* Retrieved from https://www.theguardian.com/world/2018/jan/28/fitness-tracking-app-gives-away-location-of-secret-us-army-bases

Hern, A. (2018b, Jan 29). Strava secret army bas locations heatmap public users military ban. *The Guardian.* Retrieved from https://www.theguardian.com/technology/2018/jan/29/strava-secret-army-base-locations-heatmap-public-users-military-ban

Hollister, S. (2019, May 1). An Apple lobbyist just sneakily pushed California to postpone its right-to-repair bill. *The Verge.* Retrieved from https://www.theverge.com/2019/5/1/18525542/apple-right-to-repair-bill-california-lobbyist-comptia

Humer, C., & Finkle, J. (2014). Your medical record is worth more to hackers than your credit card. *Reuters.* Retrieved from https://www.reuters.com/article/us-cybersecurity-hospitals/your-medical-record-is-worth-more-to-hackers-than-your-credit-card-idUSKCN0HJ21I20140924

Kronemyer, B. (2018). European GDPR impacts U.S. patient privacy. *Dermatology Times, 39*(12), 62, 70.

Lee, S., & Lee, K. (2018). Factors that influence an individual's intention to adopt a wearable healthcare device: The case of a wearable fitness tracker. *Technological Forecasting and Social Change, 129*, 154–163. doi:10.1016/j.techfore.2018.01.002

Levinson, C., Fewell, L., & Brosof, L. (2017). My Fitness Pal calorie tracker usage in the eating disorders. *Eating Behaviors, 27*, 14–16. doi:10.1016/j.eatbeh.2017.08.003 PMID:28843591

Liu, J. (2019). Number of Fitbit devices sold worldwide from 2010 to 2018 (in 1,000s). *Statistica.* Retrieved from: https://www.statista.com/statistics/472591/fitbit-devices-sold/

Lupton, D. (2016). *The quantified self.* Polity.

Millington, B. (2016). Fit for prosumption: Interactivity and the second fitness boom. *Media Culture & Society, 38*(8), 1184–1200. doi:10.1177/0163443716643150

Nissenbaum, H. (2011). A contextual approach to privacy online. *Daedalus, 140*(4), 32–48. doi:10.1162/DAED_a_00113

Novak, A. N. (2016). Smartest guys in the room: Framing the future of media regulation through Netflix. In K. McDonald & D. Smith-Rowsey (Eds.), *The Netflix Effect: Technology and Entertainment in the 21st Century*. Bloomsbury Press.

Nuffield Council on Bioethics. (2019). Project biological health data. *Nuffield Bioethics.org*. Retrieved from http://nuffieldbioethics.org/project/biological-health-data

Oxley, Z. M. (2018). Portrayals of PUblic Policy Discourse. In R. Browning (Ed.), *The year in C-SPAN archives research* (Vol. 4). Purdue University Press.

Patterson, J., & Monahan, E. (2017). Three emerging risks and regulations affecting fitness trackers and wearable devices. *American Bar Association*. Retrieved from https://www.americanbar.org/groups/litigation/committees/products-liability/practice/2017/three-risks-and-regulations-affecting-wearable-devices/

Pinto, M., & Yagnik, A. (2017). Fit for life: A content analysis of fitness tracker brands use of Facebook in social media marketing. *Journal of Brand Management, 24*(1), 49–67. doi:10.105741262-016-0014-4

Popkin, S., & Kabashima, I. (2007). Introduction: Changing media, changing politics. *Japanese Journal of Political Science, 8*(1), 1–6. doi:10.1017/S1468109907002538

Punj, G. (2019). Understanding individuals' intentions to limit online personal information disclosures to protect their privacy: Implications for organizations and public policy.(Report). *Information Technology Management, 20*(3), 139–151. doi:10.100710799-018-0295-2

Ramanathan, R., & Tan, B. (2015). Application of critical discourse analysis in media discourse studies. *3L, Language, Linguistics, Literature, 21*(3). Retrieved from http://search.proquest.com/docview/2257700630/

Schechner, S., & Secada, M. (2019, Feb. 22). You give apps sensitive personal information. Then they tell Facebook. *Wall Street Journal*. Retrieved from https://www.wsj.com/articles/you-give-apps-sensitive-personal-information-then-they-tell-facebook-11550851636?mod=article_inline

Seceleanu, A., & Papari, A. (2013). Presentation of media discourse of information on social issues through the construction of the Agenda Setting and Framing. *International Proceedings of Economics Development and Research, 62*, 17.

Shapiro, G. (2018). Reflection on data security. *C-SPAN*. Retrieved from https://www.c-span.org/video/?456964-1/communicators-gary-shapiro

Sherman, B. (2018). News review with Brand Sherman. *C-SPAN*. Retrieved from https://www.c-span.org/video/?442878-6/washington-journal-representative-brad-sherman-d-ca-discusses-russia-investigation

Stewart, D. (1988). Go tell it to Congress- South Carolina v. Baker, Lyng v. Northwest Indian Cemetery Protective Ass'n, Traynor v. Turnage. *ABA Journal*, 74.

Stiglbauer, B., Weber, S., & Batinic, B. (2019). Does your health really benefit from using a self-tracking device? Evidence from a longitudinal randomized control trial.(Report). *Computers in Human Behavior, 94*, 131–139. doi:10.1016/j.chb.2019.01.018

Sumra, H. (2018, Jan 29). How FDA approval affects your wearables, and how it's going to change. *Wearable.com.* Retrieved from https://www.wareable.com/wearable-tech/fda-wearables-state-of-play-239

Sydell, L. (2019, Feb. 27). Storing health records on your phone: Can apple live up to its privacy values? *NPR.* Retrieved from: https://www.npr.org/2019/02/27/697026827/storing-health-records-on-your-phone-can-apple-live-up-to-its-privacy-values

Tene, O., & Polonetsky, J. (2013). A theory of creepy: Technology, privacy, and shifting social norms. *Yale Journal of Law & Technology, 16*, 59–134.

Thune, J. (2019). Replacing the healthcare law. *C-SPAN.* Retrieved from https://www.c-span.org/video/?427815-4/representative-schweikert-health-care-law-replacement

Today, U. S. A. (2018, Feb 26). Fitbit's stock plunges after company says it's losing money. *USA Today.* Retrieved from: https://www.usatoday.com/story/tech/news/2018/02/26/fitbits-stock-plunges-after-company-says-its-losing-money/375190002/

Tonsager, L., Kraus, A., Ackerman, W., & Ponder, J. (2019). Legislation Seeks to regulate privacy and security of wearables and genetic testing kits. *Inside Privacy.* Retrieved from https://www.insideprivacy.com/data-privacy/legislation-seeks-to-regulate-privacy-and-security-of-wearables-and-genetic-testing-kits/

Wurmser, J. (2019). Wearables 2019: Advanced wearables pick up pace as fitness trackers slow. *Emarketer.* Retrieved from: https://www.emarketer.com/content/wearables-2019

## ADDITIONAL READING

Asimakopoulos, S., Asimakopoulos, G., & Spillers, F. (2017). Motivation and user engagement in fitness tracking: Heuristics for mobile healthcare wearables. *Informatics, 4*(1), 5. Advance online publication. doi:10.3390/informatics4010005

Classen, J., Wegemer, D., Patras, P., Spink, T., & Hollick, M. (2018). Anatomy of a vulnerable fitness tracking system: Dissecting the Fitbit cloud, app, and firmware. *Proceedings of the ACM on Interactive, Mobile, Wearable and Ubiquitous Technologies, 2*(1), 1–24. 10.1145/3191737

Galetsi, P., Katsaliaki, K., & Kumar, S. (2020). Big data analytics in health sector: Theoretical framework, techniques and prospects. *International Journal of Information Management, 50*, 206–216. doi:10.1016/j.ijinfomgt.2019.05.003

Gee, J. P. (2011). *An introduction to discourse analysis: Theory and method* (3rd ed.). Routledge.

Havens, T., & Lotz, A. D. (2012). *Understanding media industries.* Oxford University Press.

Lupton, D. (2016). *The quantified self.* Polity.

Tene, O., & Polonetsky, J. (2013). A theory of creepy: Technology, privacy, and shifting social norms. *Yale Journal of Law & Technology, 16*, 59–134.

Torre, I., Sanchez, O., Koceva, F., & Adorni, G. (2018). Supporting users to take informed decisions on privacy settings of personal devices. *Personal and Ubiquitous Computing, 22*(2), 345–364. doi:10.100700779-017-1068-3

## KEY TERMS AND DEFINITIONS

**C-SPAN:** Cable-Satellite Public Affairs Network which archives and broadcasts the activities of Congress and government representatives.

**Critical Media Industry Analysis:** A theoretical and methodological tool for understanding the effect of the media industry on a technological phenomenon.

**Cyber Security:** The measures used by a site, platform, or software to protect users from digital threats such as hacking.

**Data Warehouses:** Digital archives of user information including personal identifiers collected from internet use history. Data is often sold to advertisers and retailers to craft specific persuasive messages.

**Discourse Analysis:** A critical methodological tool for studying texts and analyzing patterns and meaning within a dataset.

**Hybrid Beings:** The blend of human and technological elements to create an optimal human experience.

**Platform:** A digital space that invites users to participate and engage each other.

## ENDNOTE

[1]    There is a wide variety of terminology used to describe technologies that are worn on the body to track health and fitness information. This project adopts "fitness trackers" as a term of reference, but when applicable, uses the terminology invoked in cited works. Therefore, it may appear that multiple terms are used throughout.

*This research was previously published in Privacy Concerns Surrounding Personal Information Sharing on Health and Fitness Mobile Apps; pages 240-267, copyright year 2021 by Information Science Reference (an imprint of IGI Global).*

## APPENDIX

1.  Videos and transcripts were collected using the C-SPAN Archives (https://www.c-span.org/about/videoLibrary/). Data includes all mentions of "fitness trackers" (and all variations of spelling and grammar), "wearables" (and all variations of spelling and grammar), and "smart watch" (and all variations of spelling and grammar). There were no date restrictions set for this project, and the first documented use of any of these terms was on April 1, 2012. Total collection is 341 videos (with 1120 mentions within videos).
    a.  This project equivocates each video as "one text," despite that terms may be used multiple times in one video. According to C-SPAN, videos are identified as inclusive sessions of Congressional Speech. For example, a video may be an "Open House Session" which could take up to ten hours and feature dozens of speakers. Or, a video could include the testimony of multiple individuals to a Senate committee. Based on this logic, the total video collection is 341 videos, representing 130 hours, with 1120 mentions of fitness trackers, featuring 197 unique speakers. See Table 2 in the Appendix for a description of each term and its use during each year.
2.  Researchers independently read manuscripts and watched corresponding videos to code for Gee's seven meaning making tasks (see Table 1 in the Appendix for description and examples). Videos were assigned one, two, or three practices each.
    a.  As a qualitative project, the goal is not statistical coding, but seeking out patterns of how uses invoke each task to create discourses
3.  Researchers meet to review findings and identify discourses based on the patterns of use of each meaning making task.
4.  Six frequent discourses were identified by researchers to identify how speakers invoked, constructed, and reflected on fitness trackers.
5.  Researchers independently re-read and re-watched the dataset to find examples and quotes that invoke each discourse for inclusion in the written paper

*Table 1.*

| Task | Description | Example from dataset |
|---|---|---|
| *Significance* | Text reflects importance of issue, device, or individual | "It increases their independence, it addresses a major health condition. So why does any of this really matter?" |
| *Practices* | Text describes the issue, device, or topic for other users; or engages/provides action for other users in conversation | "We are finally ready to have some overdue conversations in the privacy, data transparency and other critical issues related to social media." |
| *Identities* | Text uses nouns and adjectives to describe the issue, device, or individuals | "If personal identifiers are removed, location information could enhance a beneficial traffic mapping app" |
| *Relationships* | Text connects issue, device, or topic to other events, or foci | "We must protect our diplomats who serve our nation from any threats, including fitness trackers, for example, that expose locations" |
| *Politics* | Text reflects on the social, historical, civic, or political nature of the issue, device, or topic | "Right now, consumers do not understand what is being done with their data and current legislation does provide protection, but it's been outstripped by technological development." |
| *Connections* | Text discusses the relevance of the issue, device, or topic by comparing or relating to other issues | "From fitness trackers to smart watches to smart phones, most of us have at least one device that could be used to track us… But they could post a security risk." |
| *Sign systems and knowledge* | Text common language practices, jargon, or cultural knowledge within tweet | "We have a culture and constitution that values privacy… Google, Apple, Fitbit, Samsung…. Keep it clean, simple and honest as it goes. I don't think this is Rocket Science… The Government has to be involved to enforce some of the segments in the future." |

*Table 2.*

| Term | 2012 | 2013 | 2014 | 2015 | 2016 | 2017 | 2018 | 2019 | Total |
|---|---|---|---|---|---|---|---|---|---|
| "Fitness trackers" "fitness tracking" "fitness track" "Fitbit" "Fit bit" "Jawbone" "Strava" | 3 | 13 | 15 | 22 | 29 | 40 | 33 | 38 | 193 |
| "Wearables" "wearable devices" wear able" | 0 | 2 | 4 | 4 | 7 | 9 | 10 | 9 | 45 |
| "Smart watch" "smart-watch" "smartwatch" "Apple Watch" "iWatch" | 1 | 11 | 12 | 20 | 19 | 11 | 9 | 20 | 103 |

"Apple Watch," "Fitbit," "Strava" and "Jawbone" are the names of popular products within this time period. Future work should consider including the names of current popular products.

# Chapter 18
# Role of Wearable Technology and Fitness Apps in Obesity and Diabetes:
## Privacy, Ownership, and Portability of Data

**Shariq I. Sherwani**
*Ohio University, USA*

**Benjamin R. Bates**
*Ohio University, USA*

## ABSTRACT

*Rapid economic growth, industrialization, mechanization, sedentary lifestyle, high calorie diets, and processed foods have led to increased incidence of obesity in the United States of America. Prominently affected by the obesity epidemic are the most vulnerable such as the rural poor and those who have less access to nutritious and healthy foods due to barriers such as socioeconomic, infrastructural, and organizational. Wearable technology (WT) and health fitness applications (apps) have the potential to address some of the health disparities associated with obesity. Monitoring health parameters through WT and Apps using remote sensing technology generates personal health data which can be captured, analyzed, and shared with healthcare providers and others in social support network. Because captured data include protected health information, and breaches can occur, the concerns about health data privacy, personal ownership, and portability are addressed in this chapter.*

## INTRODUCTION

This chapter explores how wearable technology (WT) and health and fitness applications (Apps) play an important role in consumer behavior in the context of the current obesity epidemic impacting the population of the United States (US). Focusing primarily on metabolic diseases such as obesity and diabetes and comorbidities such as end stage renal disease (ESRD) and cardiovascular diseases (CVDs), the authors

DOI: 10.4018/978-1-6684-6311-6.ch018

investigate the role that WT and fitness Apps play in communicating health through (a) data capturing, (b) data storage, (c) data sharing, (d) data usage, (e) data management, (f) data privacy, (g) data portability, and (h) privacy rights (Hicks et al., 2019; Izmailova, Wagner, & Perakslis, 2018; Quesada-Gonzalez & Merkoci, 2017). The authors also consider the role that WT and Apps play in medicine and health communication within the realm of public health and organizations. The arguments within the framework of the three P's of data – privacy, personal ownership, and portability – are also outlined as these important elements are at the forefront of the debate surrounding data analytics and data confidentiality. Finally, this chapter proposes that with proper incorporation into the overall US healthcare system, WT and Apps have the potential to help in the fight against metabolic diseases instead of functioning as just a standalone weight loss option (Piwek, Ellis, Andrews, & Joinson, 2016).

## BACKGROUND

Data privacy is a major concern if the data are stored and shared carelessly despite encryption. Encryption prevents unauthorized parties from having access to intelligible data because they lack the key to decrypt the data. But, even with military encryption there are data breaches as was evident when Strava, a global positioning system (GPS)-based cycling and running App, accidentally revealed the location of US soldiers in Syria and Iraq by publishing the global "heat map," showing the movements of people who had made their data public. Strava is a digital service which calls itself the "the social network for athletes" and can be accessed and used via mobile App for personal training, monitoring, and social interactions – uploading runs, sharing updates, and following other athletes. One of the drawbacks with Strava, as with any other data-generating and management technology is that a rogue third party could easily obtain and sell the data to "shady" organizations that could compromise individual and organizational data. Regarding information protection, Strava claims:

*We take several measures to safeguard the collection, transmission and storage of the data we collect. We employ reasonable protections for your information that are appropriate to its sensitivity. The Services use industry standard Secure Sockets Layer (SSL) technology to allow for the encryption of personal information and credit card numbers. (Strava Privacy Policy, 2019)*

On the Privacy Label, Strava clearly indicates that it shares and sells aggregate information and that it retains personal data as long as necessary unless the consumer requests for deletion (Strava Privacy Policy, 2019). Given these far-reaching controls over data ownership, especially when it is shared or sold as aggregate information by entities like Strava, users have no control over it. However, users can have control over it when it comes to sharing their data, including personal health data, with third parties, only if users voluntarily and diligently remember not to give consent (opt-out) to Strava to share their data. Thus, the onus falls on the clients to opt-out, and Strava operates with the premise that many users will simply forget about it.

Individuals feel empowered in managing some of their problematic health consequences by having access to their personal data and controlling it in terms of capture, analysis, and sharing with healthcare providers and those in their social support network (SSN) such as family, friends, and colleagues (Vo, Auroy, & Sarradon-Eck, 2019). Even though data portability makes personal data interoperable between different data controllers, the individuals, technically, do not own their personal data – they can just share their data using Apps and digital services. According to the Center for Digital Democracy and the School of Communication at American University, the US consumers and their personal data are not provided the protection with regard to WT, making it vulnerable.

## METABOLIC DISEASES AND COMORBIDITIES

Obesity is a major public health issue which compromises general health, ability to accomplish normal tasks, economic opportunities, and can also be a national security issue (Popkin, 2011; Puhl & Heuer, 2010; World Health Organization [WHO], 2018). Obesity is defined as a medical condition in which unwanted fat depositions occur inside the body (WHO, 2000). Obesity a risk factor for several chronic diseases and comorbidities such as diabetes, cancers, hypertension, organ failure, cardiovascular diseases (CVD), obstructive sleep apnea (OSA), and disabilities (WHO, 2018). Obesity is the leading cause of global mortality, but it is largely a preventable disease (NCD Risk Factor Collaboration [NCD-RisC], 2019). Obesity emerges from the complex interplay of genetic susceptibility, individual behavior, ethnic background, culture, and environment including diet, physical activity, and other lifestyle choices (Centers for Disease Control and Prevention [CDC], 2009). If current growth rates of obesity are not checked, obesity will place an overwhelming burden on the US healthcare system (Hruby & Hu, 2015).

Effective obesity prevention management strategies require a collaboration among healthcare system(s), individuals, and society (Institute of Medicine [IOM], 2013). The CDC (2018) guidelines indicate that individuals with a Body Mass Index (BMI) of 25 to <30 are overweight and those with BMI of 30 or higher are obese. In the United States, as of 2011-2014, over one-third or 78.6 million (34.9%) of the adults and 12.7 million (17%) children and adolescents aged 2-19 years were obese (CDC, 2018).

Obesity has severe financial implications as it is a major burden on the US healthcare and socioeconomic system as the costs of obesity care continue to skyrocket. For example, the 1998 costs associated with obesity and overweight care included $12.8 billion out-of-pocket, $28.1 billion through private insurance, $14.1 billion through Medicaid, and $23.5 billion through Medicare, for a total cost of $78.5 billion (Finkelstein, Fiebelkorn, & Wang, 2003). The total medical costs associated with obesity care increased to $147 billion in 2008, and to a total of $344 billion in 2018, from a total of $78.5 billion in 1998 (da Luz, Hay, Touyz, & Sainsbury, 2018; Partnership to Fight Chronic Disease, 2018). The overall economic impact of obesity is described in terms of lost productivity due to illness, absences, quality-adjusted life years (QALY), disability, insurance losses, and bullying, which are expected to continue to increase in the next 10 years (Hammond & Levine, 2010). Promoting healthier lifestyle via medical monitoring while using WT and fitness Apps and regular health checkups can help with maintaining a healthier lifestyle which has potential in managing obesity and related comorbidities.

Obesity is not purely an individual, social, cultural, or medical problem rather it is a complex public health problem, so, in the public health context, it must be studied and tackled with a multi-pronged approach (Agha & Agha, 2017; Blumenthal & Seervai, 2018). Public health entities and governmental programs need to address the following determinants and risk factors such as: genetic, socioeconomic, cultural, environmental, institutional, policymaking, and resources that directly or indirectly affect obesity (Daniel, Bornstein, & Kane, 2018). As a critical public health issue, obesity has become a global epidemic and requires population-based strategies and interventions for preventing it (Gortmaker et al., 2011). There are many public health efforts and intervention programs initiated by the government, non-governmental organizations (NGO), and in public-private partnerships (PPP) but with limited success in tackling obesity (Rowe et al., 2013). Technology and technology-based interventions can provide solutions for better understanding, management, and prevention of obesity and diabetes (Coons et al., 2012). WT can empower individuals and allow them to take charge of their own health by capturing metabolic data and communicating them with individuals in their social and professional networks. Technology has been found to be associated with children's and adults' sedentary lifestyle due to video games, electronic gadgets, and wireless gaming consoles but WT has been found to motivate individuals in living and maintain a healthier lifestyle where they feel in-charge of their own health as novel WT and Apps continue to penetrate the market (Foster & Torous, 2019).

In the healthcare segment, WT and fitness Apps can be utilized as interventions in reducing, managing, and preventing obesity. The use of WT is critical as it provides a low-cost option for capturing and sharing patient data, consultations between healthcare providers, and ultimately making treatment and disease management decisions while allowing individuals to exercise control over their own biometric and health data (Godfrey et al., 2018). WT and fitness Apps continue to provide options to patients and newer opportunities for healthcare providers to treat their patients and manage treatment options (Moustafa, Kenn, Sayrafian, Scanlon, & Zhang, 2015). WT and health fitness Apps are at the forefront of helping in managing obesity and other metabolic illnesses such as diabetes, cardiovascular diseases, and sleep apnea (Mohammed, Sendra, Lloret, & Bosch, 2018; Mullington et al., 2016). The wireless body area network (WBAN), which consists of biosensors for capturing biometric data, can help in communicating important health information between patients, healthcare providers, and family members through the use of intelligent databases (Mohammed et al., 2018). The regular monitoring of health information and sharing it with their healthcare providers and those in their SSN can help motivate people in implementing weight-loss behaviors, workout sessions, and healthier lifestyles.

## WEARABLE TECHNOLOGY: FUTURE OF HEALTHCARE

Wearable technology devices are mostly computerized and often connected to the Internet while attached to the body. These devices are capable of capturing, monitoring, managing, and sharing data (Godfrey et al., 2018; Quesada-Gonzalez & Merkoci, 2017). Some common examples of WT include fitness wristbands (Fitbit, Actiwatch 2, Smartwatch, GlucoWatch Biographer), smart glasses (Google Glass, Recon Snow 2), smart clothing (Siren's Diabetic Socks and Foot Monitoring System, Nadi X yoga pants), and the smart lenses, under development by Google, which can capture glucose levels via a tear drop for diabetics. Other commonly used WT, though not as inconspicuous, is the insulin pump both for Type I diabetes (juvenile diabetes) and Type II diabetes (adult onset diabetes). The size of a small cell phone, an insulin pump is also a computerized system which automatically releases rapid-acting insulin, as a continuous flow, into the "fatty-tissue" of the body of the "wearer" of this technology. WT may be a recent phenomenon; however, the insulin pumps, especially for children (Type I), have been in use for decades without being connected to the Internet (The Endocrine Society, 2019). Now, through the use of WT and fitness Apps, data are readily available to patients and those they choose to share within their SSN.

Data captured using various digital devices have been facilitated by the emergence of wireless technologies such as WiFi, Bluetooth, and cellular networks (Quesada-Gonzalez & Merkoci, 2017). As technology continues to advance, especially in medicine and engineering, it is expected that WT will continue to evolve into miniaturized and faster devices, using high speed processors. In 2004, the FDA approved implanting of microchips (VeriChip), the size of a small grain of rice, via the pinch of a syringe in humans which are marketed by Applied Digital Solutions of Delray Beach, Florida (Halamka, Juels, Stubblefield, & Westhues, 2006). As WT continues to make inroads into our already mechanized and technologically governed lives, in the near future, it may become commonplace to implant a microchip in humans, just as in pets, under the skin, so as to capture vital statistics for various biomarkers including a patient's medical history by using a simple scanner. Microchips are already being used in humans as part of the drug delivery systems and promise to be transformative in healthcare, especially in streamlining the therapeutic processes (Eltorai, Fox, McGurrin, & Guang, 2016).

Microchips do not store medical records rather they store encrypted codes that can be revealed upon scanning and provide pertinent healthcare data (Moreno, Vallejo, Garzón, & Moreno, 2013; Wolinsky, 2006). Even with readily available Internet connectivity, computer systems do not communicate well with each other across different medical centers, hospitals, clinics, healthcare providers, pharmacies, and insurance providers. Implantable microchips can transform the healthcare system especially in drug delivery systems with implications for therapeutic and treatment options (Eltorai et al., 2016; Wolinsky, 2006). Using microchips to treat and manage diseases like diabetes and hypertension with controlled-release titrations of medications and doses will help in designing better therapy regimens (Eltorai et al., 2016). These innovative advancements provide solutions to several medical issues surrounding drug delivery systems but many questions that pervade this milestone still remain unanswered: Are implantable computer chips a medical innovation or privacy invasion? How will implanted computer chips impact privacy, confidentiality, and encryption of medical data and records? How will consumers be able to navigate the dual role that implantable microchips play – revealing data through codes while at the same time tracking movement, especially when encryption is decrypted? Who would pay for microchip implants – insurance or patients? How will patients be able to cover/afford their part of the expense (copay) necessary for microchip implants, which may cost between \$100 – \$150? (Eltorai et al., 2016). As WT continues to evolve, and prices go down, some of the answers to these questions will become clearer over time.

## PRIVACY, PERSONAL OWNERSHIP, AND PORTABILITY OF DATA

The use of WT and fitness Apps is becoming mainstream with 80% of consumers reporting that they are willing to wear fitness technology such as Fitbits, smartwatches, and wearable monitors (Phaneuf, 2020). The use of WT continues to increase within the US as it soared from 9% in 2014 to 33% in 2018, and the use of health Apps has also increased from 16% in 2014 to 48% in 2018, a three-fold increase (Accenture, 2018). In the survey by Accenture (2018), consumers shared their views on using WT as follows: (a) 75% believed that WT was beneficial to understanding their health condition while monitoring heart rate, glucose, physical activity, and sleep cycle, (b) 73% reported using WT to engage with their health, and (c) 73% reported monitoring the health of a loved one. People's perceptions are also evolving about sharing their personal data captured using health Apps. For example, consumers reported their willingness in sharing their personal data with their doctors (90%), nurses (88%), insurance provider (72%), online communities (47%), employers (38%), government agency (41%) (Accenture, 2018). The lower percentages (38% and 41%) indicate that consumers are apprehensive about sharing their personal data with employers and government agencies. Because of massive amounts of data being generated from WT and health Apps in the public health and healthcare settings and the serious consequences its breach entails, the need for data privacy, personal ownership, and portability could not be stronger.

The primary reasons for increase in the use of WT are the novelty and inquisitiveness of WT. Secondary reasons are many: they are discreet, small, universal (can be used in all environments and on all platforms); their ease of capturing, sharing, storing of data; the ability to engage in remote monitoring, and their affordability (Schukat et al., 2016). Still considered in its infancy, the global market for WT reached more than $4.5 billion in 2018 (Dias & Paulo Silva Cunha, 2018). With nearly 3 billion people expected to have access to a smartphone by 2019, the potential for the growth of this market segment appears to be unlimited (Bunn, Navalta, Fountaine, & Reece, 2018). With ever-increasing population, demands on infrastructure, and shortage of healthcare providers, the US healthcare system continues to be overwhelmed, leading to "hospital deserts" becoming a reality both in rural and urban Appalachia and other regions of the US (Sharaievska, Battista, & Zwetsloot, 2019). With poor Internet connectivity in rural and remote areas, data privacy, personal ownership, and data portability continue to be relevant issues that need to be addressed before WT can be incorporated readily in rural healthcare systems.

Legal experts continue to struggle to make sense of vast amounts of generated data, how to mine them, and how to successfully navigate data acquisition (Dimitrov, 2016). Which data are admissible in cases of intellectual, criminal, health, and other legal matters? How can consumers and experts ensure data reliability and validity during court cases and other cases of dispute? European Union (EU) requires that any organization with 250 or more employees appoint a Data Protection Officer who must regulate and safeguard all personal information and identifiable data (HIPAA Journal, 2018) but such overarching regulations do not exist in the US. Data privacy is not highly regulated or legislated in the US as there are no specific rules, regulations, or codes regarding data privacy (Frontier Technology, 2020). Federally regulated laws such as the Health Insurance Portability and Accountability Act of 1996 (HIPAA), the Children's Online Privacy Protection Act of 1998 (COPPA), and the Fair and Accurate Credit Transactions Act of 2003 (FACTA) are not all encompassing (International Comparative Legal Guides, 2019). Furthermore, despite the hundreds of US federal and state laws, personal data of consumers still remain vulnerable to ownership, privacy, and portability because of a lack of overall legal safeguards.

## Privacy of Data

Privacy issues surrounding generation, usage, storage, and ownership of healthcare data continue to be a challenge for all stakeholders – patients, participants, healthcare providers, and insurance providers. Stakeholders appear to be unaware, unsure, or unconcerned about the significant damage that healthcare data can cause if it ends up in wrong hands/places, especially through the use of unregulated health and fitness Apps (Piwek et al., 2016; Schukat et al., 2016). The HIPAA requires that protected health information (PHI) remain confidential, private, and data integrity be maintained. Despite strict HIPAA compliance regulations, the US Office of Civil Rights understands that there can be a breach of patient data and maintains a website for reporting breaches of five hundred or more individuals (U.S. Department of Health and Human Services, 2016). Despite the technological advances of the last couple of decades, especially in the area of WT and fitness Apps, the privacy and security of patient data still continues to be governed by HIPAA regulations. When HIPAA was signed into law in 1996, a majority of WT and fitness Apps were not even in existence. So, beyond HIPAA, no overarching regulations exist that cover the immense amount of data generated by WT and fitness Apps (Colorafi & Bailey, 2016). HIPAA applies to healthcare Apps, but not to consumer Apps, even though both generate and capture similar data (Downey, 2016; Quintini & Cox, 2016). Consumers are not protected against personal data breaches due to the use of WT and fitness Apps, and concerns still remain regarding certification, regulatory control, and legal implications (Boulos, Brewer, Karimkhani, Buller, & Dellavalle, 2014).

## Personal Ownership of Data

Personal ownership of data has far-reaching consequences as it allows owners the right to access, edit, and share data and how it is used as it pertains to PHI and intellectual property. Just like one does not take a property belonging to another individual without their consent, permission, and approval, similarly, personal ownership of data is of paramount importance when it comes to owning it. The problem arises when individuals, willingly, share their personal data with family, friends, and healthcare providers over unsecured platforms (Riso et al., 2017). During such instances there are increased chances of hackers (rogue individuals, parties, or organizations) stealing data and using them for nefarious purposes. Hackers represent individuals or organizations who steal PHI or credit card information and sell it to another organization, including a terrorist organization intending to inflict harm on a large number of people or to disrupt working of government(s). Data belonging to individuals, healthcare and governmental organizations including military, are prone to massive data breaches once it enters the public domain even though individuals still maintain the right to privacy related to their personal data as long as they own it (Dolezel & McLeod, 2019). But their data ceases to be their private property after it has been shared voluntarily with healthcare providers and those belonging to their SSN.

## Portability of Data

Data portability is the method through which consumers are able to transfer (port) their personal data from one service provider to the other without any problems or penalties (Vayena & Blasimme, 2017). Such data are easy to download, organize, and analyze. Data portability allows individuals and organizations to safeguard their data by keeping them separated and stored according to the type of data. Storing and managing data in individual bins, as compared to keeping it in silos, helps in easy access, decreased costs, increased efficiency, and increase the potential for innovation (Maple, 2017). Keeping and managing the data in silos, detached from different data controllers and vendors, makes the data vulnerable, difficult to access, and compromises its integrity (Maple, 2017). If data were not portable or easily transferable across different platforms, specific vendors could technically lock people out of their own data, under one pretext or the other. It is important that both personal and organizational data be portable and accessible-on-demand, allowing for interoperability by storing it in bins instead of silos. The issue of data portability continues to plague the WT and Apps healthcare segment as proponents who support easy access and easy transfer frame data portability as a matter of human rights while opponents consider this as a matter of a service being provided.

## MOBILE HEALTH AND HEALTHCARE ORGANIZATIONS

As our culture continues to be more mobile, manufacturers continue to develop and market products that cater to the needs and lifestyles of individuals who are constantly on-the-go. An ever-increasing number of people in both rural and urban communities access healthcare needs through the emerging field of mobile technology (Steinhubl, Muse, & Topol, 2015). Having 24/7 access to their digital devices, individuals feel empowered having access/control over their health and health data (Ahtinen, Isomursu, Ramiah, & Blom, 2013; Vesnic-Alujevic, Breitegger, & Guimarães Pereira, 2018). With WT and Apps, it is easier to navigate different healthcare websites, access and capture health data, and share them with friends, family, and healthcare providers. Patients and healthy individuals, truly, are becoming partners in their own health and learning to manage their health, seek interventions, and monitor progress (Pomey, Ghadiri, Karazivan, Fernandez, & Clavel, 2015).

Increasingly, people monitor their health in real-time by using WT and Apps (Lee et al., 2018). Individuals make decisions for themselves and participate in shared decision-making with healthcare providers (Vahdat, Hamzehgardeshi, Hessam, & Hamzehgardeshi, 2014). Via WT, individuals navigate healthcare portals, websites, and get instant feedback especially when they are located in remote, infrastructurally-underdeveloped areas called "hospital deserts" (Powell, 2017; Powell & Myers, 2018).

A survey conducted by Accenture (2018) showed that 75% of consumers believed that WT was beneficial to understanding their health condition while monitoring heart rate, glucose, physical activity, and sleep cycle. It appears that consumers are more cognizant of their health, health behaviors, data capture, and data sharing with family, friends, colleagues, and healthcare providers. Crossing over from health and fitness domains to leisurewear to nutrition, WT continues to evolve and is already connecting brands with their consumers (Caspi et al., 2017; Mamiya, Moodie, & Buckeridge, 2018; Sullivan & Lachman, 2017).

The US population is aging at an unprecedented rate as her citizens continue to live longer amid chronic illnesses, disabilities, and other medical and psychosocial conditions. More than 70 million Americans are predicted to be 65 years old or older by 2030, which will be double the number that was in 2000 (CDC, 2018; Gill & Morgan, 2011; IOM, 2008). Americans, 55 years and older, are the fastest growing demographic using WT, especially with health features (eMarketer, 2018). In 2019, more than 60 million Americans used WT and among them more than 8 million were 55 years or older (4.9%), while the 25-34-year-old remain the largest users (17%) of WT (eMarketer, 2018). Identifying individuals who are, or may be, early adopters of WT remains an enigma and continues to evolve with early indicators pointing toward the typical early adopters of technology – those willing to pay the "early adopter tax" (higher cost of new technology upon release) (Depasse & Lee, 2013).

Many regulatory, logistical, ethical, and data privacy problems still persist related to the use of WT. Not all WT and fitness Apps are classified as medical devices. It is important for consumers to be able to differentiate between clinical and personal uses of Apps in order to safeguard against the unethical and illegal use of data generated by such technology and devices. The ownership of captured data continues to be an intriguing question among consumers, manufacturers, brands, and organizations particularly since the regulatory approvals by the United States Food and Drug Administration (FDA) vary depending upon what specific functions these devices perform. Furthermore, there are lacunae pertaining to the accuracy of data capture, analyses, and best approach(es) to data sharing (Hicks et al., 2019; Izmailova et al., 2018).

WT helps in communicating data among various role players. These role players include consumers such as healthy individuals who are interested in taking control of their health and lives, patients, healthcare providers, and decision-makers who find themselves at the intersection of computing and sensing technology revolution. Individuals report being joyous and feeling a sense of accomplishment and satisfaction while sharing how many steps they have taken and how many calories they have burned within their SSN (Maher, Ryan, Ambrosi, & Edney, 2017). The global market for WT is expected to grow by 11.28% between 2016 and 2025 to reach a worth of $56.8 billion. There is a social component to WT where individuals often encourage, challenge, and compete with others in their SSN toward pursuing a healthier lifestyle (Lewis, Pritting, Picazo, & JeanMarie-Tucker, 2020). Sometimes individuals participate in friendly competitions and at other times they record data for individual motivation and use. They may count steps, keep precise record, share statistics, have an increased awareness of food and calorie-counting, and "check-in" via social media to enforce acceptable behaviors and motivations (Kononova et al., 2019; Simpson & Mazzeo, 2017).

Healthcare organizations incentivize their employees for participating in sanctioned activities using WT and Apps by rewarding when specific preset goals such as step-counting, weight loss, quitting smoking, lower blood pressure, and lower cholesterol are achieved. A 2018 National Business Group on Health (NBGH) survey revealed that 86% of employers offer financial incentives as part of their health and wellness programs, which was an increase of 11% from 2017. During this period, the financial incentives increased from $742 to $784 annually. Other organizations such as insurance providers also reward positive behaviors with incentives such as lower premiums for "healthy" biomarkers and punish negative behaviors with increased premiums for "unhealthy" biomarkers (Piwek et al., 2016; van Mierlo, Hyatt, Ching, Fournier, & Dembo, 2016). For example, the Healthy Rewards Program offered by WellCare (2020), an insurance provider for Medicaid and Medicare in Georgia, provides up to $125 annually if members are willing to see their primary care physician (PCP) within the first three months of signing-up. This rewarding/punishing behavior is quite prevalent across all organizations, especially, healthcare organizations where employees have reported being shamed, bullied, and coaxed into pursuing unreasonable "healthier habits" leading to negative psychosocial outcomes (Brown, 2016; Dinh-Le, Chuang, Chokshi, & Mann, 2019; Schukat et al., 2016).

Encouraging employees to incorporate healthier behaviors into their lifestyle is commendable but when employers start tracking and monitoring behaviors of their employees, it becomes discriminatory (Brown, 2016; Dinh-Le et al., 2019; Schukat et al., 2016). Large employers often contract outside firms for tracking employee data for data analytics related to medical claims, prescription use, surgeries, and pregnancy as part of monitoring employee health. Because these large data sets do not have specific employee information, or the PHI has been de-identified, the HIPAA regulations do not cover "data aggregation" activities (HIPAA, 2018). If the employees provide release of data authorization, the employer or the contracted firm on their behalf, can provide employees with pertinent healthcare information and possible options for various procedures, thus saving healthcare costs for employers. For some individuals wearing self-tracking WT can be liberating and self-motivating; however, others report feeling overwhelmed, paralyzed, and restricted by its use (Brown, 2016; Dinh-Le et al., 2019; Schukat et al., 2016).

For better productivity and healthier outcomes, and to reduce the epidemic of obesity among their employees, organizations, especially public health organizations like hospitals, strive to improve employee health, enhance quality of healthcare, and reduce costs through capturing and analyzing vast amounts of data (big data) whether from employees or consumers such as patients (Blackstone & Fuhr, 2016). Maintaining professional relationships between physicians and patients reflects upon the commitment of organizations to overall healthcare and the structures within which they operate (Meluch & Oglesby, 2015). A source of patient dissatisfaction with physicians and overall delivery of healthcare is due to insufficient information-sharing, poor communication, inadequate interactions, and incomplete instructions. Some of these inadequacies are a result of poor investment on the part of healthcare organizations in latest digital technologies. As a result, organizations lag in data capture, data sharing, and poor cloud computing services which can cause uncertainty among patients, families, and healthcare providers leading to negative health outcomes for patients and organizational breakdown.

Organizations, often, incentivize their employees by lowering their health insurance premiums if they agree to enroll in certain wellness programs – use of WT, giving-up smoking, participating in friendly step-marathons (where employees, together, try to score more steps than their competitive group). Working on the same idea, the retail giant, Target, was one of the first organizations that formed a collaboration with Fitbit to have its employees focus on their health by monitoring their health parameters and engaging in positive health behaviors (Target, 2015). This effort was targeted toward reducing obesity among its employees and saving money in terms of group plans and premiums.

The incentive that Target offered to employee groups that agreed to participate included a gift of $1 million awarded to the "Activity Challenge" winner for distribution to any charity of their choice (Target, 2015). Activity Challenge consisted of employees enrolling into the program, receiving a discounted Fitbit, and becoming a part of a group or forming a new group and, together within a group, logging daily steps (a sum total of daily steps of all group members). As Target successfully conducted the "Activity Challenge," Fitbit came to be seen as a WT helping consumers monitor their physical activity and encouraging them to implement positive behavioral changes in their lifestyles (Health Solutions, 2018). Given the high cost of medical treatment and lost productivity, Target believed that investing in preventive health measures, specifically in reducing obesity, was a better strategy.

In Target's case, the issue of data privacy was neither discussed nor revealed, but rather the employees were just offered an opportunity to participate in an organizationally sanctioned activity – use of Fitbit to capture personal data and port it to a server/platform which would provide unlimited access to Target. Individuals mistakenly believe that they own their data but do not realize that once they share their personal data, it does not remain theirs anymore – there are other partners and co-owners of their personal data.

## HEALTH MONITORING DEVICES

Almost all WT devices rely upon biosensors, whether inbuilt as in a smartphone, or worn or attached to a person for providing a precise measurement of a cell, tissue, organ, or organ system (whole person). Within the umbrella of WT, here, the authors focus on several wearable health devices (WHD) such as Actiwatch 2, GlucoWatch Biographer, wearable glucose sensor, FreeStyle Libre, and Fitbit. The issues surrounding data privacy, personal ownership, and portability across different WT and Apps platforms are also highlighted.

### Actiwatch 2

Actiwatch 2 (Manufacturer: Philips Respironics) is a noninvasive monitoring device which collects data while tracking a patient's/wearer's sleep cycle and other related polysomnographic indicators. This digital device, which looks like a Fitbit or a sleek watch, is worn on a wrist while going to bed and also during daytime as it measures the wearer's daily activity and sleep/wake cycle to try to understand the impact of natural cycle, drug-induced activity, or behavioral therapies. Actiwatch 2 is associated with the individual polysomnography to create an individual sleeping, waking, and breathing profile for the patient. Actiwatch 2 has the capability of collecting research data in a confidential manner using its Actiware software which "allows the user to configure and retrieve recorded activity data from all Actiwatch models in addition to data management, analysis and export" (Philips Respironics, 2020, para. 1).

When tied to a corporate or organizational incentive as part of OSA research, the generated data has the potential of being less confidential as it is shared and ported across different platforms and different clinical sites. Actiwatch, sometimes, is also used as a supplement to sleep test (polysomnography) as the two, together, can provide richer and more robust electronic data (Mantua, Gravel, & Spencer, 2016; Weiss, Johnson, Berger, & Redline, 2010). As the data are generated, captured, stored, edited, and shared, the issues of privacy, personal ownership, and portability persist despite HIPAA and Institutional Review Board (IRB) regulations. One of the ways in which Philip Respironics overcomes these issues is by providing each clinical site a username and password and the password is changed periodically in order to ensure that participant data remain confidential and secure. Philip Respironics appears to be cognizant of the importance of data privacy and confidentiality as is evident by its use of the secure shell (SSH) file transfer protocol (SFTP) when transferring sleep data to Sleep Reading Centers. SFTP provides additional security during access, transfer, and management of data files over any platform. Among different WT manufacturers, these safeguards put in place by Philips Respironics suggest that it does a commendable job of maintaining data privacy, confidentiality, security, and portability with regards to Actiwatch 2.

## GlucoWatch Biographer

Sometimes, the data privacy, clinical efficacy, and results reproducibility can be major reasons in whether a WT product will succeed in the market or not. The GlucoWatch Biographer, launched by the manufacturer Cygnus, Inc., in 2002, was one of the first devices to be approved by the FDA for monitoring glucose noninvasively (Med Device Online, 2001). GlucoWatch Biographer measured glucose concentrations electrochemically in skin interstitial fluid (ISF) by reverse iontophoresis (RI) (Potts, Tamada, & Tierney, 2002). It was a prescription device which provided glucose readings noninvasively three times per hour during the day and the night. It had a user-friendly interface that supported markers for insulin injections, meals, exercise, and provided an alarm if glucose fluctuations occurred below or over 35% and the accompanying software provided options for data analysis and could store up to 8500 readings (Tierney et al., 2001).

GlucoWatch Biographer had to be recalled due to skin irritation, calibration complication, and triggering false alarms 50% of the time (Diabetes Monitor, 2012). Collecting and managing accurate and complete data was challenging as Cygnus Inc., itself, warned that "skipped readings and unexpected shut offs may occur due to excessive perspiration, jarring or dislodging of the device from the skin" (Colberg, 2003, p.1). The GlucoWatch Biographer missed 75-100% data readings during intense workouts, 85-100% readings during moderate and heavy workouts, and completely shut-off 37-50% of the time. In order to restart the individual needed a new Autosensor, costing approximately $5, and it could take up to 3 hours to warm up (Colberg, 2003). So, the failed GlucoWatch Biographer had issues of data accuracy, capture, privacy, and portability which still remain major concerns at the heart of all WT. The company dissolved in 2007. The failed GlucoWatch Biographer opened the market for developing noninvasive glucose monitoring platforms which can produce accurate, reliable, and efficient data while maintaining privacy and confidentiality.

## Wearable Glucose Sensor

The development of wearable glucose sensors (WGS) has received attention in the last several years as both Type I and Type II diabetics could benefit from the use of such noninvasive electrochemical biosensing devices (Kim, Campbell, & Wang, 2018). Not the common wrist band worn WT, WGS is a temporary patch, similar to a temporary tattoo, which has biosensing devices which can measure glucose and help in management of diabetes. This screen-printed, convenient, and continuous glucose monitoring (CGM) device can capture glucose data throughout the day and night, instead of the invasive glucose monitors (Kim et al., 2018). These implantable or skin-worn devices are easy to implant (tattoo), manage, and replace.

Though still in its infancy, WGS needs to address some of the early issues such as efficiency during long-term use, biosensor performance with wireless technology, and accurate data capture, especially, during exercise due to accumulating perspiration (Lee et al., 2017). During initial testing, data have been found to be missing which can be problematic for reliable monitoring and evidence-based decision-making. Perspiration could be a result of hypoglycemia and it is during this critical time that WGS failed to capture data, compromising the diabetic patient's capability to make informed decision(s), and the data were also not available for sharing with healthcare provider for data-driven decisions. Owning personalized blood glucose data captured by biosensing devices such as WGS can benefit diabetic patients by helping them manage their diabetes proactively. The captured data can help diabetics make evidence-based decisions pertaining to their health, share their data with their healthcare providers such that evidence-based decisions can be made, while maintaining privacy, confidentiality, and security.

## Freestyle Libre

Abbot Laboratories launched the Freestyle Libre 14-day CGM system in 2017 with an accompanying Freestyle *LibreLinkUp* App (Abbot Laboratories, 2018). The wearable sensor is applied to the back of the wearer's upper arm through a minimally invasive procedure which allows for collecting micro amounts of interstitial fluid (ISF) for analyzing glucose levels. The sensor transmits real-time glucose measurements to the smartphone and the App can display present glucose levels, trends over 8-hour periods, and up to 90 days. The sensor must be replaced every 14-days. The collected data comprise of average glucose, daily patterns, charts, hypoglycemic events, and sensor usage.

Data are available for free download from FreeStyle Libre Desktop Software and LibreView Software. The FreeStyle *LibreLink* mobile App can be downloaded on a smartphone for accessing data on-the-go. Also, the *LibreLinkUp* App can be used to share data with healthcare providers and those in their SSN (up to 6 family members/friend with Family Sharing enabled). The data generated, collected, and managed by the FreeStyle *LibreLink* and *LibreLinkUp* Apps are prone to data vulnerabilities similar to other WT and Apps. First, FreeStyle Libre wearers have reported issues with sensors not recording data, being asked to get a new scanner (Reader), or changing the sensor, even when everything is brand new. Second, with *LibreLinkUp* App, people have reported the issues of non-compatibility upon upgrading their smartphones. Finally, the Reader, that comes with the system, can read the sensor, store the readings, but cannot share the readings for which an App is required. The FreeStyle *LibreLink* and *LibreLinkUp* Apps, used via smartphone, do not seem to pick up the glucose readings from the sensor for sharing. So, with data generation and collection issues like these, it is difficult to have access to personal data in real-time, trust the accuracy of the data, and have it available for sharing with others. Technically, data portability can also be a problem because, sometimes, when it is not compatible with sensor Reader and FreeStyle *LibreLink* and *LibreLinkUp* Apps, trusting the accuracy and privacy of data for patients, healthcare providers, and others in their SSN can be a challenge.

## Fitbit

As a widely used WT, Fitbit is a wirelessly enabled activity tracker which measures, captures, and manages real-time data for activities such as steps walked, floors climbed, heart rate, sleep quality, calories burned, and GPS route (Draper, 2018). Real-time data has implications in transforming management strategies for obesity and diabetes by making people aware of the strength that lies in numbers. Empowering people by giving them access to their own data from their physical activity patterns can help them better process the messages related to managing their obesity and diabetes (Brown, 2018). Data-driven messages can be more powerful and persuasive even though implementing them can still be challenging for those with sedentary lifestyles.

Fitbit data has implications for individuals, healthcare professionals, and insurance companies. Users can upload and share their valuable personal health data with their healthcare providers using Microsoft's HealthVault service. Like many organizations, the insurance company, John Hancock, rewards clients by offering them discounted insurance premiums if they are willing to wear a Fitbit and share their data for receiving rewards. Having access to personalized data can also help healthcare providers frame personalized messages such as, "this will work for you," instead of, "this is what works for an average obese and/or diabetic patient." Fitbit can show the impact of walking, sleeping, and calorie counting through captured data which can be analyzed for better management of obesity and diabetes. The data captured by Fitbit and related App are often shared across various platforms by individuals, corporate partners, and even employers. The physiological data are owned by Fitbit, with the user being able to see and manage their own data. The deidentified data are aggregated with other users' data by Fitbit for researching data trends. Because Fitbit is marketed as a consumer tech, and even though the data are used in research, HIPAA regulations do not apply to deidentified data making it vulnerable to potential breaches (National Committee on Vital Health Statistics, 2017).

## SOLUTIONS AND RECOMMENDATIONS

Obesity is a major issue of epidemic proportions with comorbidities such as diabetes, CVD, hypertension, and sleep apnea. The use of WT and Apps continues to increase as people become more aware of their health and feel empowered with access to their health data and managing it. Instead of asking their healthcare providers, patients increasingly rely upon their data for guiding and changing health behaviors for the better. WT and Apps must not share data indiscriminately, with clear understanding of how decrypted data will be used, and how such data can be encrypted for privacy, personal ownership, and portability. WT devices should be personal, must not make exaggerated claims, be of immediate applied use, and maintain data privacy.

## FUTURE RESEARCH DIRECTIONS

In the future, more people may refer to their personal health data for answers, instead of asking their healthcare providers, regarding therapies and treatment options to manage their metabolic conditions such as obesity, diabetes, CVDs, and sleep apnea (Russo, 2018). Increasingly, healthcare providers use a data-driven approach to provide disease management options. WT and data capture need to be cheaper, faster, and easily portable for easier and extensive integration in healthcare. WT manufacturers and Apps developers must address the issue of informed consent from both the medical and research perspectives as it has implications in PHI privacy and data management regulations. Presenting WT and Apps as being trendy in monitoring personal health indicators trivializes the importance and far-reaching implications of personal health data in making informed healthcare decisions. The benefits that such technologies offer in the healthcare, health communication, and public health domains can only be fully realized if personal health data remain private, confidential, and secure. In an age of health data capture and social media, unstructured data continue to be generated in large quantities and at unprecedented speeds but many challenges regarding data privacy, personal ownership, and portability still remain (Filkins et al., 2016; Ristevski & Chen, 2018).

## CONCLUSION

In order to address public health disparities associated with obesity and diabetes, WT and health fitness Apps can help reduce the impact of comorbidities such as diabetes, hypertension, cardiovascular diseases (CVD), and sleep apnea by regular monitoring of biomarkers and capturing data available for sharing and making evidence-based decisions. Data generated and captured by WT and health fitness Apps can expand and promote opportunities for physical activity by communicating and promoting healthier lifestyle choices and managing diseases. WT and fitness Apps play important roles in monitoring vital signs, calorie counts in foods and beverages, physical education programs, and links for health information while maintaining their commitment to data privacy, personal ownership, and portability for the benefit and safety of all stakeholders.

## REFERENCES

Abbot Laboratories. (2018). Introducing the freestyle libre 14-day system. Retrieved from https://www.freestylelibre.us/system-overview/freestyle-14-day.html

Accenture. (2018). Accenture study finds growing demand for digital health services revolutionizing delivery models: Patients, doctors + machines. Retrieved from https://newsroom.accenture.com/news/accenture-study-finds-growing-demand-for-digital-health-services-revolutionizing-delivery-models-patients-doctors-machines.htm

Agha, M., & Agha, R. (2017). The rising prevalence of obesity: Part A: Impact on public health. *International Journal of Surgical Oncology*, 2(7), e17. PubMed doi:10.1097/IJ9.0000000000000017

Ahtinen, A., Isomursu, M., Ramiah, S., & Blom, J. (2013). Advise, acknowledge, grow and engage: Design principles for a mobile wellness application to support physical activity. *International Journal of Mobile Human Computer Interaction*, 5(4), 20–55. doi:10.4018/ijmhci.2013100102

Blackstone, E. A., & Fuhr, J. P. Jr. (2016). The economics of medicare accountable care organizations. *American Health & Drug Benefits*, 9(1), 11–19. PubMed

Blumenthal, D., & Seervai, S. (2018). Rising obesity in the United States is a public health crisis. To the Point, The Commonwealth Fund. Retrieved from https://www.commonwealthfund.org/blog/2018/rising-obesity-united-states-public-health-crisis

Boulos, M. N., Brewer, A. C., Karimkhani, C., Buller, D. B., & Dellavalle, R. P. (2014). Mobile medical and health apps: State of the art, concerns, regulatory control and certification. *Online Journal of Public Health Informatics*, 5(3), 229. PubMed doi:10.5210/ojphi.v5i3.4814

Brown, A. (2018). Transforming diabetes through real-time data: Wearables + CGM. Retrieved from https://healthsolutions.fitbit.com/blog/transforming-diabetes-through-real-time-data-wearables-cgm/

Brown, E. A. (2016). The Fitbit fault line: Two proposals to protect health and fitness data at work. *Yale Journal of Health Policy, Law, and Ethics*, 16(1), 1–49. PubMed

Bunn, J. A., Navalta, J. W., Fountaine, C. J., & Reece, J. D. (2018). Current state of commercial wearable technology in physical activity monitoring 2015-2017. *International Journal of Exercise Science*, 11(7), 503–515. PubMed

Caspi, C. E., Lenk, K., Pelletier, J. E., Barnes, T. L., Harnack, L., ... Laska, M. N. (2017). Association between store food environment and customer purchases in small grocery stores, gas-marts, pharmacies and dollar stores. *The International Journal of Behavioral Nutrition and Physical Activity*, 14(1), 76–86. PubMed doi:10.118612966-017-0531-x

Center for Disease Control and Prevention. (2009). The power of prevention: Chronic disease…The public health challenge of the 21st century. Retrieved from https://www.cdc.gov/chronicdisease/pdf/2009-Power-of-Prevention.pdf

Center for Disease Control and Prevention. (2018). More obesity in U.S. rural counties than in urban counties. Retrieved from https://www.cdc.gov/media/releases/2018/s0614-obesity-rates.html

Colberg, S. (2003). Can you exercise while wearing a GlucoWatch Biographer? Diabetes Health. Retrieved from https://www.diabeteshealth.com/can-you-exercise-while-wearing-a-glucowatch-biographer-read-on-2/

Colorafi, K., & Bailey, B. (2016). It's time for innovation in the Health Insurance Portability and Accountability Act (HIPAA). *JMIR Medical Informatics*, 4(4), e34. PubMed doi:10.2196/medinform.6372

Coons, M. J., Demott, A., Buscemi, J., Duncan, J. M., Pellegrini, C. A., Steglitz, J., ... Spring, B. (2012). Technology interventions to curb obesity: A Systematic review of the current literature. *Current Cardiovascular Risk Reports*, 6(2), 120–134. PubMed doi:10.100712170-012-0222-8D da Luz, F. Q., Hay, P., Touyz, S., & Sainsbury, A. (2018). Obesity with comorbid eating disorders: Associated health risks and treatment approaches. *Nutrients, 10*(7), 829. PubMed doi:10.3390/nu10070829

Daniel, H., Bornstein, S. S., & Kane, G. C. (2018). Addressing social determinants to improve patient care and promote health equity: An American College of Physicians position paper. *Annals of Internal Medicine, 168*, 577–578. PubMed doi:10.7326/M17-2441

Depasse, J. W., & Lee, P. T. (2013). A model for 'reverse innovation' in health care. *Globalization and Health, 9*(40), 1–7. PubMed doi:10.1186/1744-8603-9-40

Diabetes Monitor. (2012). What happened to the GlucoWatch biographer? Retrieved from http://www.diabetesmonitor.com/glucose-meters/what-happened-to-the-glucowatch.htm

Dias, D., & Paulo Silva Cunha, J. (2018). Wearable health devices – vital sign monitoring, systems and technologies. *Sensors (Basel), 18*(8), 2414. PubMed doi:10.339018082414

Dimitrov, D. V. (2016). Medical internet of things and big data in healthcare. *Healthcare Informatics Research, 22*(3), 156–163. PubMed doi:10.4258/hir.2016.22.3.156

Dinh-Le, C., Chuang, R., Chokshi, S., & Mann, D. (2019). Wearable health technology and electronic health record integration: Scoping review and future directions. *JMIR mHealth and uHealth, 7*(9), e12861. PubMed doi:10.2196/12861

Dolezel, D., & McLeod, A. (2019). Cyber-analytics: Identifying discriminants of data breaches. Perspectives in Health Information Management, 16(Summer), 1a, 1-17.

Downey, R. (2016). Telemedicine and HIPAA compliancy. GlobalMed Telehealth Answers Blog. Retrieved from https://www.globalmed.com/telehealthanswers/telemedicine-and-hipaa-compliancy

Draper, S. (2018). How Fitbit is trying to transform healthcare, while transforming itself. Retrieved from https://www.wearable-technologies.com/2018/06/how-fitbit-is-trying-to-transform-healthcare-while-transforming-itself/

Eltorai, A. E., Fox, H., McGurrin, E., & Guang, S. (2016). Microchips in medicine: Current and future applications. BioMed Research International, 1743472. Advance online publication. PubMed doi:10.1155/2016/1743472

eMarketer. (2018). eMarketer releases new US digital user figures. Retrieved from https://www.emarketer.com/content/emarketer-release-new-us-digital-user-figures

Filkins, B. L., Kim, J. Y., Roberts, B., Armstrong, W., Miller, M. A., Hultner, M. L., ... Steinhubl, S. R. (2016). Privacy and security in the era of digital health: What should translational researchers know and do about it? *American Journal of Translational Research, 8*(3), 1560–1580. PubMed

Finkelstein, E. A., Fiebelkorn, I. C., & Wang, G. (2003). National medical spending attributable to overweight and obesity: How much, and who's paying? *Health Affairs, 22*, 219–226. PubMed

Foster, K. R., & Torous, J. (2019). The opportunity and obstacles for smartwatches and wearable sensors. Retrieved from https://pulse.embs.org/january-2019/the-opportunity-and-obstacles-for-smartwatches-and-wearable-sensors/

Frontier Technology. (2020). The differences between the United States and European Union data laws. Retrieved from https://www.frontiertechnology.co.uk/differences-between-eu-and-us-data-laws/

Gill, E. A., & Morgan, M. (2011). Home sweet home: Conceptualizing and coping with the challenges of aging and the move to a care facility. *Health Communication, 26*(4), 332–342. PubMed doi:10.1080/10410236.2010.551579

Godfrey, A., Hetherington, V., Shum, H., Bonato, P., Lovell, N. H., & Stuart, S. (2018). From A to Z: Wearable technology explained. *Maturitas, 113*, 40–47. PubMed doi:10.1016/j.maturitas.2018.04.012

Gortmaker, S. L., Swinburn, B. A., Levy, D., Carter, R., Mabry, P. L., Finegood, D. T., . . . Moodie, M. L. (2011). Changing the future of obesity: Science, policy, and action. Lancet (London, England), 378(9793), 838–847. PubMed doi:10.1016/S0140-6736(11)60815-5

Halamka, J., Juels, A., Stubblefield, A., & Westhues, J. (2006). The security implications of VeriChip cloning. *Journal of the American Medical Informatics Association: JAMIA, 13*(6), 601–607. PubMed doi:10.1197/jamia.M2143

Hammond, R. A., & Levine, R. (2010). The economic impact of obesity in the United States. *Diabetes, Metabolic Syndrome and Obesity, 3*, 285–295. PubMed doi:10.2147/DMSOTT.S7384

Health Solutions. (2018). Transforming diabetes through real-time data: Wearables + CGM. Retrieved from https://healthsolutions.fitbit.com/blog/transforming-diabetes-through-real-time-data-wearables-cgm/

Hicks, J. L., Althoff, T., Sosic, R., Kuhar, P., Bostjancic, B., King, A. C., . . . Delp, S. L. (2019). Best practices for analyzing large-scale health data from wearables and smartphone apps. NPJ Digital Medicine, 2, 45. PubMed doi:10.1038/s41746-019-0121-1

Journal, H. I. P. A. A. (2018). What is the role of the data protection officer? Retrieved from https://www.hipaajournal.com/gdpr-role-of-the-data-protection-officer/

Hruby, A., & Hu, F. B. (2015). The epidemiology of obesity: A big picture. *PharmacoEconomics, 33*(7), 673–689. PubMed doi:10.100740273-014-0243-x

Institute of Medicine. (2013). *Evaluating obesity prevention efforts: A plan for measuring progress.* The National Academies Press.

International Comparative Legal Guides. (2019). USA: Data protection 2019. Retrieved from https://iclg.com/practice-areas/data-protection-laws-and-regulations/usa

Izmailova, E. S., Wagner, J. A., & Perakslis, E. D. (2018). Wearable devices in clinical trials: Hype and hypothesis. *Clinical Pharmacology and Therapeutics, 104*(1), 42–52. PubMed doi:10.1002/cpt.966

Kim, J., Campbell, A. S., & Wang, J. (2018). Wearable non-invasive epidermal glucose sensors: A review. *Talanta, 177*, 163–170. PubMed doi:10.1016/j.talanta.2017.08.077

Kononova, A., Li, L., Kamp, K., Bowen, M., Rikard, R. V., Cotten, S., & Peng, W. (2019). The use of wearable activity trackers among older adults: Focus group study of tracker perceptions, motivators, and barriers in the maintenance stage of behavior change. *JMIR mHealth and uHealth, 7*(4), e9832. PubMed doi:10.2196/mhealth.9832

Lee, H., Song, C., Hong, Y. S., Kim, M. S., Cho, H. R., Kang, T., ... Kim, D. H. (2017). Wearable/disposable sweat-based glucose monitoring device with multistage transdermal drug delivery module. *Science Advances*, *3*(3), 1–8. doi:10.1126ciadv.1601314

Lee, M., Lee, H., Kim, Y., Kim, J., Cho, M., Jang, J., & Jang, H. (2018). Mobile App-based health promotion programs: A systematic review of the literature. *International Journal of Environmental Research and Public Health*, *15*(12), 1–13. doi:10.3390/ijerph15122838

Lewis, Z. H., Pritting, L., Picazo, A. L., & JeanMarie-Tucker, M. (2020). The utility of wearable fitness trackers and implications for increased engagement: An exploratory, mixed methods observational study. Digital Health, 6, 1–12. PubMed doi:10.1177/2055207619900059

Maher, C., Ryan, J., Ambrosi, C., & Edney, S. (2017). Users' experiences of wearable activity trackers: A cross-sectional study. *BMC Public Health*, *17*(880), 1–8. PubMed doi:10.118612889-017-4888-1

Mamiya, H., Moodie, E., & Buckeridge, D. L. (2018). A novel application of point-of-sales grocery transaction data to enhance community nutrition monitoring. AMIA ... Annual Symposium Proceedings. AMIA Symposium, 2017, 1253–1261.

Mantua, J., Gravel, N., & Spencer, R. M. (2016). Reliability of sleep measures from four personal health monitoring devices compared to research-based actigraphy and polysomnography. *Sensors (Basel)*, *16*(5), 1–11. doi:10.339016050646

Maple, C. (2017). Security and privacy in the internet of things. *Journal of Cyber Policy*, *2*(2), 155–184. doi:10.1080/23738871.2017.1366536

Med Device Online. (2001). FDA approves first non-invasive, automatic glucose monitoring system for people with diabetes. Retrieved from https://www.meddeviceonline.com/doc/fda-approves-first-non-invasive-automatic-glu-0001

Meluch, A. L., & Oglesby, W. H. (2015). Physician–patient communication regarding patients' healthcare costs in the US: A systematic review of the literature. *Journal of Communication in Healthcare*, *8*(2), 151–160. doi:10.1179/1753807615Y.0000000010

Mohammed, M. S., Sendra, S., Lloret, J., & Bosch, I. (2018). Systems and WBANs for controlling obesity. Journal of Healthcare Engineering, 2018, 1-21. 1564748.doi:10.1155/2018/1564748

Moreno, F., Vallejo, D., Garzón, H., & Moreno, S. (2013). In vitro evaluation of a passive radio frequency identification microchip implanted in human molars subjected to compression forces, for forensic purposes of human identification. *Journal of Forensic Dental Sciences*, *5*(2), 77–84. PubMed doi:10.4103/0975-1475.119766

Moustafa, H., Kenn, H., Sayrafian, K., Scanlon, W., & Zhang, Y. (2015). Mobile wearable communications. *IEEE Wireless Communications*, *22*(1), 10–11. doi:10.1109/MWC.2015.7054713

Mullington, J. M., Abbott, S. M., Carroll, J. E., Davis, C. J., Dijk, D. J., Dinges, D. F., ... Zee, P. C. (2016). Developing biomarker arrays predicting sleep and circadian-coupled risks to health. *Sleep*, *39*(4), 727–736. PubMed doi:10.5665leep.5616

National Committee on Vital Health Statistics. (2017). Health information privacy beyond HIPAA: A 2018 environmental scan of major trends and challenges. Retrieved from https://ncvhs.hhs.gov/wp-content/uploads/2018/05/NCVHS-Beyond-HIPAA_Report-Final-02-08-18.pdf

NCD Risk Factor Collaboration (NCD-RisC). (2019). Rising rural body-mass index is the main driver of the global obesity epidemic in adults. *Nature, 569,* 260–264. PubMed

Partnership to Fight Chronic Disease. (2018). New data shows obesity costs will grow to $344 billion by 2018. Retrieved from https://www.fightchronicdisease.org/latest-news/new-data-shows-obesity-costs-will-grow-344-billion-2018

Phaneuf, A. (2020). Latest trends in medical monitoring devices and wearable health technology. Business Insider. Retrieved from https://www.businessinsider.com/wearable-technology-healthcare-medical-devices

Philips Respironics. (2020). Actiware: Flexible, powerful. Retrieved from http://www.actigraphy.com/solutions/actiware/

Piwek, L., Ellis, D. A., Andrews, S., & Joinson, A. (2016). The rise of consumer health wearables: Promises and barriers. *PLoS Medicine, 13*(2), e1001953. PubMed doi:10.1371/journal.pmed.1001953

Pomey, M. P., Ghadiri, D. P., Karazivan, P., Fernandez, N., & Clavel, N. (2015). Patients as partners: A qualitative study of patients' engagement in their health care. *PLoS One, 10*(4), e0122499. PubMed doi:10.1371/journal.pone.0122499

Popkin, B. M. (2011). Is the obesity epidemic a national security issue around the globe? *Current Opinion in Endocrinology, Diabetes, and Obesity, 18*(5), 328–331. PubMed doi:10.1097/MED.0b013e3283471c74

Potts, R. O., Tamada, J. A., & Tierney, M. J. (2002). Glucose monitoring by reverse iontophoresis. *Diabetes/Metabolism Research and Reviews, 18,* S49–S53. PubMed

Powell, K., & Myers, C. (2018). Electronic patient portals: Patient and provider perceptions. Online Journal of Nursing Informatics, 22(1).

Powell, K. R. (2017). Patient-perceived facilitators of and barriers to electronic portal use: A systematic review. *Computers, Informatics, Nursing, 35*(11), 565–573. PubMed

Puhl, R. M., & Heuer, C. A. (2010). Obesity stigma: Important considerations for public health. *American Journal of Public Health, 100*(6), 1019–1028. PubMed doi:10.2105/AJPH.2009.159491

Quesada-Gonzalez, D., & Merkoci, A. (2017). Mobile phone-based biosensing: An emerging diagnostic and communication technology. *Biosensors & Bioelectronics, 92,* 549–562. PubMed

Quintini, H., & Cox, H. A. (2016). Digital health care alert: Is your health care app subject to HIPAA? Retrieved from https://www.fenwick.com/publications/pages/is-your-health-care-app-subject-to-hipaa.aspx

Riso, B., Tupasela, A., Vears, D. F., Felzmann, H., Cockbain, J., Loi, M., ... Rakic, V. (2017). Ethical sharing of health data in online platforms - which values should be considered? *Life Sciences, Society and Policy, 13*(1), 1–27. PubMed doi:10.118640504-017-0060-z

Ristevski, B., & Chen, M. (2018). Big data analytics in medicine and healthcare. *Journal of Integrative Bioinformatics*, *15*(3), 20170030. PubMed doi:10.1515/jib-2017-0030

Rowe, S., Alexander, N., Kretser, A., Steele, R., Kretsch, M., Applebaum, R., ... Falci, K. (2013). Principles for building public-private partnerships to benefit food safety, nutrition, and health research. *Nutrition Reviews*, *71*(10), 682–691. PubMed doi:10.1111/nure.12072

Russo, F. (2018). Digital technologies, ethical questions, and the need of an informational framework. *Philosophy & Technology*, *31*(4), 655–667. PubMed doi:10.100713347-018-0326-2

Schukat, M., McCaldin, D., Wang, K., Schreier, G., Lovell, N. H., Marschollek, M., & Redmond, S. J. (2016). Unintended consequences of wearable sensor use in healthcare: Contribution of the IMIA wearable sensors in healthcare. Yearbook of Medical Informatics, (1), 73–86. PubMed doi:10.15265/IY-2016-025

Sharaievska, I., Battista, R. A., & Zwetsloot, J. (2019). Use of physical activity monitoring devices by families in rural communities: Qualitative approach. JMIR Pediatrics and Parenting, 2(1), e10658. PubMed doi:10.2196/10658

Simpson, C. C., & Mazzeo, S. E. (2017). Calorie counting and fitness tracking technology: Associations with eating disorder symptomatology. *Eating Behaviors*, *26*, 89–92. PubMed doi:10.1016/j.eatbeh.2017.02.002

Steinhubl, S. R., Muse, E. D., & Topol, E. J. (2015). The emerging field of mobile health. *Science Translational Medicine*, *7*(283), 283rv3. Advance online publication. PubMed doi:10.1126citranslmed.aaa3487

Strava Privacy Policy. (2019). The privacy policy. Retrieved from https://www.strava.com/legal/privacy#full_policy

Sullivan, A. N., & Lachman, M. E. (2017). Behavior change with fitness technology in sedentary adults: A Review of the evidence for increasing physical activity. *Frontiers in Public Health*, *4*(289), 1–16. PubMed doi:10.3389/fpubh.2016.00289

Target. (2015). Target kicks off new team member wellness initiatives. Retrieved from https://corporate.target.com/article/2015/09/team-member-wellness

The Endocrine Society. (2019). New hybrid closed loop insulin pump proves hard to use for some patients with diabetes. Science Daily. Retrieved from www.sciencedaily.com/releases/2019/03/190323113741.htm

Tierney, M. J., Tamada, J. A., Potts, R. O., Jovanovic, L., Garg, S., & Team, C. R. (2001). Clinical evaluation of the GlucoWatch Biographer: A continual, non-invasive glucose monitor for patients with diabetes. *Biosensors & Bioelectronics*, *16*(9–12), 621–629. PubMed

U.S. Department of Health and Human Services Breach Portal. (2016). Notice to the secretary of HHS breach of unsecured protected health information. Retrieved from https://ocrportal.hhs.gov/ocr/breach/breach_report.jsf

Vahdat, S., Hamzehgardeshi, L., Hessam, S., & Hamzehgardeshi, Z. (2014). Patient involvement in health care decision making: A review. *Iranian Red Crescent Medical Journal*, *16*(1), e12454. PubMed doi:10.5812/ircmj.12454 van Mierlo, T., Hyatt, D., Ching, A. T., Fournier, R., & Dembo, R. S. (2016). Behavioral economics, wearable devices, and cooperative games: Results from a population-based intervention to increase physical activity. JMIR Serious Games, 4(1), e1. PubMed doi:10.2196/games.5358

Vayena, E., & Blasimme, A. (2017). Biomedical big data: New models of control over access, use and governance. *Journal of Bioethical Inquiry*, *14*(4), 501–513. PubMed doi:10.100711673-017-9809-6

Vesnic-Alujevic, L., Breitegger, M., & Guimarães Pereira, Â. (2018). 'Do-it-yourself healthcare? Quality of health and healthcare through wearable sensors. *Science and Engineering Ethics*, *24*(3), 887–904. PubMed doi:10.100711948-016-9771-4

Vo, V., Auroy, L., & Sarradon-Eck, A. (2019). Patients' perceptions of mHealth Apps: Meta-ethnographic review of qualitative studies. *JMIR mHealth and uHealth*, *7*(7), e13817. PubMed doi:10.2196/13817

Weiss, A. R., Johnson, N. L., Berger, N. A., & Redline, S. (2010). Validity of activity-based devices to estimate sleep. *Journal of Clinical Sleep Medicine: JCSM: Official Publication of the American Academy of Sleep Medicine*, *6*(4), 336–342. PubMed

WellCare. (2020). Healthy rewards program. Retrieved from https://www.wellcare.com/New-York/Members/Medicaid-Plans/Healthy-Choice/Healthy-Rewards-Program

Wolinsky, H. (2006). Tagging products and people. Despite much controversy, radiofrequency identification chips have great potential in healthcare. *EMBO Reports*, *7*(10), 965–968. PubMed doi:10.1038j.embor.7400810

World Health Organization. (2000). *Obesity: Preventing and managing the global epidemic*. World Health Organization.

World Health Organization. (2018). Noncommunicable diseases. Retrieved from https://www.who.int/news-room/fact-sheets/detail/noncommunicable-diseases

## ADDITIONAL READING

Alcántara-Aragón, V. (2019). Improving patient self-care using diabetes technologies. Therapeutic Advances in Endocrinology and Metabolism, 10. PubMed doi:10.1177/2042018818824215

Cappon, G., Vettoretti, M., Sparacino, G., & Facchinetti, A. (2019). Continuous glucose monitoring sensors for diabetes management: A review of technologies and applications. *Diabetes & Metabolism Journal*, *43*(4), 383–397. PubMed doi:10.4093/dmj.2019.0121

Dias, D., & Paulo Silva Cunha, J. (2018). Wearable health devices-vital sign monitoring, systems and technologies. *Sensors (Basel)*, *18*(8), 2414. PubMed doi:10.339018082414

Guk, K., Han, G., Lim, J., Jeong, K., Kang, T., Lim, E. K., & Jung, J. (2019). Evolution of wearable devices with real-time disease monitoring for personalized healthcare. *Nanomaterials (Basel, Switzerland)*, *9*(6), 813. PubMed doi:10.3390/nano9060813

Krummel, T. M. (2019). The rise of wearable technology in health care. JAMA Network Open, 2(2), e187672. PubMed doi:10.1001/jamanetworkopen.2018.7672

Liao, Y., Thompson, C., Peterson, S., Mandrola, J., & Beg, M. S. (2018). The future of wearable technologies and remote monitoring in health care. Care Delivery and Practice Management, 115-121.

Schwartz, F. L., Marling, C. R., & Bunescu, R. C. (2018). The promise and perils of wearable physiological sensors for diabetes management. *Journal of Diabetes Science and Technology*, *12*(3), 587–591. PubMed doi:10.1177/1932296818763228

Tong, R. K. Y. (2018). *Wearable technology in medicine and health care*. Academic Press.

Weatherall, J., Paprocki, Y., Meyer, T. M., Kudel, I., & Witt, E. A. (2018). Sleep tracking and exercise in patients with type 2 diabetes mellitus (Step-D): Pilot study to determine correlations between Fitbit data and patient-reported outcomes. *JMIR mHealth and uHealth*, *6*(6), e131. PubMed doi:10.2196/mhealth.8122

## KEY TERMS AND DEFINITIONS

**Appalachia:** A cultural and geographic region of the United States stretching from southern New York to northern Mississippi comprising of thirteen states and four hundred and twenty counties whose residents are stereotyped as impoverished, backward, isolated, and lacking healthcare and infrastructural resources and, contrary to conventional belief, the region has a distinct and rich mountain culture.

**Cardiovascular Disease:** A class of disease involving the heart and/or blood vessels. Examples include myocardial infarction (heart attack), coronary artery disease (CAD), hypertension, cardiac arrest, arrhythmia, and congestive heart failure (CHF).

**Comorbidity:** The presence of two or more (multiple comorbidities) chronic diseases or disease conditions in a patient.

**Diabetes:** It is a chronic disease in which the blood glucose (blood sugar) level of a patient is too high.

**End Stage Renal Disease:** Also known as kidney failure, end stage renal disease (ESRD) is the permanent failure of kidneys to their lowest filtration level (stage 5; 10-15%) at which point a patient requires either a dialysis treatment or a kidney transplant for survival.

**Obesity:** It is a complex disease in which a patient has excessive amount of body fat with a body mass index (BMI) of 30 or higher.

**Obstructive Sleep Apnea:** A sleep disorder in which a patient's breathing stops and starts during sleep because of the irregular opening and closing of the airway throat muscles. Examples include snoring and daytime sleepiness.

**Portability:** The right/feature that allows a user to transfer (port) their personal/health data across different platforms or from one service provider (organization) to another.

*This research was previously published in Privacy Concerns Surrounding Personal Information Sharing on Health and Fitness Mobile Apps; pages 31-59, copyright year 2021 by Information Science Reference (an imprint of IGI Global).*

# Chapter 19
# DeTER Framework:
## A Novel Paradigm for Addressing Cybersecurity Concerns in Mobile Healthcare

**Rangarajan (Ray) Parthasarathy**
*University of Illinois at Urbana-Champaign, USA*

**David K. Wyant**
*Belmont University, USA*

**Prasad Bingi**
*Purdue University, Fort Wayne, USA*

**James R. Knight**
*The Ohio State University, USA*

**Anuradha Rangarajan**
*Indiana State University, USA*

## ABSTRACT

*The use of health apps on mobile devices by healthcare providers and receivers (patients) is proliferating. This has elevated cybersecurity concerns owing to the transmittal of personal health information through the apps. Research literature has mostly focused on the technology aspects of cybersecurity in mobile healthcare. It is equally important to focus on the ethical and regulatory perspectives. This article discusses cybersecurity concerns in mobile healthcare from the ethical perspective, the regulatory/ compliance perspective, and the technology perspective. The authors present a comprehensive framework (DeTER) that integrates all three perspectives through which cybersecurity concerns in mobile healthcare could be viewed, understood, and acted upon. Guidance is provided with respect to leveraging the framework in the decision-making process that occurs during the system development life cycle (SDLC). Finally, the authors discuss a case applying the framework to a situation involving the development of a contact tracing mobile health app for pandemics such as COVID-19.*

DOI: 10.4018/978-1-6684-6311-6.ch019

## INTRODUCTION

Mobile devices and healthcare apps are routinely used today in the healthcare industry by doctors, nurses, and other healthcare professionals to view, transmit and share patient-related healthcare data and information. One of the most common mobile devices in use around the world today is the smartphone. It is predicted that there will be more than 5 billion smartphone users by the year 2020 (Ericsson Mobility Report, 2016; Population Pyramids Report, 2016). A study in 2015 reported that there were more than 160,000 mHealth apps in use worldwide including 103,000 multiple platform apps by 45,000 different publishers (Research2Guidance, 2015). A nationwide study in the US found that considering adults who had smartphones or tablets, 36% used mHealth apps. Among respondents using apps, 60% reported that mHealth apps were useful in achieving specific health behavior goals, 35% reported that apps helped with medical care decision-making, and 38% reported using apps for asking questions of their physicians or for seeking a second opinion (Bhuyan et. al., 2016a, 2016b). It is reasonable to conclude that the public are taking an increased interest in monitoring their own health through the use of mobile devices, smartphones and health apps. Offering of interventions for specific diseases such as diabetes, mental health and cardiovascular health through the use of smartphones is becoming increasingly common around the world, especially in the United States (Boulos et al., 2014; Fatehi, Gray & Russell, 2017; Firth et al., 2017; Kelli, Witbrodt & Shah, 2017; Lyles et al., 2011; Seto et al., 2017). The ideal of ubiquitous and pervasive healthcare using mobile devices, which would enable healthcare for everyone everywhere at all times, is poised to become a reality in the not-so-distant future (Haluza & Jungwirth, 2018; Varshney, 2013).

The practice of using mobile devices to view, transmit and share healthcare data and information is referred to as 'mobile health' or 'mHealth' in research and practitioner literature (Van Heerden et al., 2012). The global observatory for electronic health of the World Health Organization (WHO) defines mobile health as follows:

*medical and public health practice supported by mobile devices, such as mobile phones, patient monitoring devices, personal digital assistants, and other wireless devices (Van Heerden et al., 2012).*

A generic definition of cybersecurity refers to the harm caused through the misuse of network access and hardware to transmit virus and other harmful software-based code (Collard et al., 2017; Schatz, Bashroush & Wall, 2017; Talens et al., 2017). Such misuse may be with a view to intentionally harm through enticement leading to deviation from secure operation of electronic devices (such as computers and mobile devices), or by intentional or unintentional access of data by users who should not have access to it (Collard et al., 2017; Schatz, Bashroush & Wall, 2017; Talens et al., 2017). There are multiple definitions of the term 'cybersecurity' in research literature, some of which are as follows:

*Cybersecurity is the collection of tools, policies, security concepts, security safeguards, guidelines, risk management approaches, actions, training, best practices, assurance and technologies that can be used to protect the cyber environment and organization and user's assets. (International Telecommunications Union, 2008)*

*The state of being protected against the criminal or unauthorized use of electronic data, or the measures taken to achieve this. (Oxford University Press, 2014)*

*The body of technologies, processes, practices and response and mitigation measures designed to protect networks, computers, programs and data from attack, damage or unauthorized access so as to ensure confidentiality, integrity and availability. (Public Safety Canada, 2014)*

*The activity or process, ability or capability, or state whereby information and communications systems and the information contained therein are protected from and/or defended against damage, unauthorized use or modification, or exploitation. (DHS, 2014)*

While cybersecurity generally refers to behaviors and activity when using the cyber environment (i.e.) the internet, data security refers specifically to the security of data and information (Von Solms & Van Niekerk, 2013). Researchers and practitioners agree that cybersecurity and data security are intertwined and behaviors and activity that find coverage under cybersecurity impact data security as well, which some scholars have collectively referred to as "Information and Communication Technology Security" (Von Solms & Van Niekerk, 2013).

Research literature has discussed the importance and relevance of cybersecurity in mobile devices and healthcare applications (Appari & Johnson, 2010; Bhuyan et al, 2017; DesRoches et al., 2008; Gritzalis, 1998; Gritzalis, 1997; MacKinnon & Wasserman, 2009; McGinn et al., 2011; Palvia et al., 2015; Vaast, 2007; Wilkowska & Ziefle, 2012; Malvey & Slovensky, 2014). Increased use of electronic devices and adoption of technologies such as cloud computing in healthcare has led to cybersecurity concerns for obvious reasons (Aljawarneh & Yassein, 2016; Jang-Jaccard & Nepal, 2014). Snedakar (2016) went to the extent of arguing that information security is required as a core capability in healthcare organizations. Olenik and Reynolds (2012) provided an overview of security threats and controls in healthcare information technology (HIT).

Three perspectives of cybersecurity pertaining to patient-related healthcare data/information transmittal over the internet have been mentioned in research literature. These are the ethical perspective (Albrecht and Fangerau, 2015, Kotz et al., 2016), regulatory and compliance perspective (Lhotska et al., 2016), and the technology perspective (Hoglund, 2017; Morera et al., 2016; Munos et al., 2016). Past research has investigated the cybersecurity challenges and concerns relating to the storage, transmittal and use of patient-related healthcare data/information with respect to the three perspectives (Albrecht and Fangerau, 2015, Hoglund, 2017, Kotz et al., 2016, Lhotska et al., 2016).

While each of the three perspectives have been independently incorporated into past research work, there is no integrated framework in existence which comprehensively takes into account the interplay between these perspectives. This is a research gap which is addressed by this article. When the three perspectives are integrated into a framework, the impact of the interplay between these perspectives on cybersecurity becomes clearer, and the scope of the solution for decision-makers becomes broader. This article views the cybersecurity challenges and concerns relating to the storage, transmittal and use of patient-related healthcare data/information using mobile devices through a comprehensive framework lens comprising all three perspectives and, in this respect, is unique and innovative. By doing so, it bridges a research gap and makes a contribution to research literature.

# DISCUSSION OF CYBERSECURITY CONCERNS FROM AN ETHICAL PERSPECTIVE

Ethics are less formal than laws developed by nongovernment sources (e.g. professional societies), often matters of personal choice, and often interpreted by the person/authority concerned. With respect to matters concerning information security in cyberspace (cybersecurity), Pfleeger and Pleeger (2008) mentioned distinctions between ethics and laws. Laws are formal documents developed by legislatures, applicable to everyone, and interpreted and enforced by the courts. For example, the Health Insurance Portability and Accountability Act of 1996 (HIPAA) establishes legal boundaries for patient privacy. By contrast, ethics in a business context are rules, standards, codes, or principles which provide guidelines for morally right behavior and truthfulness in specific situations (Lewis, 1985).

Harmen (2013) provided details of the evolution of ethical standards through the contributions of professional societies in the field of health information management. Kotz et al. (2016) delved into multiple ethical facets of mobile health (mHealth) considering the data security challenges which impact and are impacted by ethical aspects. In a scenario involving the use of health information management systems, explicit patient consent for the collection and use of personal health information (PHI) is usually obtained. However, in mobile health (mHealth) situations wherein multiple parameters pertaining to an individual's physiology, physical activity, and social behavior may be continuously monitored, recorded, transmitted and stored using mobile devices, it is not typical to obtain patient consent covering each and every aspect of such activity because the monitoring process is likely to be automated and continuous. Due to this, individual patients may not have the opportunity to deny access to one or more parts of the data collection which they consider to be private and confidential. Such situations often blur the line of explicit consent and raise questions with respect to the level of consent the individual concerned has implicitly provided. Other concerns pertain to how, when and with whom the collected data is shared. A major ethical concern in automated and continuous monitoring using mobile devices is the possibility of unmitigated access to all parts of the healthcare receiver's sensitive information in the event of unauthorized access or security breach. When explicit consent is not obtained for recording and storing multiple health parameters using mobile devices, there arises the question of whether the risks associated with data collection based on all of the multiple parameters were properly understood during the process of implicit consent. The foregoing presentation should have made it clear that continuous health monitoring through the use of mobile devices give rise to complex ethical and legal challenges that are not easy to address. Bhuyan et al. (2016a, 2016b) discussed approaches pertaining to the involvement of the healthcare receivers in the consent process. They pointed out that healthcare providers and healthcare receivers often don't realize that patient information is routinely viewed by a number of nonclinical staff employed by healthcare facilities such as billing staff, insurance employees, and registry workers and not just by physicians and nurses, which alleviates security and privacy concerns.

Sharp and Sullivan (2017) emphasized ethical aspects of data collection, storage and use such as the need to identify when data access in a cloud computing environment is involved, the need to know the origins of the data when it is combined with other data for purposes of research, and the need to protect against selling data and confidential patient information to third parties. It is relatively easy today to take a photograph with mobile devices, a facility which could be misused and prove to be detrimental to the privacy of the healthcare receivers. Sharp and Sullivan (2017) pointed to ethical issues such as patient identification, image clarity, and data protection associated with the use of clinical photographs of patients for diagnosis, treatment, education, research, and for other medical purposes.

It may be surmised from the above presentation that preserving patient anonymity while continuing to collect granular data assumes the form of a dichotomy, and one that needs to be appropriately addressed by researchers and developers alike. Mobile devices such as smart phones are often equipped with location-sensing features such as Global Positioning Systems (GPS) which could reveal places a user has visited. Users may not want such information revealed for reasons pertaining to the safeguarding their privacy and security (McKenzie et al., 2016; Piwek et al., 2016). Wearable sensors, while capturing user's health status, food consumption behaviors, and sedentary patterns, may inadvertently capture audio or video pertaining to private, conversational, and emotional characteristics which the users may desire to protect and not reveal (Kotz et al., 2016; Shrestha & Saxena, 2017; Steil et al., 2019).

Albrecht and Fangerau (2015) referred to the ethical values of the 'patient economy', which include the 'right to know' when mobile devices are used for recording physiological parameters. They alluded to the implications of such situations on physician-patient relationships. They observed that the questions arising from the target-based approach which is typical of medical practice sometimes stand in contrast to value-rational principles of medical ethics. They contended that the code of ethics for health information professionals put forth by the International Medical Informatics Association (IMIA) should be the ideal starting point for developing a comprehensive ethics guideline pertaining to mobile health (mHealth), and that such mHealth code should include the elements of autonomy, justice, non-maleficence, and good scientific practice.

Morera et al. (2016) discussed the 'serious problem' of mHealth app security or rather the lack of it. Based on a review of mobile health apps sought out in virtual stores, they presented a guide that included information about the elements of security and its' implementation at different levels for all types of mobile health apps, based on the data each app manipulates, the associated calculated risk as a likelihood of occurrence, and the threat level resulting from its vulnerabilities. They suggested that developers implant features like "remote wipe" in apps, which would provide the ability to eliminate any patient health information on the server once the objective of the app has been fulfilled, and simultaneously assist in situations involving lost or stolen mobile devices. When discussing ethical challenges in telemedicine and telehealth, Kaplan and Litewka (2008) emphasized the ethics related challenges arising from security breaches.

Karcher and Presser (2018) acknowledged that there are many avenues for mobile devices and mHealth to serve as adjunct tools in psychotherapy, but highlighted the ethical issues involving text messaging and mHealth apps which they contended are not secure mediums. They pointed to how mHealth data could be obtained through malware software such as Trojan Horse, spyware, phishing, and/or installation of apps such as 'TextGuard' on client phones (which then allow the third party to monitor all text messages received by the client). It should be noted here that TextGuard software enables monitoring and logging of Short Message Service (SMS) and other communications, and allows users to access and search the messaging archives. In addition, there is always the risk of mobile devices being hacked, especially when used on unsecured Wi-Fi networks. Karcher and Presser (2018) also emphasized the importance of ethics in cybersecurity by considering the regulation of electronic patient health information (ePHI) (such as patient names, birth dates, e-mail addresses and other identifying information) by HIPAA.

According to Chatzipavlou et al. (2016), mobile device and apps designers must consider key elements of user satisfaction such as navigability, interactivity, and customizability from the point of view of an average user, but to be fully ethical, also from the point of view of the less able users with physical handicaps and other handicaps. Chatzipavlou et al. (2016) contended that ethical considerations should dictate user autonomy in controlling what information about them is being recorded (and for what purpose) and the ability to prevent such recording.

## DISCUSSION OF CYBSERSECURITY CONCERNS FROM A REGULATORY AND COMPLIANCE PERSPECTIVE

Despite the proliferation of health apps for mobile devices, their design and use are currently leniently regulated at best, thereby creating threats for data security and privacy (Boulos et al., 2014; Kao & Liebovitz, 2017; Terry & Gunter, 2018; Wolf et al., 2013). The few regulations that do exist do not provide a strong framework for satisfactory risk assessment and re-design (Boulos et al., 2014; Kao & Liebovitz, 2017; Terry & Gunter, 2018; Wolf et al., 2013). There is no security certification process mandated by law in the healthcare industry (Abraham et al., 2019). There is a growing concern that the structure, content and use of mobile phone health apps are not scrutinized or regulated to the extent they ought to be due to which their use could (inadvertently or otherwise) compromise the health and safety of the public (m-Health-Intelligence Report, 2016; Semigran et al., 2015). Such concerns have become more pronounced in the light of the fact that many such apps enable patients to make healthcare related decisions based on the information contained within the apps without direct clinical oversight.

Petersen and DeMuro (2015), while discussing legal and regulatory considerations associated with the use of patient-generated health data from social media and mHealth devices, stated that a reason why the United States Food and Drug Administration (FDA) regulates medical devices and health apps (used with mobile devices) is that patients and other users may experience severe consequences should the devices/apps lack adequate data protection or be hacked into. In the United States, the mHealth app guidance issued by the FDA focuses on two categories of mobile apps. The first category pertains to apps that are used with regulated medical devices. The second category pertains to apps that help to convert a mobile device such as a smartphone into a medical device of sorts. Other categories of apps are not the focus of this FDA guidance. This level of oversight has been deemed to be inadequate by the healthcare providers. In fact, surveys involving healthcare providers in the United States have revealed that many healthcare providers hesitate to recommend the use of mobile devices and health apps to their patients because of the lack of adequate oversight by reputed agencies such as the FDA (Boruff & Storie, 2014; Gauntlett et al., 2013; Hussain et al., 2015). In addition, the major focus of FDA regulations is on the manufacturers of medical devices and not on their users. Licensed practitioners who manufacture mobile medical apps for use in their professional practice, but do not label or promote their medical apps for use by other licensed practitioners and others do not meet FDA's definition of a manufacturer, thus placing them outside the purview of FDA's regulatory policy (Kramer, Kinn & Mishkind, 2015).

HIPAA applies to safeguarding medical information and contains provisions for data security and data privacy. Amatayakul (2013) provided a summary of the HIPAA privacy rule and the HIPAA security rule, which included a discussion of the changes on account of the Omnibus rule that was finalized in January 2013. Rinehart-Thompson (2017a, 2017b) provided a two-part overview of the HIPAA privacy law. Part I deals with the composition of the law and rules concerning disclosure of patient information. Part II details individual rights, breaches and breach notification, requirements for researchers, preemption and administrative requirements. Reynolds and Brodnik (2017) provided an in-depth discussion of the security rule. Trotter and Uhlman (2013) provided a list of recommendations concerning policies to help comply with the security rule. For example, they noted that encryption is sometimes labelled a data loss prevention strategy whereas in reality, it only mitigates data loss. They also pointed to the importance of updating policies from time to time to reflect the constantly changing Health Information Technology (HIT) environment. With respect to the problems caused due to the aggregation of data from multiple sources through the use of mobile health, Tan and Hung (2005) presented an insightful discussion about designing the mobile health architecture to best protect security for various types of electronic health data aggregation. For instance, when the number of records is below a certain threshold, it may become easier to identify a particular record (picking a particular record from ten records is easier than picking it from a thousand records). Besides being quantity dependent, aggregation could be made time dependent, context dependent or functionality dependent for enhanced data security and privacy.

Rinehart-Thompson and Harmen (2015) discussed the implications of mobile health in the light of HIPAA, including possible problems due to social media integration and use. In the context of using mobile devices, smartphones, and healthcare apps for exchange of electronic healthcare data and information, concerns exist pertaining to how healthcare providers can receive and store health data from patients in a HIPAA compliant manner, and actions the healthcare provider must take in situations where patient-transmitted healthcare data indicates a potential for harm to the patient or others (Kramer, Kinn & Mishkind, 2015). A related problem stems from the fact that HIPAA applies only to 'covered entities', and patients are not considered covered entities under HIPAA rules. This leads to a situation wherein patients are free to do whatever they want (with respect to storage and transmittal) with Protected Health Information (PHI), but the healthcare provider who receives the Protected Health Information (PHI) must ensure compliance with HIPAA (Kramer, Kinn & Mishkind, 2015; Luxton, Kayl & Mishkind, 2012; Luxton et al., 2011).

Petersen and DeMuro (2015) discussed yet another important aspect of transmittal of Protected Health Information (PHI) using mobile phones and health apps. Though Protected Health Information (PHI) which is in the possession of health providers (and certain other covered entities) is protected with respect to privacy under HIPAA, it is not protected when transmitted between individuals and organizations who are not covered under HIPAA. They also discussed interesting situations such as Patient-Generated Health Data (PGHD) being treated as the data of the patient when a patient checks such data with his/her mobile device, but assumes coverage under HIPAA if the patient uses his/her mobile device to transmit such information to a health care provider for the purposes of health monitoring.

Many healthcare laws and legislations around the world including those pertaining to the appropriate design and use of mobile devices and health apps for healthcare are equivocal (Lhotska et al., 2016, Petersen & DeMuro, 2015). This could result in incorrect and inconsistent interpretations of each during the design and manufacture of mobile devices and health apps, which in-turn could lead to information security and privacy being compromised. For instance, the European Union does not have clear and binding rules as to the delimitation between lifestyle and well-being apps, and likewise between medical devices and in-vitro diagnostic medical devices (Lhotska et al., 2016). As of 2016, the Food and Drug Administration (FDA) in the United States had formally approved only about 100 of 100,000 healthcare apps in use in the United States (Lhotska et al., 2016). Such lack of delineation and formal approval by regulatory agencies could lead to an absence of or inconsistency in security and privacy features available in mobile healthcare devices and apps, which then opens the doors for a wide variety of cybersecurity attacks.

Though steps have begun to be taken to address such gaps by the United States and other countries in recent times, a lot remains to be done from a regulatory and compliance perspective. For instance, the United States Federal Communications Commission (FCC) has extended its jurisdiction to cover certain smartphone applications used as biosensors and certain medical devices using radio technology such as Bluetooth technology. Per the breach notification rules of the United States Federal Trade Commission (FTC), when the security of data gathered, stored and transmitted by mHealth apps is breached, the entity responsible for developing the app is required to notify the users about the breach within 60 days (Munos et al., 2016). Per guidelines issued by the health informatics unit of the Royal College of Physicians of the United Kingdom, a mobile device or healthcare app used for medical purposes is classified as a medical device, and any app that uses patient specific information needs a *Conformité Européenne* (CE) mark.

Brooks (2006) suggested a number of metrics for measuring the management of information security. Although the list targets the general issue of IT service management, some of the metrics could prove to be useful in managing a mobile environment as well. One example is measuring the time it takes to implement security patches, which is as applicable to a mobile device use as it is to any other IT situation. Knapp (2010) notes that when service level agreements (SLAs) which include mobile devices are specified between service desks and functional units, security policies must be specified.

## DISCUSSION OF CYBSERSECURITY CONCERNS FROM A TECHNOLOGY PERSPECTIVE

Multiple technology factors need to be addressed to successfully defend against cyber threats. One challenge pertains to preserving data authenticity and accuracy. Snedaker (2013, 2016) described mobile devices as "the bane of every IT shop" because of the difficultly of managing (privacy and security) in a 'bring your own device' (BYOD) environment. Cornelius, Harmen and Mullen (2015) noted that the presence of multiple points of entry for mobile information increases vulnerability. Kotz et al. (2016) stated that in a typical mHealth setting, data passes through multiple layers involving processing, filtering and summarization. This combination of factors (multiple platforms, multiple data sources, multiple layers of processing) could expose data to various forms of cyberattacks, which makes the need to preserve contextual information critical.

The body of research concerning the embedding of appropriate measures to protect patient and user data privacy is nascent. For example, Snedaker (2013, 2016) stated that there are "no solid answers to mobile device management in healthcare IT". Hoglund (2017) presented an overview of the current wireless medical device security landscape. He emphasized the need for the healthcare industry needs to address unique yet multifaceted cybersecurity requirements – that of increasing productivity while providing secure connections for mobile devices. Though device manufacturers employ authentication mechanisms as "biomedical interfaces" on wireless devices, Hoglund (2017) provided examples of hidden malware in devices that are not activated until the device is powered. He underscored the importance of a strong risk management practice to holistically address this complex problem.

Technologies such as Blockchain are finding their way into the broader mHealth ecosystem. Data tampering is a critical security issue that needs to be addressed from a multitude of perspectives such as securing patient data while in transit and tamper-proofing data once it reaches its intended destination. Blockchain technology ensures tamper resistance by maintaining a continuously growing list of transactional records organized into blocks known only to the sender and receiver, which is cryptographically signed by the sender. Ichikawa, Kashiyama, & Ueno (2017) developed and evaluated a tamper-resistant mHealth system for cognitive behavioral therapy for insomnia using a smart phone app. Patient data comprised of subjective data (e.g. clinical indicators of sleep) and objective psychomotor vigilance data captured using a smart phone. This was transmitted on a daily basis to a cluster of servers running a distributed Blockchain platform. To validate tamper resistance, the authors injected network faults. Results showed that patient data was successfully registered and updated in the database despite these faults.

In the information technology and information security scenario of today where stealing of data through hacking and other means is becoming alarmingly common, it is imperative that any health data transmitted through mobile devices, smartphones and health apps be appropriately encrypted. Concerns include lack of adequate security measures in mobile devices, smartphones, and health apps to prevent third party attacks and interception of health information, disabled security features on the mobile devices belonging to individual users which may facilitate theft of health information, and lack of HIPAA compliant encryption features on mobile devices (Kramer, Kinn & Mishkind, 2015; Luxton et al., 2012).

Morera et al. (2016) provided a comprehensive analysis of security solutions which must ideally be incorporated into the design of mHealth apps for smartphones and other mobile devices. They summarized the top ten vulnerabilities affecting mobile application security by perusing best-in-class books, industry standards, and standards published by organizations such as the FTC. This comprehensive analysis is a valuable guidebook for the technology professional and the technology user alike, which should help to raise awareness and also to train professionals who are tasked with developing secure yet scalable mHealth apps. Chatzipavlou et al. (2016) emphasized the need for developers with considerable technical expertise to work on developing health apps so that the health apps developed would include the highest levels of data protection and data integrity by taking into account all relevant laws, while at the same time being user-friendly by considering the needs of the users of the markets where the health apps will be used. It is apt to state that maintainability, portability and user safety are aspects that have a bearing on both the technology perspective and the ethical perspective (Abbas et al., 2017; Albrecht & von-Jan, 2017; Fatehi, Gray & Russell, 2017).

## DeTER FRAMEWORK BASED ON ETHICAL, REGULATORY AND TECHNOLOGY PERSPECTIVES

It should be clear from the foregoing discussion that a paradigm for viewing, discussing, and addressing cybersecurity concerns in mobile healthcare should include all three perspectives, viz. ethical, regulatory, and technology perspectives, because these perspectives act together with significant interplays rather than as individual entities in the cybersecurity context. With this in mind, the authors developed the DeTER framework, which is an integrated and comprehensive framework with which to view and address cybersecurity concerns in mobile healthcare. The DeTER framework is presented in Figure 1. This framework offers the following advantages: 1) it is of immense value to health app designers and developers and assists them with incorporating the salient aspects of each perspective into their design and development, 2) it is a useful tool for benchmarking health apps and mobile healthcare, and 3) it provides an enhanced understanding of the interplay between the perspectives and the combined impact on the end-product. The integrated framework, in addition to containing the core blocks of ethical perspectives, regulatory/compliance perspectives, and technology perspectives, also considers the overlaps between the core blocks. The overlapping areas contain the cybersecurity issues that impact more than one core block.

*Figure 1. DeTER Framework*

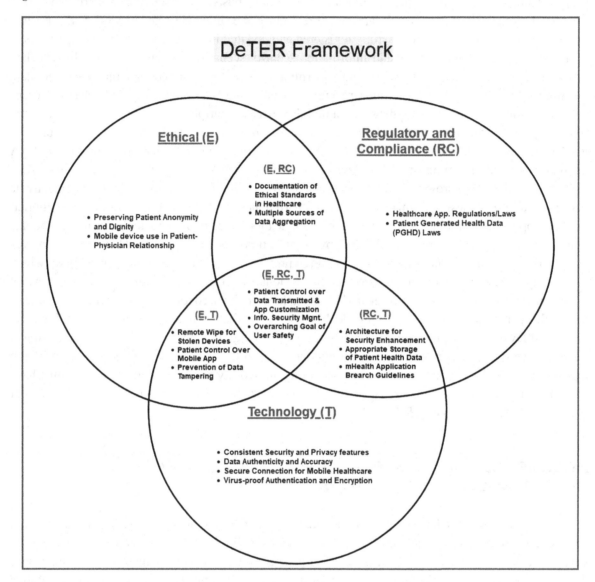

The ethical block plays an important role in mobile healthcare situations and is primarily concerned with preserving patient anonymity and dignity, and appropriate mobile device use in patient-provider relationships. A major component of the ethical block covers the grey area of explicit versus implicit patient consent with respect to personal health information (PHI) in continuous health monitoring in mobile health (mHealth). Patients need to be made aware of the PHI being collected through mHealth, and have the opportunity to accept or deny the collection of all of or certain parts of the PHI being collected. Such explicit consent should be obtained after ensuring that the patient has understood the implications of hacking, unauthorized access, and/ or security breach situations on the collection, retention, and use of PHI. In such instances, ethics would place a greater value on a well-informed patient's explicit consent than an ill-informed patient's implicit consent. The above is especially important in a continuous health monitoring process using mobile devices and health apps. The ethical block should be considered on the basis of its own merits when using mobile devices and health apps, but may well have interaction effects with other blocks in such situations. Hence it is important to consider the interplay between the Ethical and Regulatory/Compliance Block, Technology and Ethical Block, and the Ethical, Regulatory/Compliance and Technology Block.

The regulatory and compliance block is primarily concerned with laws and policies concerning the use of healthcare apps in mobile healthcare and PGHD laws. With regard to the interplay between ethics and regulatory/compliance, regulatory/compliance laws and policies should cover all aspects of mobile health use including regulation of all apps used in mobile devices while considering the ethical impacts at the same time. For example, it would be unethical to approve the use of apps that have continuous monitoring enabled if such apps do not take into account the desire of the users to not have their movements through the day monitored. Another example would be a situation involving multiple sources of data aggregation which inadvertently or otherwise reveal more information about particular users than they themselves would care to reveal.

The technology block with respect to mobile healthcare is concerned with implementing security/privacy features in all mobile devices and apps, ensuring data authenticity and accuracy, enabling secure connections for mobile healthcare with a view to eliminating hacking and data stealing, and virus-proofed authentication and encryption. The intertwining of the technology block with the regulatory/compliance block reveals itself in aspects such as designing an appropriate architecture for security enhancement which simultaneously assists with compliance, storage of patient health data in a manner that safeguards against data breaches and thus protects patient health information, and the design of mHealth apps with enhanced security and privacy features which would address breach guidelines stated in regulatory/compliance laws and policies. The collaboration between the technology block and the ethical block could lead to the development of mobile healthcare which is immensely beneficial for individual and public health improvement, while also addressing ethics concerns. Examples of how technology features in mobile healthcare could address ethical issues include a remote wipe software feature which could help to prevent data theft from stolen devices, greater patient control over mobile apps whereby they could safeguard their own privacy by limiting access to data they do not want to share, and effective technology controls in devices that prevent data tampering thereby helping to safeguard protected health information.

There is also a degree of interplay between all the blocks. Such interplay between the technology, ethical, and regulatory/compliance blocks would lead to an end-result comprising of features/controls such as app customization to enable healthcare receivers to have a great degree of control over what, when, and how healthcare data is transmitted, innovative features for information security management such as two factor authentication and AES-256 encryption, and continuous improvement of healthcare apps as regulatory/compliance laws and policies change, and as the field of information security/cybersecurity develops.

Using the DeTER framework will benefit healthcare receivers who are mobile healthcare users, information technology professionals who are involved in the design and development of mobile healthcare (both hardware and software), and law/policy makers involved in law/policy making for mobile healthcare, and provide the overall effect of making mobile healthcare robust and safe for use by all concerned due to the addressal of inter-disciplinary issues as already explained. This will hopefully also result in efficiency and effectiveness in mobile healthcare development, which is an integral part of information technology strategy (IT strategy).

*Figure 2. Mapping of mHealth app concerns to ethical principles, laws and regulations, and security standards*

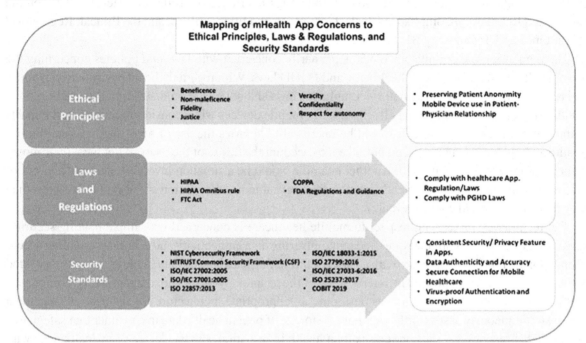

## IMPLEMENTING THE DeTER FRAMEWORK

This section provides guidance to mHealth app designers and app developers on applying the DeTER framework to their work, and seamlessly integrating it into the system development lifecycle (SDLC). Figure 2 illustrates how the salient aspects of each block in the DeTER framework could be mapped to guiding ethical principles, laws, and security standards.

### Applying Ethical Principles Using the Framework

Researchers have studied and cataloged key ethical principles pertaining to the healthcare context (Gelling, 1999). Several of these ethical principles are applicable in the context of mobile healthcare app development. The DeTER framework applies seven of these ethical principles (beneficence, non-maleficence, fidelity, justice, veracity, confidentiality, respect for autonomy) that have most often been discussed in research literature to cybersecurity in mobile healthcare, and more specifically health app development.

Beneficence is the requirement that the output/outcome benefits the patient (Gelling, 1999). Physicians are primarily guided by the Hippocratic Oath that states "I will use the treatment to help the sick according to my ability and judgement, but never with a view to injury and wrongdoing." Physicians need to exercise due diligence and apply the Hippocratic oath to their recommendations of mobile healthcare apps to their patients. This implies that it is the physicians' responsibility to ensure that the recommended app will not cause injury or harm in any form or manner to their patients, whether inadvertently or otherwise. It also implies that when the physician is unable to ascertain this, he/she would be well-advised not to recommend or endorse the health app. Though the equivalent of the Hippocrates

Oath does not exist for designers and developers of health apps, it should be possible to create one at the beginning of the system development life cycle which may then be utilized as an ethical compass to guide the design and development of the app.

Non-maleficence stipulates that no harm should come to the patient or research participant as a result of taking part in a study (Faden & Beauchamp, 1986; Garity, 1995). Applying this to a health app development context, the implication is to ensure patient safety and security are never compromised due to the use of the health app. For instance, a design specification that the health app healthcare app record, transmit, and store patient's real-time geographical location must be critically examined with regard to the tradeoffs between the risks to patients/health app users and the health-related benefits that may accrue through such monitoring.

Fidelity is the principle concerned with the building of trust between the researcher and the participants (Parahoo, 1997). The research participants entrust themselves to the researcher, who subsequently has an obligation to safeguard the participants and their welfare in the research situation (Garity, 1995). When applied to the design and development of health apps in mobile healthcare, this implies taking all steps not to betray the trust placed by the users on the health apps, which in turn translates to the app designers and developers including all features in the app to safeguard user privacy and security and preventing harm to the users. This will require a significant amount of thought and reflection on the part of the app designers and developers. In addition, since patients generally trust their physician's advice and tend to unconditionally follow their guidance, patients may treat their physician's suggestion to consider using a health app as a strong recommendation vouching for certain health apps. To eliminate such misunderstanding, it is important that the patients receive the following information up-front and in a transparent manner in order for them to make an informed decision: (1) what personal data would be captured along with the periodicity of capture, (2) how such data will be used for the patient's benefit in terms of improved healthcare, and (3) where the patients would report their concerns should they suspect that their personal data has been stolen or compromised. Doing so can not only build trust, but make patients better informed and be prepared to handle any unforeseen exigencies.

The principle of justice requires the researcher to be fair to the participants (Parahoo, 1997). When applied to the design and development of health apps in mobile healthcare, this implies that the app designers and developers understand the patient demographic that would use the app and incorporate features best suited to protect the demographic as well as make them comfortable with using the health app. The millennial generation is arguably more comfortable with utilizing mobile and hand-held technologies compared to baby-boomers. It is the ageing population in the latter demographic that may have a pressing need to utilize health apps for alternate forms of healthcare delivery. The app designers and developers may do well to solicit input from a wide demographic keeping such needs in mind in order to ensure that the app addresses the needs of each demographic in as fair a manner as possible.

The research principle of veracity highlights the obligation of the researcher to tell the truth about the research, even if it deters potential participants from entering the study (Garity, 1995; Parahoo, 1997). Along these lines, healthcare app designers and developers must disclose all aspects of the features and functionality to potential patients/users. This should not be limited to initial use of the app. If patients are uncomfortable with newer feature enhancements, they will be well within their rights to stop utilizing the app and such a possibility should not deter the app designers from disclosing the whole truth. While it is understandable that health app designers, developers, and marketers would want to grow their user-base in order to sustain their business, this should be done in an ethical manner with veracity and not otherwise.

Respect for autonomy is an ethical principle which is associated with several different concepts including privacy, voluntariness, self-mastery, free choice, choosing one's own moral position, and accepting responsibility for one's own choices (Gelling, 1999). It is defined as the personal rule of self by adequate understanding, while remaining free from controlling influences by others and from personal limitations that prevent choice (Faden & Beauchamp, 1986). Gillion (1985a) further classified this into three types (1) autonomy of thought – this includes a wide range of intellectual activities that are described as thinking for oneself, (2) autonomy of will – this involves the freedom of an individual to do something based on their own deliberations, and (3) autonomy of action – this implies that the individual making the decision should be able to act as he/she wishes, after the decision has been made. It may be argued that in the context of mobile healthcare app development, this is perhaps one of the most important albeit complicated ethical principles to adhere to. When a health app does continuous monitoring and real-time data collection, patients need to be made aware of all the PHI being collected, and must have the ability to allow or deny the collection of all or certain parts of it. Furthermore, such decisions of patients must be transferrable to future versions of the health app. Designers and developers of mobile healthcare apps should incorporate such granular level of authorization into their technical design even if this results in increased time and costs upfront.

The ethical principle of confidentiality requires two conditions to exist: (1) one person must undertake not to disclose information considered to be secret and (2) a different person must disclose to the first person information that they consider to be secret (Burns & Grove, 1995; Gillon, 1985b). This may be applied to mobile healthcare app development in several ways. Patients who are concerned about the violation of confidentiality when using health apps may be unwilling to use the apps or interact with it in a way other than intended. Physicians are governed by their professional code of conduct in physician-patient relationships and hence may have a relatively better understanding of confidentiality. Due to the absence of such a code of conduct for the designers and developers of mobile healthcare apps, they should incorporate the principle of confidentiality through actions such as including as many features as possible for safeguarding patient confidentiality, making available a detailed user-guide with the option of a help-line, proactively contacting patients if there is an observed abnormality in PHI data patterns, preemptively alerting patients to potential data breaches, and following up with patients through periodic communications. Such actions, besides duly incorporating the principle of confidentiality, would also increase patients' trust and positively impact patients' perception of confidentiality.

## Applying Laws and Regulations Using the Framework

When designing and developing mobile healthcare apps, it is important to understand the geographic scope of use based on the intended demographic. This is because the local laws and regulations with respect to health data transmission and storage will vary based on the users' geographic locations which may have an impact on the software architecture and design. For example, the architecture and design of mobile health apps used in the United States will be impacted by the HIPAA rules. HIPAA protects the privacy of digital health information. Healthcare providers, health plans, healthcare clearing houses and business associates (BA) are subject to the 'Privacy Rule' provision in HIPAA. The HIPAA 'Security Rule' requires that all covered entities 1) ensure confidentiality, integrity, and availability of electronic PHI, 2) detect and safeguard anticipated security threats to the information, 3) protect against anticipated impermissible uses or disclosures, and 4) certify compliance by their workforce (U.S. Department of Health and Human Services, 2020). The HIPAA 'Omnibus Rule; extends the definition of BA to include personal health record vendors engaged by physicians as well as electronic data storage providers. These entities are independently responsible to the Office for Civil Rights (OCR) for complying with all aspects of HIPAA. The Omnibus Rule mandates that all covered entities, following the discovery of a breach of protected health information, notify each individual whose data has been compromised within 60 calendar days after discovery workforce (U.S. Department of Health and Human Services, 2020). In the mHealth context, app designers need to validate whether they are operating as one of the covered entities and implement corresponding operational controls to adhere to the appropriate HIPAA rules (Centers for Disease Control and Prevention, 2018). Complying with the Omnibus Rule requires careful consideration of PHI data storage and access policies during the design and implementation phases of mHealth apps development

The Federal Trade Commission (FTC) Act grants to the FTC the authority to oversee mHealth apps. The FTC calls for companies handling consumer data to adhere to three core principles 1) privacy by design: mobile healthcare app developers must build in privacy at every stage of development, 2) simplified consumer choice: mobile healthcare app developers must provide consumers context-and-time relevant choices when operating outside of a transaction relationship, and 3) adherence to greater transparency: companies must disclose details about their collection and use of consumer information. The FTC has taken selective enforcement actions against at least seven mobile healthcare app developers in this regard for reasons ranging from unsubstantiated health-related claims to lack of calibration of the mHealth technology to billing practices which are misleading (Wagner, 2020). The United States Congress enacted the Children's Online Privacy Protection Act (COPPA) which forbids mobile app developers from gathering personal information of children under 13 without the express consent (permission given specifically, most often in writing) of their parents (Federal Trade Commission, 2015). Personal information includes information such as online contact information, telephone number, and geolocation information sufficient to identify street name and city name. For the above reasons, it is important for mobile healthcare app developers to take the time and make the effort to ensure adherence to all principles specified by the FTC.

As of September 2019, the Food and Drug Administration (FDA) of the United States has issued additional nonbinding recommendations for mobile medical applications. The FDA refers to software functions that are device functions as "device software functions." Device software functions may include "Software as a Medical Device (SaMD)" and "Software in a Medical Device (SiMD)". Software functions that meet the definition of a device may be deployed on mobile platforms. Furthermore, if a software function is intended for use in performing a medical device function (i.e. for diagnosis of disease or other conditions, or the cure, mitigation, treatment, or prevention of disease) it is a considered to be the equivalent of a medical device and will hence be regulated by FDA (FDA Guidance Reference). For example, mobile apps running on smart phones which analyze and interpret EKG waveforms to detect heart function irregularities would be FDA regulated. The FDA has further provided clarification on software functions for which it intends to exercise enforcement discretion. Examples include software functions that help patients with diagnosed psychiatric conditions maintain their behavioral coping skills, software functions that use patient's PHI to provide preventive recommendations from established authorities, and apps that use GPS location information to alert asthmatics (Food and Drug Administration, 2019). The FDA has emphasized that the guidance provided does not establish legally enforceable responsibilities. Rather, it is necessary that mobile healthcare app developers take all the above into account during SDLC.

Laws surrounding data collection and retention requirements pose unique constraints for mHealth apps that integrate PHI data with a patient's electronic medical record (EMR). The HIPAA Privacy Rule does not set standards for retaining medical records. However, nearly every state in the United States has statutes or regulations that set such requirements. For hospitals, state laws impose retention periods ranging from 5 years from the date of discharge, to "permanently" – typically amounting to a 10-year retention period. For medical doctors, a shorter schedule ranging from 3 to 10 years is specified, but is typically 7 years (White & Daniel, 2009). The HIPAA privacy rule allows the disclosure of an individual's PHI without the need to seek institutional review board (IRB) approval as long as three conditions are met – it's use is solely for research purposes, documentation pertaining to the death of subjects used in the study can be provided, and it has been proved that the data is absolutely necessary for the research (Gostin et al., 2009). Use of PHI for non-research purposes is also governed by the HIPAA rules. As of January 2013, the HIPAA 'Privacy Rule' has shortened the period for the protection of personal health information from an indefinite interval to a period of fifty years after death. However, state laws have the option of extending this timeline. The state of Hawaii still mandates 'infinite protection' i.e. for an indefinite period (Haw. Rev. Stat. section 323C-43) (Huser & Cimino, 2013). As stated earlier, mobile healthcare app designers and developers must be cognizant of the above discussed laws/rules and be sure to apply them to their designs and end-products to be legally compliant and also to protect the end-users (patients specifically).

## Applying Security Standards Using the Framework

While ethical principles and laws and regulations provide a roadmap for *What* are important considerations for mHealth app development, adherence to security standards and related technical frameworks guide *How* apps need to be implemented. These can serve as useful guiding posts to mHealth app designers and developers throughout SDLC.

The National Institute of Standards and Technology (NIST) has put forth a compilation of standards, guidelines, and best practices to manage cybersecurity risk (National Institute of Standards and Technology, 2020). The framework comprises of three components: 1) The Framework Core, 2) The Framework Implementation Tiers, and 3) The Framework Profile. The 'Framework Core' provides a comprehensive listing of functions to assist with managing cybersecurity risk. The 'Framework Implementation Tiers' provide a measurement of how organizations view and manage this risk. The 'Framework Profile' provides a means to align an organization's implementation scenarios to the core functions and implementation tiers. The Control Objectives for Information and Related Technology (COBIT) framework was created by the Information Systems Audit and Control Association (ISACA) for IT management and governance. It allows technical managers to bridge the gap between control requirements, technical issues, and business risks (Akowuah et al., 2013). The COBIT 2019 framework provides for integration with NIST's Cybersecurity Framework to comprehensively address IT governance in the rapidly evolving cybersecurity landscape. It is important for organizations (particularly healthcare providers) to utilize these frameworks to assess their current and desired cybersecurity risk management posture. This can then assist with making technical decisions that holistically align to cybersecurity principles during SDLC.

The Health Information Trust Alliance (HITRUST ®) founded in 2007 has championed programs that safeguard sensitive health information in collaboration with information security leaders across public and private sectors (The Health Information Trust Alliance [HITRUST], 2020a). The HITRUST Common Security Framework (CSF ®) is based on the International Organization of Standards (ISO) and Electrotechnical Commission (IEC) standards 27001:2005 and 27002:2005, and incorporates several healthcare information security-related regulations and standards to provide comprehensive and prescriptive guidance (HITRUST, 2020b). It contains 13 security Control Categories and 42 Control Objectives that allow healthcare technology organizations to contextually and effectively identify, define, and manage their people, process, and technology resources for cybersecurity needs.

The 'ISO 22857:2013 Health Informatics – Guidelines on data protection to facilitate trans-border flows of personal health data' standard provides guidance on data protection requirements to facilitate the transfer of personal health data across national or jurisdictional borders (The International Standards Organization [ISO], 2013). This standard covers both, the data protection principles that apply to international or trans-jurisdictional transfers, and the security policy which an organization adopts to ensure compliance with those principles. This standard can be particularly important in the context of mobile healthcare app development involving apps whose scope of use spans national boundaries, or in cases where PHI is not stored on premises within an organization but stored in a cloud infrastructure that spans multiple geographies. The 'ISO 27799:2016 Health Informatics – Information Security Management in Health Using ISO/IEC 27002' standard was published in 2016. By implementing ISO 27799:2016, healthcare organizations and other custodians of health information will be able to ensure a minimum requisite level of security that maintains confidentiality, integrity, and availability of PHI (ISO, 2016). The 'ISO 25237:2017 Health informatics — Pseudonymization' standard contains principles and requirements for privacy protection using pseudonymization services for the protection of personal health information (ISO, 2017). Pseudonymization is data de-identification, such that data belonging to an individual in the clinical environment still belongs to the same individual in the de-identified version for secondary use (Noumeir et al., 2007).

The 'ISO/IEC 27033-6:2016 Information technology — Security techniques — Network security' standard provides guidance for the selection, implementation, and monitoring of technical controls necessary to provide secure communications using wireless networks (ISO, 2016b). The 'ISO/IEC 18033-1:2015 Information technology — Security techniques — Encryption algorithms' standard provides significant insights on encryption techniques to protect confidentiality of transmitted or stored data (ISO, 2015). These standards must be applied by mobile healthcare app developers to their app design and developments to ensure network security and data/information security respectively.

The DeTER framework will guide mobile healthcare app developers with respect to applying the standards presented in the preceding paragraphs so as to ensure that their software is resilient to malicious attacks which target (especially) PHI during data transmission or when 'at rest'.

## APPLICATION OF THE DeTER FRAMEWORK TO BUILDING A CONTACT TRACING APP FOR COVID-19

The application of the integrated and comprehensive DeTER framework to building a Contact Tracing app to combat the novel coronavirus disease 2019 (COVID-19) pandemic is presented in this section.

The COVID-19 global pandemic represents an urgent public health crisis (Yasaka et al., 2020). Several countries have been faced with the dilemma of choosing an appropriate public health response (Ferguson et al). According to Abeler et al. (2020), it is not adequate to quarantine people after they exhibit COVID-19 symptoms because data collected to date informs that about half of the infections occur before the symptoms of fever or persistent cough appear. In addition, though strategies such as social distanc-

*Figure 3. Framework application for COVID-19 Contact Tracing mHealth app*

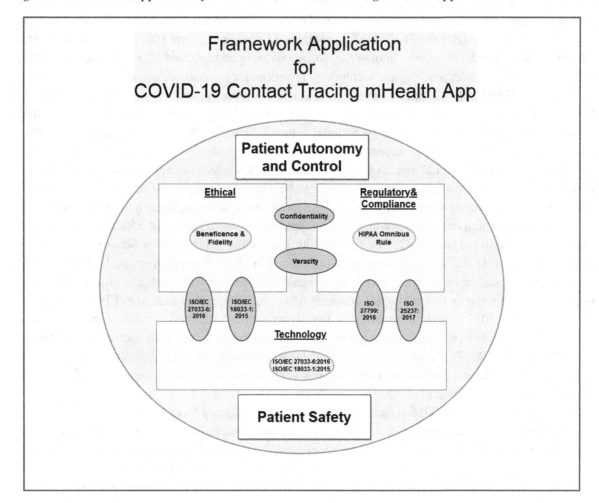

ing help to a certain extent, long term social distancing for the entire population of states and countries until a vaccine becomes available is rather impractical and will cause significant economic loss. As an alternative to drastic measures, healthcare researchers have been exploring the use of technological solutions such as a contact tracing smartphone app technology (Ferguson et al., Yasaka; Abeler, 2020).

Contact tracing is the process of tracing potential transmission routes of an infection through a population for the purposes of isolating those who may have been exposed, and thus reducing further transmission (Yasaka et al., 2020). Building a mHealth app for this purpose requires complex decision-making from an ethical, regulatory, and technology standpoint. The framework presented in this study can assist mHealth app designers and developers navigate these concerns as depicted in Figure 3.

While all elements of the ethical, regulatory, and technology perspective would be quite relevant to such an app, a sub-set will play a prominent role in this scenario. For instance, beneficence and fidelity (which have been discussed in preceding sections) would be highly important in a contract tracing app for COVID-19. Due to the humanitarian impact of COVID-19, a health app developed in this scenario may not be readily adopted by the public/users unless they have trust in it and believe it is for their ultimate benefit. This means the principle of fidelity (which has been discussed in preceding sections) has to be upheld at all times. From a regulatory standpoint, the HIPAA Omnibus rule assumes prominence in this context. It is foreseeable that data collected from such mHealth app will be utilized for secondary research purposes. This places the mHealth app developer in the role of the BA who is subject to the OCR. Therefore, additional due diligence needs be performed on safeguarding PHI. From a technology perspective, mHealth app developers can benefit from adhering to the ISO standards ISO/IEC 27033-6:2016 and ISO/IEC 18033-1:2015, to make possible the confidentiality, integrity, and availability of the data being collected.

The concerns/issues which overlap various perspectives can also be effectively addressed by applying the DeTER framework. By being cognizant of the confidentiality principle, app developers can seek to uphold the inherent trust placed in them. Veracity is an important virtue to uphold as it is highly likely that patients' adoption of mobile healthcare apps would be heavily influenced by the disclosure of the PHI being collected. Related ethical principles are reflected in the HIPAA Omnibus regulation which formalizes the need for adhering to such principles. The technology standards ISO 27799:2016 and ISO 25237:2017 play an important role in designing and implementing confidentiality and pseudonymiza-tion features within mHealth apps. Closing the loop between the ethical and technology perspectives is the adherence to ISO/IEC 27033-6:2016 and ISO/IEC 18033-1:2015, which address confidentiality and non-maleficence. Underpinning this ecosystem is the ethical principle of respect for patient autonomy while maintaining patient safety at all times, whereby patients need to be provided the option of selectively turning off the recording of PHI data. We believe that the use of the DeTER framework will help in the successful development of an efficient and effective COVID-19 tracing app incorporating all the perspectives discussed in this article.

## CONTRIBUTIONS, LIMITATIONS AND FUTURE RESEARCH

Three specific and very important perspectives of cybersecurity, namely the ethical perspective, the regulatory and compliance perspective, and the technology perspective were considered in this article. To the best of our knowledge, no other body of work has both, considered these three perspectives in an integrated and comprehensive manner as this article has, and also presented a framework for practical implementation (for practitioners) such as the DeTER framework presented in this article. In consideration of the COVID-19 pandemic the world is facing today, this article presents an application of the DeTER framework to a COVID-19 related app, which the authors believe is timely and pertinent. Frameworks and models are theoretical representations of the way systems or processes work, and they tend to reduce complexities in practical implementations (Callen et al., 2008). In that regard, a strength of this article and the DeTER framework presented herein is that it synthesizes three important and vast viewpoints into an integrated and comprehensive single view. However, there could well be other perspectives pertaining to cybersecurity which this article does not consider. This article is mostly based on the state of healthcare, cybersecurity, and mobile health app development in the United States. The ethical, regulatory/compliance, and technical perspectives pertaining to cybersecurity and mobile health app development in other countries may be different from what they are in the United States. In terms of future research possibilities, the discussion and conclusions presented in this article could be validated through an empirical assessment. Also, exploring how the framework presented in this article drives decision-making in each phase of SDLC may be worth exploring.

# CONCLUSION

The use of mobile devices and apps for healthcare related uses is rapidly on the rise in the information technology world we live in today. From an ethical perspective, the question of implied consent should be addressed when developing apps for mobile health. This is especially true in situations that could lead to unauthorized access involving continuously and automatically monitored patient health information. When developing mHealth applications, developers should include security features which prevent access to the information which the consumer or healthcare receiver has not explicitly consented to share. For example, global positioning systems used in mobile devices and mobile healthcare should have inbuilt options to prevent the automatic transmission of all daily and hourly movements of the user without explicit consent, as otherwise there could arise a situation involving invasion of privacy. From a regulatory and compliance perspective, laws must unequivocally define the absolute minimum level of privacy and security for consumers, especially as these apply to mobile devices. From a technology perspective, the combination of multiple platforms, multiple data sources, and multiple layers of processing in mobile health exposes data to multiple forms of cyberattacks, which enhances the need for security. When the rights of the user and the perspectives discussed in this article are incorporated into the design and development of mobile healthcare, it could become an effective tool with which to achieve public health improvement and well-being both, in the short-term and in the long-term. Healthcare technology will then become a great boon to the world.

# REFERENCES

A Glossary of Common Cybersecurity Terminology. (2014). http://niccs.us-cert.gov/glossary#letter_c

Abbas, R. M., Carroll, N., Richardson, I., & Beecham, S. (2017). The Need for Trustworthiness Models in Healthcare Software Solutions. In HEALTHINF (pp. 451-456). doi:10.5220/0006249904510456

Abeler, J., Bäcker, M., Buermeyer, U., & Zillessen, H. (2020). COVID-19 Contact Tracing and Data Protection Can Go Together. *JMIR mHealth and uHealth*, 8(4), e19359. doi:10.2196/19359 PMID:32294052

Akowuah, F., Yuan, X., Xu, J., & Wang, H. (2013). A survey of security standards applicable to health information systems. *International Journal of Information Security and Privacy*, 7(4), 22–36. doi:10.4018/ijisp.2013100103

Albrecht, U. V., & Fangerau, H. (2015). Do Ethics Need to be Adapted to mHealth? In ICIMTH (pp. 219-222). Academic Press.

Albrecht, U. V., & von Jan, U. (2017). Safe, sound and desirable: Development of mHealth apps under the stress of rapid life cycles. *mHealth*, 3, 3. doi:10.21037/mhealth.2017.06.05 PMID:28828374

Aljawarneh, S. A., & Yassein, M. O. B. (2016). A conceptual security framework for cloud computing issues. *International Journal of Intelligent Information Technologies*, 12(2), 12–24. doi:10.4018/IJIIT.2016040102

Amatayakul, M. K. (2013). *Electronic health records: A practical guide for professionals and organizations* (5th ed.). American Health Information Management Association.

Appari, A., & Johnson, M. E. (2010). Information security and privacy in healthcare: Current state of research. *International Journal of Internet and Enterprise Management, 6*(4), 279–314. doi:10.1504/IJIEM.2010.035624

Bhuyan, S. S., Bailey-DeLeeuw, S., Wyant, D. K., & Chang, C. F. (2016b). Too Much or Too Little? How Much Control Should Patients Have Over EHR Data? *Journal of Medical Systems, 40*(7), 174. doi:10.100710916-016-0533-2 PMID:27272134

Bhuyan, S. S., Kim, H., Isehunwa, O. O., Kumar, N., Bhatt, J., Wyant, D. K., ... Dasgupta, D. (2017). Privacy and security issues in mobile health: Current research and future directions. *Health Policy and Technology, 6*(2), 188–191. doi:10.1016/j.hlpt.2017.01.004

Bhuyan, S. S., Lu, N., Chandak, A., Kim, H., Wyant, D., Bhatt, J., & Chang, C. F. (2016a). Use of mobile health applications for health-seeking behavior among US adults. *Journal of Medical Systems, 40*(6), 153. doi:10.100710916-016-0492-7 PMID:27147516

Boruff, J. T., & Storie, D. (2014). Mobile devices in medicine: A survey of how medical students, residents, and faculty use smartphones and other mobile devices to find information. *Journal of the Medical Library Association: JMLA, 102*(1), 22–30. doi:10.3163/1536-5050.102.1.006 PMID:24415916

Boulos, M. N. K., Brewer, A. C., Karimkhani, C., Buller, D. B., & Dellavalle, R. P. (2014). Mobile medical and health apps: State of the art, concerns, regulatory control and certification. *Online Journal of Public Health Informatics, 5*(3), 229. PMID:24683442

Brooks, P. (2006). *Metrics for IT service management.* Van Haren.

Callen, J. L., Braithwaite, J., & Westbrook, J. I. (2008). Contextual implementation model: A framework for assisting clinical information system implementations. *Journal of the American Medical Informatics Association, 15*(2), 255–262. doi:10.1197/jamia.M2468 PMID:18096917

Centers for Disease Control and Prevention. (2018). *Health Insurance Portability and Accountability Act of 1996.* https://www.cdc.gov/phlp/publications/topic/hipaa.html#one

Chatzipavlou, I. A., Christoforidou, S. A., & Vlachopoulou, M. (2016). *A recommended guideline for the development of mHealth Apps.* Academic Press.

Collard, G., Ducroquet, S., Disson, E., & Talens, G. (2017). A definition of Information Security Classification in cybersecurity context. In *Research Challenges in Information Science (RCIS), 2017 11th International Conference on* (pp. 77-82). IEEE. 10.1109/RCIS.2017.7956520

Cornelius, F. H., Harmen, L. B., & Mullen, V. L. (2015). Future Challenges and Opportunities. In Ethical Health Informatics (3rd ed.). Jones & Bartlett Publishers.

Cybersecurity | Definition of cybersecurity in English by Oxford Dictionaries. (n.d.). http://www.oxford-dictionaries.com/definition/english/Cybersecurity

DesRoches, C. M., Campbell, E. G., Rao, S. R., Donelan, K., Ferris, T. G., Jha, A., & Blumenthal, D. (2008). Electronic health records in ambulatory care—A national survey of physicians. *The New England Journal of Medicine, 359*(1), 50–60. doi:10.1056/NEJMsa0802005 PMID:18565855

Faden, R. R., & Beauchamp, T. L. (1986). *A history and theory of informed consent*. Oxford University Press.

Fatehi, F., Gray, L. C., & Russell, A. W. (2017). Mobile health (mHealth) for diabetes care: Opportunities and challenges. *Diabetes Technology & Therapeutics*, *19*(1), 1–3. doi:10.1089/dia.2016.0430 PMID:28099051

Federal Trade Commission. (2015). *Complying with COPPA: Frequently Asked Questions*. https://www.ftc.gov/tips-advice/business-center/guidance/complying-coppa-frequently-asked-questions

Ferguson, N. M., Laydon, D., & Nedjati-Gilani, G. (2020). *Impact of non-pharmaceutical interventions (NPIs) to reduce COVID-19 mortality and healthcare demand*. Imperial College COVID-19 Response Team.

Firth, J., Torous, J., Nicholas, J., Carney, R., Rosenbaum, S., & Sarris, J. (2017). Can smartphone mental health interventions reduce symptoms of anxiety? A meta-analysis of randomized controlled trials. *Journal of Affective Disorders*, *218*, 15–22. doi:10.1016/j.jad.2017.04.046 PMID:28456072

Food and Drug Administration. (2019). *Policy for Device Software Functions and Mobile Medical Applications*. Author.

Garity, J. (1995). Ethics in research. *Principles and Practice of Nursing Research*, 35-54.

Gauntlett, C., MacCarthy, J., Tindall, M., Buck, S., & Connery, G. (2013). *Patient apps for improved healthcare: from novelty to mainstream*. IMS Institute for Healthcare Informatics.

Gelling, L. (1999). Ethical principles in healthcare research. *Nursing Standard*, *13*(36), 39–42. doi:10.7748/ns1999.05.13.36.39.c2607 PMID:10497544

Gillon, R. (1985a). Deontological foundations for medical ethics? *British Medical Journal (Clinical Research Ed.)*, *290*(6478), 1331–1333. doi:10.1136/bmj.290.6478.1331 PMID:3922480

Gillon, R. (1985b). Confidentiality. *British Medical Journal (Clinical Research Ed.)*, *291*(6509), 1634–1636. doi:10.1136/bmj.291.6509.1634 PMID:3935216

Gostin, L. O., Levit, L. A., & Nass, S. J. (Eds.). (2009). *Beyond the HIPAA privacy rule: enhancing privacy, improving health through research*. National Academies Press.

Gritzalis, D. (1997). A baseline security policy for distributed healthcare information systems. *Computers & Security*, *16*(8), 709–719. doi:10.1016/S0167-4048(97)00009-6

Gritzalis, D. A. (1998). Enhancing security and improving interoperability in healthcareinformation systems. *Informatics for Health & Social Care*, *23*(4), 309–323. PMID:9922951

Haluza, D., & Jungwirth, D. (2018). ICT and the future of healthcare: Aspects of pervasive health monitoring. *Informatics for Health & Social Care*, *43*(1), 1–11. doi:10.1080/17538157.2016.1255215 PMID:28005444

Harmen, L. B. (2013). Ethical Issues in Health Information Management. In Health information management: Concepts, principles, and practice (4th ed.). AHIMA.

Hoglund, D. H. (2017). Secure and Reliable Wireless Medical Device and Mobile Connectivity. *Biomedical Instrumentation & Technology*, *51*(2), 130–134. doi:10.2345/0899-8205-51.2.130 PMID:28296442

Huser, V., & Cimino, J. J. (2013). Don't take your EHR to heaven, donate it to science: Legal and research policies for EHR post mortem. *Journal of the American Medical Informatics Association*, *21*(1), 8–12. doi:10.1136/amiajnl-2013-002061 PMID:23966483

Hussain, M., Al-Haiqi, A., Zaidan, A. A., Zaidan, B. B., Kiah, M. L. M., Anuar, N. B., & Abdulnabi, M. (2015). The landscape of research on smartphone medical apps: Coherent taxonomy, motivations, open challenges and recommendations. *Computer Methods and Programs in Biomedicine*, *122*(3), 393–408. doi:10.1016/j.cmpb.2015.08.015 PMID:26412009

Ichikawa, D., Kashiyama, M., & Ueno, T. (2017). Tamper-Resistant Mobile Health Using Blockchain Technology. *JMIR mHealth and uHealth*, *5*(7), e111. doi:10.2196/mhealth.7938 PMID:28747296

International Telecommunication Union. (2008). *X.1205: Overview of cybersecurity*. https://www.itu.int/rec/T-REC-X.1205-200804-I

Jang-Jaccard, J., & Nepal, S. (2014). A survey of emerging threats in cybersecurity. *Journal of Computer and System Sciences*, *80*(5), 973–993. doi:10.1016/j.jcss.2014.02.005

Kao, C. K., & Liebovitz, D. M. (2017). Consumer mobile health apps: Current state, barriers, and future directions. *PM & R*, *9*(5), S106–S115. doi:10.1016/j.pmrj.2017.02.018 PMID:28527495

Kaplan, B., & Litewka, S. (2008). Ethical challenges of telemedicine and telehealth. *Cambridge Quarterly of Healthcare Ethics*, *17*(4), 401–416. doi:10.1017/S0963180108080535 PMID:18724880

Karcher, N. R., & Presser, N. R. (2018). Ethical and Legal Issues Addressing the Use of Mobile Health (mHealth) as an Adjunct to Psychotherapy. *Ethics & Behavior*, *28*(1), 1–22. doi:10.1080/10508422.2016.1229187

Kelli, H. M., Witbrodt, B., & Shah, A. (2017). THE future of mobile health applications and devices in cardiovascular health. *European Medical Journal. Innovations*, *2017*, 92. PMID:28191545

Knapp, D. (2010). *A guide to service desk concepts*. Nelson Education.

Kotz, D., Gunter, C. A., Kumar, S., & Weiner, J. P. (2016). Privacy and security in mobile health: A research agenda. *Computer*, *49*(6), 22–30. doi:10.1109/MC.2016.185 PMID:28344359

Kramer, G. M., Kinn, J. T., & Mishkind, M. C. (2015). Legal, regulatory, and risk management issues in the use of technology to deliver mental health care. *Cognitive and Behavioral Practice*, *22*(3), 258–268. doi:10.1016/j.cbpra.2014.04.008

Lewis, P. V. (1985). Defining 'business ethics': Like nailing jello to a wall. *Journal of Business Ethics*, *4*(5), 377–383. doi:10.1007/BF02388590

Lhotska, L., Cheshire, P., Pharow, P., & Macku, D. (2016, April). Non-technical Issues in Design and Development of Personal Portable Devices. In *Transforming Healthcare with the Internet of Things: Proceedings of the EFMI Special Topic Conference 2016* (*Vol. 221*, p. 46). IOS Press.

Luxton, D. D., Kayl, R. A., & Mishkind, M. C. (2012). mHealth data security: The need for HIPAA-compliant standardization. *Telemedicine Journal and e-Health*, *18*(4), 284–288. doi:10.1089/tmj.2011.0180 PMID:22400974

Luxton, D. D., McCann, R. A., Bush, N. E., Mishkind, M. C., & Reger, G. M. (2011). mHealth for mental health: Integrating smartphone technology in behavioral healthcare. *Professional Psychology, Research and Practice*, *42*(6), 505–512. doi:10.1037/a0024485

Lyles, C. R., Harris, L. T., Le, T., Flowers, J., Tufano, J., Britt, D., Hoath, J., Hirsch, I. B., Goldberg, H. I., & Ralston, J. D. (2011). Qualitative evaluation of a mobile phone and web-based collaborative care intervention for patients with type 2 diabetes. *Diabetes Technology & Therapeutics*, *13*(5), 563–569. doi:10.1089/dia.2010.0200 PMID:21406018

MacKinnon, W., & Wasserman, M. (2009, January). Integrated electronic medical record systems: Critical success factors for implementation. In *System Sciences, 2009.HICSS'09. 42nd Hawaii International Conference on* (pp. 1-10). IEEE.

Malvey, D., & Slovensky, D. J. (2014). mHealth: transforming healthcare. Springer.

McGinn, C.A., Grenier, S., Duplantie, J., Shaw, N., Sicotte, C., Mathieu, L., Leduc, Y., Légaré, F., & Gagnon, M. P. (2011). Comparison of user groups' perspectives of barriers and facilitators to implementing electronic health records: A systematic review. BMC Medicine, 9(1), 1. doi:10.1186/1741-7015-9-46 PMID:21524315 doi:10.1186/1741-7015-9-46 PMID:21524315

McKenzie, G., Janowicz, K., & Seidl, D. (2016). Geo-privacy beyond coordinates. In *Geospatial Data in a Changing World* (pp. 157–175). Springer. doi:10.1007/978-3-319-33783-8_10

mHealthIntelligence Report. (2016). *Doctors Still Don't Trust mHealth Apps*. Available at https://mhealthintelligence.com/news/doctors-stilldont-trust-mhealth-apps

Morera, E. P., de la Torre Díez, I., Garcia-Zapirain, B., López-Coronado, M., & Arambarri, J. (2016). Security recommendations for mHealth apps: Elaboration of a developer's guide. *Journal of Medical Systems*, *40*(6), 152. doi:10.100710916-016-0513-6 PMID:27147515

Munos, B., Baker, P. C., Bot, B. M., Crouthamel, M., Vries, G., Ferguson, I., ... Ozcan, A. (2016). Mobile health: The power of wearables, sensors, and apps to transform clinical trials. *Annals of the New York Academy of Sciences*, *1375*(1), 3–18. doi:10.1111/nyas.13117 PMID:27384501

National Institute of Standards and Technology. (2020). *Cybersecurity Framework*. https://www.nist.gov/cyberframework/frequently-asked-questions/framework-basics#framework

Noumeir, R., Lemay, A., & Lina, J. M. (2007). Pseudonymization of radiology data for research purposes. *Journal of Digital Imaging*, *20*(3), 284–295. doi:10.100710278-006-1051-4 PMID:17191099

Olenik, K., Brodnik, M. S., Reynolds, R. B., & Rinehart-Thompson, L. A. (2012). Security Threats and Controls. In Fundamentals of law for health informatics and information management. American Health Information Management Association.

Palvia, P., Jacks, T., & Brown, W. (2015). Critical issues in EHR implementation: Provider and vendor perspectives. *Communications of the Association for Information Systems*, *36*(1), 36. doi:10.17705/1CAIS.03636

Petersen, C., & DeMuro, P. (2015). Legal and regulatory considerations associated with use of patient-generated health data from social media and mobile health (mHealth) devices. *Applied Clinical Informatics*, *6*(1), 16–26. doi:10.4338/ACI-2014-09-R-0082 PMID:25848410

Pfleeger, C. P., & Pfleeger, S. L. (2008). *Security in computing*. Prentice Hall of India.

Piwek, L., Ellis, D. A., Andrews, S., & Joinson, A. (2016). The rise of consumer health wearables: Promises and barriers. *PLoS Medicine*, *13*(2), e1001953. doi:10.1371/journal.pmed.1001953 PMID:26836780

Population Pyramids of the World from 1950 to 2100. (n.d.). Available at https://populationpyramid.net

Public Safety Canada. (2014). *Terminology Bulletin 281: Emergency Management Vocabulary*. Ottawa: Translation Bureau, Government of Canada. http://www.bt-tb.tpsgcpwgsc.gc.ca/publications/documents/urgence-emergency.pdf

Rebar, C. R., & Macnee, C. L. (2011). *Understanding nursing research*. Wolters Kluwer/Lippincott Williams & Wilkins Health.

Report, E. M. (2016). Available at https://www.ericsson.com/mobility-report

Research2Guidance. (2015). *mHealth app developer economics 2015*. https://research2guidance.com/r2g/r2g-mHealth-App-Developer-Economics-2015.pdf

Reynolds, R. B., & Brodnik, M. (2017). The HIPAA Security Rule. In Fundamentals of law for health informatics and information management (3rd ed.). American Health Information Management Association.

Rinehart-Thompson, L. A. (2017a). The HIPAA Privacy Rule: Part I. In Fundamentals of law for health informatics and information management (3rd ed.). American Health Information Management Association.

Rinehart-Thompson, L. A. (2017b). The HIPAA Privacy Rule: Part II. In Fundamentals of law for health informatics and information management (3rd ed.). American Health Information Management Association.

Rinehart-Thompson, L. A., & Harmen, L. B. (2015). Privacy and Confidentiality. In Ethical Health Informatics (3rd ed.). Jones & Bartlett Publishers.

Schatz, D., Bashroush, R., & Wall, J. (2017). Towards a more representative definition of cyber security. *Journal of Digital Forensics, Security and Law*, *12*(2), 8.

Semigran, H. L., Linder, J. A., Gidengil, C., & Mehrotra, A. (2015). Evaluation of symptom checkers for self diagnosis and triage: audit study. *BMJ*, *351*, h3480.

Seto, E., Ware, P., Logan, A. G., Cafazzo, J. A., Chapman, K. R., Segal, P., & Ross, H. J. (2017). Self-management and clinical decision support for patients with complex chronic conditions through the use of smartphone-based telemonitoring: Randomized controlled trial protocol. *JMIR Research Protocols*, *6*(11), e229. doi:10.2196/resprot.8367 PMID:29162557

Sharp, M., & O'Sullivan, D. (2017). Mobile medical apps and mHealth devices: A framework to build medical apps and mHealth devices in an ethical manner to promote safer use-a literature review. *Studies in Health Technology and Informatics*, *235*, 363–367. PMID:28423815

Shrestha, P., & Saxena, N. (2017). An offensive and defensive exposition of wearable computing. *ACM Computing Surveys*, *50*(6), 1–39. doi:10.1145/3133837

Snedaker, S. (2013). *Business continuity and disaster recovery planning for IT professionals*. Newnes.

Snedaker, S. (2016). *Leading Healthcare IT: Managing to Succeed*. Productivity Press. doi:10.1201/9781315181417

Steil, J., Koelle, M., Heuten, W., Boll, S., & Bulling, A. (2019, June). Privaceye: privacy-preserving head-mounted eye tracking using egocentric scene image and eye movement features. In *Proceedings of the 11th ACM Symposium on Eye Tracking Research & Applications* (pp. 1-10). 10.1145/3314111.3319913

Talens, G., Disson, E., Collard, G., & Ducroquet, S. (2017, May). A Definition of Information Security Classification in Cybersecurity Context. *Eleventh International Conference on Research Challenges in Information Science*.

Tan, J., & Hung, P. (2005). E-Security Frameworks for Privacy and Security in E-Health Data Integration and Aggregation. In E-health care information systems: an introduction for students and professionals. John Wiley & Sons.

Terry, N. P., & Gunter, T. D. (2018). Regulating mobile mental health apps. *Behavioral Sciences & the Law*, *36*(2), 136–144. doi:10.1002/bsl.2339 PMID:29659069

The Health Information Trust Alliance. (2020a). *About Us*. https://hitrustalliance.net/about-us/

The Health Information Trust Alliance. (2020b). *CSF Assurance Program*. https://hitrustalliance.net/csf-assurance/

The International Standards Organization. (2013). *ISO 22857:2013(en)*. https://www.iso.org/obp/ui/#iso:std:iso:22857:ed-2:v1:en

The International Standards Organization. (2015). *ISO/IEC 18033-1:2015 (en)*. https://www.iso.org/obp/ui/#iso:std:iso-iec:18033:-1:ed-2:v1:en

The International Standards Organization. (2016). *ISO 27799:2016(en)*. https://www.iso.org/obp/ui/#iso:std:iso:27799:ed-2:v1:en

The International Standards Organization. (2016b). *ISO/IEC 27033-6:2016 (en)*. https://www.iso.org/obp/ui/#iso:std:iso-iec:27033:-6:ed-1:v1:en

The International Standards Organization. (2017). *ISO ISO 25237:2017(en)*. https://www.iso.org/obp/ui/#iso:std:iso:25237:ed-1:v1:en

Trotter, F., & Uhlman, D. (2013). *Hacking healthcare: A guide to standards, workflows, and meaningful use*. O'Reilly Media, Inc.

U.S. Department of Health and Human Services. (2013). *Breach Notification Rule*. https://www.hhs.gov/hipaa/for-professionals/breach-notification/index.html

U.S. Department of Health and Human Services. (2020). *Summary of the HIPAA Security Rule*. https://www.hhs.gov/hipaa/for-professionals/security/laws-regulations/index.html

Vaast, E. (2007). Danger is in the eye of the beholders: Social representations of Information Systems security in healthcare. *The Journal of Strategic Information Systems*, *16*(2), 130–152. doi:10.1016/j.jsis.2007.05.003

Van Heerden, A., Tomlinson, M., & Swartz, L. (2012, May). Point of Care in Your Pocket: A Research Agenda for the Field of M-Health. *Bulletin of the World Health Organization*, *90*(5), 393–394. doi:10.2471/BLT.11.099788 PMID:22589575

Varshney, U. (2007). Pervasive healthcare and wireless health monitoring. *Mobile Networks and Applications*, *12*(2-3), 113–127. doi:10.100711036-007-0017-1

Von Solms, R., & Van Niekerk, J. (2013). From information security to cyber security. *Computers & Security, 38*, 97-102.

Wagner, J. K. (2020). The Federal Trade Commission and Consumer Protections for Mobile Health Apps. *The Journal of Law, Medicine & Ethics, 48*(1_suppl), 103-114.

White, J., & Daniel, J. (2009, August). *Privacy and Security Solutions for Health Information Exchange*. Report on State Medical Record Access Laws. https://www.healthit.gov/sites/default/files/290-05-0015-state-law-access-report-1.pdf

Wilkowska, W., & Ziefle, M. (2012). Privacy and data security in E-health: Requirements from the user's perspective. *Health Informatics Journal*, *18*(3), 191–201. doi:10.1177/1460458212442933 PMID:23011814

Wolf, J. A., Moreau, J. F., Akilov, O., Patton, T., English, J. C., Ho, J., & Ferris, L. K. (2013). Diagnostic inaccuracy of smartphone applications for melanoma detection. *JAMA Dermatology*, *149*(4), 422–426. doi:10.1001/jamadermatol.2013.2382 PMID:23325302

Yasaka, T. M., Lehrich, B. M., & Sahyouni, R. (2020). Peer-to-Peer Contact Tracing: Development of a Privacy-Preserving Smartphone App. *JMIR mHealth and uHealth*, *8*(4), e18936. doi:10.2196/18936 PMID:32240973

*This research was previously published in the International Journal of Intelligent Information Technologies (IJIIT), 17(2); pages 1-24, copyright year 2021 by IGI Publishing (an imprint of IGI Global).*

# Chapter 20

# A Lightweight Three-Factor Anonymous Authentication Scheme With Privacy Protection for Personalized Healthcare Applications

**Mengxia Shuai**

*University of Science and Technology of China, Anhui, China*

**Nenghai Yu**

*University of Science and Technology of China, Anhui, China*

**Hongxia Wang**

*Southwest Jiaotong University, Chengdu, China*

**Ling Xiong**

*Xihua University, Chengdu, China*

**Yue Li**

*Southwest Jiaotong University, Chengdu, China*

## ABSTRACT

*Security and privacy issues in wireless medical sensor networks (WMSNs) have attracted lots of attention in both academia and industry due to the sensitiveness of medical system. In the past decade, extensive research has been carried out on these security issues, but no single study exists that addresses them adequately, especially for some important security properties, such as user anonymity and forward secrecy. As a step towards this direction, in this paper, the authors propose a lightweight three-factor anonymous authentication scheme with forward secrecy for personalized healthcare applications using only the lightweight cryptographic primitives. The proposed scheme adopts pseudonym identity technique to protect users' real identities and employs one-way hash chain technique to ensure forward secrecy. Analysis and comparison results demonstrate that the proposed scheme can not only reduce execution time by 34% as compared with the most effective related schemes, but also achieve more security and functional features.*

DOI: 10.4018/978-1-6684-6311-6.ch020

*Figure 1. A typical structure of WMSNs*

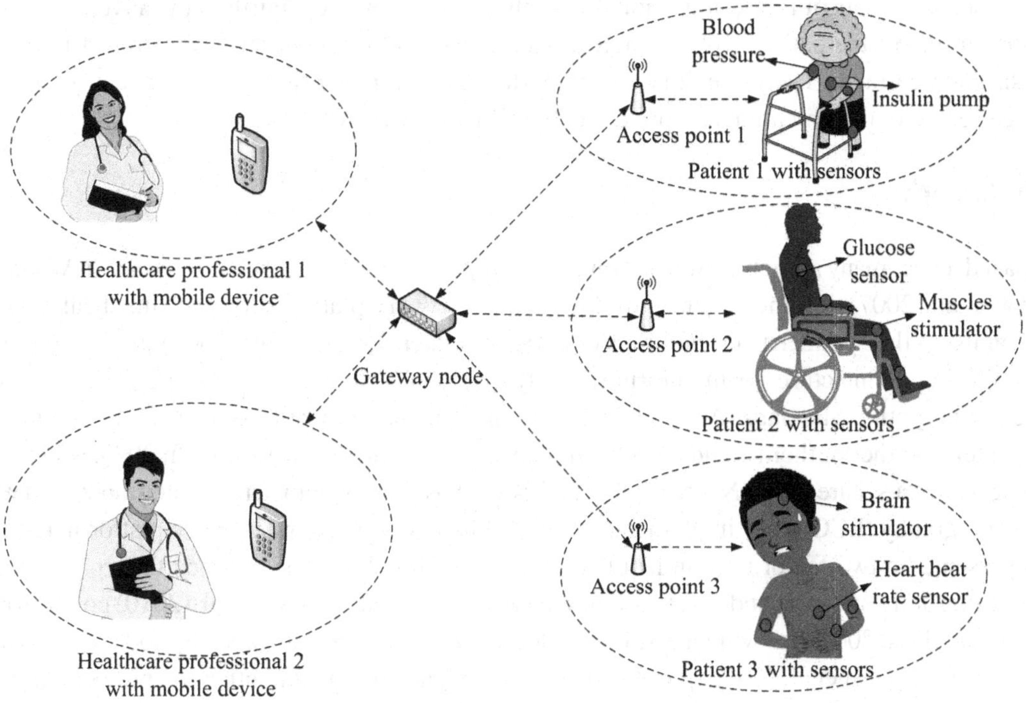

## INTRODUCTION

The Internet of Things (IoT) is an emerging mode of modern wireless telecommunications, which allows objects to be sensed or controlled remotely over existing network infrastructure. By combining with cloud computing and fog computing (Qi, Zhang, Dou, & Ni, 2017; Gill, Chana, & Buyya, 2017; Qi, Yu, & Zhou, 2017; Gong, Qi, & Xu, 2018; Qi et al., 2018a), IoT devices can be used to build many service-based applications, such as smart devices (Cui, Zhang, Cai, Liu, & Li, 2018; Cheng, Xu, Tang, Sheng, & Cai, 2018), smart home (Liu, et al., 2018) and security-related applications (Wang, Li, Shi, Lian, & Ye, 2016; Qi, Zhou, Yu, & Liu, 2017; Ma, Luo, Li, Bao, & Zhang, 2018; Zhang, Qin, Zhang, Liu, & Luo, 2018; Qi et al., 2018b). IoT devices can also be used to enable remote health monitoring, which is a new field known as wireless medical sensor networks (WMSNs). WMSNs have attracted lots of attention in both academia and industry because of the potential in improving the quality of medical services (Walczak & Mann, 2010; Lee, Ghapanchi, Talaei-Khoei, & Ray, 2015). Through WMSNs, healthcare professionals are able to access the patients' sensitive data collected from the medical sensor nodes which are placed on/in patients' bodies, and provide remote medical treatment, emergency medical assistance or give some constructive advice on the patients' further treatment.

A typical structure of WMSNs for personalized healthcare applications is demonstrated in Figure 1. Although WMSNs bring a lot of convenience to people's life (Siddesh et al., 2017), security and privacy issues in WMSNs are becoming great challenges due to the sensitiveness of medical system (Ameen, Liu, & Kwak, 2012; Xu, Qi, Dou, & Yu, 2017). The medical data collected from the medical sensor nodes is sensitive, and the privacy of these data is protected legally. Due to the open feature of wireless communication, an adversary can intercept and alter the transmitted messages easily. Once obtaining these sensitive data, an adversary may acquaint the disease what the patient has and profit financially by selling sensitive data, it is a serious violation of the patient's privacy. Further, the adversary can even misreport or distort the patient's physiological data to cause physical harm, it may result in improper diagnosis and treatment. Therefore, it is very important to design an effective authentication scheme to guarantee secure communication and protect patients' privacy in WMSNs.

## Related Work

In the past decade, many authentication schemes are proposed to solve the security issues in WMSNs. In 2007, Hu et al. (2007) designed a telecardiology sensor network platform for real-time healthcare data collection using the symmetric cryptography. Two years later, Huang et al. (2009) presented a health-care monitoring architecture for monitoring elderly or chronic patients in their residence, which used Advanced Encryption Standard (AES) algorithm to provide authentication and secret communication. Unfortunately, neither of them could achieve mutual authentication successfully. In 2009, Malasri et al. (2009) designed a secure WMSN system for healthcare based on symmetric cryptography and elliptic curve cryptography (ECC), they implemented their mechanisms on a wireless mote platform. Later, Das (2009) presented a two-factor user authentication protocol for WSN and claimed their protocol could provide strong authentication and resist various attacks. Unfortunately, Khan et al. (2010) pointed out that Das's scheme (Das, 2009) was vulnerable to privileged-insider attack and Gateway node (GWN) bypass attack. In 2012, Kumar et al. (2012) presented an efficient and strong authentication protocol, named E-SAP, for healthcare application using WMSNs. They demonstrated that their protocol was more secure against many practical attacks. But later, He et al. (2015) in 2015 pointed out that the scheme proposed by Kumar et al. failed to resist some known attacks, liking off-line password guessing attack and privileged insider attack. To overcome their security shortcomings, they proposed a robust anonymous authentication protocol for healthcare applications using WMSNs. One year later, Li et al. (2016) pointed out that He et al.'s scheme (He et al., 2015) was not only incorrect in authentication and session key agreement phase, but also lacked wrong password detection mechanism. Further, they proposed a new user anonymous authentication protocol based on WMSNs. In their scheme, the biometric was introduced as the third authentication factor. Similarly, Mir et al. (2017) also showed that He et al.'s scheme (He et al., 2015) still suffered from various security flaws, including inefficient login phase, password guessing attack, forward secrecy. They also proposed an improved scheme and claimed that their scheme was secure in forward secrecy. However, the authors find out their scheme is still prone to forward secrecy attack. An adversary can guess the user identity offline through the transmitted message if GWN's secret key is compromised, the adversary can further compute the session key. Hence, Mir et al.'s scheme (Mir et al., 2017) failed to achieve forward secrecy. At the same year, Wu et al. (2017) also claimed that He et al.'s scheme (He et al., 2015) still had some vulnerabilities, including off-line password guessing attack, the impersonation attack and the sensor node capturing attack. Hence, they proposed an energy-efficient scheme with a lightweight design for WMSNs. But later, Srinivas et al. (2017) observed that Wu et al.'s scheme was not only failed to resist various attacks, such as off-line guessing attack, privileged insider attack and new smart card issue attack, but also not suitable for practical applications. To compensate for these defects, they designed a symmetric key based authentication protocol for WMSNs environment using only computationally efficient operations to achieve lightweight attribute. Unfortunately, the authors find that all these schemes cannot achieve forward secrecy effectively.

## Motivation and Contributions

User anonymity and forward secrecy are two indispensable security properties of the authentication scheme (Gope & Hwang, 2016), especially for some scenarios containing real-time sensitive data, such as health monitoring. If the long-term keys are obtained by an adversary, it may cause the disclosure of the session key used in previous communications. Further, the content of previous communications may be revealed. The adversary can access the patients' physiological data and assess the patients' health status, it is devastating for the patients' privacy. To the best of our knowledge, none of the existing scheme can achieve user anonymity and forward secrecy at the same time. In particular, it is disturbing to find that forward security has not been considered even when designing authentication schemes (He et al., 2015; Li et al., 2016; Srinivas et al., 2017). In fact, forward secrecy is present in several major protocol implementations, such as SSH and IPsec. In addition, forward secrecy has also been seen as an important security feature and provided to users by several large internet information providers, such as Google, Twitter, Facebook and Apple. It is a consensus to take forward security into consideration in the design of an effective lightweight anonymous authentication scheme (Mir et al., 2017; Khan & Kumari, 2013; Jin et al., 2015). As a step towards this direction, in this paper, the authors adopt pseudonym identity technique to protect healthcare professional's real identity, and employ one-way hash chain technique (Gope & Hwang, 2016) to ensure forward secrecy. The contributions of this paper are summarized mainly as follows:

1. The authors present a novel and lightweight three-factor anonymous authentication scheme with privacy protection for personalized healthcare applications using only the lightweight cryptographic primitives, which is easy to carry out in practical applications.
2. The authors use Burrows-Abadi-Needham (BAN) logic (Burrows, Abad, & Needham, 1989) to prove that the proposed scheme is secure and fulfills mutual authentication successfully.
3. The authors conduct a formal verification of the proposed scheme using the widely-accepted tool ProVerif (Burrows, 2001, pp. 82-96).
4. The security analysis shows that the proposed scheme can not only provide user anonymity and forward secrecy, but also resist various malicious attacks, such as smart card loss attack, replay attack and wrong password login attack.
5. The authors evaluate the performance of the proposed scheme with other related schemes, and the results show that the proposed scheme can reduce the computational cost substantially.

## PRELIMINARY KNOWLEDGE

In this section, the authors briefly introduce security requirements for healthcare applications and adversary attack model.

### Security Requirements for Healthcare Applications

Since the communications between the health professional and the medical sensor nodes are done via public channel, the designed authentication scheme must be secure and efficient. Here the authors describe some important requirements for a secure anonymous authentication scheme in WMSNs:

- **User anonymity:** The first indispensable attribute of the authentication scheme for WMSNs is user anonymity, which mainly comprises two properties. The first one is user identity-protection which means the real identity of the user cannot be figured out by the adversary. Untraceability is another important property, which guarantees the adversary neither determining who the user is nor telling apart whether two sessions are executed by the same user (Wang & Wang, 2014). Therefore, the anonymous authentication scheme is very crucial to address privacy problem in WMSNs.

- **Forward secrecy:** If the long-term keys used to generate the session key are obtained by an adversary, it may cause the disclosure of the session key used in previous communications. Further, the content of previous communications may be revealed. The adversary can access the patients' physiological data and assess the patients' health status, it is devastating for the patients' privacy. Therefore, anonymous authentication scheme must achieve forward secrecy.

- **Mutual authentication:** Mutual authentication among the health professional, GWN and the medical sensor node is needed, it is an essential requirement for all authentication schemes.

- **Session key agreement:** After mutual authentication, further communications should be encrypted using the shared session key to achieve confidentiality. Therefore, the proposed scheme should provide session key agreement.

- **Attacks resistance:** To ensure secure communication, the designed authentication scheme is able to resist various attacks, liking smart card loss attack, replay attack and wrong password login attack.

## Adversary Attack Model

In this paper, the authors propose an authentication scheme based on the Dolev-Yao threat model (Dolev & Yao, 1983), which is the most widely accepted attacker model in the analysis of security protocols. According to this model, any two communicating parties communicate over an insecure channel and the endpoint entities are not considered as trusted entities. Based on this threat model and real application environments, the abilities of an adversary $A$ are summarized as follows:

1. $A$ may be a legitimate but malicious health professional in WMSNs.
2. $A$ may be a legitimate but malicious medical sensor node.
3. $A$ can intercept and modify the transmitted messages over insecure public communication channel easily (Ameen et al., 2012).
4. $A$ can acquire all the secret values stored in the smart card using side-channel attacks (Kocher, Jaffe, & Jun, 1999).
5. $A$ can get the long-term secret keys when forward secrecy is evaluated.
6. $A$ is a probabilistic polynomial time attacker. That is to say, $A$ can guess the low-entropy password and identity information within polynomial time.
7. There is no tamper-resistant hardware equipped in medical sensor nodes. In other words, $A$ can extract all the sensitive data stored in medical sensor nodes.

## THE PROPOSED SCHEME

In this section, the authors present a lightweight three-factor anonymous authentication scheme for personalized healthcare applications using WMSNs, which not only achieves the required security attributes, liking user anonymity and forward secrecy, but also withstands various attacks. The proposed scheme is divided into four phases: registration phase, login and authentication phase, password change phase. For ease of presentation, some intuitive abbreviations and notations mentioned in the proposed scheme are listed in Table 1.

*Table 1. Notations*

| Notation | Descriptions |
|---|---|
| $U_i$ | Remote health professional |
| $GWN$ | Gateway node |
| $SN_j$ | Medical sensor node |
| $ID_i$ | Unique identity of $U_i$ |
| $PW_i$ | Password of $U_i$ |
| $fg_i$ | Biometric information of $U_i$ |
| $HID_i$ | Pseudonym identity of $U_i$ |
| $SID_j$ | Unique identity of $SN_j$ |
| $E_k[.]/D_k[.]$ | Symmetric encryption/decryption with key k |
| $R, R_A$ | Random number |
| $T_1, T_2, T_3, T_4$ | Current time stamp |
| $\Delta T$ | The maximum of the transmission delay time |
| $K$ | Secret key generated by GWN |
| $SK$ | Session key |
| $h(.)$ | One-way hash function |
| $BH(.)$ | Biohash function |
| $X\|Y$ | Concatenate operation |
| $\oplus$ | XOR operation |

## Registration Phase

The registration phase is divided into two parts, i.e., health professional registration phase and medical sensor node registration phase.

## Health Professional Registration

When a new health professional wants to be a legitimate user in WMSNs, he/she must register in GWN first. The procedure of professional's registration is described as follows:

**Step 1:** The health professional $U_i$ chooses his/her identity $ID_i$, password $PW_i$ and imprints its biometrics $fg_i$ via a sensor, and generates a random number $m_i$. Then $U_i$ computes $MB_i = BH(m_i \| fg_i)$, $MPW_i = h(ID_i \| PW_i \| MB_i \| m_i)$ Ui sends the message $\{ID_i, MPW_i\}$ and his/her personal credential to GWN through a secure channel.

**Step 2:** Upon receiving the message, GWN generates three random integers $n_i$, $r_i$, $K_1$ and computes $HID_i = ID_i \oplus r_i$, $X_i = h(ID_i \| K \| n_i)$, $Y_i = X_i \oplus MPW_i$, $V_i = h(X_i \| MPW_i)$. After that, GWN stores $\{ID_i, HID_i, n_i, K_1\}$ into its own database and also maintains a health professional personal credential table. Finally, GWN writes $\{HID_i, Y_i, V_i, K_1, h(.), BH(.)\}$ into smart card and issues it to $U_i$ via a private channel.

**Step 3:** Upon receiving the smart card, $U_i$ writes $m_i$ into the smart card. Finally, the smart card contains $\{HID_i, Y_i, V_i, K_1, m_i, h(.), BH(.)\}$.

## Medical Sensor Node Registration

The procedure of medical sensor node registration is outlined as follows:

**Step 1:** The medical sensor node $SN_j$ selects the identity $SID_j$ and transmits it to GWN via a secure channel.

**Step 2:** Upon receiving $SID_j$, GWN first checks whether $SID_j$ exists in the medical sensor node information table. If it exists, GWN refuses the medical sensor node registration request. Otherwise, GWN generates a random integer $K_2$ and stores $\{SID_j, K_2\}$ into its sensor node information table. After that, GWN sends $K_2$ to $SN_j$ via a private channel.

**Step 3:** Upon receiving the message from GWN, $SN_j$ stores $K_2$ into its memory secretly.

## Login and Authentication Phase

When a health professional $U_i$ wants to access a medical sensor node, he/she needs to login in GWN first. As shown in Figure 2, the procedure of health professional's login and authentication phase is described as follows:

**Step 1:** The health professional $U_i$ inserts his smart card into a card reader and inputs the identity $ID_i$, the password $PW_i$ and enters the fingerprint $fg_i$ at the sensor device. Then, the smart card computes

$$MB_i^* = BH\left(m_i \parallel fg_i\right), \quad MPW_i^* = h\left(ID_i \parallel PW_i \parallel MB_i^* \parallel m_i\right), \quad X_i^* = Y_i \oplus MPW_i^*, \quad V_i^* = h\left(X_i^* \parallel MPW_i^*\right)$$

and compares $V_i^*$ with the stored value $V_i$. If they are not equal, the smart card terminates the session. Otherwise, the smart card proceeds to the next step.

**Step 2:** After verifying the legitimacy of health professional $U_i$, the smart card generates a random number $R$ and gets the current time $T_1$. After that, $U_i$ selects the identity $SID_j$ of the medical sensor node $SN_j$ that he/she wants to access, and the smart card computes $UG = h(HID_i \parallel X_i \parallel K_1)$, $M_1 = E_{UG}(R \parallel SID_j)$, $CK_1 = h(ID_i \parallel R \parallel X_i \parallel HID_i \parallel K_1 \parallel T_1)$. Then $U_i$ sends the login message $\{HID_i, M_1, CK_1, T_1\}$ to GWN through a public channel.

**Step 3:** Upon receiving the login request message, GWN first checks the validity of the time stamp. GWN gets the current time $T_1^*$ and compares with the received time $T_1$. If the matching score $|T_1^*-T_1|$ is beyond a predefined threshold value $\Delta T$, GWN terminates the session. Then, GWN extracts $ID_i, n_i$ and $K_1$ from user information database corresponding to pseudonym identity $HID_i$. Next, GWN computes $X_i = h(ID_i \parallel K \parallel n_i)$, $UG = h(HID_i \parallel X_i \parallel K_1)$, $R^* \parallel SID_j = D_{UG}(M_1)$, $CK_1^* = h(ID_i \parallel R^* \parallel X_i \parallel HID_i \parallel K_1 \parallel T_1)$ and compares $CK_1^*$ with the received value $CK_1$. If they are not equal, GWN terminates the session. Otherwise, GWN believes the legitimacy of $U_i$. What's more, GWN generates a random number $T_2$, a session key $SK$ and computes $M_2 = (SK \parallel ID_i) \oplus h(K_2 \parallel SID_j)$, $CK_2 = h(ID_i \parallel SID_j \parallel SK \parallel K_2 \parallel T_2)$. Finally, GWN transmits the message $\{M_2, CK_2, T_2\}$ to the sensor node $SN_j$ via open channel.

**Step 4:** Upon receiving the message $\{M_2, CK_2, T_2\}$, $SN_j$ first checks the validity of the time stamp $|T_2^* - T_2| < \Delta T$ and computes

$$(SK \parallel ID_i) = M_2 \oplus h(K_2 \parallel SID_j), \quad CK_2^* = h(ID_i \parallel SID_j \parallel SK \parallel K_2 \parallel T_2).$$

Then, the sensor node $SN_j$ compares $CK_2^*$ with the received value $CK_2$. If it is satisfied, $SN_j$ generates a random number $T_3$ and computes $CK_3 = h(SID_j \parallel ID_i \parallel SK \parallel T_3)$. At last, $SN_j$ updates $K_2$ with $K_2 = h(K_2)$ and sends the message $\{CK_3, T_3\}$ to GWN through a public channel.

**Step 5:** GWN first checks the freshness of the time stamp $T_3$ and computes $CK_3^* = h(SID_j \parallel ID_i \parallel SK \parallel T_3)$. Then, the GWN checks whether $CK_3^*$ matches with the received $CK_3$. If it does not hold, GWN terminates the session. Otherwise, GWN generates two random numbers $r_i^*$, $T_4$ and computes $HID_i^* = ID_i \oplus r_i^*$, $GU = h(R \parallel HID_i \parallel X_i \parallel K_1)$, $M_3 = E_{GU}(SK \parallel HID_i^* \parallel SID_j)$, $CK_4 = h(ID_i \parallel SK \parallel HID_i \parallel T_4)$. After that, GWN updates $K_1, K_2, HID_i$ with $K_1 = h(K_1)$, $K_2 = h(K_2)$, $HID_i = HID_i^*$, respectively. Finally, GWN sends the message $\{M_3, CK_4, T_4\}$ to $U_i$ through a public channel.

**Step 6:** Upon receiving the message from GWN, $U_i$ first checks the time stamp $T_4$. If $T_4$ is fresh, GWN computes $GU = h(R \parallel HID_i \parallel X_i \parallel K_1)$,

$$(SK \parallel HID_i^* \parallel SID_j) = D_{GU}(M_3), \quad CK_4^* = h(ID_i \parallel SK \parallel HID_i \parallel T_4).$$

Then, $U_i$ checks whether $CK_4^*$ matches with the received value $CK_4$. If it holds, $U_i$ updates $K_1, HID_i$ with $K_1 = h(K_1)$, $HID_i = HID_i^*$ and completes the authentication. Otherwise, $U_i$ fails to authenticate GWN.

## Password Change Phase

If a health professional $U_i$ wants to change his/her password, he/she needs to run as follows:

**Step 1:** $U_i$ first inserts his/her smart card into a card reader and inputs the identity $ID_i$, the password $PW_i$ and imprints its biometrics $fg_i$ via a sensor device. Then, the smart card computes $MB_i = BH(m_i \parallel fg_i)$, $MPW_i = h(ID_i \parallel PW_i \parallel MB_i \parallel m_i)$, $X_i = Y_i \oplus MPW_i$, $V_i^* = h(X_i \parallel MPW_i)$. $U_i$ compares $V_i^*$ with $V_i$ which is stored in the smart card. If they are not equal, the smart card rejects the password change request. Otherwise, the smart card believes the legitimacy of $U_i$ and allows $U_i$ to input a new password $PW_i^*$.

**Step 2:** The smart card computes

*Figure 2. Login and authentication phase of the proposed scheme*

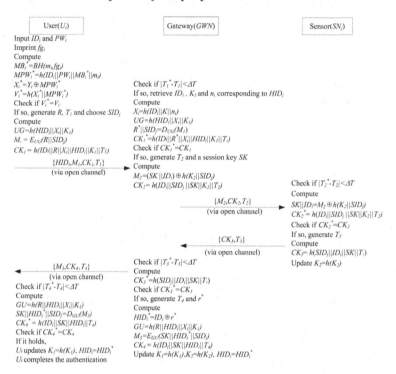

$$MPW_i^* = h(ID_i \parallel PW_i^* \parallel MB_i \parallel m_i), \quad Y_i^* = X_i \oplus MPW_i^* = Y_i \oplus MPW_i \oplus MPW_i^*, \quad V_i^* = h(X_i \parallel MPW_i^*).$$

**Step 3:** At last, $Y_i^*$ and $V_i^*$ are stored in the smart card to replace $Y_i$ and $V_i$, respectively.

## SECURITY ANALYSIS OF THE PROPOSED SCHEME

In this section, the authors first analyze the proposed scheme using the widely-accepted BAN logic (Burrows et al., 1989). In addition, the authors conduct a formal verification of the proposed scheme with Proverif (Blanchet, 2001, pp. 82-96). Finally, the authors discuss the possible attacks on the proposed scheme.

### Authentication Proof Based on the BAN Logic

The BAN logic (Burrows et al., 1989) is an efficient way to analyze the security of a protocol, which is widely-used in many works, such as (Odelu, Das, & Goswami, 2015; He, Kumar, Lee, & Sherratt, 2014). For convenience, all the notations used in the BAN logic are given in Table 2.

Some primary rules of BAN logic are as given below:

*Table 2. Notations in BAN logic*

| Notation | Implication |
|---|---|
| $P \lhd X$ | Principal $P$ sees a statement $X$ |
| $P\mid\equiv X$ | Principal $P$ believes a statement $X$ |
| $P\mid\Rightarrow X$ | Principal $P$ has jurisdiction over statement $X$ |
| $P\mid\sim X$ | Principal $P$ once said a statement $X$ |
| $\#(X)$ | Statement $X$ is fresh |
| $(X,Y)$ | Statement $X$ or $Y$ is one part of statement $(X,Y)$ |
| $X_K$ | Statement $X$ is encrypted with the key $K$ |
| $<X>_Y$ | Statement $X$ is combined with statement $Y$ |
| $(X)_K$ | Statement $X$ is hashed with the key $K$ |
| $P \xleftarrow{\ K\ } Q$ | Principal $P$ and principal $Q$ communicate with the shared key $K$ |

Message-meaning rule: $\dfrac{P \mid\equiv P \xleftarrow{\ K\ } Q, P \lhd X_K}{P \mid\equiv Q \mid\sim X}$

Nonce-verification rule: $\dfrac{P \mid\equiv \#(X), P \mid\equiv Q \mid\sim X}{P \mid\equiv Q \mid\equiv X}$

Jurisdiction rule: $\dfrac{P \mid\equiv Q \mid\Rightarrow X, P \mid\equiv Q \mid\equiv X}{P \mid\equiv X}$

Freshness-conjuncatenation rule: $\dfrac{P \mid\equiv \#(X)}{P \mid\equiv \#(X,Y)}$

The proposed scheme should satisfy following four goals:

**Goal 1:** $U_i \mid\equiv (U_i \xleftarrow{\ SK\ } SN_j)$

**Goal 2:** $U_i \mid\equiv SN_j \mid\equiv (U_i \xleftarrow{\ SK\ } SN_j)$

**Goal 3:** $SN_j \mid\equiv (U_i \xleftarrow{\ SK\ } SN_j)$

**Goal 4:** $SN_j \mid\equiv U_i \mid\equiv (U_i \xleftarrow{\ SK\ } SN_j)$

First of all, messages exchanged in the proposed scheme are transformed into idealized forms as follows:

**Msg1:**$U_i{\rightarrow}GWN$: $< ID_i, SID_j, R, HID_i, T_1, U_i \xleftrightarrow{X_i} GWN >_{U_i \xleftrightarrow{K_1} GWN}$

**Msg2:**$GWN{\rightarrow}SN_j$: $< ID_i, SID_j, T_2 >_{GWN \xleftrightarrow{K_2} SN_j}$

**Msg3:**$SN_j{\rightarrow}GWN$: $< ID_i, SID_j, T_3 >_{SN_j \xleftrightarrow{K_2} GWN}$

**Msg4:**$GWN{\rightarrow}U$: $< ID_i, SID_j, HID_i, T_4 >_{GWN \xleftrightarrow{K_1} U_i}$

Second, some initial assumptions about the proposed scheme are listed below:

A1: $GWN \mid\equiv \#(T_1)$
A2: $SN_j \mid\equiv \#(T_2)$
A3: $GWN \mid\equiv \#(T_3)$
A4: $U_i \mid\equiv \#(T_4)$
A5: $U_i \mid\equiv U_i \xleftrightarrow{K_1} GWN$
A6: $GWN \mid\equiv U_i \xleftrightarrow{K_1} GWN$
A7: $SN_j \mid\equiv SN_j \xleftrightarrow{K_2} GWN$
A8: $GWN \mid\equiv SN_j \xleftrightarrow{K_2} GWN$
A9: $U_i \mid\equiv SN_j \mid\Rightarrow U_i \xleftrightarrow{SK} SN_j$
A10: $SN_j \mid\equiv U_i \mid\Rightarrow U_i \xleftrightarrow{SK} SN_j$

Third, based on the BAN logic rules and assumptions, the main proofs are performed as follows. According to the Msg1, the authors get:

S1: $GWN \triangleleft < ID_i, SID_j, R, HID_i, T_1, U_i \xleftrightarrow{X_i} GWN >_{U_i \xleftrightarrow{K_1} GWN}$

Based on assumption A6, S1 and message-meaning rule, the authors have:

S2: $GWN \mid\equiv U_i \mid\sim (ID_i, SID_j, R, HID_i, T_1, U_i \xleftrightarrow{X_i} GWN)$

From A1 and freshness-conjuncatenation rule, the authors get:

S3: $GWN \mid\equiv \#(ID_i, SID_j, R, HID_i, T_1, U_i \xleftrightarrow{X_i} GWN)$

From S3, S2 and nonce-verification rule, the authors get:

S4: $GWN \mid\equiv U_i \mid\equiv (ID_i, SID_j, R, HID_i, T_1, U_i \xleftrightarrow{X_i} GWN)$

According to the Msg2, the authors get:

S5: $SN_j \lhd < ID_i, SID_j, T_2 >_{GWN \xleftarrow{K_2} SN_j}$

From A7, S5 and message-meaning rule, the authors have:

S6: $SN_j \equiv GWN \mid\sim (ID_i, SID_j, T_2)$

From A2 and freshness-conjuncatenation rule, the authors get:

S7: $SN_j \equiv \#<ID_i, SID_j, T_2>$

From S7, S6 and nonce-verification rule, the authors get:

S8: $SN_j \equiv GWN \equiv <ID_i, SID_j, T_2>$

According to the Msg3, the authors get:

S9: $GWN \lhd < ID_i, SID_j, T_3 >_{SN_j \xleftarrow{K_2} GWN}$

From A8, S9 and message-meaning rule, the authors have:

S10: $GWN \equiv SN_j \mid\sim (ID_i, SID_j, T_3)$

From A3 and freshness-conjuncatenation rule, the authors get:

S11: $GWN \equiv \#(ID_i, SID_j, T_3)$

From S11, S10 and nonce-verification rule, the authors get:

S12: $GWN \equiv SN_j \equiv (ID_i, SID_j, T_3)$

According to the Msg4, the authors get:

S13: $U_i \lhd < ID_i, SID_j, HID_i, T_4 >_{GWN \xleftarrow{K_1} U_i}$

From A5, S13 and message-meaning rule, the authors have:

S14: $U_i \equiv GWN \mid\sim <ID_i, SID_j, HID_i, T_4>$

From A4 and freshness-conjuncatenation rule, the authors get:

S15: $U_i \mathrel{|\!\equiv} \#(ID_i, SID_j, HID_i, T_4)$

From S15, S14 and nonce-verification rule, the authors get:

S16: $U_i \mathrel{|\!\equiv} GWN \mathrel{|\!\equiv} (ID_i, SID_j, HID_i, T_4)$

From S12, S16 and the session key $SK$, the authors have:

S17: $U_i \mathrel{|\!\equiv} SN_j \mathrel{|\!\equiv} (U_i \xleftrightarrow{SK} SN_j)$ (Goal2)

From S4, S8 and the session key $SK$, the authors have:

S18: $SN_j \mathrel{|\!\equiv} U_i \mathrel{|\!\equiv} (U_i \xleftrightarrow{SK} SN_j)$ (Goal4)

From S17, A9 and jurisdiction rule, the authors have:

S19: $U_i \mathrel{|\!\equiv} (U_i \xleftrightarrow{SK} SN_j)$ (Goal1)

From S18, A10 and jurisdiction rule, the authors have:

S20: $SN_j \mathrel{|\!\equiv} (U_i \xleftrightarrow{SK} SN_j)$ (Goal3)

According to Goal1-Goal4, the authors conclude that the proposed scheme can achieve mutual authentication successfully.

## Formal Security Verification Using ProVerif

ProVerif (Blanchet, 2001, pp. 82-96) is a formal verification tool which is widely used in many works, such as (Xiong, Peng, Peng, Liang, & Liu, 2017; Jiang, Zeadally, Ma, & He, 2017). Privacy and security of authentication schemes can be verified by ProVerif which supports many cryptographic primitives, including digital signatures, hash functions, encryption, Diffie-Hellman key agreements, and so on. In this subsection, the authors use ProVerif to analyze the security of the proposed scheme.

First of all, the authors define two public channels and basic types of variables. Secondly, the authors model the cryptographic functions of the proposed scheme, and the secret keys, events and authentication queries are defined. Thirdly, the authors model the process of the health professional, GWN and the medical sensor node, respectively. Finally, the authors model the whole process of the proposed scheme. The execution codes of the proposed scheme are placed on GitHub (Shuai, 2018), and the simulation results with ProVerif version 1.96 are given in Figure 3.

The results demonstrate that the proposed scheme fulfills the secrecy of session key and achieves mutual authentication successfully.

*Figure 3. The simulation results with the ProVerif*

```
Completing...
Starting query not attacker(snameA[])
RESULT not attacker(snameA[]) is true.
Starting query not attacker(snameB[])
RESULT not attacker(snameB[]) is true.
Starting query not attacker(snameC[])
RESULT not attacker(snameC[]) is true.
Starting query not attacker(snameD[])
RESULT not attacker(snameD[]) is true.
-- Query inj-event(SGend(x_2072)) ==> inj-event(SGbegin(x_2072))
Completing...
Starting query inj-event(SGend(x_2072)) ==> inj-event(SGbegin(x_2072))
RESULT inj-event(SGend(x_2072)) ==> inj-event(SGbegin(x_2072)) is true.
-- Query inj-event(GSend(x_4178)) ==> inj-event(GSbegin(x_4178))
Completing...
Starting query inj-event(GSend(x_4178)) ==> inj-event(GSbegin(x_4178))
RESULT inj-event(GSend(x_4178)) ==> inj-event(GSbegin(x_4178)) is true.
-- Query inj-event(GHend(x_6181)) ==> inj-event(GHbegin(x_6181))
Completing...
Starting query inj-event(GHend(x_6181)) ==> inj-event(GHbegin(x_6181))
RESULT inj-event(GHend(x_6181)) ==> inj-event(GHbegin(x_6181)) is true.
-- Query inj-event(HGend(x_8172)) ==> inj-event(HGbegin(x_8172))
Completing...
Starting query inj-event(HGend(x_8172)) ==> inj-event(HGbegin(x_8172))
RESULT inj-event(HGend(x_8172)) ==> inj-event(HGbegin(x_8172)) is true.
```

## Analysis of Security Properties

In this section, the authors look at how the proposed scheme provides user anonymity, forward secrecy, mutual authentication, session key agreement, security against smart card loss attack and replay attack.

### The Proposed Scheme Provides User Anonymity

In the proposed scheme, the authors adopt pseudonym identity technique to protect health professional's real identity. The pseudonym identity generated randomly by GWN is updated during every session, so the transmitted messages in current session are also different from other session. In addition, the health professional's real identity is protected by one-time hash function, the adversary cannot get it even if he/she intercept the transmitted messages. Therefore, the proposed scheme can not only protect the health professional's real identity, but also provide untraceability.

### The Proposed Scheme Provides Forward Secrecy

In the proposed scheme, even if an attacker obtains the long-term keys $K_1$, $K_2$ and $X_i$, he/she cannot get the session key which was used in previous communications. The reason is that the long-term keys $K_1^*$ and $K_2^*$ are updated by $K_1=h(K_1^*)$ and $K_2=h(K_2^*)$ after each session. The attacker cannot get $K_1^*$ and $K_2^*$ from $K_1$ and $K_2$ because hash function is irreversible. Therefore, the proposed scheme provides forward secrecy.

## The Proposed Scheme Achieves Mutual Authentication

In the proposed scheme, mutual authentication between health professional and GWN will be achieved by checking $CK_1^* = CK_1$ and $CK_4^* = CK_4$. Similarly, mutual authentication between GWN and the medical sensor node will be achieved by checking $CK_2^* = CK_2$ and $CK_3^* = CK_3$. Therefore, the proposed scheme achieves mutual authentication successfully.

## The Proposed Scheme Provides Session Key Agreement

In the execution of the proposed scheme, health professional, GWN and the medical sensor node establish a shared session key $SK$ to protect future communications in WMSNs. Therefore, the proposed scheme provides session key agreement.

## The Proposed Scheme is Resistant to Smart Card Loss Attack

Suppose the smart card is lost/stolen, an attacker can get the stored secret values $\{HID_i, Y_i, V_i, K_1, m_i, h(.), BH(.)\}$, where $V_i = h(X_i \| MPW_i)$, $X_i = h(ID_i \| K \| n_i)$, $Y_i = X_i \oplus MPW_i$, $HID_i = ID_i \oplus r_i$, $MB_i = BH(m_i \| fg_i)$, $MPW_i = h(ID_i \| PW_i \| MB_i \| m_i)$, $MB_i = BH(m_i \| fg_i)$. Here, the authors also suppose that the transmitted messages via open channels can be eavesdropped by the attacker. Using these values, the attacker can launch a smart card loss attack and try to guess the health professional's real identity and password. However, the attack will be failed without knowing the health professional's personal biometric $fg_i$, GWN's secret key $K$ and the high entropy random integer $n_i$ generated by GWN. Therefore, the proposed scheme is resistant to smart card loss attack.

## The Proposed Scheme Resists Replay Attack

The proposed scheme adopts the time stamp to avoid the replay attack. In the replay attack, an adversary cannot pass the time stamp checking process because all transmitted messages including current time stamp values, i.e., $T_1, T_2, T_3, T_4$. Therefore, the proposed scheme resists replay attack.

## The Proposed Scheme Resists Wrong Password Login Attack

In the proposed scheme, the value $V_i$ stored in the smart card is used to verify the legality of health professional, where

$$V_i^* = h\left(X_i^* \| MPW_i^*\right), \quad X_i^* = Y_i \oplus MPW_i^*, \quad MPW_i^* = h\left(ID_i \| PW_i \| MB_i^* \| m_i\right), \quad MB_i^* = BH\left(m_i \| fg_i\right).$$

If the health professional inputs a wrong password $PW_i^*$, the values $V_i^*$ and $V_i$ will be not equal. At this moment, the smart card rejects the health professional's login request. Therefore, the proposed scheme resists wrong password login attack.

## PERFORMANCE ANALYSIS

In this section, the authors compare the computational costs of the proposed scheme with other related schemes (He et al., 2015; Li et al., 2016; Srinivas et al., 2017). In order to evaluate the computational costs, the authors define two computational notations $T_h$ and $T_{cr}$, where $T_h$ denotes the time complexity of a one-way hash function operation, and $T_{cr}$ denotes the time complexity of general symmetric-key encryption/decryption operation. According to the existing experimental results (He, Kumar, Lee, & Sherratt, 2014), the execution time of a one-way hash function operation and general symmetric-key encryption/decryption operation are 0.00032s and 0.0056s, respectively. The simulations are achieved on a machine characterized by a processing rate of 3.2 GHz and a memory of 4 GB, the results are averaged over 300 randomised simulation runs. The comparison results between the proposed scheme and other related schemes are shown in Table 3.

In WMSNs, medical sensor nodes are limited in terms of computation capabilities and thus, the user authentication scheme must be lightweight in terms of computation. The proposed scheme only uses the lightweight cryptographic primitives including one-way hash function and symmetric encryption/decryption algorithm, which are efficient. Although the proposed scheme increases the number of hash operations slightly, it reduces the number of symmetric encryption/decryption operations substantially. Comparison demonstrates that the proposed scheme performs better than He et al.'s scheme (He et al., 2015), Li et al.'s scheme (Li et al., 2016) and Srinivas et al.'s scheme (Srinivas et al., 2017). It is valuable to note that the proposed scheme achieves the required security attributes and is more suitable for personalized healthcare applications.

*Table 3. Performance comparison between the proposed scheme and other related schemes*

| Scheme | He et al.'s scheme (He et al., 2015) | Li et al.'s scheme (Li et al., 2016) | Srinivas et al.'s scheme (Srinivas et al., 2017) | The proposed scheme |
|---|---|---|---|---|
| Users | $4T_h+3T_{cr}$ | $7T_h+2T_{cr}$ | $8T_h+3T_{cr}$ | $8T_h+2T_{cr}$ |
| GWN | $2T_h+5T_{cr}$ | $7T_h+6T_{cr}$ | $4T_h+2T_{cr}$ | $10T_h+2T_{cr}$ |
| Sensor node | $1T_h+2T_{cr}$ | $5T_h+2T_{cr}$ | $5T_h+2T_{cr}$ | $4T_h$ |
| Total cost | $7T_h+10T_{cr}$ | $19T_h+10T_{cr}$ | $17T_h+7T_{cr}$ | $22T_h+4T_{cr}$ |
| Execution time | 0.05824s | 0.06208s | 0.04464s | 0.02944s |

## CONCLUSION

With the wide use of WMSNs in healthcare applications, security and privacy issues have become a great challenge. In order to securely transmit physiological data collected from patients, the authors propose a novel and lightweight three-factor anonymous authentication scheme with privacy protection for personalized healthcare applications using only the lightweight cryptographic primitives. Using the BAN logic, the authors have proved that the proposed scheme fulfills mutual authentication successfully. In addition, the authors evaluated the security of the proposed scheme with ProVerif, and the simulation results show that the proposed scheme is secure. Through the heuristic way, the authors prove that the proposed scheme can not only provide user anonymity and forward secrecy, but also resist various malicious attacks, such as smart card loss attack and replay attack. Finally, the authors evaluate the performance of the proposed scheme with other related schemes, and the results show that the proposed scheme reduces the computational cost substantially and is more suitable for personalized healthcare applications.

## ACKNOWLEDGMENT

This work was supported by the National Natural Science Foundation of China (NSFC) under the grant No. U1536110.

## REFERENCES

Ameen, M. A., Liu, J. W., & Kwak, K. S. (2012). Security and privacy issues in wireless sensor networks for healthcare applications. *Journal of Medical Systems*, *36*(1), 93–101. doi:10.100710916-010-9449-4 PMID:20703745

Blanchet, B. (2001). An efficient cryptographic protocol verifier based on prolog rules. *IEEE Computer Security Foundations Workshop*, *1*, 82-96. 10.1109/CSFW.2001.930138

Burrows, M., Abad, M., & Needham, R. M. (1989). A logic of authentication. *Proceedings of the Royal Society of London A: Mathematical, Physical and Engineering Sciences, 426*(1871), 233-271. 10.1145/74850.74852

Cheng, J. R., Xu, R. M., Tang, X. Y., Sheng, V. S., & Cai, C. T. (2018). An abnormal network flow feature sequence prediction approach for DDoS attacks detection in big data environment. *Computers Materials & Continua*, *55*(1), 95–119.

Cui, J. H., Zhang, Y. Y., Cai, Z. P., Liu, A. F., & Li, Y. Y. (2018). Securing display path for security-sensitive applications on mobile devices. *Computers Materials & Continua*, *55*(1), 17–35.

Das, M. L. (2009). Two-factor user authentication in wireless sensor networks. *IEEE Transactions on Wireless Communications*, *8*(3), 1086–1090. doi:10.1109/TWC.2008.080128

Dolev, D., & Yao, A. (1983). On the security of public key protocols. *IEEE Transactions on Information Theory*, *29*(2), 198–208. doi:10.1109/TIT.1983.1056650

Gill, S. S., Chana, I., & Buyya, R. (2017). IoT based agriculture as a cloud and big data service: The beginning of digital India. *Journal of Organizational and End User Computing*, *29*(4), 1–23. doi:10.4018/JOEUC.2017100101

Gong, W. W., Qi, L. Y., & Xu, Y. W. (2018). Privacy-aware multi-dimensional mobile service quality prediction and recommendation in distributed fog environment. *Wireless Communications and Mobile Computing*, *4*, 1–8.

Gope, P., & Hwang, T. (2016). A realistic lightweight anonymous authentication protocol for securing real-time application data access in wireless sensor networks. *IEEE Transactions on Industrial Electronics*, *63*(11), 7124–7132. doi:10.1109/TIE.2016.2585081

He, D. B., Kumar, N., Chen, J. H., Lee, C. C., Chilamkurti, N., & Yeo, S. S. (2015). Robust anonymous authentication protocol for health-care applications using wireless medical sensor networks. *Multimedia Systems*, *21*(1), 49–60. doi:10.100700530-013-0346-9

He, D. B., Kumar, N., Lee, J. H., & Sherratt, R. S. (2014). Enhanced three-factor security protocol for consumer USB mass storage devices. *IEEE Transactions on Consumer Electronics*, *60*(1), 30–37. doi:10.1109/TCE.2014.6780922

Hu, F., Jiang, M., Wagner, M., & Dong, D. C. (2007). Privacy-preserving telecardiology sensor networks: Toward a low-cost portable wireless hardware/software codesign. *IEEE Transactions on Information Technology in Biomedicine*, *11*(6), 619–627. doi:10.1109/TITB.2007.894818 PMID:18046937

Huang, Y. M., Hsieh, M. Y., Chao, H. C., Hung, S. H., & Park, J. H. (2009). Pervasive, secure access to a hierarchical sensor-based healthcare monitoring architecture in wireless heterogeneous networks. *IEEE Journal on Selected Areas in Communications*, *27*(4), 400–411. doi:10.1109/JSAC.2009.090505

Jiang, Q., Zeadally, S., Ma, J. F., & He, D. B. (2017). Lightweight three-factor authentication and key agreement protocol for internet-integrated wireless sensor networks. *IEEE Access: Practical Innovations, Open Solutions*, *5*, 3376–3392. doi:10.1109/ACCESS.2017.2673239

Jin, C. H., Xu, C. X., Zhao, X. J., & Zhao, J. N. (2015). A secure RFID mutual authentication protocol for healthcare environments using Elliptic Curve Cryptography. *Journal of Medical Systems*, *39*(3), 24. doi:10.100710916-015-0213-7 PMID:25666925

Khan, K., & Kumari, S. (2013). An authentication scheme for secure access to healthcare services. *Journal of Medical Systems*, *37*(4), 9954. doi:10.100710916-013-9954-3 PMID:23828650

Khan, M. K., & Alghathbar, K. (2010). Cryptanalysis and security improvements of two-factor user authentication in wireless sensor networks. *Sensors (Basel)*, *10*(3), 2450–2459. doi:10.3390100302450 PMID:22294935

Kocher, P., Jaffe, J., & Jun, B. (1999). Differential power analysis. *Advances in Cryptology-CRYPTO'99*, *1666*, 388-397.

Kumar, P., Lee, S. G., & Lee, H. J. (2012). E-SAP: Efficient-strong authentication protocol for healthcare applications using wireless medical sensor networks. *Sensors (Basel)*, *12*(2), 1625–1647. doi:10.3390120201625 PMID:22438729

Lee, T., Ghapanchi, A. H., Talaei-Khoei, A., & Ray, P. (2015). Strategic information system planning in healthcare organizations. *Journal of Organizational and End User Computing*, *27*(2), 1–31. doi:10.4018/joeuc.2015040101

Li, X., Niu, J. W., Kumari, S., Liao, J. G., Liang, W., & Khan, K. (2016). A new authentication protocol for healthcare applications using wireless medical sensor networks with user anonymity. *Security and Communication Networks*, *9*(15), 2643–2655. doi:10.1002ec.1214

Liu, W. Y., Luo, X. Y., Liu, Y. M., Liu, J. Q., Liu, M. H., & Shi, Y. Q. (2018). Localization algorithm of indoor Wi-Fi access points based on signal strength relative relationship and region division. *Computers Materials & Continua*, *55*(1), 71–93.

Ma, Y. Y., Luo, X. Y., Li, X. L., Bao, Z. K., & Zhang, Y. (2018). Selection of rich model steganalysis features based on decision rough set α-positive region reduction. *IEEE Transactions on Circuits and Systems for Video Technology*, *99*, 1–1.

Malasri, K., & Wang, L. (2009). Design and implementation of a securewireless mote-based medical sensor network. *Sensors (Basel)*, *9*(8), 6273–6297. doi:10.339090806273 PMID:22454585

Mir, O., Munilla, J., & Kumari, S. (2017). Efficient anonymous authentication with key agreement protocol for wireless medical sensor networks. *Peer-to-Peer Networking and Applications*, *10*(1), 79–91. doi:10.100712083-015-0408-1

Odelu, V., Das, A. K., & Goswami, A. (2015). A secure biometrics-based multi-server authentication protocol using smart cards. *IEEE Transactions on Information Forensics and Security*, *10*(93), 1953–1966. doi:10.1109/TIFS.2015.2439964

Qi, L. Y., Meng, S. M., Zhang, X. Y., Wang, R. L., Xu, X. L., Zhou, Z. L., & Dou, W. C. (2018a). An exception handling approach for privacy-preserving service recommendation failure in a cloud environment. *Sensors (Basel)*, *18*(7), 2037. doi:10.339018072037 PMID:29949893

Qi, L. Y., Yu, J. G., & Zhou, Z. L. (2017). An invocation cost optimization method for web services in cloud environment. *Scientific Programming*, *11*, 1–9. doi:10.1155/2017/4358536

Qi, L. Y., Zhang, X. Y., Dou, W. C., Hu, C. H., Yang, C., & Chen, J. J. (2018b). A two-stage locality-sensitive hashing based approach for privacy-preserving mobile service recommendation in cross-platform edge environment. *Future Generation Computer Systems*, *88*, 636–643. doi:10.1016/j.future.2018.02.050

Qi, L. Y., Zhang, X. Y., Dou, W. C., & Ni, Q. (2017). A distributed locality-sensitive hashing based approach for cloud service recommendation from multi-source data. *IEEE Journal on Selected Areas in Communications*, *35*(11), 2616–2624. doi:10.1109/JSAC.2017.2760458

Qi, L. Y., Zhou, Z. L., Yu, J. G., & Liu, Q. (2017). Data-sparsity tolerant web service recommendation approach based on improved collaborative filtering. *IEICE Transactions on Information and Systems*, *100*(9), 2092–2099. doi:10.1587/transinf.2016EDP7490

Shuai, M. X. (2018, July 9). *The execution code of a lightweight three-factor anonymous authentication scheme with privacy protection for personalized healthcare applications*. Retrieved from https://github.com/smx12345/code/blob/master/wmsns.pv

Siddesh, G. M., Srinivasa, K. G., Kaushik, S., Varun, S. V., Subramanyam, V., & Patil, V. M. (2017). Internet of things (IOT) solution for increasing the quality of life of physically challenged people. *Journal of Organizational and End User Computing*, *29*(4), 72–83. doi:10.4018/JOEUC.2017100104

Srinivas, J., Mishra, D., & Mukhopadhyay, S. (2017). A mutual authentication framework for wireless medical sensor networks. *Journal of Medical Systems*, *41*(5), 80. doi:10.100710916-017-0720-9 PMID:28364358

Walczak, S., & Mann, R. (2010). Utilization and perceived benefit for diverse users of communities of practice in a healthcare organization. *Journal of Organizational and End User Computing*, 22(4), 24–50. doi:10.4018/joeuc.2010100102

Wang, D., & Wang, P. (2014). On the anonymity of two-factor authentication schemes for wireless sensor networks: Attacks, principle and solutions. *Computer Networks*, 73, 41–57. doi:10.1016/j.comnet.2014.07.010

Wang, J. W., Li, T., Shi, Y. Q., Lian, S. G., & Ye, J. Y. (2016). Forensics feature analysis in quaternion wavelet domain for distinguishing photographic images and computer graphics. *Multimedia Tools and Applications*, 76(22), 1–17.

Wu, F., Xu, L. L., Kumari, S., & Li, X. (2017). An improved and anonymous two-factor authentication protocol for health-care applications with wireless medical sensor networks. *Multimedia Systems*, 23(2), 195–205. doi:10.100700530-015-0476-3

Xiong, L., Peng, D. Y., Peng, T., Liang, H. B., & Liu, Z. C. (2017). A lightweight anonymous authentication protocol with perfect forward secrecy for wireless sensor networks. *Sensors (Basel)*, 11(11), 2681. doi:10.339017112681 PMID:29160861

Xu, Y. W., Qi, L. Y., Dou, W. C., & Yu, J. G. (2017). Privacy-preserving and scalable service recommendation based on simHash in a distributed cloud environment. *Complexity*, 2, 1–9. doi:10.1155/2017/3437854

Zhang, Y., Qin, C., Zhang, W. M., Liu, F. L., & Luo, X. Y. (2018). On the fault-tolerant performance for a class of robust image steganography. *Signal Processing*, 146, 99–111. doi:10.1016/j.sigpro.2018.01.011

*This research was previously published in the Journal of Organizational and End User Computing (JOEUC), 33(3); pages 1-18, copyright year 2021 by IGI Publishing (an imprint of IGI Global).*

# Chapter 21
# My Health Record and Emerging Cybersecurity Challenges in the Australian Digital Environment

**Anita Medhekar**

 https://orcid.org/0000-0002-6791-4056

*Central Queensland University, Australia*

## ABSTRACT

*The main aim of embracing evolutionary digital e-health technologies such as 'My Health Records' is to transform and empower the patients to control their health records, access, choose the right healthcare provider and suitable treatment, when required. It has been a challenge for the healthcare practitioners, hospital staff, as well as patients to accept, embrace, and adopt transformative digital e-health technologies and manage their healthcare records amidst concerns of slow adoption by the patient due to data privacy and cybersecurity issues. Australia, since COVID-19, has stressed the importance of secure online connectivity for the government, business, and the consumers. It is essential that My Health Record platform is cyber-safe, and user-friendly so that consumers feel conformable, safe and secure regarding their personal health records. This chapter discussed the challenges of embracing e-health digital technologies and assurance of advancing cybersecurity of online My Health Record, which will transform e-health provision and empower patients and healthcare providers.*

## INTRODUCTION

In the 21st century, developed countries such as Australia, has adopted digital transformation of healthcare records or e-health revolution for advancing cybersecurity, by implementing My Health Records to empower patients, and improve healthcare practice for clinicians and medical professionals, and provide positive experience to consumers at large. It has been a challenge for the healthcare practitioners, hospital staff as well as patients to accept, embrace, advance, and adopt digital e-health technologies and manage their healthcare records amidst concerns of slow adoption by the patient due to data privacy, security, security of technical devices, user authentication, and Cybersecurity issues (Chandrakar, 2021; Coven-

DOI: 10.4018/978-1-6684-6311-6.ch021

try & Branley, 2018; Office of Australian Information Commissioner, 2021a; OAIC, 2021b; Pandey & Litoriya, 2020; Tanwar, Tyagi, & Kumar 2019). The main aim of advancing and embracing innovative digital e-health technologies such as health informatics and 'My health Records' is to transform and empower the patients to control their health records, choose the right healthcare provider and suitable treatment, without compromising the safety, privacy and security of private health data. Further, adoption of e-health records, helps in digitizing, maintaining and storing e-health records, and introduces ease of communication between the various healthcare departments through electronic data interchange for sharing information between the patient and the healthcare providers (Baldwin et al., 2017; Bhuyan et al., 2020; Kim & Johnston, 2002; Medhekar & Nguyen, 2020; Queensland Health, 2017; Sittig, 2002).

Given that the e-health revolution is driven by innovators of healthcare technologies, entrepreneurs, medical professionals, healthcare providers and government policy makers to bring about a transformative change in healthcare ecosystems. It is essential that e-health innovation such as My health Record platform is cyber-safe and user-friendly so that consumers as patients feel comfortable, safe, and secure regarding protection of their personal health-care records and diagnostic reports by the hospitals cloud system (Tanwar et al., 2019). Assurance of cybersecurity related to My Health Record' will help to change the patient experience and empower them to embrace e-health digital technologies and empower the patients to manage their own health records with positive healthcare experience and digitally transform health care delivery (Bhuyan et al., 2016; Coventry & Branley, 2018; Medhekar & Nguyen, 2020; Medhekar, 2021). On the 26th of November 2018, the Australian parliament passed the My Health Records amendment bill to protect the privacy of the people using the digital e-health system to meet the multi-layered privacy and cybersecurity standards and to protect the electronic health records system from malicious attacks from online hackers and cyber-criminals (Australian Digital Health Agency {ADHA}, 2019; Aunger, 2020). Since COVID-19 pandemic on one hand governments, business and consumers are increasingly depending on online delivery of business, goods and services; on the other hand cyber criminals are busy attacking the internet cloud information systems from all over the world, stealing money, identities, and sensitive finance, government, business, defense data, research facilities and healthcare data for ransom or stealing patient privacy (Bhuyan et al., 2020; Department of Home Affairs, 2020; Sharma & Purohit, 2018; William, Chaturvedi, & Chakravarthy, 2020).

My health records can only be accessed by the patient and the healthcare provider involved in treating patients, and registered with My Health Record System Operator, who are allowed by law to access patients My Health Record (Wood et al., 2013). For example, patients GP, specialist physician/surgeon, pharmacies for prescription medicine, pathology, hospitals, and allied healthcare professionals. The Queensland health has identified four key roles for digital technologies or e-health system. **(i)** *Promoting wellbeing* by thorough healthy behaviour to improving health of Queenslanders. **(ii)** *Delivering healthcare* by emphasizing access, equity, and quality in healthcare delivery for all. **(iii)** *Connecting healthcare* by tackling funding, policy, and delivery barriers, to make the health system work better for consumers and communities. **(iv)** *Pursuing innovation* by developing evidence-based models that work, promoting research and translating it into better healthcare practice (Queensland Health, 2017). Therefore, patient's healthcare data privacy and two- factor based user authentication is essential for data security, from cyber-attacks as it hinders patient care at all levels (Bhuyan et al., 2020; Chandrakar, 2021; Ehrenfeld, 2017; Jalali & Kaiser, 2018). According to William et al. (2020) in COVID-19 period cyber threats have increased fivefold and by the end of 2021, "cybersecurity threats are estimated to cost the world US $6 trillion" and healthcare organisations and health industry as a whole need to protect the sensitive health research and patient data from cyber-crimes. Healthcare organisations pay huge fines to department of justice for cybercrime related patients personal data breaches.

According to Harman et al. (2012) there are three major ethical requirements for electronic health records of the patients **(i)** privacy and confidentiality, **(ii)** security, and **(iii)** data integrity and availability for patient and providers use. Further, the global healthcare emergent COVID-19 pandemic, has also raised concerns of cybersecurity challenges, where the cyber-criminals are targeting healthcare providers, pharmaceuticals companies, medical research, academics, and government health departments to collect personal information, health related intellectual property which aligns with countries national security priorities (Aunger, 2020; William et al., 2020). According to HIPPA Journal (2019) USA, reported that in 2019, more than 500 healthcare data breaches took place from department of health and human services office, with an increase of 196% from 2018 breaches, where healthcare records of 12.55% of US population was exposed, disclosed or stolen by cybercrime attacks.

Digital transformation of the healthcare system records, and diagnostic reports has its benefits and opportunities of digitisation of health reports and records, for longitudinal studies, research, ease of communication between health departments and patient's history. However, it has to face many costs or challenges for keeping confidential private health records safe from cyber-threats and cyber-attacks from hackers, who could misuse the data for a ransom. Literature review also indicates publications on healthcare transformation to digitization of health reports and cybersecurity of digital health/e-health reports and My Health Records ' of healthcare organisations is relatively an emerging new area of research globally and in Australia (Jalali et al., 2019; Tanwar et al., 2019).

The key objective of this chapter is to explore the importance and significance of cybersecurity of e-health records and my health records of the patients. This chapter is structured as follows. The first introductory section of the chapter introduces the growing importance and significance of digital or e-health adoption and Cybersecurity concerns in Australia. Section two provides the literature review on e-health related My Health Record and Cybersecurity risk assessment and management. Section three discusses the example of Australia in adopting e-health strategies such as My Health Records and related Cybersecurity concerns. Section four discusses the challenges of my health records from cybersecurity threats, recommendations to improve cybersecurity of healthcare records, and policy implications proposing a *My Health Record and Cybersecurity Empowerment Model,* which can be empirically tested in the future with the proposed hypothesis. This is followed by future research directions to advance the knowledge in the field Cybersecurity of electronic My Health Records and conclusion.

## Background: Literature Review

Medical records of the patients were traditionally paper, or file based with the doctor, in a legible handwriting. These medical records were in control of the hospital and the doctors who used for patient's treatment, clinical research, administrative and financial reason. Paper based records also had limitations in terms of storage and security (Harman, Flite, & Bond, 2012). Patients as well kept the information related to prescription medicines, x-ray, and reports of diagnostic tests. According to Greenlalgh et al. (2010) as we move from information-age to industrial-age, adoption of 'My Health Record' is a move from specialists-driven to patient-driven self-managed care, with an interactive digital platform of communication between the patient and the healthcare provider which is patient-centered care at all levels.

Since health informatics systems and digital e-health was introduced, patient data related to visits, prescriptions, diagnostic test results, treatment was electronically saved on healthcare providers super computers, and was easily accessed by the treating doctor and further there was electronic data interchange between the clinic and the diagnostic centers, which made it easy for healthcare decision making based on documentation of the patient's treatment.

Online My Health Record System was launched in Australia in 2018, where the consumers had the choice to opt-in or opt-out, as the history and treatment of patient is available on My Health Record system (ADHA, 2019), which could be susceptible to cyber-crime or cyber-attack hindering patient care (Bogle, 2018; Coventry & Branley, 2018; Ehrenfeld, 2017). A study by Torrens and Walker (2017) found that females were more likely to register and use the online My Health Records than males. Moreover, middle-aged males, older females and adolescents of both sexes had lowest registration and uptake of My Health Record due to digital literacy and online security concerns. Therefore, cybersecurity, safety, and privacy of patient's personal health records, is of concern to the patients as consumers, medical professionals, health informatics managers, and government healthcare system.

## My Health Record

My Health Record is defined by ADHA (2019), as an online summary of key health information of the patients, which can be recorded and tracked over time in a safe online environment. These electronic health records can be viewed in a secure online environment from anywhere in the world and can be accessed on any device with an internet connection. When a patient visits a doctor, or is in an emergency, unable to talk, healthcare providers can access the information related to patients' allergies, prescription medicine, health history, medical conditions, medical images and pathology diagnostic tests results to provide appropriate treatment for getting the best outcomes for the patient. Healthcare providers and doctors can access patient's important health care information if they cannot talk under anesthetic, to know about patient's prescription medicine, allergies, family history of diseases, pathology and radiology tests results and medical condition for diagnosis and treatment plan (ADHA, 2019).

My Health Record system was originally called as the personally administered electronic health record (PCEHR), of the Australian citizens, which was launched by the Australian Government nationwide in July 2012, with an opt-in or opt-out model provided by National E-Health Transition Authority. By the end of 2012, nearly 2.6 million (11%) had registered, and since March 2016, it was relaunched as 'My Health Record' an opt-out model operated by Digital Health Agency (Department of Health, 2016). My health record is covered by four key regulatory acts introduced by the Australian Commonwealth Government for administration related to use, privacy and regulation of 'My Health Records' system. **(i)** *Healthcare Identifier Act 2010,* **(ii)** *My Health Record Act 2012',* **(iii)** *My Health Record Regulations 2012, and* **(iv)** *My Health Record Rule 2016, and Privacy Act 1988* to provide access, identify the user, privacy and confidentiality of patient records, and the rules governing the electronic health records (Australian Government, 2016a; Commonwealth of Australia, 2012 & 2015). In 2019, Amendment to the Privacy Act 1988 was passed by the Morrison Government to tighten the cybersecurity. In 2020, the Morrison government introduced the 2020- Cyber Security Strategy, replacing the 2016-Cyber Security Strategy which has been a catalyst for change, launching a series of government and private sector activities and responses to cyber-security and cyber-crime challenges (Department of Home Affairs, 2020).

The Australian national participation rate for uptake of My Health Record as at 28th of July 2019, reported by the Australian Government was 90.1 percent. This is the rate of people who chose not to opt-out as a percentage of those who meet the eligibility criteria for Medicare (Australian Government, 2019). State wise participation rate and uptake of My Health Records across Australia is as follows: Northern

Territory (93.6%), Queensland (91.2%), Western Australia (90.4%), Tasmania (90.3), New South Wales (90.2%), South Australia (89.3%), Victoria (89.3), and Australian Capital Territory (86.7%). Overall an approximate number of 16,400 healthcare provider organisations have registered with My Health Record (Australian Government, 2019). The number and types of health care providers organisation registered are as follows: General Practice Organisations (7,240), Pharmacies (4770), Other Categories of healthcare providers Including Allied Health (2960), Public Hospitals and Health Services (832), Aged Care Residential Services (239), Private Hospitals and Clinics (190), Pathology and Diagnostic Imaging Clinics (119) Services (Australian Government, 2019).

Electronic health reports on My Health Record, shares confidential patient information with all healthcare staff involved in treating a patient at all levels of care. It helps to improve the flow of information between the Doctor-GP, the specialists and the patients. This may also help to improve patient treatment outcomes. Patients can choose to share the information with their healthcare providers, manage My Health Records by deleting or adding information, choosing privacy and security settings by adding personal notes regarding allergies, care-plan, set access control to restrict access to who can and cannot see your health information, review healthcare information that doctors can see and set-up e-mail and SMS notification. This helps to provide detail picture of health history, diagnosis, and treatment plan (ADHA, 2019). Concerns have been raised by the public regarding cybersecurity of personal data on My Health Record since the one and a half million Singaporean nationals, including the prime ministers my health personal records were hacked in July 2018 as reported by the British Broadcasting Corporation (BBC, 2010). Therefore protecting the privacy and security of patients My Health Record from misuse, cyber-attack, and cyber-crimes is crucial.

## Cybersecurity

Cybersecurity is defined by Merriam-Webster dictionary as "measure taken to protect a computer or computer system on the internet against unauthorized access or attack". Cybersecurity of patients online 'My Health Records' which is an electronic record of patient's meetings with the general practitioner, specialist, nursing staff, results of diagnostic reports, blood tests, x-ray, allergies, prescription medicine records at one central place. These sensitive health records stored in cloud can be accessed on demand by the medical practitioner and the patients with access to internet, on any device, anytime, anywhere in the world. It helps to keep check on our health over our lifetime (Regola & Chawla, 2013; Varadharajan, 2018). Electronic health records therefore can be accessed and viewed by many stakeholders at the same time, using various information technology and electronic tools in a timely manner to improve patient treatment outcomes. However, the rich healthcare information of the organisations and sensitive patient data is susceptible to cyber security breaches of patient privacy and safety and for financial gains by the hackers (Conaty-Buck, 2017; Perakslis, 2020; Rowe, Lunt, & Ekstrom, 2011).

These personal e-health or 'My health Records' are managed by the patients to restrict access to some, or all health records stored. However, in an emergency the doctor can override the safeguard to access information to provide the best care to the patient. This also requires everyone to have access to internet connection, smart phones, and laptop. Two studies- Zurita and Nøhr (2004) in New Zealand and Chhanabhai and Holt (2007) in Denmark, found that patients were concerned about the privacy, safety, and security of their personal e-health records from cyber-attackers. Fernández-Alemán, Carrión Señor, Lozoya and Toval (2013) conducted a systematic review of literature around security of e-health record, and concluded from 49 articles that, security and privacy of patient's electronic health records and regulation around security and privacy policy is a concern given that countries are moving away from paper-based to online integrated electronic health records.

According to Kelly (2020), healthcare sector in Australia reported in 2018 the highest incidence of health data security breaches, because Australia does not have US-Style mandatory security standards and regulations for the protection of private electronic health information. The costs to the patient in terms of loss of trust in organisations in protecting their privacy and safety of sensitive personal health data, including the healthcare organisations of cybersecurity breaches are enormous. Conaty-Buck (2017) has summarized the costs of cybersecurity breaches to United States electronic healthcare records systems, in terms of fines, and the average cost of breach per record is US $380. For example **(i)** Advocate health care had four stolen laptops, and data of 4 million patients was breached, and had to incur a fine of US $5.55 million. **(ii)** Anthem in Indiana state paid fine of US $115 million, as 80 million patients' private data was breached containing social security, birthdates, names, address, e-mail, employment, and income information. **(iii)** Alaska department of health and social services was fined 1.7 million due to stolen USB drive containing patient's personal health information. **(iv)** New York, Presbyterian hospital and Columbia University was fined 4.8 Million, because a physician left data insecure in an attempt to deactivate a personal computer. **(v)** Oregon Health and Science University was fined US $ 2.7 million for cyber security breaches of 7000 patient's health records from stolen laptops and data stored in an unapproved and insure google cloud system.

Therefore patients are concerned about the safety and privacy of their e-health records in terms of who has access and permission to use their personal health records and for what purposes as justified by a study conducted by Atienza et al. (2015). Consumers as patients are concerned about unauthorized access, control, misuse and sharing of their confidential health data with healthcare providers in a trustworthy manner. Further, a quantitative survey in Queensland by Gajanayake and Sahama (2014), where they surveyed 750 Australian participants, up to the age of 65. These participants had opted out and not used My Health Records due to the lack of trust in the e-health system, perceived risk of cybersecurity issues, involved in using and sharing the online health record system, and privacy and confidentiality breaches by healthcare providers and users of their personal health records.

Moreover, technologies developed by Australia Cyber–Security Engineering Research Centre can be used to protect the personal health records data by encryption and at the same time allow the users that is the patients and the healthcare providers to access the data, and the administrator of the cloud can have access to data only if provided by the patient (Pavithra & Chandrasekaran, 2021; Regola & Chawla, 2013; Zhou, Varadharajan, & Gopinath, 2016). The global patients or medical travelers also have to exchange medical data and diagnostic health reports via shared cloud storage provided by the international hospitals treating foreign patients which is password protected, before they travel abroad for surgery. Patients therefore have to have internet knowledge regarding uploading files, reports and security identification (Medhekar & Wong, 2020). Further, Varadharajan (2018) also mentions about the literacy of the users of my health records that is the patients and provider's literacy and healthcare stakeholders, capability and competency in setting preferences and strong privacy controls by default, to protect the data from cyberattack.

Further, a qualitative pilot study by Kerai, Wood, and Martin (2014), where they interviewed 80 senior citizens in Australia to know their perspective on usage of electronic health record. Kerai et al. (2014) study found that due to lack of knowledge of online usage of My Health Records, 84% of the participants were not ready to take on the responsibility of using the system and preferred their general practitioner's medical practice to manage their health records. Furthermore, from clinician's perspective, an Australian study with 26 clinicians from three large hospitals found that hospital clinician staff were not trained to use and understand the information and regulation related to privacy and security implementation effectively and identify confidential and sensitive private information of the patients. This resulted in suboptimal patient safety, security of patient private data, and healthcare outcomes (Fernando & Dawson, 2009). Therefore, cyber-attackers can demand ransom from hospitals, resulting in appointments being cancelled, delayed surgeries impacting the total healthcare system- as it happened in 2017 in United Kingdom, putting the patients in life and death situation (Bogle, 2018).

Various articles have discussed the application and benefits of innovative and transformative blockchain technology in bio-medical and healthcare industry for security, privacy of patient information, transparency, and integrating consumers health records and efficient access by the users – healthcare providers and the patients (Kuo, Kim, & Ohno-Machado, 2017; Krawiec & White 2016; Schumacher, 2017; Tanwar Parekh & Evans, 2020; Zhang et al., 2018). In terms of innovation in cybersecurity systems, Pandey and Litoriya (2020), provide a conceptualized ecosystem of blockchain technology in digital healthcare design in their research and suggest that a centralised system of keeping health records is more vulnerable and easy single point of contact for cyber-crime and failure of communication. Whereas a complex decentralized and innovative blockchain technology is computationally expensive using cryptographic algorithms, with multiple coordinator nodes, which can maintain communication, if one fails, or is hacked. In the age of data insecurity, decentralized blockchain technology distribution system is therefore more reliable in providing patient centered care in terms of security, transparency, privacy, safety and inter-operationality of patient's e-healthcare data in the healthcare system, which is continuously updated and securely stored.

Qualitative research by Jalali and Kaiser (2018), where they interviewed 19 participants such as hospitals chief medical officers, and hospital cyber security officers and cyber security experts to understand hospitals cybersecurity capabilities to protect hospital and patient's data from cyber-crime. They found that the risk of cyber-attack in the hospital comes from end point complexity and internal hospital users/stakeholder's alignment. Therefore cybersecurity capabilities-gap can be closed if all hospitals not only devote equitable mount of resources to enhance and upgrade the entire healthcare industry cybersecurity infrastructure to protect e-health records from cyber-crime, but also reduce end point complexity and improve internal hospital users/stakeholder's alignment of hospitals and patient's healthcare data from cyber-attackers.

Given the cybersecurity issues since COVID-19 has come to the forefront of all countries including the Australian government's overall security strategy, on the 6th of August 2020, the Australian Government released the Australia's Cyber Security Strategy-2020. The strategy aims to invest Aus $1.67 billion over the 10 years to create a cyber-secure and safe online environment for the Australian citizens, businesses and the three levels of government. Australia's Cyber Security Strategy-2020 was a consultative process, face-to-face, workshops, roundtables and bilateral meetings. It is to be implemented through actions taken by the Australian government, business and the community to ensure and protect the essential services of all Australians, by upgrading the security and resilience of critical cyber security online infrastructure facilities of national significance (Department of Home Affairs, 2020). **(i)** Governments action to strengthen the protection of Australians, businesses and critical infrastructure from the most sophisticated threats. **(ii)** Businesses action to secure their products and services and protect their customers from known cyber vulnerabilities. **(iii)** Community action to practice secure online behaviours and make informed purchasing decisions (Department of Home Affairs, 2020).

## Cybersecurity- AustrAlia My Health Records

My Health Records shares information with patents and physician/clinicians, which also engages patients in managing their healthcare issues and records related to sickness, diagnostic results x-rays, and prescribed medications. It is essential that patients have e-health literacy in the use of internet and eHealth record portals to engage and manage their online health records to improve self-management of healthcare (Baldwin et al., 2017; Coughlin et al., 2018; Greenlee, 2021). Medical imaging devices for example ultra-sound, CT-scan and MRI machines have also gone through digital transformation and innovation and link digital images and reports of diagnostic tests of the patients with My Health Records and can be obtained from computer desktop. Therefore, digital imaging technology should be built with cybersecurity firewalls in place, as diagnostic reports are also faced with cyber-threats from cyber-attackers' who may steal private sensitive patient data for a ransom. These attacks can range from insider threats, data breaches, e-mail scams, phishing attacks, ransomware and distributed denial of service attack (Greenlee, 2021; Langer, 2017; Nigrin, 2014).

A mixed methods study in England by Greenlalgh et al. (2010) found that patients perceived online Health- Space neither useful nor easy to use to self-manage their health records. Policy makers according to their study hoped that adopting HealthSpace will empower patients, lower NHS costs, provide better quality of data, personalize healthcare, and improve patient health literacy. Australian study found that, protection of private data, ease of use of e-Health records, lack of interest and lack of integration of health records with the existing health systems, privacy and security of personal information of the patent is critical for the health consumer and healthcare professionals (Andrews et al., 2014; Lehnbom, McLachlan, & Brien, 2012).

Findings from Australian Commission on Safety and Quality in Health Care {ACSQHC}, commissioned report by Shaw, Hines, and Kielly-Carroll (2017) identified five key areas of digital health interventions: **(i)** electronic patient portals, **(ii)** Electronic patient reminders on mobile phone technologies, **(iii)** information-sharing by electronic discharge summaries, **(iv)**computerized provider order entry and electronic prescription, and **(v)** clinical decision support systems. Given these high levels of e-health and digital intervention, it is essential to build trust, for safety and security to protect patients e-health data from cyber-crime and online-hackers, better planning by healthcare organizations and government health departments is required to prevent cyber breaches.

Bhuyan et al. (2020), have identified seven types of health organisation related cyber-attacks and motivation of cyber-criminals behind these attacks. **(i)** *Denial-of-Services* (DoS), which is prevent access by shutting down the entire network of healthcare organizations for example 2014 Boston's children's hospitals DoS attack, disrupting network of various healthcare organizations sharing information. **(ii)** *Privilege Escalation Attacks* are vertical and horizontal to have access to highest level of information, compromising patient's safety. **(iii)** *Eavesdropping Attack* or man in the middle (MITM), when communication is intercepted by a third party compromising the integrity of the healthcare data communicated, by gaining access to patients' confidential information for blackmail. **(iv)** *Cryptographic Attack,* to decrypt encrypted information which can be understood by the sender and the receiver. **(v)** *Structured Query Language (SQL)* can be exploited by the hackers to alter the information of the patients in the database, affecting availability, integrity and authenticity of the healthcare information stored in hospital information system. **(vi)** *Malware or malicious software attack* .The examples of *Malware/ malicious software* are *Virus, Trojans, spyware, ransomware, Phishing, and worms.* They are designed to harm the computer system without the knowledge of the user and infect virus on other computer systems through user activation, by deleting and corrupting files and stored data. For example in 2017, malware attack shut down the Medical Centre at Erie country New York.

There are many benefits of adopting e-health technologies to the clinicians as well as to empower the patients to manage their own health records. However, there are also many challenges in terms of internet health literacy, and key stakeholders' responsibility in ensuring privacy and Cybersecurity of patient's personal health history and data (ADHA, 2019; Russo et al., 2016; Sittig, Belmont, & Singh, 2018). According to Davidson (2019), My Health Record failed to manage cybersecurity and privacy risk audit. Literature review indicates publications on Cybersecurity of My Health Records from cyber criminals is relatively an emerging new area of research. The Vision of Cyber Security Strategy-2020 is to provide "A more secure online world for Australians, their businesses and the essential services upon which we all depend". This cybersecurity is to be delivered by complementary action taken by the government, businesses and community to protect accessing of sensitive defense, health, research, information and data for financial gains, dark-web crimes, exploitation of children and vulnerable people, and other crime by cyber-criminals and hackers. The next section summaries challenges of cybersecurity and provides few recommendations to deal with the issues related to cybersecurity of My Health Records (Department of Home Affairs, 2020).

## SOLUTIONS AND RECOMMENDATIONS

### Emerging Cybersecurity Challenges

Medical practice is increasingly depending on information systems and becoming information-intensive using various applications for doctors' appointments to medical alerts and notification including, My Health Records. Information Systems managers, Cybersecurity managers, healthcare providers and patients face many challenges of securing sensitive private healthcare records from misuse by cyber-criminals.

1. *Technological and Digital Competency:* General practitioners, physicians, nurses and specialist surgeons need to have skills and expertise in clinical practice as well as be technologically competent. Therefore, continuous information systems skilling and training is requited to be able to use the information system and various electronic health records and applications.
2. *Back-up Digitized Health Records:* Digitized personal health records are prone to cyber-crime and security issues. It is essential, that digitized health records are backed-up in more than one place to prevent loss of healthcare records and data required for treatment and medical research.
3. *Cybersecurity and Privacy:* With increasing digitization of health records and automation of health-related appointments and applications the downside is the cybersecurity and privacy issues related with the My Health Records of the patients.
4. *Medical Imaging Devices and Cybersecurity: M*edical imaging devices have improved patient care and healthcare outcomes. However, medical imaging technology and equipment such as CT-scan and MRI machines need to have built-in innovative cybersecurity alerts, multi-layered protection, and firewalls to protect the personals sensitive healthcare and medical-imaging data from cyber-threats, e-mail scams and phishing attacks.
5. *My Health Record User Literacy, training and Empowerment:* The stakeholders and users of My Health Records, are continuously updated by the user and cyber security policy which empowers

them to keep or delete and provide access to their personal health records such as general practitioners. Therefor consumers have to be aware of the definitions of the following terms and how cyber-crime hackers attack the internet devices using various tools: such as **(i)** *Virus* which infects software and reproduces copies when it is opened; **(ii)** *Worm* infects software and spreads without the user taking any actions. **(iii)** *Trojan* contains malware, which acts when downloaded and opened. **(iv)** *Ransom-ware*, allows the users to access their system or encrypts files until a ransom has been paid. (v) *Rootkits* hide malware from antivirus detection and removal programs. (vi) *Keystroke* logger program records user keystrokes, to acquire passwords. (vii) *Adware* produces a code which automatically download malware.

6. *Public-Private- Partnerships (PPPs)*: Challenge of partnerships between the key stakeholder's government, regulators, healthcare organisations, community, individuals for cybersecurity regulation, planning and implementation are required to prevent health organisations cyber-breaches of sensitive healthcare data.

## RECOMMENDATIONS

The following recommendations in dealing with the issues, controversies, or problems presented in the preceding section can be made related to cybersecurity of My Health Records.

1. *Cybersecurity Alarm:* In case of cybercrime or hacking of the personal healthcare records, the information system to check cyber -crime thoroughly, should have a built-in system for alerting the user via a firewall alarm, so that all systems automatically close down to protect the data from cybercrime, prevent data manipulation, and preserve sensitive health records along with backup facilities.

2. *Alerts for Health Data Entry Errors:* It is important that health data entry by the healthcare professionals is correct when it is shared through electronic data interchange (EDI) system between different healthcare departments such as doctors' clinics, hospital, diagnostic clinics, rehab centers and aged-care institutions and health systems for accurate data integrity at all levels. Cyber-attack alerts set in place can warn any suspicious cyber-criminal attack.

3. *Software Menu Choices:* Various items related to drop down menu choices available in the software have to be increased, so clinicians can make an appropriate choice of the problem as per the diagnosis, so that the original health data is preserved and there are no system errors due to incorrect choice made in a hurry from the drop-down menu.

4. *Innovative Data System:* Continuous innovation and improvement in the e-health data systems and cyber-security software will result in security of e-health records, better healthcare outcomes, greater efficiency in healthcare delivery and more effective research into e-healthcare and digital health.

5. *Digital Health Partnerships:* Australian Digital Health Authority could seek global partnerships in order to engage with Global Digital Health, for implementing and ensuring cybersecurity and safety of patient's e-health records, including cyber-security related education and training.

6. *Cybersecurity Training:* Consumers, clinicians, health-care professional staff and administrators need to go through online education and security training of usage and protection related to cyber security of healthcare data. Regular upgrade training and alerts should be made available to the

users, confirmation with a tick that the information or training has been completed, with a small quiz, before we access or log-on to My Health Records platform for cybersecurity education and training.

7.  *Re-Engineering Healthcare Cybersecurity:* National government should invest to continuously re-engineer and improve e-health cybersecurity. Funds should be allocated for cybersecurity education provided by cybersecurity experts and professionals. It is also essential to have updated innovation and technological improvement to protect healthcare data from cyber-threat and hackers. Hospitals and healthcare clinics are at greater risk due to shortage of funds allocated to keep up-to-date with the latest cyber-security technology, software upgrade and training.

8.  *Cybersecurity Awareness Culture:* Healthcare professionals and workers at the clinics, diagnostic centers, hospitals, aged-care institutions, need to embed a culture of awareness of cybersecurity of healthcare reports, data and medical imaging records with the aim to protect patient privacy, prevent cyber-crime, preserve records, and back-up healthcare reports and records.

9.  *Cybersecurity Awareness and Education:* Consumers as users of My Health Records, online banking, shopping, and using other internet applications and cloud storage, should build cyber-security awareness as part of their daily life when using internet applications, and acquire online cyber-security awareness education and information related to cybersecurity, antivirus software program and protecting their data from unauthorized access and cyber- crime. Most of the government health departments, provide cybersecurity related resources for individuals and use by the professionals in organizations. Various tips and steps for cybersecurity awareness of My Health Records are necessary to follow as suggested by Conaty-Buck (2017) as it is everyone's business to be aware of cybercrime and be safe. Such as: choosing a secure password, not opening and therefore deleting e-mails and attachments from unknown people, using data encryptions for all internet connected devices, downloading security updates, educate oneself and others, reporting any suspicious e-mails to organisations information technology (IT) department, and while accessing resources "Stop, Think and Connect" steps to be followed, to be safe and secure from cyber-crime.

10. *Adoption of Blockchain Technology in Healthcare:* Sharing peer-to-peer healthcare related data between pharmaceuticals industry, healthcare providers and hospitals, health insurance providers and consumers in a secure manner, without the fear of breach can be done by adopting blockchain technology. It can save healthcare sector millions of dollars in costs related to cybercrime data breaches in operations, IT costs, support services, and personnel. Blockchain technology can help the health sector in recording accurately each and every medical and cash transaction, storing and securely data sharing, and transfer between devices and healthcare providers, thus ensuring cybersecurity and preventing sensitive data breaches. It also helps to find right patients for medical trials for the pharmaceutical companies and enhances healthcare related supply chain operations management (Tanwar et al., 2019).

The following hypothesis is proposed for future research on My Health Record Cybersecurity survey based on Figure-1.

H-1: *Technological and Digital Competency will positively improve My Health Record Cybersecurity Empowerment.*

H-2: *Cybersecurity Awareness Culture will positively improve My Health Record Cybersecurity Empowerment.*

H-3: *Cybersecurity Training will positively improve My Health Record Cybersecurity Empowerment.*

H-4: *Cybersecurity Alarm Recognition will positively improve My Health Record Cybersecurity Empowerment.*

H-5: *My Health Record Cybersecurity Stakeholder Communication will positively improve My Health Record Cybersecurity Empowerment.*

H-6: *My Health Record Cybersecurity Digital Health Partnerships will enhance and positively improve My Health Record Cybersecurity Empowerment.*

Figure-1 provides a model for My Health Record and Cybersecurity, which can be tested via qualitative interviews with the stakeholders and quantitative survey for future research. Figure-1 illustrates that My Health Records cybersecurity depends on the six dimensions such as **(i)** Technological and Digital Competency, **(ii)** Cybersecurity Awareness Culture, **(iii)** Cybersecurity Training, **(iv)** Cybersecurity Alarm Recognition, **(v)** MHR-Cybersecurity Stakeholder Communication, and **(vi)** MHR- Cybersecurity Digital Health Partnerships between the regulators, three levels of government, businesses, and the community.

*Figure 1. My Health Record and Cybersecurity Empowerment Model*
*Source: Developed for this Chapter*

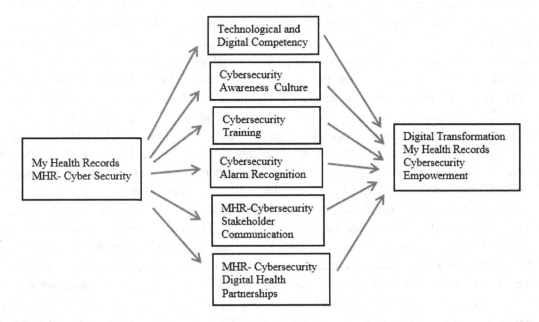

## FUTURE RESEARCH DIRECTIONS

Given the reliance of consumers, business and governments on internet technology and its devices such computers, iPad and mobile phones including various applications, safety and cybersecurity of personal, business and government data is a very challenging issue. All the sectors such as My Health Records, banking, finance, defense, education, businesses corporations, tax office, including governments have gone through digital transformation in context of the use of the internet for online business transactions and cloud computing data storage. The use of internet and various applications has increased since March

2020 pandemic and increasingly businesses and retails sector have shown online presence to sell goods and services to reach out to their customers during lockdown and keep their business afloat. Similarly various health, general practitioners, education and legal consulting services are also relying heavily on the internet and communication technologies, various applications and cloud storage to share documents with the customers. The future and emerging trends is all about cybersecurity of internet transactions, sensitive documents, personal data of health records, and data storage. Future research opportunities can focus on conducting one to one interview with Step-1: the key stakeholders'- users of My Health Record system from the health sector such as health informatics, information technology maintenance staff responsible for Cybersecurity, information health-care providers, doctors, nurses, and administrators. Step-2 one to one interview with consumers as stakeholders and users of My Health Records. Step 3: Applying the Conceptual Model of My Health Record and the proposed hypothesis, by developing the items to operationalize the cybersecurity constructs related to My Health Record and conducting an online survey.

## CONCLUSION

The chapter covers consumer's personal health data on 'My Health Record' related cybersecurity issues and challenges in Australia. Many Australians have opted out of My Health Record, due to concerns related to Cybersecurity issues personal and sensitive health data related privacy, confidentiality on the internet and possibility of cyber-criminals hacking the personal health information of millions of citizens. Cybersecurity is on the agenda of all the governments since 2020, COVID -19 year, given the changing geo-political environment to protect the strategic government data, business data and individual citizens My Health Records, finance and other personal data with tax and social security systems.

This chapter covered increasing adoption of digital e-health technologies such as health informatics and 'My Health Records' to transform and empower the patients to control their health records, have access choose the right healthcare provider and suitable treatment, when required. It has been a challenge for the healthcare practitioners, hospital staff as well as patients to accept, embrace and adopt transformative digital e-health technologies and manage their healthcare records amidst concerns of slow adoption by the patient due to data privacy and cybersecurity issues. This chapter discussed the challenges of embracing e-health digital technologies and assurance of advancing cybersecurity of individuals My Health Record', which will transform e-health provision and experience for patients and the healthcare providers. It is time to continually re-engineer and upgrade cybersecurity firewalls and technology with the aim to meet patients and health sectors needs to protect patient privacy and confidential healthcare data and medical images from cyber-crime. Professional staff of information technology and cybercrime division along with healthcare professionals, government, regulators, businesses and community should work in partnership to protect health information without sacrificing and compromising patient's data privacy and security, and strengthen cyber security at all levels.

# REFERENCES

Andrews, L., Gajanayake, R., & Sahama, T. (2014). The Australian general public's perceptions of having a personally controlled electronic health record. *International Journal of Medical Informatics*, *83*(12), 889–900. doi:10.1016/j.ijmedinf.2014.08.002 PMID:25200198

Atienza, A. A., Zarcadoolas, C., Vaughon, W., Hughes, P., Patel, V., Chou, W.-Y., & Pritts, J. (2015). Consumer Attitudes and Perceptions on mHealth Privacy and Security: Findings from a Mixed-Methods Study. *Journal of Health Communication*, *20*(6), 673–679. doi:10.1080/10810730.2015.1018560 PMID:25868685

Aunger, C. (2020). *It's Time to Re-engineer Healthcare Cybersecurity. Forbes Technology Council.* Available from www.forbes.com/sites/forbestechcouncil/2020/08/05/its-time-to-re-engineer-health-care-cybersecurity/?sh=e74c6f412784

Australian Digital Health Agency (ADHA). (2019). *My Health Record.* Available from https://www.myhealthrecord.gov.au/for-you-your-family/what-is-my-health-record

Australian Government. (2016). *MyHRCs Rule 2016.* Available from https://www.legislation.gov.au/Details/F2016C00607

Australian Government. (2019). *My Health Record Statistics*. Available from https://www.myhealthrecord.gov.au/sites/default/files/my_health_record_dashboard_-_28_july_2019.pdf?v=1565831963

Baldwin, J. L., Singh, H., Sittig, D. F., & Giardina, T. D. (2017). Patient portals and health apps: Pitfalls, promises, and what one might learn from the other. *Health Care*, *5*(3), 81–85. PMID:27720139

Bhuyan, S. S., Bailey-DeLeeuw, S., Wyant, D. K., & Chang, C. F. (2016). Too Much or Too Little? How Much Control Should Patients Have Over EHR Data? *Journal of Medical Systems*, *40*(7), 174. doi:10.100710916-016-0533-2 PMID:27272134

Bhuyan, S. S., Kabir, U. Y., Escarino, J. M., Ector, K., Palakodeti, S., ... Dobalian, A. (2020). Transforming Healthcare Cybersecurity from Reactive to Proactive: Current Status and Future Recommendations. *Journal of Medical Systems*, *44*(98), 98. Advance online publication. doi:10.100710916-019-1507-y PMID:32239357

Bogle, A. (2018). *Healthcare data a growing target for hackers, cybersecurity experts warn*. Available from https://www.abc.net.au/news/science/2018-04-18/healthcare-target-for-hackers-experts-warn/9663304

Chandrakar, P. (2021). A Secure Remote User Authentication Protocol for Healthcare Monitoring Using Wireless Medical Sensor Networks. In *Research Anthology on Telemedicine Efficacy* (pp. 549–572). Adoption, and Impact on Healthcare Delivery. www.igi-global.com/chapter/a-secure-remote-user-authentication-protocol-for-healthcaremonitoring-using-wireless-medical-sensor-networks/

Commonwealth of Australia. (2012). *MyHRCs Act 2012 (Australia)*. Available from https://www.legislation.gov.au/Series/C2012A00063

Commonwealth of Australia. (2015). *MyHRCs Regulation 2012 (Australia)*. Available from https://www.legislation.gov.au/Details/F2016C00093

Conaty-Buck, S. (2017). Cyber security and healthcare records. Tips for ensuring patient safety and privacy. *American Nurse Today*, *12*(9), 62–65.

Coventry, L., & Branley, D. (2018). Cybersecurity in healthcare: A narrative review of trends, threats and ways forward. *Maturitas*, *113*, 48–52. doi:10.1016/j.maturitas.2018.04.008 PMID:29903648

Davidson, H. (2019). My Health Record failed to manage cybersecurity and privacy risk- audit finds. *The Guardian*. Available from https://www.theguardian.com/australia-news/2019/nov/25/my-health-record-failed-to-manage-cybersecurity-and-privacy-risks-audit-finds

Department of Health. (2016, March). MyHRC *Stastics*. Canberra: Australian Government. Available from https://myhealthrecord.gov.au/internet/mhr/publishing.nsf/

Department of Home Affairs. (2020). *Australia's Cyber Security Strategy*. Available from https://www.homeaffairs.gov.au/about-us/our-portfolios/cyber-security/strategy

Ehrenfeld, J. M. (2017). WannaCry, Cybersecurity and Health Information Technology: A time to act. *Journal of Medical Systems*, *41*(7), 104. doi:10.100710916-017-0752-1 PMID:28540616

Fernández-Alemán, J. L., Carrión Señor, I., Lozoya, P. L. O., & Toval, A. (2013). Security and privacy in electronic health records: A systematic literature review. *Journal of Biomedical Informatics*, *46*(3), 541–562. doi:10.1016/j.jbi.2012.12.003 PMID:23305810

Fernando, J., & Dawson, L. (2009). The health information system security threat lifecycle: An informatics theory. *International Journal of Medical Informatics*, *78*(12), 815–826. doi:10.1016/j.ijmedinf.2009.08.006 PMID:19783203

Greenlalgh, T., Hinder, S., Stramere, K., Bratan, T., & Russell, J. (2010). Adoption, non-adoption, and abandonment of a personal electronic health record: Case study of HealthSpace. *Biomedical Journal*, *341*, c5814. doi:10.1136/bmj.c581 PMID:21081595

Greenlee, M. (2021). *Cybersecurity for Healthcare: Addressing Medical Image Privacy*. Available from https://securityintelligence.com/articles/cybersecurity-for-healthcare-problems-and-solutions/

Harman, L. B., Flite, C. A., & Bond, K. (2012). Electronic Health Records: Privacy, Confidentiality, and Security. *AMA Journal of Ethics*, *14*(9), 712–719. doi:10.1001/virtualmentor.2012.14.9.stas1-1209 PMID:23351350

HIPPA Journal. (2019). *2019 Healthcare Data Breach Report*. Available from https://www.hipaajournal.com/2019-healthcare-data-breach-report/

Jalali, M. S., & Kaiser, J. P. (2018). Cybersecurity in Hospitals: A Systematic, Organizational Perspective. *Journal of Medical Internet Research*, *20*(5), e10059. doi:10.2196/10059 PMID:29807882

Jalali, M. S., Razak, S., Gordon, W., Perakslis, E., & Madnick, S. (2019). Health care and cybersecurity: Bibliometric analysis of the literature. *Journal of Medical Internet Research*, *21*(2), e12644. doi:10.2196/12644 PMID:30767908

Kelly, J. M. (2020). Australia would benefit from US-Style health Information Security regulation. *The Journal of Law and Technology*, *1*(2), 1–24.

Kerai, P., Wood, P., & Martin, M. (2014). A pilot study on the views of elderly regional Australians of personally controlled electronic health records. *International Journal of Medical Informatics*, *83*(3), 201–209. doi:10.1016/j.ijmedinf.2013.12.001 PMID:24382474

Kim, M. I., & Johnston, K. B. (2002). Personal Health Records: Evaluation of Functionality and Utility. *Journal of the American Medical Informatics Association: JAMIA*, *9*(2), 171–180. doi:10.1197/jamia. M0978 PMID:11861632

Krawiec, R., & White, M. (2016). *Blockchain: Opportunities for health care*. Available from: https://www2.deloitte.com/content/dam/Deloitte/us/Documents/public-sector/us-blockchainopportunities-for-health-care.pdf

Kuo, T. T., Kim, H. E., & Ohno-Machado, L. (2017). Blockchain distributed ledger technologies for biomedical and health care applications. *Journal of the American Medical Informatics Association: JAMIA*, *24*(6), 1211–1220. doi:10.1093/jamia/ocx068 PMID:29016974

Langer, G. (2017). Cybersecurity Issues in Healthcare Information Technology. *Journal of Digital Imaging*, *30*(1), 117–125. doi:10.100710278-016-9913-x PMID:27730416

Lehnbom, E. C., McLachlan, A., & Brien, J. A. (2012). A qualitative study of Australians' opinions about personally controlled electronic health records. *Studies in Health Technology and Informatics*, *178*, 105–110. PMID:22797027

Medhekar, A. (2021). Digital Health Innovation Enhancing Patient Experience in Medical Travel. In *Research Anthology on Telemedicine Efficacy, Adoption, and Impact on Healthcare Delivery. Edition1* (pp. 199–223). IGI Global. doi:10.4018/978-1-7998-8052-3.ch011

Medhekar, A., & Nguyen, J. (2020). My Digital Healthcare Record: Innovation, Challenge and Patient Empowerment. In K. Sandhu (Ed.), *Opportunities and Challenges in Digital Healthcare Innovation* (pp. 131–150). IGI Global., doi:10.4018/978-1-7998-3274-4.ch008

Medhekar, A., & Wong, H. (2020). Medical Travellers' Perspective on Factors Affecting Medical Tourism to India. *Asia Pacific Journal of Tourism Research*, *25*(12), 1295–1310. doi:10.1080/10941665.2 020.1837893

Merriam-Webster. (2021). *Cybersecurity*. Available from https://www.merriam-webster.com/dictionary/cybersecurity

Nazi, K. M., Hogan, T. P., Wagner, T. H., McInnes, D. K., Smith, B. M., Haggstorm, D., Chumbler, N. R., Gifford, A. L., Charters, K. G., Saleem, J. J., Weingardt, K. R., Fischetti, L. F., & Weaver, F. M. (2010). Embracing a Health Services Research Perspective on Personal Health Records: Lessons Learned from the VA My HealtheVet System. *Journal of General Internal Medicine*, *25*(1), 62–67. doi:10.100711606-009-1114-6 PMID:20077154

Nigrin, D. J. (2014). When "Hacktivists" Target Your Hospital. *The New England Journal of Medicine*, *371*(5), 393–395. doi:10.1056/NEJMp1407326 PMID:25075830

OAIC. (2021b). *Tips to protect My Health Record*. Available from https://www.oaic.gov.au/privacy/health-information/my-health-record/tips-to-protect-your-my-health-record/

Office of Australian Information Commissioner (OAIC). (2021a). *Health Information Privacy*. Available from https://www.oaic.gov.au/privacy/health-information/

Pandey, P., & Litoriya, R. (2020). Securing and authenticating healthcare records through blockchain technology. *Cryptologia*, *44*(4), 341–356. doi:10.1080/01611194.2019.1706060

Pavithra, V., & Chandrasekaran, J. (2021). Developing Security Solutions for Telemedicine Applications: Medical Image Encryption and Watermarking. In *Research Anthology on Telemedicine Efficacy, Adoption, and Impact on Healthcare Delivery* (pp. 612-631). Retrieved from www.igi-global.com/chapter/developing-security-solutions-for-telemedicineapplications/

Perakslis, E. D. (2014). Cybersecurity in Health Care. *The New England Journal of Medicine*, *371*(5), 395–397. doi:10.1056/NEJMp1404358 PMID:25075831

Queensland Health. (2017). *Digital Health Strategic Vision for Queensland 2026*. Retrieved from https://www.health.qld.gov.au/__data/assets/pdf_file/0016/645010/digital-health-strat-vision.pdf

Regola, N., & Chawla, N. V. (2013). Storing and Using Health Data in a Virtual Private Cloud. *Journal of Medical Internet Research*, *15*(3), e63. doi:10.2196/jmir.2076 PMID:23485880

Rowe, D. C., Lunt, B. M., & Ekstrom, J. J. (2011). *The Role of Cyber-Security in Information Technology Education*. SIGITE'11, West Point, NY, USA. .2047628 doi:10.1145/2047594

Russo, E., Sittig, D. F., Murphy, D. R., & Singh, H. (2018). Challenges in patient safety improvement research in the era of electronic health records. *Health Care*, *4*(4), 285–290. PMID:27473472

Schumacher, A. (2017). *Reinventing healthcare: Towards a global, blockchain-based precision medicine ecosystem*. Available from: https://www.researchgate.net/publication/317936859_Blockchain_Healthcare_-_2017_Strategy_Guide

Sharma, R., & Purohit, M. (2018). Emerging Cyber Threats and the Challenges Associated with them. *International Research. Journal of Engineering Technology*, *5*(2). https://www.irjet.net/archives/V5/i2/IRJET-V5I2127.pdf

Shaw, T., Hines, M., & Kielly-Carroll, C. (2017). *Impact of Digital Health on the Safety and Quality of Health Care*. Sydney: ACSQHC. Available from https://www.safetyandquality.gov.au/

Sittig, D. F. (2002). Personal health records on the internet: A snapshot of the pioneers at the end of the 20th Century. *International Journal of Medical Informatics*, *65*(1), 1–6. doi:10.1016/S1386-5056(01)00215-5 PMID:11904243

Sittig, D. F., Belmont, E., & Singh, H. (2018). Improving the safety of health information technology requires shared responsibility: It is time we all step up. *Health Care*, *6*(1), 7–12. PMID:28716376

Tanwar, S., Parekh, K., & Evans, R. (2020). Blockchain-based electronic healthcare record system for healthcare 4.0 applications. *Journal of Information Security and Applications*, *50*, 102407. Advance online publication. doi:10.1016/j.jisa.2019.102407

Tanwar, S., Tyagi, S., & Kumar, N. (2019). Security and Privacy of Electronic Health Records. London, UK: The Institution of Engineering and Technology.

Varadharajan, V. (2018). *Cybersecurity and privacy issues surrounding My health records*. Retrieved from https://www.newcastle.edu.au/newsroom/research-and-innovation/my-health-record

William, C. M., Chaturvedi, R., & Chakravarthy, K. (2020). Cybersecurity Risks in a Pandemic. *Journal of Medical Internet Research*, *22*(9), e23692. doi:10.2196/23692 PMID:32897869

Wood, S., Schwartz, E., Tuepker, A., Pres, N. A., Nazi, K. M., Turvery, C., & Nichol, W. P. (2013). Patient Experiences with Full Electronic Access to Health Records and Clinical Notes Through the My HealtheVet Personal Health Record Pilot: Qualitative Study. *Journal of Medical Internet Research*, *15*(3), e65. doi:10.2196/jmir.2356 PMID:23535584

Zhang, P., Schmidt, D., White, J., & Lenz, G. (2018). Blockchain technology use cases in healthcare. In *Advances in Computers*. Elsevier.

Zhou, L., Varadharajan, V., & Gopinath, K. (2016). A Secure Role-Based Cloud Storage System for Encrypted Patient-Centric Health Records. *The Computer Journal*, *59*(11), 1593–1611. doi:10.1093/comjnl/bxw019

## ADDITIONAL READING

Al-Muhtadi, J., Shahzad, B., Saleem, K., Jmeel, W., & Orgun, M. A. (2017). Cybersecurity and privacy issues for socially integrated mobile healthcare applications operating in a multi-cloud environment. *Health Informatics Journal*, *25*(2), 315–329. doi:10.1177/1460458217706184 PMID:28480788

Amatayakul, M. K. (2012). *Electronic Health Records: A Practical Guide for Professionals and Organizations* (5th ed.). American Health Information Management Association.

Ayala, L. (2016). *A Guide to Detection and Prevention*. Springer. Available from https://link.springer.com/content/pdf/10.1007/978-1-4842-2155-6.pdf

Bray, K., & Mihm, U. (2019). M*y Health Record- what you need to know- stay in or opt out*. Retrieved from https://www.choice.com.au/health-and-body/health-practitioners/online-health-advice/articles/my-health-record-and-what-you-need-to-know

Burke, W., Oseni, T., Jolfraei, A., & Gongal, I. (2019). Cybersecurity Indexes for eHealth. *Proceedings of the Australasian Computer Science Week Multiconference*. Article No. 17, 1-18 10.1145/3290688.3290721

Clauson, K., Breeden, E., Davidson, C., & Mackey, T. (2018). Leveraging Blockchain Technology to Enhance Supply Chain Management in Healthcare. *Blockchain in Healthcare Today*, *10*. Advance online publication. doi:10.30953/bhty.v1.20

Coventry, L., & Branley, D. (2018). Cybersecurity in healthcare: A narrative review of trends, threats and ways forward. *Maturitas*, *113*, 48–52. doi:10.1016/j.maturitas.2018.04.008 PMID:29903648

Offner, K. L., Sitnikova, E., Joiner, K., & MacIntyre, C. R. (2020). Towards understanding cybersecurity capability in Australian healthcare organisations: A systematic review of recent trends, threats and mitigation. *Intelligence and National Security*, *35*(4), 556–585. doi:10.1080/02684527.2020.1752459

Webb, T., & Dayal, S. (2017). Building the wall: Addressing cybersecurity risks in medical devices in the U.S.A. and Australia. *Computer Law & Security Review*, *33*(4), 559–563. doi:10.1016/j.clsr.2017.05.004

Wirth, A. (2020). Cyberinsights: COVID-19 and What It Means for Cybersecurity. *Biomedical Instrumentation & Technology*, *54*(3), 216–219. Advance online publication. doi:10.2345/0899-8205-54.3.216 PMID:32442003

## KEY TERMS AND DEFINITIONS

**Blockchain Technology:** Blockchain technology is defined as an effective technology of chain of transactions or datasets, chained together by a cryptographic signature, stored in a shared ledger and supported by a network of connected nodes or processes, which are continuously updated, and data synced. Blockchain technology can help to prevent data breaches in the healthcare industry, as it is a secure method of recording, storing, sharing, and updating sensitive data of the patients.

**Confidentiality:** Personal health records of the patients, must be protected from being misused by those who are not concerned with it. The information of the patient must be released only with patient's formal consent and authorized medical persons have access to the information for clinical treatment or research purposes.

**Cybersecurity Risk:** Measures taken by an organsiation such as banks, hospitals, universities, schools, businesses, governments, and individuals to protect their own computer or computer systems in an organsiation as a whole from internet hackers, malwares or cyber-attacks.

**Digital Health Technology:** Digital health technology also known as e-health technology is convergence of digital technologies and internet with healthcare records and reports, mobile-phones, apps, tablets and computer vis the internet to improve people's health and maximise impact. Digital health helps to enhance efficiency in healthcare service delivery for effective and positive healthcare outcomes, providing personalized and precise healthcare plan.

**Digital Transformation:** Digital transformation is the process of using internet based digital technologies to create, improve and transform existing business processes that is re-engineering and innovating digital health technology applications continuously. This will not only manage risk from cyber-threat but also improve consumer use experience and value by the patients and the healthcare providers, to meet changing healthcare needs of the consumers, hospitals and healthcare organisations efficiency.

**Healthcare Data Integrity:** Data integrity related to accuracy of healthcare data. Due to electronic data interchange and exchange of information between the diagnostic clinics and general practitioners, clinicians or relevant medical professionals between healthcare organisations, data can be changed or tampered with as it moves between healthcare organisations, resulting in poor documentation integrity and errors in medical records.

**Information Security:** Information security can be defined as preserving and protecting patient's data in terms of confidentiality, integrity, and availability of patients' personal health information data by the hospital, healthcare providers, healthcare professionals such as doctors, clinicians, physicians, nurses and allied healthcare staff. The back-up of electronic data is essential in case of cyber-attack.

**My Health Record:** My Health Record is a personal health record and summary of individuals key health information in an electronic or digital format on a patient portal. Patients can maintain, manage and provide access to their personal health information to healthcare providers such as their doctor or hospital regarding medication, allergies and diagnostic tests results. This e-health information is private, and protected, in a secure confidential online digital environment.

*This research was previously published in the Handbook of Research on Advancing Cybersecurity for Digital Transformation; pages 79-98, copyright year 2021 by Information Science Reference (an imprint of IGI Global).*

# Section 3
# Securing Medical Images

# Chapter 22
# Secure Access to Biomedical Images

**Tariq Javid**
*Hamdard University, Pakistan*

## ABSTRACT

*This chapter introduces a framework for secure access to biomedical images. Biomedical images are acquired using a vast array of imaging techniques depending upon the specific application. A magnetic resonance spatial domain image is acquired by taking inverse weighted Fourier transform of raw frequency domain data generated by the modality. After correction, these images are stored in a standard format. The access to these stored images is typically subjected to authorization. Medical information in biomedical images needs to be protected in both stored form and in transmission. Encryption technologies are used to secure information whereas compression technologies are used to reduce the information without affecting the contents. In this chapter, a cryptocompression system is proposed which integrates both encryption and compression to fulfill the requirements of electronic protected health information records.*

## INTRODUCTION

Biomedical images are generally imagined images that are acquired by the application of physical principles. These images are often valuable and typically require implementation of information security measures for authorized access. This chapter introduces a framework for secure access to biomedical images.

Images are acquired, stored, transferred from one place to another, and processed. Information and communication technologies play an important role to accomplish these tasks. Commercial systems use intensive computing resources to apply complex image processing and analysis algorithms in order to produce desired results. These results are useful for further examination by medical experts or computer-based expert systems.

Biomedical images are acquired using a vast array of imaging techniques depending upon the specific application. A magnetic resonance spatial domain image is acquired by taking inverse weighted Fourier

DOI: 10.4018/978-1-6684-6311-6.ch022

transform of raw frequency domain data generated by the modality. After correction, these images are stored in a standard format. Access to these stored images is typically subjected to authorization.

Information security measures are helpful in order to provide a controlled access to biomedical images. These security measures ensure protection of useful information in images from unauthorized access, manipulation, and deletion. These aspects of information security are referred to as information confidentiality, integrity, and availability – the CIA triad model. The model provides useful insights on how information needs to be protected in the presence of a wide variety of threats.

Encryption and compression standards are useful when images are archived and retrieved over a network medium. Compression is used optionally to lower the impact of encryption overhead. In this chapter, components and function of a proposed cryptocompression system with advanced encryption standard and joint photographic experts group 2000 standard for biomedical image processing are described. The structure and objectives of this chapter are as follows:

- Provide an overview of fundamental security concepts, CIA triad model, framework, and related standards helpful to provide secure access to biomedical images.
- Briefly review information security research that enabled the protection of digital images in general and biomedical images in particular.
- Explain proposed framework components and function.
- Outline challenges and future research trends.

## BACKGROUND

### Information Security

Information security (INFOSEC) refers to the protection of information contents and information systems against unauthorized access and modification in stored form, during processing, or in transmission channel (Kissel, 2013). It ensures information availability to authorized users by preventing denial of service attacks. It includes security measures that are necessary to detect, document, and counter threats. INFOSEC ensures confidentiality, integrity, and availability of information – known as the confidentiality, integrity, and availability (CIA) triad model. Figure 1 shows the CIA triad model. This model is designed to guide INFOSEC policies in organizations. The model terms are briefly defined with implementation technologies as follows:

- Confidentiality refers to authorized access and is implemented with cryptographic techniques.
- Integrity refers to consistency and is implemented with digital signatures and hash algorithms.
- Availability refers to timely and reliable access and is implemented with secure redundant systems and networks.

*Table 1. Acronyms*

| Acronym | Term |
|---|---|
| AE | Application Entity |
| AES | Advanced Encryption Algorithm |
| AWS | Amazon Web Services |
| ePHI | Electronic Protected Health Information |
| CIA | Confidentiality, Integrity, and Availability |
| CSA | Compressed and Secure Archive |
| CT | Computed Tomography |
| DES | Data Encryption Standard |
| DHCP | Dynamic Host Configuration Protocol |
| DICOM | Digital Imaging and Communications in Medicine |
| EHR | Electronic Health Record |
| FSAMI | Framework for Secure Access to Medical Images |
| INFOSEC | Information Security |
| HIPAA | Health Insurance Portability and Accountability Act |
| HIS | Hospital Information System |
| HL7 | Health Level Seven |
| ISCL | Integrated Secure Communication Layer |
| JPEG | Joint Photographic Experts Group |
| LDAP | Lightweight Directory Access Protocol |
| MRI | Magnetic Resonance Imaging |
| NEMA | National Electrical Manufacturers Association |
| NIST | National Institute of Standards and Technology |
| PHI | Protected Health Information |
| PGM | Portable Gray Map |
| RIS | Radiology Information System |
| TLS | Transport Layer Security |
| WAF | Web Application Firewall |

*Figure 1. Confidentiality, integrity, and availability (CIA) triad model*

## Cryptography

Cryptology refers to data storage and communication in a secret manner (Simmons, 2016). It includes both cryptography and cryptanalysis. Cryptography refers to key-controlled transformations of information that is either impossible or computationally infeasible to decipher. Cryptanalysis refers to the art of recovering ciphered information without the knowledge of key. Cryptographic systems are generally classified as cipher systems, key cryptosystems, and block or stream ciphers. A short description of each term is as follows:

- Cipher systems generally use mathematical operations: transpositions and substitutions.
- Key cryptosystems employ either symmetric key or asymmetric keys.
- Block or stream ciphers break plaintext into blocks or streams for encryption.

Encryption at transmitter and decryption at receiver require significant computing resources. An approach to lower the effect of computational overhead is to use compression for data communication. Two main encryption standards are advanced encryption standard (AES) (Daemen & Rijmen, 2011) and data encryption standard (DES) (Paar, & Plzl, 2010). Both AES and DES are block cipher based on symmetric encryption and published as national institute of standards and technology (NIST) standards.

Figure 2 shows a public-private key cryptosystem. The public key of receiving entity is used at transmitter to encrypt plaintext. The receiving entity uses the private key to decrypt the received cipher text. As the name suggests, the public key is available to everyone; however, only receiver has access to the private key to see the information in plaintext.

*Figure 2. Public-private key cryptosystem*

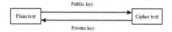

## Compression

Compression refers to data encoding using fewer bits. Data compression is an important area with applications in almost every field. The task is accomplished by identifying and exploiting following principle types of data redundancies (Gonzalez & Woods, 2008).

- Coding redundancy is reduced using code words assigned to various symbols.
- Spatial and temporal redundancy is reduced by exploiting similarity in nearby pixels and frames.
- Irrelevant information is reduced by exploiting information ignored by the human visual system.

Compression plays an important role in case of image data storage and transmission. Consider a typical case in which ten times reduction in image size is possible without affecting the information perception. In this case time required for image transmission reduces ten times. This saving is significant especially for a large image data set.

Compression include both lossy and up to lossless techniques. These techniques can be combined to compress part(s) of an image using lossless method whereas the rest of image is compressed in a lossy manner. Figure 3 shows transmission with compressed data. The transmitter sends compressed data which is decompressed at receiver.

*Figure 3. Transmission with compressed data*

## Cryptocompression System

A cryptocompression system has both cryptographic and compression modules. The system uses encryption, compression for at transmitter and decryption, decompression at receiver. Such a system is capable of providing both data security and data reduction at the same time. The computational cost is high at both transmitter and receiver. Both transmission time and storage requirements are reduced within a secure environment.

The decryption techniques do not tolerate a bit change in the encrypted cipher text for faithful data recovery. This poses a real constraint on conventional image transmission networks which are designed to preserve image quality without affecting the human perception. The introduction of bit change(s) in the received cryptocompressed data will result in useless decryptocompressed plain text. Therefore reliable transfer is essential requirement for faithful recovery of cryptocompressed data.

Two cryptocompression systems for secure transfer of medical images are proposed by Borie, Puech, and Dumas (2004). Their proposed systems are based on block cipher using tiny encryption algorithm (Wheeler & Needham, 1995) and stream cipher based on Vigenere's ciphering with the compression based on run length coding. Ali, Aziz, Akhtar, and Bhatti (2009) proposed a framework for secure access to medical images (FSAMI). Their developed algorithm used region-of-interest based cryptocompressed data with AES and joint photographic experts group (JPEG) 2000 standard. Figure 4 shows the FSAMI framework.

In FSAMI framework DICOM images are acquired either from modality or from archive. These images are converted to portable gray map (PGM) format. The region-of-interest is marked by the interactive process. The JJ2KEncoder is used to generate the compressed data. The compressed data contains region-of-interest compressed with lossless scheme whereas background is compressed with lossy scheme. These encryption schemes are defined in JPEG 2000 standard. After compression step, AES encryption is applied on lossless part. The cryptocompressed data is transmitted. There is an option to save this information in compressed and secure archive. The steps at receiver side are self-explanatory. Figure 5 shows resulting images at various stages of framework.

*Figure 4. Framework for secure access to medical images (Ali, Aziz, Akhtar, & Bhatti, 2009)*

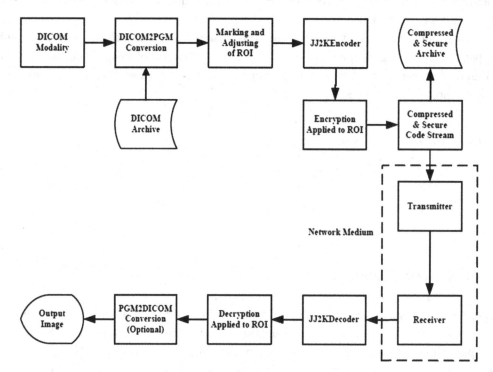

*Figure 5. Resulting images in the FSAMI framework (Ali, Aziz, Akhtar, & Bhatti, 2009)*

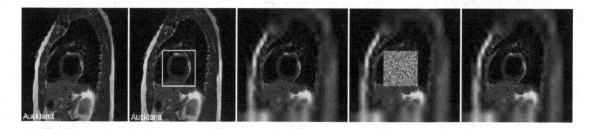

## Biomedical Images

An image is record of a scene captured at specific time. Presently, information shared on social media is mostly in the form of digital images. These images are taken by digital cameras. These cameras have imagining sensors that record incoming light intensity values in the form of an array of numbers. Biomedical images are internal anatomic records that provide biochemical and physiological analysis of tissues and organs (Collection Development Manual of the National Library of Medicine, 2004). These image are obtained by using medical imaging modalities, for example, computed tomography (CT), digital X-ray imaging, magnetic resonance imaging (MRI), molecular and cellular imaging, and scanning microscopies. Figure 6 shows an example of a biomedical image.

*Figure 6. Example of a biomedical image visualization (Arena, Rueden, Hiner, Wang, Yuan, & Eliceiri, 2016)*

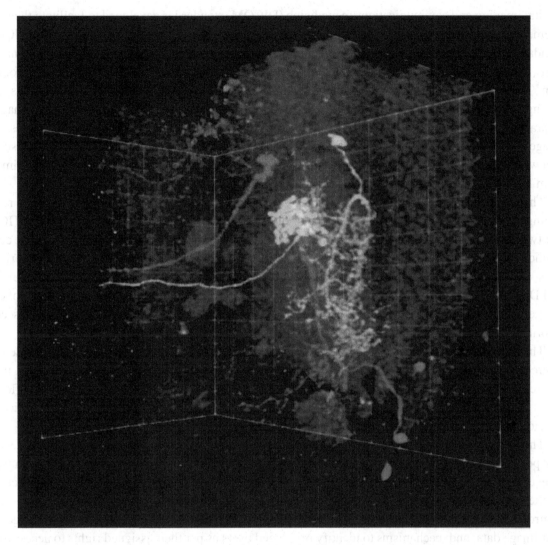

Biomedical images are important part of biomedical big data. Depending upon the nature and application, these images may have significant value for an organization. In such a case, there is a need to ensure secure access to authorized users. The security system implements required measures as per INFOSEC definition. Encryption technologies are considered primarily for secure storage and secure communication of important information.

Biomedical images are usually part of a clinical examination conducted by the radiology department of a healthcare organization as per recommendation by the consultant. A study may consist of several hundred images out of which fewer images may have relatively more diagnostic value. These diagnostically important images are marked jointly by the radiographer and medical expert during preparation of the study and at report sign-off by another medical expert. The marked images need to be accessible only to authorized users to ensure privacy of health information.

## Digital Imaging and Communication in Medicine

Digital imaging and communications in medicine (DICOM) standard is developed to facilitate the management and communication of medical images and related health records (NEMA, 2017). The DICOM standard provides interoperability for medical imaging devices and equipment for network communications, syntax and semantics of commands, media communication, and mandatory compliance information. The standard does not outline implementation details, overall set of features and functions, and testing/validation procedure. The standard is developed with an emphasis on diagnostic medical imaging as practiced in cardiology, dentistry, ophthalmology, pathology, radiology, and related disciplines, and image-based therapies such as interventional radiology, radiotherapy and surgery. It is also well suited to a wide range of information exchanged in healthcare environments. Figure 7 shows extracted image from DICOM format in R programming language using oro.dicom package (Whitcher, 2015).

The DICOM standard specify system management and security profiles which are defined by referencing externally developed standard protocols, such as dynamic host configuration protocol (DHCP), lightweight directory access protocol (LDAP), transport layer security (TLS) and integrated secure communication layer (ISCL). These protocols may use security techniques like public keys, public-private keys, and smart cards. There are a number of data encryption standardized available, for example AES and DES. The DICOM standard provides mechanisms that can be used to implement security policies to interchange objects and leaves the responsibility to establish and enforce appropriate policy to secure information on local administrator.

The DICOM standard specifies application specific subsets referred as application profiles used for interchange of medical images and related information on DICOM storage for specific clinical uses. These profiles follow the framework defined in the DICOM standard for the interchange of different types of information. An application profile has associated security settings that enable selection of cryptographic techniques to use with the secure media storage.

The DICOM standard only outlines mechanisms that may be used to implement appropriate security policies with regard to the DICOM objects interchange between application entities. For example, a security policy may enforce some level of access control. The standard assumes that the application entities (AEs) involved in a DICOM interchange have appropriate security policies which include access control, audit trails, physical protection, maintaining the integrity and confidentiality of both image and non-image data, and mechanisms to identify privileged users as per their assigned rights to access data. Essentially, each AE must insure security of local environment before initiating secure communications with other AEs.

## Health Level Seven Standards

Health information in electronic form is preferred due ease of access. Health Level Seven International (HL7) is a not-for-profit, ANSI-accredited organization. HL7 standards provide a framework to manage electronic health information. It is applicable on exchange, integration, sharing, and retrieval of such information. The set of standards defines how information is assembled for communication from one host computer to another, language, structure and data types required for interoperability between information systems. Figure 8 shows security labeling service (Jorgenson, Pyette, Davis, Connor, & Blobel, 2014). HL7 standards support clinical practice and the management, delivery of health services and evaluation. These standards are categories in following categories:

*Figure 7. DICOM image displayed using R (Javid, 2017)*

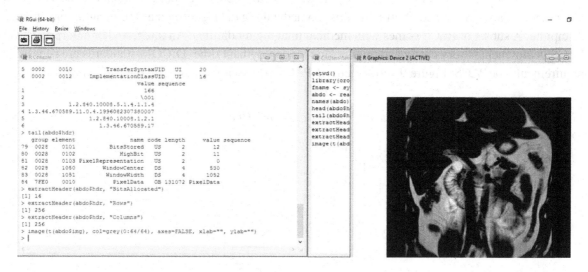

- Primary standards that are more frequently used in health organizations.
- Foundational standards define fundamental tools and building blocks to implement technology.
- Clinical and administrative domains contain messaging and document standards.
- Electronic health record (EHR) profiles provide functional models to manage medical information.
- Implementation guides to support and supplement standards implementation.
- Rules and references provide technical specification and programming structures.
- Education and awareness for adoption of HL7 standards.

*Figure 8. HL7 security labeling service (Jorgenson, Pyette, Davis, Connor, & Blobel, 2014)*

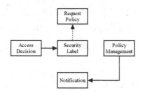

## Picture Archiving and Communication System

Picture archiving and communication system (PACS) based on digital, communication, display, and information technologies has revolutionized the practice of radiology and medicine (Huang, 2014). It includes digital imaging modalities to lower patient exposure to radiations, speed-up healthcare delivery, and reduction in overall medical operation costs. A digital radiology department has the following components:

- Radiology information system (RIS) as a subset of hospital information system (HIS).
- Digital imaging system like PACS that includes medical imaging modalities.

PACS contains high volume of radiographic data useful to improve quality patient care services and outcome. The art and science of utilizing this biomedical big data is termed as the imaging informatics discipline. A subset of PACS comes with medical imaging modalities. An integrated or enterprise level PACS deployment is very costly and requires longer deployment time. DICOM standards are necessary requirements for PACS. Figure 9 shows generic PACS components and basic dataflow model.

*Figure 9. Generic PACS components and basic data flow (Huang, 2014)*

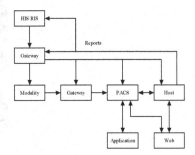

## HIPAA Compliance

Patient confidentiality is a serious concern for medical data and especially for images. This is the mandate of Health Insurance Portability and Accountability Act (HIPAA). The intent behind this act was to reform the healthcare industry by cost reduction, simplification of administrative processes and lowering burdens, and improving the security and privacy of medical health information. HIPAA act provides a conceptual framework for medical records security and integrity and enforce significant penalties in case of noncompliance. However, the guidelines provided by the act do not outline specific technical solutions. There is a consistent emphasis on the need for flexible solutions appropriate for a variety of clinical scenarios. Figure 10 shows an example of Amazon Web Services Web Application Firewall (AWS WAF) which is part of Amazon's HIPPA compliant cloud offerings.

The HIPAA privacy rule focused on the storage, access, and sharing of medical information of any individual. More specifically it outlines security standards to protect electronic health data records. These records are also known as electronic protected health information (ePHI). HIPAA compliance requires the following safeguards in place for ePHI:

- Physical safeguards include facility access and control with authorized access.
- Technical safeguards require access control with unique login credentials and security measures.
- Technical policies to ensure integrity and disaster recovery mechanism.
- Network, or transmission, security to protect information and information system from unauthorized access.

The HIPAA security rule requires covered entities (CEs) that are similar to DICOM AEs to maintain suitable administrative, technical, and physical safeguards for ePHI. Specifically, CEs must have the following measures in place (HHS.gov, 2013):

- Ensure the confidentiality, integrity, and availability of ePHI.
- Identify and protect against security threats.
- Protect against impermissible uses or disclosures.
- Ensure compliance by their workforce.

*Figure 10. HIPAA compliant Amazon Web Services Web Application Firewall (AWS WAF)*

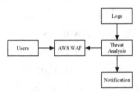

## PROPOSED FRAMEWORK

The proposed cryptocompression system for secure access to biomedical images is based on use of generic PACS components and data flow model in Huang (2014) with the framework for secure access to medical images (FSAMI) by Ali, Aziz, Akhtar, and Bhatti (2009). Figure 11 shows an integrated PACS and FSAMI system that has the ability to use cryptocompressed data for both storage and transmission. The compressed and secure archive (CSA) is accessible through FSAMI framework. Though other formulations for image data flow with cryptocompression are possible, the focus of discussion here is on the proposed formulation.

The FSAMI framework is connected to the PACS server, host, Web server, and modality. The communication from medical imaging modality is through the acquisition gateway.

*Figure 11. Proposed formulation for secure access to biomedical images with framework for secure access to medical images (FSAMI) and compressed and secure archive (CSA)*

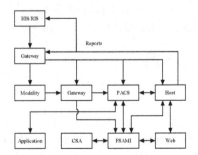

## Challenges

Data privacy and security is a big challenge and especially when data size is huge. This is especially true for the case of biomedical images. When encryption and compression schemes are applied to large size data, the computation overhead increases considerably.

A number of standards exist to provide guidance on privacy and security of medical information. However, the task to provide authorized access requires considerable efforts due persistent nature of challenges faced primarily due digital nature of biomedical images.

Cryptocompression systems need to be deployed and maintained in physically secure locations with limited physical access. However, the case of software is different. Their protection requires application of updates which are known to have effect on the overall reliability of system.

Both compression and encryption schemes require an ideal communication channel with no loss of information in transit. Loss of a single bit can result in significant quality degradation for complete or part of the image received. The multimedia networks for audio and video are known to tolerate information loss to a certain extent. However, this is not the case for a cryptocompression system.

Medical and radiographic experts are not convinced to use technologies which limit their ability to visualize beyond region-of-interest, compressed in a lossless manner. Author has many discussions with medical experts on use of compression for medical images. Most of them are not convinced to use such technology. The main reason stated was that all parts of a medical image are important at some point in time. The possibility of valuable diagnostic information loss has to be avoided in all cases. This mindset is a big challenge.

## FUTURE RESEARCH DIRECTIONS

The proposed formulation is a typical case which is a mere attempt to make the FSAMI framework fit for a hospital PACS deployment. Other formulations to integrate this cryptocompression system within the PACS environment are possible.

The proposed FSAMI framework may be used as a software plugin within PACS server and host workstation.

A hardware implementation of the optimized version of proposed formulation is also possible.

Author was unable to convince a medical expert while at BCBGC-09 conference, Orlando, USA; on why to apply such a technique only on the image part of DICOM file? Medical expert insisted to manipulate the DICOM header information in order to protect privacy. A valuable suggestion still awaited to be explored.

## CONCLUSION

This chapter has presented a possible practical implementation of a cryptocompression system for biomedical images. The proposed setup was explained by the introduction of an earlier developed framework for secure access to medical images in a hospital PACS environment. Cryptocompression systems offer an attractive choice to take care of privacy and security part of electronic protected health information.

Despite many challenges, the future is promising for both compression and encryption technologies for upcoming biomedical Big Data setups.

## ACKNOWLEDGMENT

Author would like to acknowledge Prof. Dr. Vali Uddin, Dean Faculty of Engineering Sciences & Technology, Hamdard University, Karachi Campus, Pakistan for his valuable suggestion toward this work which is closely related to author's research interests and industry experience.

## REFERENCES

Ali, T. J., Aziz, A., Akhtar, P., & Bhatti, M. I. (2009). A framework for secure access to medical images. *2009 International Conference on Bioinformatics, Computational Biology, Genomics and Chemoinformatics (BCBGC-09)*.

Arena, E. T., Rueden, C. T., Hiner, M. C., Wang, S., Yuan, M., & Eliceiri, K. W. (2016). Quantitating the cell: Turning images into numbers with ImageJ. *Wiley Interdisciplinary Reviews. Developmental Biology*, 6(2). doi:10.1002/wdev.260 PMID:27911038

Borie, J. C., Puech, W., & Dumas, M. (2004). Crypto-Compression System for Secure Transfer of Medical Images. *2nd Medical Image and Signal Processing*.

*Collection Development Manual of the National Library of Medicine*. (2004). 4th ed.). Bethesda, MD: U.S. Dept. of Health and Human Services, Public Health Service, National Institutes of Health, National Library of Medicine.

Daemen, J., & Rijmen, V. (2011). *The design of Rijndael: AES - the advanced encryption standard*. Berlin: Springer.

Gonzalez, R. C., & Woods, R. E. (2008). *Digital Image Processing* (3rd ed.). Pearson.

HHS.gov. (2013). *Summary of the HIPAA Security Rule*. Retrieved July 29, 2017, from https://www.hhs.gov/hipaa/for-professionals/security/laws-regulations/index.html

Huang, H. K. (2014). *PACS and Imaging Informatics: Basic Principles and Applications* (2nd ed.). Wiley-Blackwell.

Javid, T. (2017). How to read DICOM in R with oro.dicom? [Web log post]. Retrieved July 30, 2017, from http://tariqjavid72.blogspot.com/2017/07/how-to-read-dicom-in-r-with-orodicom.html

Jorgenson, D., Pyette, P., Davis, J. M., Connor, K., & Blobel, B. (2014). *HL7 Standard: Privacy, Access and Security Services (PASS) - Security Labeling Service, Release 1.0*. Academic Press.

Kissel, R. (Ed.). (2013). *Glossary of key information security terms*. Gaithersburg, MD: U.S. Dept. of Commerce, National Institute of Standards and Technology. doi:10.6028/NIST.IR.7298r2

NEMA PS3 / ISO 12052. (2017). *Digital Imaging and Communications in Medicine (DICOM) Standard*. Rosslyn, VA, USA: National Electrical Manufacturers Association (NEMA). Available at http://medical.nema.org/

Paar, C., & Pelzl, J. (2010). *Understanding Cryptography: A Textbook for Students and Practitioners*. Berlin: Springer Berlin. doi:10.1007/978-3-642-04101-3

Simmons, G. J. (2016). Cryptology. In *Encyclopædia Britannica*. Encyclopædia Britannica, Inc.

Wheeler, D., & Needham, R. (1995). TEA, a tiny encryption algorithm. In *Proceedings of the 1995 Fast Software Encryption Workshop*. Springer-Verlag.

Whitcher, B. (2015). Rigorous - DICOM Input / Output [R package oro.dicom version 0.5.0]. Retrieved July 31, 2017, from https://CRAN.R-project.org/package=oro.dicom

## ADDITIONAL READING

*Amazon Web Services, Inc.* (2017). Architecting for HIPAA Security and Compliance on Amazon Web Services.

*Announcing the Advanced Encryption Standard (AES)*. (2001). United States: National Institute of Standards and Technology.

Dey, N., Das, P., Chaudhuri, S. S., & Das, A. (2012). Feature analysis for the blind-watermarked electroencephalogram signal in wireless telemonitoring using Alattar's method. *Proceedings of the Fifth International Conference on Security of Information and Networks (SIN'12)*, 87-94. 10.1145/2388576.2388588

Dey, N., Mukhopadhyay, S., Das, A., & Chaudhuri, S. (2012). Analysis of P-QRS-T components modified by blind watermarking technique within the electrocardiogram signal for authentication in wireless telecardiology using DWT. *International Journal of Image, Graphics and Signal Processing, 4*(7).

Dey, N., Roy, A., Das, A., & Chaudhuri, S. (2012). Stationary Wavelet Transformation Based Self-recovery of Blind-Watermark from Electrocardiogram Signal in Wireless Telecardiology. *Recent Trends in Computer Networks and Distributed Systems Security*, 347-357. Introduction to HL7 Standards. (n.d). Retrieved July 29, 2017, from http://www.hl7.org/implement/standards

Dey, N., & Santhi, V. (2017). *Intelligent Techniques in Signal Processing for Multimedia Security*. Cham: Springer International Publishing. doi:10.1007/978-3-319-44790-2

Masmoudi, A., & Puech, W. (2014). Lossless chaos-based crypto-compression scheme for image protection. *IET Image Processing, 8*(12), 671–686. doi:10.1049/iet-ipr.2013.0598

Mhetre, N. A., Deshpande, A. V., & Mahalle, P. N. (2016). Trust Management Model based on Fuzzy Approach for Ubiquitous Computing. *International Journal of Ambient Computing and Intelligence, 7*(2), 33–46. doi:10.4018/IJACI.2016070102

National Institute of Standards and Technology. (1999). *FIPS PUB 46: Data Encryption Standard*. Washington, D.C.: U.S. Dept. of Commerce, National Bureau of Standards.

Sarkar, M., Banerjee, S., Badr, Y., & Sangaiah, A. K. (2017). Configuring a Trusted Cloud Service Model for Smart City Exploration Using Hybrid Intelligence. *International Journal of Ambient Computing and Intelligence*, 8(3), 1–21. doi:10.4018/IJACI.2017070101

Tamane, S., Solanki, V. K., & Dey, N. (2017). *Privacy and security policies in Big Data*. Hershey, PA: IGI Global, Information Science Reference. doi:10.4018/978-1-5225-2486-1

Yamin, M., & Sen, A. A. (2018). Improving Privacy and Security of User Data in Location Based Services. *International Journal of Ambient Computing and Intelligence*, 9(1), 19–42. doi:10.4018/IJACI.2018010102

## KEY TERMS AND DEFINITIONS

**Application Entity:** Application entity is a functional unit in DICOM. The imaging modality, server, or workstation in the PACS have unique application entities.

**Cryptocompression System:** A system which implements both encryption and compression technologies to generate cryptocompressed text from plain text.

**Cryptography:** Cryptography refers to key-controlled transformations of information that is either impossible or computationally infeasible to decipher.

**Cryptosystem:** A system which converts plain text to cipher text or cipher text to plain text by the application of encryption or decryption algorithm. The key generation for encryption and decryption algorithms is also part of a cryptosystem.

**Denial of Service (DoS) Attack:** A situation in which service is not available to an authorized user. A typical case of in which a malicious software code makes services inaccessible by overloading computing and network resources.

**Digital Imaging and Communications in Medicine:** Digital imaging and communications in medicine (DICOM) is the standard for the communication and management of medical images and related data.

**Distributed DoS Attack:** A distributed denial-of-service attack is a botnet attack in which multiple locations are used to attack on a service.

**Information Security:** Information security (INFOSEC) refers to the protection of information and information systems against unauthorized access and modification of information in storage, processing, or in transit.

**National Institute of Standards and Technology:** The National Institute of Standards and Technology (NIST) was founded in 1901 and is now part of the U.S. Department of Commerce.

**Picture Archiving and Communication System:** Picture archiving and communication system (PACS) includes digital imaging modalities to lower patient exposure to radiations, speed-up healthcare delivery, and reduction in overall medical operation costs.

*This research was previously published in the Handbook of Research on Information Security in Biomedical Signal Processing; pages 38-53, copyright year 2018 by Information Science Reference (an imprint of IGI Global).*

# Chapter 23
# Medical Signal Security Enhancement Using Chaotic Map and Watermarking Technique

**Ajita Sahay**
*KIIT University, India*

**Chittaranjan Pradhan**
*KIIT University, India*

**Amandip Sinha**
*West Bengal University of Technology, India*

## ABSTRACT

*This chapter explores medical signal security enhancement using chaotic map and watermarking techniques. This new approach provides security to both the medical image and also maintains the confidentially of both the patient and doctor. Medical image encryption is done by using 2D Gaussian iterated map and BARCODE ECC200. Personal data is encoded in barcode. The encrypted image and barcode are embedded using DCT and DWT, which provides high PSNR values and higher NC value, which help to provide more security.*

## INTRODUCTION

As a fast growing world, everyone uses internet for their communication where they exchange personal information, text, audio, still images, animation video etc. The transmission has been done through channel which arises the word security because it may be possible while image transferred through channel some hacker try to interrupt the channel and get the image or he can even modify the image. Hence, everyone wants security in every field. Thus, many new approaches have been developed to ensure the

DOI: 10.4018/978-1-6684-6311-6.ch023

security proof of originality and authentication. Image encryption is one of the method which has been proposed last few decades which deals with the modification of pixels of digital image (Wang, Ding, Zhang, & Ding, 2008).

In medical field, hospital – treatment – patient – doctors – disease are very common terms which are being used in this field but besides this, there is one more term which is called security in parallel moving in every one's mind whether he/she is a patient or doctor, because in any treatment hospital updates their database with patient full information like phone number, photo, age, identity proof, mail id, and the disease from which patient suffer, his/her diagnosis etc. Hospital also maintains their database for doctors which contains all information about doctors and also their patient names, their prescriptions to the patients. All these things are updated in their database. All these things are stored on a computer, which may be accessed illegally and someone may misuse the information to make fake identity etc. So, healthcare providers must take proper measures for patient data safety (Agrawal, & Sharma, 2016). PHI i.e. Patient health information referred as from an unofficial access and breaking of privacy and confidentiality. Hence, encryption is the best form of protection of such issues and to preserve the privacy confidentiality. So many different techniques are already introduced for the encryption. The federal government requires the secure handling of electronic media and PHI with standards put forth by the Health Insurance Portability and Accountability Act i. e. called HIPAA of 1996.

On the other hand, when patient visit first time for checkup to the consultant doctor, then that doctor first go through the previous record and documents of that patient before starting the treatment. One possible way is to send medical images along with a specialist report, over a computer network. Computer networks are complex and may be spying by the third party. That time the security problem may arise when patient data is sent over the network. Since security is our first concern and the security issues arise here, the medical imagery cannot be sent. Hence, to avoid such issues, the encryption technique is preferable for the protection of these data. So many different techniques are already introduced for the encryption because it is the best form of protection. Thus, in this chapter we try to provide security to both personnel as well as medical image.

Images are categorized as raster images and vector images. Raster images are defined as bitmap images, which are made up of bits, pixels. Each bit can be visualized as a dot which is defined by number of pixels per unit of measurement and it determines the resolution of the image, which is represented by ppi (pixel per inch) or dpi (dots per inch). Vector images are mathematical arrangements of points, where each point is connected by mathematical formulae. Most of the images are connected by straight lines.

Chittaranjan Pradhan et. al. (2014) explains digital watermarking is the technique which protects the data from being compromised or redistribution. It preserves the integrity and authenticity of the digital data. Digital watermarking technique is divided into two groups on the basis of feature set the watermark is embedded in; i.e. Spatial domain watermarking or Frequency domain (or Transform domain) watermarking. Spatial domain type deals with the image Matrix; whereas transform domain deals with the rate of which pixels value are changing in spatial domain.

## BACKGROUND

Different approaches have been proposed for providing security to medical images. Like medical image encryption, authors generate pseudo random numbers by using chaotic maps and applying XOR operation with each bit of image pixels. Some approaches provide security to both personnel and medical image at the same time. The following section deals with the work done by different researchers in this area.

A. Giakoumaki et. al. (2003) proposed a medical image watermarking scheme based on wavelet transform. This paper addressed the problems of medical confidentiality protection and both origin and data authentication. William Puech et. al. (2005) proposed a crypto-compression of medical images by selective encryption of DCT. This paper presented a method of partial or selective encryption for JPEG images. Yin Dai et. al. (2012) proposed a medical image encryption technique based on a composition of logistic maps and Chebyshev maps.

Amarit Nambutdee et. el. (2015) proposed a medical image encryption based on DCT-DWT domain combining 2D- Data matrix barcode. They used scrambling algorithm to hide the patient information and required unique patient password to access a real image. Muath AlShaikh et. al. (2016) proposed a novel CT scan image watermarking scheme in DWT transform coefficients. Ritu Agrawal et. al. (2016) proposed a medical image watermarking technique in the application of e-diagnosis using M-ary modulation. The proposed model was robust and lossless in nature. Amit Kumar Singh et. al. (2017) presented a comprehensive review of medical image watermarking techniques in both spatial and transform domain.

## IMAGE WATERMARKING

Digital watermarking is the process where information is inserted into digital signal, where signal may be video, audio, images etc. Digital watermarking is of four types (Pradhan, Rath, & Bisoi, 2012):

1. Perceptible Digital Watermarking
2. Imperceptible Digital watermarking
3. Blind Digital watermarking
4. Non-Blind Digital watermarking

Image watermarking technique is defined as some information in the form of image is embedded into original image. The embedded information may be visible or invisible. This hidden information is used to provide security to original image and also protect from illegal copying or misuse the information. The watermarking can be done in two ways as:

1. Spatial domain watermarking
2. Transform domain watermarking

## 1. Spatial Domain Technique

It deals with the pixels values of image by modifying it and generally analyze it with respect to time. This is one of the simplest way to embed the watermark. In spatial domain watermarking, the authors choose a pseudo random of pixel set and to modify the least significant bit. The major disadvantage of this technique is that it is very sensitive to noise and common signal. Hence it cannot be used in practical application generally (Abraham & Paul, 2014). One example of spatial domain are:

$$g(x,y) = \sum_{s=-a}^{a}\sum_{t=-b}^{b} \omega(s,t) f(x-s, y-t) \tag{1}$$

where, f (x, y) and g (x, y) are the input and output images respectively. The convolution kernel is w (s, t). The output image be generated by using the following equation.

$$g = \omega * f \tag{2}$$

*Figure 1. First level*

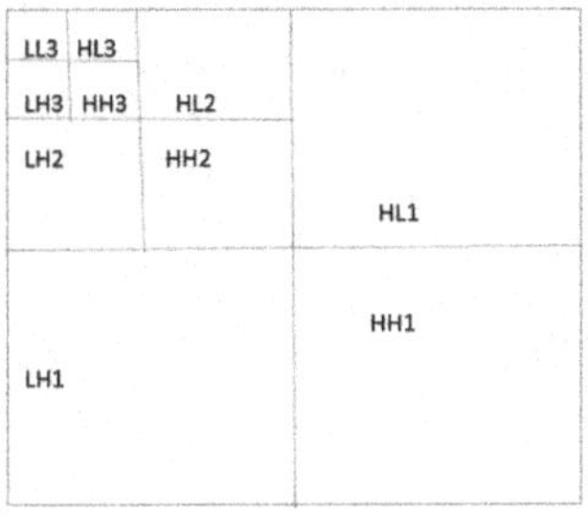

## 2. Transform Domain Technique

In Transform domain watermarking technique, digital image is processed by using specific transformation. This technique can be applied to either the whole image or the smaller blocks of it. The block size can be of 8 x 8 or 16 x 16 size. This technique (also known as frequency domain technique) analyzes with respect to frequency. In terms of transform domain, the image is split into various frequency bands. Frequency domain transform uses the techniques like DCT (Discrete Cosine Transform), DWT (Discrete Wavelet Transform) etc. to transfer an image to its frequency representation.

## a. DCT (Discrete Cosine Transform)

It helps to divide the image into two parts with respect to image's optical quality. It transforms the image from spatial domain to frequency domain (Abraham & Paul, 2014) as shown in Figure 5.

The general equation of DCT for one dimension is:

$$F(U) = \left(\frac{2}{N}\right)^{\frac{1}{2}} \sum_{i=0}^{N-1} \Delta(i) \cdot \cos\left[\frac{\pi.\mu}{2.N}(2i+1)\right] f(i) \tag{3}$$

The respective inverse 1D DCT transform is simple $F^{-1}(U)$ i.e.

*Figure 2. Second level*

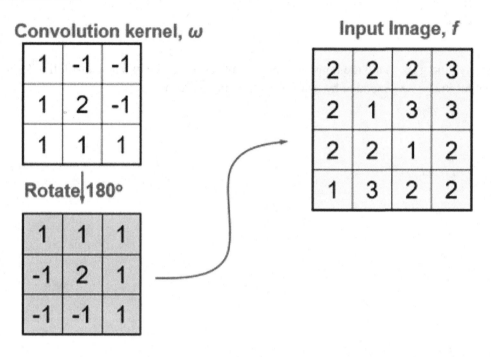

*Figure 3. Third level*

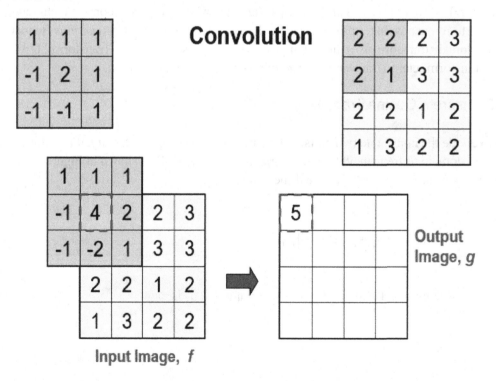

*Figure 4. Fourth level*

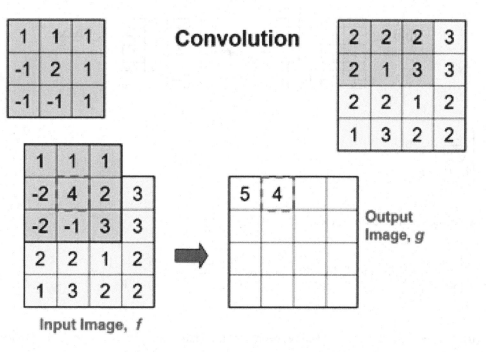

*Figure 5. DCT in block*

| 5 | 4 | 4 | -2 |
|---|---|---|---|
| 9 | 6 | 14 | 5 |
| 11 | 7 | 6 | 5 |
| 9 | 12 | 8 | 5 |

**Final output Image, *g***

*Figure 6. Cameraman image*

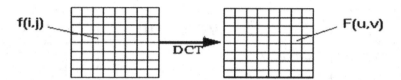

$$\Delta\left(i\right) = \begin{cases} \dfrac{1}{\sqrt{2}}, \varepsilon = 0 \\ 1, otherwise \end{cases} \tag{4}$$

The two dimension version of DCT is:

$$F\left(u,v\right) = \left(\dfrac{2}{\sqrt{UV}}\right) T\left(U\right) T\left(V\right) \sum_{X=0}^{U-1}\sum_{Y=0}^{V-1} f\left(x,y\right) x \cos\left(\dfrac{2x+1}{2U}\right)\pi u \cos\left(\dfrac{2y+1}{2V}\right)\pi v \tag{5}$$

where T(u), T(v) =1/ $\sqrt{2}$ , F(u, v) and F(x, y) represent the pixel value in DCT domain and spatial domain. M x N is the image's size. In many researches transform image by DCT then divided into non-overlapped M x M block. The inverse DCT equation is represented as:

$$F\left(x,y\right) = \left(\dfrac{2}{\sqrt{UV}}\right) \sum_{X=0}^{U-1}\sum_{Y=0}^{V-1} F\left(u,v\right) T\left(u\right) T\left(v\right) x \cos\left(\dfrac{2x+1}{2U}\right)\pi u \cos\left(\dfrac{2y+1}{2V}\right)\pi v \tag{6}$$

Following are the features of using DCT:

- It helps us to see what sine waves makeup our underlying signal. The more complex sine wave will more complex graph.
- Filtering involves like attenuating or removing certain frequencies.
- It is very efficient for multimedia compression.

Figure 6 represents the original cameraman image. After applying DCT to this image, the transformed image is represented by Figure 7. When inverse DCT is applied to this, the reconstructed image is generated as shown in Figure 8.

## b. DWT (Discrete Wavelet Transform)

According to the Fourier transformation concept, the signal is defined as sum of the information series of cosines and sines. This summation is also called Fourier expansion. This expansion is based on only frequency resolution and there is no time resolution involved. That means we are able to determine all the present frequency in the signal but we are unable to detect when they are present. To overcome this

*Figure 7. DCT converted image*

disadvantage of Fourier transform, discrete wavelet transform comes to the picture. DWT is able to represent a signal in time and frequency domain at the same time (Liu & Li, 2010; Pradhan, Rath, & Kumar Bisoi, 2012).

According to the Mallat-tree decomposition or Mallat algorithm, DWT is decomposed into successively by low pass filter and high pass filter (as shown in Figure 9).

Where, f is the signal, G denotes the low pass filter and H denotes the high pass filter. At each level of decomposition, the low pass filter gives coarse approximation and the high level gives detailed information.

The wavelet decomposition is always split into four parts i.e. horizontal direction, vertical direction, diagonal direction and low frequency part, and it can be decomposed on and on. The wavelet transformed image has a low frequency band LL3 and high frequency bands LHi, HLi, HHi where i=1 .. 3 (as shown in Figure 10). By taking Baboon image as the input, Figure 10 represents the three level DWT decomposition of it. The low frequency part with a few in horizontal, vertical and diagonal parts [G, H] concentrated the main energy.

## Data Matrix

Data matrix is also called as Two-Dimensional Barcode. Data matrix is mainly used for encoding large amount of data. Data may be in text format or in numeric format. Usually data size ranges from few bytes

*Figure 8. Reconstructed image*

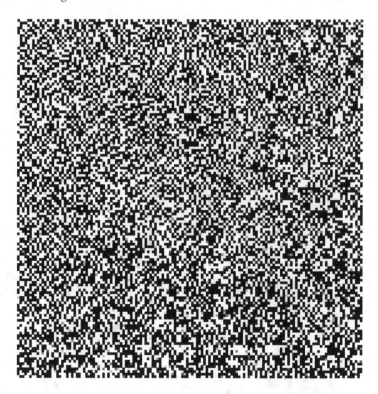

to 1556 bytes and the barcode size depends on the encoded message. In two dimensional barcode, it consist of only combination of two colors i.e. white and black. The shape of barcode is generally square or rectangle which represents the bits. The cells are categorized into two types: light or dark. Light cell is expressed as 0 and dark cell is expressed as 1 or vice versa.

Data matrix is made up of two solid adjacent boundaries borders in an L shape which is called finder path and other two borders consisting alternative light and dark cells which is called timing pattern. The encoded information are stored between these two boundaries of rows and column. Both the boundaries have their own responsibilities. For location and orient the symbols, finder path is used; whereas timing pattern is used to count the number of rows and columns in the symbol. Each code is unique which makes the barcode more secure. Error correction helps to increase the reliability of the barcode by making it readable even after damage of one or more cells because error correction enables reconstruction of the original data using different ways. Data matrix barcode are used in various purpose to prove originality, confidentiality, and authentication (Nambutdee & Airphaiboon, 2015). It is used in various fields like Paytm to accept payment, post office when parcel has been dispatched, industrial engineering, food industry etc.

New version of Data matrix of two dimensional barcode ECC 200 used in Reed-Solomon codes for error and recovery. ECC added some more extra features as compare to data matrix like:

- It provides light images on a dark background which is called inverse reading symbols.
- It extended channel interpretation i.e. specification of the character set.
- It uses rectangular symbols; whereas data matrix generally used square symbols.

*Figure 9. Mallat tree decomposition*

- It provides the structure which can link up to 16 different symbols for encoding large amount of data.

## Gauss Iterated Map

Chaotic map is very useful to ensure security. It has the properties like deterministic in nature, easy to generate and difficult to estimate. Gauss iterated map is one type of chaotic map which also generate a pseudo random number (Zhou, Shi, Bao, & Yang, 2010; Zhou, Bao, & Chen, 2014). It is a nonlinear iterated map of the reals into real interval as provided by Gaussian function:

$$X_{N+1} = \exp\left(-\alpha X_N^2\right) + \beta \tag{7}$$

where, $\alpha$ and $\beta$ are real parameters. Gauss iterated map shows best result when the value of $\alpha$ has some positive value lies between +1 to +6 and $\beta$ value lies between -1 to +1 (Zhou, Shi, Bao, & Yang, 2010). The bell shaped Gaussian function map is similar to logistic map. Figure 11 shows the Gaussian map with $\alpha$=4.9 and $\beta$= -1 to +1 which resembles like mouse, that's why it is also called as mouse map.

The basic feature of Gauss map which makes it different from logistic map are:

*Figure 10. Three levels of decomposition*

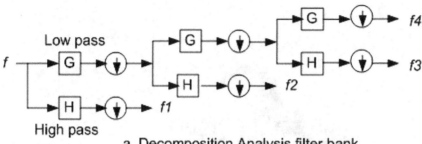

a. Decomposition Analysis filter bank

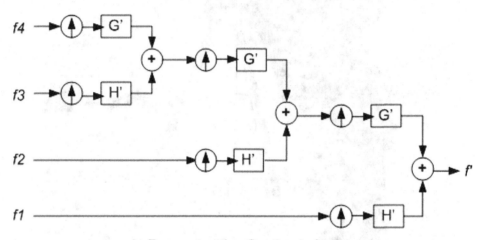

b. Reconstruction Synthesis filter bank

- Reverse period
- Coexisting Attractor
- Doubling
- Two parameters, i.e. $\propto$ and $\beta$

The analysis of its behavior of long term iterators and becomes more complicated than the logistic map. Let's consider an image with size M × M and generate a sequence up to image size, i.e. M x M iteration using Equation 7 and then quantized to binary format by using Equation 8.

$$S(i) = \begin{cases} 0, 0 < X(n) \le 0.5 \\ 1, 0.5 < X(n) \le 1 \end{cases} \qquad (8)$$

Where, X(n) is a random number in sequence and S(i) is quantized sequence. Then S (i) is XOR with each bit of M x M image to produce the encrypted image. The initial value lies between 0 and 1.

*Figure 11. 1D Gauss iterated map*

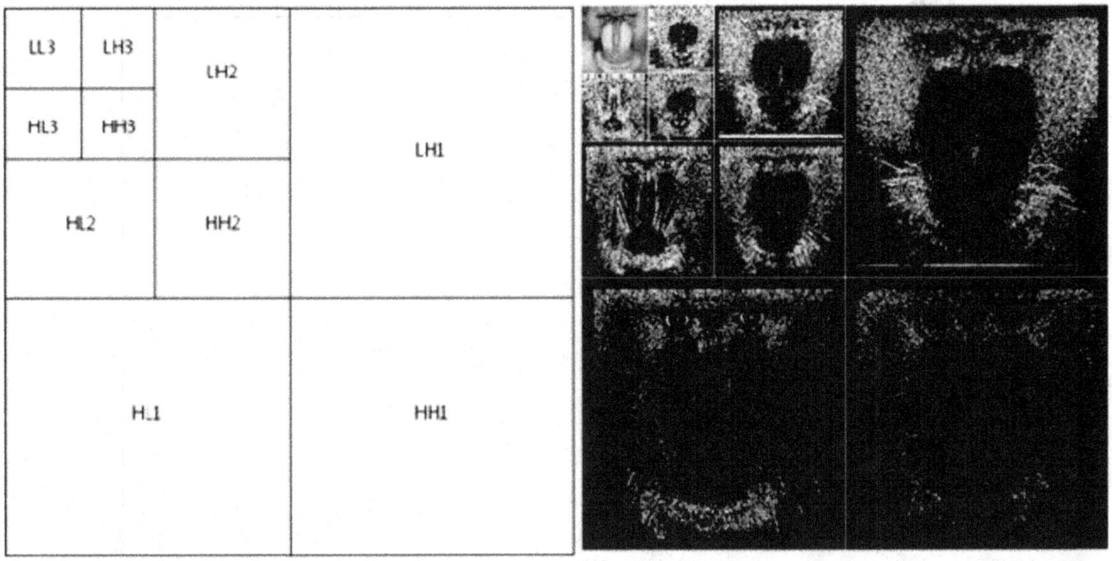

a. 3-level DWT decomposition          b. 3-level DWT decomposition of Image

## 2D Gauss Iterated Map

2D Gauss iterated map has come to overcome the disadvantage of 1D Gauss iterated map as well as 2D Logistic map. It has been developed by using more number of parameters and key spaces to make it more complex, robust and secure in nature (Pisarchik & Zanin, 2012; Sahay & Pradhan, 2017).

$$A[X,Y] = \begin{array}{l} X_{N+1} = \exp\left(-\alpha_1 X_N^2\right) + \beta_1 + \gamma_1 X_N^2 \\ Y_{N+1} = \exp(-\alpha_2 Y_N^2 + \beta_2 + \gamma_2 X_N^2 Y_N^2 \end{array} \tag{9}$$

where, N=1, 2, 3……. $\alpha 1, \beta 1, \gamma 1,_{\alpha} 2, \beta 2, \gamma 2_{\alpha}$ are the system control parameter. X0, Y0 are the initial conditions. The values of parameters range are

$$0 < X_N, Y_N \leq 1; 1.75 \leq \alpha_1 \leq 4.5; -1 \leq \beta_1 \leq 1; 3 \leq \gamma_1 \leq 5.5; 2 \leq \alpha_2 \leq 4.5; -1 \leq \beta_2 \leq 1; 3 \leq \gamma_2 \leq 4$$

Figure 12 shows the graph by taking

$$\alpha_1 = 2.9, \beta_1 = -0.56, \gamma_1 = 4.75, \alpha_2 = 3.53, \beta_2 = -0.81, \gamma_2 = 3.45, X_0 = 0.12, Y_0 = 0.34$$

As we can see the above graph has very complex structure which helps to provide more security during encryption process. The quantization function used to convert the decimal points to binary bits is:

*Figure 12. 2D Gauss iterated map*

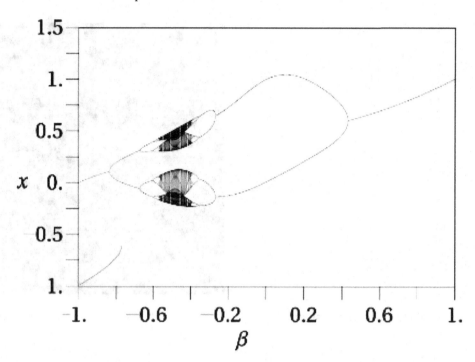

$$S(t) = \begin{cases} 0, 0 < 2K(i,j) \le 0.5 \\ 1, 0.5 < 2K(i,j) \le 1 \end{cases} \tag{10}$$

where, 2K(i, j) is a random number in sequence and S(t) is quantized sequence. In 2D Gauss iterated map, 1D matrix multiplied with Y transposed matrix to generate 2D Matrix. Which is called 2K Matrix (Kumar Kabi, Saha, Pradhan, & Bisoi, 2014).

## PROPOSED METHOD

In this proposed approach, we are embedding the information and provide security to personal information as well as medical image. The steps for embedding are:

- First patient updates his/her information in hospital database. The information is encoded using barcode ECC200. Then encode the information into data matrix.

1. Take the patient medical image and embed the barcode into that medical image by generating pseudo random sequence Gauss 2D iterated map (Liu, & Miao, 2016). The final embedding process has been done by using image watermarking.

## Watermark Embedding Process

The steps for watermark embedding are:

- First convert the personal data of patient in encrypted form by using two dimensional barcode i.e. ECC200 which helps to improve the high capacity of watermark W1.
- Then scrambling of pixels is done by using 2D Gauss iterated map on the original watermark image using Equation 9.
- Then second scrambling is performed by using 1D Gauss iterated map which is given in Equation 7. By the second scrambling we will make it more complex and follow the new sequence of sorting in ascending order defined in Equation 11 and Equation 12.

$$\text{New Sequence} = \text{Sort}_{\text{Ascending}}(X_i) \tag{11}$$

$$W_{s2} = W_{s1}(\text{New Sequence}) \tag{12}$$

- Apply DCT technique in the original cover image into 8 x 8 non overlapping blocks with N x N size of an original image, we get $A_{DCT}$ by using Equation 13.

$$A_{DCT}\left(P\right) = DCT\left(A_{D(i,j)}\right) \tag{13}$$

where, P=1, 2... N/8.

- Separate the original cover image into non overlapping block size 8 x 8. After that we apply DWT to the original image up to two level of decomposition to get the coefficient $DWT_{cff}$.
- By using the Equation 13, we store the value of the position (1, 2) in position (1, 1). DCT will use for comparison the position (1, 2) in next position which decide the considerable area for embed the information.
- $DWT_{cff\,(index)}$ is the matrix size N/8 x 1. Z is the matrix size of N/8 x N/8 as given in Equation 14.

$$T(\text{index}) = DWT_{eff(1,2)} \tag{14}$$

$$C\left(i\right) = \begin{cases} 0, if \ I_{DCT}\left(i\right) > T\left(i\right) \\ 1, if \ I_{DCT}\left(i\right) \le T\left(i\right) \end{cases} \tag{15}$$

$$B = \left[ DWT_{cff}\left(1\right), DWT_{cff}\left(2\right), \cdots DWT_{cff}\left(\frac{N}{8}\right) \right] \qquad (16)$$

where, index i =1, 2 ... N/8.

$$\operatorname{Re} m\left(i\right) = \begin{cases} 0, if\, C\left(i\right) = W_{s2}\left(i\right) \\ 1, if\, I_{DCT}\left(i\right) \le L\left(i\right) \end{cases} \qquad (17)$$

- Then apply IDWT up to two levels of decomposition and replace the value of T (i) in DWT$_{cff}$ using fifth step. I$_e$ is the image after embedment of the information. Hence image encryption has been done.

2. Watermark Extraction Process

The watermark can be extracted by performing the extraction process which is the reverse of embedding process. Then confirm barcode readability.

## Experimental Results

We have taken MATLAB 2013a simulator for the demonstration purpose using 'x_ray.bmp' image of size 64 x 64 as shown in Figure 15. We have used Visual Basic 2012 for barcode decoding. The details of patient Aditi Sahay has been taken (as shown in Figure 13) and barcode has been generated as shown in Figure 14. After embedding the medical image with encrypted patient information, we got Figure 16.

The process of generating medical information and patient information from the extracted watermark is shown in the figures (Figure 17 to 20).

To detect the similarity between two images and extraction watermark images, we are using two parameters i. e. Peak Signal to Noise Ratio (PSNR) and Normal Correlation (NC) which is given in the Equations 18 and 20.

$$PSNR = 10 log_{10}\left( \frac{N * N}{MSE} \right) \qquad (18)$$

$$MSE = \frac{1}{N * N} \sum_{I=0}^{M-1}\sum_{j=0}^{N-1}\left[ \left\{ x\left(i,j\right) - y\left(i,j\right) \right\}^2 \right] \qquad (19)$$

*Figure 13. Patient information*

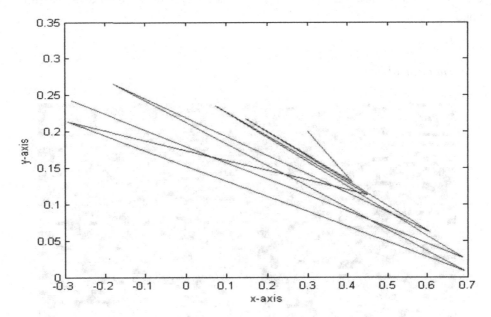

$$NC = \frac{1}{W_H W_H} \sum_{i=1}^{W_H} \sum_{j=1}^{W_W} W(i,j) * W'(i,j) \tag{20}$$

*Figure 14. Encrypted patient information*

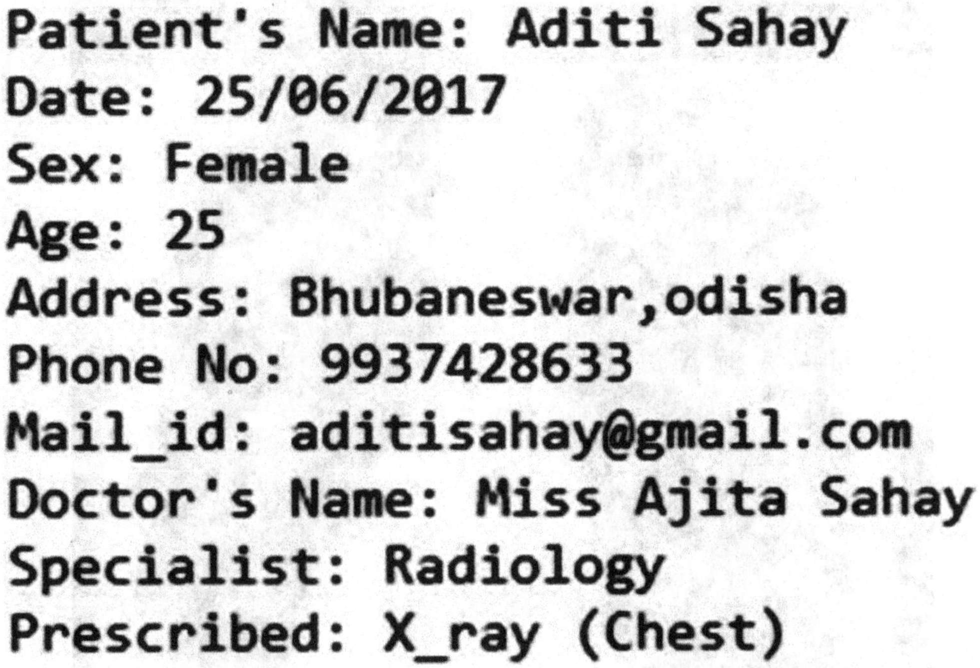

**Patient's Name: Aditi Sahay**
**Date: 25/06/2017**
**Sex: Female**
**Age: 25**
**Address: Bhubaneswar,odisha**
**Phone No: 9937428633**
**Mail_id: aditisahay@gmail.com**
**Doctor's Name: Miss Ajita Sahay**
**Specialist: Radiology**
**Prescribed: X_ray (Chest)**

N x N is the size of image and MSE stands for mean square error between extracted image and the original image

*Figure 15. Patient medical image*

*Figure 16. Embedment of medical image with encrypted patient information*

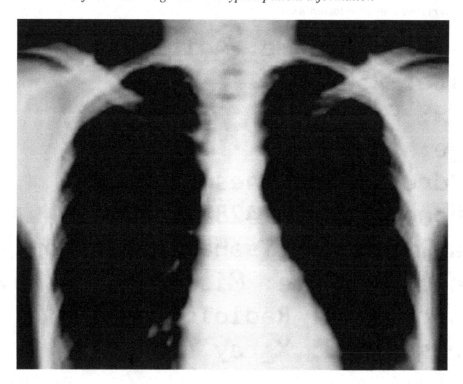

*Figure 17. Final encrypted image*

For experimental purpose we take a data set of patient personal details and encode that details by using bar code ECC200. The encoded form is then embedded as watermarked image by using DCT and DWT. This helps to provide the more security in the medical fields. The result analysis is given in Table 1.

*Figure 18. Extracted medical image*

*Figure 19. Extracted barcode*

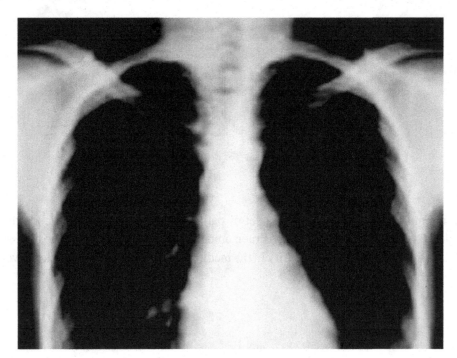

## CONCLUSION

This model helps us to achieve increased embedding capacity with maintaining high PSNR values which shows the details of the embedded information by using DCT and DWT. Image encryption is done by using 2D Gaussian iterated map and BARCODE ECC200. Here, the personal data is encoded in barcode whereas the medical image is encrypted using 2D Gauss iterated function. Then the encrypted image

*Figure 20. Extracted patient information*

*Table 1. Result Analysis*

| Patient Information | Medical Image | PSNR | NC |
|---|---|---|---|
| Patient's Name: Aditi Sahay<br>Date: 25/06/2017<br>Sex: Female<br>Age: 25<br>Address: Bhubaneswar,odisha<br>Phone No: 9937428633<br>Mail_id: aditisahay@gmail.com<br>Doctor's Name: Miss Ajita Sahay<br>Specialist: Radiology<br>Prescribed: X_ray (Chest) | | 47.15 | 0.925 |
| Patient's Name: Riya Sahay<br>Date: 29/06/2017<br>Sex : Female<br>Address : Banagalore,Marathahalli<br>Phone no: 09945327844<br>Mail_id : riya1234@gmal.com<br>Doctor's name: Miss Ajita Sahay<br>Specialist: Gynecologist<br>Prescribed : Ultra Sound | | 47.20 | 0.940 |
| Patient's Name: Sonali Sahay<br>Date: 25/06/2017<br>Sex : Female<br>Address : Banagalore,BTM first phase<br>Phone no: 09946490799<br>Mail_id : riya1234@gmal.com<br>Doctor's name: Miss Dimpi Sahay<br>Specialist: Gynecologist<br>Prescribed : Ultra Sound | | 47.80 | 0.917 |

and barcode are embedded using DCT and DWT. On the basis of experimental result which gives higher PNSR value and higher NC value proves that our approach provides better security.

## REFERENCES

Abraham, J., & Paul, V. (2014). Image Watermarking using DCT in Selected Pixel Regions. *IEEE International Conference on Control, Instrumentation, Communication and Computational Technologies*, 398-402. 10.1109/ICCICCT.2014.6992994

Agrawal, R., & Sharma, M. (2016). Medical Image Watermarking Technique in the Application of E-diagnosis using M-Ary Modulation. *Elsevier International Conference on Computational Modelling and Security, Procedia Computer Science*, 85, 648-655.

AlShaikh, M., Laouamer, L., Nana, L., & Pascu, A. (2016, January). A Novel CT Scan Images Watermarking Scheme in DWT Transform Coefficients. *International Journal of Computer Science and Network Security*, *16*(1), 62–71.

Dai, Y., & Wang, X. (2012). Medical Image Encryption based on a Composition of Logistic Maps and Chebyshev Maps. *IEEE International Conference on Information and Automation*. 10.1109/ICInfA.2012.6246810

Giokoumaki, A., Pavlopoulos, S., & Koutouris, D. (2003). A Medical Image Watermarking Scheme based on Wavelet Transform. *IEEE International Conference on Engineering in Medicine and Biology Society*. 10.1109/IEMBS.2003.1279900

Kabi, K. K., Saha, B. J., Pradhan, C., & Bisoi, A. K. (2014). Comparative Study of Image Encryption using 2D Chaotic Map. *IEEE International Conference on Information Systems and Computer Networks*, 105-108. 10.1109/ICISCON.2014.6965227

Liu, L., & Miao, S. (2016, March). A New Image Encryption Algorithm based on Logistic Chaotic Map with Varying Parameter. *SpringerPlus*. PMID:27066326

Liu, X., & Li, S. (2010). An Adaptive Chaotic Encrypted Binary Image Digital Watermarking Algorithm based on DCT. *IEEE International Conference on Intelligent Computing and Integrated Systems*, 149-153. 10.1109/ICISS.2010.5656801

Nambutdee, A., & Airphaiboon, S. (2015). Medical Image Encryption based on DCT-DWT Domain Combining 2D-Data Matrix Barcode. *IEEE Biomedical Engineering International Conference*.

Pisarchik, A. N. (2012). *Chaotic Map Cryptography and Security. In Horizons in Computer Science* (Vol. 4). Springer.

Pradhan, C., Rath, S., & Bisoi, A. K. (2012). Non Blind Digital Watermarking Technique using DWT and Cross Chaos. *Elsevier International Conference on Communication, Computing & Security, Procedia Technology*, 6, 897-904. 10.1016/j.protcy.2012.10.109

Pradhan, C., Saha, B. J., & Kabi, K. K. (2014). Blind Watermarking Techniques using DCT and Arnold 2D Cat Map for Color Images. *IEEE International Conference on Communication and Signal Processing*, 26-30.

Puech, W., & Rodrigues, J. M. (2005). Crypto-Compression of Medical Images by Selective Encryption of DCT. *European Signal Processing Conference*.

Sahay, A., & Pradhan, C. (2017). Multidimensional Comparative Analysis of Image Encryption using Gauss Iterated and Logistic Maps. *IEEE International Conference on Communication and Signal Processing*.

Singh, Kumar, Singh, & Mohan. (2017). *Medical Image Watermarking*. Springer.

Wang, Q., Ding, Q., Zhang, Z., & Ding, L. (2008). Digital Image Encryption Research based on DWT and Chaos. *IEEE International Conference on Natural Computation*, 494-498. 10.1109/ICNC.2008.105

Zhou, Y., Bao, L., & Philip Chen, C. L. (2014). A New 1D Chaotic System for Image Encryption. *Signal Processing, Elsevier*, *97*(Apr), 172–182. doi:10.1016/j.sigpro.2013.10.034

Zhou, Z., Shi, W., Bao, Y., & Yang, M. (2010). A Gaussian Function based Chaotic Neural Network. *IEEE International Conference on Computer Application and System Modeling*, 203-206.

# Index

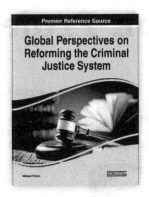

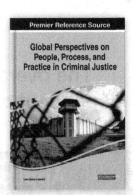

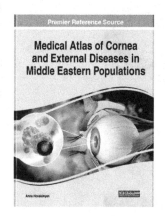
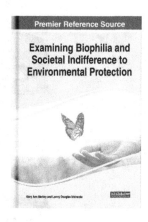
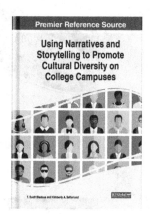

Printed in the United States
by Baker & Taylor Publisher Services